New National Framework

MATHEMATICS 8★

M. J. Tipler J. Douglas

Published in 2004 by:
Nelson Thornes Ltd
Delta Place
27 Bath Road
CHELTENHAM
GL53 7TH
United Kingdom

04 05 06 07 08 / 10 9 8 7 6 5 4 3 2 1

A catalogue record for this book is available from the British Library

ISBN 0 7487 8527 2

Illustrations by Harry Venning
Page make-up by Mathematical Composition Setters Ltd

Printed and bound in Spain by Graficas Estella

Acknowledgements

The publishers thank the following for permission to reproduce copyright material.

Casio: 8, 50, 91; Corel (NT): 2, 135, 282, 285, 322, 332, 340; Corel 1 (NT): 118; Corel 24 (NT): 73; Corel 184 (NT): 37; Corel 205 (NT): 19; Corel 604 (NT): 201; Corel 612 (NT): 232; Photodisc 22 (NT): 105; Digital Stock: 132, 269; Digital Vision: 205, 294; Digital Vision 6 (NT): 300; Digital Vision 12 (NT): 26, 76; Digital Vision 15 (NT): 66, Image 100 (NT): 70, 292; Photodisc 26 (NT): 116; Photodisc 31 (NT): 356, 358.

The publishers have made every effort to contact copyright holders but apologise if any have been overlooked.

Contents

Contents

Introduction

We hope that you enjoy using this book. There are some characters you will see in the chapters that are designed to help you work through the materials.

These are    

This is used when you are working with information.

This is used where there are hints and tips for particular exercises.

This is used where there are cross references.

This is used where it is useful for you to remember something.

These are blue in the section on number.

These are green in the section on algebra.

These are red in the section on shape, space and measures.

These are yellow in the section on handling data.

Number Support

Place value – whole numbers

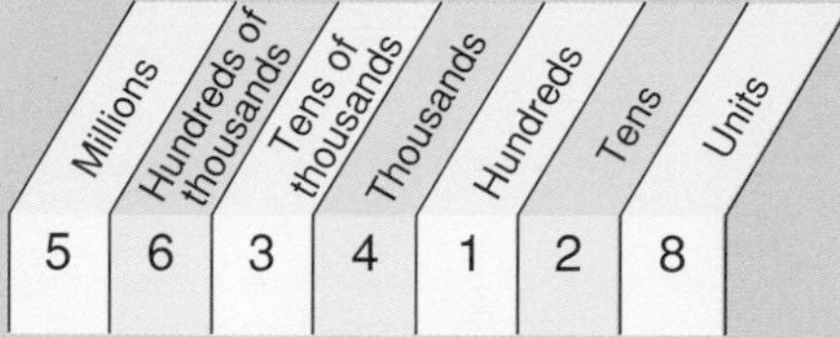

This chart shows **place value.**

In 5 634 128 the value of the 5 is 5 millions or 5 000 000
the value of the 6 is 6 hundreds of thousands or 600 000
the value of the 3 is 3 tens of thousands or 30 000
the value of the 4 is 4 thousands or 4000
the value of the 1 is 1 hundred or 100
the value of the 2 is 2 tens or 20
the value of the 8 is 8 units or 8.

Practice Questions 1, 2, 9, 25, 27

Reading and writing numbers

Large numbers are **read** and **written** in groups of three.

MILLIONS			THOUSANDS					
Hundreds	Tens	Units	Hundreds	Tens	Units	Hundreds	Tens	Units
		9	6	7	4	1	0	8

The number 9 674 108 is read as 'nine million, six hundred and seventy-four thousand, one hundred and eight'.

3·56 is said as 'three point five six' **not** 'three point fifty-six'.

Practice Questions 5, 6, 8

Multiplying and dividing whole numbers by 10, 100 and 1000

When we **multiply by 10, 100 or 1000** the digits move to the **left** by one place for 10, two places for 100 and three places for 1000.

When we **divide by 10, 100 or 1000** the digits move to the **right** by one place for 10, two places for 100 and three places for 1000.

60 × 1000 = 60 000

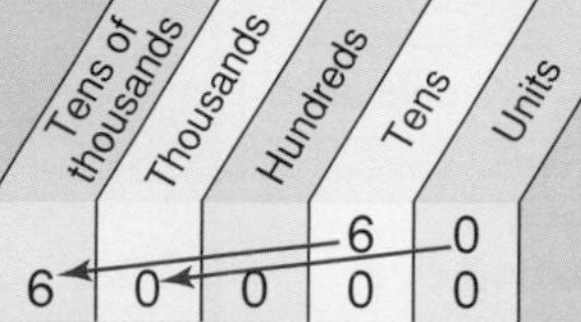

56 000 ÷ 100 = 560

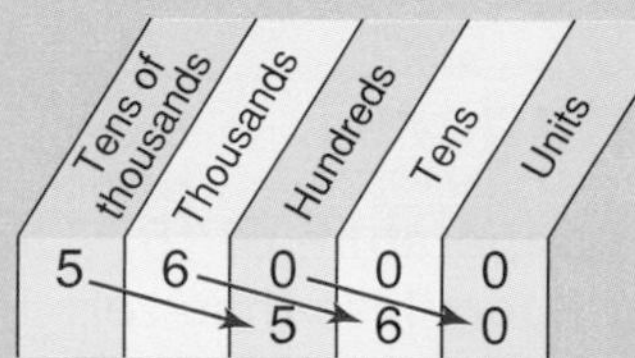

Practice Question 20

Putting whole numbers in order

To **put numbers in order** we look at digits in the same place or column
We start at the left.

Example Put 8356, 8563 and 8536 in order from largest to smallest.

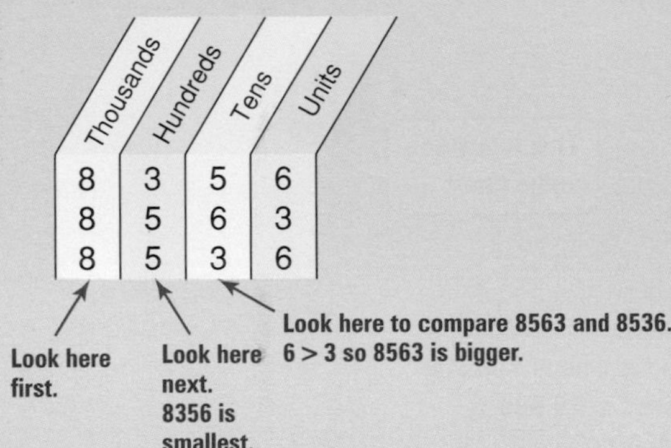
Thousands
Hundreds
Tens
Units
8 3 5 6
8 5 6 3
8 5 3 6
Look here first.
Look here next. 8356 is smallest.
Look here to compare 8563 and 8536. 6 > 3 so 8563 is bigger.

The numbers in order are **8563, 8536, 8356**.

Practice Questions 14, 42, 47

Rounding

Rounding to the nearest 10 or 100

27 cm is closer to 30 cm than to 20 cm.
27 cm **rounded** to the nearest 10 cm is 30 cm.

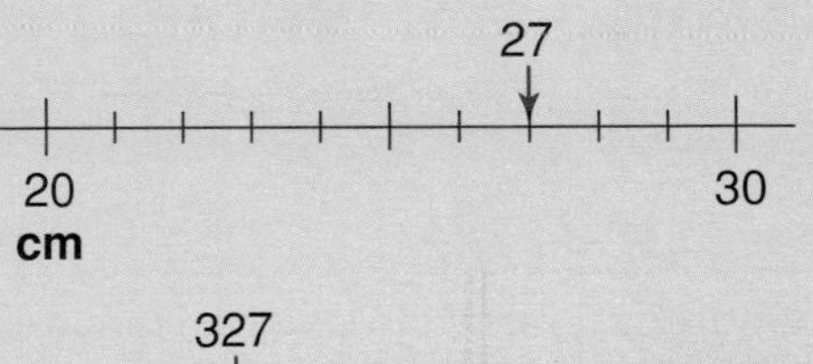
27
20
30
cm

327 mm is closer to 300 mm than to 400 mm.
327 mm **rounded** to the nearest 100 mm is 300 mm.

327
300
400
mm

Numbers exactly **halfway** between are rounded up.
465 to the nearest 10 is 470.
250 to the nearest 100 is 300.

Rounding to the nearest whole number

3·7 is closer to 4 than to 3.
3·7 rounded ot the nearest whole number is 4.

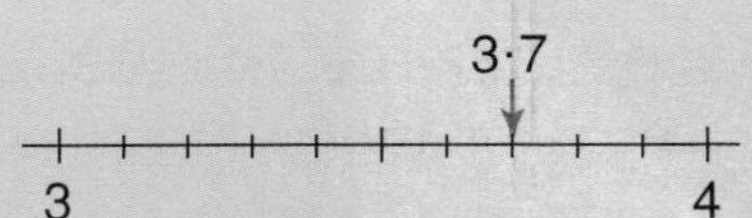
3·7
3
4

Practice Questions 17, 26

Integers

It's cold here.

A temperature of ⁻5 °C means 5 °C below zero.
Numbers less than zero are called **negative numbers**.
The number ⁻4 is read as 'negative 4'.

..., $^-4$, $^-3$, $^-2$, ... are called integers.
We can show these on a number line.

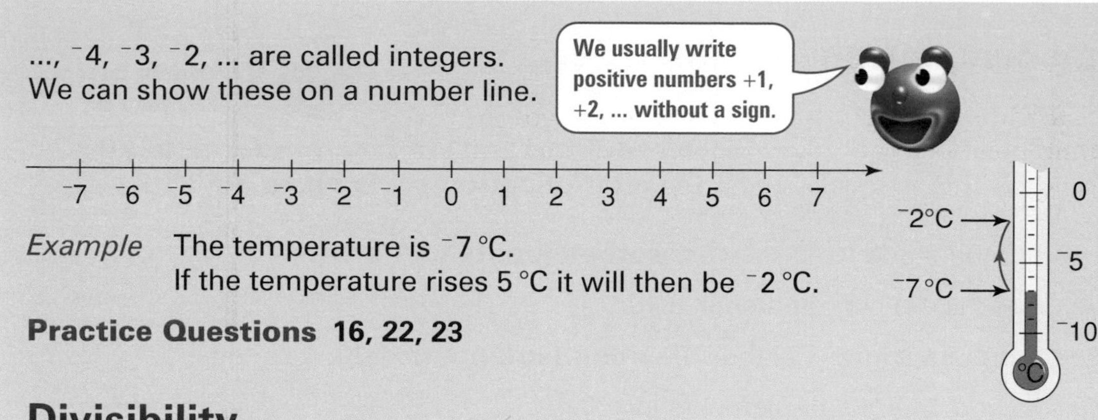

Example The temperature is $^-7$ °C.
If the temperature rises 5 °C it will then be $^-2$ °C.

Practice Questions 16, 22, 23

Divisibility

A number is **divisible by 2** if it is an even number.

A number is **divisible by 3** if the sum of its digits is divisible by 3.
Example 72 is divisible by 3 since $7 + 2 = 9$ and 9 is divisible by 3.

A number is **divisible by 4** if the last two digits are divisible by 4.
Example 124 is divisible by 4 because 24 is divisible by 4.

A number is **divisible by 5** if its last digit is 0 or 5.

A number is **divisible by 9** if the sum of its digits is divisible by 9.
Example 126 is divisible by 9 since $1 + 2 + 6 = 9$.

A number is **divisible by 10** if the last digit is 0.

Practice Question 21

Multiples, factors, primes, squares

The **multiples** of a number are found by multiplying the number by 1, 2, 3, 4, 5, 6, ...

Example The multiples of 6 are 6, 12, 18, 24, 30, 36, ...

1 is not a prime number because it has only got one factor.

The **factors** of a number are all of the numbers that will divide into that number leaving no remainder.

Example The factors of 24 are 1, 2, 3, 4, 6, 8, 12 and 24.

A **prime number** has just two factors, itself and 1.
1 is not a prime number.

Example 17 can only be divided by 17 and 1 so it is a prime number.

The prime numbers less than 20 are 2, 3, 5, 7, 11, 13, 17 and 19.

A whole number when multiplied by itself, gives a **square number**.
Example $4 \times 4 = 16$. 16 is a square number.

The first 10 square numbers are 1, 4, 9, 16, 25, 36, 49, 64, 81 and 100.

Practice Questions 7, 15, 24, 34

Mental calculation

You should be able to quickly recall the **addition and subtraction facts to 20**.
You should be able to quickly recall the **multiplication facts up to 10 × 10**.

When two numbers add to 10 they are **complements in 10**.

Example 6 and 4 are complements in 10.

When two numbers add to 100 they are **complements in 100**.

Example 36 and 64 are complements in 100.

Adding and Subtracting

When adding or subtracting mentally we can use these ways:

1 Partitioning

Examples

$$67 + 58 = 60 + 7 + 50 + 8 = 60 + 50 + 7 + 8 = 110 + 15 = \mathbf{125}$$

$$73 - 38 = 73 - 30 - 8 = 43 - 8 = \mathbf{35}$$

2 Nearly numbers

Example

$$67 + 58 = 70 + 60 - 3 - 2 = 130 - 5 = \mathbf{125}$$

3 Adding or subtracting too much then compensating

Examples

$$67 + 58 = 67 + 60 - 2 = 127 - 2 = \mathbf{125}$$

$$73 - 38 = 73 - 40 + 2 = 33 + 2 = \mathbf{35}$$

4 Counting up

Examples 67 + 58 73 − 38 = **35**

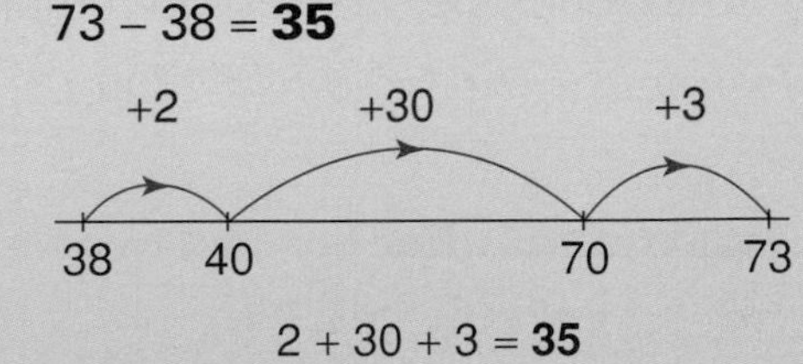

67 + 58 = **125** 2 + 30 + 3 = **35**

Multiplying

When multiplying mentally we can use these ways:

1 Partitioning

Example

$$25 \times 6 = (20 + 5) \times 6 = 20 \times 6 + 5 \times 6 = 120 + 30 = \mathbf{150}$$

2 Factors

Example $25 \times 6 = 5 \times 5 \times 2 \times 3$
$= 5 \times 10 \times 3$
$= 50 \times 3$
$= \mathbf{150}$

Dividing

When dividing mentally we can use these ways:

1 Partitioning

Example $84 \div 4 = (80 \div 4) + (4 \div 4)$
$= 20 + 1$
$= \mathbf{21}$

2 Factors

Example $84 \div 4 = \mathbf{21}$ $\quad 84 \div 2 = 42$
$42 \div 2 = \mathbf{21}$

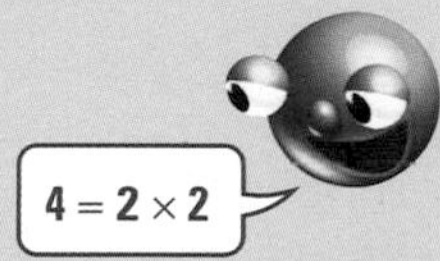

Practice Questions 3, 4, 10, 12, 37, 39, 40, 41, 57

Order of operations

We work out operations in this order:
Brackets then
Division and Multiplication then
Addition and Subtraction.

Example $7 + 3 \times 2 = 7 + 6$
$= \mathbf{13}$

Do first.

$2(9 - 4) = 2 \times 5$
$= \mathbf{10}$

Work out the brackets first.

Practice Question 43, 58

Estimating

Always **estimate** the answer to a calculation first.

Example 23 + 89
23 is about 20. 89 is about 90.
20 + 90 = 110
We estimate the answer to 23 + 89 is about 110.
The actual answer to 23 + 89 is 112.

Practice Questions 28, 35

Written calculation

Adding and Subtracting

We can **add and subtract** whole numbers by lining up the units column.

Example 386 + 427

386 + 427 is about 400 + 400 = 800.

Estimate first.

$$\begin{array}{r} 386 \\ +\,427 \\ \hline 813 \\ \hline {\scriptstyle 1\,1} \end{array}$$

Example 526 − 87

526 − 87 is about 500 − 100 = 400.

$$\begin{array}{r} {\scriptstyle 4\,11\,1} \\ \not{5}\not{2}6 \\ -\;\;87 \\ \hline 439 \\ \hline \end{array}$$

Multiplying

We can **multiply** whole numbers in different ways.

Example
527 × 2

527 × 2 is approximately equal to 500 × 2 = 1000.

This is called the grid method.

	500	**20**	**7**	
2	1000	40	14	= **1054**

or

$$\begin{array}{r} 527 \\ \times\;\;\;2 \\ \hline \mathbf{1054} \\ \hline {\scriptstyle 1} \end{array}$$

Example
56 × 24

56 × 24 is approximately equal to 60 × 20 = 1200.

	50	**6**	
20	1000	120	**1120**
4	200	24	**224**
			1344

or

$$\begin{array}{rl} 56 & \\ \times\;\;24 & \\ \hline 1120 & \leftarrow 56 \times 20 \\ 224 & \leftarrow 56 \times 4 \\ \hline 1344 & \\ \hline \end{array}$$

Dividing

Example 343 ÷ 7

$$\begin{array}{rl} 7\overline{)343} & \\ -280 & \quad 7 \times 40 \\ \hline 63 & \\ -63 & \quad 7 \times 9 \\ \hline 0 & \end{array}$$

Answer 40 + 9 = **49**

Checking Answers

We can check using **inverse operations**.

Example 351 − 72 = 279 **is correct because 72 + 279 = 351**

22 × 15 = 330 **is correct because 330 ÷ 22 = 15**

Practice Questions 13, 30, 33, 44, 50, 52, 55

Fractions

$\frac{2}{5}$ is read as 'two-fifths' and means 2 out of every 5.

$\frac{2}{5}$ ← numerator ← denominator

Example

3 out of 7 or $\frac{3}{7}$ of these horses are red.

Some fractions are **equivalent**.

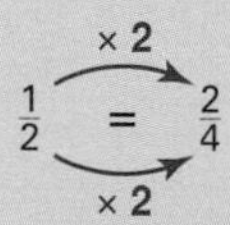

$$\frac{1}{2} \underset{\times 2}{\overset{\times 2}{=}} \frac{2}{4}$$

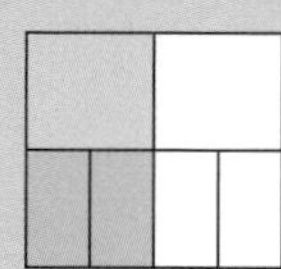

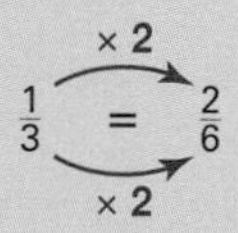

$$\frac{1}{3} \underset{\times 2}{\overset{\times 2}{=}} \frac{2}{6}$$

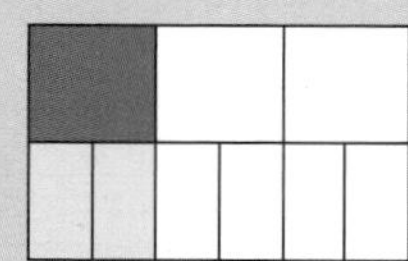

$\frac{1}{2}$ and $\frac{2}{4}$ are equivalent.

$\frac{1}{3}$ and $\frac{2}{6}$ are equivalent.

Decimals

We can write **fractions as decimals**.
You should know these.

$\frac{1}{2} = 0{\cdot}5$ $\frac{1}{4} = 0{\cdot}25$ $\frac{3}{4} = 0{\cdot}75$ $\frac{1}{5} = 0{\cdot}2$

$\frac{1}{10} = 0{\cdot}1$
$\frac{2}{10} = 0{\cdot}2$
$\frac{3}{10} = 0{\cdot}3$ and so on

$\frac{1}{100} = 0{\cdot}01$
$\frac{2}{100} = 0{\cdot}02$
$\frac{53}{100} = 0{\cdot}53$ and so on

Improper fractions and mixed numbers

An **improper fraction** has a larger numerator than denominator.

Example $\frac{17}{8}$

A **mixed number** has a whole number and a fraction.

Example $1\frac{3}{5}$

We often change between mixed numbers and improper fractions.

Examples $\frac{7}{2}$ is the same as $7 \div 2$.
$7 \div 2 = 3$ with 1 left over
$\frac{7}{2} = \mathbf{3\frac{1}{2}}$

$1\frac{3}{4}$ is the same as $1 + \frac{3}{4}$.
$1 + \frac{3}{4} = \frac{4}{4} + \frac{3}{4}$
$= \mathbf{\frac{7}{4}}$

Fraction of

We can find a **fraction of a quantity**.

Examples $\frac{1}{10}$ of $40 = 40 \div 10$
$= 4$

$\frac{1}{5}$ of $35 = 35 \div 5$
$= 7$

We find $\frac{1}{10}$ by dividing by 10, and $\frac{1}{5}$ by dividing by 5.

Practice Questions 11, 18, 29, 31, 32, 48, 49, 56

Percentages

7% is read as 'seven per cent' and means 7 out of 100 or $\frac{7}{100}$ or 0·07.

Rachel got 69 out of 100 in her maths test.
This is 69% or $\frac{69}{100}$ or 0·69.

You should know these.
100% = 1   50% = $\frac{1}{2}$ = 0·5   25% = $\frac{1}{4}$ = 0·25   75% = $\frac{3}{4}$ = 0·75   10% = $\frac{1}{10}$ = 0·1

Fractions and decimals can be changed to percentages by writing them with a denominator of 100.

Examples

$0{\cdot}32 = \frac{32}{100} = 32\%$

u	t	h
0	3	2

$\frac{1}{5} = \frac{20}{100} = 20\%$ (× 20)

Practice Questions 46, 51, 53, 54

Ratio and proportion

There are four red squares for every five blue squares.
The ratio red to blue can be written 4 : 5.

Ratio compares part to part.
Proportion compares part to whole.

In the above diagram
the proportion of red squares is $\frac{4}{9}$
the proportion of blue squares is $\frac{5}{9}$.

We can **solve ratio and proportion problems**.

Example Jack gets 3 apples for every 2 apples that Mary gets.
If Jack gets 12 apples (3 × **4**) then Mary gets 8 apples (2 × **4**).

Practice Questions 19, 36, 38, 45

Using a calculator

We use a calculator to find the answers to difficult calculations.
Always try to use a mental or written method first.

display
memory
clear
divide by
subtract
equals
multiply by
add

Always ask yourself if you could do it using a mental or written method instead.

Practice Questions 59, 60, 61, 62

Practice Questions

1 What is the value of the 8 in these?
a 34 859 **b** 584 392 **c** 123 468 **d** 4 348 213 **e** 8 050 712

2 Which digit in each of the numbers in question **1** has a place value of tens of thousands?

3 Partition these numbers.
a 72 **b** 86 **c** 420 **d** 571 **e** 967

4 Find the complements in 100 of these.
a 37 **b** 81 **c** 56 **d** 49 **e** 62 **e** 78

5 Write these in words.
a 6·75 **b** 10·2 **c** 22·16 **d** 15·05

6 Write these in figures.
a four hundred and eighty
b sixty-two thousand, five hundred and four
c five hundred and two thousand, four hundred and twenty
d three million, four hundred thousand, eight hundred
e six hundred and thirty thousand and twelve

7 Write down the first 6 multiples of these.
a 7 **b** 9

8 Write these in words.
a 7521 **b** 12 045 **c** 250 018 **d** 25 482 134 **e** 5 062 011

9 Which is bigger, 5 thousands or 51 hundreds?

10 Do these mentally.
a 9×7 **b** 8×5 **c** 9×6 **d** 8×6 **e** 7×8
f 60×2 **g** 80×2 **h** 40×3 **i** 70×5 **j** 300×5
k 600×4 **l** 900×8 **m** 600×7

11 What fraction of these is coloured?
a

b
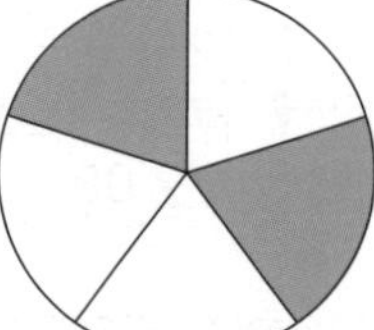
c

12 Find the answer to these mentally.

a 42 ÷ 7 **b** 80 ÷ 10 **c** 45 ÷ 9 **d** 72 ÷ 8
e 48 ÷ 6 **f** 320 ÷ 8 **g** 360 ÷ 6 **h** 280 ÷ 7

13 What goes in the gaps?

a 64 – 37 = 27 so 27 + ___ = 64
b 115 + 132 = 247 so 247 – ___ = 132
c 26 × 17 = 442 so 442 ÷ ___ = 26
d 2645 ÷ 23 = 115 so 115 × ___ = 2645
e $\frac{1}{3}$ of 54 = 18 so 3 × ___ = 54

14 Which of these are true?

a 596 > 634 **b** 407 032 < 407 049 **c** 10 000 > 9999

15 Write down the factors of these.

a 8 **b** 20 **c** 45 **d** 60

T **16**

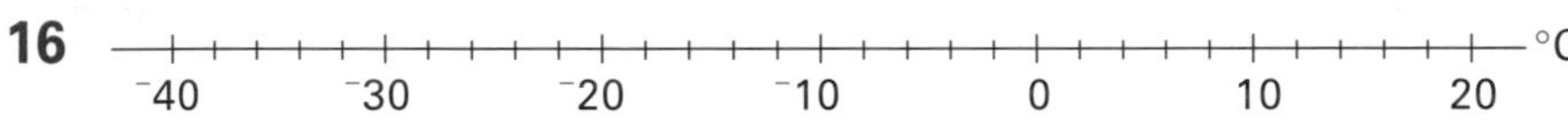

Use a copy of this number line.
Mark these temperatures.

a $^{-}40$ °C **b** 12 °C **c** $^{-}25$ °C **d** $^{-}8$ °C

17 This list gives the number of people at an art gallery. Round them
a to the nearest 10 **b** to the nearest 100.

Monday 89 Tuesday 124 Wednesday 189 Thursday 173
Friday 364 Saturday 757 Sunday 650

18 What goes in the boxes?

a $\frac{1}{2} = \frac{4}{\square}$ (× 4, × 4) **b** $\frac{1}{3} = \frac{2}{\square}$ (× 2, × 2) **c** $\frac{1}{4} = \frac{\square}{\square}$ (× 5, × 5)

19 Lamb should be cooked for 80 minutes for each kilogram.
How long does it take to cook a 2 kg piece of lamb?

20 Calculate these.

a 52 × 10 **b** 750 ÷ 10 **c** 2 × 100
d 46 000 ÷ 100 **e** 820 × 100 **f** 73 × 1000
g 56 000 ÷ 1000 **h** 50 × 1000 **i** 72 000 ÷ 10

21 Which of the numbers in the box are divisible by
a 2 **b** 5 **c** 4 **d** 9?

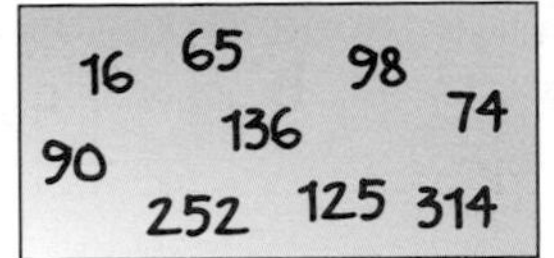

22 A diver is 20 m below sea level.
This is written as $^{-}20$ m.
Write the depth if she
a goes down a further 10 m
b comes up 10 m.

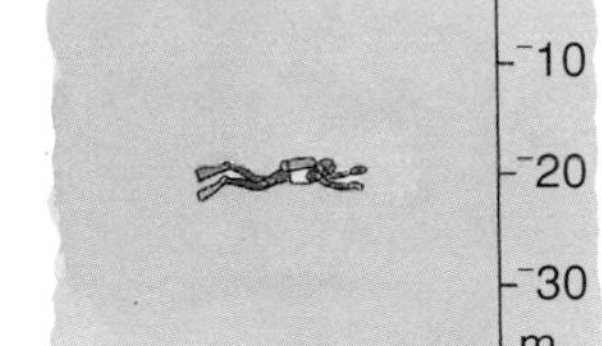

23 Andy has £25 in his bank account.
Write his new bank balance as a positive or negative number if
a he withdraws £30 **b** he deposits £30.

24 Write down the first seven prime numbers.

25 What is
a 100 more than 5824 **b** 10 less than 7269 **c** 1000 less than 60 427
d 1000 more than 29 842 **e** 100 less than 6080 **f** 10 less than 14 007?

26 Round these to the nearest whole number.
a 6·7 **b** 2·3 **c** 4·5 **d** 16·8 **e** 21·4 **f** 65·6 **g** 89·5

27 Find the number halfway between these.
a 38 and 40 **b** 45 and 55 **c** 260 and 280 **d** 3500 and 4500

28 There were 884 men and 703 women at a concert.
Rory estimated there were 1400 people altogether.
Explain why Rory is wrong.

29 Find these.
a $\frac{1}{4}$ of £16 **b** $\frac{1}{2}$ of £10 **c** $\frac{1}{10}$ of 80 m **d** $\frac{1}{5}$ of 40 ℓ **e** $\frac{1}{3}$ of 27 g

30
a $\begin{array}{r} 146 \\ +233 \\ \hline \\ \hline \end{array}$ **b** $\begin{array}{r} 659 \\ -236 \\ \hline \\ \hline \end{array}$ **c** $\begin{array}{r} 369 \\ -\ 95 \\ \hline \\ \hline \end{array}$ **d** $\begin{array}{r} 4812 \\ +\ 379 \\ \hline \\ \hline \end{array}$

e 462 + 89 **f** 614 − 38 **g** 1306 + 421 **h** 925 − 98

31 Write these improper fractions as mixed numbers.
a $\frac{5}{2}$ **b** $\frac{4}{3}$ **c** $\frac{6}{5}$ **d** $\frac{9}{7}$

32 Write these mixed numbers as improper fractions.

a $1\frac{1}{2}$ **b** $2\frac{1}{4}$ **c** $4\frac{1}{5}$ **d** $3\frac{1}{6}$

33 Calculate these.

a $\begin{array}{r} 34 \\ \times\ 8 \\ \hline \end{array}$ **b** $\begin{array}{r} 64 \\ \times\ 7 \\ \hline \end{array}$ **c** 42×6 **d** 121×4 **e** 342×6

34

2	4	6	8	11	16	18	19	21	24	25	30	49	60	64	290

From the box, write down

a the multiples of 3

b the numbers that can be divided by 10

c the prime numbers less than 20

d the factors of 16

e the square numbers.

35 Estimate the answers to these.

a $86 + 29$ **b** $96 - 51$ **c** 52×6 **d** 37×7 **e** $66 \div 8$

36 What goes in the gap?

a There is one blue square for every ___ white squares.

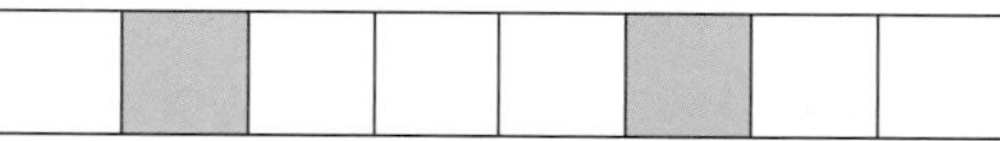

b There are ___ blue squares for every one white square.

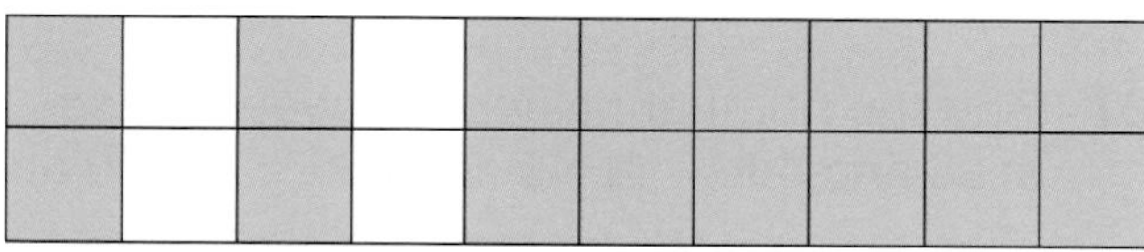

37 Find the answers to these mentally.

a $52 + 65$ **b** $89 - 46$ **c** $48 + 65$ **d** $72 - 38$

e $87 + 28$ **f** $63 - 37$ **g** $79 + 84$ **h** $94 - 69$

38 For every 1 kg of berries, Mrs Thorn makes four jars of jam. How many jars does 3 kg of berries make?

39 Find the missing numbers mentally.

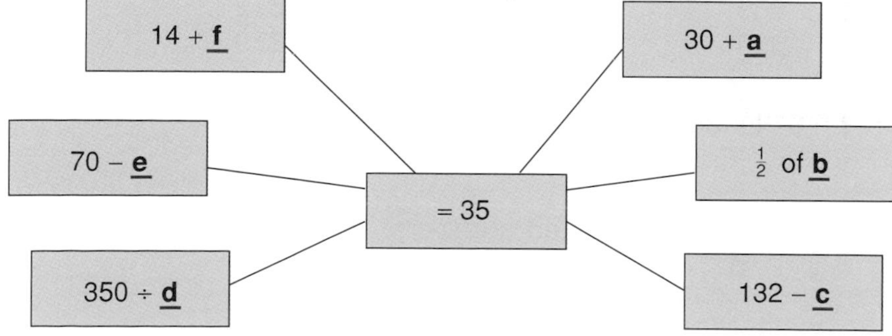

40 Find the answers to these mentally.

a 12×6 **b** 15×8 **c** 25×8 **d** 16×5
e 35×8 **f** 48×6 **g** $125 \div 5$ **h** $128 \div 8$
i $144 \div 4$ **j** $162 \div 6$ **k** $234 \div 9$ **l** $\frac{189}{7}$

41 Find the answers to these mentally.

a Gerri got 36 and 9 with two darts.
What was her total?

b Gerri threw 4 darts and hit the same number each time.
Her total was 64.
What number did she hit each time?

42 Write the numbers in these lists in order from the smallest to the largest.

a 3041, 3401, 3104, 3410 **b** 82 345, 82 352, 82 435, 82 325

43 **a** $1 + 3 \times 2$ **b** $5 + 2 \times 6$ **c** $5 \times 10 - 8$ **d** $20 - 2 \times 4$
e $2 \times (3 + 6)$ **f** $3 \times (5 - 1)$ **g** $4(3 + 7)$ **h** $(10 - 5) \times 2$

44 Eight people paid a total of £128 for a mini bus tour.

a How much change did they get from £150?
b What was the cost for each person?

45 In Lisa's class there are 2 boys for every 3 girls.

a If there are 4 boys, how many girls are there in Lisa's class?
b If there are 10 boys, how many girls are there?

46 Out of every 100 students, 19 have a Saturday job.
What percentage of students is this?

47 If $4160 < \square < 4180$, write down three whole numbers that could go in the box.

48 Which fractions from the box are equivalent to

a $\frac{1}{2}$ **b** $\frac{1}{4}$ **c** $\frac{1}{3}$?

$\frac{4}{8}$	$\frac{3}{12}$	$\frac{5}{20}$	$\frac{10}{20}$	$\frac{4}{12}$	$\frac{5}{15}$	$\frac{50}{100}$	$\frac{25}{100}$

49 Write these as decimals.

a $\frac{1}{2}$ **b** $\frac{1}{4}$ **c** $\frac{3}{4}$ **d** $\frac{1}{10}$ **e** $\frac{1}{100}$

50 Copy these.
Find the answers.

a $\begin{array}{r} 52 \\ \times 12 \\ \hline \\ \hline \end{array}$ **b** $\begin{array}{r} 36 \\ \times 19 \\ \hline \\ \hline \end{array}$ **c** $\begin{array}{r} 82 \\ \times 14 \\ \hline \\ \hline \end{array}$ **d** $\begin{array}{r} 39 \\ \times 58 \\ \hline \\ \hline \end{array}$ **e** $\begin{array}{r} 72 \\ \times 27 \\ \hline \\ \hline \end{array}$

51 Which of these is the same as 100%?
A 100 **B** $\frac{1}{100}$ **C** 1 **D** $\frac{1}{10}$

52 Cass bought 36 of these small cakes.
How much did she pay?

53 Write these as percentages.
a $\frac{1}{2}$ **b** $\frac{1}{4}$ **c** $\frac{3}{4}$ **d** $\frac{1}{10}$

54 Write these as percentages.
a 0·5 **b** 0·75 **c** 0·36 **d** 0·06

55 There are 7 boxes of books.
3 of the boxes have 48 books each.
The other boxes have 36 books each.
How many books are there altogether?

56 Wasim had 30 bars of chocolate.
He gave $\frac{1}{5}$ of these to his sister.
He gave $\frac{1}{4}$ of the rest to his brother.
How many did he have left?

57 Melanie has these coins.

Write down all the different ways she could pay for these.

a

50p per slice

b

45p each

c

38p each

58 Copy and complete this to make the answer 20.
You may use any of these operations: $+ \quad - \quad \times \quad \div$

14 __ 12 __ 2 = 20

Use your calculator to answer questions 59, 60, 61 and 62.

59 Calculate these.

a 25×36 **b** 189×17 **c** $1045{\cdot}1 \div 7$ **d** $83{\cdot}7 \times 5{\cdot}4$

e $219{\cdot}18 \div 39$ **f** $56{\cdot}72 \times 8{\cdot}3$ **g** £2·65 × 14 **h** £440 ÷ 16

60 **a** How many diaries can be bought with £20?
b How much change is there from £20 if one calculator and one diary is bought?

Calculators	£4.95
Diaries	£1.89

61 **a** Fourteen people ate a meal at this cafe.
How much did it cost altogether?
b A group all had the special.
It cost £92·65 altogether.
How many were in the group?
c One morning 27 people ate breakfast at the cafe.
How much did this cost altogether?

62 Find some different ways of completing

1 Place Value, Ordering and Rounding

You need to know

Key vocabulary

compare, decimal place, one decimal place (1 d.p.), ⩽ less than or equal to, ⩾ greater than or equal to

Sticks and stones

One of the first people to use place value, the Mayans, used sticks and stones to show numbers.

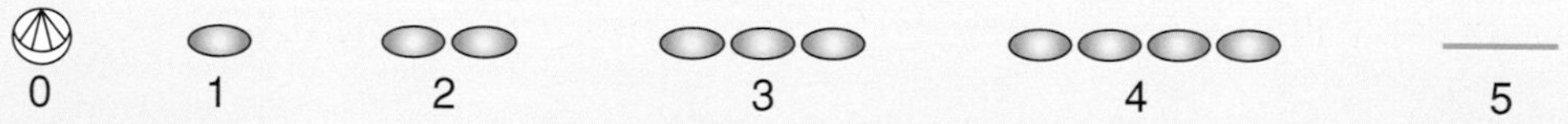

0 1 2 3 4 5

6 was written as (5 and 1)

7 was written as  (5 and 2)

We count in lots of 10.

The Mayans counted in lots of 20.

Place value was shown by putting one place above the other.

28 was written as **1 lot of 20** ***and***
1 lot of 5 and 3 ones (8)

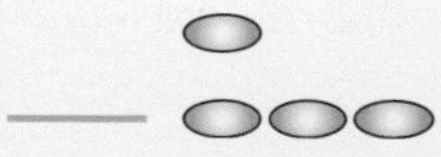

60 was written as **3 lots of 20**
0

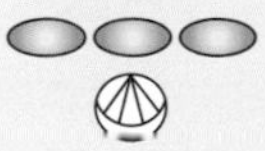

47 was written as **2 lots of 20 (40)**
1 lot of 5 and 2 ones (7)

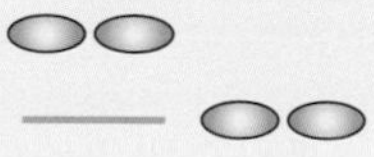

Write these numbers like the Mayans would.

9 16 23 57 34

Place value

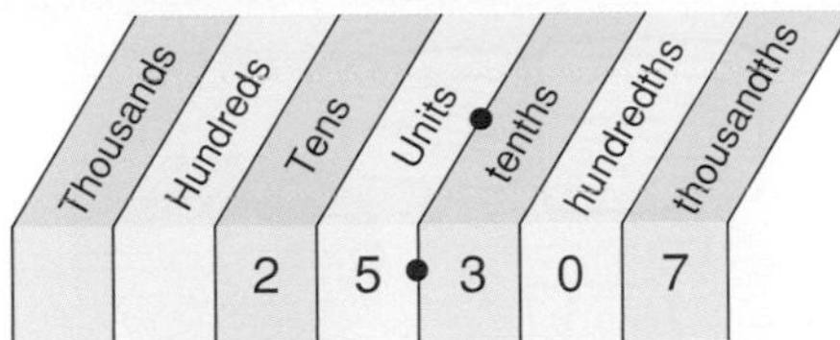

In the number 25·307 **the 2 is 2 tens**
the 5 is 5 units
the 3 is 3 tenths
the 0 is 0 hundredths
the 7 is 7 thousandths

Worked Example
What is the value of the 6 in 304·564?

Answer
The 6 is in the hundredths place.
The value of the 6 is **6 hundredths** or $\frac{6}{100}$.

Exercise 1

1 What is the value of the 9 in these numbers?

a	609·32	**b**	586·394	**c**	734·629	**d**	50·93
e	82·913	**f**	403·009	**g**	386·09	**h**	5926·3

2 What is the value of the 3 in each of the numbers in **question 1**?

3 Write each of these with a decimal point so that the value of the 4 is 4 hundredths.

a	86349	**b**	93247	**c**	9864	**d**	546
e	7841	**f**	234	**g**	84	**h**	4

***4** **a** Make the largest number you can with Mark's cards.
There must be at least one digit after the decimal point.
The last digit must not be zero.

b Make the smallest number you can with Mark's cards.
There must be at least one digit before the decimal point.
The first digit must not be zero.

c How many different decimal numbers can you make using all of Mark's cards?
Each must have two decimal places
The last digit must not be zero.
Write them down.

Puzzle

__ __ · __ __

I am a decimal number.
Just two of my digits are the same.
My tens digit is smaller than my units digit.
My units digit is the same as my tenths digit.
My tens digit is one less than my hundredths digit.
My digits add up to 11.
What number am I?

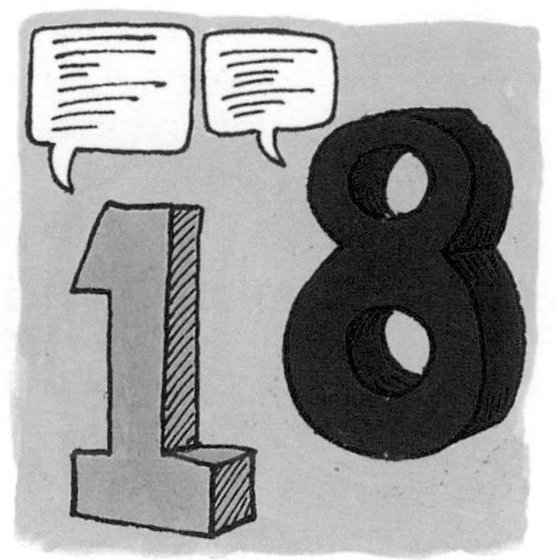

Reading and writing numbers

Remember

We say 8 306 402 as 'eight million, three hundred and six thousand, four hundred and two'.

We say 7·86 as 'seven point eight six' **not** 'seven point eighty-six'.

Discussion

We write seventeen thousand and four and twenty-one hundredths as 17004·21.
I think we write it as 17004·021.

Louise Damien

Who is right? **Discuss.**
Use this place value chart to help you decide.

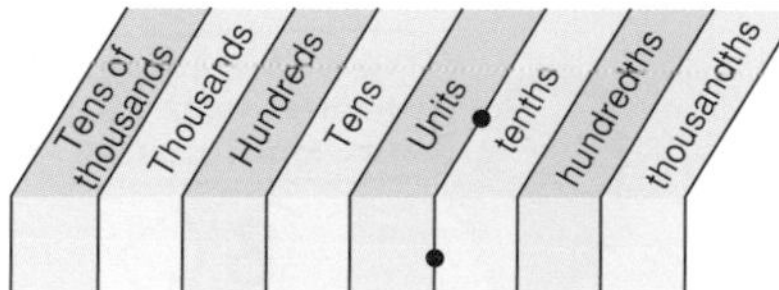

How do we write

a six thousand and twenty and thirty-four thousandths?
b thirty thousand, one hundred and five and forty-six hundredths?

Exercise 2

1 Write in words what
- **a** Pip got on the beam
- **b** Rebecca got on the floor
- **c** Tammy got on the beam
- **d** Pip got on the floor
- **e** Tammy got on the floor
- **f** Rebecca got on the beam

Gymnastics marks		
	Floor	Beam
Pip	7·86	9·24
Rebecca	8·93	8·90
Tammy	5·02	7·43

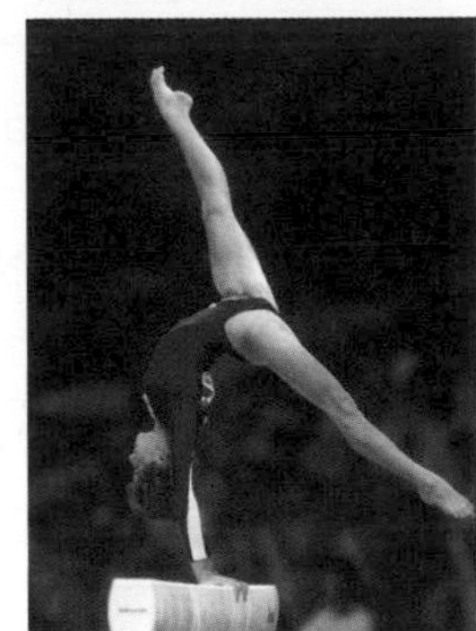

2 Write these in figures.
- **a** ninety point seven
- **b** twenty-one point six five
- **c** one thousand and three point zero seven
- **d** thirty-three thousand point two zero nine
- **e** five hundred and six thousand and ten point zero zero eight
- **f** two million, sixty-four thousand and five point zero one five

T

3

		N						N
0·72	702·086	**203·5**	0·72	18·009	2030·05	0·086	0·72	**203·5**

18·9	0·72	302·13	302·03	0·72	7020·86	72·86	32·3	7002·806

25 000   7002·806   302·03   302·03   7002·806   18·9

Use a copy of this box.
Write these as decimal numbers.
Write the letter that is beside each question above its answer.

- **N** two hundred and three and five tenths = **203·5**
- **U** thirty-two and three tenths
- **H** eighteen and nine tenths
- **E** three hundred and two and three hundredths
- **L** two thousand and thirty and five hundredths
- **I** eighteen and nine thousandths
- **A** seventy-two hundredths
- **C** eighty-six thousandths
- **V** three hundred and two and thirteen hundredths
- **O** seventy-two and eighty-six hundredths
- **T** seven thousand and two and eight hundred and six thousandths
- **S** seven hundred and two and eighty-six thousandths
- **B** seven thousand and twenty and eighty-six hundredths

***4** Write these in words and then as decimal numbers.

a $4\frac{7}{10}$ **b** $216\frac{1}{10}$ **c** $12\frac{59}{100}$ **d** $3\frac{8}{100}$ **e** $114\frac{77}{100}$

f $6\frac{451}{1000}$ **g** $42\frac{367}{1000}$ **h** $805\frac{29}{1000}$ **i** $617\frac{2}{1000}$

Adding and Subtracting 0·1 and 0·01

We can use place value to **add or subtract 0·1 and 0·01**.

0·1 is one tenth and 0·01 is one hundredth.

u	•	t	h	th
0	•	1		
0	•	0	1	

Example 4·**3**6 m – 0·**1** m = 4·**2**6 m **subtract one tenth from the tenths**

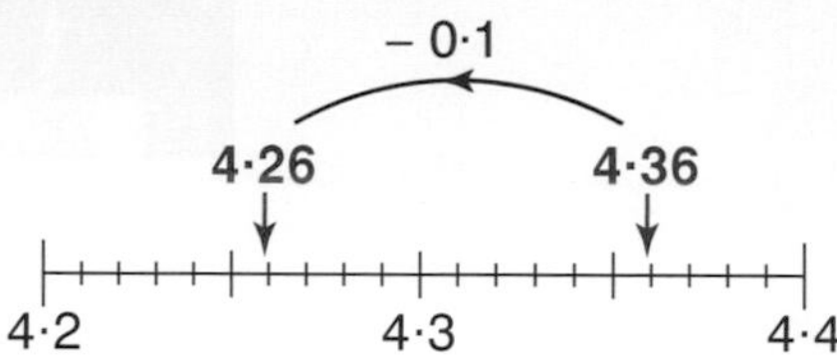

Example 4·0**9** + 0·0**1** = 4·**10** **add one hundredth to the hundredths**

Exercise 3

1 Write down the first six numbers if you

a count on in 0·1s from 3·5

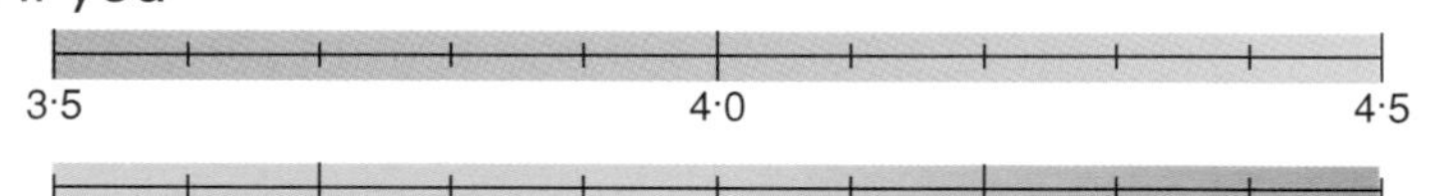

b count back from 12·6 in 0·1s

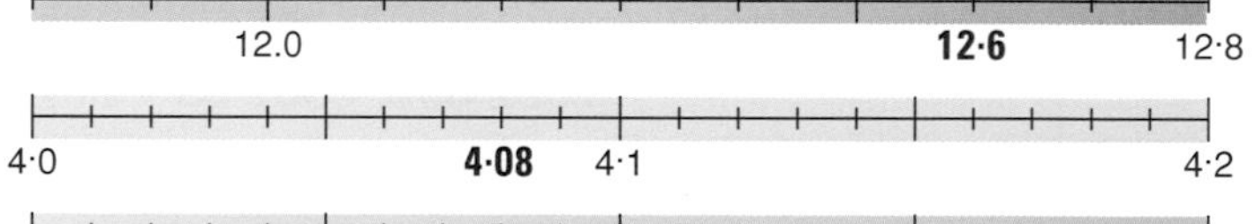

c count on in 0·01s from 4·08

***d** count back from 2·13 in 0·01s

***e** count back from 12 in 0·01s.

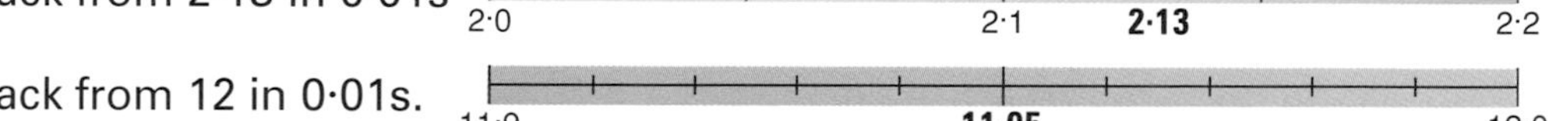

2 What length is 0·1 m less than **a** 7·6 m **b** 4·2 m **c** 3·9 m ***d** 4 m?

3 What length is 0·01 m greater than **a** 5·72 m **b** 8·65 m **c** 3·01 m ***d** 8·69 m?

4 Graham wanted a length of wood 1·83 m long.
He measured a piece he had in the garage.
It was 0·1 m too short.
How long was the piece in the garage?

***5** **a** Find the sum of 18·642 and 0·01.
b Find the difference between 13·056 km and 0·1 km.

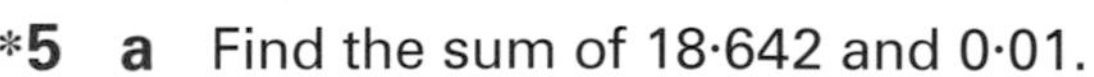

*6 What must be added or subtracted to the first number to get the second?
The answer to **a** is **add 0·1**.
a 8·6, 8·7 **b** 9·73, 9·63 **c** 0·88, 0·89 **d** 62·037, 61·937

Multiplying and dividing by 10, 100 and 1000

Remember

To **multiply** by 10, 100 or 1000, move each digit one place to the left for **each** zero in 10, 100 or 1000.

To **divide** by 10, 100 or 1000, move each digit one place to the right for **each** zero in 10, 100 or 1000.

Examples

4·82 × 10 = 48·2

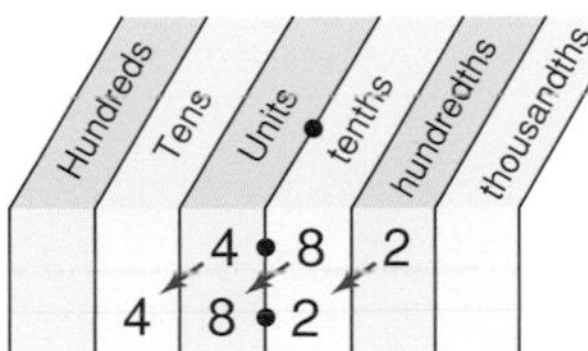

8·37 × 1000 = 8370

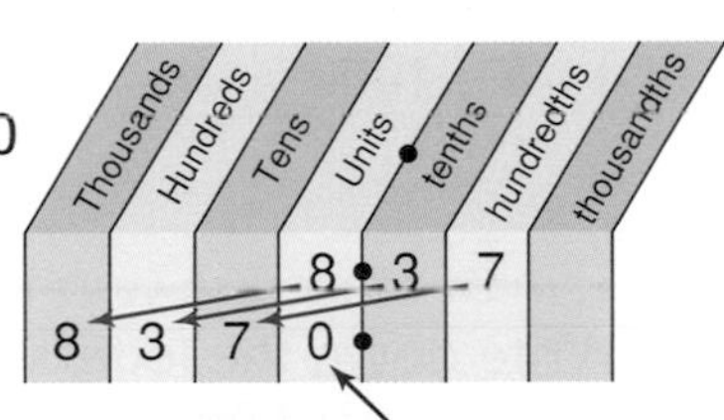

Use a zero, not a space, to show there are no units.

8·6 ÷ 10 = 0·86

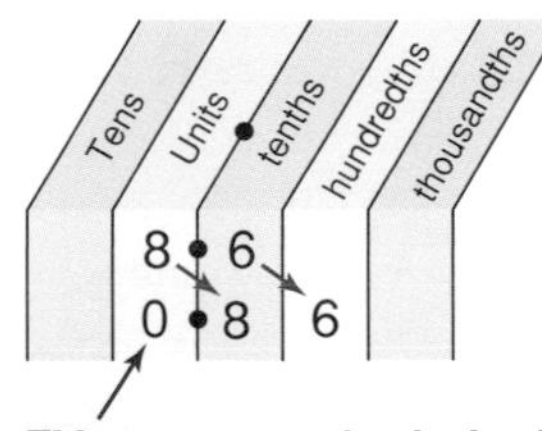

This zero stops the decimal point getting lost.

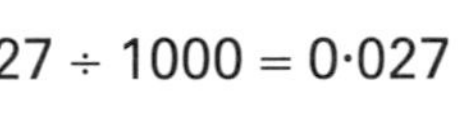
27 ÷ 1000 = 0·027

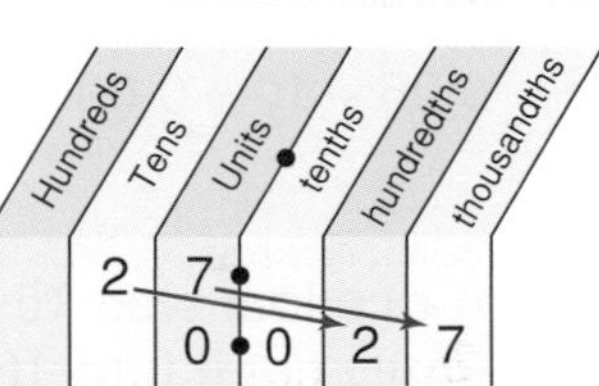

Worked Example

a 203·6 × 100 **b** 2·7 × 1000
c 462 ÷ 100 **d** 2·7 ÷ 1000

Answer

a 20 360 **Move each digit two places to the left.**
b 2700 **Move each digit three places to the left.**
c 4·62 **Move each digit two places to the right.**
d 0·0027 **Move each digit three places to the right.**

Exercise 4

1 Which of 10, 100 or 1000 goes in the box?
a 4080 ÷ ☐ = 408 **b** 84 ÷ ☐ = 8·4 **c** 70 ÷ ☐ = 0·7 **d** 3·56 × ☐ = 356
e 5·7 × ☐ = 5700 **f** 0·81 × ☐ = 810 **g** 6 ÷ ☐ = 0·006 **h** 7·2 ÷ ☐ = 0·072

T

2

4824	0·02		4824	0·02	0·008		**C** **4200**	4824	0·02
4·2	3800	0·002	0·008		0·002	3800	0·002	0·008	0·038
0·008	3800	0·351	642	6·42		3800	0·008	6·42	
380	72 430	0·02		0·351	4824	6·42	6·42		

Use a copy of this box.
Find the answers to these.
Write the letter that is beside each question above its answer.

C 42 × 100 = **4200**
Y 3·8 ÷ 100
W 724·3 × 100
T 8 ÷ 1000
L 42 ÷ 10
E 6·42 × 100
F 0·02 ÷ 10
O 3·8 × 100
S 64·2 ÷ 10
A 48·24 × 100
I 3·8 × 1000
M 351 ÷ 1000
N 2 ÷ 100

3 Five of these are wrong.
Write down the letters that are beside them.
Make a word from your five letters.

O 81·6 × 100 = 8160
B 0·32 ÷ 10 = 0·032
I 0·05 ÷ 10 = 0·005
T 62·4 ÷ 1000 = 0·624
M 56·3 ÷ 100 = 5·63
H 1·8 ÷ 100 = 0·018
S 52·3 × 10 = 5·23
A 6·84 × 1000 = 684
R 86 ÷ 1000 = 0·86

4 **a** A rice loaf was 16·5 cm long.
Emily cut it into 10 slices.
How thick was each slice?

b Rubbish bags cost £0·35 each.
Tom bought 100 of them.
How much did this cost?

c Tariq bought 100 ℓ of paint for his work.
It cost £982.
How much did each litre cost?

***5** A sheet of paper is 0·25 mm thick.
How high would a pile of 500 sheets of paper be?

***6** Grace has these cards.
She made the number 45·3 with four of her cards.

a Use some of Grace's cards to show the number 10 times as big as 45·3.

b Use some of Grace's cards to show the number 100 times as big as 45·3.

*7 **a** Explain what happens when we multiply a number by
i 10 **ii** 1000.
b Explain what happens when we divide a number by
i 100 **ii** 1000.

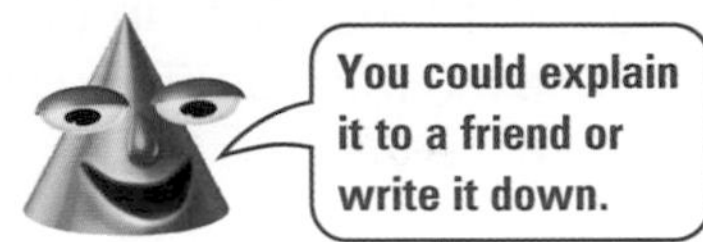

You could explain it to a friend or write it down.

*8 Mel multiplied 40×30 like this.
Use Mel's method to find the answers to these.
a 60×20 **b** 60×40 **c** 80×70
d 200×40 **e** $5{\cdot}2 \times 30$

$$40 \times 30 = 4 \times 3 \times 10 \times 10$$
$$= 12 \times 10 \times 10$$
$$= 1200$$

Putting numbers in order

Remember
To **put numbers in order**:
Compare the digits with the same place value.
Start at the left.

Worked Example
Put these numbers in order, from biggest to smallest.
5·06 5·6 5·065 5·142

Answer
The units are the same in all the numbers.
Compare the tenths.
5·6 is biggest
5·142 is next.
Then compare the hundredths for 5·06 and 5·065.
They are the same.
Compare the thousandths. $5 > 0$
The numbers from biggest to smallest are
5·6 5·142 5·065 5·06

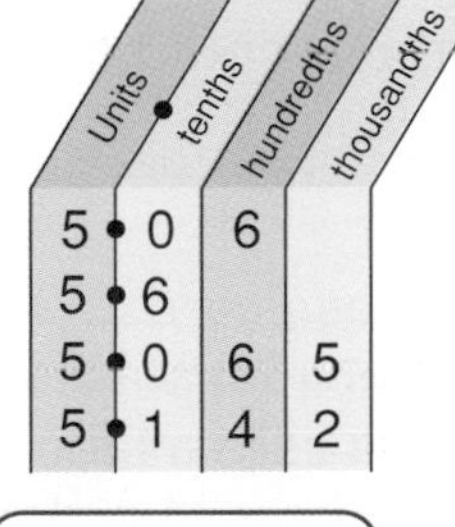

Units
tenths
hundredths
thousandths
5 • 0 6
5 • 6
5 • 0 6 5
5 • 1 4 2

5·06 is the same as 5·060.

Exercise 5

1 Which is bigger?
a 9·6 or 9·4 **b** 3·54 or 3·45 **c** 7·307 or 7·37
d 16·65 or 16·605 **e** 0·064 or 0·046 **f** 5·112 or 5·121

T **2** Use a copy of this.
Which number is smaller?
Shade it on your diagram.
a 6·03 or 6·30 **b** 9·61 or 9·16 **c** 5·34 or 5·4
d 4·7 or 4·71 **e** 1·0 or 0·92 **f** 6·08 or 6·09
g 5·64 or 5·72 **h** 5·30 or 5·80 **i** 8·02 or 8·20
What letter does your shading make?

6·03	0·92	6·08	4·7	5·34
6·4	8·2	5·64	9·07	8·20
6·30	9·6	8·02	4·8	9·61
4·71	5·72	9·16	7·9	5·4
5·80	6·09	5·30	1·0	4·0

3 Put these lists in order from largest to smallest.

a 0·9 ℓ, 0·89 ℓ, 0·92 ℓ, 0·88 ℓ

b 1·04 m, 1·403 m, 0·904 m, 1·43 m

c 6·23 kg, 5·32 kg, 6·213 kg, 6·312 kg

d 7·011 m, 7·2 m, 7·101 m, 7·11 m

4 This table shows the distances 5 girls ran.
Put these distances in order from longest to shortest.

Sudi	Nina	Joy	Julie	Gwen
2·63 km	3·04 km	2·7 km	2·6 km	2·75 km

5 Which of <, > or = goes in the box?

a 850 mℓ ☐ 8 ℓ

b 5·5 ℓ ☐ 550 mℓ

c 3500 m ☐ 3·5 km

***d** 8350 g ☐ 8·305 kg

Remember:
When comparing measurements they must be in the same units.
1 kg = 1000 g
1 ℓ = 1000 mℓ
1 km = 1000 m

6 **a** Change all the measurements in each list to the same unit.

i 0·5 kg, 600 g, 531 g, 0·53 kg

ii 160 m, 1·6 km, 1·62 km, 1602 m

iii 7610 mℓ, 716 mℓ, 7·6 ℓ, 0·71 ℓ

iv 4·02 kg, 402 g, 4·2 kg, 4220 g

b Put the lists in **a** in order from smallest to largest.

***7** $32.4 \leqslant \square \leqslant 32.6$
What number could go in the box if the number has one decimal place?

⩽ means is less than or equal to.

***8** Fran has these cards. Write down all the numbers with two decimal places she could make with them.
Do not have zero as the first or last digit.
Put the numbers in order from largest to smallest.

8
0
6
4
·

T

Puzzle

25 paths	**Excellent**
20 paths	**Very good**
15 paths	**Good**
10 paths	**Keep trying**

Use some copies of this.

Start at the top and move to the bottom.

You may move to any square that has a **smaller** number in it.

You may move → ← ↓ but

not ↑ or ↘ or ↙ or ↗ or ↖

Your path must go through just one number on the bottom row.

START

					10					
				9·6	9·4	9·2				
			8·63	9·18	9·1	9·03	9·0			
		8·3	8·36	8·41	9·08	8·8	7·9	7·89		
	7·04	7·29	7·31	7·13	7·2	7·18	7·81	7·63	7·5	
7·4	7·01	7·16	7·24	7·31	7·18	7·12	7·2	7·51	7·48	7·36

Find as many paths as you can.

Decimal ladders – game for a group

You will need a copy of this ladder for each player.

To play

- Choose someone to start.
- This person writes down five numbers between 4 and 5, without letting anyone see.

Example **Lyn wrote down these numbers.**
4·63 4·12 4·5 4·86 4·07

- This person then calls them out **one** at a time.
- As each number is called, the other players choose where to write it on their ladder
The numbers must be written in order from largest to smallest.

Example **Lyn called 4·63.**
Bryn wrote it here.
Lyn called 4·07.
Bryn wrote it as shown.
Lyn called 4·5.
Bryn wrote it as shown.
Lyn called 4·86.
Bryn wrote it as shown.
Lyn called 4·72.
Bryn could not write it on his ladder because it should go between 4·63 and 4·86.

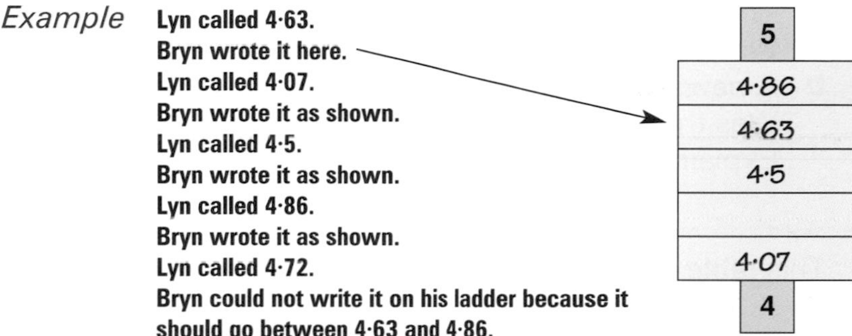

- The players with the most numbers written **in order** on their ladder take 5 points.
- The winner is the player with the most points after 10 rounds.

Rounding to the nearest 10, 100 or 1000

The population of Stroud is about 37 820.

37 820 to the nearest 100 is 37 800.

37 800 to the nearest 1000 is 38 000.

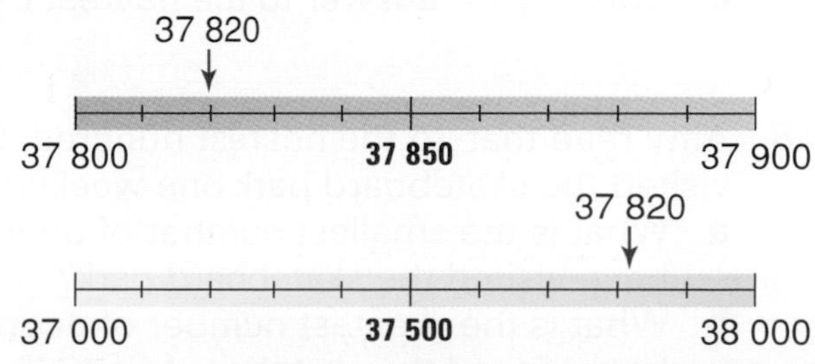

Exercise 6

Except for questions 6 and 7.

1 Round these to the nearest 10.
a 83 **b** 124 **c** 314·8 **d** 255·5

2 Round these to the nearest 100.
a 402 **b** 586 **c** 850·3 **d** 922·9

3 Round these to the nearest 1000.
a 860 **b** 952 **c** 1248 **d** 1864 **e** 3049
f 8650 **g** 4205·25 **h** 6500·75

4 There were 8723 people at a cricket match.
a The radio report said that there were about 9000 people at the match. Was this rounded to the nearest thousand or nearest hundred?
b A newspaper report said that nearly 10 000 people were at the match. Was the newspaper correct? Explain.

5 This table shows the length of some of the longest coastlines in km.

China	Indonesia	Canada	Greenland	New Zealand	Australia
14 508	54 716	90 908	44 087	15 134	25 760

a Round each distance to the nearest 100 km.
b Put the coastlines in order, longest first.
c Which two coastlines are the same length to the nearest 1000 km?

6 Alice and her friends walked 13 km each day for 11 days. To the nearest 10 km, how far is this in total?

You will need to do a calculation before you round.

7 Manuel bought 19 tables for his café at £49·99 each.
a How much did this cost altogether?
b Round your answer to the nearest £10.
c Round your answer to the nearest £100.

***8** Amy read that 'to the nearest hundred, 500 people visited the skateboard park one weekend'.
a What is the smallest number of people who might have visited the skateboard park?
b What is the greatest number of people who might have visited the skateboard park?

*9 The population of Hereford, to the nearest thousand, is 48 000.
  a What is the smallest number of people who might live there?
  b What is the greatest number of people?

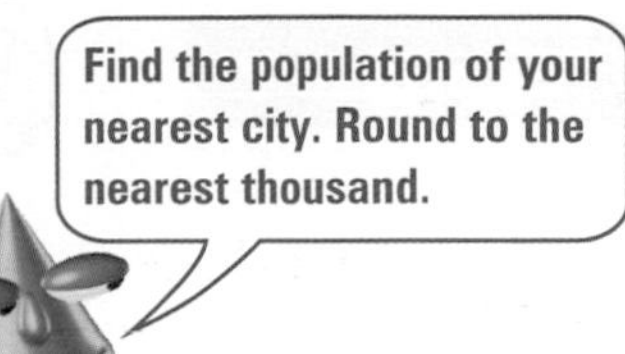

Find the population of your nearest city. Round to the nearest thousand.

*10 How long is this string to the nearest
  a 10 cm b cm c 100 cm d mm?

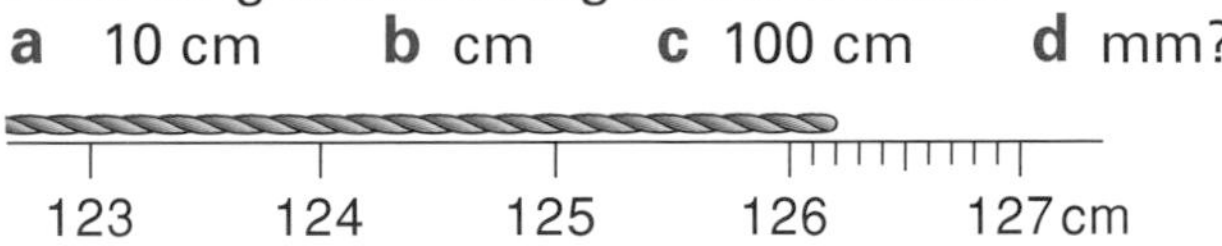

Rounding to the nearest whole number and one decimal place

Remember
To **round** to the **nearest whole number** we look at the digit in the tenths column.
If this digit is 5 or more we round up.
Otherwise we leave the whole number as it is.

Example 5·8 km to the nearest whole number is **6 km**.

This digit is bigger than 5 so we round 5·8 up to 6.

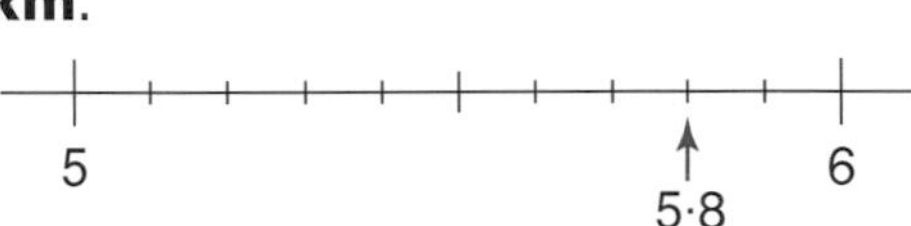

To **round** to **one decimal place** we look at the digit in the hundredths column.
If this digit is 5 or more we round up.
Otherwise we leave the number in the tenths column as it is.

Examples 4·682 to one decimal place is **4·7**.

5 or more so round the first decimal place up.

18·349 to one decimal place is **18·3**.

Less than 5 so leave the first decimal place the same.

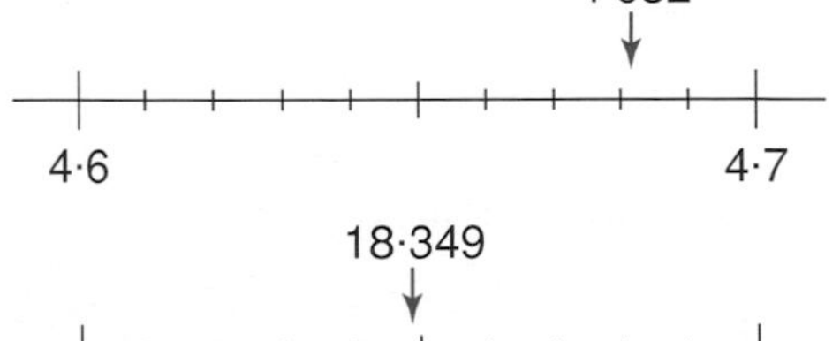

4·97 to one decimal place is **5·0**.

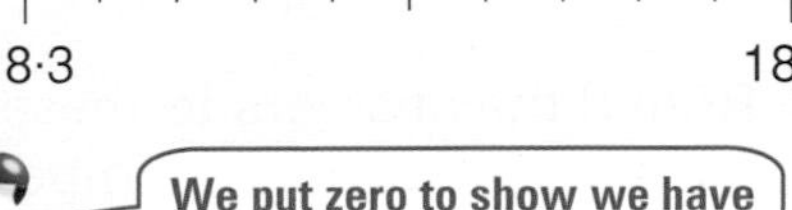

We put zero to show we have rounded to one decimal place.

Decimal place is often written as **d.p.**

Example 8·69 to 1 d.p. is 8·7.

Exercise 7

Except for question 6.

T

1 Use a copy of this.
Fill in the table.

	Number	Nearest 10	Nearest whole number	to 1 d.p.
(a)	14·71			
(b)	8·34			
(c)	17·205			
(d)	19·684			
(e)	62·867			
(f)	13·50			
(g)	26·285			
(h)	633·851			

2 Round these to the nearest whole number.
a 526·4 g **b** 82·913 kg **c** 904·56 m **d** 350·67 m
e 1086·71 mm **f** 1492·03 ℓ

3 Round the numbers in **question 2** to one decimal place.

Look at the second decimal place.

4 What goes in the gaps?
a 4·98 rounded to the nearest whole number is ___ and to 1 d.p. is ___.
b 0·96 rounded to the nearest whole number is ___ and to 1 d.p. is ___.

5 This table shows the points given to the five dogs in the final of the 'most lovable pooch' competition.

Name	Misty	Dougal	Katie	Hound Dog	Muss
Points	93·42	86·87	91·95	88·60	92·00

Round each to
a the nearest whole number
b one decimal place.

***6** Round the answers to these to
i the nearest whole number **ii** one d.p.
a 56 ÷ 17 **b** 824 ÷ 26
c 9174 ÷ 824 **d** 96·8 ÷ 3·2

Rounding up or down

Worked Example
A lift can carry 12 people at most.
How many times must the lift go up to take 75 people?

Answer
$\frac{75}{12} = 6{\cdot}25$ Key 75 ÷ 12 to get 6.25

To round down is not sensible because after the lift has taken 6 trips there will still be some people left over.
This is shown by the decimal part of the answer.
The lift must go up **7** times.

Exercise 8

1 Would the answers to each of these be rounded up or rounded down?
Find the answers.

a A school hired mini buses for 100 students.
Each mini bus could hold 16 students.
How many mini buses were needed?

b 90 students want to play netball.
They are put into teams of 7.
How many full teams can be made?

2 'Coachline' coaches can carry only 52 people.
How many coaches are needed for

a 126 people **b** 207 people **c** 270 people?

3 Jason had a holiday job packing chocolates.
A box holds 48 chocolate cremes.
How many boxes can be filled with

a 72 chocolate cremes **b** 186 chocolate cremes?

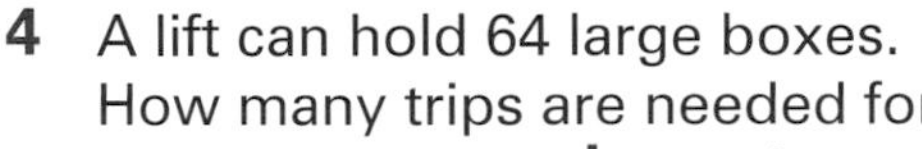

4 A lift can hold 64 large boxes.
How many trips are needed for

a 187 boxes **b** 271 boxes **c** 385 boxes?

5 Trees at 'Evergreen' are all £11.

a Simon had £100 to buy trees for his new garden.
How many trees could he buy?

b How many trees could be bought with £240.

c How many trees could be bought with £472?

Summary of key points

This chart shows **place value**.

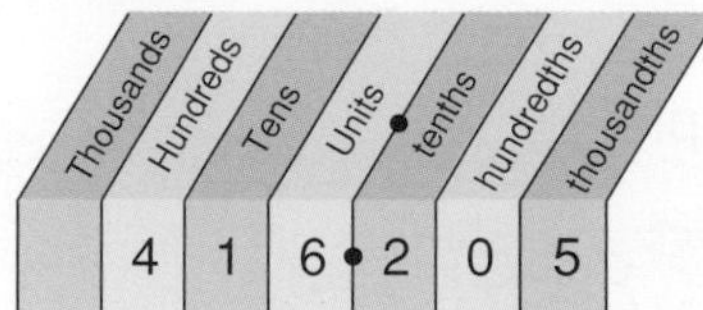

In the number 416·205

the 4 is	**4 hundreds**
the 1 is	**1 ten**
the 6 is	**6 units**
the 2 is	**2 tenths**
the 0 is	**0 hundredths**
the 5 is	**5 thousandths.**

416·205 is said as 'four hundred and sixteen point two zero four'.
Three and forty-two hundredths is written as 3·42.

We use place value to **add and subtract 0·1 and 0·01**.

Examples 5·**6**3 – 0·**1** = 5·**5**3 **subtract one tenth from the tenths**

2·0**8** + 0·0**1** = 2·0**9** **add one hundredth to the hundredths**

To **multiply by 10, 100 or 1000** move each digit one place to the left for each zero in 10, 100 or 1000, ...

Examples 46 × 10 = 460 0·8 × 100 = 80 0·520 × 1000 = 520

To **divide by 10, 100 or 1000** move each digit one place to the right for each zero in 10, 100 or 1000, ...

Examples 530 ÷ 10 = 53 4·8 ÷ 100 = 0·048 834 ÷ 1000 = 0·834

To **put numbers in order** look at the digits in the same place or column.
Start at the left.

Example 4·63 > 4·528
The units digits are both 4.
The tenths digits are 6 and 5.
6 is bigger than 5.

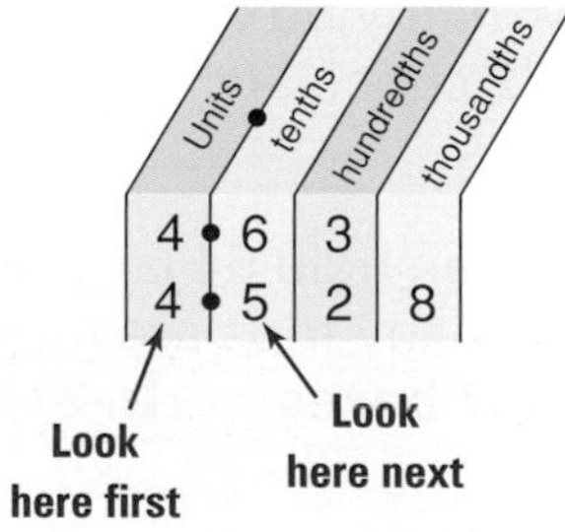

Rounding to the nearest 10, 100 or 1000

Example 76 542 to the nearest 100 is 76 500.

76 500 — 76 542 — 76 600

76 542 to the nearest 1000 is 77 000.

76 000 — 76 542 — 77 000

To **round to the nearest whole number** we look at the digit in the tenths column.

If this digit is 5 or more we round up.

Otherwise the whole number stays the same.

Example 16·54 to the nearest whole number is 17.

The tenths digit is 5 so 16 becomes 17.

To **round to one decimal place** we look at the digit in the hundredths column.

If this digit is 5 or more we round up.

Otherwise the digit in the tenths column stays the same.

Examples 4·58 to 1 d.p. is 4·6.

4·82 to 1 d.p. is 4·8.

In some problems we must decide whether to **round up** or **round down**.

Test yourself

1 What is the value of the 7 in these? **A**

a 43 725 **b** 607·82 **c** 286·74 **d** 43·07 **e** 6·197

2 Make the largest number you can with these cards. 

You must have at least one digit after the decimal point.

The last digit must not be zero.

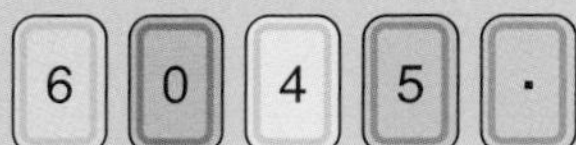

3 Write these in words. **B**

a 25·08 **b** 72·018 **c** $6\frac{3}{100}$ **d** $4\frac{273}{1000}$

4 Write these as decimal numbers. (B)
- **a** forty-nine and six hundredths
- **b** three thousand and two and thirty-five hundredths
- **c** six hundred and ten and twenty-five thousandths

5 Find the answers to these. 

a 8·7 + 0·1 **b** 14·06 – 0·1 **c** 3·98 + 0·01 **d** 5·00 – 0·01

6 
- **a** What mass is 0·1 kg less than 28·352 kg?
- **b** Find the sum of 8·647 km and 0·01 km.
- **c** Find the difference between 18·072 ℓ and 0·1 ℓ.

T **7** (D)

_	_	A	_	_	_		A	_	_
1·2	0·12	620	14	12	1·2		620	14	6200

_	_	_		_	_	_	_
6·2	0·12	6200		0·062	62	140	1·4

_	_	_	_		_	_	A	_
0·0012	0·62	1·2	0·12		6·2	0·12	620	6·2

_	A	_		_	_	_	_	_
0·14	620	62		120	140	0·62	62	12

Use a copy of this box.
Find the answers to these in the box. Write the letter above the answer.
The first one is done.

A	62 × 10 = 620	**E**	62 × 100	**O**	0·62 ÷ 10	**T**	6200 ÷ 1000
N	0·062 × 1000	**I**	62 ÷ 100	**L**	1·4 × 100	**Y**	14 ÷ 10
C	140 ÷ 1000	**R**	0·014 × 1000	**F**	1·2 ÷ 1000	**H**	12 ÷ 100
S	0·012 × 100	**K**	0·012 × 1000	**B**	1·2 × 100		

8 (D)
- **a** Sara planted 100 seeds in 13 minutes. How long did she take to plant each seed?
- **b** Ralph bought 10 cakes for £0·45 each. How much did these cost altogether?

9 Which is bigger? 

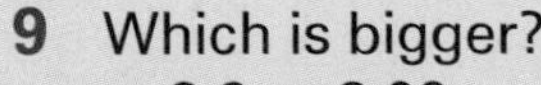

a 8·6 or 8·06 **b** 7·257 or 7·527 **c** 4·23 or 4·231 **d** 8·36 or 8·036

10 Put these in order from smallest to largest. 

a 4·1, 4·12, 4·214, 3·99 **b** 0·864, 0·87, 0·86, 0·684, 0·846

11 This table shows the amount of pocket money Wayne's friends get. 
Who gets the most pocket money?
Put the amounts in order from biggest to smallest.

Jon	Sam	Tim	Nick
£1·25	£1·10	£2·05	£1·50

12 Round these to the nearest 100. 
a 640 **b** 790 **c** 81 **d** 1249 **e** 3150

13 £15 386 was raised at a charity evening.
a How much, to the nearest £100, was raised?
b How much, to the nearest £1000, was raised?
c Was the headline in The Mail correct? Explain.
d At another charity evening, £15 000 to the nearest thousand pounds was raised. What are the greatest and least amounts, to the nearest pound, that could have been raised?

THE MAIL
Nearly £20 000 raised at charity evening

14 This table shows the distances, in metres, five people threw in a 'welly throwing' competition.

Name	B. Smith	R. Johns	M. Carter	S. Patel	M. Read
Distance (m)	17·23	20·49	16·58	19·98	18·00

Round each distance to
a the nearest whole number **b** one d.p.

15 A mini bus can carry 15 people. How many mini buses are needed for 
a 84 people **b** 107 people **c** 186 people?

16 Iced buns cost 35p. How many can be bought for
a 90p **b** £2 **c** £4·25?

2 Integers, Powers and Roots

You need to know

Key vocabulary

divisibility, factor, highest common factor (HCF), integer, lowest common multiple (LCM), prime, prime factor

To the dungeon!

Game for 2 players

You will need 13 markers (you could use chalk marks, paper or chairs)
a cube with numbers 1, 2, 3, $^{-}1$, $^{-}2$, $^{-}3$ on the faces.

To Play: In an old fairy story, a rich King played a game with his people.
Each person who played had a chance to win gold.
The King had a staircase with 13 steps. He put a person on the middle step, then tossed a dice with 1, 2, 3 and $^{-}1$, $^{-}2$, $^{-}3$ on it.
Each time the dice was tossed the person would move up or down the staircase that number of steps.
If the person reached the bottom the game was over and he or she was thrown in the dungeon.
If the person reached the top, he or she was given gold.
Make your own staircase with markers or chairs.
Play this game.

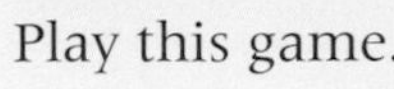

Integers

Remember
The numbers ..., $^{-}4$, $^{-}3$, $^{-}2$, $^{-}1$, 0, 1, 2, 3, 4, ... are called **integers**.
We can put the integers on a number line.

$^{-}4$ $^{-}3$ $^{-}2$ $^{-}1$ 0 1 2 3 4

The further left a number is on the number line, the smaller it is.

Worked Example
Put the integers $^{-}1$, $^{-}4$, 2, 0, $^{-}3$, in order from smallest to largest.

Answer
We can show these integers on a number line.

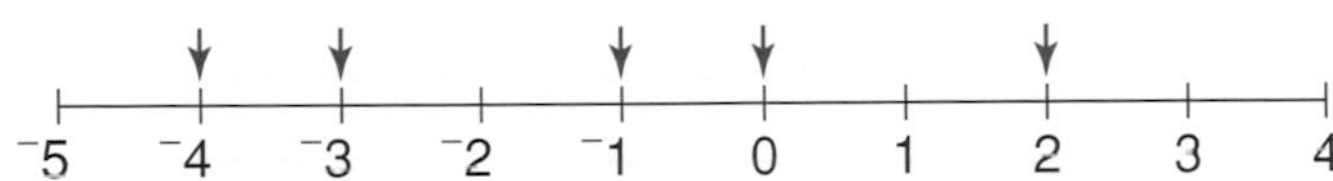

In order, these integers are **$^{-}$4, $^{-}$3, $^{-}$1, 0, 2**.

Exercise 1

1 Are these true or false?
a $^{-}3$ °C > 0 °C **b** $^{-}2$ °C < 2 °C
c $^{-}2$ °C > $^{-}5$ °C **d** $^{-}2$ °C < $^{-}3$ °C

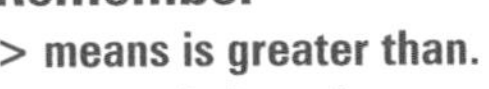

Remember
> means is greater than.
< means is less than.

2 Which of > or < goes between these?
a 2 °C $^{-}2$ °C **b** $^{-}1$ °C 1 °C **c** $^{-}8$ °C 0 °C
d $^{-}9$ °C $^{-}4$ °C **e** $^{-}14$ °C $^{-}7$ °C

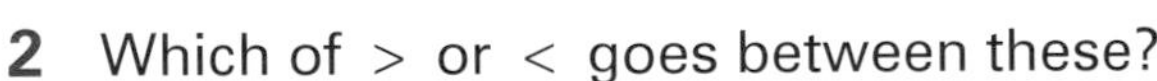

3 Put these temperatures in order from coldest to warmest.
a $^{-}1$ °C, $^{-}3$ °C, 1 °C, 0 °C, $^{-}7$ °C
b $^{-}2$ °C, 4 °C, 9 °C, $^{-}4$ °C, $^{-}8$ °C, $^{-}3$ °C

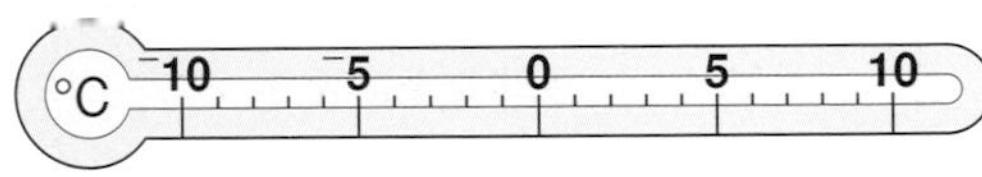

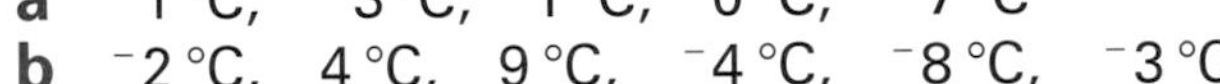

4

One of the integers given is at A and the other is at B.
Which is at A?
a $^{-}7$ or $^{-}3$ **b** $^{-}20$ or $^{-}4$ **c** $^{-}3$ or $^{-}10$ **d** $^{-}25$ or $^{-}35$

5 Which of the three integers is closest to zero?
a $^{-}4$, $^{-}3$, $^{-}5$ **b** $^{-}6$, $^{-}8$, $^{-}3$ **c** $^{-}2$, $^{-}1$, $^{-}8$

6 These were the temperatures at midnight on 12 February.

Beijing	$^{-}5$ °C	Kiev	$^{-}2$ °C	New York	$^{-}6$ °C
Calgary	$^{-}22$ °C	Montreal	$^{-}24$ °C	Warsaw	$^{-}3$ °C
Jerusalem	$^{-}1$ °C	Moscow	$^{-}8$ °C		

a Which city had the coldest night?
b Which city had the warmest night?
c Which was the colder, Moscow or New York?
d Write the temperatures in order, from coldest to warmest.

7 Put the integers $^{-}7$, $^{-}3$, $^{-}6$, $^{-}2$ on a number line.
Which number is halfway between these?
a $^{-}7$ and $^{-}3$ **b** $^{-}6$ and $^{-}2$

Using integers

We often use **negative numbers**.

Example The diver is at about $^{-}18$ m.
This is 18 m below sea level.

Exercise 2

1 **a** What is at about 20 m?
b What is at about $^{-}10$ m?
c The top of the submarine is at about $^{-}25$ m.
Where will it be if it
i rises 10 m
ii rises 20 m
iii sinks 5 m?
d The deck of the boat is at about 5 m.
About how far below the deck is
i the fish **ii** the top of the submarine?
e What depth will the stingray be if it starts at
i $^{-}20$ m and rises 5 m **ii** $^{-}30$ m and rises 20 m
iii $^{-}10$ m and goes down 5 m **iv** $^{-}5$ m and goes down 10 m?

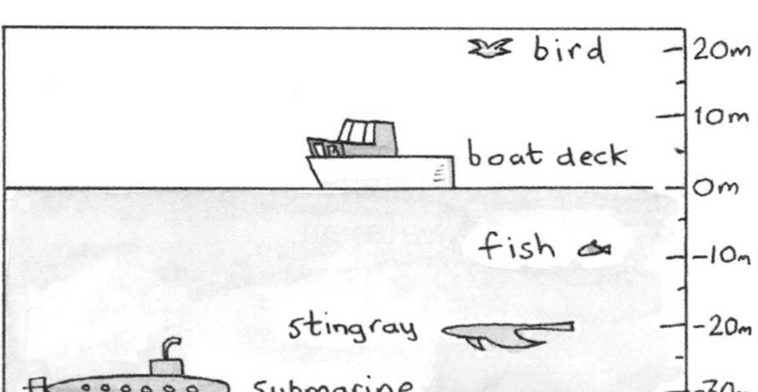

T

2 Use a copy of this.
Use the thermometer to help you fill in this table.

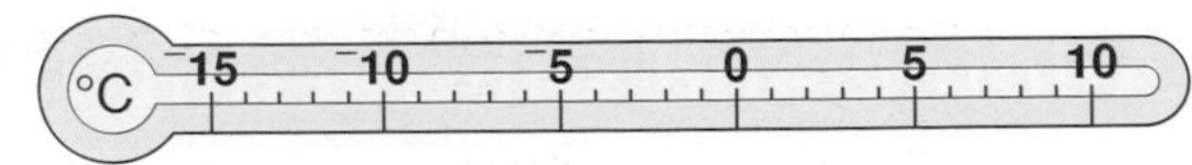

Temperature at 12 p.m	Change in Temperature	Temperature at 3p.m
a $^{-}3$°C	rises by 4°C	
b 2°C	falls by 5°C	
c 0°C	falls by 7°C then rises by 4°C	
d $^{-}4$°C	rises by 7°C then falls by 8°C	
e 2°C	falls by 12°C then rises by 6°C	

3 Use the thermometer in **question 2** to help.
What is the difference between these night and day temperatures?
a night $^{-}4$ °C, day 2 °C **b** night $^{-}4$ °C, day 0 °C **c** night $^{-}10$ °C, day 2 °C
d night $^{-}3$ °C, day $^{-}1$ °C **e** night $^{-}9$ °C, day $^{-}2$ °C **f** night $^{-}14$ °C, day $^{-}7$ °C

4 A diver is at $^{-}15$ m.
He goes down another 4 m then up 11 m.
Where is he now?

5 These were the temperatures in 8 places.

London 1 °C   Moscow $^{-}15$ °C   Rome 13 °C   Paris $^{-}3$ °C
Oslo $^{-}9$ °C   New York $^{-}4$ °C   Warsaw 2 °C   Montreal $^{-}26$ °C

a How much **colder** was it in
i Oslo than London   **ii** New York than Rome
iii Oslo than New York   **iv** Montreal than Oslo?
b How much **warmer** was it in
i Rome than Oslo   **ii** Warsaw than Montreal?

***6** The depth below sea level of a prawn, a sea spider and a sea snail is shown.
a What is the difference in depth between the prawn and the sea snail?
b How much higher is the sea spider than the sea snail?

Creature	Depth
prawn	– 6400 m
sea spider	– 7400 m
sea snail	– 10 400 m

***7** In a board game, Victoria has scored 5 points.
What will Victoria's score be, if on the next three turns she
a gains 2 points, loses 4 points and gains 1 point
b loses 8 points, gains 2 points and gains 4 points
c gains 1 point, loses 9 points and loses 3 points
d loses 4 points, gains 3 points and loses 7 points?

$^{-}10$ $^{-}5$ 0 5 10

Adding and subtracting integers

We can use a **number line** to add and subtract.

To **add a positive integer** we move **to the right**.
To **add a negative integer** we move **to the left**.

Examples $3 + {}^{-}4$

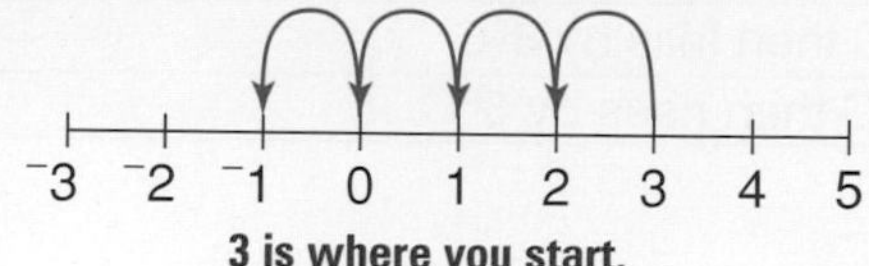

3 is where you start.
$+{}^{-}4$ means move left 4.
The answer is $^{-}1$.

$^{-}2 + 5$

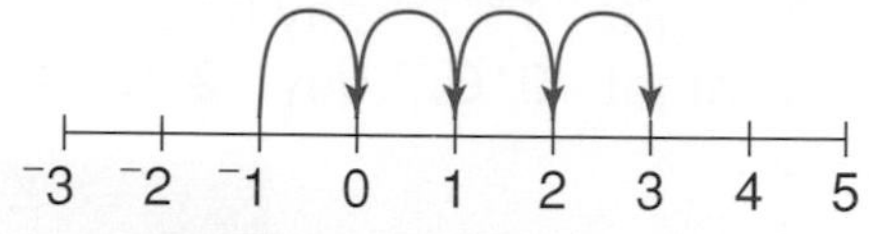

$^{-}2$ is where you start.
$+5$ means move right 5.
The answer is 3.

$^{-}1 + {}^{-}2$

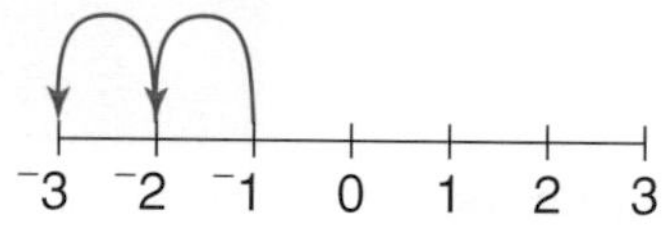

$^{-}1$ is where you start.
$+{}^{-}2$ means move left 2.
The answer is $^{-}3$.

To **subtract a positive integer** we move **to the left**.
To **subtract a negative integer** we move **to the right**.

Examples $2 - 6$

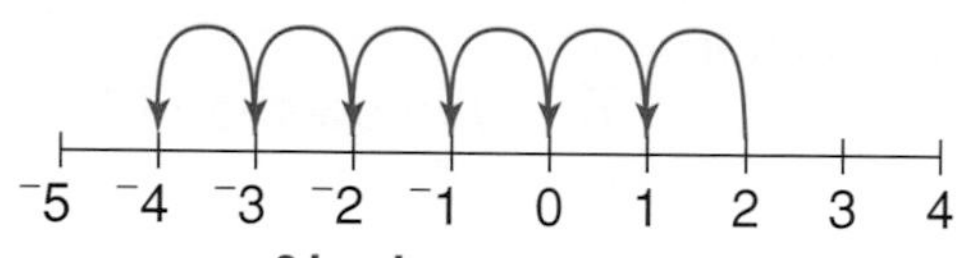

2 is where we start.
$^{-}6$ means move left 6.
The answer is $^{-}4$.

$^{-}3 - {}^{-}4$

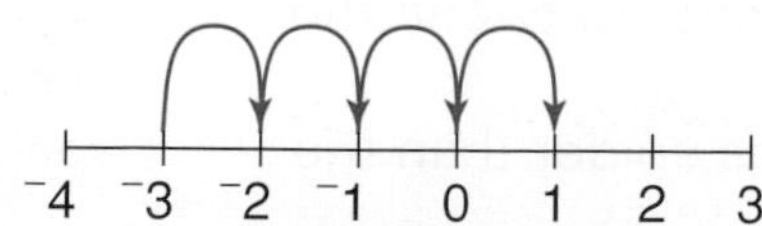

$^{-}3$ is where we start.
$-{}^{-}4$ means move right 4.
The answer is 1.

$1 - {}^{-}2$

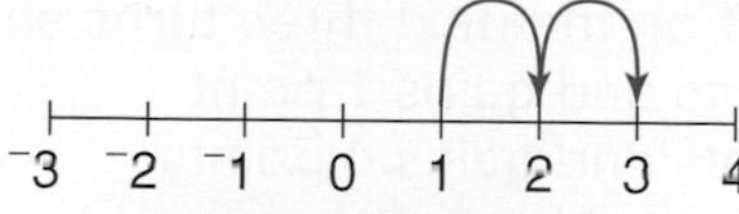

1 is where we start.
$-{}^{-}2$ means move right 2.
The answer is 3.

Exercise 3

$^{-}8$ $^{-}7$ $^{-}6$ $^{-}5$ $^{-}4$ $^{-}3$ $^{-}2$ $^{-}1$ 0 1 2 3 4 5 6 7 8

Use the number line to help you find the answers to questions 1 and 2.

1 **a** $^{-}3 + 4$ **b** $^{-}5 + 2$ **c** $^{-}1 + 4$ **d** $^{-}2 + 6$ **e** $2 + {}^{-}5$
f $3 + {}^{-}2$ **g** $1 + {}^{-}3$ **h** $^{-}2 + {}^{-}3$ **i** $^{-}3 + {}^{-}1$

2 **a** $^{-}2 - 5$ **b** $^{-}1 - 5$ **c** $2 - 4$ **d** $3 - 4$ **e** $2 - {}^{-}1$
f $3 - {}^{-}2$ **g** $0 - 3$ **h** $0 - {}^{-}3$ **i** $^{-}2 - {}^{-}3$ **j** $^{-}3 - {}^{-}2$
k $^{-}1 - {}^{-}4$

T

3 Use a copy of this table.
Fill in the green shaded section first.
Use the pattern to fill in the rest of the table.

second number (columns); first number (rows)

+	$^{-}3$	$^{-}2$	$^{-}1$	0	1	2	3
3						5	6
2							5
1							
0							
$^{-}1$							
$^{-}2$							
$^{-}3$							

4 Use the table you completed in **question 3** to help answer these.
a $1 + {}^{-}2$ **b** $2 + {}^{-}1$ **c** $3 + {}^{-}2$ **d** $^{-}2 + 3$ **e** $^{-}3 + 3$
f $^{-}1 + 3$ **g** $^{-}2 + {}^{-}1$ **h** $^{-}3 + {}^{-}1$ **i** $0 + {}^{-}2$ **j** $^{-}2 + {}^{-}3$
k $^{-}3 + {}^{-}3$

***5** 3 $^{-}4$ 0 8 $^{-}7$ 2 $^{-}6$

a Choose a number card to give the answer 5.

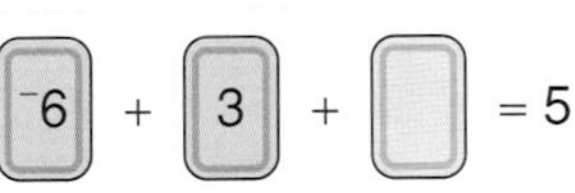

b Choose a card to give the lowest possible total.
What is this total?

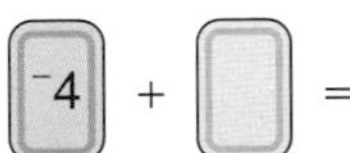

T

***6** Use a copy of this.
The numbers in the squares add to the number in the circle between them.
a Find the numbers in the circles, A, B, C, D and E.
b What is the total of the numbers in the circles?
c What is the total of the numbers in the squares?
d Subtract the total of the squares from the total of the circles.

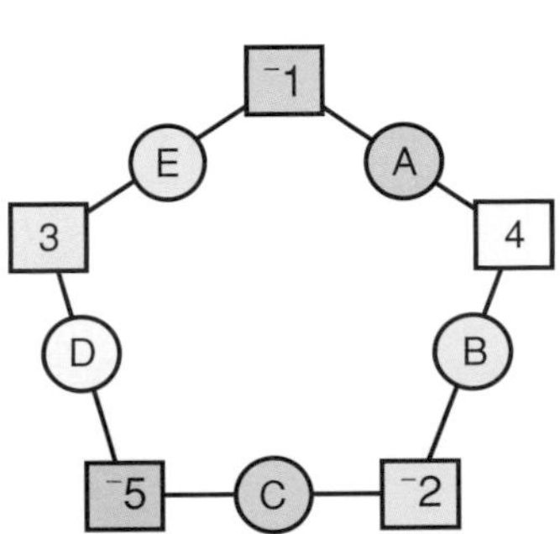

Puzzle

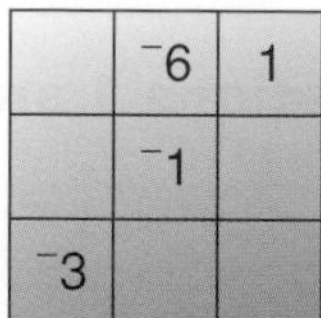

	-6	1
	-1	
-3		

Use a copy of this magic square.

Remember Each row, each column and each diagonal must add to the same number.

a What does the diagonal 1, -1, -3 add up to?
b Complete the magic square.

Double dice – a game for 2 players

You will need a blue dice and a white dice, the board below and different coloured counters for each player.

To play
- Take turns to throw the dice.
- Subtract the number on the blue dice from the number on the white dice.
- Put a counter on the answer on the board. If the other player has a counter on the answer already, you can take it off and put your counter on.
- The winner is the first person to get 3 counters in a row.

Examples

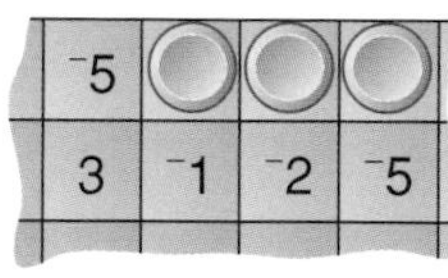

4	0	-4	-5	5	5	2	3	-4	-1	1
2	1	4	3	-1	-2	-5	-3	4	-2	5
-3	-1	0	-5	-3	-4	2	1	0	3	-2

Divisibility

Remember

A number is **divisible by 2** if it is an even number.

A number is **divisible by 3** if the sum of its digits is divisible by 3.
Example 261 is divisible by 3 since $2 + 6 + 1 = 9$ and 9 is divisible by 3.

A number is **divisible by 4** if the last two digits are divisible by 4.
Example 436 is divisible by 4 since 36 is divisible by 4.

A number is **divisible by 5** if its last digit is 0 or 5.

A number is **divisible by 9** if the sum of its digits is divisible by 9.
Example 648 is divisible by 9 since $6 + 4 + 8 = 18$ and 18 is divisible by 9.

A number is **divisible by 10** if the last digit is 0.

A number is **divisible by 6** if it is divisible by both 2 and 3.
Example 456 is divisible by 2 since it is an even number.
456 is divisible by 3 since $4 + 5 + 6 = 15$ and 15 is divisible by 3.
So 456 is divisible by 6.

A number is **divisible by 8** if half of it is divisible by 4.
Example Half of $432 = 216$.
216 is divisible by 4 so 432 os divisible by 8.

Exercise 4

T

1 Use a copy of this table.

80	19	105	162	54
96	94	136	211	635
39	116	102	164	104
87	77	65	76	321
370	121	432	53	126
114	91	111	42	215

Shade the squares with numbers that are
a divisible by 5
b divisible by 3
c divisible by 8.
What number does the shading give?

2 **a** Which two of 84, 92, 162 and 432 are divisible by both 3 and 4?
b Which of 108, 161, 234 and 342 are divisible by both 2 and 9?

3 Which of 116, 125, 143, 216, 224 and 360 are divisible by
a 2 **b** 3 **c** 4 **d** 5 **e** 6 **f** 8 **g** 9 **h** 10?

*__4__ Choose a number from 168, 174, 177, 200, 388, 418, 423 for each gap.
Use each number only once.
a ___ is divisible by 2. **b** ___ is divisible by 3. **c** ___ is divisible by 4.
d ___ is divisible by 5. **e** ___ is divisible by 6. **f** ___ is divisible by 8.
g ___ is divisible by 9.

Investigation

Divisibility by 4

The sum of four even numbers is divisible by 4.
When is this true? When is it false? **Investigate**.

To help you answer this:
Choose four even numbers.
Work out **how many** of these numbers are divisible by 4.
Find their sum.
Work out if this sum is divisible by 4.
Repeat this again and again.

Hint: If just one of the numbers is divisible by 4 then the total isn't.

Multiples and Lowest Common Multiple

Remember
The numbers 4, 20, 28 and 36 are all multiples of 4 because they are all divisible by 4.

To find the **multiples** of a number we multiply by 1, 2, 3, 4, 5, 6, ...
All the multiples of 4 are divisible by 4.

Example The multiples of 6 are 6, 12, 18, **24**, 30, 36, 42, 48, ... $1 \times 6 = 6$, $2 \times 6 = 12$, ...

The multiples of 8 are 8, 16, **24**, 32, 40, 48, 56, ... $1 \times 8 = 8$, $2 \times 8 = 16$, ...

24 is the smallest multiple of both 6 and 8.

24 is called the **Lowest Common Multiple (LCM)** of 6 and 8.
It is the smallest number that is a multiple of both 6 and 8.

Exercise 5

1 a Write down the first ten multiples of 3.
  b Write down the first ten multiples of 4.
  c What is the Lowest Common Multiple of 3 and 4?

2 Find the LCM of these.

a 2 and 5	b 3 and 8	c 3 and 7	d 7 and 10	e 4 and 5
f 4 and 6	g 6 and 5	h 6 and 9	i 8 and 10	

3 Use a copy of this.
  a Shade all the multiples of 4.
    Shade all the multiples of 7.
    Which letter have you made?
  *b Which number in the grid is the LCM of 4 and 7?

37	24	59	21	27
34	49	54	42	45
13	32	56	14	61
18	36	26	63	47
57	28	38	35	43

Prime numbers

Remember

A **prime number** is divisible by only two numbers. These are itself and 1.

1 is not a prime number.

Example 13 can only be divided by 13 and 1.
13 is a prime number.

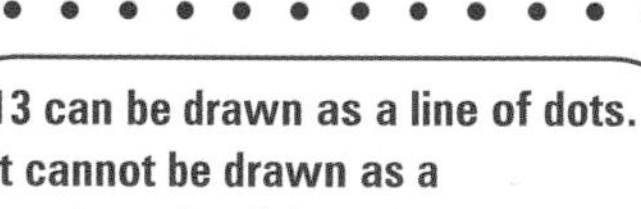

13 can be drawn as a line of dots. It cannot be drawn as a **rectangle** of dots.

The **prime numbers less than 30** are 2, 3, 5, 7, 11, 13, 17, 19, 23 and 29.

To **test if a number is prime**, try to divide it by each of the prime numbers in turn.

Example To test if 149 is prime, try dividing it by 2, 3, 5, 7 and 11.

Exercise 6

Except for question 3.

1 For which of these numbers can you only draw a rectangle of dots that is just a straight line?

5 7 9 12 13 17 19 21 23 27 29

2 In each list there is one number which is not prime. Which number?
  a 1, 2, 3, 5, 7 b 2, 3, 5, 9, 11 c 7, 11, 13, 27
  d 2, 5, 11, 21, 23 e 7, 11, 17, 23, 25, 29

3 Test whether these numbers are prime.

a 33	**b** 41	**c** 45
d 47	**e** 63	**f** 81

Investigation

Primes

1 a $6 = 1 + 5$

6 is an even number.
1 and 5 are prime numbers.
Investigate to see if other even numbers bigger than 4 are the sum of two prime numbers.

b 6 is double 3.
5 is a prime number between 6 and 3.
Investigate to see if there is a prime number between every number from 3 to 50 and its double.

2 $2 = 5 - 3$
$3 = 5 - 2$
$4 = 7 - 3$
$5 = 7 - 2$

List of prime numbers

2	3	5	7	11	13	17
19	23	29	31	37	41	43
47	53	59	61	67	71	73
79	83	89	97			

2, 3, 4 and 5 are whole numbers.
Each of them has been made by finding the difference between two prime numbers.
Try and make the numbers 6, 7, 8, 9, 10 and 11 by finding the difference between two prime numbers.
Use the list of prime numbers to help you.
Try and make more whole numbers by subtracting two primes.

Puzzle

1 I am a prime number.
I have 2 digits.
My digits add to 10.
What number might I be?

There are 3 possible answers to question 1.

2 I am a prime number less than 50.
The number after me is a multiple of 8.
The number before me is a multiple of 10.
What number am I?

Highest Common Factor

Remember
The **factors** of 8 are 1, 2, 4 and 8. 8 is divisible by each of these factors.
A **factor** divides exactly into the given number.

A factor that is a prime number is a **prime factor**.

Worked Example
What is the Highest Common Factor (HCF) of 18 and 42?

Answer
The factors of 18 are 1, **2**, 3, 6, 18.
The factors of 42 are 1, **2**, 3, 6, 7, 14, 21, 42.
The **common factors** of 18 and 42 are 1, 2, 3 and 6.
The Highest Common Factor is 6.

6 is called the **Highest Common Factor (HCF)** of 18 and 42.

Exercise 7

T

1 Use a copy of this diagram. Colour all the parts with
- **a** factors of 15
- **b** factors of 28
- **c** multiples of 9.

Which number is not coloured?

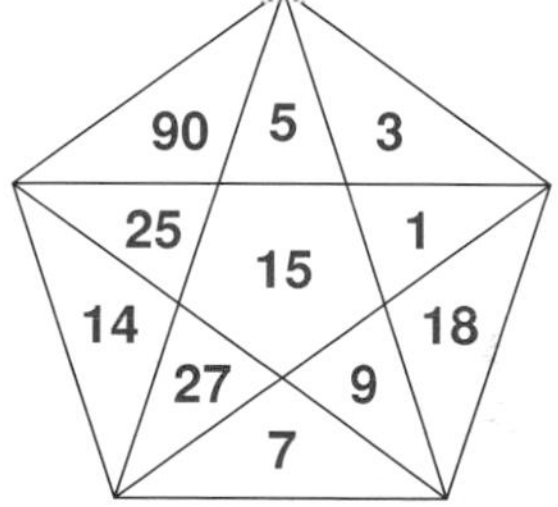

2 **a** What are the factors of 12?
- **b** Write down the prime factors of 12.
- **c** Write down the prime factors of 30.

3 **a** Write down the factors of 8.
- **b** Write down the factors of 20.
- **c** 2 is a common factor of 8 and 20.
  Write down all the other common factors of 8 and 20.
- **d** What is the Highest Common Factor of 8 and 20?

4 **a** Write down the factors of 16.
- **b** Write down the factors of 40.
- **c** 4 is a common factor of 16 and 40.
  Write down all the other common factors of 16 and 40.
- **d** What is the Highest Common Factor of 16 and 40?

5 Find the HCF of these.
a 6 and 10 **b** 16 and 36 **c** 40 and 25 **d** 6 and 18

*6 a What is the HCF of 20 and 36?
b Copy and complete $\frac{20}{36} = \frac{4 \times 5}{4 \times \_\_}$.
c Use **b** to write $\frac{20}{36}$ in its lowest terms.

This is called cancelling. There is more about cancelling on page 100.

Puzzle

I am a factor of 24.
I am a factor of 56.
I am greater than the third smallest prime number.
What number am I?

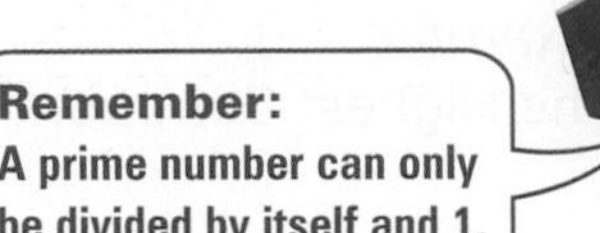

Remember:
A prime number can only be divided by itself and 1.

Triangular numbers

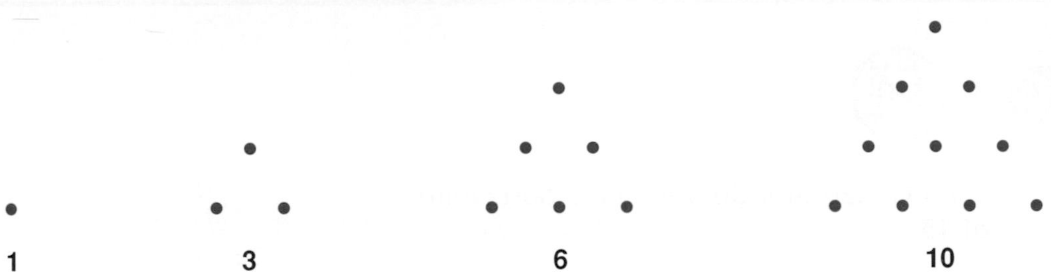

1, 3, 6, 10 are **triangular numbers**.

Exercise 8

You could use triangular dotty paper.

1 1, 3, 6, 10 are the first four triangular numbers.
Draw the next triangle in the pattern shown in the screen above.
What is the next triangular number after 10?

2

1 3 6 10

1 + 2 = 3 1 + 2 + 3 = 6 1 + 2 + 3 + 4 = 10

Continue this pattern to find the next three triangular numbers.

*3 1 ＼ 2 ／ 3 ＼ 3 ／ 6 ＼ 4 ／ 10 ＼ 5 ／ 15

$3 - 1 = 2$
$6 - 3 = 3$
$10 - 6 = 4$
$15 - 10 = 5$

The difference between 15 and the next triangular number will be **6**.

$15 + \mathbf{6} = 21$

The next triangular number must be 21.
Continue this pattern to show that 28, 36, 45 and 55 are triangular numbers.

*4 Some triangular numbers can be written as the sum of two other triangular numbers.
Find the three smallest triangular numbers that can be written like this.

Practical

Begin with 2 students
then 3 students
then 4 students
then 5 students
and so on.

Count the number of handshakes if every student shakes hands with every other student.
Put your answers in a table like this.

Number of students	Number of handshakes
2	1
3	
4	
5	
⋮	

What do you notice about the numbers you get?

Square numbers

Remember
When we multiply a number by itself the answer is a **square number**.

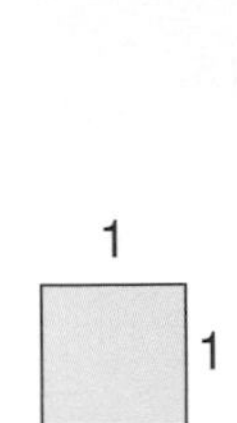

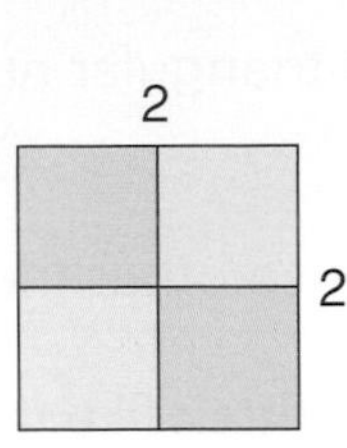

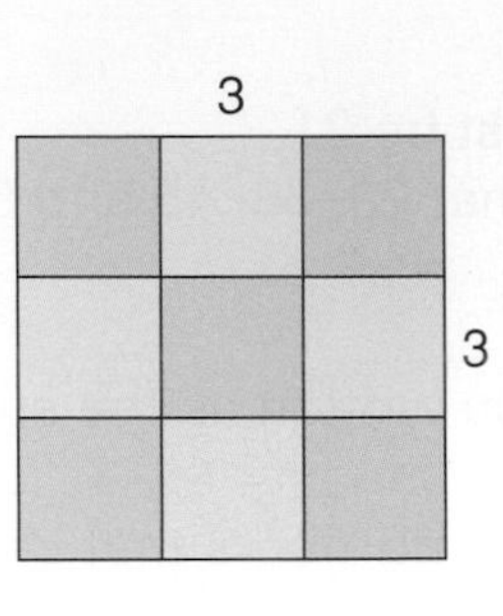

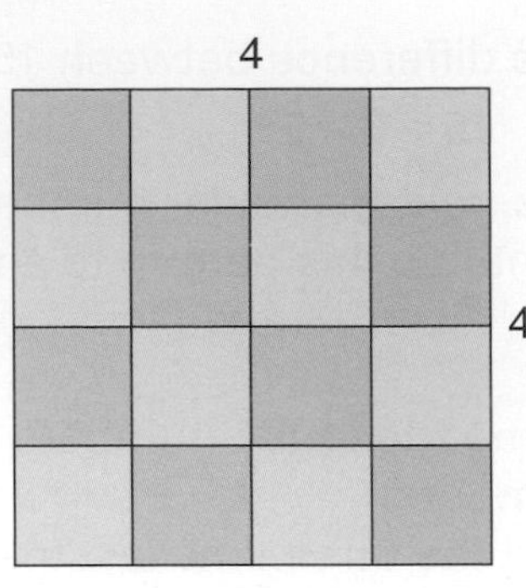

$1 \times 1 = 1$ $2 \times 2 = 4$ $3 \times 3 = 9$ $4 \times 4 = 16$

The first twelve square numbers are shown in bold.

$1 \times 1 =$ **1** $2 \times 2 =$ **4** $3 \times 3 =$ **9** $4 \times 4 =$ **16** $5 \times 5 =$ **25** $6 \times 6 =$ **36**
$7 \times 7 =$ **49** $8 \times 8 =$ **64** $9 \times 9 =$ **81** $10 \times 10 =$ **100** $11 \times 11 =$ **121** $12 \times 12 =$ **144**

We write 3×3 as 3^2.
We read 5^2 as '5 squared'. $5^2 = 5 \times 5 = 25$

Exercise 9

T

1 Use a copy of this.
Shade all the square numbers.
What letter have you made?

24	49	64	100	42
84	144	82	60	82
2	16	36	54	18
66	1	120	38	77
90	121	131	6	96

2 Pick out the square number in each list.
a 5, 12, 16, 24, 30
b 2, 8, 15, 25, 33
c 1, 11, 22, 66, 83
d 28, 36, 48, 53, 60
e 48, 53, 64, 72, 80
f 38, 55, 85, 99, 100

3 Find the answers to these.
a 8^2 **b** 3^2 **c** 4^2 **d** 6^2 **e** 7^2
f 12^2 **g** 10^2 **h** 9^2 **i** 11^2

***4** Calculate mentally.
a $3^2 + 6$ **b** $5^2 + 7$ **c** $4^2 + 9$ **d** $(2 + 4)^2$
e $(3 + 4)^2$ **f** $3^2 + 2^2$ **g** $6^2 + 8^2$ **h** $8^2 - 9$
i $6^2 - 11$ **j** $10^2 - 5^2$ **k** $9^2 - 4^2$

In **d** and **e** work out the bracket first.

Investigation

Square patterns

$1 = 1$

$1 + 3 = 4$ adding the first two odd numbers

$1 + 3 + 5 = 9$ adding the first three odd numbers

$1 + 3 + 5 + 7 = 16$ adding the first four odd numbers

1, 4, 9 and 16 are all square numbers.

Does adding the first **five** odd numbers also give you a square number?

Does adding the first **six** odd numbers also give you a square number?

Does this pattern carry on?

Square roots

The answer to 'What number squared gives 9?' is 3.
3 is called the **square root** of 9.
The sign for a square root is $\sqrt{\ }$.
$\sqrt{9}$ means 'the square root of 9'. The answer is 3.

Squaring and finding the square root are inverse operations. One 'undoes' the other.

Example $3^2 = 9$ and $\sqrt{9} = 3$.

3 → square → 9

3 ← square root ← 9

Exercise 10

T **1** Use a copy of this table.
Fill it in.

$\sqrt{1}$	$\sqrt{4}$	$\sqrt{9}$	$\sqrt{16}$	$\sqrt{25}$	$\sqrt{36}$	$\sqrt{49}$	$\sqrt{64}$	$\sqrt{81}$	$\sqrt{100}$	$\sqrt{121}$	$\sqrt{144}$
1	2										

2 **a** The square root of 36 is ___.
b 4 is the square root of ___.
c The square root of ___ is 7.
d ___ is the square root of 9.
e 12 is the square root of ___.
f ___ is the square root of 1.
g The square root of 100 is ___.
h 5 is the square root of ___.
i ___ is the square root of 4.

3 **a** $4^2 = 16$ and $\sqrt{16} =$ ___
b $5^2 =$ ___ and $\sqrt{25} = 5$
c $3^2 =$ ___ and $\sqrt{9} = 3$
d $7^2 = 49$ and ___ $= 7$
e $6^2 = 36$ and ___ $= 6$
f ___ $= 81$ and $\sqrt{81} = 9$
g ___ $= 1$ and $\sqrt{1} = 1$
h $8^2 = 64$ and ___ $= 8$
i $10^2 = 100$ and $\sqrt{100} =$ ___
j $2^2 = 4$ and $\sqrt{4} =$ ___

***4** Calculate mentally.
a $\sqrt{1+3}$ **b** $\sqrt{4+5}$ **c** $\sqrt{9+7}$ **d** $\sqrt{24+12}$ **e** $\sqrt{20-4^2}$

***5** Which is bigger, the square root of the sum of 9 and 16 or the sum of the square roots of 9 and 16?

Calculator squares and square roots

Squares on a calculator

To find 7^2 **Key** [7] [x^2] [=] to get 49.

To find $6{\cdot}3^2$ **Key** [6] [·] [3] [x^2] [=] to get 39·69.

Square roots on a calculator

To find $\sqrt{5{\cdot}29}$ **Key** [√] [5] [·] [2] [9] [=] to get 2·3.

To find $\sqrt{29}$ **Key** [√] [2] [9] [=] to get 5.385164807

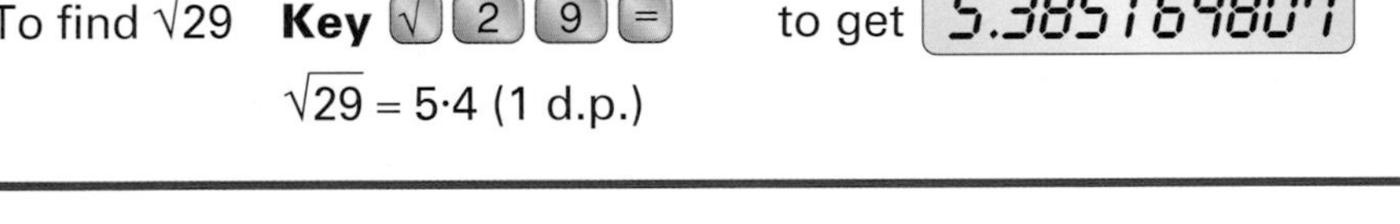

$\sqrt{29} = 5{\cdot}4$ (1 d.p.)

Exercise 11

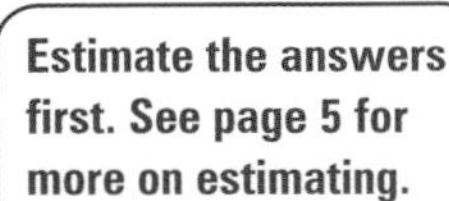

Estimate the answers first. See page 5 for more on estimating.

1 Calculate these.
a 11^2 **b** 5^2 **c** 18^2 **d** 24^2
e 87^2 **f** 113^2 **g** $7{\cdot}9^2$ **h** $9{\cdot}3^2$

2 Calculate these.
a $\sqrt{196}$ **b** $\sqrt{484}$ **c** $\sqrt{1156}$ **d** $\sqrt{2{\cdot}25}$
e $\sqrt{21{\cdot}16}$ **f** $\sqrt{62{\cdot}41}$ **g** $\sqrt{0{\cdot}16}$ **h** $\sqrt{0{\cdot}04}$

3 Give the answers to these to 1 d.p.
a $\sqrt{54}$ **b** $\sqrt{94}$ **c** $\sqrt{104}$ **d** $\sqrt{964}$

***4** Give the answer to these to the nearest tenth.

a $\sqrt{19}$ **b** $\sqrt{27}$ **c** $\sqrt{71{\cdot}4}$ **d** $\sqrt{92{\cdot}8}$

***5** $1^2 = 1$

$11^2 = 121$

$111^2 = 12321$

a Use your calculator to find the next line of this pattern.

b Without using your calculator, write down the answers to 11111^2 and 111111^2.

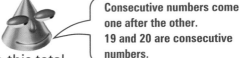

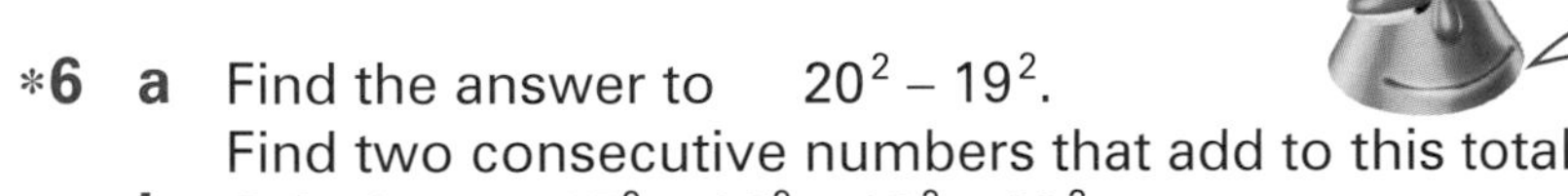

Consecutive numbers come one after the other.
19 and 20 are consecutive numbers.

***6** **a** Find the answer to $20^2 - 19^2$.
Find two consecutive numbers that add to this total.

b Calculate $15^2 - 14^2 + 13^2 - 12^2$.
Find four consecutive numbers that add to this total.

c Which four consecutive numbers do you think add to the answer to $32^2 - 31^2 + 30^2 - 29^2$?

d What about $66^2 - 65^2 + 64^2 - 63^2$?

Summary of key points

The numbers ... $^{-}3$, $^{-}2$, $^{-}1$, 0, 1, 2, 3, 4, ... are the **integers**.

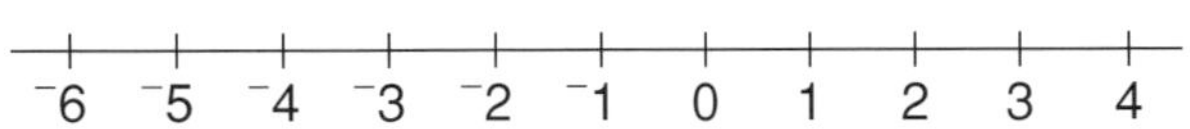

On the number line the further to the left an integer is the smaller it is.

Example $^{-}5 < {}^{-}3$

We can **add and subtract integers** using a number line.

To **add a positive integer**, we move **to the right**.

$^{-}2 + 4 = 2$

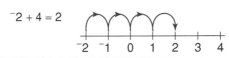

To **add a negative integer**, we move **to the left**.

$3 + {}^{-}5 = {}^{-}2$

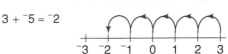

To **subtract a positive integer**, we move **to the left**.

$3 - 4 = {}^{-}1$

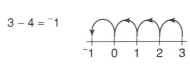

To **subtract a negative integer**, we move **to the right**.

$^{-}4 - {}^{-}1 = {}^{-}3$

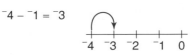

A number is **divisible by 6** if it is divisible by both 2 and 3.

A number is **divisible by 8** if half of it is divisible by 4.

The **Lowest Common Multiple (LCM)** of 4 and 5 is the smallest number that is a multiple of both 4 and 5.

The multiples of 4 are 4, 8, 12, 16, **20**, 24, ...

The multiples of 5 are 5, 10, 15, **20**, 25, ...

20 is the Lowest Common Multiple of 4 and 5.

Prime numbers are only divisible by themselves and 1.
1 is not a prime number.
The prime numbers less than 30 are 2, 3, 5, 7, 11, 13, 17, 19, 23 and 29.
You need to know these.

We can use divisibility tests to test if other numbers are prime.

The **Highest Common Factor (HCF)** of two numbers is the largest number that is a factor of both the numbers.

Example The factors of 18 are 1, 2, 3, 6, **9**, 18.
The factors of 27 are 1, 3, **9**, 27.
9 is the Highest Common Factor of 18 and 27.

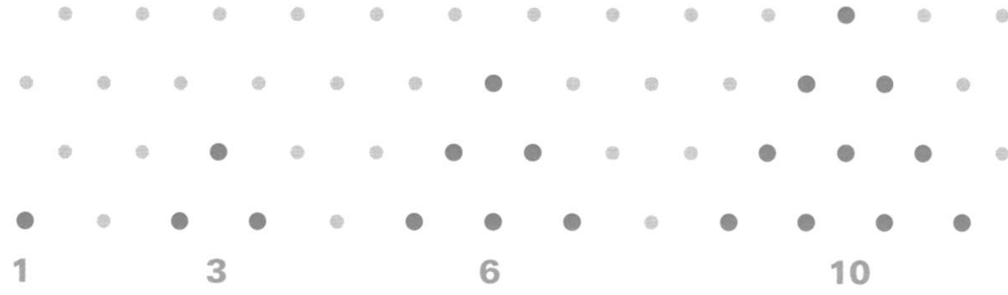

The first four **triangular numbers** are 1, 3, 6 and 10.

8×8 can be written as 8^2 and is said as '8 **squared**'. $8^2 = 64$
8 is the **square root** of 64 and is written as $\sqrt{64} = 8$.
Squaring and finding the square root are **inverse operations**.

To **square a number** using a **calculator** use the x^2 key.

Example $5{\cdot}1^2$ is keyed as 5 · 1 x^2 = to get 26·01.

To find the **square root** of a number using a **calculator** use the √ key.

Examples $\sqrt{324}$ is keyed as √ 3 2 4 = to get 18.
$\sqrt{56}$ is keyed as √ 5 6 = to get 7·483314774 = 7·5 (1 d.p.).

Test yourself

Except for questions 8, 15 and 16.

1 3 $^-1$ $^-4$ 0 1 $^-6$
Put these integers in order from smallest to largest.

Use a number line.

A

2 The noon temperature at Bristol was $^-2$ °C.
The midnight temperature was $^-8$ °C.
a Which temperature was colder?
b What is the difference between these temperatures?

A B

3 Use the number line to help you answer these.

$^-10$ $^-5$ 0 5 10

a $2 + 3$ **b** $^-4 + 2$ **c** $5 + {}^-2$ **d** $3 + {}^-4$
e $^-2 + {}^-4$ **f** $^-1 + {}^-5$

A

4

$^-4$	2
3	$^-1$

Both counters might land on the same square.

Two counters are dropped onto this board.
The numbers are added to get the score.
Write down all the possible scores.

B

5 Which of 75, 150, 188, 220, 235, 240, 336 and 522 are divisible by
a 5 **b** 3 **c** 4 **d** 10 **e** 2 **f** 6 **g** 8 **h** 9

C

6 Find the LCM of these.
a 2 and 9 **b** 4 and 7 **c** 3 and 5 **d** 4 and 10

D

7 Write down all the prime numbers between 8 and 24.

E

8 Test whether these numbers are prime.
a 36 **b** 37 **c** 49 **d** 67

E

9 Two prime numbers are added.
The answer is 24.
What could the numbers be?

Find all the possible answers.

E

T

10 Use a copy of this grid.
Shade
a the prime numbers
b the numbers that have 3 as a factor
c the factors of 56
d the multiples of 7.
What shape does the shading make?

65	100	76	82	92	44
87	29	15	8	42	99
35	6	28	60	11	56
300	21	17	7	30	33
77	4	1	63	72	14
110	55	74	40	200	76

11 Find the HCF of these.
a 16 and 24 **b** 20 and 45.

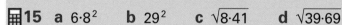

12

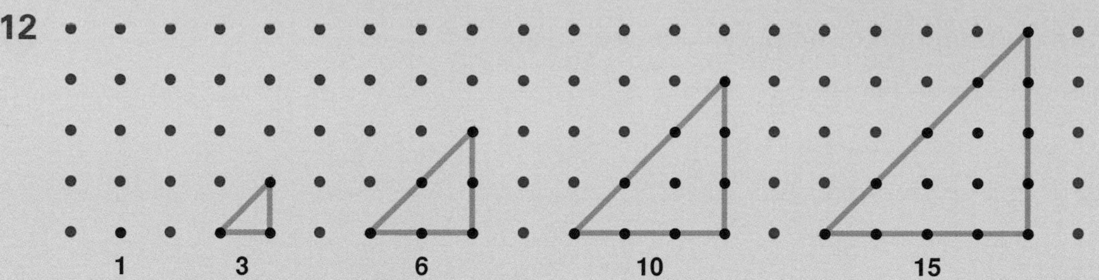

The first 5 triangular numbers can be shown like this.
Draw the next triangle in this pattern.
What is the next triangular number after 15?

13 **a** ___ squared is 64.
b 25 is the square of ___.
c The square root of 81 is ___ .
d 4 is the square root of ___.
e The square root of 9 is ___.
f The square root of ___ is 6.

14 **a** 4^2 **b** $\sqrt{100}$ **c** 7^2 **d** $\sqrt{49}$

15 **a** $6{\cdot}8^2$ **b** 29^2 **c** $\sqrt{8{\cdot}41}$ **d** $\sqrt{39{\cdot}69}$

16 Give the answers to 1 decimal place.
a $\sqrt{21}$ **b** $\sqrt{33}$ **c** $\sqrt{109}$

3 Mental Calculation

You need to know

Key vocabulary

approximately, compensation, complements, difference, double, estimate, factor, operation, order of operations, partition, product

A star is born

You can use these two charts to work out the day of the week someone was born.

Month	Jan	Jan (leap yr)	Feb	Feb (leap yr)	Mar	Apr	May	Jun	Jul	Aug	Sep	Oct	Nov	Dec
Month number	8	7	11	10	11	7	9	5	7	10	6	8	11	6

Remainder	0	1	2	3	4	5	6
Day	Saturday	Sunday	Monday	Tuesday	Wednesday	Thursday	Friday

Follow these steps: *Example* **Robbie Williams 13 February 1974**

Step 1 Write down the last two digits of the year the person was born. **74**
Step 2 Divide this number by 4 (ignore the remainder). **18**
Step 3 Write down the number for the day the person was born. **13**
Step 4 Write down the number for the month the person was born. Use the chart above. **11**
Step 5 Add up the numbers you wrote for steps 1–4.
74 + 18 + 13 + 11 = 116
Step 6 Divide the answer to step 5 by 7. **116 ÷ 7 = 70 ÷ 7 + 46 ÷ 7 = 10 + 6 R 4**
= 16 R 4
Step 7 Write down the remainder. **4**
Step 8 Find the day using the chart above. **Wednesday**

This method only works for birthdays in the 1900s.

Robbie Williams was born on a Wednesday.

Find what day some other people were born. Try these:

Michael Jackson 29 August 1958
Steven Spielberg 18 December 1947

Work them out mentally. Use jottings if you need to.

Adding and subtracting whole numbers

Here are some ways to **add and subtract mentally**.

Mentally means 'in your head'. These boxes explain ways you could do it.

Example 417 + 388

417 + 388 = 400 + 10 + 7 + 300 + 80 + 8 = 400 + 300 + 10 + 80 + 7 + 8 = 700 + 90 + 15 = 790 + 15 = **805**	417 + 388 = 400 + 400 + 17 − 12 = 800 + 17 − 12 = 817 − 12 = **805**	417 + 388 = 420 + 390 − 3 − 2 = 810 − 3 − 2 = **805**
Partitioning	**Nearly doubles**	**Nearly numbers**

Example 605 − 293

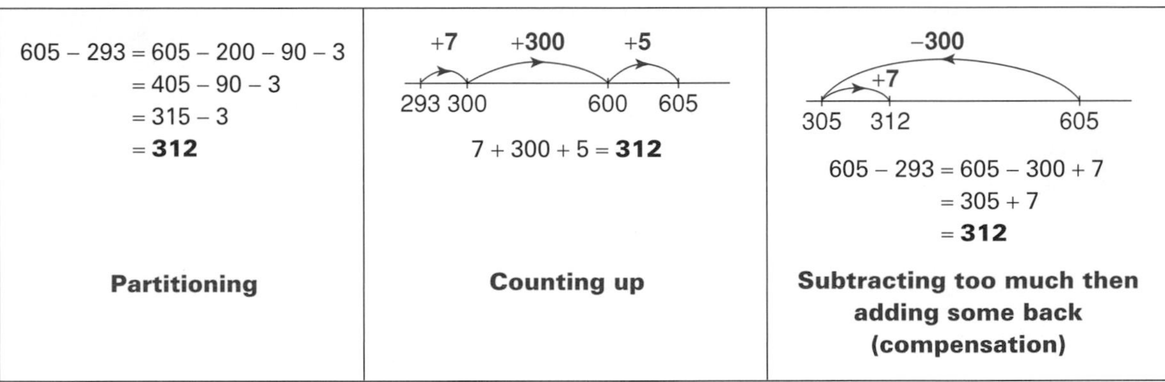

605 − 293 = 605 − 200 − 90 − 3 = 405 − 90 − 3 = 315 − 3 = **312**	+7 +300 +5 293 300 600 605 7 + 300 + 5 = **312**	−300 +7 305 312 605 605 − 293 = 605 − 300 + 7 = 305 + 7 = **312**
Partitioning	**Counting up**	**Subtracting too much then adding some back (compensation)**

Look for **complements**.

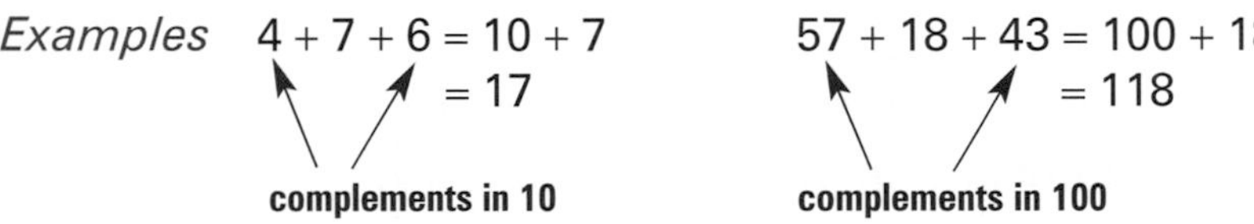

Examples 4 + 7 + 6 = 10 + 7
= 17

57 + 18 + 43 = 100 + 18
= 118

Exercise 1

This exercise is to be done mentally.

1 **a** 3 + 8 + 12 **b** 7 + 12 + 18 **c** 14 − 7 + 6 − 2
d 18 − 6 + 12 − 13 + 8 **e** 13 + 12 − 8 + 16 − 15

2 **a** 50 + 20 − 10 **b** 80 − 20 − 10 **c** 80 + 40 − 40 **d** 100 − 60 + 40
e 60 + 50 − 30 **f** 160 − 50 **g** 130 + 70 + 40

3 **a** 36 + 20 **b** 86 − 30 **c** 57 + 48 **d** 93 − 54 **e** 37 + 89
f 36 + 23 **g** 89 − 35 **h** 58 − 33 **i** 96 − 8 **j** 86 − 19

T

4 Use a copy of this magic square.
Fill it in.

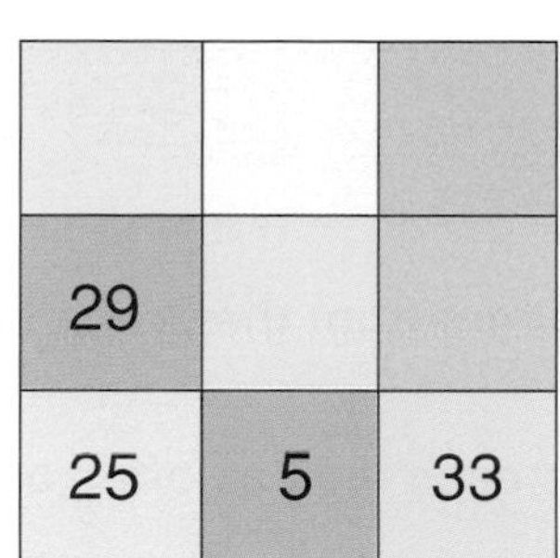

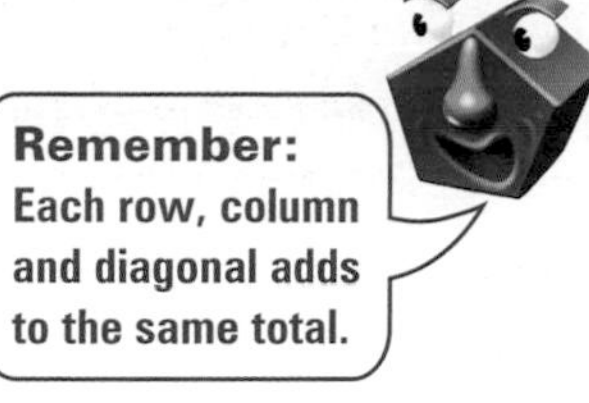

Remember:
Each row, column and diagonal adds to the same total.

You may need to use jottings for some of these.

5 **a** 543 + 57 **b** 486 + 23 **c** 196 − 23 **d** 388 − 36
e 285 − 32 **f** 293 − 57 **g** 597 − 79 **h** 894 + 27

6 **a** 520 − 360 **b** 830 − 470 **c** 740 + 470 **d** 840 − 390
e 925 − 402 **f** 586 + 278 **g** 350 − 289 **h** 630 − 376
i 327 + 366 ∗**j** 1064 + 2387 ∗**k** 7013 − 4875 ∗**l** 5860 + 3429

7 **a** Find the sum of 86 and 47.
b Find the difference between 94 and 68.
c Increase 146 by 77.
d Decrease 184 by 57.

8

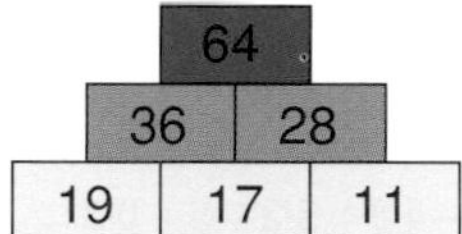

In this pyramid, to get each number we added the two numbers below it.

Find the number that goes in the red square.

a

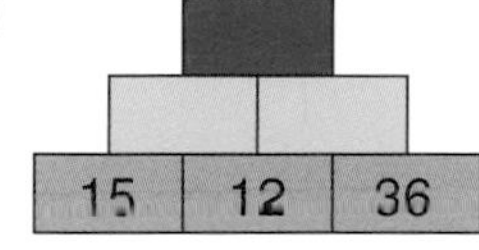

b

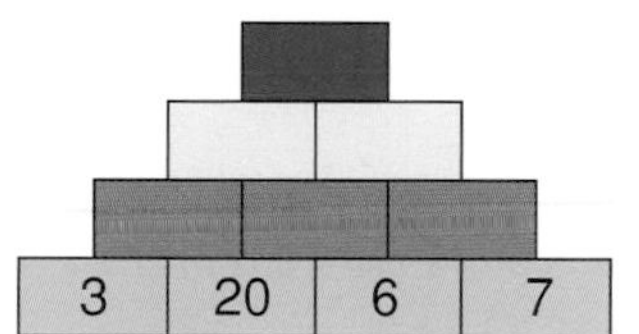

c

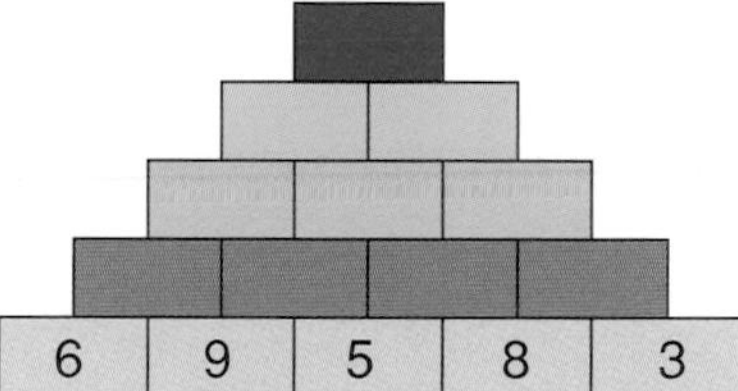

∗**9** **a** Three consecutive numbers add to 81.
What are they?
b 7, 9, 11, 13 are four consecutive odd numbers.
Find four consecutive odd numbers which add to 80.
c Is it possible to find four consecutive odd numbers which add to 511?
Explain your answer.

Consecutive numbers come one after the other.

Puzzle

Choose numbers from the green box to make these true.

You may use each digit as often as you like.

a ☐☐ + ☐☐ = 114 **b** ☐☐ + ☐☐ = 90 **c** ☐☐ + ☐☐ = 172

Note There is more than one answer for each.

Adding and subtracting decimals

Here are some ways to **add and subtract decimals mentally**.

Example 5·2 + 4·8

5·2 + 4·8 = 5 + 0·2 + 4 + 0·8 = 5 + 4 + 0·2 + 0·8 = 9 + 1 = **10** **Partitioning**	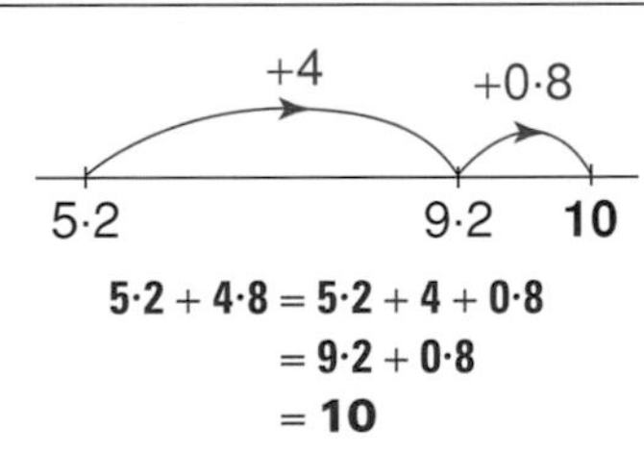 **5·2 + 4·8 = 5·2 + 4 + 0·8** **= 9·2 + 0·8** **= 10** **Counting up**	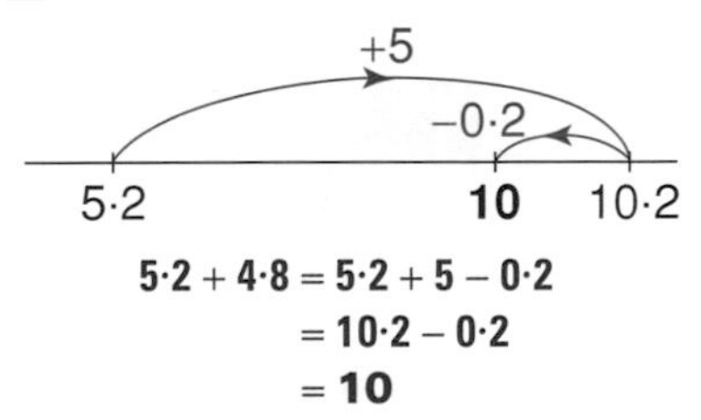 **5·2 + 4·8 = 5·2 + 5 − 0·2** **= 10·2 − 0·2** **= 10** **Adding too much then taking some away (compensation)**

You could also add these using **nearly numbers**.

5·2 + 4·8 = 5 + 5 − 0·2 + 0·2 **5·2 is nearly 5 and 4·8 is nearly 5**
= **10**

Example 14·4 − 7·6

14·4 − 7·6 = 14·4 − 7 − 0·6 = 7·4 − 0·6 = 7·4 − 0·4 − 0·2 = 7 − 0·2 = **6·8** **Partitioning**	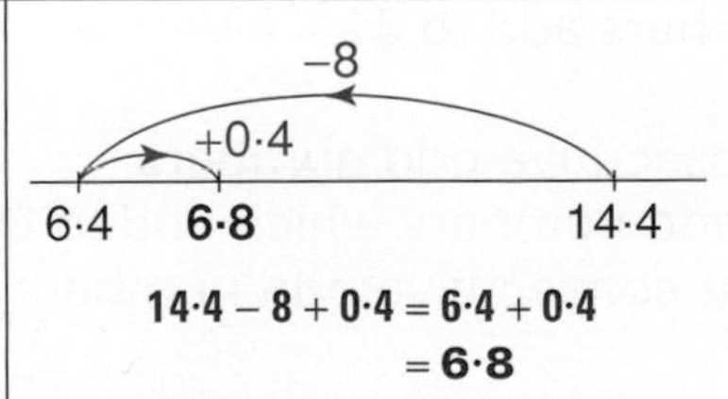 **14·4 − 8 + 0·4 = 6·4 + 0·4** **= 6·8** **Subtracting too much then adding some back**	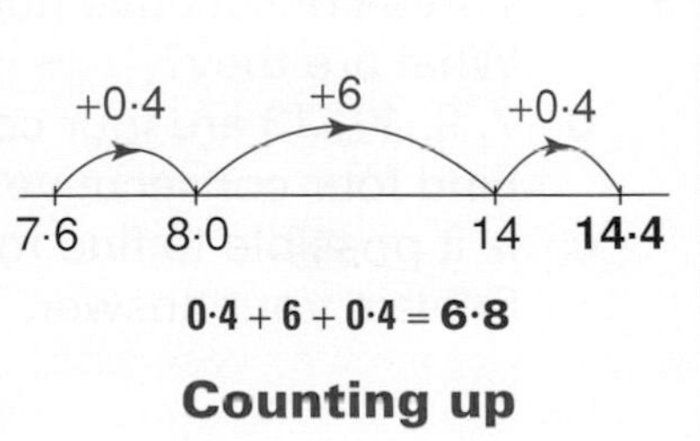 **0·4 + 6 + 0·4 = 6·8** **Counting up**

Exercise 2

This exercise is to be done mentally.

Remember to look for complements.

1 **a** 0·7 + 0·8 **b** 0·9 + 0·8 **c** 1·3 + 0·4 **d** 2·9 + 0·8
e 0·7 + 1·3 **f** 2·8 + 2·9 **g** 0·41 + 0·57 ***h** 0·97 + 0·68

2 **a** 0·8 – 0·5 **b** 0·9 – 0·4 **c** 1·8 – 0·9 **d** 1·3 – 0·7
e 5·6 – 3·2 **f** 3·9 – 1·5 **g** 9·4 – 2·8 **h** 7·3 – 3·8
i 3 – 0·7 **j** 7 – 5·2 ***k** 0·78 – 0·39 ***l** 0·65 – 0·36

3 What goes in the box?
a 8·6 + ☐ = 10 **b** 3·7 + ☐ = 11 **c** 5·4 + ☐ = 12 **d** 7·8 + ☐ = 14
e 12·2 + ☐ = 20 ***f** ☐ + 14·7 = 25 ***g** ☐ + 16·4 = 24 ***h** 17·8 + ☐ = 36

4 What is the answer to 10·2 – 6·8?

T

5

		R							R	
2·6	15·8	7·7	13·3	0·8	13·3	21·4	19·5	7·7	13·3	
20·2	4·1	13·3	21·4	19·5	10·5	13·3	21·4	9·3	7·9	13·3

	R					R		
14·5	7·7	2·6	10·5	3·5	9·3	7·7	20·2	4·1

Use a copy of this box.
Find the answer to these.
Write the letter beside the question above its answer in the box.

R 6·3 + 1·4 = 7·7 **U** 8·6 + 7·2 **A** 15·3 + 4·2 **H** 8·3 – 4·2
Y 6·3 – 5·5 **S** 17·8 + 3·6 **I** 6·4 + 2·9 **O** 8·3 – 5·7
T 16·4 + 3·8 **F** 11·9 + 2·6 **Z** 12·8 – 4·9 **M** 18·1 – 7·6
B 5·0 – 1·5 **E** 16·0 – 2·7

You may need to use jottings for some of these.

***6** Find ways to fill in each box with one digit to make these true.

a ☐·☐ + ☐·☐ = 14·6 **b** ☐·☐ – ☐·☐ = 1·3

Investigation

Highest Total

Start at the top.
You must move to a triangle that touches the side of the one you are in.
You can only go to a triangle once.

Example

If you are in this triangle you can only move to one of the blue triangles.

Start

1·3
1·2
1·0 2·3
1·8 2·9
2·4 1·3 3·2
2·8 2·1 1·0
1·6 3·2 1·7 3·5

Investigate to find the path to a red triangle which has the highest total.

Note Once you have reached a red triangle you must stop.

Multiplying and dividing whole numbers

Here are **some ways to multiply mentally**.

Example 21×9

$$\begin{aligned} 21 \times 9 &= 21 \times 3 \times 3 && \text{using factors} \\ &= 63 \times 3 \\ &= (60 \times 3) + (3 \times 3) && \text{partitioning 63} \\ &= 180 + 9 \\ &= \mathbf{189} \end{aligned}$$

We can multiply in any order.

Example 15×12

Partitioning	Using factors	Doubling one number and halving the other
$15 \times 12 = 15 \times (10 + 2)$ $= (15 \times 10) + (15 \times 2)$ $= 150 + 30$ $= \mathbf{180}$ **or** $15 \times 12 = (10 + 5) \times 12$ $= (10 \times 12) + (5 \times 12)$ $= 120 + 60$ $= \mathbf{180}$	$15 \times 12 = 3 \times 5 \times 4 \times 3$ $= 3 \times 20 \times 3$ $= 60 \times 3$ $= \mathbf{180}$ **or** $15 \times 12 = 15 \times 2 \times 6$ $= 30 \times 6$ $= \mathbf{180}$	$15 \times 12 = 30 \times 6$ $= 180$ **Double 15 is 30** **Half of 12 is 6**

Discussion

Marcy multiplied 38×5 and 18×25 like this.
How could you use Marcy's method to work these out?

46×5 $\quad$ 16×25
240×5 $\quad$ 116×25

38 × 10 = 380
380 ÷ 2 = 190
so 38 × 5 = 190.
18 × 100 = 1800
1800 ÷ 4 = 450
so 18 × 25 = 450.

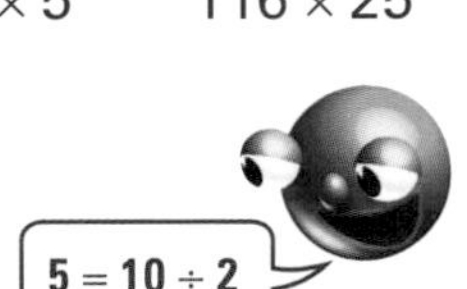

5 = 10 ÷ 2

25 = 100 ÷ 4

Exercise 3

This exercise is to be done mentally.

1 Sophie worked out 5×800 like this.

$5 \times 8 = 40$
$5 \times 80 = 400$
$5 \times 800 = 4000$

Write down the answers to these.

a $9 \times 6 =$ ___ $9 \times 60 =$ ___ $9 \times 600 =$ ___ $9 \times 6000 =$ ___

b $7 \times 8 =$ ___ $7 \times 80 =$ ___ $7 \times 800 =$ ___ $7 \times 8000 =$ ___

c $9 \times 7 =$ ___ $9 \times 70 =$ ___ $9 \times 700 =$ ___ $9 \times 7000 =$ ___

2 **a** 40×30 **b** 50×60 **c** 200×40 **d** 300×60

3 **a** $2 \times 3 \times 4$ **b** $8 \times 5 \times 3$ **c** $5 \times 4 \times 2$ **d** $12 \times 2 \times 2$
e $6 \times 9 \times 3$ **f** $4 \times 3 \times 5 \times 4$ **g** $6 \times 2 \times 5 \times 7$ **h** $4 \times 7 \times 3 \times 5$

4 What goes in the box?
a $2 \times \square \times 4 = 40$ **b** $3 \times 6 \times \square = 36$ **c** $7 \times \square \times 3 = 63$
d $5 \times \square \times 6 = 150$ **e** $\square \times 7 \times 2 = 28$

T **5**

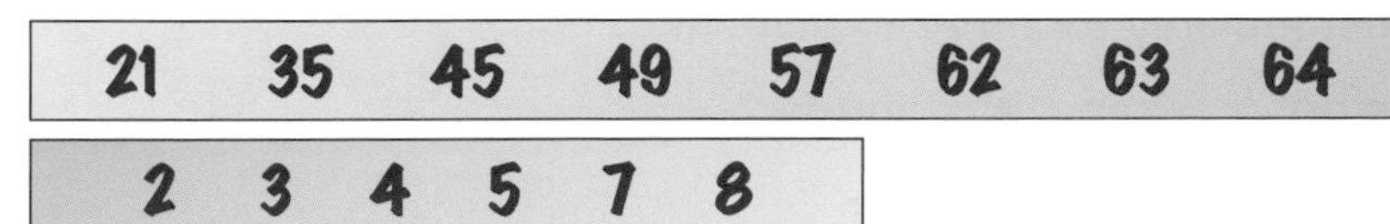

21 35 45 49 57 62 63 64
2 3 4 5 7 8

Choose one number from each box to multiply together to give these.
a 90 **b** 175 **c** 320 **d** 228 **e** 496
f 441 **g** 245 **h** 147

6 **a** 540 × 2 **b** 860 × 2 **c** 370 × 2 **d** 590 × 2 **e** 830 × 2
f 1500 × 2 **g** 1700 × 2 **h** 120 × 3 **i** 140 × 4 **j** 250 × 8

7 **a** 24 × 50 **b** 150 × 20 **c** 52 × 40 **d** 32 × 30 **e** 120 × 60
f 37 × 40 **g** 58 × 60 **h** 156 × 50 **i** 138 × 50

8 64 × 17 = 1088.
What is the answer to 1088 ÷ 17?

9 **a** 72 × 11 **b** 45 × 12 **c** 25 × 16 **d** 75 × 12
e 23 × 11 ***f** 23 × 21 ***g** 42 × 25 ***h** 24 × 31

***10** **a** Find the product of 29 and 19.
b Find the product of 16 and 11.

Remember:
We find the ***product*** by multiplying the numbers together.

11 Find ways of filling in the box and the circle.
■ × ● = 216.

Puzzle

1 Choose numbers from the oval to put in the boxes below.
Use each number only once in each question.

1 2 3
4 5 6

a □ × □ − □ = 2 **b** (□ + □) × □ = 24

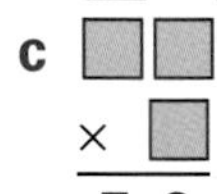

c
□□
× □
7 2

Note There is more than one way for each.

T **2** Use a copy of the diagram.
Put one of the numbers 1, 2, 4, 6, 8 and 12 in each circle.
Use each number only once.
The three numbers along each side of the triangle must multiply together to give 48.

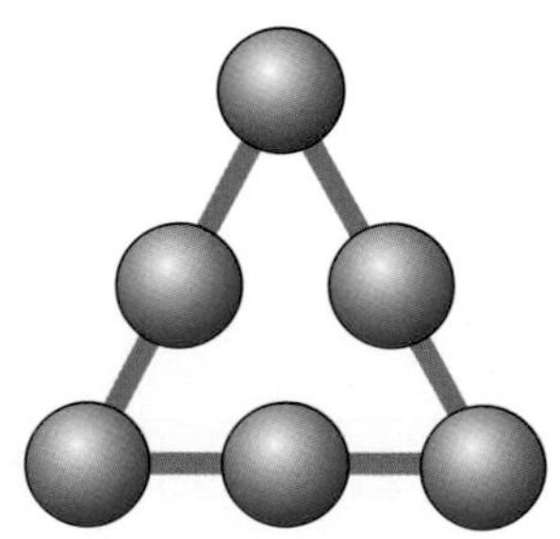

* **3** What digits do ▲, ■ and ★ stand for?

a ▲2 × 3 = 18▲ **b** ■■ × 4 = 396 **c** 2★ × ★ = 224

Here are **some ways to divide mentally**.

Example 168 ÷ 8

168 ÷ 8 = (160 ÷ 8) + (8 ÷ 8) = 20 + 1 = **21** **Partitioning**	168 ÷ 8 → 168 ÷ 2 = 84 84 ÷ 2 = 42 42 ÷ 2 = **21** 168 ÷ 8 = **21** **Using factors**

Exercise 4

This exercise is to be done mentally.

1 Akbar worked out 7200 ÷ 9 like this:

72 ÷ 9 = 8
720 ÷ 9 = 80
7200 ÷ 9 = 800

Write down the answers.

a
48 ÷ 6 = ___
480 ÷ 6 = ___
4800 ÷ 6 = ___
48 000 ÷ 6 = ___

b
63 ÷ 7 = ___
630 ÷ 7 = ___
6300 ÷ 7 = ___
63 000 ÷ 7 = ___

c
8000 ÷ 4 = ___
8000 ÷ 40 = ___
8000 ÷ 400 = ___
8000 ÷ 4000 = ___

2 **a** 900 ÷ 300 **b** 800 ÷ 40 **c** 600 ÷ 20 **d** 4000 ÷ 200

3

a 72 ÷ 9	**b** 54 ÷ 6	**c** 56 ÷ 8	**d** 63 ÷ 7
e 84 ÷ 2	**f** 92 ÷ 2	**g** 120 ÷ 4	**h** 200 ÷ 5
i 246 ÷ 6	**j** 328 ÷ 8	**k** 147 ÷ 7	**l** 360 ÷ 9

4

a 420 ÷ 5	**b** 208 ÷ 8	**c** 196 ÷ 4	**d** 900 ÷ 6
e 156 ÷ 6	**f** 940 ÷ 2	**g** 340 ÷ 2	**h** 580 ÷ 2
i 1700 ÷ 2	**j** 5600 ÷ 2	***k** 128 ÷ 16	***l** 180 ÷ 15

? Puzzle

Choose numbers from the oval to put in the boxes.

Use each number only once.

Find as many different ways as you can.

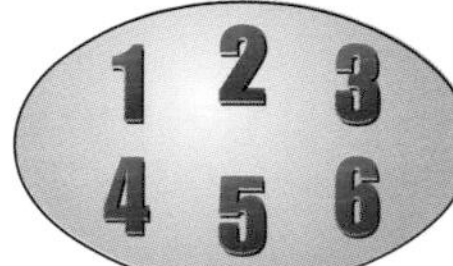

(□ + □) ÷ (□ + □) = 1

Multiplying and dividing decimals

Discussion

Rod and Alan worked out $2{\cdot}3 \times 40$ like this.

Rod

$2{\cdot}3 \times 40 = 2 \times 40 + 0{\cdot}3 \times 40$
$= 80 + 12$
$= 92$

$3 \times 40 = 120$
$0{\cdot}3 \times 40 = 12$

Alan

$2{\cdot}3 \times 40 = 2{\cdot}3 \times 4 \times 10$
$= 2{\cdot}3 \times 2 \times 2 \times 10$
$= 4{\cdot}6 \times 2 \times 10$
$= 9{\cdot}2 \times 10$
$= 92$

Which way do you like best? **Discuss.**

How else could you work out $2{\cdot}3 \times 40$? **Discuss.**

Here are **some ways to multiply and divide decimals mentally.**

Example $4{\cdot}6 \times 5$

Partitioning	Multiply then divide
$4{\cdot}6 \times 5 = 4 \times 5 + 0{\cdot}6 \times 5$ $= 20 + 3$ $= \mathbf{23}$ ($6 \times 5 = 30$, $0{\cdot}6 \times 5 = 3$)	$4{\cdot}6 \times 5 = 4{\cdot}6 \times 10 \div 2$ $= 46 \div 2$ $= \mathbf{23}$

Exercise 5

This exercise is to be done mentally.

1 **a** $1{\cdot}2 \times 2$ **b** $3{\cdot}1 \times 3$ **c** $2{\cdot}6 \times 2$ **d** $4{\cdot}3 \times 3$
e $7{\cdot}5 \times 6$ **f** $4{\cdot}7 \times 2$ ***g** $4{\cdot}9 \times 7$ ***h** $2{\cdot}3 \times 9$

T **2** Use a copy of this.
Shade the answers to these in the box.
a $0{\cdot}2 \times 8$ **b** $0{\cdot}3 \times 4$
c $4 \times 0{\cdot}5$ **d** $0{\cdot}3 \times 6$
e $0{\cdot}02 \times 6$ **f** $0{\cdot}05 \times 3$
g $8 \times 0{\cdot}04$ **h** $6 \times 0{\cdot}05$

2	0·16	0·03	0·32
0·2	1·8	1·6	0·012
0·18	0·15	0·3	3·2
1·2	0·03	1·5	0·12

3 What goes in the box?
a $\square \times 0{\cdot}2 = 1$ **b** $\square \times 0{\cdot}2 = 10$ **c** $5 \times \square = 0{\cdot}5$ **d** $3 \times \square = 1{\cdot}2$

4 Choose one number from each box to multiply together to give these.
a 24 **b** 62 **c** 255 **d** 72

1·2	3·1	5·1

20	50	60

5 **a** 4·1 × 11 **b** 3·2 × 12 **c** 5·2 × 14 **d** 7·5 × 12

6 Joe found 4·8 ÷ 8 in these two ways.

4·8 ÷ 8 = 4·8 ÷ 2 ÷ 2 ÷ 2
= 2·4 ÷ 2 ÷ 2
= 1·2 ÷ 2
= 0·6

4·8 ÷ 8

48 ÷ 8 = 6
So 4·8 ÷ 8 = 0·6

Work these out.

a 2·4 ÷ 4 **b** 3·6 ÷ 6 **c** 2·5 ÷ 5 **d** 3·2 ÷ 8
e 4·5 ÷ 5 **f** 4·8 ÷ 6 **g** 8·4 ÷ 2 **h** 5·4 ÷ 2

You could use a different way from Joe if you like.

T

7

A										'				
8·6	57·2		86	0·45	2·1	4·5	8·4	45	30	0·45		2·4	108	2·4

											A	
8·4	0·45		0·8	8·4	0·7	0·7	2·4	4·5		2·1	30	8·6	57·2

						A		
8·4	2·1	0·45		0·8	4·5	8·6	8·4	57·2

Use a copy of this box.
Write the letter beside each question above its answer in the box.

A 4·3 × 2 = 8·6 **I** 1·4 × 6 **T** 0·3 × 7 **S** 9 × 0·05 **O** 4·3 × 20
Y 3·6 × 30 **N** 5·2 × 11 **H** 2·5 × 12 **C** 0·9 × 50 **E** 4·8 ÷ 2
R 1·5 × 3 **G** 5·6 ÷ 8 **B** 7·2 ÷ 9

8 3 × 2·6 = 7·8
What does 7·8 ÷ 3 equal?

***9** ■ × ● = 3·6
Find ways of filling in the box and the circle.

Solving problems mentally

You must decide whether to **add, subtract, multiply or divide** to solve problems.

Worked Example
126 people went kart racing one day.
They were put into groups of exactly 6.
How many groups were there?

Answer
We must divide 126 by 6.
Here is one way to do this: 126 ÷ 6 = 126 ÷ 2 ÷ 3
= 63 ÷ 3
= **21**

There were **21** groups altogether.

Exercise 6

This exercise is to be done mentally.
You may use jottings.

1 Tim saved £68 one month and £182 the next month.
How much did he save altogether?

2 104 pupils went swimming. 57 were boys.
How many were girls?

3 Joel saved £262.
He buys a tennis racket for £89 and some tennis balls for £8.
How much does he have left?

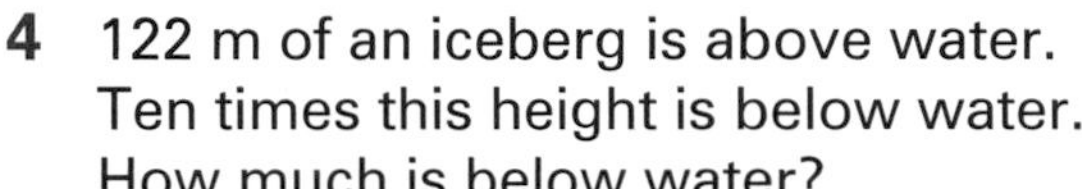

4 122 m of an iceberg is above water.
Ten times this height is below water.
How much is below water?

5 144 km^2 of the world's forest is cut down every 6 hours.
- **a** How much is cut down each hour?
- ***b** How much is cut down each day?

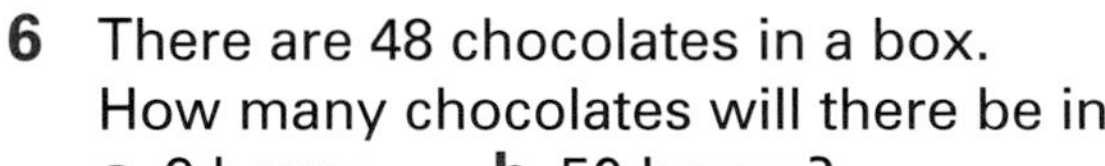

6 There are 48 chocolates in a box.
How many chocolates will there be in
a 9 boxes **b** 50 boxes?

7 Write the answer to these as quickly as possible.
- **a** What is one less than six and a half million?
- **b** How many millilitres are there in 4·5 ℓ?
- **c** How many minutes are there in 2·25 hours?
- **d** How many days are there in 60 hours?
- **e** How many hours and minutes are there in 155 minutes?
- **f** Two angles join to make a straight line. One is 124°. What is the other?
- **g** The area of a square is 25 m^2. What is the length of one side?

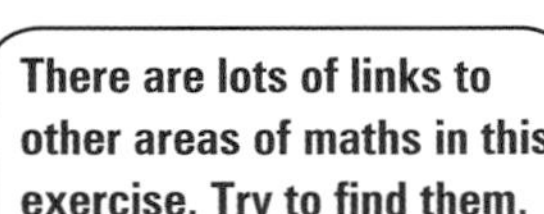

There are lots of links to other areas of maths in this exercise. Try to find them.

8 Brad ran 6·5 km one day and 3·8 km the next day.
How far did he run altogether?

9 Lucy had 4·6 kg of chicken pieces.
She used 2·8 kg for a party.
How many kilograms did she have left?

10 A pelican eats about 14·7 kg of fish each week.

a About how much does it eat each day?

b About how much fish would it eat in four days?

11 Melissa had a piece of rope 3·5 m long.
She cut it into five equal pieces.
How long was each piece?

Order of operations

Remember

We work out operations in this order.

Brackets
Indices
Division and Multiplication
Addition and Subtraction

You will learn about this on page 5.

We use the word **BIDMAS** to help us remember the order.

Examples $16 \div (6 + 2) = 16 \div 8$
$= \mathbf{2}$

Work out the bracket first.

$4 \times 6 - 3 \times 2 = 24 - 6$
$= \mathbf{18}$

Do the multiplications first.

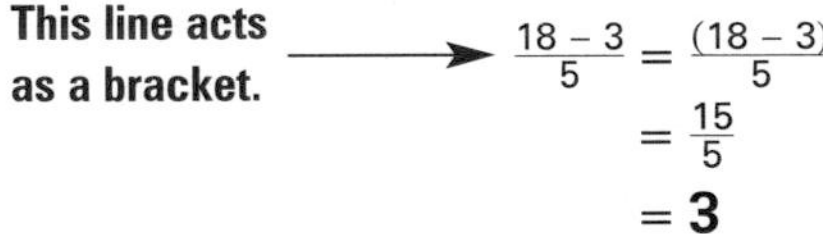

This line acts as a bracket.

$$\frac{18 - 3}{5} = \frac{(18 - 3)}{5}$$
$$= \frac{15}{5}$$
$$= \mathbf{3}$$

Exercise 7

This exercise is to be done mentally.

1 **a** $3 + 5 \times 2$ **b** $4 \times 5 + 7$ **c** $12 - 4 \times 2$ **d** $24 - 3 \times 5$
e $6 \times 2 + 4 \times 5$ **f** $7 \times 2 + 4 \times 4$ **g** $7 \times 8 + 6 \times 2$ **h** $12 \div 3 \div 2$
i $12 + 8 \div 4$ **j** $11 + 16 \div 4$ **k** $7 \times 9 - 3 \times 10$ **l** $5 + 2 \times 3 - 1$

2 **a** $2(3 + 5)$ **b** $7(6 - 2)$ **c** $6(9 - 4)$ **d** $8(7 - 1)$
e $(16 - 4) \times 2$ **f** $(7 - 2) \times 6$ **g** $(7 + 9) \times 2$ **h** $15(22 - 2)$
i $6 \times (15 + 10 - 15)$ **j** $(16 + 7 - 13) \times 3$ **k** $2(20 - 2 \times 4)$ **l** $3(12 - 4 \times 2)$

3 **a** $\frac{16 + 4}{2}$ **b** $\frac{8 + 12}{4}$ **c** $\frac{5 + 9}{7}$ **d** $\frac{24}{3 \times 8}$
e $\frac{100}{2 \times 5}$ **f** $\frac{100}{5 \times 5}$ **g** $\frac{14}{6 - 4}$ **h** $\frac{7 + 9}{10 - 6}$

T **4**

5	28	5	1	45	16	42	7	72		16	14	5		7	45	5
3	42	28	6		16	42	4	10	16	28	72					
7	45	16	7		C 21	16	42	7		12	32	10	1			

Use a copy of this box.
Write the letter that is beside each question above its answer.

C	$7(2+1) = \mathbf{21}$	**N**	$6(10-3)$	**R**	$2(9-2)$	**L**	$(5+9)\times 2$
U	$(11-3)\times 4$	**S**	$8(10-4+3)$	**H**	$5(1+2\times 4)$	**A**	$2(14-2\times 3)$
O	$21-2(3\times 3)$	**Y**	$\frac{8+4}{2}$	**T**	$\frac{20+8}{4}$	**I**	$\frac{32-4}{7}$
M	$\frac{80}{2\times 4}$	**E**	$\frac{26+4}{2\times 3}$	**P**	$(20-16)\div(9-5)$	**J**	$36-2(3\times 4)$

***5** **a** $3\times 4-2(5-1)$ **b** $5\times 4-3(6-3)$ **c** $9\times 8+3(2\times 2)$
d $5\times 4+6(3\times 0)$ **e** $6\times 2+4(3+0)$ **f** $5\times 8-3(8-2\times 2)$

***6** $2+3\times 6=20$ $3(6-2)=12$
Both of these are made using 2, 3 and 6.
What other answers can you make using 2, 3 and 6?
You may use $+, -, \times, \div$ and brackets.
What is the biggest answer you can make?

We work out **squares** (indices) **before** multiplication and division but after brackets.

Example

$$3\times 4^2 = 3\times 16 = 3\times(10+6) = 3\times 10+3\times 6 = 30+18 = \mathbf{48}$$

$$\frac{3^2-1}{2^2} = \frac{(3^2-1)}{2^2} = \frac{9-1}{4} = \frac{8}{4} = \mathbf{2}$$

$$(3^2-2^2)^2 = (9-4)^2 = 5^2 = \mathbf{25}$$

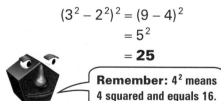

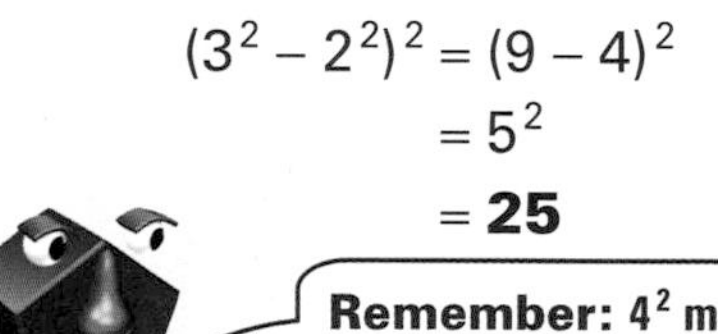
Remember: 4^2 means 4 squared and equals 16.

Exercise 8

This exercise is to be done mentally.

1 **a** 2×3^2 **b** 5^2-2 **c** 4×2^2
d $3^2\times 2-3$ **e** $4^2\div 4+2$ **f** $5^2-12\div 3$
***g** $(2^2+1^2)^2$ ***h** $\frac{5^2-1}{10-2}$ ***i** $\frac{3\times 2^2}{2^2-1}$

Calculation Full House – a game for a group

You will need these calculations which have the numbers 1 to 20 as answers.

1 $= 3 + 4 + 5 - 11$	**2** $= 8 \times 3 - 22$	**3** $= 21 - 9 \times 2$
4 $= 14 - 2 \times 5$	**5** $= 12 \div 2 - 1$	**6** $= 18 - 3 \times 4$
7 $= \frac{20-6}{6-4}$	**8** $= 32 \div 2 \div 2$	**9** $= (7-4)^2$
10 $= 2^2 + 6$	**11** $= \frac{17+5}{8-6}$	**12** $= 3(5 \times 4 - 16)$
13 $= \frac{20+6}{2}$	**14** $= 6 \times 4 - 5 \times 2$	**15** $= 5^2 - 10$
16 $= 2(14 - 3 \times 2)$	**17** $= 5^2 - 4 \times 2$	**18** $= 2(5^2 - 16)$
19 $= 4^2 + 15 \div 5$	**20** $= 4 \times 2 + 3 \times 4$	

To Play

- Choose a leader.
- Everyone, except the leader, writes down five numbers from 1 to 20.
- The leader calls out one of the calculations (but not the answer), making sure the players can't see this page.
- If the answer to the calculation is one of the five numbers a player has, they cross it out.

Example Pete had the numbers 2, 3, 8, 10 and 18.
The leader called out the calculation $2^2 + 6$.
The answer is 10.
Pete crossed out 10.

- The first student to cross out all five numbers is the winner. This student is the leader for the next round.

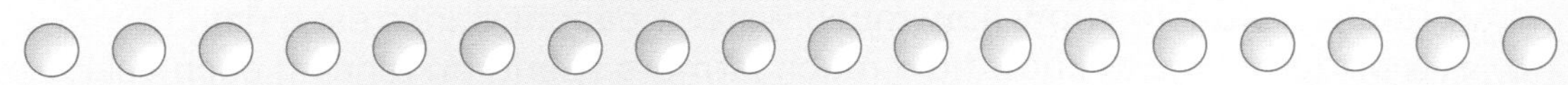

Investigation

Number Chains

Begin with any number.

If the number is even, divide it by 2.
If the number is odd, multiply it by 3 and then add 1.

Keep doing this until you get the digit 1.

Example If we begin with 20 we get

$$20 \div 2 = 10$$
$$10 \div 2 = 5$$
$$5 \times 3 + 1 = 16$$
$$16 \div 2 = 8$$
$$8 \div 2 = 4$$
$$4 \div 2 = 2$$
$$2 \div 2 = 1$$

The number chain is

There are seven numbers in this chain.

Find all the pairs of numbers from 10 to 20 which have number chains of the same length.
For example, 12 and 13 have number chains of length 9.

Making estimates

Sometimes we don't need an exact answer to a question. Often an **estimate is good enough**.

Examples How many people were at the school fair?
How many burgers does a typical teenager eat in a year?

We make the **best estimate** possible.

Example Amanda was asked to estimate the number of times her sister said 'um' in a 10-minute phone call.
She counted the number of times her sister said 'um' in 1 minute. She got 11.
She multiplied 11 by 10 to get 110.
We would probably say Amanda's sister said 'um' **about 100** times.

In this example the estimate only needs to be a rough estimate.

Exercise 9

1 For which of these would an estimate be good enough?
- **a** A reporter wants to know how many people were at a football match.
- **b** The accountant wants to know how much profit was made at the school fair.
- **c** A doctor wants to know how much water a patient drinks each day.
- **d** A reporter wants to know how much farmers spend on fencing each year.
- **e** A football club manager wants to know the number of wins, draws and losses for the first division team.

Practical

Find the best estimate you can for these.
Explain how you got your estimate.

1. The number of litres of water your household uses in a day to the nearest 10 litres.
2. The distance your family car travels in one year to the nearest 1000 miles.
3. The distance you travel to school and back in one year to the nearest 10 miles.
4. The number of people in this picture.

Estimating answers to calculations

Remember
Always **estimate** the answer to a calculation first.

Example 185 × 23 is about 200 × 20 which is 4000.

Discussion

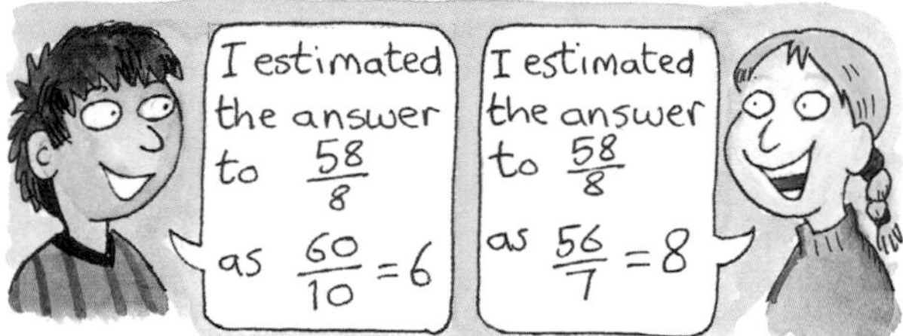

I estimated the answer to $\frac{58}{8}$ as $\frac{60}{10} = 6$
I estimated the answer to $\frac{58}{8}$ as $\frac{56}{7} = 8$

Are the estimates that Ralph and Sudi got both correct? **Discuss**.

Exercise 10

This exercise is to be done mentally.

1 Which is the best approximation for these?

a	281 + 496	**A** 300 + 500	**B** 200 + 400	**C** 250 + 450
b	91 − 47	**A** 100 − 40	**B** 90 − 50	**C** 90 − 40
c	411 − 182	**A** 500 − 200	**B** 400 − 100	**C** 400 − 200
d	33 × 57	**A** 30 × 60	**B** 40 × 50	**C** 40 × 60
e	942 ÷ 32	**A** 1000 ÷ 30	**B** 900 ÷ 40	**C** 900 ÷ 30
f	748 × 26	**A** 800 × 30	**B** 700 × 30	**C** 700 × 20
g	324 ÷ 53	**A** 300 ÷ 60	**B** 300 ÷ 50	**C** 400 ÷ 50

2 Estimate the answers to these.

a 804 − 396 **b** 3524 + 973 **c** 39 × 42 **d** 804 ÷ 9
e 8·18 + 3·81 **f** 50·8 − 39·7 **g** 596 ÷ 61 **h** 550 × 69

3 Write down two ways to find an approximate answer for each of these.

a 815 − 254 **b** 862 + 303 **c** 44 × 19 **d** 9·23 + 8·5

Practical

You will need a partner.

Work out an estimate for each of these.

Explain to your partner why you found the estimate the way you did.

649 − 347 $\frac{37}{5}$ 56 × 2·4 34 × 19

Summary of key points

A Some ways of **adding and subtracting mentally** are:

- **partitioning**
- **counting up**
- **adding too much then taking some away**
- **nearly doubles**
- **nearly numbers**
- **subtracting too much then adding back**
- **recognising complements**

B Some ways of **multiplying and dividing mentally** are:

- **partitioning**
- **using factors**
- **doubling one number and halving another**
- **multiplying then dividing**

C We can **solve problems** mentally.

D This is the order in which we do operations.

Brackets
↓
Squares (**I**ndices)
↓
Division and **M**ultiplication
↓
Addition and **S**ubtraction

Use BIDMAS to help you remember.

Examples **a** $7 + 20 \div 5 = 7 + 4$
$= 11$

This line acts as a bracket.

$\frac{80}{4 \times 5} = \frac{80}{(4 \times 5)}$
$= \frac{80}{20}$
$= 4$

E Sometimes an **estimate** is a good enough answer to a question.
Example How many people went to a concert?

F Always **estimate the answer to a calculation**.
An estimate is an approximate answer.
Example $348 + 197$ is approximately
$300 + 200 = 500$

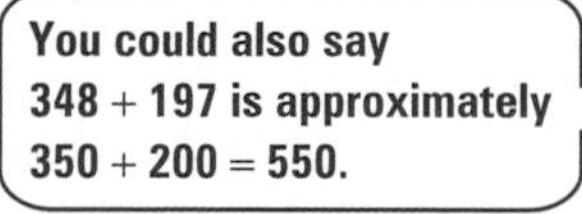
You could also say
348 + 197 is approximately
350 + 200 = 550.

Test yourself

Find the answers mentally. You may use jottings.

1 **a** 15 + 3 − 11 + 16 − 2 **b** 100 − 50 + 20 

2 **a** 90 − 50 **b** 36 + 14 **c** 76 − 52 **d** 83 + 17 **e** 59 + 58 
f 186 + 39 **g** 486 − 57 **h** 411 − 379 **i** 5200 − 384

3 **a** 0·9 + 0·8 **b** 2·7 − 0·8 **c** 2·9 + 6·9 **d** 5·2 − 3·5 **e** 4·7 + 8·9 
f 16·3 − 4·7 **g** 1·9 + 3·2 **h** 19·0 − 5·8

T **4** Use a copy of these. Fill them in.

a

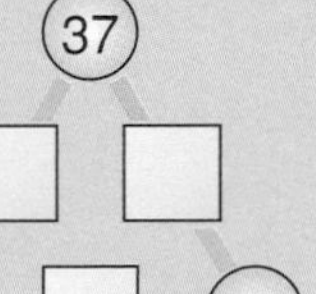

b

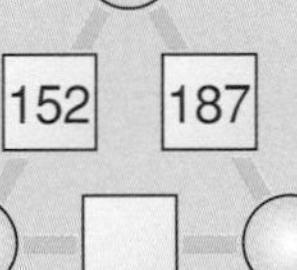

The numbers in the circles add to the number in the square between them.

5 Write down the answers that go in the gaps.

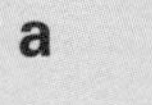

a 8 × 9 = 72
8 × 90 = ___
8 × 900 = ___
8 × 9000 = ___

b 56 ÷ 8 = ___
560 ÷ 8 = ___
5600 ÷ 8 = ___
56 000 ÷ 8 = ___

6 **a** 3 × 5 × 4 **b** 82 × 5 **c** 150 × 3 **d** 78 ÷ 2 
e 128 ÷ 4 **f** 40 × 20 **g** 120 × 30 **h** 82 × 11
i 390 ÷ 3 **j** 36 × 50

7 **a** 1·3 × 2 **b** 4·3 × 5 **c** 4·8 ÷ 2 **d** 6·3 ÷ 9 
e 0·3 × 8 **f** 9 × 0·6 **g** 1·8 ÷ 3 **h** 4·3 × 30
i 5·3 × 50 ∗**j** 4·7 × 13

8 **a** Find the sum of 3·5 + 8·9. 
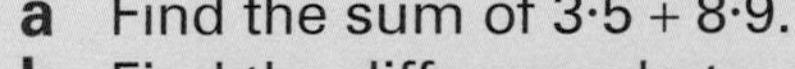
b Find the difference between 671 and 289.
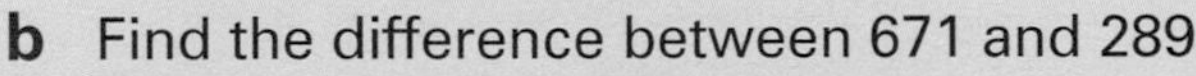
∗**c** Find the product of 5 and 119.
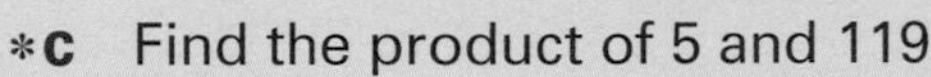

9 A bag was filled with 3·5 kg of apples and 2·7 kg of oranges. How many kilograms of fruit were in the bag? 

10 A turtle can move 26 m each minute. How far could the turtle move in 
a 2 minutes **b** 5 minutes
c 8 minutes ∗**d** 1 hour?

11 Chris stacked 96 bricks into 4 equal piles. How many were in each pile? 

12 **a** $14 - 3 \times 2$ **b** $4 \times 3 + 7 \times 2$ **c** $9 + 20 \div 4$ **d** $6(8 + 2)$ 
e $\frac{9+6}{5}$ **f** $\frac{24}{3 \times 2}$ **g** 2×5^2 **h** $3(4^2 - 8)$
i $\frac{3^2 - 1}{2}$ **j** $\frac{25+5}{7-2}$ ***k** $3(4^2 - 10)$ ***l** $12 + 3 \times 2^2$

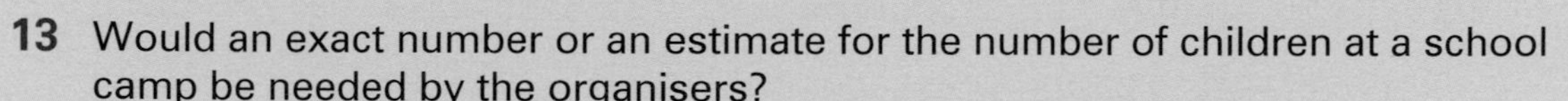

13 Would an exact number or an estimate for the number of children at a school camp be needed by the organisers?

14 Which is the **best** approximation for these?

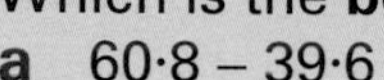

a	60·8 – 39·6	**A** 60 – 39	**B** 608 – 396	**C** 61 – 40	**D** 6·0 – 3·9
b	8·14 × 4·91	**A** 9 × 4	**B** 8 × 5	**C** 9 × 5	**D** 8 × 4

15 Write down two ways to find an approximate answer for these. 
a 451 + 187 **b** 3·47 × 4·96 **c** 962 – 359

4 Written and Calculator Calculation

You need to know

Key vocabulary

approximately, brackets, calculator, difference, equivalent calculation, estimate, inverse operations, order of magnitude, remainder, sum

Back to front

373 reads the same from left to right as it does from right to left.

It is a **palindromic number**.

Other examples are 88, 1441 and 36 763.

Many palindromic numbers can be made like this:

Begin with any number, say	168
Reverse the digits	+ 861
Add	1029
Reverse the digits	+ 9201
Add	10230
Reverse the digits	+03201
Add	13431

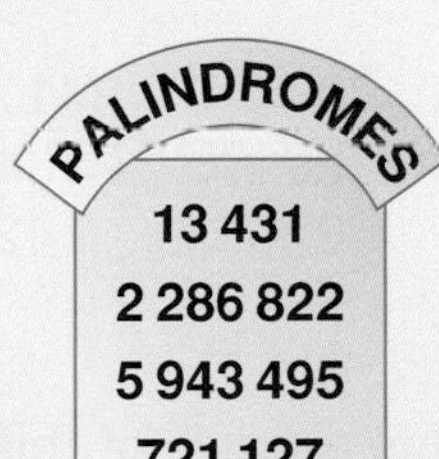

PALINDROMES
13 431
2 286 822
5 943 495
721 127

It took 3 reversals of digits to make the palindromic number 13 431.

Find the number of reversals needed to make palindromic numbers from other starting numbers.

Adding and subtracting

Remember

We **add and subtract whole numbers** by lining up the units column.

$$\begin{array}{r} {}^{2}3{}^{1}1{}^{5}6{}^{1}5 \\ -\ 727 \\ \hline 2438 \\ \hline \end{array}$$

We **add and subtract decimals** by lining up decimal points.
Always estimate the answer first.

Example Scott weighed 52·74 kg
His motorbike weighed 138·6 kg.
He added the masses.
52·74 + 138·6 is about 50 + 150 = 200

$$\begin{array}{r} 52{\cdot}74 \\ +138{\cdot}6 \\ \hline 191{\cdot}34 \\ \hline {\scriptstyle 1\,1}\phantom{{\cdot}34} \end{array}$$

They weighed 191·34 kg in total.

Exercise 1

Estimate first then calculate the answer.

1 a $\begin{array}{r} 365 \\ +142 \\ \hline \\ \hline \end{array}$ b $\begin{array}{r} 1416 \\ +\ 378 \\ \hline \\ \hline \end{array}$ c $\begin{array}{r} 629 \\ -417 \\ \hline \\ \hline \end{array}$ d $\begin{array}{r} 2416 \\ -\ 127 \\ \hline \\ \hline \end{array}$

e 623 + 748 f 517 – 329 g 637 + 2195 h 3261 + 2977
i 2782 – 359 j 1044 – 139 k 7635 + 4186 l 5030 – 2741

2 a 79 + 26 + 341 b 52 + 561 + 2106
c 369 + 52 + 1043 + 2 d 53 + 862 + 1957 + 2841
e 562 + 39 – 142 f 316 + 2416 – 816

T 3 Use a copy of this.
The number in any square is found by adding the numbers in the two circles on either side of the square.

Find the missing numbers.

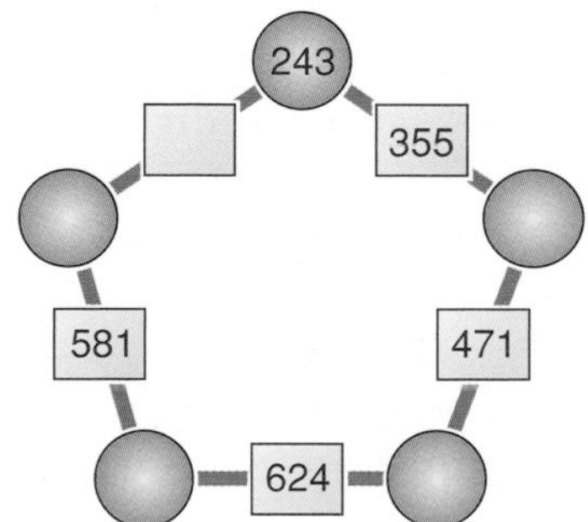

T

4

___ 29·91	___ 21·68	___ 104·8	___ 520·61	___ 3959·93	___ 3325·76	
___ 1598·13	___ 211·78	___ 5470·25	___ 520·61			
___ 3325·76	___ 29·91	___ 3959·93	___ 21·68	___ 104·16	___ 520·61	___ 1·87
___ 3325·76	K 698·7	___ 21·68	___ 298·81			

Use a copy of the box.
Find the answers to these.
Write the letter beside each question above its answer in the box.

K 643·7 + 55 = 698·7   **V** 5371·8 + 98·45   **D** 2·41 − 0·54   **N** 304·6 − 5·79

H 72·03 + 1526·1   **E** 521·3 − 0·69   **R** 4086·5 − 126·57
A 179 + 32·78   **G** 184 − 79·2   **T** 29·06 + 0·85
S 34·69 + 3291·07   **I** 28 − 6·32   **P** 257 − 152·84

5 **a** 4·76 + 62·4 + 3·7   **b** 51·8 + 183·9 + 46·39   **c** 9·74 + 25·1 + 19

6 **a** Find the sum of 86·3 and 5·27.
b Find the difference between 298·03 and 36·47.
***c** The sum of two numbers is 864·27.
What might the numbers be?
***d** The difference between two numbers is 18·64.
What might the numbers be?

7 In Science, Rainer began with 5 ℓ of a blue solution.
He used 1·38 ℓ of it for one experiment and 2·6 ℓ of it for another.
How much did he have left?

8 This is the tuck shop price list at Lucy's school.
a Rachel buys a roll, a doughnut and an apple.
How much does this cost?
How much change does she get from £5?
b Joshua bought 3 different things from the tuck shop and spent £3·60.
What might he have bought?
Find 4 different answers.
c You have £3·50. Write down what you would buy for lunch.
How much change would you get?

PRICE LIST

Sandwiches	£1·25	Apple	40p
Rolls	£1·80	Banana	35p
Meat Pie	£1·60	Chips	£1·00
Apple Pie	£1·20	Yoghurt	80p
Pizza Slice	£1·80	Juice	£1·10
Doughnut	90p	Chocolate Milk	£1·50

9 □□□ + □□ = 213 □□·□ − 12·3 = □□·□

Find at least three ways to fill in these boxes.
Put one digit in each box.

Puzzle

Where should the decimal points be placed to make these true?

a 36 + 12 = 372 **b** 136 − 4 = 96 **c** 281 + 12 − 145 + 31

You may add a zero at the start or end of any number.
Is there more than one answer for each?

*Investigation

Decimal Magic Square
Is this a magic square?

Would it be a magic square if each number had a decimal point? **Investigate**.

155	150	250	125
450	105	95	750
850	65	550	115
350	135	145	50

Multiplying

Multiplying by a 1-digit number

Always **estimate** the answer first.

Example 32·9 × 6 is about 30 × 6 = 180.
32·9 × 6 is the same as 329 × 6 ÷ 10.

32·9 × 6 = 329 ÷ 10 × 6
= 329 × 6 ÷ 10

```
  329
×   6
 1974
  1 5
```

and 1974 ÷ 10 = 197·4.

So 32·9 × 6 = **197·4**

Check that the decimal point is in the right place by comparing with the estimate.

or 32·9 × 6

	30	2	0·9
6	180	12	5·4

180 + 12 + 5·4 = **197·4**

Exercise 2

Estimate first then calculate the answers.

T

1 Use a copy of this crossnumber.
Fill it in.

Across	**Down**
1. 159 × 3 = **477**	**1.** 122 × 4
3. 128 × 7	**2.** 153 × 5
5. 165 × 5	**3.** 177 × 5
6. 176 × 3	**4.** 167 × 4
7. 152 × 3	**7.** 81 × 6
9. 127 × 5	**8.** 94 × 7
11. 216 × 3	**9.** 108 × 6
12. 106 × 8	**10.** 142 × 4

[1] 4	7	[2] 7	■	[3]		[4]
	■		■		■	
[5]			■	[6]		
■	■	■	■	■	■	■
[7]		[8]	■	[9]		[10]
	■		■		■	
[11]			■	[12]		

2 Sam the snail crawls 41 cm an hour.
How far would Sam crawl in a week?

T

3 Use a copy of this.

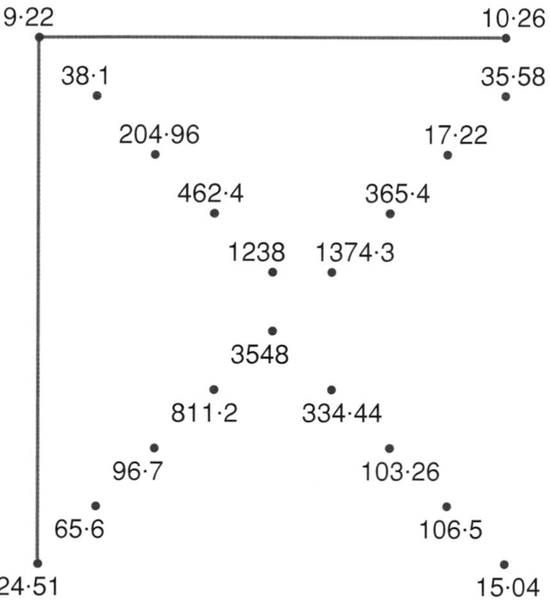

Find the answers to these.
Join the answers in order. The first two lines have been drawn.

a	3·42 × 3	**b**	4·61 × 2	**c**	8·17 × 3	**d**	3·76 × 4	**e**	5·93 × 6
f	12·7 × 3	**g**	16·4 × 4	**h**	21·3 × 5	**i**	2·46 × 7	**j**	25·62 × 8
k	19·34 × 5	**l**	17·21 × 6	**m**	121·8 × 3	**n**	115·6 × 4	**o**	135·2 × 6
p	83·61 × 4	**q**	152·7 × 9	**r**	309·5 × 4	**s**	443·5 × 8		

4 Shabir measured one of her paces as 78·3 cm.
Her bedroom is six paces long and four paces wide.
What is the length and width of Shabir's bedroom?

5 Jack bought six packets of blank CDs.
How much did they cost?

6 Jarad found 58 × 0·7 like this.

58 × 7 = 406
so 58 × 0·7 = 40·6

$$\begin{array}{r} 58 \\ \times\ 7 \\ \hline 406 \\ \hline _5 \end{array}$$

Find the answer to these the same way.

a 794 × 0·5 **b** 584 × 0·6 **c** 329 × 0·9 **d** 486 × 0·6
***e** 396 × 0·03 ***f** 634 × 0·09 ***g** 825 × 0·04

Multiplying by a 2-digit number

Remember

Example 834 × 27 is about 800 × 30 = 24 000.

$$\begin{array}{r} 834 \\ \times\ 27 \\ \hline 16680 \\ 5838 \\ \hline \mathbf{22518} \\ \hline _{111} \end{array}$$

16680 ← **834 × 20**
5838 ← **834 × 7**

or

	800	30	4
20	16 000	600	80
7	5600	210	28

Answer 16 000 + 600 + 80 + 5600 + 210 + 28 = **22 518**

Exercise 3

1 **a** 21 × 18 **b** 83 × 16 **c** 21 × 33 **d** 27 × 24
e 32 × 51 **f** 54 × 36 **g** 25 × 18 **h** 56 × 24
i 73 × 32 **j** 68 × 54 **k** 790 × 68 **l** 532 × 41
m 666 × 66 **n** 432 × 41 **o** 846 × 34 **p** 612 × 27

2 Selma worked these out.
There is a mistake in each of them.
Find the mistake.
Then find the correct answer.

a
$$\begin{array}{r} 721 \\ \times\ 63 \\ \hline 2163 \\ 4326 \\ \hline 6489 \\ \hline \end{array}$$

b
$$\begin{array}{r} 386 \\ \times\ 82 \\ \hline 772 \\ 30\,880 \\ \hline 30\,552 \\ \hline \end{array}$$

c
$$\begin{array}{r} 306 \\ \times\ 75 \\ \hline 1530 \\ 2520 \\ \hline 4050 \\ \hline \end{array}$$

3 **a** Tim's class went on a day's outing to a Wildlife Park.
To raise money they sold 48 cans of soup for 65p each.
How much money did they get in total?

b There are 29 pupils in Tim's class.
They each paid £12 to get into the park.
How much did they pay altogether?

4 A train holds 536 people.
One week, every trip it made was full.

a How many people did it carry each day?

b How many people did it carry that week?

c If each person paid £15 for the trip, how much money was paid in total on the Sunday?

Day	Number of trips
Sun	6
Mon	15
Tue	13
Wed	17
Thur	14
Fri	18
Sat	11

***5**

180 30 245 75 56 100 25 194 146

a Which two numbers in the box will give 2250 when multiplied together?

b Which two numbers in the box will give 5820 when multiplied together?

c Which two numbers in the box will give 13 720 when multiplied together?

d Which two numbers in the box will give 8176 when multiplied together?

e Which three numbers in the box will give 135 000 when multiplied together?

*Puzzle

1 In these sums, some of the digits got covered by ink. Work out what the missing digits are.

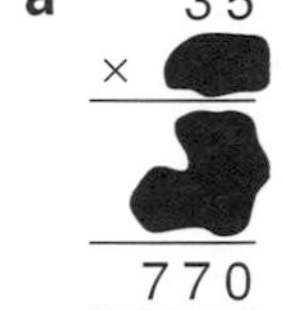

a

```
   35
 × ■
  ■
  770
```

b

```
   ■
 × 3■
  ■7
  ■1
  52■
```

2 ●▲ is a 2-digit number.
The digits add up to 7.

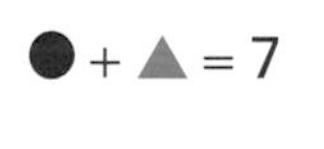

●+▲=7

```
     ●▲
   × ▲●
    102
   1360
   1462
```

What are the digits ● and ▲?

3 Put the digits 3, 4, 5, 6 and 7 in the boxes to make each true.
Use each digit only once.

a □□□ × □□ = 25 228 **b** □□□ × □□ = 24 310

Discussion

```
   42
×  16
  420   ←— 10 × 42
  252   ←— 6 × 42
  672
```

How can we use the answer to 42 × 16 to find the answer to 4·2 × 16? **Discuss.**

Exercise 4

1. a 32 × 1·3 b 24 × 1·5 c 29 × 3·6 d 3·6 × 21
   e 59 × 4·2 f 2·4 × 42 g 49 × 6·3 h 96 × 5·7

2. Rachel makes picture frames.
   Each frame uses 1·6 m of wood.
   How much wood does she need to make 35 frames?

3. Bertha has 42 birds.
   She gives each bird 1·3 kg of food each month.
   How much food is given to the birds each month?

*4 Make up a word problem for this calculation.
   2·6 × 35

Dividing

Dividing by a 1-digit number

Example 27·3 ÷ 7 is about 28 ÷ 7 = 4.

```
7)27·3
 −21·0   7 × 3
   6·3
   6·3   7 × 0·9
   0·0
```

Answer **3·9**

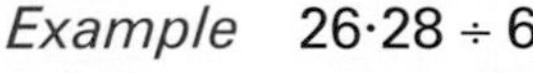

Example 26·28 ÷ 6

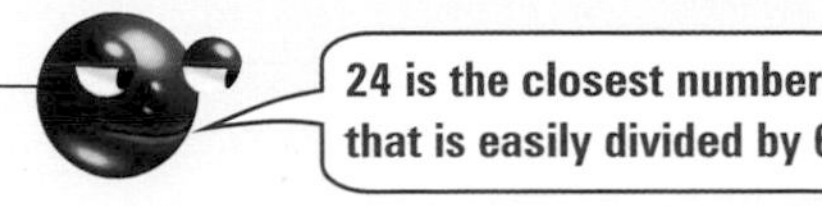
24 is the closest number that is easily divided by 6.

26·28 ÷ is approximately 24 ÷ 6 = 4

Notice that the decimal points line up.

```
6)26·28
 −24·00     6 × 4
   2·28
 − 1·80     6 × 0·3     because 6 × 3 = 18
   0·48
 − 0·48     6 × 0·08    because 6 × 8 = 48 and 6 × 0·8 = 4·8
   0·00
```

Answer **4·38**

or

$$6\overline{)26{\cdot}{}^{2}2{}^{4}8}\quad 4{\cdot}38$$

Exercise 5

Estimate first then calculate the answer.

T

1

65·55	9·1	99·37		206·59	95·36	146·3	146·3	56·2	
9·1	95·36	146·3		83·24	56·7	83·24	206·59	Y 1·1	
1·21	146·3	83·24	65·55	95·36	146·3		206·59	3·39	146·3	Y 1·1
3·39	9·1	12·48	146·3		9·1	65·32	65·55	95·36	1·34	56·2

Use a copy of this box.
Put the letter that is beside the division above its answer. The first one is done.

Y 5·5 ÷ 5 = 1·1	**H** 6·78 ÷ 2	**B** 4·84 ÷ 4	**A** 45·5 ÷ 5
N 9·38 ÷ 7	**V** 74·88 ÷ 6	**S** 393·4 ÷ 7	**I** 510·3 ÷ 9
E 438·9 ÷ 3	**T** 826·36 ÷ 4	**R** 762·88 ÷ 8	**F** 499·44 ÷ 6
C 457·24 ÷ 7	**O** 589·95 ÷ 9	**K** 496·85 ÷ 5	

2 Eight equal sized books were piled on top of one another.
The pile was 49·6 cm high.
How thick was each book?

3 Nine people shared the cost of a meal equally.
The meal cost £239·22.
How much did each pay?

***4** Five people stood on a bridge. Their total mass was 384·25 kg.
a What was the average mass of each person?
b The bridge mass limit is 700 kg.
Can nine people of the average mass you found in **a** safely stand on the bridge?

There is more about the average (mean) on page 317.

Puzzle

What values might A, B and C have?

1

$$\begin{array}{r} A \cdot B \\ \times\ BA \\ \hline BC \cdot B \end{array}$$

2

$$\begin{array}{r} A \cdot A \\ \times\ BB \\ \hline BC \cdot B \end{array}$$

Dividing by a 2-digit number

Worked Example

Jody put 910 magazines into 26 piles.
How many were in each pile?

Answer

We need to **divide** 910 by 26.
910 ÷ 26 is about 900 ÷ 30 = 30.

$$\begin{array}{rll} 26\overline{)910} & & \\ -780 & 26 \times \mathbf{30} & \text{because } 26 \times 3 = 78 \\ \hline 130 & & \\ -130 & 26 \times \mathbf{5} & \\ \hline 0 & & \end{array}$$

Answer **35**

Exercise 6

Estimate first then calculate the answer.

1 **a** 512 ÷ 16 **b** 738 ÷ 18 **c** 540 ÷ 15 **d** 696 ÷ 12
e 782 ÷ 23 **f** 800 ÷ 32 **g** 868 ÷ 28 **h** 893 ÷ 19
i 576 ÷ 18 **j** 416 ÷ 26 **k** 770 ÷ 35 **l** 522 ÷ 29

2 There are 29 pupils in 8NT.
They walked a total of 551 km for a fundraiser.
If each pupil walked the same distance, how far did each walk?

3 At a sweet factory, 912 sweets are made each hour.
They are put into bags of 24.
How many full bags are made each hour?

4 23 people shared a prize of £828 equally.
How much money did each person get?

***5** 304 people live in an area of 16 square miles.
What is the mean number of people per square mile?

This is linked to mean on page 317 and geography.

***6** Make up a word problem for this.

756 ÷ 18

Puzzle

Copy this diagram.

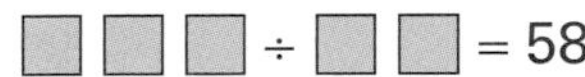

Put the numbers 1, 2, 6, 8 and 9 in your boxes to make this true.

Checking if answers are sensible

We can **check an answer** using one of these methods.

1 Check that the answer is sensible

Example Jan wrote down the rainfall each day one week.
0 mm 7 mm 12 mm 0 mm 5 mm 8 mm 3 mm
She found the average rainfall that week and got 70 mm.
This is not sensible because much less rain than this fell each day.

Example Bill calculated that the floor area of his garden shed was 186 m^2.
This is not sensible as it is about the size of a house.

2 Estimate first then check if the answer is the right order of magnitude

Example Ray bought 8 packets of chips at £1·89 a packet.
8 × £1·89 is about 10 × £2 = £20.
Ray was asked to pay £24·60.
He knew this was wrong because it should be less than his estimate of £20.

Exercise 7

1 Veronica worked out the answers to these.
Her answers are given in the blue boxes.
Are her answers sensible?
If not, explain why not.

a Mary eats a 125 g packet of crisps each day.
How many grams of crisps does she eat each week? | 8·8 g |

b A packet of 4 small cakes costs £3·85.
How much does each cake cost? | £9·63 |

c These are the heights of Veronica's four brothers.
Calculate the mean of these heights. | 159·75 m |

1·46 m   1·63 m   1·58 m   1·72 m

2 Rebecca wrote down how much she had earned doing jobs for her parents.

£4·50   £5·25   £8·70   £9·85

She added these up and got £82·50.
Is she correct or incorrect? Say why.

3 Mikey can run 100 m in 15 seconds.
He worked out it would take him 16 minutes 15 seconds to run 650 m.
Could this answer be right? Explain your answer.

4 Maha bought a pie for £2·68, a muffin for £1·20 and a drink for 84p.
She gave £10 and got £2·26 change.
Is this correct or incorrect? Say why.

***5** Pete multiplied 864×529 and got 447 534.
How can you tell this answer is wrong?

***6** Nick multiplied 783×467 and got 36 810.
How can you tell this answer is wrong?

Checking answers using inverse operations

We can check an answer to a calculation using **inverse operations.**

Addition and **subtraction** are **inverse operations.**
Multiplication and **division** are **inverse operations.**

Remember: Inverse operations undo each other.

Examples Check 2·4 × 6 = 14·4 using 14·4 ÷ 6 or 14·4 ÷ 2·4.
Check 6 ÷ 7 = 0·8571428 ... using 7 × 0·8571428.
Check 96·3 + 5·89 = 102·19 using 102·19 − 5·89 or 102·19 − 96·3.

* Sometimes we check the answer to a calculation using **estimating** *and* **inverse operations**.

Examples

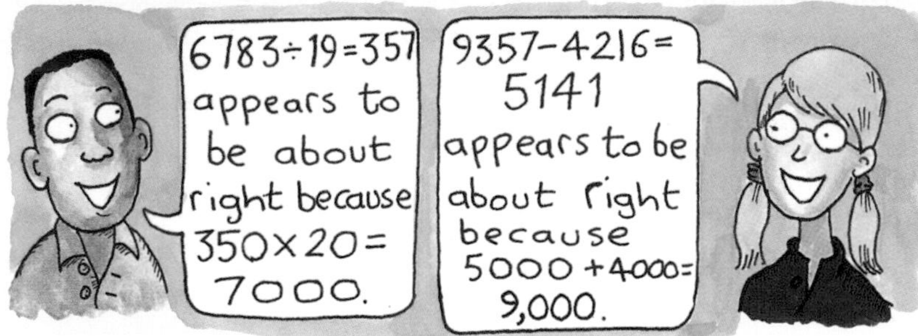

Exercise 8

1 Find the missing numbers.

a Check 3864 − 258 = 3606 using 3606 + ☐ = 3864.
b Check 9432 + 4176 = 13 608 using 13 608 − ☐ = 4176.
c Check 563 × 14 = 7882 using 7882 ÷ ☐ = 563.
d Check 3705 ÷ 65 = 57 using ☐ × 65 = 3705.

2 **i** Find the answer to these.
ii Write down a calculation using inverse operations that you could do to check your answer.

a 9613 + 9423 **b** 5873 − 1659 **c** 321 × 89 **d** 2080 ÷ 65
e 20·7 ÷ 9 **f** 834·62 + 93·1 **g** 97 − 3·842 **h** 92·3 × 4·1

3 Neroli wanted to know how much 18 bags of crisps would cost.
Each bag costs £1·49.

a What calculation does she need to do?
b How much would 18 bags of crisps cost?
c What calculation could she do to check her answer?

***4** What calculation could you do to check these?
Use estimation *and* inverse operations.

a 80 231 − 4975 = 75 256 **b** 5421 ÷ 65 = 83·4 **c** 89·6 − 30·5 = 59·1
d 242·73 ÷ 2·9 = 83·7 **e** 581 × 62 = 36 022 **f** 9842 + 3754 = 13 596

Puzzle

Using the numbers in the squares write

four divisions such as $16 \div 2 = 8$
four multiplications such as $8 \times 3 = 24$
four additions such as $16 + 2 = 18$
and four subtractions such as $12 - 2 = 10$.

Each square must be used only once.

The 16 calculations will use *all* of the numbers.

16	8	2	2	8	6
5	6	18	16	4	40
6	18	2	6	10	32
32	2	24	3	3	4
8	4	6	8	24	8
18	32	5	8	2	3
12	18	40	6	10	24
12	24	2	9	6	12

* Checking answers using an equivalent calculation

We can check an answer to a calculation by doing an **equivalent calculation**.

Example $494 \times 5 = 2470$ can be checked by doing one of these calculations.

$(500 - 6) \times 5 = 500 \times 5 - 6 \times 5$

or $494 \times 10 \div 2$

or $400 \times 5 + 90 \times 5 + 4 \times 5$

Example $20{\cdot}8 \div 8 = 2{\cdot}6$ can be checked by doing one of these calculations.

$20{\cdot}8 \div 4 \div 2$

or $20 \div 8 + 0{\cdot}8 \div 8$

Exercise 9

1 Check the answers to these by doing an equivalent calculation.
If the answers are wrong give the correct answer.
Write down the calculation you did.

a $304 \times 5 = 1520$ **b** $893 \times 6 = 5358$
c $52 \times 40 = 2080$ **d** $705 \times 50 = 35\,250$
e $388 \div 4 = 48{\cdot}5$ **f** $495 \div 5 = 99$
g $86 \times 20 = 1270$ **h** $45 \times 98 = 4410$

Using a calculator

Jan did a calculation on her calculator.

She got 45.2

How she writes down the answer depends on what the question was.

Question	**Answer**
Pip bought five pictures for £226. How much did each cost?	**£45·20**
Madhu took 226 minutes to run five laps. How long did she take to run each lap?	45·2 minutes is 45 minutes and 0·2 of a minute. A minute is 60 seconds. $0{\cdot}2 \times 60 = 12$ The answer is **45 minutes and 12 seconds**.
Peter bought five lengths of fencing. Each length was 9·04 m long. What is the total length he bought?	45·2 m is 45 m and 0·2 of a metre. There are 100 centimetres in a metre. The answer is **45 m and 20 cm**.

Exercise 10

Always check your answer.

1 Robert paid £164 for five tickets to a show.
How much did each ticket cost?

2 Chloe bought 164 cm of ribbon. She cut it into five equal pieces.
How long, in cm and mm, was each piece?

3 Freda took 164 minutes to walk round the block five times.
How long did she take to walk round once? Give the answer in minutes and seconds.

4 Helen did a calculation and got the answer 16·4.
What should she write down if the question asked for
a £ **b** cm and mm **c** minutes and seconds
d hours and minutes **e** mm and cm?

***5** Tiffany measured one of her pet stick insects.
It was 3 cm and 4 mm long.
If eight of these stick insects lined up one behind the other, how long would the line be?

* **Discussion**

- 51 ÷ 8 = 6 **remainder** 3 or 6 R 3
  The calculator gives the answer to 51 ÷ **8** as 6·375.

  Sally said she could get the remainder 3 on the calculator. She subtracted 6 from 6·375 to get 0·375 on the screen. Then she multiplied by **8**. Does this give the remainder, 3? **Discuss.**

  0.375

  What do you need to key to give the remainder in these? $\frac{34}{8}$ $\frac{71}{4}$ $\frac{102}{5}$ **Discuss**.

- **Discuss** how to write 259 minutes in hours and minutes
  259 weeks in years and weeks
  259 months in years and months.

* **Exercise 11**

1 Find the remainder.
a $\frac{154}{5}$ b $\frac{261}{8}$ c $\frac{342}{4}$ d $\frac{411}{6}$ e $\frac{279}{16}$

2 Change these.
a 227 hours to days and hours
b 1862 hours to days and hours
c 527 minutes to hours and minutes
d 613 minutes to hours and minutes
e 426 weeks to years and weeks
f 379 weeks to years and weeks
g 195 months to years and months

3 Simone took 569 minutes to play the same CD six times.
How long does the CD take to play?
Give your answer in minutes and seconds.

Brackets on the calculator

Discussion

- $\frac{24}{6+2}$
  Emily and Tom did this on a calculator.
  Emily keyed [2] [4] [÷] [6] [+] [2] [=] and got the answer 6.
  Tom keyed [2] [4] [÷] [(] [6] [+] [2] [)] [=] and got the answer 3.
  Who is right? **Discuss.**

- $\dfrac{12 + 6}{3 - 1}$

  Janita, Asad, Mel and Peter did this on a calculator.
  Janita got 5.
  Asad got 9.
  Mel got 13.
  Peter got 15.

  Who is right. **Discuss**.

Sometimes to find the answer to a calculation, we need to use the **brackets** on a calculator.

brackets

Worked Example
Calculate these.

a $3{\cdot}7 - (2{\cdot}09 - 1{\cdot}6)$

b $\dfrac{8{\cdot}2}{9{\cdot}6 - 5{\cdot}5}$

Remember: The horizontal line acts as a bracket.

Answer

a Key 3 · 7 − (2 · 0 9 − 1 · 6) = to get **3·21**.

b Key 8 · 2 ÷ (9 · 6 − 5 · 5) = to get **2**.

Both the numerator and denominator must have brackets.

Exercise 12

1 **a** $7 + 3(14 + 8)$ **b** $48 - 2(3 + 11)$ **c** $47 \times (396 - 72)$
d $52 \times (851 - 36)$ **e** $(7 + 14) \times (23 + 28)$ **f** $(52 + 81) \times (37 - 19)$
g $314 - (827 - 619)$ **h** $816 - (327 - 214)$

2 Calculate these.
a $5{\cdot}2 \times (9{\cdot}6 - 3{\cdot}85)$ **b** $7{\cdot}2 \times (15{\cdot}73 - 8{\cdot}6)$ **c** $8{\cdot}2 + 5(6{\cdot}4 + 1{\cdot}04)$

3 Calculate these.
a $\frac{135}{5 + 4}$ **b** $\frac{120 + 15}{21 - 6}$ **c** $\frac{10{\cdot}5}{7{\cdot}6 - 4{\cdot}1}$ **d** $\frac{7{\cdot}6 + 10{\cdot}6}{0{\cdot}9 + 1{\cdot}7}$

Summary of key points

We **add and subtract decimals** by lining up the decimal points.

Examples

```
  32·35        5 11 1
 +16·9          162·39
 ------       -  54·62
  49·25        -------
  1             107·77
```

Multiplying by a 1-digit number

Example 21·6 × 7 is about 20 × 7 = 140

21·6 × 7 = 216 × 7 ÷ 10

21·6 × 7 = 216 ÷ 10 × 7
= 216 × 7 ÷ 10

```
   216
 ×   7
 -----
  1512
   14
```

and 1512 ÷ 10 = **151·2**

Multiplying by a 2-digit number

Example 5·6 × 14 is about 6 × 10 = 60.

5·6 × 14 is the same as 56 ÷ 10 × 14 = 56 × 14 ÷ 10.

```
   56
 × 14
 ----
  560     56 × 10
  224     56 × 4
 ----
  784
```

and 784 ÷ 10 = **78·4**

Dividing by a 1-digit number

Example 20·8 ÷ 8 is about 20 ÷ 10 = 2.

```
8)20·8
 −16·0    8 × 2
 -----
   4·8
  −4·8    8 × 0·6
  ----
     0
```

Answer **2·6**

```
  18
 × 3
 ---
  54
```

Dividing by a 2-digit number

Example 594 ÷ 18 is about 600 ÷ 20 = 30.

```
18)594
  −540    18 × 30
  ----
    54
   −54    18 × 3
   ---
     0
```

Answer **33**

- Always **check that an answer is sensible**.
- Always **estimate** the answer to calculations.

We can check the answer to a calculation using **inverse operations**.

Addition and **subtraction** are **inverse operations**.

Multiplication and **division** are **inverse operations**.

Examples $1184 - 397 = 787$ so $787 + 397 = 1184$

$197 \times 31 = 6107$ so $6107 \div 31 = 197$ and $6107 \div 197 = 31$

Sometimes we need to **interpret** the answer given by a calculator.

Example [5.6] might be £5·60 or 5 hours 36 minutes or 5 metres 60 centimetres and so on.

Sometimes we use **brackets** on a calculator.

Example 4·2 – (3·6 – 1·2)

Key [4] [·] [2] [–] [(] [3] [·] [6] [–] [1] [·] [2] [)] [=] to get **1·8**.

In a fraction, the horizontal line acts as a bracket.

Example $\dfrac{8{\cdot}6}{4{\cdot}5 - 3{\cdot}8}$

Key [8] [·] [6] [÷] [(] [4] [·] [5] [–] [3] [·] [8] [)] [=]

to get **12·3** to 1 d.p.

Test yourself

Except questions 13, 14 and 15.

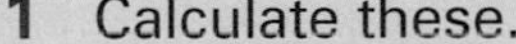

1 Calculate these.

a 6423 + 865	**b** 7·96 + 8·3	**c** 17·07 + 8·65	**d** 36·8 + 5·79
e 9806 – 394	**f** 20·6 – 19·24	**g** 314·7 – 19·64	**h** 800·5 – 3·69

2 **a** 8·36 + 52·9 + 4 + 0·23 **b** 16 – 5·83 – 4·27 + 14·9

3 Amy bought trainers for £79·60 and socks for £4·72.
How much did these cost altogether?

4 a 34×45 b 56×89 c 278×56 d 445×38 C

5 Sari needed 5 m of lace for a tablecloth she was making for design and technology.
How much did it cost, to the nearest penny? B

Lace
£1·89
per m

6 a $52{\cdot}7 \times 8$ b $3 \times 4{\cdot}63$ c $5{\cdot}74 \times 4$ d $16 \times 11{\cdot}4$ B

7 Tennis balls are packed in tubes of 15.
There are 154 tubes in a crate.
How many balls are there altogether? C

8 a $24{\cdot}8 \div 4$ b $122{\cdot}4 \div 8$ c $226{\cdot}8 \div 7$ D

9 A block of apricot cheese is to be divided into eight equal pieces.
The block weighs 98·4 g.
How much will each piece weigh? D

10 a $210 \div 14$ b $336 \div 24$ c $592 \div 16$ d $420 \div 28$ E

11 Marilyn ran round a 3·6 km track 18 times.
She worked out she had run 648 km.
Is this answer sensible? F

12 Check each calculation by looking at the size of the answer.
If the answer is wrong, explain how you can tell.
a $5{\cdot}2 \times 6{\cdot}3 = 2{\cdot}9$ b $8{\cdot}3 \div 0{\cdot}4 = 2{\cdot}075$ c $89 \div 6{\cdot}8 = 197$ F

13 Using inverse operations, write down a calculation you could do to check the answer to these.
a $836 \times 42 = 35\,112$ b $364{\cdot}8 \div 1{\cdot}9 = 192$ c $8{\cdot}36 + 19{\cdot}72 = 28{\cdot}08$ G

14 Calculate. Give the answer to 1 d.p. if you need to round.
a $(53 + 21) \times 75$ b $4{\cdot}2 + (6{\cdot}8 - 0{\cdot}87)$ c $\frac{8{\cdot}3 + 4{\cdot}2}{8{\cdot}3}$ d $\frac{17{\cdot}6}{4{\cdot}2 + 3{\cdot}7}$ I

15 Convert
a 186 hours to days and hours b 373 seconds to minutes and seconds. H

5 Fractions

You need to know

✓	fractions	– mixed numbers, improper fractions	page 7
✓		– equivalent fractions	
✓		– finding a fraction of	
✓	decimals		page 7

Key vocabulary

cancel, convert, lowest terms, simplest form, unit fraction

The whole sound of music

Music is written in 'bars'.
In a bar the note values often add up to one whole note.
The possible notes are:

𝅝 = one whole note (semibreve)

𝅗𝅥 = half note

♩ = quarter note

♪ = eighth note

𝅘𝅥𝅯 = sixteenth note

1 Which of these bars do **not** have notes which add to one whole note?

2 Write the bars for these notes.
a $\frac{1}{2}, \frac{1}{4}, \frac{1}{4}$ **b** $\frac{1}{4}, \frac{1}{8}, \frac{1}{8}, \frac{1}{4}, \frac{1}{4}$ **c** $\frac{1}{16}, \frac{1}{16}, \frac{1}{16}, \frac{1}{16}, \frac{1}{8}, \frac{1}{8}, \frac{1}{4}, \frac{1}{8}, \frac{1}{8}$

3 Write four bars of your own music. Make each bar add to one whole note.

Fractions of shapes

Unit fractions have numerator 1.

Example $\frac{1}{5}$, $\frac{1}{8}$, $\frac{1}{15}$ are unit fractions.

$\frac{2}{3}$, $\frac{3}{7}$, $\frac{5}{12}$ are not.

Investigation

T

Unit fractions

This rectangle has 24 small squares.
It is divided into three parts.

$\frac{1}{2}$ is blue (12 squares).

$\frac{1}{3}$ is red (8 squares).

$\frac{1}{6}$ is yellow (4 squares).

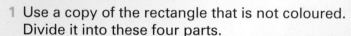

1 Use a copy of the rectangle that is not coloured.
Divide it into these four parts.

$\frac{1}{2}$ $\frac{1}{3}$ $\frac{1}{8}$ $\frac{1}{24}$

2 Divide it into four parts in a different way.
Each part should be one of these fractions.

$\frac{1}{2}$ $\frac{1}{3}$ $\frac{1}{4}$ $\frac{1}{6}$ $\frac{1}{8}$ $\frac{1}{12}$ $\frac{1}{24}$

*3 Divide it into five parts.
Each part should be one of these fractions.

$\frac{1}{2}$ $\frac{1}{3}$ $\frac{1}{4}$ $\frac{1}{6}$ $\frac{1}{8}$ $\frac{1}{12}$ $\frac{1}{24}$

Hint: Two of them are $\frac{1}{2}$ and $\frac{1}{8}$.

Example We can **estimate** from this pie chart that
about $\frac{1}{3}$ of calcium comes from milk
about $\frac{1}{6}$ comes from cereal.

Calcium in the British diet

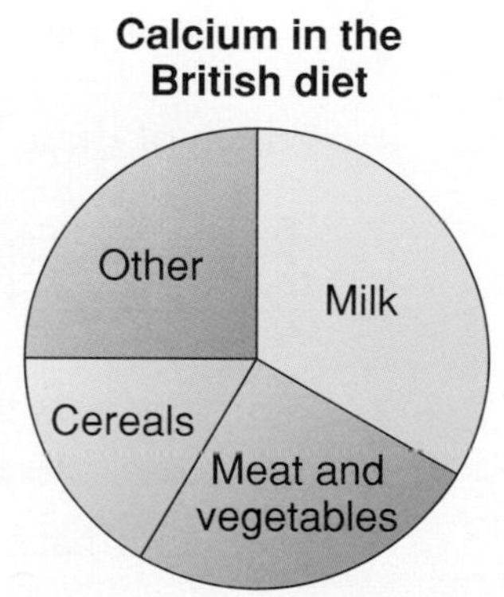

Exercise 1

1 What fraction of each shape is shaded?

a

b

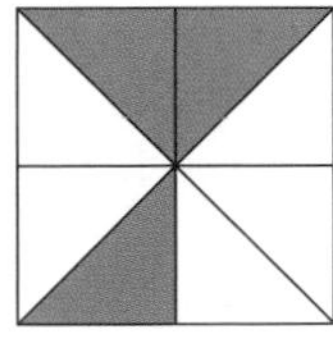

***c**

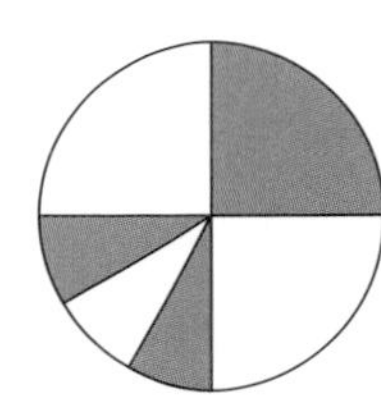

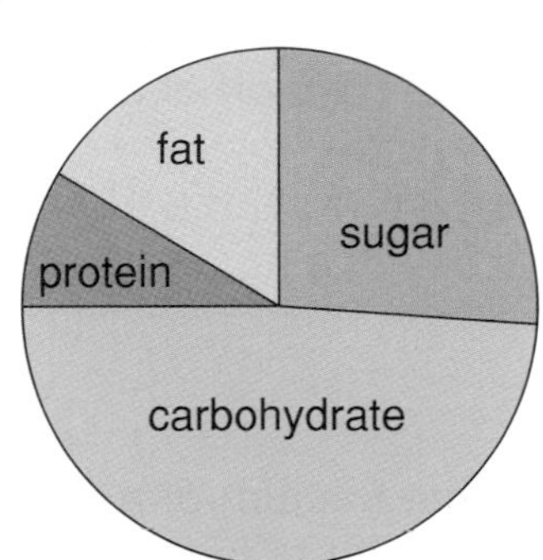

2 The pie chart shows what is in a muesli bar.
Estimate the fraction of the muesli bar that is
a sugar
b fat.

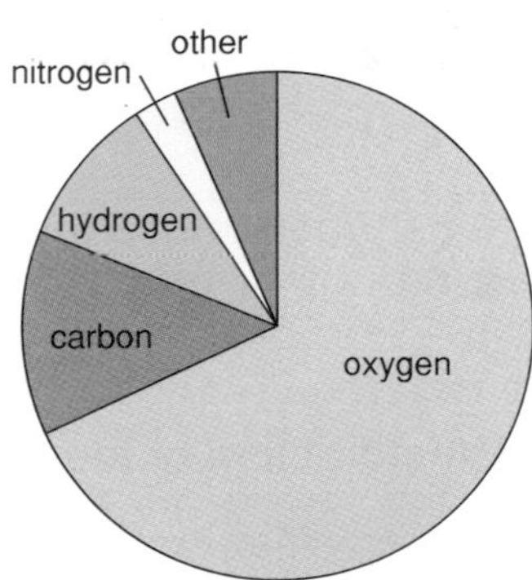

3 The pie chart shows what a human body is made of.
Estimate the fraction of the human body that is
a oxygen
b carbon.

One number as a fraction of another

Jason had a piece of wood 1 m long.
He cut off 43 cm.

1 metre = 100 centimetres

43 cm as a fraction of a metre = $\frac{43}{100}$

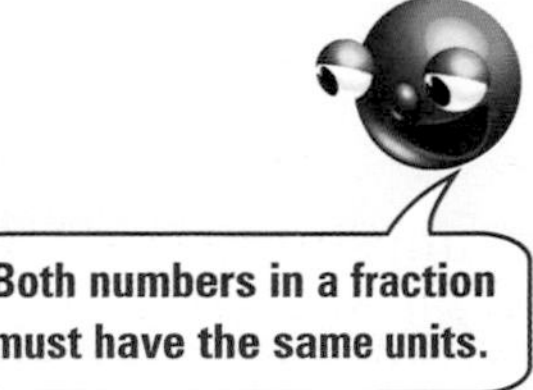

Both numbers in a fraction must have the same units.

Example Nick wants to know what fraction of a turn the minute hand turns through between 6:25 p.m. and 6:40 p.m.

Between 6:25 p.m. and 6:40 p.m. the hand turns through 15 minutes.
This is $\frac{1}{4}$ of a turn.

Exercise 2

1 What fraction of

a 1 metre is 51 centimetres
b 1 kilogram is 37 grams
c 1 hour is 13 minutes
d 1 metre is 17 centimetres
e £2 is 87p
f 1 yard is a foot
g 1 litre is 183 millilitres?

2 What fraction of a turn does the minute hand turn through between

a 8 p.m. and 8:15 p.m.
b 2:20 a.m. and 2:40 a.m.
c 11:10 a.m. and 11:40 a.m.?

3 What fraction of a turn takes you from facing

a north to facing south
*__b__ north to facing north-west
*__c__ north to facing south-west?

N
NW NE
W E
SW SE
S

4 What fraction of a turn is

a 90° **b** 120° ***c** 36°?

*__5__ What fraction of the large shape is the small one?

a  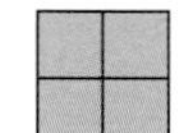 **b** 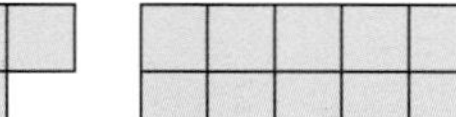 **c** 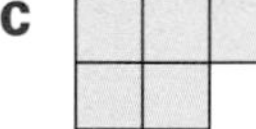

Equivalent fractions

Practical

The shaded diagram shows that $\frac{1}{2}$, $\frac{2}{4}$, $\frac{4}{8}$, $\frac{8}{16}$ are equal.

Use two copies of the unshaded diagram.

Fill them in to show that these sets of fractions are equal.

1 $\frac{1}{2}$, $\frac{3}{6}$, $\frac{5}{10}$, $\frac{6}{12}$

2 $\frac{1}{4}$, $\frac{2}{8}$, $\frac{3}{12}$, $\frac{4}{16}$

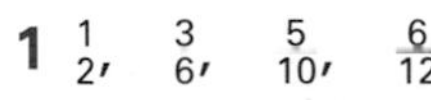

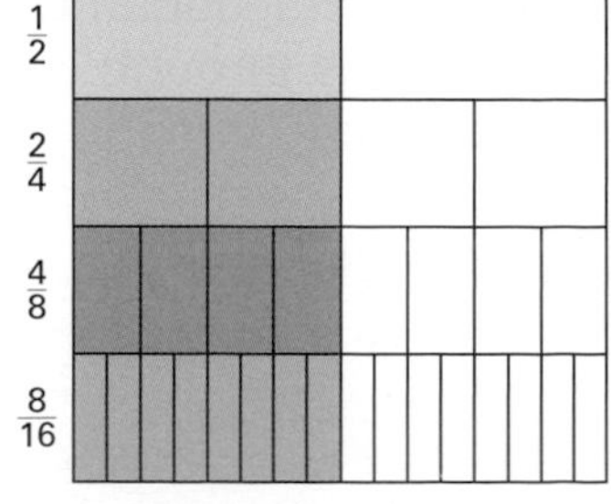

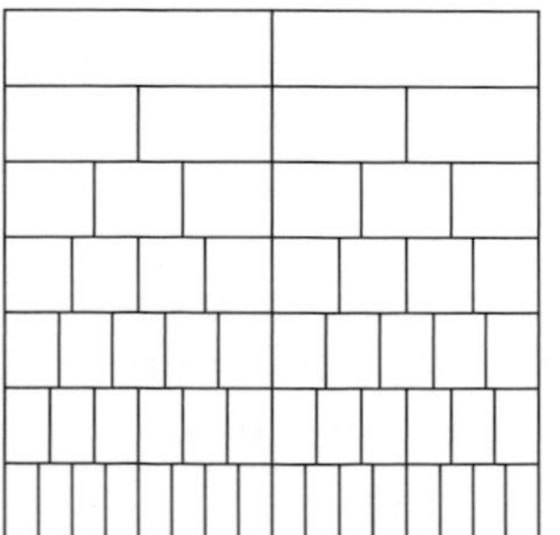

Equal fractions are called **equivalent fractions**.

Examples $\frac{1}{2}, \frac{2}{4}, \frac{4}{8}, \frac{6}{12}, \frac{50}{100}$ are equivalent fractions.
They all equal $\frac{1}{2}$.

$\frac{1}{1}, \frac{4}{4}, \frac{8}{8}, \frac{100}{100}$ all equal 1.

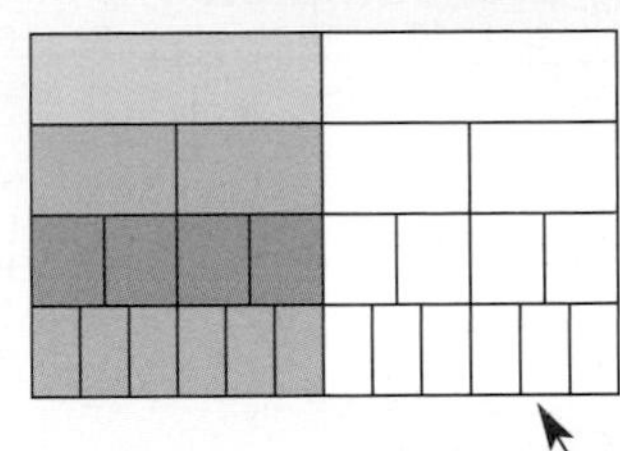

This diagram shows that $\frac{1}{2}, \frac{2}{4}, \frac{4}{8}$ and $\frac{6}{12}$ are all equal.

We make equivalent fractions by multiplying or dividing both the numerator and denominator by the same number.

Example

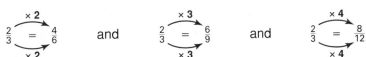

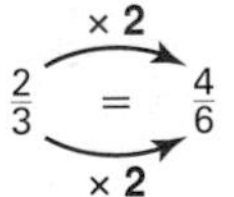

$\frac{2}{3} = \frac{4}{6}$ (× 2)

and

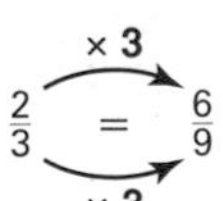

$\frac{2}{3} = \frac{6}{9}$ (× 3)

and

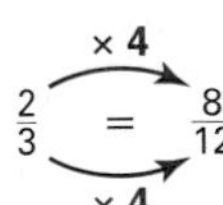

$\frac{2}{3} = \frac{8}{12}$ (× 4)

$\frac{2}{3} = \frac{4}{6} = \frac{6}{9} = \frac{8}{12}$

Example

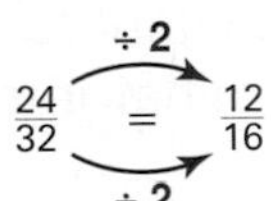

$\frac{24}{32} = \frac{12}{16}$ (÷ 2)

and

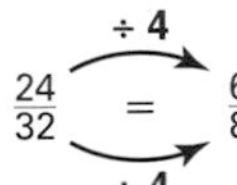

$\frac{24}{32} = \frac{6}{8}$ (÷ 4)

and

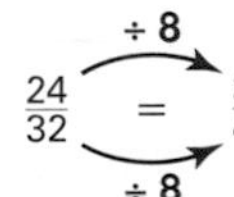

$\frac{24}{32} = \frac{3}{4}$ (÷ 8)

$\frac{24}{32} = \frac{12}{16} = \frac{6}{8} = \frac{3}{4}$

Exercise 3

This exercise is to be done mentally.

1 What number goes in the box to make an equivalent fraction?

a $\frac{1}{8} = \frac{\square}{16}$ (× 2)

b $\frac{1}{5} = \frac{3}{\square}$ (× 3)

c $\frac{4}{18} = \frac{\square}{9}$ (÷ 2)

d

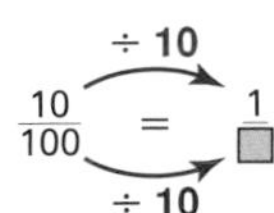

$\frac{10}{100} = \frac{1}{\square}$ (÷ 10)

e

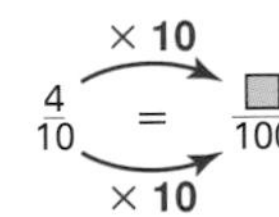

$\frac{4}{10} = \frac{\square}{100}$ (× 10)

f $\frac{6}{15} = \frac{2}{\square}$ (÷ 3)

g

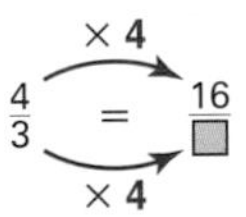

$\frac{4}{3} = \frac{16}{\square}$ (× 4)

h

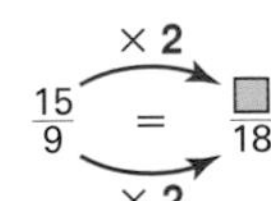

$\frac{15}{9} = \frac{\square}{18}$ (× 2)

i

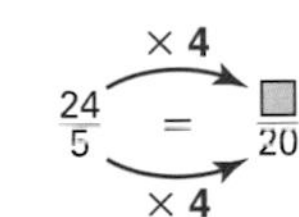

$\frac{24}{5} = \frac{\square}{20}$ (× 4)

j

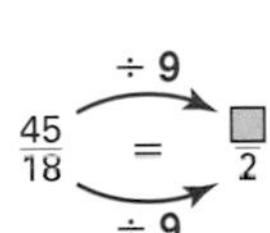

$\frac{45}{18} = \frac{\square}{2}$ (÷ 9)

k $\frac{24}{20} = \frac{\square}{5}$ (÷ 4)

T **2**

			A					A			A		
24	35	2	4	8	64	12	4	8	3	4	8	12	

				–	A				
2	12	7	20	6	4	1	5	12	5

Use a copy of this box.
What goes in the box?
Write the letter beside each fraction, above an equivalent fraction in the box.

A $\frac{1}{2} = \frac{2}{4}$ **S** $\frac{6}{10} = \frac{\square}{5}$ **L** $\frac{8}{12} = \frac{\square}{3}$ **D** $\frac{12}{15} = \frac{4}{\square}$ **N** $\frac{28}{28} = \frac{1}{\square}$ **T** $\frac{25}{100} = \frac{5}{\square}$ **E** $\frac{4}{9} = \frac{\square}{27}$

P $\frac{5}{8} = \frac{15}{\square}$ **O** $\frac{7}{10} = \frac{\square}{50}$ **R** $\frac{4}{15} = \frac{\square}{30}$ **B** $\frac{6}{16} = \frac{24}{\square}$ **F** $\frac{63}{81} = \frac{\square}{9}$ **H** $\frac{35}{42} = \frac{5}{\square}$

3 Copy and complete.

a $\frac{2}{5} = \frac{\square}{10} = \frac{10}{\square} = \frac{16}{\square}$ **b** $\frac{3}{8} = \frac{6}{\square} = \frac{\square}{24} = \frac{\square}{40} = \frac{\square}{80}$ **c** $\frac{2}{3} = \frac{\square}{9} = \frac{12}{\square} = \frac{\square}{12}$

***4** Write two equivalent fractions for each of these.

a $\frac{1}{3}$ **b** $\frac{1}{6}$ **c** $\frac{3}{8}$ **d** $\frac{3}{4}$ **e** $\frac{5}{6}$

You can use jottings for **questions 4** and **5** if you need to.

***5** Write the equivalent fraction which has a denominator of 24.

a $\frac{1}{2}$ **b** $\frac{2}{3}$ **c** $\frac{3}{4}$ **d** $\frac{5}{6}$ **e** $\frac{3}{8}$

Puzzle

1 I am equivalent to $\frac{2}{3}$.
My denominator is 10 more than my numerator.
What fraction am I?

2 I am equivalent to $\frac{80}{100}$.
My denominator is a prime number.
What fraction am I?

Cancelling a fraction to its lowest terms

$\frac{2}{3}$ is in its **lowest terms**.

Sometimes we call it 'simplest form'.

2 and 3 have no common factors other than 1.

$\frac{8}{12}$ is **not** in its lowest terms.
8 and 12 can both be divided by 4.

We write a fraction in its lowest terms by **cancelling**.

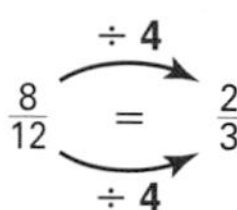

We divide 8 and 12 by 4.
4 is the Highest Common Factor (HCF) of 8 and 12.

Examples $\frac{{}^{3}\cancel{15}}{{}_{4}\cancel{20}} = \frac{3}{4}$ **We divide 15 and 20 by 5.**
5 is the HCF of 15 and 20.

$\frac{6}{42} = \frac{1}{7}$ **We divide 6 and 42 by 6.**
6 is the HCF of 6 and 42.

There is more about HCF on page 000.

If you find it hard, you could cancel in steps.

Example $\frac{\cancel{28}^{4}}{\cancel{42}^{6}} = \frac{4}{6}$ **We divide 28 and 42 by 7.**
We can cancel again.

$\frac{\cancel{4}^{2}}{\cancel{6}^{3}} = \frac{2}{3}$ **We divide 4 and 8 by 2.**
2 is the Highest Common Factor of 4 and 6.

Exercise 4

1 Cancel these to their simplest form.

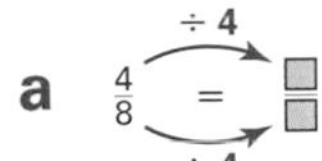

a $\frac{4}{8} = \frac{\square}{\square}$ (÷ 4)

b $\frac{2}{6} = \frac{\square}{\square}$ (÷ 2)

c $\frac{3}{15} = \frac{\square}{\square}$ (÷ 3)

d $\frac{4}{12} = \frac{\square}{\square}$ (÷ 4)

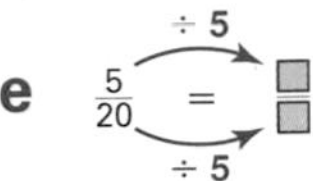

e $\frac{5}{20} = \frac{\square}{\square}$ (÷ 5)

f $\frac{6}{18}$ g $\frac{6}{8}$ h $\frac{8}{12}$ i $\frac{15}{60}$ j $\frac{16}{20}$

k $\frac{24}{40}$ l $\frac{15}{25}$ *m $\frac{15}{18}$ *n $\frac{24}{36}$ o $\frac{35}{42}$

p $\frac{56}{63}$ q $\frac{56}{72}$ r $\frac{36}{96}$ s $\frac{48}{108}$

2 Give the answers as fractions in their lowest terms.

Hollydale School is organising a fair.

a 4 of the 28 outside stalls are to be covered. What fraction will be covered?

b 15 of the 21 inside stalls need two tables. What fraction is this?

*3 Write these as fractions of an hour in their simplest form.

a 30 minutes b 20 minutes c 45 minutes d 27 minutes

Fractions and decimals

Remember

$0{\cdot}1 = \frac{1}{10}$

$0{\cdot}2 = \frac{2}{10}$

$0{\cdot}3 = \frac{3}{10}$

$1{\cdot}7 = 1\frac{7}{10}$

units	tenths
0	1

one tenth or $\frac{1}{10}$

$0{\cdot}01 = \frac{1}{100}$

$0{\cdot}02 = \frac{2}{100}$

$0{\cdot}03 = \frac{3}{100}$

units	tenths	hundredths
0	0	1

one hundredth or $\frac{1}{100}$

$0{\cdot}25 = \frac{1}{4}$

$0{\cdot}5 = \frac{1}{2}$

$0{\cdot}75 = \frac{3}{4}$

To **convert a decimal to a fraction** make the denominator 10 or 100. Cancel, if possible, to give the fraction in its simplest form.

Examples $0{\cdot}6 = \frac{\cancel{6}^3}{\cancel{10}_5} = \frac{3}{5}$ $0{\cdot}71 = \frac{71}{100}$ $1{\cdot}25 = 1\frac{\cancel{25}^1}{\cancel{100}_4} = 1\frac{1}{4}$

Exercise 5

1 Write these as fractions.

a 0·3 b 0·9 c 0·7 d 0·1 e 0·41

f 0·73 g 0·83 h 1·9 i 1·75 j 2·37

T **2**

$\frac{1}{4}$	$\frac{4}{25}$	**1932**	$\frac{2}{5}$	$\frac{3}{5}$	**E** $\frac{1}{5}$		$\frac{4}{25}$	$\frac{1}{4}$	$\frac{1}{2}$	$\frac{9}{20}$	$\frac{1}{2}$	$\frac{3}{4}$	$\frac{1}{2}$

$\frac{13}{20}$	$\frac{1}{2}$	$1\frac{3}{5}$	$1\frac{3}{5}$	$\frac{4}{5}$	$\frac{13}{20}$	$\frac{3}{4}$	$\frac{11}{50}$	$\frac{3}{20}$	**E** $\frac{1}{5}$	$\frac{4}{5}$	$\frac{11}{50}$	$1\frac{3}{5}$	$\frac{1}{4}$	$\frac{87}{100}$

Use a copy of this box.
Write these as fractions in their lowest terms.
Write the letter beside each above its answer.

E $0{\cdot}2 = \frac{2}{10} = \frac{1}{5}$	**D** 0·87	**S** 0·8	**T** 0·4	**H** 0·6
O 0·22	**N** 0·16	**I** 0·25	**R** 0·75	**Z** 0·15
A 0·5	**F** 0·65	**G** 0·45	**L** 1·6	

T **3** Use a copy of these diagrams. Beside each is a decimal.
Show the decimal number by shading the diagram.

a 0·3

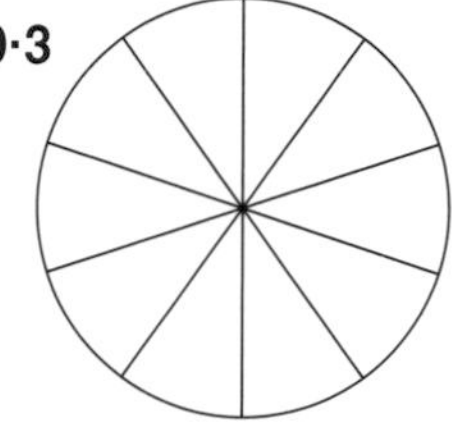

b 0·25

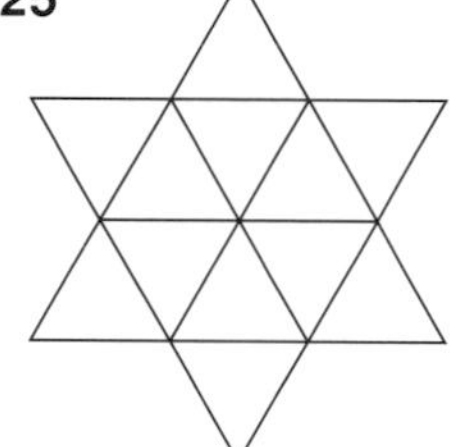

c 0·75

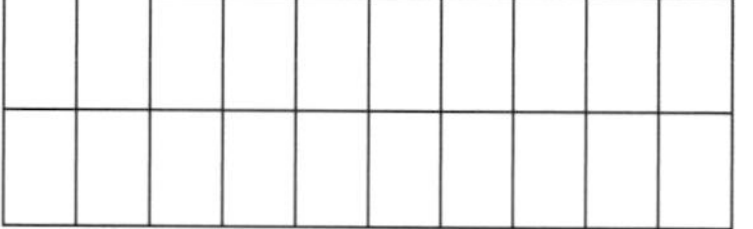

*__4__ Which of the following does *not* show 0·6?

a

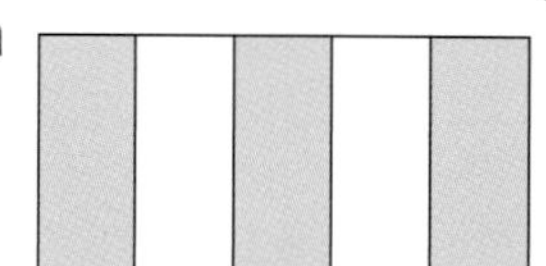

b

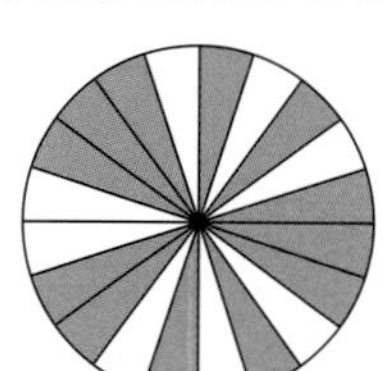

c

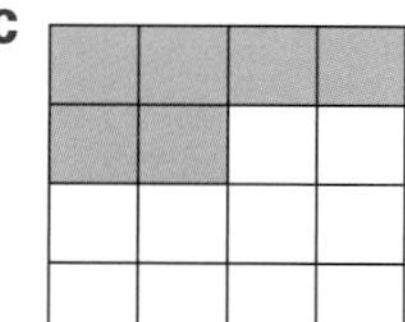

d

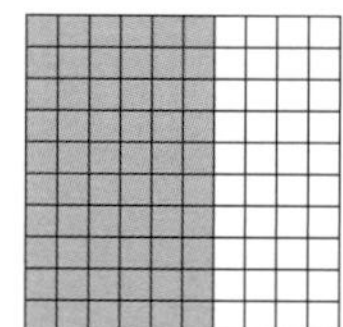

Remember

$\frac{1}{2} = 0{\cdot}5$ $\quad \frac{1}{4} = 0{\cdot}25$ $\quad \frac{3}{4} = 0{\cdot}75$ $\quad \frac{1}{5} = 0{\cdot}2$

To **convert a fraction to a decimal** we can

1 use one of the facts above

$\frac{2}{5} = 2 \times \frac{1}{5}$
$= 2 \times 0{\cdot}2$
$= 0{\cdot}4$

$\frac{1}{8} = \frac{1}{4} \div 2$
$= 0{\cdot}25 \div 2$
$= 0{\cdot}125$

$\frac{9}{12} = \frac{3}{4}$
$= 0{\cdot}75$

2 make an equivalent fraction with denominator 10 or 100

$\frac{7}{20} \overset{\times 5}{=} \frac{35}{100}$
$= 0{\cdot}35$

$\frac{12}{40} = \frac{3}{10}$
$= 0{\cdot}3$

See page 27 for rounding to 1 d.p.

3 use a calculator.

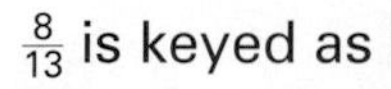

$\frac{8}{13}$ is keyed as [8] [÷] [13] [=] to get 0·615 384 615
We round this to 1 d.p. to get 0·6.

Exercise 6

Except for question 5.

1 Write these as decimals.

a $\frac{7}{10}$ **b** $\frac{3}{10}$ **c** $\frac{81}{100}$ **d** $\frac{63}{100}$

e $\frac{4}{100}$ **f** $1\frac{9}{10}$ ***g** $\frac{25}{10}$ ***h** $\frac{216}{100}$

2 Convert these to decimals. Use a fact from the box to help.
Find the answers mentally.

a $\frac{1}{2}$ **b** $\frac{3}{4}$ **c** $\frac{4}{5}$ **d** $\frac{5}{20}$

e $\frac{1}{8}$ **f** $2\frac{1}{4}$ **g** $3\frac{3}{6}$ ***h** $\frac{12}{16}$

$\frac{1}{2} = 0{\cdot}5$ $\frac{1}{4} = 0{\cdot}25$
$\frac{1}{5} = 0{\cdot}2$

3 Write these as decimals by first writing them with a denominator of 10 or 100.

a $\frac{4}{20} = \frac{}{10} =$ **b** $\frac{4}{5} = \frac{}{10} =$ **c** $\frac{14}{20} = \frac{}{10} =$ **d** $\frac{7}{50} = \frac{}{100} =$

e $\frac{40}{200} = \frac{}{100} =$ **f** $\frac{8}{40} = \frac{}{10} =$ ***g** $\frac{36}{60} = \frac{}{10} =$ ***h** $\frac{9}{30} = \frac{}{10} =$

4 What fraction of each shape is shaded?
Write your answer as a decimal?

a

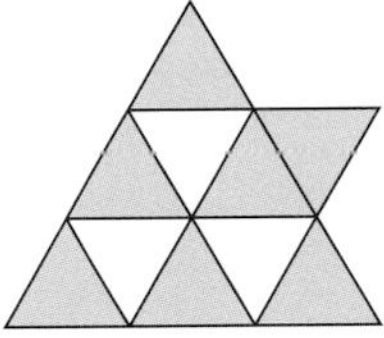

b

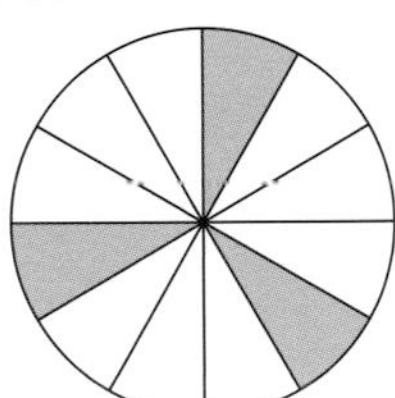

c

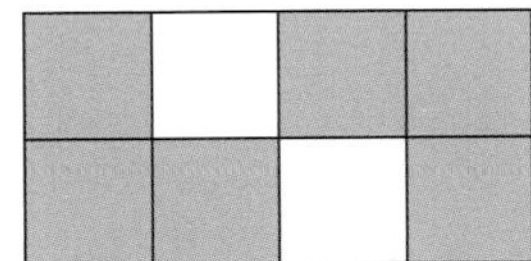

5 Use your calculator to convert these to decimals.
Round your answers to 1 decimal place.

a $\frac{3}{13}$ **b** $\frac{4}{17}$ **c** $\frac{5}{19}$ **d** $\frac{15}{26}$ **e** $\frac{17}{23}$ **f** $\frac{15}{17}$

Ordering fractions

A diagram is a good way to **compare fractions**.

We can see from this diagram that

$\frac{1}{2} > \frac{1}{3} > \frac{1}{4} > \frac{1}{5} > \frac{1}{6} > \frac{1}{7} > \frac{1}{8}$.

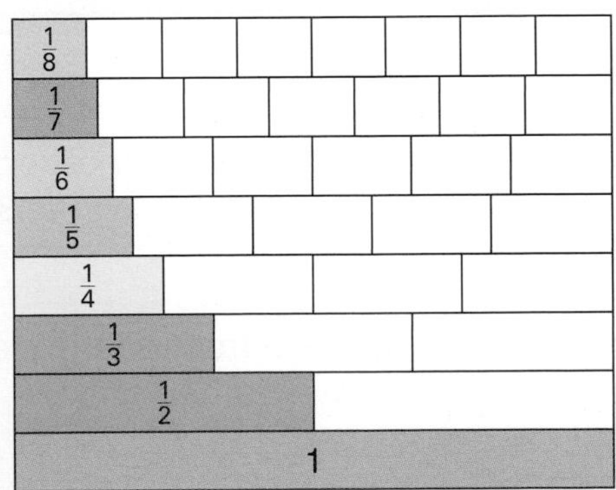

We could also use lines divided into parts.

Worked Example

Write these fractions in order, smallest to largest.

$\frac{3}{4}$, $\frac{4}{5}$, $\frac{2}{3}$

Answer

We can see from the lines that the fractions in order from smallest to largest are $\frac{2}{3}$, $\frac{3}{4}$, $\frac{4}{5}$.

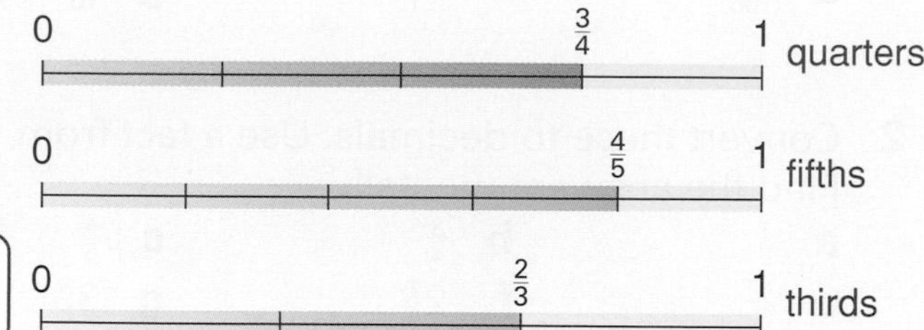

A line of 60 mm is easy to divide up.

Exercise 7

Use the diagram on the previous page to answer **question 1**.

1 Which of < or > goes in the box.

a $\frac{1}{2}$ ☐ $\frac{2}{3}$ **b** $\frac{3}{5}$ ☐ $\frac{1}{2}$ **c** $\frac{5}{8}$ ☐ $\frac{1}{2}$ **d** $\frac{3}{5}$ ☐ $\frac{2}{3}$ **e** $\frac{7}{8}$ ☐ $\frac{5}{6}$

2 Write these fractions in order from smallest to largest.
Use the number lines to help.

a $\frac{1}{2}$, $\frac{3}{8}$, $\frac{1}{4}$ **b** $\frac{5}{6}$, $\frac{6}{7}$, $\frac{2}{3}$ **c** $\frac{7}{8}$, $\frac{3}{4}$, $\frac{4}{5}$ **d** $\frac{1}{4}$, $\frac{2}{5}$, $\frac{3}{8}$

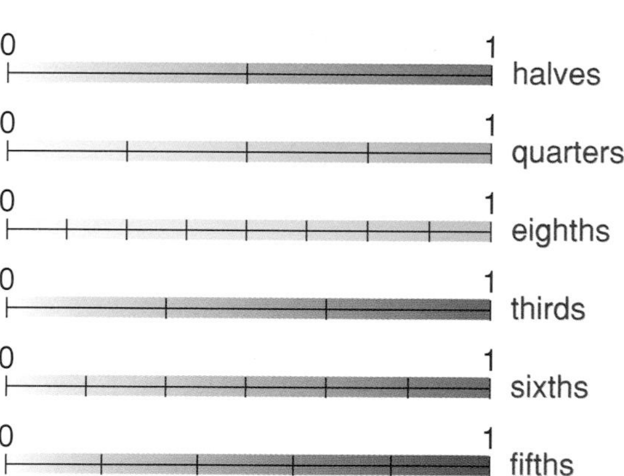

3 Write these fractions in order, smallest first.

a $1\frac{1}{4}$, $1\frac{1}{2}$, $1\frac{2}{3}$ **b** $3\frac{1}{4}$, $3\frac{3}{8}$, $3\frac{2}{5}$, $3\frac{1}{5}$ **c** $2\frac{3}{10}$, $1\frac{7}{8}$, $2\frac{3}{5}$, $1\frac{3}{5}$, $1\frac{5}{6}$

***4** Which of these fractions is closer to 1?
Explain how you can tell.

a $\frac{3}{4}$ or $\frac{4}{3}$ **b** $\frac{7}{8}$ or $\frac{8}{7}$

Adding and subtracting fractions

We can **add and subtract simple fractions mentally.**

$\frac{1}{4} + \frac{1}{2} = \frac{3}{4}$

$\frac{1}{4}$ + $\frac{1}{2}$ = $\frac{3}{4}$

$\frac{3}{4} + \frac{3}{4} = 1\frac{1}{2}$

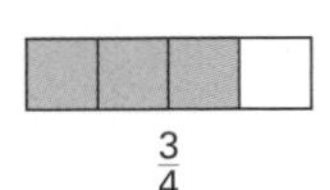

$\frac{3}{4}$ + $\frac{3}{4}$ =

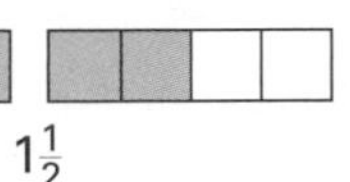

$1\frac{1}{2}$

$\frac{1}{8} + \frac{1}{8} = \frac{1}{4}$

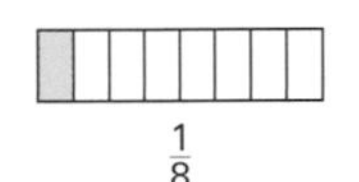

$\frac{1}{8}$ + $\frac{1}{8}$ = $\frac{1}{4}$

It is easy to add and subtract fractions when the **denominators are the same.**

Examples $\frac{2}{5} + \frac{1}{5} = \frac{2+1}{5}$ $= \frac{3}{5}$

$\frac{3}{10} - \frac{1}{10} = \frac{3-1}{10}$ $= \frac{\not{2}^1}{\not{10}^5}$ $= \frac{1}{5}$

Always cancel fractions if you can.

$\frac{6}{9} + \frac{5}{9} - \frac{1}{9} = \frac{6+5-1}{9}$ $= \frac{10}{0}$ $= \frac{9}{9} + \frac{1}{9}$ $= 1\frac{1}{9}$

Change improper fractions to mixed numbers.

Exercise 8

1 Find the answers to these mentally. Use diagrams to help.

a $\frac{1}{2} + \frac{1}{4}$ **b** $\frac{3}{4} + \frac{1}{2}$ **c** $\frac{1}{2} - \frac{3}{8}$ **d** $\frac{3}{4} - \frac{1}{2}$ **e** $\frac{1}{8} + \frac{1}{8} + \frac{1}{8}$

f $\frac{1}{2} - \frac{1}{8}$ **g** $\frac{1}{8} + \frac{1}{8} + \frac{1}{4}$ **h** $\frac{3}{4} + \frac{1}{8}$ **i** $\frac{5}{8} - \frac{1}{4}$

2 Calculate these.

a $\frac{1}{5} + \frac{2}{5}$ **b** $\frac{3}{14} + \frac{5}{14}$ **c** $\frac{7}{8} - \frac{5}{8}$ **d** $\frac{11}{15} + \frac{14}{15}$ **e** $\frac{11}{12} + \frac{5}{12}$ **f** $\frac{7}{16} + \frac{9}{16}$

3 **a** $\frac{1}{8} + \frac{1}{8} + \frac{3}{8}$ **b** $\frac{7}{10} + \frac{3}{10} + \frac{1}{10} + \frac{4}{10}$ **c** $\frac{3}{12} + \frac{5}{12} + \frac{7}{12} + \frac{4}{12}$

d $\frac{5}{20} + \frac{17}{20} + \frac{8}{20} + \frac{6}{20}$ **e** $\frac{4}{15} + \frac{7}{15} + \frac{1}{15} + \frac{3}{15}$

4 **a** $\frac{7}{10} + \frac{2}{10} - \frac{4}{10}$ **b** $\frac{3}{12} + \frac{5}{12} + \frac{4}{12} - \frac{3}{12}$ **c** $\frac{6}{15} + \frac{7}{15} - \frac{8}{15}$

d $\frac{11}{12} + \frac{11}{12} + \frac{5}{12} - \frac{1}{12}$ **e** $\frac{19}{20} + \frac{3}{20} - \frac{7}{20}$ **f** $\frac{8}{10} + \frac{3}{10} - \frac{5}{10}$

5 Debs had $\frac{7}{12}$ of her bus card left.
She used another $\frac{3}{12}$ of it.
What fraction did she have left then?

We **add and subtract fractions with different denominators** using equivalent fractions.

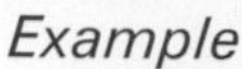

Example $\frac{1}{3}+\frac{5}{6}$ ← **different denominators**

$=\frac{2}{6}+\frac{5}{6}$ ← **make both denominators the same**

$=\frac{7}{6}$

$=1\frac{1}{6}$

$\frac{1}{3} \xrightarrow{\times 2} \frac{2}{6}$

Example $\frac{7}{8}-\frac{1}{4}=\frac{7}{8}-\frac{2}{8}$

$=\frac{7-2}{8}$

$=\frac{5}{8}$

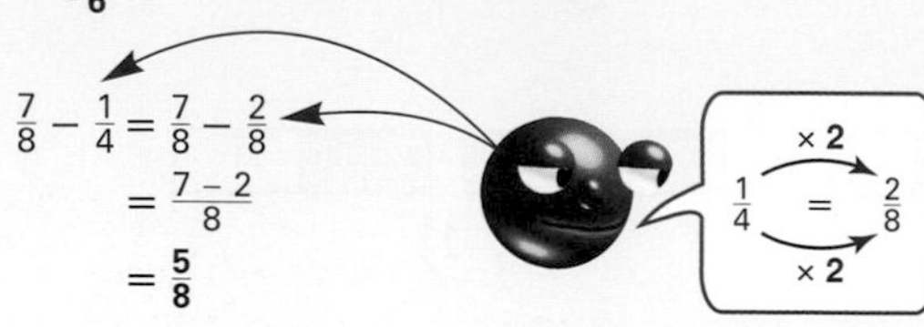

Exercise 9

1 Copy these and fill in the gaps?

a $\frac{1}{2}+\frac{3}{10}=\frac{}{10}+\frac{3}{10}$ (×5)

$=\frac{}{10}$

$=$ ___

b $\frac{1}{3}+\frac{1}{6}=\frac{}{6}+\frac{1}{6}$ (×2)

$=\frac{}{6}$

$=$ ___

c $\frac{3}{7}+\frac{5}{14}=\frac{}{14}+\frac{5}{14}$

$=\frac{}{14}$

d $\frac{7}{10}-\frac{1}{5}=\frac{7}{10}-\frac{}{10}$

$=\frac{}{10}$

$=$ ___

e $\frac{9}{10}-\frac{1}{2}=\frac{9}{10}-\frac{}{10}$

$=\frac{}{10}$

$=$ ___

f $\frac{5}{12}-\frac{1}{6}=\frac{5}{12}-\frac{}{12}$

$=\frac{}{12}$

$=$ ___

2 **a** $\frac{1}{3}+\frac{1}{12}$ **b** $\frac{3}{5}+\frac{3}{10}$ **c** $\frac{1}{2}+\frac{1}{10}$ **d** $\frac{7}{10}-\frac{1}{5}$

e $\frac{11}{12}-\frac{2}{3}$ **f** $\frac{3}{16}+\frac{1}{4}$ **g** $\frac{14}{15}-\frac{2}{3}$ **h** $\frac{7}{20}-\frac{1}{10}$

3 **a** $\frac{3}{10}+\frac{2}{5}+\frac{1}{10}$ **b** $\frac{3}{4}+\frac{1}{8}-\frac{1}{4}$ **c** $\frac{5}{9}+\frac{1}{3}-\frac{2}{9}$ **d** $\frac{7}{20}-\frac{1}{5}+\frac{1}{4}$

4 Fran bought $\frac{2}{5}$ m of ribbon and then another $\frac{3}{10}$ m.
What fraction of a metre did she buy altogether?

5 $\frac{1}{4}$ of a park is grass and $\frac{3}{8}$ is a playground.
What fraction of the park is this altogether?

Fraction of

Remember

To find $\frac{1}{5}$ we divide by 5. $\frac{1}{5}$ of $30 = 30 \div 5 = 6$

To find $\frac{1}{8}$ we divide by 8. $\frac{1}{8}$ of $56 = 56 \div 8 = 7$

Example Harry sat a science test.
It was out of 50.
Harry got $\frac{4}{5}$ of the possible marks.

$\frac{1}{5}$ of $50 = 50 \div 5$
$= 10$

$\frac{4}{5}$ of $50 = \mathbf{4} \times 10$
$= \mathbf{40}$

You can do ones like this mentally.

Worked Example

Find $\frac{1}{8}$ of 280.

Answer

Find $\frac{1}{4}$ of 280, then halve it.

$\frac{1}{4}$ of $280 = 280 \div 4 = 70$

$\frac{1}{2}$ of $70 = \mathbf{35}$

Exercise 10

T **1**

_ _ _ _ _ _ _ _   _ N _ _
20 40 36 16 180 180 63 21   15 4 8 9

_ _ _ _ _   **5**   _ _ N _ _ _ _
21 8 63 63 30   27 40 4 45 6 63 21

_ _ _ _
16 14 16 9

Use a copy of this box.
Find the answers to these mentally.
Write the letter that is beside each question above its answer.

N $\frac{1}{6}$ of 24 = 4	**L** $\frac{1}{7}$ of 56	**D** $\frac{2}{5}$ of 35	**T** $\frac{3}{7}$ of 14	**O** $\frac{3}{10}$ of 50
A $\frac{2}{3}$ of 24	**M** $\frac{3}{4}$ of 36	**I** $\frac{2}{5}$ of 100	**S** $\frac{3}{8}$ of 56	**U** $\frac{5}{6}$ of 54
Y $\frac{3}{7}$ of 21	**E** $\frac{7}{9}$ of 81	**R** $\frac{4}{5}$ of 45	**P** $\frac{1}{8}$ of 240	
G $\frac{1}{7}$ of 140	**F** $\frac{3}{8}$ of 480			

2 **a** $1\frac{1}{2}$ of 20 kg   **b** $1\frac{1}{4}$ of 40 cm   **c** $1\frac{1}{4}$ of 36 g   **d** $2\frac{1}{2}$ of 10 p

3 Anju found 0·75 of 48 like this.

$0{\cdot}75 = \frac{3}{4}$

$0{\cdot}75 \text{ of } 48 = \frac{3}{4} \text{ of } 48$

$\frac{1}{4} \text{ of } 48 = 48 \div 4$
$= 12$
$\frac{3}{4} \text{ of } 48 = 3 \times 12$
$= 48$

Use Anju's method to find these.

a 0·5 of 18 **b** 0·5 of 28 **c** 0·25 of 24 **d** 0·75 of 32

4 **a** In the story Peter Pan, the children spent $\frac{1}{8}$ of a day in Never-Never Land.
How many hours was this?

b A Jupiter day is about $\frac{3}{8}$ of an Earth day.
About how many hours are there in a Jupiter day?

c On the moon, a person's weight is about $\frac{1}{6}$ of their weight on earth.
About how many kilograms would a person weigh on the moon if their weight on earth is 54 kg?

***5** **a** $\frac{3}{10}$ of £120 **b** $\frac{7}{10}$ of 210 km **c** $\frac{3}{5}$ of 350 m **d** $\frac{5}{9}$ of 450 cm

You may need to write some things down to do these.

***6** **a** Write $\frac{3}{10}$ of 1 cm in millimetres.

b Write $\frac{7}{1000}$ of 1 metre in millimetres.

T

Puzzle

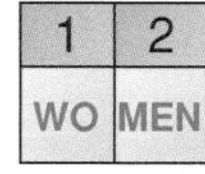

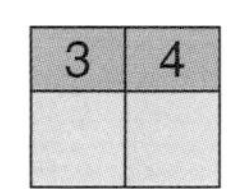

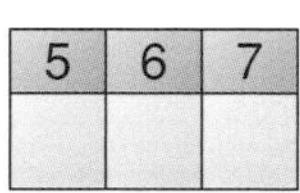

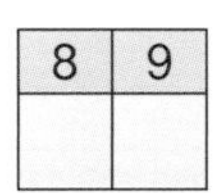

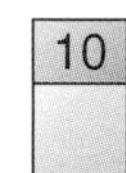

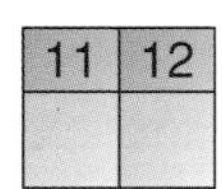

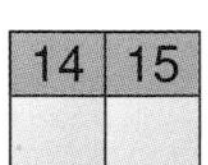

Use a copy of the chart.
Use the clues below to fill it in. The first one is done.

1 First two fifths of *women*.
2 First three quarters of *mend*.
3 First quarter of *blankets*.
4 Last three fifths of *think*.
5 Second half of *lane*.
6 Last two thirds of *car*.
7 Last third of *really*.
8 First two thirds of *two*.
9 Last three quarters of *nice*.
10 Middle third of *Alaska*.
11 First two fifths of *munch*.
12 Last third of *crunch*.
13 First two thirds of *ask*.
14 Last third of *Sam*.
15 Last fifth of *chairwomen*.

Multiplying fractions and integers

$\frac{1}{4}$ of 20 = $\frac{1}{4} \times 20$ = $20 \div 4$

$\frac{1}{4}$ of 20, $\frac{1}{4} \times 20$ and $20 \div 4$ all give the same answer.

Examples $\frac{1}{8} \times 24 = \frac{1}{8}$ of 24
$= 24 \div 8$
$= \mathbf{3}$

$\frac{3}{8} \times 16 = \frac{3}{8}$ of 16
$\frac{1}{8}$ of 16 $= 16 \div 8$ find $\frac{1}{8}$ first
$= 2$
$\frac{3}{8}$ of 16 $= 3 \times 2$ now multiply by 3 to find $\frac{3}{8}$
$= \mathbf{6}$

Exercise 11

1 Write true or false for these.
a $\frac{1}{4}$ of $16 = \frac{1}{4} \times 16$ **b** $\frac{1}{3}$ of $18 = 18 \times 3$ **c** $\frac{1}{4} \times 24 = 24 \div 4$

2 Calculate these.
a $\frac{1}{5} \times 20$ **b** $\frac{1}{3} \times 24$ **c** $\frac{1}{6} \times 30$ **d** $\frac{1}{7} \times 42$
e $\frac{3}{5} \times 20$ **f** $\frac{3}{8} \times 16$ **g** $\frac{7}{10} \times 40$ **h** $\frac{5}{6} \times 24$

***3** Amy wanted to find $\frac{3}{5} \times 4$.
She wrote $\frac{3}{5} \times 4 = 3 \times \frac{1}{5} \times 4$
$= 3 \times 4 \times \frac{1}{5}$ I can multiply in any order.
$= 12 \times \frac{1}{5}$ 12 lots of $\frac{1}{5}$ is $\frac{12}{5}$.
$= \frac{12}{5}$ or $2\frac{2}{5}$
Use Amy's way to find the answers to these.

a $2 \times \frac{1}{3} = 2$ lots of $\frac{1}{3}$
= ___
b $3 \times \frac{1}{5} = 3$ lots of $\frac{1}{5}$
= ___
c $5 \times \frac{1}{6}$ **d** $5 \times \frac{1}{8}$
e $\frac{1}{4} \times 3$ **f** $\frac{2}{5} \times 3$ **g** $\frac{3}{8} \times 5$ **h** $\frac{5}{6} \times 5$

Summary of key points

Unit fractions have a numerator of 1.
Examples $\frac{1}{8}, \frac{1}{12}, \frac{1}{16}$

Five out of six parts are shaded.
We write this as $\frac{5}{6}$.

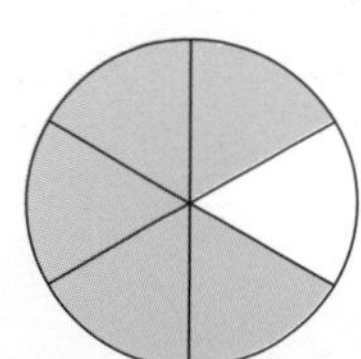

When **writing one number as a fraction of another**, make sure the numerator and denominator have the same units.

Example 37 minutes as a fraction of an hour is $\frac{37}{60}$. **1 hour is 60 minutes.**

$\frac{2}{3}, \frac{4}{6}, \frac{6}{9}, \frac{8}{12}, \frac{10}{15}, \ldots$ are **equivalent fractions**.

We find **equivalent fractions** by multiplying or dividing both the numerator and denominator by the same number.

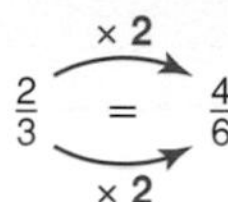

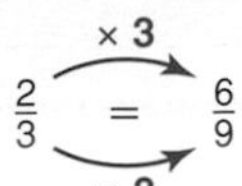

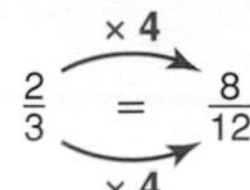

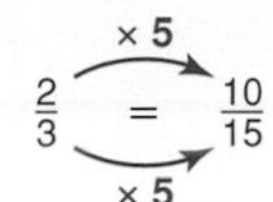

We simplify a fraction to its lowest terms by **cancelling**.

Example $\frac{24^4}{30^5} = \frac{4}{5}$ **Both 24 and 30 have been divided by 6. 6 is the Highest Common Factor of 24 and 30.**

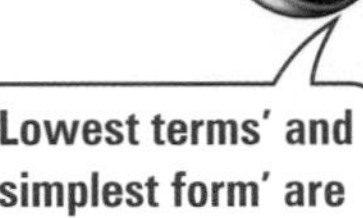

'Lowest terms' and 'simplest form' are the same.

To convert a **decimal to a fraction**, write it as tenths or hundredths and then cancel.

$0{\cdot}8 = \frac{8^4}{10^5} = \frac{4}{5}$ $\quad 0{\cdot}93 = \frac{93}{100}$ $\quad 1{\cdot}65 = 1\frac{65}{100} = 1\frac{13}{20}$

Cancel the fraction to its simplest form if possible.

We can write **a fraction as a decimal**

1 using **facts we already know**

Example $\frac{4}{5} = 4 \times \frac{1}{5}$

$= 4 \times 0{\cdot}2$

$= 0{\cdot}8$

2 by making an **equivalent fraction** with denominator 10 or 100

Example $\frac{3}{20} = \frac{15}{100}$

$= 0{\cdot}15$

Multiply numerator and denominator of $\frac{3}{20}$ by 5.

3 using a **calculator**.

Example $\frac{5}{13}$ is keyed as 5 ÷ 1 3 = to get 0·384615384.

We round this to 1 d.p. to get 0·4.

We can use this diagram to **order fractions**.

We can also divide lines of the *same length* into parts.

Example

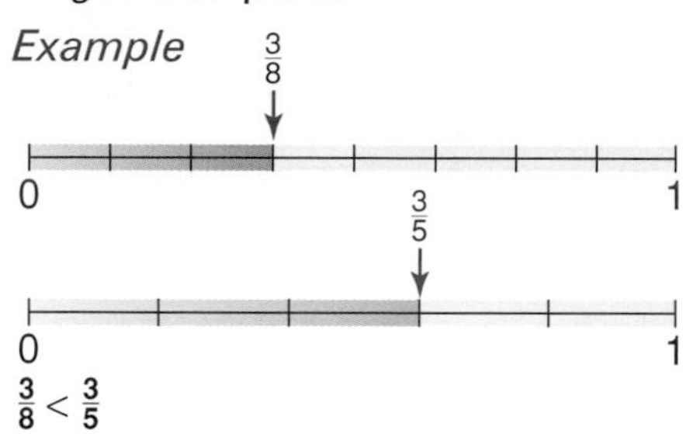

$\frac{3}{8} < \frac{3}{5}$

$\frac{1}{8}$							
$\frac{1}{7}$							
$\frac{1}{6}$							
$\frac{1}{5}$							
$\frac{1}{4}$							
$\frac{1}{3}$							
$\frac{1}{2}$							
1							

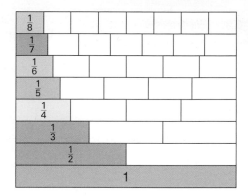

We can **add (or subtract) fractions** which have the **same denominator** as follows.

Example $\frac{3}{5} + \frac{4}{5} = \frac{3+4}{5}$ ← **keep the denominator**

$= \frac{7}{5}$

$= \mathbf{1\frac{2}{5}}$

To **add (or subtract) fractions** which have **different denominators** change to equivalent fractions with the same denominator.

Example $\frac{1}{2} + \frac{3}{10} = \frac{5}{10} + \frac{3}{10}$

$= \frac{5+3}{10}$

$= \frac{8}{10}$

$= \mathbf{\frac{4}{5}}$

$\frac{1}{2} = \frac{5}{10}$

Fraction of a quantity

Example To find $\frac{3}{5}$ of £45.

$\frac{1}{5}$ of £45 = £45 ÷ 5

= £9

$\frac{\mathbf{3}}{5}$ of £45 = **3** × £9

= £27

$\frac{1}{3}$ of 12, $\frac{1}{3} \times 12$, $12 \times \frac{1}{3}$, $12 \div 3$ are all equivalent.

Examples $\frac{2}{3} \times 6 = 2 \times \frac{1}{3} \times 6$

$= 2 \times 2$

$= 4$

$\frac{1}{7} \times 5 = 5 \times \frac{1}{7}$ **5 lots of $\frac{1}{7}$.**

$= \frac{5}{7}$

Test yourself

Except for question 10

1 What fraction of this shape is shaded? 

2 The pie chart shows the time of day at which burglaries took place in one year. 
Estimate the fraction that took place
a at night **b** in the afternoon.

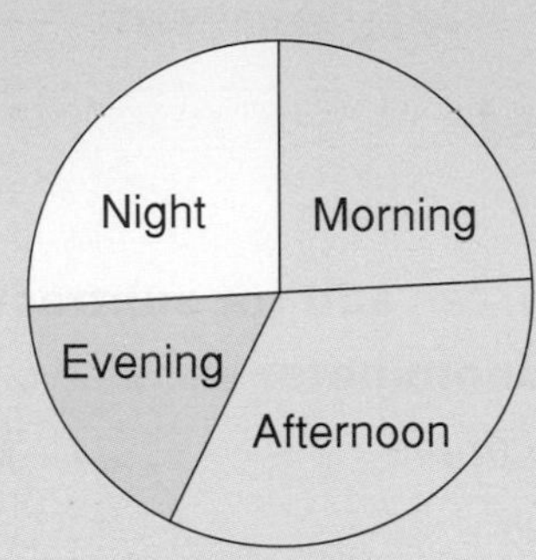

3 What fraction of 
a 1 metre is 51 centimetres **b** 1 kilogram is 49 grams
c 1 hour is 43 minutes?

4 Copy and complete. 
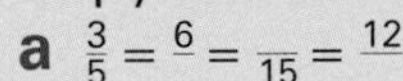
a $\frac{3}{5} = \frac{6}{\ } = \frac{\ }{15} = \frac{12}{\ }$ **b** $\frac{5}{8} = \frac{\ }{16} = \frac{\ }{24} = \frac{20}{\ } = \frac{25}{\ }$ **c** $\frac{2}{7} = \frac{4}{\ } = \frac{\ }{21} = \frac{\ }{28} = \frac{\ }{35}$

5 Write two equivalent fractions for each of these. 
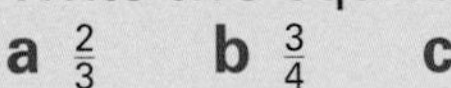
a $\frac{2}{3}$ **b** $\frac{3}{4}$ **c** $\frac{1}{8}$

6 Use cancelling to write these fractions in their lowest terms. 
a $\frac{7}{21}$ **b** $\frac{6}{8}$ **c** $\frac{16}{20}$ **d** $\frac{10}{15}$ **e** $\frac{18}{24}$ **f** $\frac{15}{40}$

7 Give the answers to these as fractions in their lowest terms.
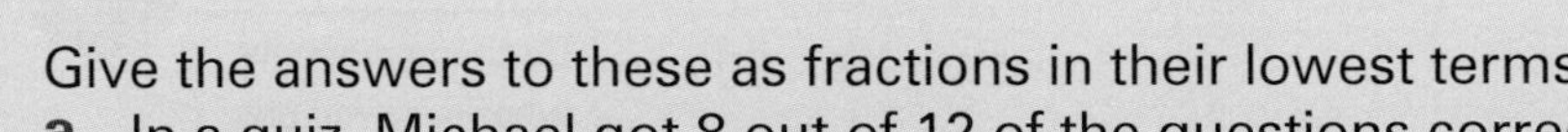
a In a quiz, Michael got 8 out of 12 of the questions correct.
What fraction did he get *wrong*?
b On Monday 48 animals were seen by a vet.
36 were dogs.
What fraction is this?

8 Write these as fractions.
a 0·5 **b** 0·3 **c** 0·6 **d** 0·43 **e** 0·45 **f** 0·28

9 Write these as decimals. 
a $\frac{1}{5}$ **b** $\frac{6}{8}$ **c** $\frac{79}{100}$ **d** $\frac{4}{100}$ **e** $\frac{6}{25}$ **f** $1\frac{1}{2}$

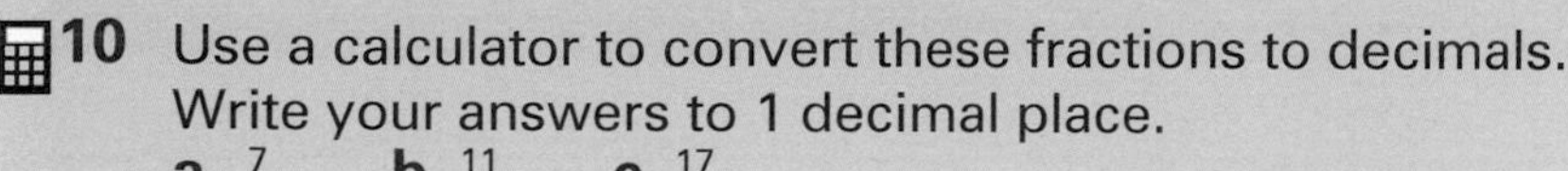

10 Use a calculator to convert these fractions to decimals. 
Write your answers to 1 decimal place.
a $\frac{7}{13}$ **b** $\frac{11}{17}$ **c** $\frac{17}{26}$

11 Write these fractions in order, largest first.
a $\frac{1}{4}, \frac{2}{5}, \frac{3}{4}, \frac{3}{8}, \frac{1}{6}$ **b** $1\frac{4}{5}, 1\frac{3}{4}, 1\frac{7}{8}, 1\frac{5}{8}$

Use the number lines in question 2 on page 104 to help you.

12 **a** $\frac{3}{5}+\frac{1}{5}$ **b** $\frac{1}{8}+\frac{3}{8}+\frac{1}{8}$ **c** $\frac{3}{4}-\frac{1}{2}$ **d** $\frac{7}{8}-\frac{3}{8}$ **e** $\frac{4}{9}+\frac{5}{9}$ 

13 Find the answers to these. 
The first one has been started.
a $\frac{1}{5}+\frac{1}{10}=\frac{2}{10}+\frac{1}{10}$ **b** $\frac{7}{8}-\frac{1}{2}$ **c** $\frac{2}{3}+\frac{5}{6}$ **d** $\frac{7}{8}-\frac{3}{4}$

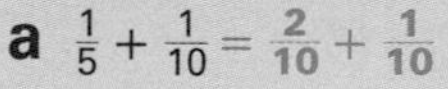

14 **a** $\frac{2}{3}$ of £36 **b** $\frac{5}{8}$ of 56 cm **c** $\frac{3}{7}$ of 21 m **d** $\frac{5}{8}$ of 240 g

Do as many as possible mentally.

15 Jake had 18 plums.
He ate $\frac{2}{3}$ of them and gave the rest away.
How many did he give away?

16 **a** $\frac{1}{3}\times 24$ **b** $16\times\frac{1}{4}$ **c** $\frac{3}{8}\times 32$ ***d** $\frac{1}{5}\times 2$

6 Percentages, Fractions, Decimals

You need to know

✓ fractions page 7

✓ decimals page 7

✓ percentages page 8

Key vocabulary

decimal, discount, interest, percentage (%)

How much?!

- We often estimate percentages.

  About what percentage of the petrol tank is full?

  About what percentage of this file has downloaded?

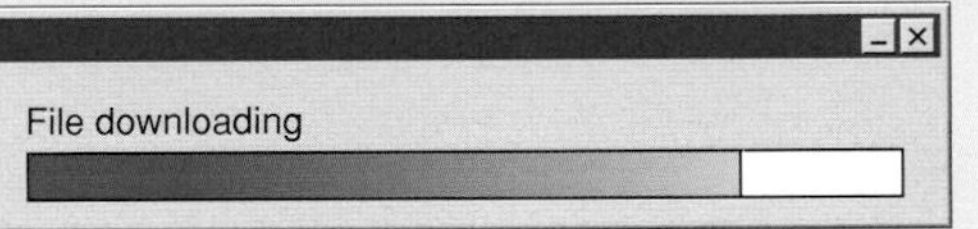

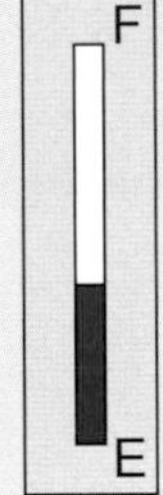

  Think about other times we estimate percentages.

- We often give proportions of a whole as percentages.

Age	%
11	17%
12	21%
13	19%
14	22%
15	17%
16	4%

  What should the total add up to in each case?

  Think about other times we divide a whole into percentages.

- How are percentages used to help sell goods?

Converting fractions, decimals and percentages

Percentages to decimals and fractions

Remember
'Per cent' means 'out of 100'.
67% means 67 out of 100 or $\frac{67}{100}$ or 0·67.

u	t	h	th
0 •	6	7	

We always **cancel** fractions if we can.

Example Mani got 80% in her ballet exam.

$80\% = \frac{\cancel{80}^{\,4}}{\cancel{100}_{\,5}}$

$= \mathbf{\frac{4}{5}}$

You could cancel $\frac{80}{100}$ in steps.
$\frac{80}{100} = \frac{40}{50} = \frac{20}{25} = \frac{4}{5}$

You need to know these.

$100\% = 1$ $25\% = \frac{1}{4}$ $50\% = \frac{1}{2}$ $75\% = \frac{3}{4}$

$10\% = \frac{1}{10}$ $1\% = \frac{1}{100}$ $33\frac{1}{3}\% = \frac{1}{3}$

Exercise 1

1 Write these as fractions.
a 37% **b** 21% **c** 53% **d** 91%

2 Write these as decimals.
a 14% **b** 62% **c** 51% **d** 35%

3 Write these as fractions in their lowest terms.
a 1% **b** 25% **c** 50% **d** 30% **e** 70%
f 75% **g** 90% **h** $33\frac{1}{3}\%$ **i** 5% **j** 45%
k 62% **l** 120%

T **4**

$\frac{11}{20}$ $\frac{16}{25}$ 0·35 $\frac{16}{25}$ $\frac{9}{25}$ 0·15 $\frac{87}{100}$ (A) $\frac{9}{20}$ 0·46 $\frac{6}{25}$ $\frac{87}{100}$ (A) $\frac{17}{100}$ $\frac{9}{20}$

$\frac{17}{100}$ 0·1   0·35 $\frac{17}{100}$ 0·25 $\frac{16}{25}$ $\frac{11}{20}$ $\frac{4}{5}$

$\frac{3}{25}$ 0·35 $\frac{6}{25}$ $\frac{22}{25}$ 0·35 $\frac{9}{20}$ $\frac{11}{20}$ $\frac{47}{50}$ $\frac{87}{100}$ (A) $\frac{11}{20}$ 0·35 $\frac{6}{25}$

Use a copy of the box on the previous page.
Write these as fractions in their lowest terms.
Write the letter that is beside each question above its answer.

A 87% = $\frac{87}{100}$ **I** 17% **Y** 80% **H** 64% **W** 94%
N 45% **C** 88% **P** 12% **T** 55% **R** 24%
U 36%

Write these as decimals.

S 10% **G** 25% **E** 35% **M** 15% **B** 46%

5 78% of people in Britain listen to tapes, records or CDs.
What fraction is this?

6 In a survey it was found that 95% of Americans had been to McDonald's in the last year.
Write 95% as a **a** decimal **b** fraction.

Fractions and decimals to percentages

Remember

Fractions and decimals can be converted to percentages by writing them with a denominator of 100.

Examples $0{\cdot}85 = \frac{85}{100} = 85\%$ $0{\cdot}07 = \frac{7}{100} = 7\%$

$\frac{2}{5} = \frac{40}{100} = 40\%$ (× 20 top and bottom) $\frac{7}{25} = \frac{28}{100} = 28\%$ (× 4 top and bottom)

Exercise 2

1 Write these as percentages.

a 1 **b** 0·25 **c** 0·5 ***d** 0·8 ***e** 0·45
f 0·65 **g** 0·08 **h** 0·03 **i** 1·25 **j** 1·6

2 Which of these percentages is the same as the fraction?

a $\frac{4}{5}$	**A** 8%	**B** 40%	**C** 80%
b $\frac{9}{10}$	**A** 90%	**B** 19%	**C** 9%
c $\frac{7}{20}$	**A** 70%	**B** 7%	**C** 35%
d $\frac{9}{25}$	**A** 18%	**B** 36%	**C** 90%

T

3 Use a copy of this.
Write these fractions as percentages.
Shade the percentage in the grid.

a $\frac{3}{4}$ **b** $\frac{1}{10}$ **c** $\frac{1}{2}$ **d** $\frac{3}{10}$
e $\frac{1}{100}$ **f** $\frac{1}{3}$ **g** $\frac{7}{10}$ **h** $\frac{49}{100}$
i $\frac{17}{50}$ **j** $\frac{13}{20}$ **k** $\frac{11}{25}$

What letter does the shading make?

60%	50%	65%	$33\frac{1}{3}$%	27%
100%	49%	56%	25%	5%
90%	30%	70%	10%	17%
7%	44%	3%	20%	39%
94%	1%	75%	34%	33%

4

40%	75%	30%	20%	50%	60%	25%	80%	70%

Find a percentage from the purple box for each sentence.

a Seven out of ten people watch the news on TV.
b One out of every two people who eat at McDonald's is under 12.
c In a survey it was found that maths was the favourite subject for three quarters of students.
d Two out of every five people go abroad for their summer holiday.
e Six out of every twenty students play a musical instrument.

5 These diagrams show how much petrol is left in the tanks of four cars.

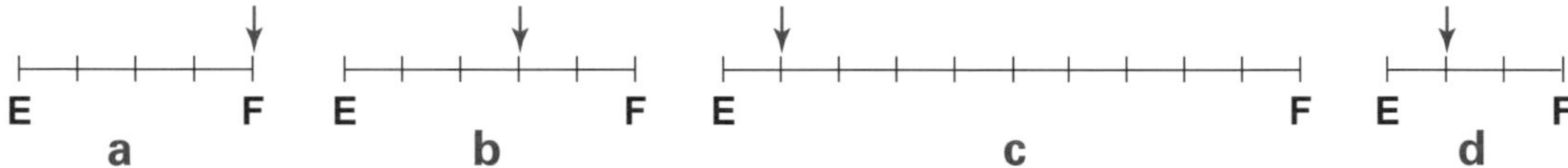

E is empty. **F** is full.
What percentage is left in each case?

6 **a** 5p in 100p.
What percentage is this?
b 25p in £1.
What percentage is this?

***7** **a** What fraction of this shape is red?
b What percentage is red?
c What percentage is *not* red?

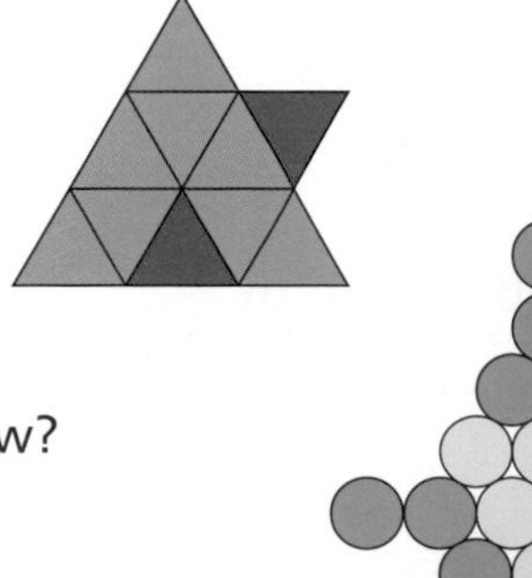

***8** **a** What fraction of the circles are yellow?
b Write this as a percentage.
c Write this as a decimal.

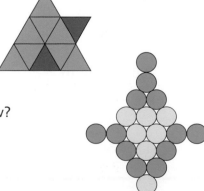

Practical

Ask 20 people these questions.

- Have you ever been to Spain?
- Do you think you should be allowed fires on Guy Fawkes?
- Have you seen Prince William in person?
- Have you been on a yacht?
- Do you like Robbie Williams' music?

Work out the percentage who said 'Yes' to each.

Percentage of – mentally

Remember
10% = $\frac{1}{10}$

We sometimes use facts like these to find percentages mentally.

Example To find 5% of 42 m, find 10% and halve it.

10% of 42 m = 42 ÷ 10
= 4·2 m
$\frac{1}{2}$ of 4·2 m = **2·1 m**

Example Broomfield School raised £5600.
11% of this went to the RSPCA.
11% of £5600 = **£616**

10% of £5600 = £560
1% of £5600 = £56
11% of £5600 = £560 + £56 **11% = 10% + 1%**
= £616

Example 30% of 180 m = **54 m**

10% of 180 = 18
30% = 3 × 18
= 54

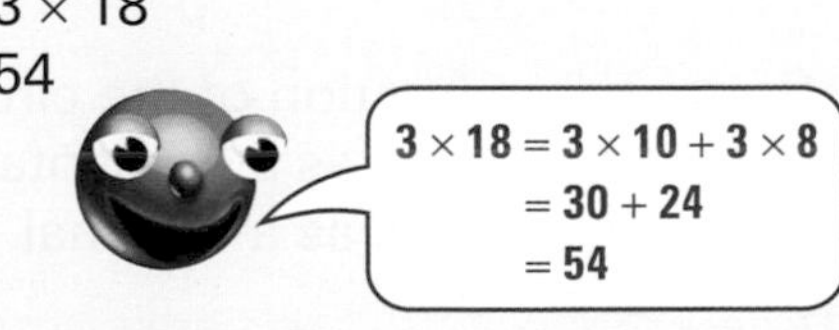

Exercise 3

T

1 Use a copy of this chart.

					y																
52	1	17	71	52	8		28	17	12	75	17	71	52		30	40		52	1	31	

52	30	3	17	40		52	17	71		28	17	12	75	17	71	52

Find the answer to these. Write the letter beside the question above the answer in the chart.

Y 10% of 80 = 8
C 30% of 250
N 50% of 142
E 100% of 17
R 10% of 120
I 20% of 150
M 15% of 20
P 70% of 40
S 25% of 160
O 25% of 124
W 5% of 20
T 65% of 80

2 Find these.

a 10% of 50
b 20% of 30
c 25% of 24
d 5% of 300
e $33\frac{1}{3}$% of 120
f 40% of 120
g 25% of 48
h 75% of 16
i 20% of 25
j 15% of 60
***k** 11% of 7200
***l** 11% of 8500

3 There are 240 pupils in a school.
15% went on a skiing holiday.
How many pupils went?

4 Ella borrowed £80.
She had to pay 5% interest.
How much interest did she pay?

5 How much would Perry save on a shirt in the sale?

***6** Jane said that 30% of £45 is the same as 45% of £30.
Is she correct?

Percentage of – using a calculator

76% = 0·76 = $\frac{76}{100}$

We find 76% of £120 by keying

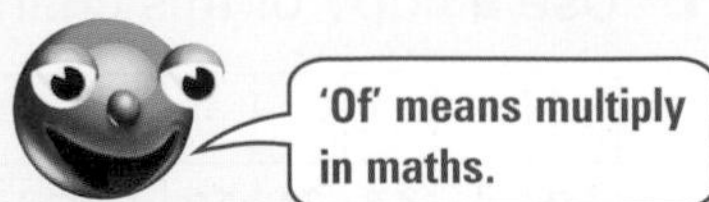
'Of' means multiply in maths.

 to get 91·2 **using decimals**

or 7 6 ÷ 1 0 0 × 1 2 0 = to get 91·2. **using fractions**

The answer is **£91·20**.

Exercise 4

T

1

£267·12	£1033·20	£87·78		£37·96	£87·78	£27·20	£253·80	£1752

£267·12 £1033·20 £87·78   £37·96 £87·78 £27·20 £253·80 £1752

£121·80 **S** £2304   £1022 £1033·20 £121·80 £267·12 £87·78

£1022 £121·80 £267·12 £1033·20

£27·20 £64·98 £1752 £419·60 £792·40

S £2304 £267·12 £253·80 £121·80 £3·96 £87·78 **S** £2304

Use a copy of this box.
Find the answers to these.
Write the letter beside each question above its answer.
Use fractions to find these.

S 32% of £7200 = **£2304**
A 48% of £3650
H 63% of £1640
E 19% of £462
R 54% of £470
K 14% of £5660
W 28% of £3650

Use decimals to find these.

L 18% of £361
T 36% of £742
C 80% of £524·50
I 84% of £145
B 40% of £68
P 9% of £44
Z 8% of £474·50

2 Mary bought a house for £135 000.
She sold it 5 years later and made a 45% profit.
How much profit did Mary make?

3 Daniel paid a 30% deposit on a £45·50 coat.
How much deposit was this?

4 Sinita bought a bike for £75.
When she sold it, she made a 35% loss.
How much did Sinita lose when she sold the bike?

5 16% of a 125 g pot of 'Fruit Delight' is fruit.
How many grams is *not* fruit?

6

Mark bought these three things in the sale.
How much did he save altogether?

***7** Which of these is true?
A 85% of £9 < 90% of £8·50
B 85% of £9 > 90% of £8·50
C 85% of £9 = 90% of £8·50

T

Percentage of – a game for two players

You will need a copy of these boards, 2 counters and a calculator.

10%	30%	5%
100%	15%	50%
25%	1%	20%

percentage

200	160	60
64	800	50
80	120	320

amount

To play

- One player drops a counter onto each board.
- That player then finds the **percentage** of the **amount** mentally.
  Example Hien got 1% and 64.
  1% of 64 = $\frac{1}{100}$ of 64
  = 0·64
- The other player checks the answer with a calculator.
- If the first player got it right, he/she writes the answer down.
- After four turns each, both players add up their four answers. The player with the higher total wins.

Summary of key points

To write a **percentage as a fraction or decimal**, write the percentage as the number of parts per hundred.

Examples $93\% = \frac{93}{100}$ $\quad$ $85\% = \frac{85}{100}$ (85 and 100 crossed out and replaced by 17 and 20)

$= 0{\cdot}93$ $\quad$ $= \frac{17}{20}$

B To write a **fraction or decimal as a percentage** write it with denominator of 100.

Examples $0{\cdot}31 = \frac{31}{100}$

$= 31\%$

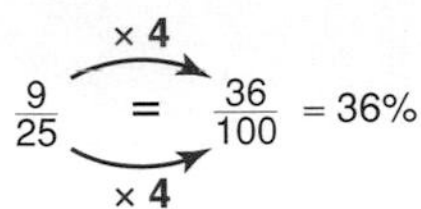

You need to know these.

$100\% = 1$ $\quad$ $25\% = \frac{1}{4}$ $\quad$ $50\% = \frac{1}{2}$ $\quad$ $75\% = \frac{3}{4}$

$10\% = 0{\cdot}1 = \frac{1}{10}$ $\quad$ $1\% = 0.01 = \frac{1}{100}$ $\quad$ $33\frac{1}{3}\% = \frac{1}{3}$

5% is half of 10%. $\quad$ 25% is $\frac{1}{4}$.

We sometimes use these facts **to find the percentage of a quantity mentally**.

Examples 25% of 84 g = 21 g $\quad$ **finding $\frac{1}{4}$**

5% of 120 m = 6 m $\quad$ **finding 10%, then halving this to find 5%**

We can find the **percentage of a quantity using a calculator**.

Example 65% of 155 m = 100·75 m

key [·] [6] [5] [×] [1] [5] [5] [=] to get 100·75

or key [6] [5] [÷] [1] [0] [0] [×] [1] [5] [5] [=]

to get 100·75.

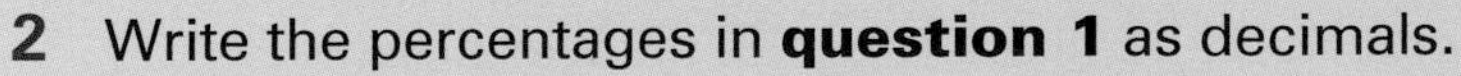

Test yourself  **Except for questions 12 and 13.**

1 Write these as fractions in their lowest terms. 
a 30% **b** 27% **c** 75% **d** 35%

2 Write the percentages in **question 1** as decimals. 

3 In a survey it was found that 48% of pupils stayed in England for their holidays. 
What fraction is this?

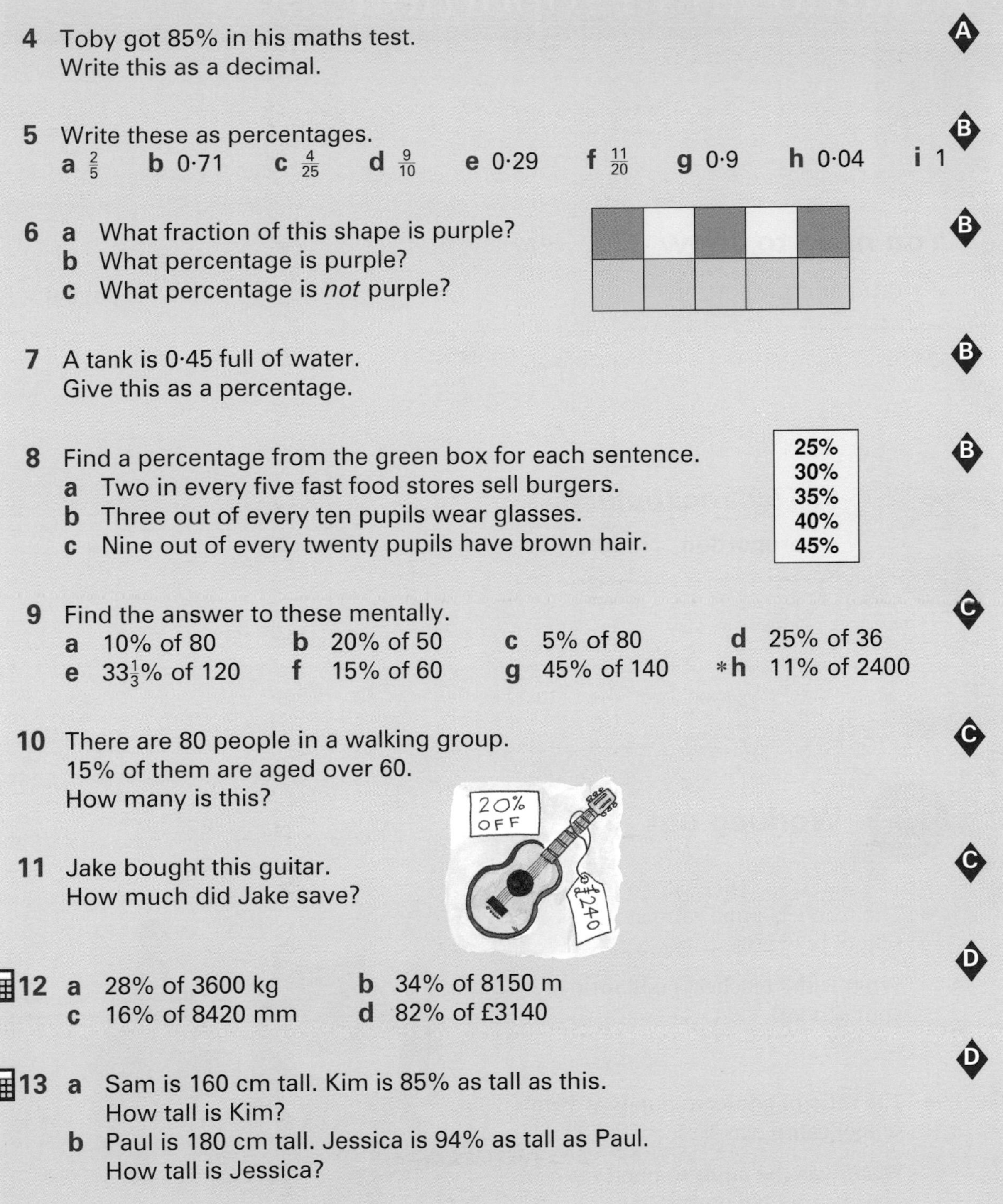

4 Toby got 85% in his maths test. **A**
Write this as a decimal.

5 Write these as percentages. **B**
a $\frac{2}{5}$ **b** 0·71 **c** $\frac{4}{25}$ **d** $\frac{9}{10}$ **e** 0·29 **f** $\frac{11}{20}$ **g** 0·9 **h** 0·04 **i** 1

6 **a** What fraction of this shape is purple? **B**
b What percentage is purple?
c What percentage is *not* purple?

7 A tank is 0·45 full of water. **B**
Give this as a percentage.

8 Find a percentage from the green box for each sentence. **B**
a Two in every five fast food stores sell burgers.
b Three out of every ten pupils wear glasses.
c Nine out of every twenty pupils have brown hair.

25%
30%
35%
40%
45%

9 Find the answer to these mentally. **C**
a 10% of 80 **b** 20% of 50 **c** 5% of 80 **d** 25% of 36
e $33\frac{1}{3}$% of 120 **f** 15% of 60 **g** 45% of 140 ***h** 11% of 2400

10 There are 80 people in a walking group. **C**
15% of them are aged over 60.
How many is this?

11 Jake bought this guitar. **C**
How much did Jake save?

12 **a** 28% of 3600 kg **b** 34% of 8150 m **D**
c 16% of 8420 mm **d** 82% of £3140

13 **a** Sam is 160 cm tall. Kim is 85% as tall as this. **D**
How tall is Kim?
b Paul is 180 cm tall. Jessica is 94% as tall as Paul.
How tall is Jessica?

7 Ratio and Proportion

You need to know

✓ ratio and proportion page 8

Key vocabulary

proportion, ratio

Working out

- The teacher–pupil ratio at Pam's school is 1 : 20.

  What is the teacher–pupil ratio at your school?

- The ratio of adults to pupils at Pam's school camp was 1 : 5.

  What was the adult to pupil ratio on your last school outing?

Proportion

We often **find the cost of one first** when solving proportion problems.

Worked Example
5 pies cost £10·50.
What will 3 pies cost?

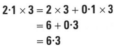

When we find the cost of **one** first this is called the **unitary** method

Answer
Find the cost of 1 pie first.
1 pie costs $\frac{£10·50}{5}$ = £2·10
3 pies cost £2·10 × 3 = £6·30

$2·1 \times 3 = 2 \times 3 + 0·1 \times 3$
$= 6 + 0·3$
$= 6·3$

Exercise 1

1 4 chocolate bars cost £1·40.
How much will these cost?
a 8 bars **b** 12 bars **c** 20 bars **d** 36 bars

2 £1 is worth 175 Japanese yen.
How many yen will you get for
a £30 **b** £50 **c** £150 **d** £225?

3 **a** 8 rolls cost £24.
What will 6 rolls cost?

b 10 filled mushrooms cost £20.
What will 6 cost?

c 8 milk shakes cost £16.
What will 3 cost?

d 9 tickets to see a band cost £270.
What will 5 cost?

e 7 afternoon teas cost £35.
What will 15 cost?

f 7 chocolate bars cost £2·80.
What will 11 cost?

g 6 chairs cost £162.
What will 8 cost?

h 12 nights accommodation cost £672.
What will 7 nights cost?

* **i** 6 fruit and nut bars cost £4·80.
Joni has £24.
How many fruit and nut bars can she buy?

* **j** 9 pens cost £5·40. Ross has £10.
How many pens can he buy?

*4 Sara used this recipe to make apple crumble.
She wants to make it for 10 people.
How much of these does she need?
a flour **b** sugar **c** butter

Apple crumble
for 4 people

4 large apples
50 g butter
100 g sugar
200 g flour

Simplifying ratios

Remember
If there are 12 boys and 16 girls on a bus, the ratio of boys to girls is written as 12 : 16.
In its simplest form this is 3 : 4.

We can simplify a ratio to its **simplest form** by **cancelling**.

Example

$$\begin{array}{rcl} 12 & : & 16 \\ \downarrow \div 4 & & \downarrow \div 4 \\ = 3 & : & 4 \end{array}$$

This is linked to cancelling. See page 100.

Exercise 2

1 Write each ratio in its simplest form.

a 3 : 6 ($\div 3$, $\div 3$) = __ : __
b 5 : 15 ($\div 5$, $\div 5$) = __ : __
c 2 : 8 ($\div 2$, $\div 2$) = __ : __
d 4 : 16 ($\div 4$, $\div 4$) = __ : __

e 5 : 25 **f** 6 : 30 **g** 4 : 6 **h** 8 : 12
i 10 : 4 **j** 15 : 3 **k** 20 : 36 **l** 48 : 36

2 On a bus there were 4 adults and 12 children.
Write the ratio of adults to children in its simplest form.

3 Mary had 3 pens and 18 pencils.
a Write the ratio of pens to pencils in its simplest form.
b Write the ratio of pencils to pens in its simplest form.

4 Julie shot 12 goals and Ella shot 20 goals in a netball game.
Write the ratio of goals shot by Julie to goals shot by Ella in its simplest form.

5 This table shows the colour of hats sold.
Write these as ratios in their simplest forms.

Red	24
Green	16
Blue	21
Black	30

a red hats to green hats **b** green hats to black hats
c blue hats to black hats **d** black hats to red hats

***6** Cycling uses 2700 kJ an hour. Slow walking uses 300 kJ an hour.
Write the ratio of kJ used cycling to kJ used slow walking in its simplest form.

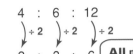

kJ are a measure of energy.

***7** Todd simplified 4 : 6 : 12 like this.

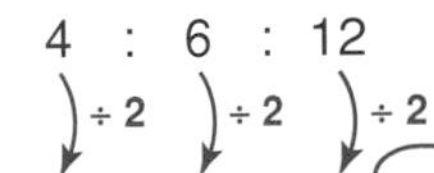

All parts of the ratio have been divided by 2.

Use Todd's way to simplify these.
a 6 : 4 : 10 **b** 8 : 16 : 4
c 12 : 9 : 15 **d** 24 : 8 : 32

Practical

Find these ratios for your class.
Simplify the ratios if you can.

right-handed pupils : left-handed pupils
boys : girls
own a dog : don't own a dog

Ratio and proportion

Remember
Ratio compares part to part.
Proportion compares part to whole.

Worked Example
There are 20 jelly beans in a jar.
14 are black and 6 are blue.

a Write the ratio of black jelly beans to blue jelly beans in its simplest form.
b Write the proportion of blue jelly beans as a percentage.

Answer
a ratio of black to blue

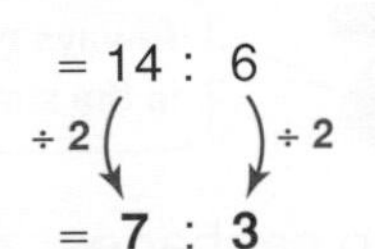

Always give fractions and ratios in their simplest form.

b 6 out of 20 are blue
$\frac{6}{20} = \frac{3}{10}$ $\frac{3}{10} = \frac{30}{100} = 30\%$
30% are blue.

Exercise 3

Except for question 6.

1 A pet shop has 12 kittens needing homes.
4 are black and 8 are grey.
- **a** What proportion of the kittens are black? Give your answer as a fraction.
- **b** What proportion of the kittens are grey? Give your answer as a fraction.
- **c** What is the ratio of black to grey kittens?

2 There were 10 accidents on a busy road last month.
7 were car accidents and 3 were cycle accidents.
- **a** Give the proportion of car accidents as a fraction.
- **b** Give the proportion of cycle accidents as a percentage.
- **c** What is the ratio of car to cycle accidents?

3
- **a** What is the ratio of blue to red on this rod?

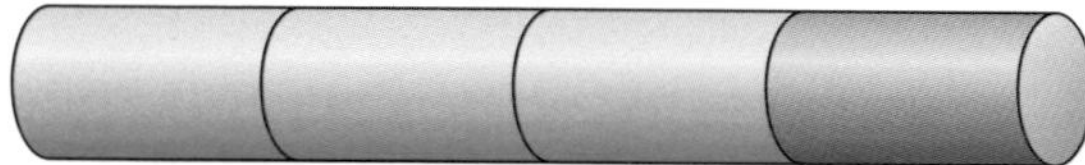

- **b** What proportion of the rod is blue? Give the answer as a fraction.
- **c** What proportion of the rod is red? Give the answer as a percentage.

4 Paul asked 20 people if they liked summer or winter best.
15 said they liked summer and 5 said they liked winter.
- **a** Write, in its simplest form, the ratio of people who said summer to people who said winter.
- **b** What proportion said summer? Give your answer as a fraction.
- **c** What proportion said winter? Give your answer as a percentage.
- **d** Give the answer to **c** as a decimal.

*5 One-fifth of Juliet's friends went rock climbing.
- **a** What is the ratio of friends who went rock climbing to those who didn't?
- **b** What proportion went rock climbing?

*6 Bernie planted these 48 plants.
4 tomato plants
5 leeks
3 cabbages

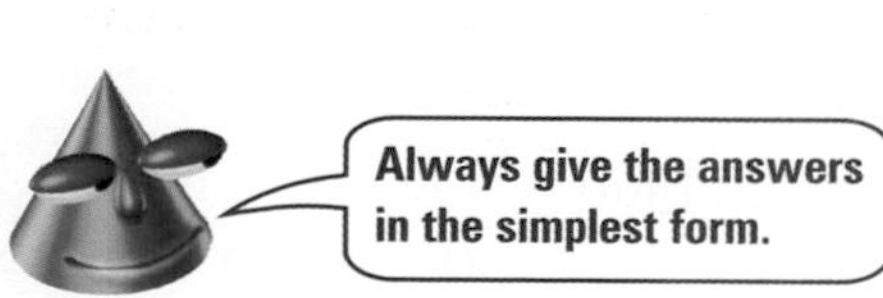

Always give the answers in the simplest form.

- **a** Write the ratio of tomato plants to leeks to cabbages.
- **b** What proportion of the plants were tomato?
- **c** What proportion were cabbages?
- **d** What proportion were either leeks or cabbages?

*7 On Thursday and Friday Brett counted the number of pupils who had lunch at school and the number of those who had sandwiches.

	Total number	Number who had sandwiches
Thursday	189	21
Friday	216	27

On which day did the greater proportion of pupils have sandwiches.

Practical

Make a ratio and proportion poster about the people living in your house.

You could include the ratio of males to females
ratio of over 30s to under 30s
proportion who wear glasses
proportion who are right-handed.

You could do this for all your relatives instead.

Solving ratio and proportion problems

Worked Example
Marie makes felt hats.
She always makes 6 red hats then 5 blue hats.
Last week she made 48 red hats.
How many blue hats did she make?

Answer
48 red hats is **8** lots of 6 red hats.
So there must be **8** lots of 5 blue hats.
There are $8 \times 5 =$ **40 blue hats**.

Worked Example
The ratio of boys to girls in a drama class is 2 : 5.
There are 30 girls in the class.
How many boys are there?

Answer
For every 2 boys there are 5 girls.
30 girls is **6** lots of 5 girls.
So there must be **6** lots of 2 boys or **12** boys.

Exercise 4

1 A recipe for a salad has 2 peppers for every 7 tomatoes.
Ruth makes the salad and uses 6 peppers.
How many tomatoes does she use?

2 There are 3 girls for every 4 boys in a class.
There are 15 girls in the class.
How many boys are there?

3 For every US$8 you get £5.
How many pounds would you get for US$48?

4 A class voted between going to the cinema and going to the beach.
The ratio of cinema to beach was 5 : 3.
If 20 pupils voted for the cinema, how many voted for the beach?

Anti-Freeze

Mix in the ratio
3 parts water to
2 parts anti-freeze

5 How much anti-freeze should be added to 6 litres of water?

6 The ratio of non-smokers to smokers in a café was 10 : 2.
There were 120 non-smokers.
How many smokers were there?

*7 The ratio of protein to carbohydrate in a burger is 2 : 3.
There are 39 g of carbohydrate in a burger.
How many grams of protein are there?

Puzzle

Lena is aged between 20 and 50.

a The ratio of Lena's age to her daughter Anthea's age is 4 : 1.
What are all the possible ages to the nearest year Lena and Anthea could be?

*b If in four years time the ratio of their ages will be 3 : 1, how old are Lena and Anthea now?
How old will Lena and Anthea be in four years time?

Dividing in a given ratio

Discussion

Emma and Ashok won £42.
They shared it in the ratio 4 : 3.
Emma wrote

4 : 3 means there are 4 + 3 = 7 shares in total.
I get 4 out of 7.
Ashok gets 3 out of 7.
I get $\frac{4}{7}$ of £42.

$$\frac{1}{7} \text{ of } £42 = £42 \div 7 = £6$$

$$\frac{4}{7} \text{ of } £42 = 4 \times £6 = £24$$

What might Ashok write to work out his share? **Discuss.**

Worked Example

A box of 40 chocolates had milk and dark chocolates in the ratio **2** : **3**.
How many were milk chocolates?

Answer

2 + **3** = 5 **add the parts of the ratio to get the total parts**

Out of every 5 chocolates,
2 were milk and 3 were dark.
$\frac{2}{5}$ were milk chocolates.

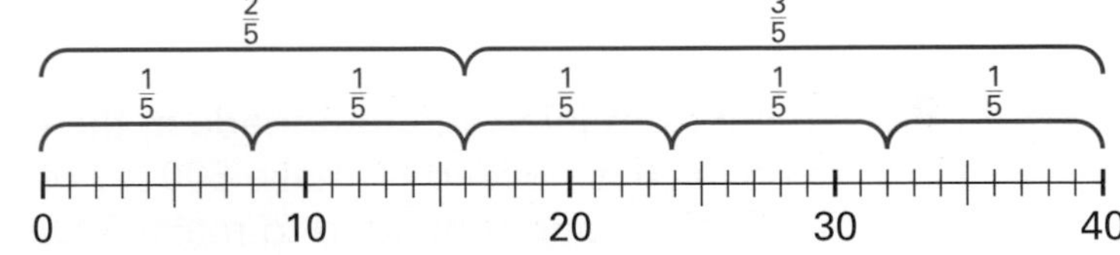

$\frac{1}{5}$ of 40 = 40 ÷ 5
= 8

$\frac{2}{5}$ of 40 = 2 × 8
= 16

16 chocolates were milk chocolates.

Would we have got the same answer if milk and dark chocolates were divided in the ratio 3 : 2?

Exercise 5

1 Jessie had £40.
She spent it on clothes and sports gear in the ratio 1 : 4.

- **a** How many parts in total are there in the ratio 1 : 4?
- **b** What fraction of the total did Jessie spend on clothes?
- **c** How much did Jessie spend on clothes?

2 20 people visited a museum in one hour.
The ratio of adults to children was 1 : 3.

a How many parts are there in total in the ratio 1 : 3?
b What fraction of the total were children?
c How many children were there?

3 A school has Indian and Asian pupils in the ratio 3 : 2.
There are 50 Indian and Asian pupils altogether.

a How many parts are there in total in the ratio 2 : 3?
b How many Indian and how many Asian pupils are there?

4 Asad spent £120 on CDs and a stereo in the ratio 1 : 5.

a How many parts are there in total in the ratio 1 : 5?
b Out of every £6, how much did he spend on each?
c How much in total did he spend on each?

5 To make purple paint you mix red and blue paint in the ratio 2 : 7.
How much of each colour do you need to make
a 9 ℓ **b** 27 ℓ **c** 4·5 ℓ **d** 36 ℓ?

6 A drink is made from juice and lemonade in the ratio 2 : 3.

a How much juice is needed to make 500 mℓ of the drink?
b How much lemonade is needed to make 500 mℓ of the drink?
c Answer **a** and **b** again if the ratio of juice and lemonade is 3 : 2.
Do you get the same answers? Explain.

7 To make Jo's salad dressing you mix oil and vinegar in the ratio 3 : 1.
How much of each do you need to make these amounts of dressing?
a 4 ℓ **b** 40 mℓ **c** 400 mℓ **d** 800 mℓ
e Todd made some salad dressing.
He mixed the oil and vinegar in the ratio 1 : 3.
Would it taste the same as Jo's? Explain.

***8** Kate spend £44 in the holidays.
She spent three times as much on clothes as she did on food.
How much did she spend on food?

Summary of key points

We can solve **proportion problems**.

Example 3 bags of crisps cost £2·70.

1 bag of crisps costs £2·70 ÷ 3 = £0·90

10 bags of crisps cost £0·90 × 10 = £9.

A ratio should be written in its **simplest form**.

We write a ratio in its simplest form by cancelling.

Example

$$10 : 25 \quad \xrightarrow{\div 5} \quad = 2 : 5$$

Proportion compares part to whole.

Ratio compares part to part.

Example 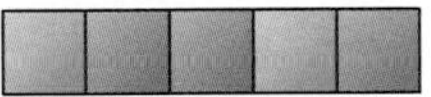

The ratio of red to blue is 3 : 2.

The proportion of red is 3 parts out of 5 or $\frac{3}{5}$ or 60% or 0·6.

We can solve **ratio and proportion** problems.

Example The ratio of boys to girls in a cricket club is 5 : 3.

If there are 20 boys then we can work out the number of girls.

20 is **4** lots of 5.

There must be **4** lots of 3 or **12** girls.

We can **divide in a given ratio**.

Example There are 45 pupils in the badminton club.

The ratio of boys to girls is 4 : 5.

Out of every 9 pupils, 4 are boys.

$\frac{4}{9}$ are boys.

$\frac{1}{9}$ of 45 = 5

$\frac{4}{9}$ of 45 = 4 × 5

= 20

There are 20 boys in the badminton club.

We add the parts of the ratio together: 4 + 5 = 9. This is the total number of parts.

Test yourself

Expect for question 2.

1 5 kg of apples cost £6.
How much will these cost?
a 10 kg **b** 15 kg **c** 25 kg **d** 40 kg

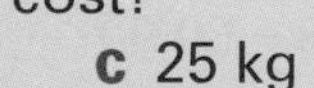

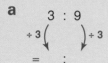

2 How many grams of meat would be needed to make curry for 3 people?

CURRY
for 2 people
250 g meat
1 onion
1 cup curry sauce
2 tbsp sultanas

3 Write these ratios in their simplest forms.
a 3 : 9 **b** 4 : 24 **c** 8 : 20 **d** 18 : 30

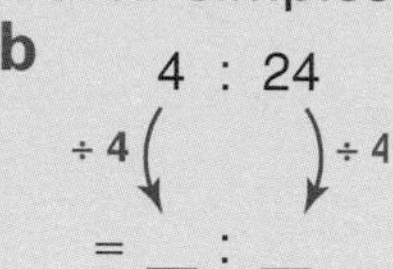

4 8 adults and 12 children went for a picnic.
Write the ratio of adults to children in its simplest form.

5 **a** What is the ratio of red to green squares?
Give your answer in its simplest form.
b What proportion of the squares are red?
Give your answer as a percentage.
c What proportion of the squares are green?
Give your answer as a decimal.

6 A recipe for fertiliser says to add 5 litres of water to every 2 litres of fertiliser.
How much water should be added to 6 litres of fertiliser?

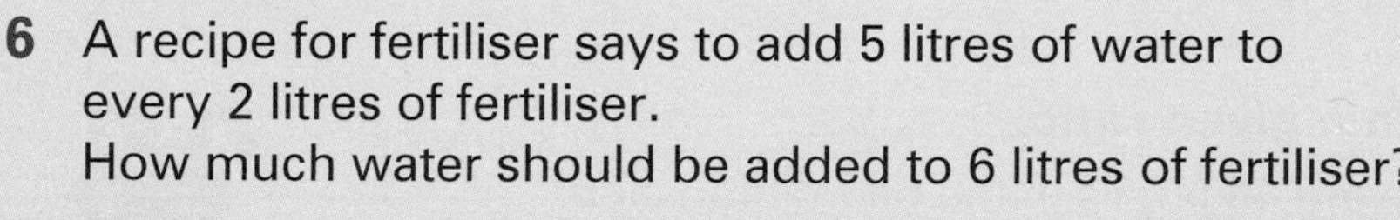

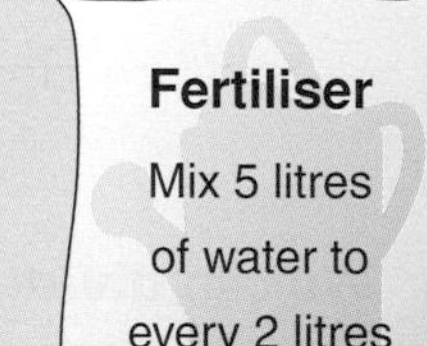

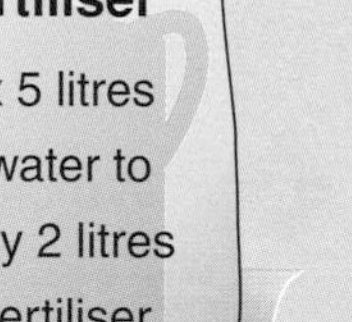

Fertiliser
Mix 5 litres
of water to
every 2 litres
of fertiliser

7 The ratio of nurses to children in a children's ward at a hospital is 2 : 5.
How many nurses are needed if there are 20 children?

8 Manzoor has 80 books.
The ratio of fiction to non-fiction is 3 : 1.
a What fraction is fiction books?
b How many fiction books does he have?

Remember to find
the total number
of parts first.

9 A 35 cm length of lace is cut into two pieces in the ratio of 2 : 3.
What is the length of the longer piece?

Algebra Support

Expressions, formulae, unknowns and inverses

Expressions

In **algebra** letters stand for numbers.

Example In $x + 4$, x stands for any number.

In algebra **letters follow the same rules as numbers do in arithmetic.**

Example $4 + 4 = 2 \times 4$ $a + a = 2 \times a$
$= 2a$

We write $2 \times a$ as $2a$.

Example $x + x + x + x = 4x$

We call this **collecting like terms.**

We can find the value of $n + 3$ if we know the value of n.

Example If $n = 2$ then $n + 3 = 2 + 3$
$= 5$

Formulae

A **formula** is a rule for working something out.

Example time in seconds = time in minutes × 60

Unknowns

In each of these, ▢ stands for an **unknown.**

$7 + ▢ = 12$ $3 \times ▢ = 12$

Inverses

Adding and subtracting are **inverse operations.**
Multiplying and dividing are also inverse operations.

The inverse of adding 4 is subtracting 4.
The inverse of multiplying by 4 is dividing by 4.

Practice Questions 3, 5, 7, 9, 10, 11

Sequences

3, 6, 9, 12, ... is a **number sequence**.

1st term 3rd term These three dots tell us the sequence continues forever.

We can make a number sequence by counting on or back.

Example Starting at 0 and counting on in threes gives 0, 3, 6, 9, 12, ...

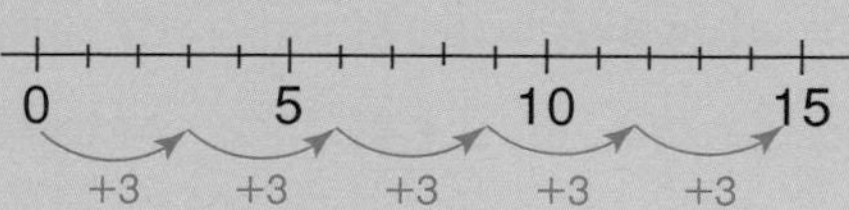

We can find a sequence if we are **given a rule**.

Example **first term** 1, **rule for finding next term** add 2
This gives the sequence 1, 3, 5, 7, 9, ...

Practice Questions 1, 2, 8, 12, 14

Functions

We can find the **output** of a function machine if we are given the **input**.

Example

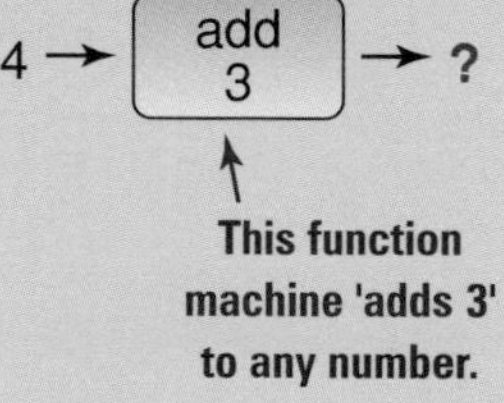

The output will be **7**. 4 + 3 = 7.

We can find the **input** using an inverse function machine.

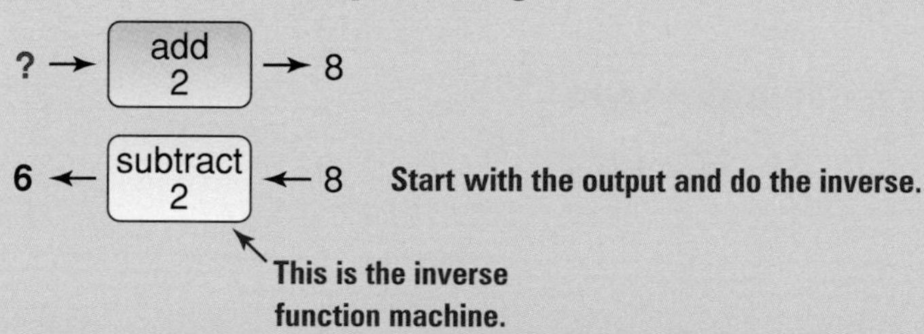

The input was **6**.

Practice Questions 6, 16

Coordinates and graphs

Coordinates

(2, 3) is a **coordinate pair**.

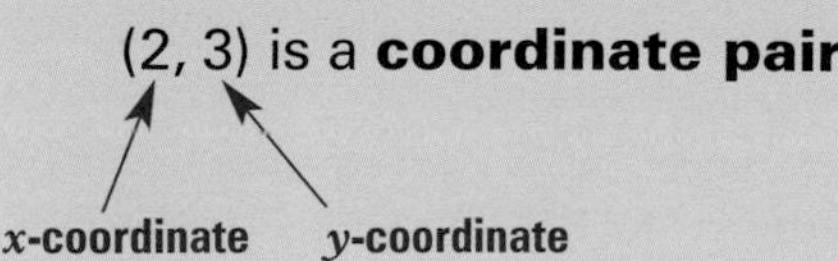

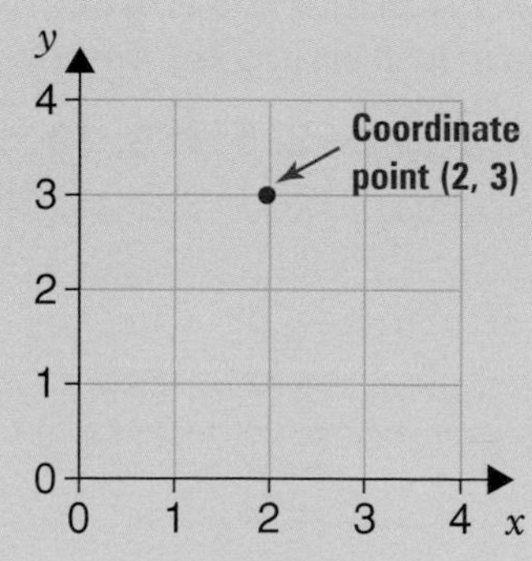

Graphs

Coordinate pairs can be used to **draw a graph**.

Example $y = x + 2$
Each y-coordinate is the x-coordinate plus 2.

x-coordinate	working (add 2 to x)	y-coordinate
0	0 + **2**	2
1	1 + **2**	3
2	2 + **2**	4
3	3 + **2**	5

The coordinate pairs are (0, 2), (1, 3), (2, 4) and (3, 5).

We plot them and draw a line through them.

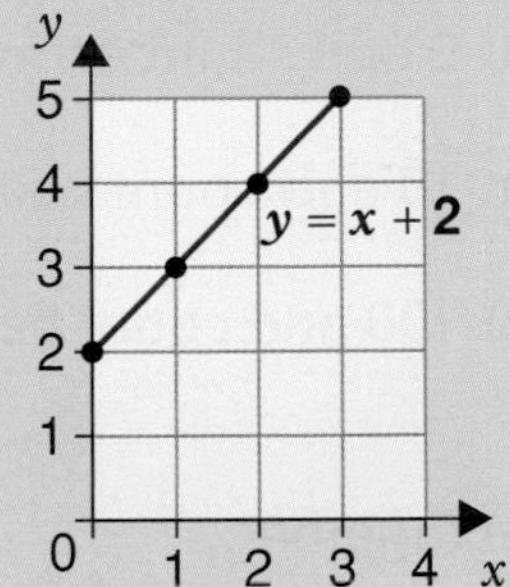

Real-life graphs

We can plot and read **real-life graphs**.

Example This graph can be used to find the cost of mints.

Mass in grams	0	1000	4000
Cost in £	0	3	12

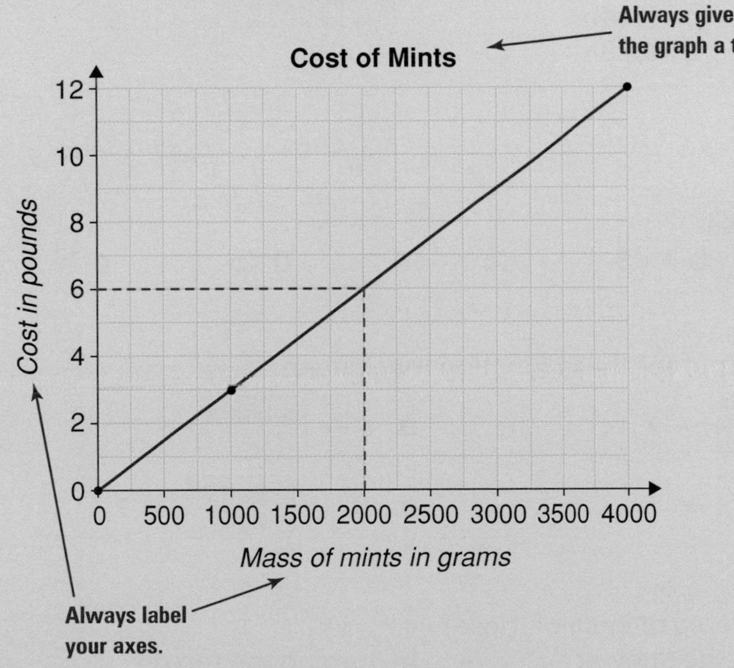

Example To find the cost of 2000 g of mints, draw the --- dashed line from 2000 g up to the line.
Then draw the blue dashed line across to the cost.
2000 g costs about £6.

Practice Questions 4, 13, 15, 17

Practice Questions

1 Which is the 3rd term in these sequences?

a 2, 4, 6, 8, ... **b** 20, 17, 14, 11, 8, ...
c 1, 3, 9, 27, ... **d** 100, 93, 86, 79, 72, ...

2 Write down the first six numbers you get when you

a start at 0 and count on in twos
b start at 0 and count on in fives
c start at 10 and count back in twos
d start at 100 and count back in tens.

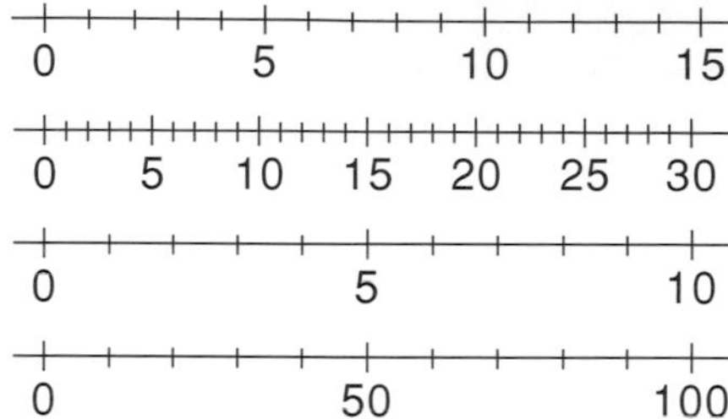

3 Add these together.

a $a + a + a$ **b** $b + b + b + b$ **c** $x + x + x + x + x + x$
d $m + m + m + m + m$ **e** $2x + 3x$ **f** $2a + 4a$

T

4 Use a copy of this grid.
Plot these coordinate pairs.
Label them.

a (1, 2) **b** (1, 4)
c (4, 1) **d** (3, 3)

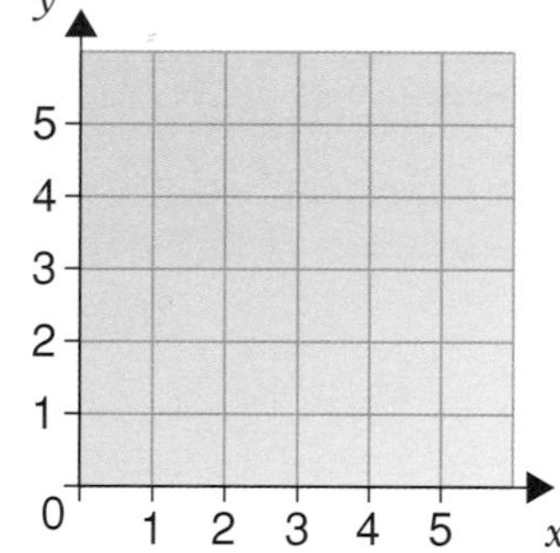

5 If $b = 2$ find these.

a $b + 2$ **b** $b + 3$ **c** $b - 1$ **d** $2b$ **e** $3b$

6 What is the output for these function machines?

a 2 → [add 6] → ? **b** 5 → [subtract 2] → ?
c 4 → [multiply by 3] → ? **d** 10 → [divide by 2] → ?

7 What is the inverse of each of these?

a getting into the shower **b** turning the tap off

8 What is the next number?

a 2, 4, 6, ... **b** 4, 8, 12, ... **c** 25, 20, 15, ...
d 2, 4, 8, ... **e** 3, 9, 27, ... **f** 10 000, 1000, 100, ...

9 Sam has $m + 3$ model cars.
How many has he got if m is equal to
a 1 **b** 2 **c** 5?

10 What number does ■ stand for?
a ■ + 6 = 10 **b** 7 + ■ = 16 **c** 13 + ■ = 29 **d** 4 × ■ = 28
e 5 × ■ = 45 **f** 7 × ■ = 63 **g** $\frac{■}{6} = 10$ **h** $\frac{■}{9} = 8$

11 What is the inverse of each of these?
a adding 3 **b** multiplying by 2
c dividing by 4 **d** subtracting 5

12 The first term and rule for the next term are given.
Write down the first 5 terms of these sequences.
a **first term** 1, **rule** add 2
b **first term** 10, **rule** subtract 2

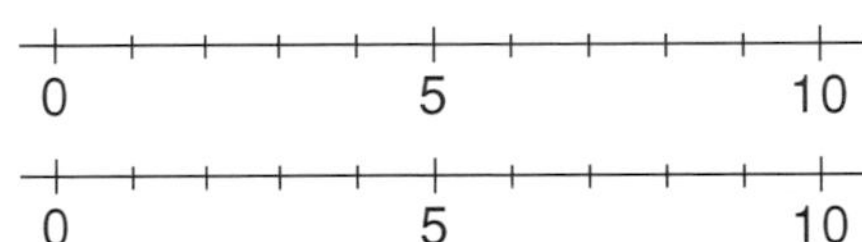

T **13** Use a copy of this.
a Fill in the gaps in the table for the rule $y = x + 1$.

x-coordinates	working (add 1 to x)	y-coordinates
0	0 + 1	1
1		
3		

b Fill in the coordinates.
(0, ___), (1, ___), (3, ___)

c Plot the three points.
Draw the line through them.
Label it $y = x + 1$.

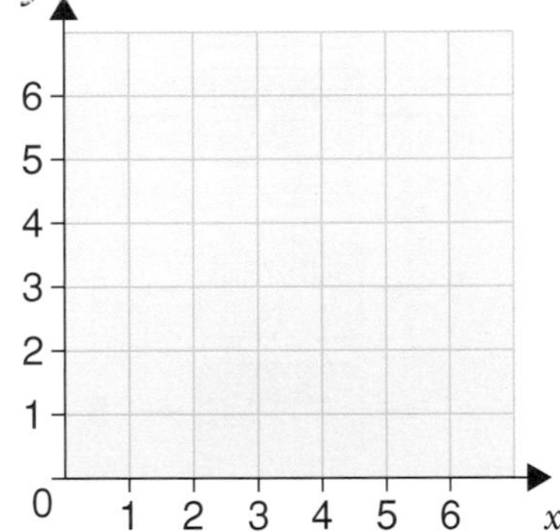

14

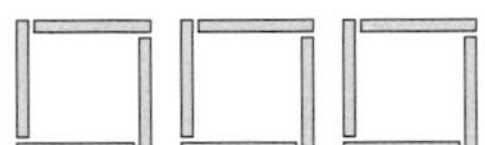

1 square **2 squares** **3 squares**

This pattern is made with sticks.
a What two numbers go in the gaps in the table?
How did you find them?
b What rule goes in the box?

Number of squares	1	2	3	4	5
Number of sticks	4	8	12	__	__

15 Sarah drew this graph to show the cost of ribbon.

a How much does it cost for 1 metre?
b How much does it cost for 3 metres?
c Sarah paid £10 for some ribbon.
How many metres did she buy?

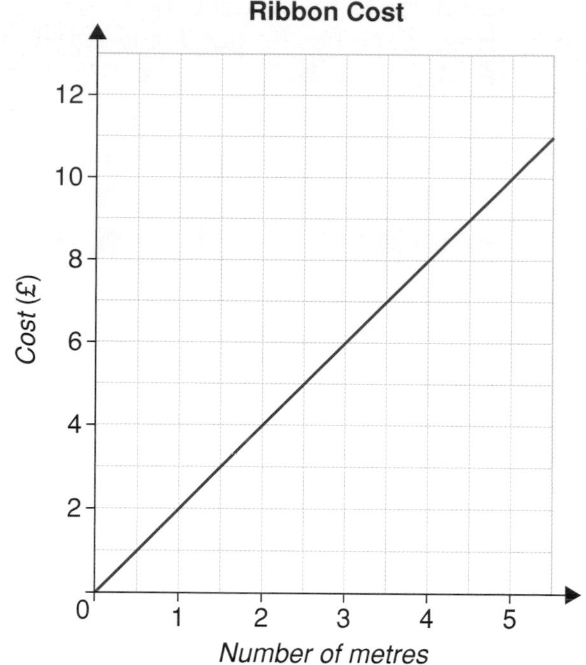

16 Find the input for these.
Use the inverse function machines to help you.

a ? → [add 2] → 10
← [subtract 2] ← 10

b ? → [divide by 3] → 4
← [multiply by 3] ← 4

c ? → [subtract 1] → 5
← [add 1] ← 5

d ? → [divide by 3] → 7
← [multiply by 3] ← 7

T **17** Use a copy of this.
Peter heated some water.
This table shows the temperature of the water.

Time (minutes)	1	4	7
Temperature (°C)	30	60	90

a Plot the points on your grid.
b Draw a straight line through your points.
c Give your graph a title.
d Use your graph to estimate the temperature after 5 minutes.

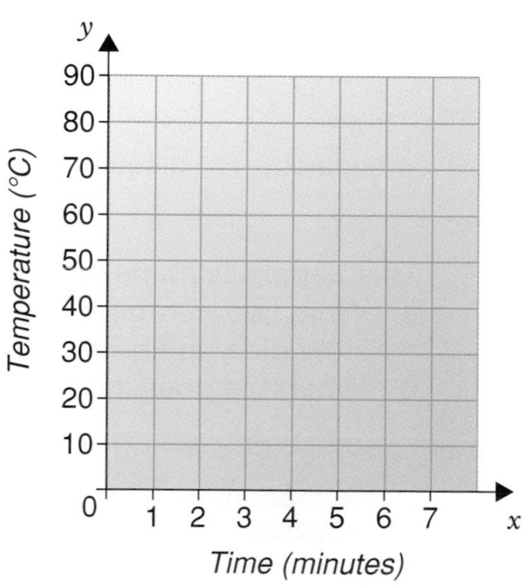

8 Expressions, Formulae and Equations

You need to know

Key vocabulary

brackets, collect like terms, evaluate, expression, formula, formulae, inverse operations, solution, substitute, symbol, verify

Stand ins

1 This square is on the door of a safe.

The letters A, B, C, D and E stand for whole numbers.

The red numbers show the sum of each row and column.

$E = 3$

To unlock the safe you must know what number the other letters stand for.

What do they stand for?

2 This square is on another safe door.

The letters P, Q, R, S and T stand for whole numbers.

The red numbers show the sum of each row and column.

$T = 4$

What number do the other letters stand for?

Understanding algebra

Expressions

Brian borrowed some videos.
We don't know how many.
He also has 8 of his own.
We could say he has n + **8**.

unknown number of borrowed videos (↑ n) — his own videos (↑ **8**)

$n + 8$ is an **expression**.
n stands for an unknown number.

Writing expressions

I think of a number. Call it n

	expression
I multiply it by 2.	$2 \times n$ or $2n$
I add 5 to it.	$n + 5$
I subtract 3 from it.	$n - 3$
I multiply it by 2 then add 1.	$2 \times n + 1$ or $2n + 1$
I subtract 3 from it then multiply by 2.	$(n - 3) \times 2$ or $2(n - 3)$
I multiply it by itself.	$n \times n$ or n^2

We write $3 \times p$ as $3p$.
$1 \times p$ as p.

We write expressions without a multiplication sign.

Exercise 1

1 Write these without a multiplication sign.

a $3 \times x$ **b** $4 \times b$ **c** $n \times 3$ **d** $h \times 5$ **e** $9 \times (x + 3)$
f $(n - 4) \times 3$ **g** $5 \times (m - 3)$ **h** $n \times n$ **i** $p \times p$

2 Write these **with** a multiplication sign.

a $4n$ **b** $5x$ **c** $12c$ **d** $8p$ **e** $4(x + 3)$
f $8(n - 2)$ **g** $7(p + 3)$ **h** x^2 **i** q^2

3 Write an expression for these. Let the unknown number be n.

a subtract 5 from a number **b** add 6 to a number
c multiply a number by 9 **d** divide a number by 8
e multiply a number by 5 then add 4
***f** subtract 3 from a number then multiply by 4
***g** multiply a number by itself

Write your expressions without a multiplication sign.

*4 Explain the difference between these.
 a $3p$ and $p+3$ b n^2 and $2n$ c $5(n+2)$ and $5n+2$

Remember
Letters follow the same rules as numbers.

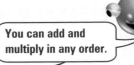

You can add and multiply in any order.

Arithmetic	**Algebra**
$4+5=5+4$	$a+b = b+a$
$4 \times 5=5 \times 4$	$a \times b = b \times a$ or $ab = ba$
$2+(4+5)=(2+4)+5$	$a+(b+c) = (a+b)+c$
$2 \times (4 \times 5)=(2 \times 4) \times 5$	$a \times (b \times c) = (a \times b) \times c$ or $a(bc) = (ab)c$

Exercise 2

T

1 Use a copy of this.
Draw a line between expressions that have the same meaning.

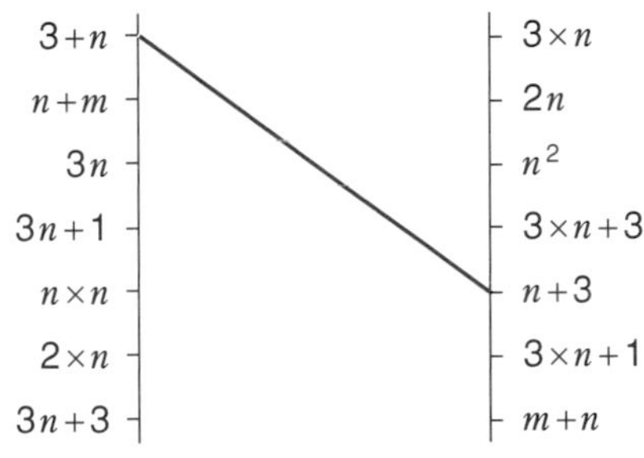

2 Write down another way of writing these expressions.
 a ab b $a+b$ c $2a+1$

Collecting like terms

We can simplify expressions by adding and subtracting **like terms**.
This is called **collecting like terms**.

Arithmetic	**Algebra**
$4+4+4=3 \times 4$	$a+a+a = 3a$
$\mathbf{3} \times 6+ \mathbf{4} \times 6=\mathbf{7} \times 6$	$3c+4c = 7c$
$\mathbf{5} \times 4- \mathbf{2} \times 4=\mathbf{3} \times 4$	$5d-2d = 3d$

Examples

$a+b+b+c = a+2b+c$

$5a+2a-6a = 7a-6a$
$= a$

$1a = a$.

$p+q+3p+4q = p+3p+q+4q$
$= 4p+5q$

$7a+6-4a-2 = 7a-4a+6-2$
$= 3a+4$

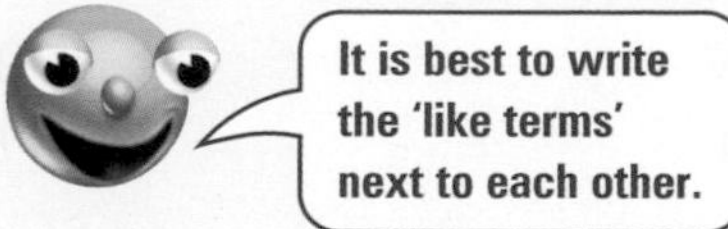

Exercise 3

T

1

			E						E
$7a$	$3a$	$10a$	$4a$	$9a$	$14a$		$3a$	$13a$	$4a$

$5a$ $8a$ $13a$ $15a$ $6a$ $18a$ $11a$ $2a$ $8a$ $12a$ $11a$

$2a$ $12a$ $10a$ a $14a$

Use a copy of this.
Simplify these expressions.
Write the letter that is beside each expression above the answer in the box.

E $a+a+a+a = 4a$	**U** $9a+3a$	**O** $9a-a$	**N** $4a+11a$
P $7a-6a$	**H** $10a-8a$	**B** $8a-3a$	**I** $9a+2a+7a$
M $9a+3a-2a$	**T** $10a+4a-3a$	**W** $11a+2a-7a$	**A** $16a-7a-6a$
R $15a-a-a$	**S** $20a-2a-4a$	**C** $19a-5a-7a$	**L** $17a-6a-2a$

2 Simplify these.
Remember to only add like terms.

a $b+b+a+a$	**b** $p+p+p+q+q$	**c** $2c+3c+d$	**d** $f+g+2g$
e $2m+3m+4n+3n$	**f** $5p+2p+4q+q$	**g** $3a+2a+2b+b$	**h** $3x+x+8y+y$
i $4t+3s+2t+7s$	**j** $3a+2b+4a+b$	**k** $4p+3q+7p+8q$	**l** $11c+d+12c+d$

3 The number in each box is found by adding the numbers in the two boxes below it.
Write an expression for the red box.
Write the expression as simply as possible.

a

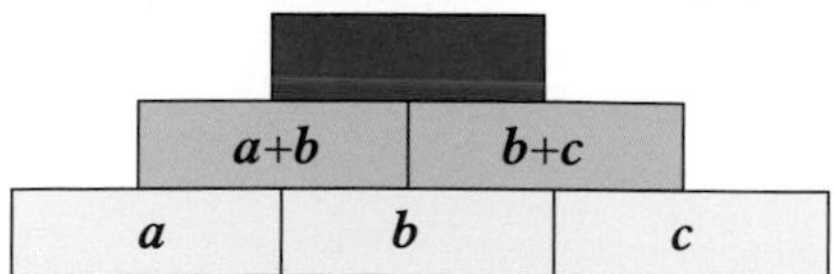

b

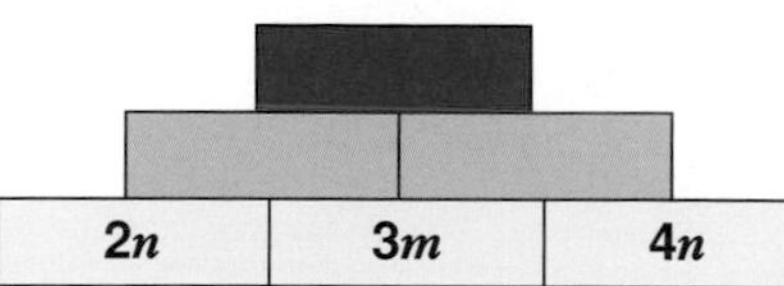

*4 Here are some cards.

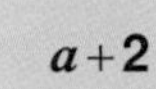

$a+2$	$a \div 2$	$2a-1$	$2a+a$	$2a$
$a-2$	a^2	$a+a$	$2a+2$	$3a+3$

a Which card will always give the same answer as
i $\frac{a}{2}$ **ii** $2+a$ **iii** $3a-a+2$ **iv** $5a-2a+3$ **v** $a \times a$?

b Which two cards will always give the same answer as $2 \times a$?

c When the expressions on two cards are added they can be simplified to $5a+2$. Which two cards are they?

d Write a new card that will always give the same answer as
i $4a+2a$ **ii** $3a+5a$ **iii** $8a-3a$.

Simplifying expressions by cancelling

We can **simplify expressions** by **cancelling**.

Arithmetic	**Algebra**	
$\frac{4}{4} = 1$	$\frac{n}{n} = 1$	
$\frac{\cancel{3}^1 \times 4}{\cancel{3}^1} = 4$	$\frac{\cancel{3}^1 n}{\cancel{3}^1} = n$	Divide numerator and denominator by 3.
$\frac{\cancel{8}^2 \times 5}{\cancel{4}^1} = 2 \times 5$	$\frac{\cancel{8}^2 n}{\cancel{4}^1} = 2n$	Divide numerator and denominator by 4.
$\frac{5 \times \cancel{6}^1}{\cancel{6}^1} = 5$	$\frac{5\cancel{a}^1}{\cancel{a}^1} = 5$	Divide numerator and denominator by a (6 in the arithmetic example).
$\frac{\cancel{10}^5 \times 7}{\cancel{6}^3} = \frac{5 \times 7}{3}$	$\frac{\cancel{10}^5 a}{\cancel{6}^3} = \frac{5a}{3}$	Divide numerator and denominator by 2.

Exercise 4

1 Simplify these expressions.

a $\frac{m}{m}$ **b** $\frac{c}{c}$ **c** $\frac{y}{y}$ **d** $\frac{3a}{3}$ **e** $\frac{6b}{6}$

f $\frac{7m}{7}$ **g** $\frac{9y}{9}$ **h** $\frac{8n}{4}$ **i** $\frac{10p}{2}$ **j** $\frac{14n}{7}$

k $\frac{54b}{9}$ **l** $\frac{42m}{7}$ **m** $\frac{35a}{7}$ **n** $\frac{21b}{b}$ **o** $\frac{72x}{9}$

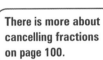

T

2

		A					A						
$9x$	$3x$	1	$7x$	$4x$	$9x$	$2x$	1	$3x$	$9x$	$4x$	$5x$	$5x$	4

										A		
6	2	12	$8x$	$10x$	12	$5x$	$5x$	3	$5x$	1	12	$9x$

								A				
5	$7x$	$8x$	$10x$	2	10	$8x$	$5x$	1	$8x$	$7x$	$3x$	$6x$

Use a copy of this.
Simplify these expressions by cancelling.
Write the letter that is beside each expression above the answer in the box.

A $\frac{x}{x} = 1$	**O** $\frac{2w}{w}$	**F** $\frac{6x}{x}$	**U** $\frac{10x}{x}$	**R** $\frac{12x}{x}$
N $\frac{6x}{2}$	**C** $\frac{20x}{10}$	**H** $\frac{20x}{2}$	**T** $\frac{24x}{3}$	**G** $\frac{30x}{5}$
I $\frac{42x}{6}$	**L** $\frac{16x}{4}$	**E** $\frac{25x}{5}$	**S** $\frac{27x}{3}$	***P** $\frac{24x}{6x}$
***W** $\frac{30x}{6x}$	***Y** $\frac{12x}{4x}$			

Brackets

We can write an **expression without brackets**.

Arithmetic

$6 \times 52 = 6 \times (50 + 2)$

	50	+2
6	300	+12

$6 \times (50 + 2) = (6 \times 50) + (6 \times 2)$
$= \mathbf{300 + 12}$

Algebra

$a(b + c) = a \times (b + c)$

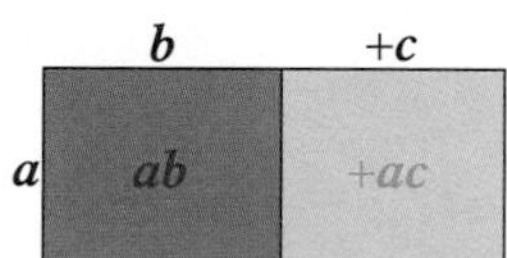

$a \times (b + c) = (a \times b) + (a \times c)$
$= \mathbf{ab} + ac$

Examples $2(a + 5) = \mathbf{2a + 10}$

	a	+5
2	$2a$	+10

$3(x + 7) = 3x + 21$

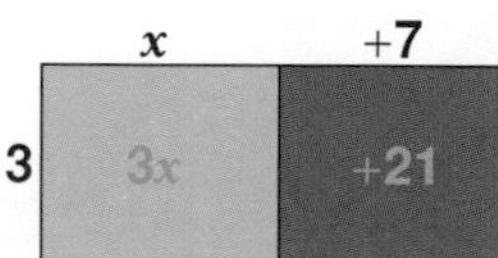

Exercise 5

T

1 Use a copy of this.
Write these expressions without brackets.
Use the grids to help.

a $3(a+2)$

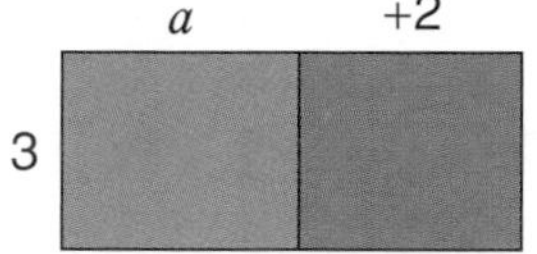

b $5(n+4)$

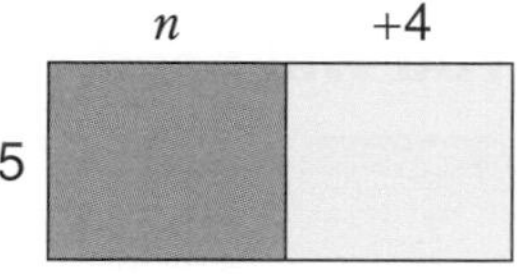

c $3(m+6)$

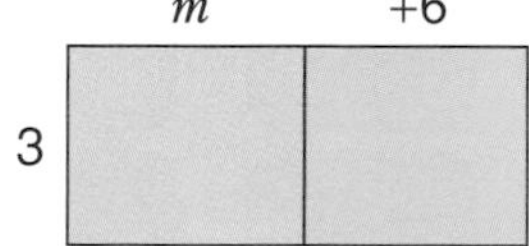

d $2(x+5)$

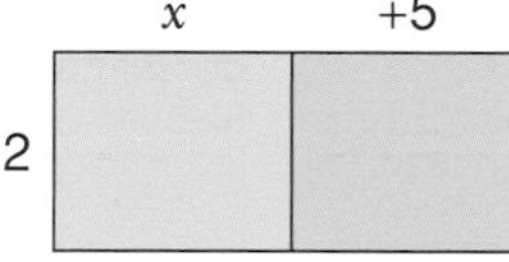

e $4(p+10)$

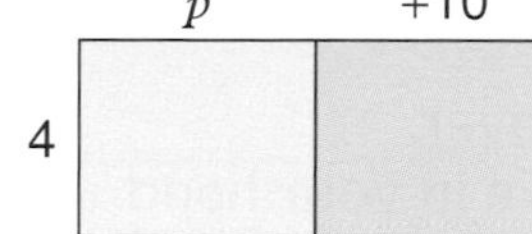

2 Write these without brackets.

a $4(a+2)$ **b** $5(y+3)$ **c** $9(a+4)$ **d** $7(n+1)$
e $6(b+5)$ **f** $14(p+2)$ **g** $24(n+1)$ **h** $3(n+12)$

T

***3** Use a copy of the diagram.
Write each expression without brackets.
Find your answer in the diagram. Cross out the letter above it.
What three word sentence do the letters that are left make?

$4(n+3)$ $7(n+5)$ $9(n+3)$ $36(n+1)$ $2(n+4)$

$3(n+6)$ $5(n+8)$ $10(n+4)$ $6(n+6)$ $8(n+1)$

C	R	A	A	T	Y	S	F	I	C	S	A	N	H	T	E	V	O	A	M	T	I	T
$3n+18$	$9n+12$	$5n+40$	$3n+9$	$4n+3$	$4n+12$	$3n+6$	$8n+8$	$7n+35$	$8n+1$	$10n+40$	$9n+3$	$7n+5$	$9n+27$	$5n+8$	$36n+36$	$10n+4$	$10n+14$	$6n+36$	$36n+1$	$2n+8$	$2n+4$	$4n+7$

Mixed simplifying

T

Card Pairs – a game for 2 players

You will need a set of cards like this.

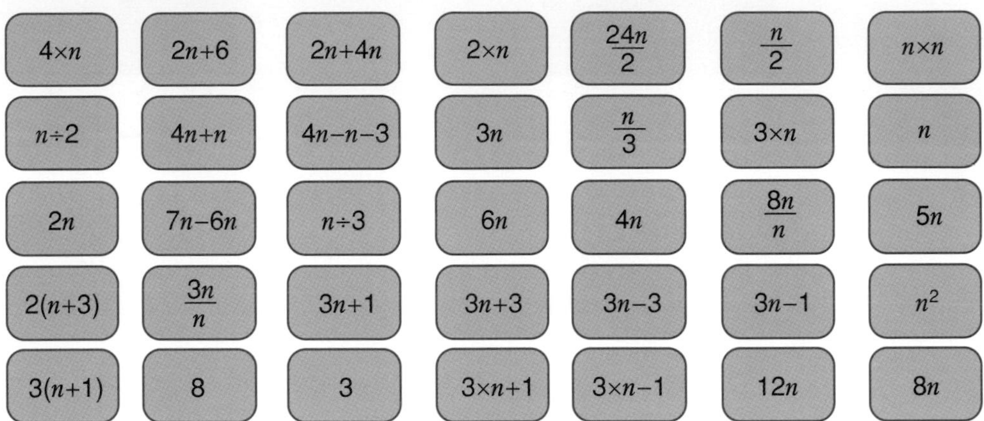

$4\times n$	$2n+6$	$2n+4n$	$2\times n$	$\frac{24n}{2}$	$\frac{n}{2}$	$n\times n$
$n\div 2$	$4n+n$	$4n-n-3$	$3n$	$\frac{n}{3}$	$3\times n$	n
$2n$	$7n-6n$	$n\div 3$	$6n$	$4n$	$\frac{8n}{n}$	$5n$
$2(n+3)$	$\frac{3n}{n}$	$3n+1$	$3n+3$	$3n-3$	$3n-1$	n^2
$3(n+1)$	8	3	$3\times n+1$	$3\times n-1$	$12n$	$8n$

To play
- Shuffle the cards.
- Deal half of them to each player.
- Find all of the **pairs** you have in your hand.
  A pair is made from two cards which match.

Example $n \times n$ and n^2 are a pair.

- Put your pairs down in a pile beside you.
- Take turns to choose a card from your partner's hand.
  Try to match it with a card in your hand to make a pair.
- The player who has the most pairs at the end is the winner.

Substituting

Remember
Letters stand for numbers.

Lauren made n ham and 10 egg sandwiches.
She made $n + 10$ sandwiches.
She said 'I made **12** ham sandwiches'.

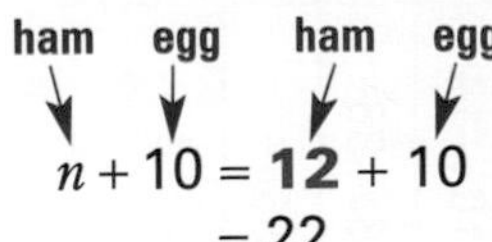

$n + 10 = \mathbf{12} + 10$
$= 22$

12 has been put in place of n.
We call this **substitution**.

We **evaluate** an expression by **substituting** for the unknown in the expression.

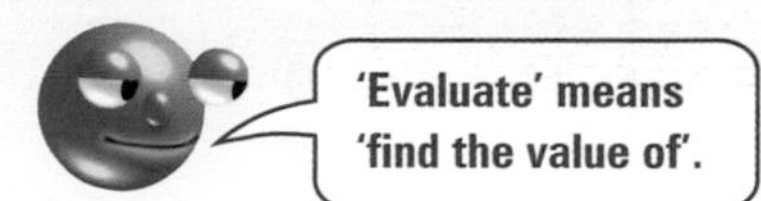
'Evaluate' means
'find the value of'.

The **order of operations** is the same as for arithmetic.

Brackets
Indices (squares)
Division and **M**ultiplication
Addition and **S**ubtraction

Examples If $n = \mathbf{6}$ then

$$\begin{aligned} 2n &= 2 \times n \\ &= 2 \times \mathbf{6} \\ &= \mathbf{12} \end{aligned}$$

$$\begin{aligned} 2n + 3 &= 2 \times n + 3 \\ &= 2 \times \mathbf{6} + 3 \\ &= 12 + 3 \\ &= \mathbf{15} \end{aligned}$$

If $a = \mathbf{4}$ and $b = \mathbf{2}$ then

$$\begin{aligned} a + b &= \mathbf{4} + \mathbf{2} \\ &= \mathbf{6} \end{aligned}$$

$$\begin{aligned} a(8 - b) &= a \times (8 - b) \\ &= \mathbf{4} \times (8 - \mathbf{2}) \\ &= 4 \times (6) \\ &= \mathbf{24} \end{aligned}$$

Exercise 6

1 If $x = 1$ copy and finish these.

a $3x = 3 \times x$
$= 3 \times$ __
$=$ __

b $5x = 5 \times x$
$= 5 \times$ __
$=$ __

c $x + 7 =$ __ $+ 7$
$=$ __

d $2x + 1 = 2 \times x + 1$
$= 2 \times$ __ $+ 1$
$=$ __

e $3x + 2 = 3 \times x + 2$
$= 3 \times$ __ $+ 2$
$=$ __

2 If $y = 2$ find the value of these.

a $5 \times y$ **b** $y + 6$ **c** $3 \times y + 4$ **d** $2 \times y - 1$ **e** $7 \times y - 5$

3 If $y = 4$ find the value of these.

a $2y + 2$ **b** $12 - y$ **c** $3y + 4$
d $20 - 2y$ **e** $3(y + 2)$ **f** $4(y - 2)$

4 If $p = 2$ and $q = 4$ evaluate these.

a $p + q$ **b** $p + q - 1$ ***c** $2p + q$ ***d** $3q - p$
***e** $2p + 3q$ ***f** $p(6 - q)$

5 The expression $3d + 2$ gives the total number of dots needed to make a row with d blue dots.

How many dots in total are needed to make a row with 15 blue dots?

T ***6**

11	22	0	8		10	9	1		4	7	1	13	22		10	9	1	2

12	1	15	15	10		3	9	0	13		2	0	18

I			I		
5	8	13	5	18	0

Use a copy of this box.
If $p = 2$, $q = 5$, $r = 7$ evaluate these.
Write the letter that is beside each expression above the answer in the box.

I	$r - p = 7 - 2 = 5$	**E**	$p + q - r$	**W**	$2p + r$	**H**	$3q + r$
O	$2r - q$	**D**	$2(p + r)$	**S**	$3q - p$	**N**	$\frac{16}{p}$
T	$2(p + 4)$	**Y**	$2(r - p)$	**G**	$\frac{3q}{5}$	**L**	$\frac{r}{7} + 6$
R	$\frac{3p}{2} - 1$	**U**	$\frac{10p}{5} - 3$	**B**	$2(r - q)$	**M**	$q(10 - r)$

Substitution Totals – a game for a group

You will need
a dice,
a copy of the board and different colour counters for each player.

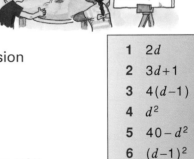

To play

- Throw the dice.
  This gives you the number of your expression from the box.
- Throw it again.
  This gives you the number to substitute.
- Work out the answer.
- Put a counter on the answer.
- If there is already a counter on this number, you can't put your counter there.
- At the end of the game (your teacher will tell you when to stop), add up all the numbers with your counters on them.
  The highest total wins.

1	$2d$
2	$3d+1$
3	$4(d-1)$
4	d^2
5	$40-d^2$
6	$(d-1)^2$

Example Chloe threw a 4 first.
Her expression is d^2.

Then she threw a **3**.
$d^2 = \mathbf{3}^2$
$= 9$
She put a counter on 9.

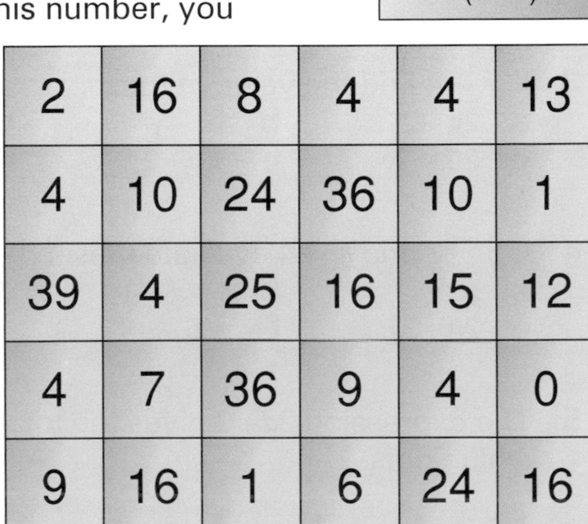

2	16	8	4	4	13
4	10	24	36	10	1
39	4	25	16	15	12
4	7	36	9	4	0
9	16	1	6	24	16
19	25	0	31	20	8

Substituting into formulae

The area of this sail is

$$A = \frac{b \times h}{2}.$$

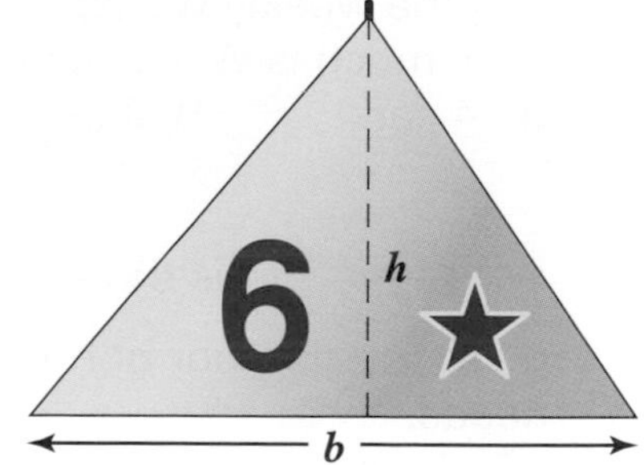

If $b = \mathbf{8}$ mm and $h = \mathbf{10}$ mm,

$A = \frac{b \times h}{2}$ — **Write the formula down first.**

$= \frac{\mathbf{8} \times \mathbf{10}}{2}$ — **Substitute the values.**

$= \frac{80}{2}$

$= \mathbf{40\ mm^2}$ — **Remember the units.**

Exercise 7

1 This is a formula for finding force. **Force** $= m \times a$

Find F if **a** $m = 5$ and $a = 8$ **b** $m = 12$ and $a = 4$.

2 This is a formula for finding speed. **Speed** $= \frac{d}{t}$

Find speed if

a $d = 15$ and $t = 5$

b $d = 32$ and $t = 4$.

3 The perimeter of this trampoline is given by

$P = 2l + 2w$

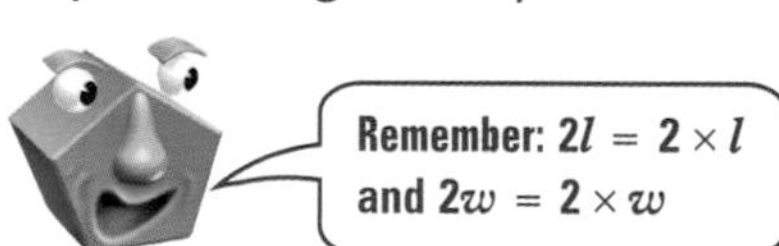

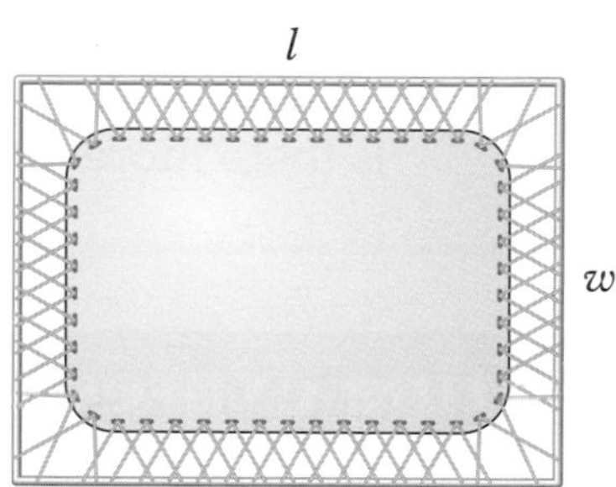

Find the perimeter if

a $l = 3$ m, $w = 2$ m

b $l = 4$ m, $w = 3$ m

c $l - 6$ m, $w = 4$ m.

4 $V = IR$ This is the formula for the voltage, V, in an electrical circuit with current I and resistance R.

Find V if **a** $I = 2$ $R = 12$ **b** $I = 6$, $R = 3$ ***c** $I = 1{\cdot}5$, $R = 8$.

5 The mean length of 4 guinea pigs is given by this formula.

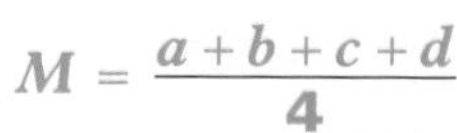

There is more about the mean (average) on page 317.

M is the mean length.

a, b, c and d are the lengths of the guinea pigs.

Find M if $a = 17$ cm, $b = 16$ cm, $c = 16{\cdot}5$ cm, $d = 18{\cdot}5$ cm.

6 The weekly wage of a car salesperson is worked out using this formula.

$w = 200 + 100n$

n is the number of cars sold.
w is the weekly wage, in pounds.
How much is Will's weekly wage if he sells

a 4 cars **b** 3 cars **c** no cars **d** 1 car **e** 6 cars?

***7** $h = \frac{28 - a}{2}$ is thought to be a formula which gives the number of hours of sleep that a child needs.
h is the number of hours of sleep.
a is the age, in years, of the child.
Copy and fill in this table.

a	2	4	6	8	10	12
h	13					

* Puzzle

Replace each of the letters with one of the digits 0, 1, 2, 3, 4, 5, 6, 7, 8, 9 so that the addition is correct.

```
   S O M E
 +   C A N
 ---------
   H E A R
```

Is there more than one possible answer?

Writing expressions

I have n books.

Mike has twice as many.
He has $2 \times n$ or $2n$ books.

Ramesh has 5 fewer than me.
He has $n - 5$.

I share my books among 3 people.
Each gets $\frac{n}{3}$.

Exercise 8

1 There are n seats in a row.
How may seats will there be in 30 rows?

2 There are n coins in this pile.
Write an expression for the number of coins in a pile that has

a two more coins
b five fewer coins
c four times as many coins
d half as many coins.

3 You have d sweets.

a Milly has four more than you.
How many does Milly have?

b Shabir has twice as many as you.
How many does Shabir have?

c You give away three sweets.
How many do you have left?

4 Sam had p trees in his garden.
Write an expression for the number of trees someone has if they have

a three more than Sam
b ten fewer than Sam
c four times as many as Sam
d half as many as Sam.

5 The picture shows some packets of rice and a 5 kg weight.
Each packet of rice weighs n kg.
The total mass in the weighing pan is $\mathbf{3} \times \boldsymbol{n} + \mathbf{5}$ or $\mathbf{3}\boldsymbol{n} + \mathbf{5}$.

Write an expression for the total mass in each of these.

Pan 1

Pan 2

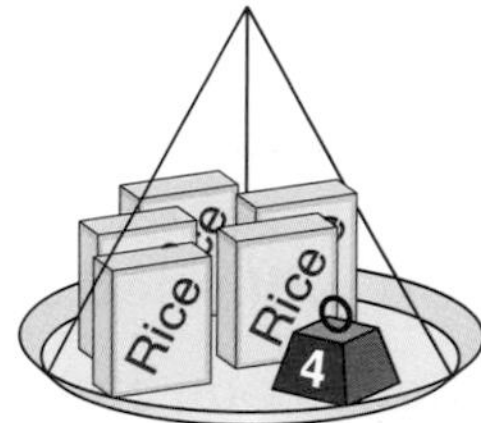

Pan 3

***6** In a sale, a comic costs c pence.
Hadley gives £3 to pay for 4 comics.
Which of these expressions gives his change in pence?

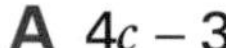

A $4c - 3$ **B** $4c - 300$ **C** $2 - 4c$ **D** $300 - 4c$

Writing formulae

There are 60 seconds in a minute.
We can **write a formula** for finding the number of seconds in any number of minutes. In words, the formula is:

number of seconds = 60 times the number of minutes

Using S for the number of seconds and m for the number of minutes we write:

$S = 60 \times m$ **or** $60m$

Exercise 9

1 Write a formula for these. The answer to **a** is $c = 35 \times n$ or $35n$.

- **a** the cost, c, of n chocolate bars at 35p each $c =$ ___
- **b** the cost, c, of m pencils at 21p each $c =$ ___
- **c** the cost, c, of l buttons at 17p each $c =$ ___
- **d** the cost, c, of h hair ties at £2 each $c =$ ___
- **e** the total money raised, r, in a sponsored walk at 20p per kilometre, k $r =$ ___
- **f** the total number of cans of baked beans, b, eaten by a boy who eats 6 cans a week for w weeks $b =$ ___
- **g** the total weight, w, of a cat weighing c kg and a dog weighing 20 kg $w =$ ___
- **h** the total length, l of a caravan of length c m and a car of length 4 m $l =$ ___
- **i** the cost, c, per person if a meal costing m pounds is shared by 6 people $c =$ ___
- ***j** the final length, l, of a 4 m piece of wood with c cm cut off $l =$ ___
- ***k** the final length, l, of an 8 m piece of wood with c cm cut off $l =$ ___

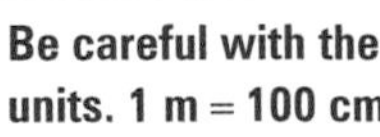

Be careful with the units. 1 m = 100 cm.

* Practical

1 You will need a spreadsheet.

Choose one of these formulae or a formula of your own.
Use a spreadsheet to print a table of values.

pints = gallons × 8

speed $= \dfrac{\textbf{distance}}{\textbf{time}}$

perimeter of rectangle $= 2l + 2w$

area of rectangle $= lw$

Example pints = gallons × 8

	A	B	C	D	E	F
1	gallons	1	= B1 + 1	⟶	copy across	
2	pints	= B1 * 8	⟶	copy across		

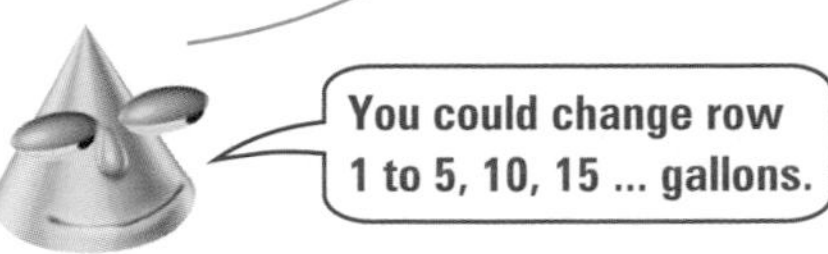

Investigation

Diagonals

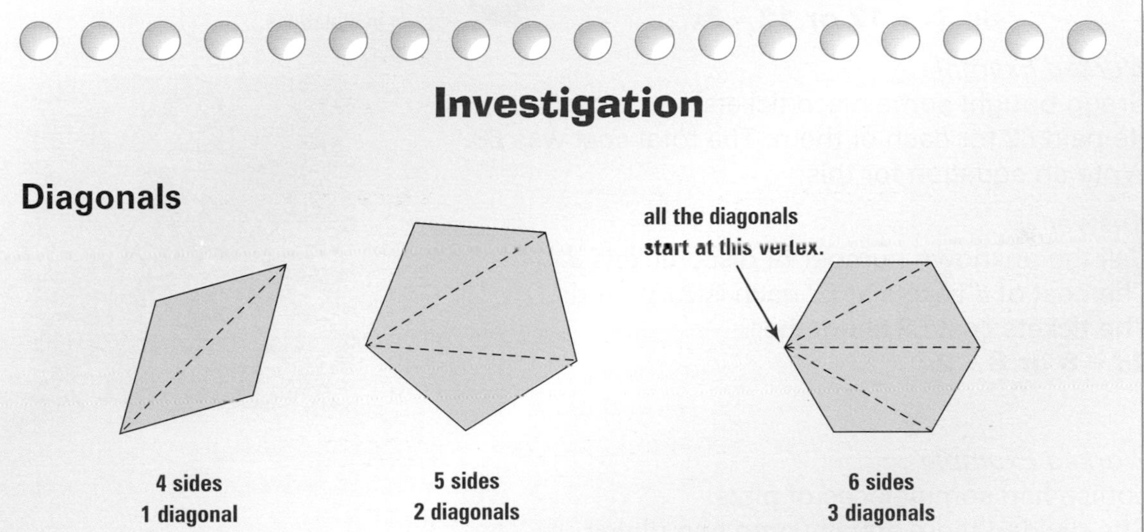

Polly drew these shapes and diagonals.
She wanted to know if there was a formula for finding the number of diagonals from *one* vertex of a shape with s sides.

Draw some shapes with 7, 8, 9, ... sides.
Draw the diagonals.
Begin all the diagonals at one vertex.
Copy and fill in this table.

Number of sides, s	4	5	6	7	8	9	10	...
Number of diagonals, d	1	2	3					...

The number of diagonals = number of sides ____.
So $d = s$____.

Writing equations

$x + 4 = 9$ is an **equation**.
An equation always has an equals sign.

Examples $n + 7 = 10$
$2n + 1 = 4$

Example I think of a number and multiply it by 3.
The answer is 12.

Call the number I think of x.
x multiplied by 3 is $3x$.
So $\mathbf{3x = 12}$ **or** $\mathbf{12 = 3x}$.

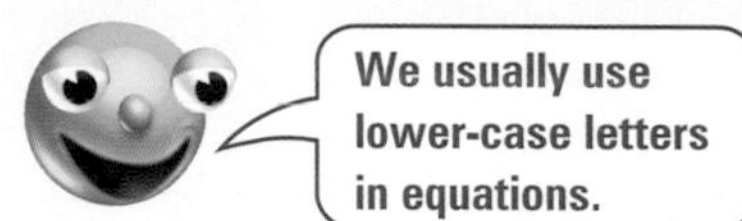

We usually use lower-case letters in equations.

Worked Example
Gregg bought some disco tickets.
He paid £2 for each of them. The total cost was £8.
Write an equation for this.

Answer
Call the unknown number of disco tickets d.
The cost of d tickets at £2 each is $2d$ pounds.
The tickets cost £8 altogether.
$\mathbf{2d = 8}$ **or** $\mathbf{8 = 2d}$

Worked Example
Louise had some pieces of pizza.
She divided them equally onto two plates.
There were eight pieces on each plate.
Write an equation for this, using p for the number of pieces of pizza.

Answer
p is divided by 2 to get $\frac{p}{2}$.
The number of pieces on each plate is 8.
$\mathbf{\frac{p}{2} = 8}$ **or** $\mathbf{8 = \frac{p}{2}}$

Exercise 10

1 Write an equation for each of the following.
Use n as the unknown.

a I think of a number.
I subtract 11.
The answer is 9.

b I think of a number.
I add 5.
The answer is 23.

c I think of a number.
I divide it by 4.
The answer is 6.

d I think of a number.
I multiply it by 5 and then add 4.
The answer is 34.

2 Write an equation for each of the following. Use n as the unknown.
a I think of a number, multiply it by 3 and then add 7. The answer is 19.
b I think of a number, multiply it by 4 and then add 8. The answer is 20.
c I think of a number, multiply it by 6 and then subtract 5. The answer is 13.
d I think of a number, multiply it by 8 and then subtract 20. The answer is 20.
e When a number is multiplied by 3 the answer is 15.

***3** When Allanah doubles her lucky number and then adds 4, she gets an answer of 30.
Write an equation for n, Allanah's lucky number.

***4** Simon bought some peanut bars.
They cost £2 each.
The total cost was £16.
Write an equation for n, the number of peanut bars.

***5** Bianca bought some bags of sweets at £1 each and a drink for £2.
The total cost was £6.
Write an equation for n, the number of bags of sweets.

Writing and solving equations

Discussion

I think of a number, add 4 and the answer is 16. What number did I think of?
I need to "undo" what Marty did. He added 4 So I need to subtract 4 from the answer. 16 − 4 = 12. It's 12!
Marty
Rani

Is Rani correct? **Discuss**.

We can use **inverse operations** and **function machines** to **solve equations**.

Example I think of a number, n, add 8 and the answer is 24.
The function machine for this is

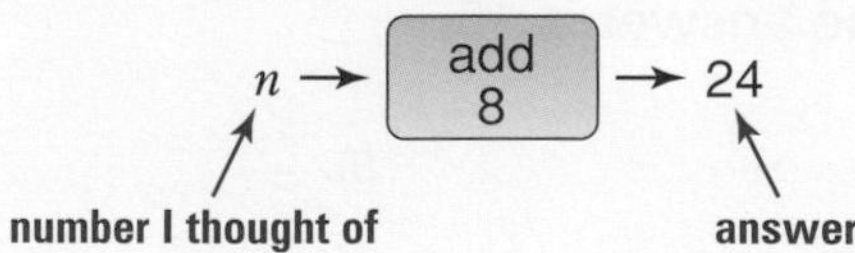

We can draw an inverse function machine to find n.

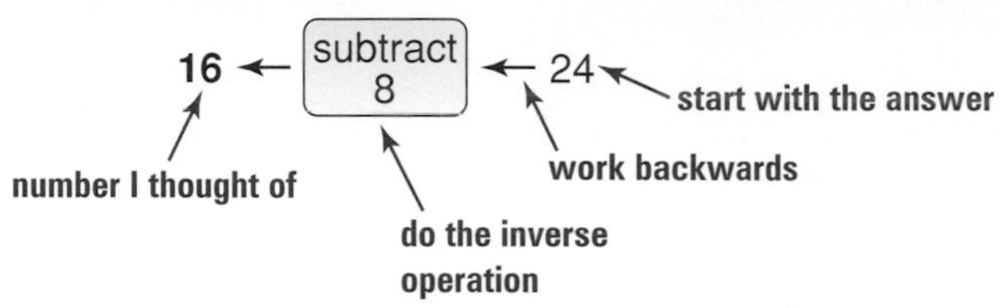

Worked Example
Solve $n+7 = 12$.

$n \rightarrow$ add 7 $\rightarrow 12$

Answer

$n+7 = 12$
$n = 12 - 7$
$n = \mathbf{5}$

$5 \leftarrow$ subtract 7 $\leftarrow 12$

Exercise 11

1 Write equations for these. Solve them.

a I think of a number.
I multiply this number by 5.
The answer is 30.
What is the number?

$n \rightarrow$ multiply by 5 $\rightarrow 30$

$\leftarrow$ divide by 5 $\leftarrow$

b I think of a number.
I subtract 6 from this number.
The answer is 30.
What is the number?

$n \rightarrow$ subtract 6 $\rightarrow 30$

$\leftarrow$ add 6 $\leftarrow$

2 Solve these equations. The first four are started for you.

a $x+8 = 11$
$x = 11$ __
$x =$ __

b $y+7 = 24$
$y = 24$ __
$y =$ __

c $9+p = 23$
$p = 23$ __
$p =$ __

d $70 = 60+p$
70 __ $= p$
__ $= p$

e $n-3 = 7$ **f** $20 = a-3$ **g** $6a = 54$ **h** $7a = 84$

i $\frac{n}{6} = 3$ **j** $\frac{n}{17} = 5$ **k** $72 = p-27$

*3 Write and solve equations for these.
Let the unknown be n.

a Ross bought some CDs at 'Sounds'.
He bought two more at 'CD Warehouse'.
Altogether he bought 8 CDs.
How many did he buy at 'Sounds'? $n + \_\_ = \_\_$

b Caroline bought some packets of muesli bars.
They cost £3 each.
The total cost was £12. How many did she buy?

c 20 copies of the same book are piled on top of one another.
The stack is 35 cm high.
How thick is one book?

Discussion

In the morning I put on my socks and then my shoes. At night I must take my shoes off first because I put them on last.

Discuss Steven's statement.

Example To find the **solution** (answer) to $3y + 4 = 19$, use **inverse operations**.

$y \rightarrow$ [multiply by 3] $\xrightarrow{3y}$ [add 4] $\rightarrow 3y + 4$

$5 \leftarrow$ [divide by 3] $\xleftarrow{15}$ [subtract 4] $\leftarrow 19$ **Start with 19 and work backwards doing the inverse.**

$y = \mathbf{5}$

We can solve equations without drawing the function machines.

Example

$9x + 3 = 21$

$9x = 21 - 3$ **The inverse of adding 3 is subtracting 3.**

$9x = 18$

$x = 18 \div 9$ **The inverse of multiplying by 9 is dividing by 9.**

$= \mathbf{2}$

Exercise 12

T **1** Use a copy of this.

Find the answer to these using inverse operations.

n → divide by 4 → add 6 → 9

← [ ] ← [ ] ← 9

a I think of a number, n
I divide by 4, then add 6. The answer is 9.
What is the number?

b I think of a number, n.
When I multiply by 3, then add 5 the answer is 23.
What is the number?

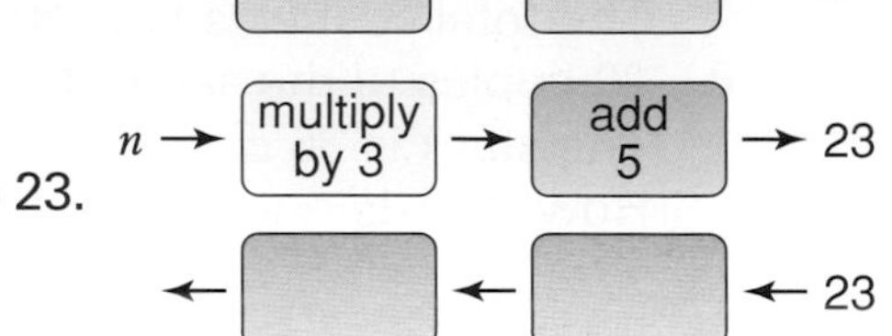

c I think of a number.
I add 5 then divide by 2.
The answer is 10.
What is the number?

***d** I think of a number.
I add 2·7 then multiply it by 5.
The answer is 24·5.
What is the number?

T **2** Use a copy of this.

Fill in the gaps to solve these equations.

a $2n + 4 = 10$

n → multiply by 2 → add 4 → $2n + 4$

___ ← [___] ⇌ [___] ← 10

b $3y + 4 = 22$

y → multiply by 3 → add 4 → $3y + 4$

___ ← [___] ⇌ [___] ← 22

c $4x - 7 = 1$

x → [___] → [___] → $4x - 7$

___ ← [___] ⇌ [___] ← 1

d $9p - 7 = 20$

p → [___] → [___] → $9p - 7$

___ ← [___] ⇌ [___] ← 20

e $7m + 8 = 29$
$7m = 29 -$ ___
$=$ ___
$m =$ ___
$=$ ___

f $5p + 6 = 31$
$5p = 31 -$ ___
$=$ ___
$p =$ ___
$=$ ___

***g** $4x + 3 = 63$
$4x = 63 -$ ___
$=$ ___
$x =$ ___
$=$ ___

3 Solve these equations.

a	$8b - 6 = 10$	**b**	$9a + 3 = 30$	**c**	$7x + 2 = 30$	**d**	$2 + 3n = 14$
e	$4a - 1 = 11$	**f**	$2y + 9 = 19$	***g**	$20 = 8n - 4$	***h**	$18 = 5x - 7$

*4 Write and solve equations for these.

a Jesse had saved £29.
Her aunt gave her £5 of this.
The rest she got from working for a neighbour for £3 an hour.
Finish writing this equation.

$$5 + 3 \times h = \_\_\_$$

Solve it to find the number of hours work she did.

b Sam bought some cakes for £3 each and one bag of biscuits for £2.
The total cost was £14.
How many cakes did Sam buy?

**Worked Example*

Worked Example

In this diagram the number in each box is found by adding the two numbers above it.

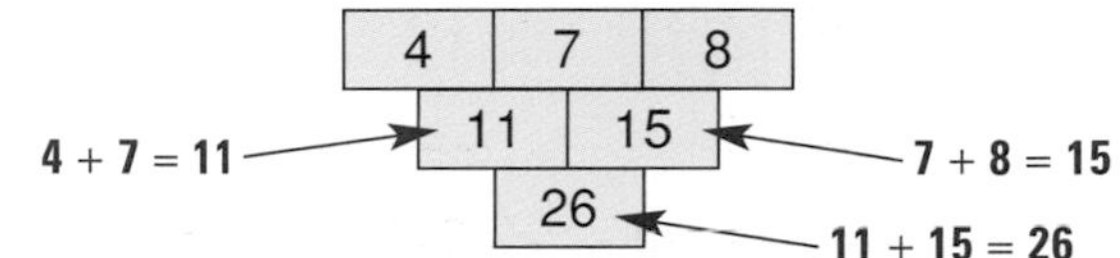

What are the missing numbers in this diagram?

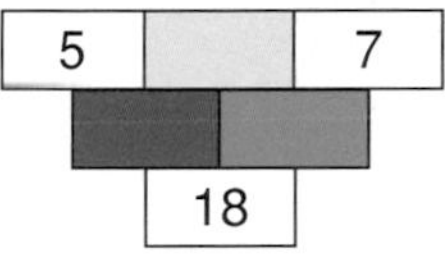

Answer

Let n be the number in the yellow box.

red box $= n + 5$

blue box $= n + 7$

18 = red box + blue box

$$18 = n + 5 + n + 7$$
$$= n + n + 5 + 7$$
$$= 2n + 12$$

$2n + 12 = 18$

$\therefore \quad 2n = 18 - 12$ **the inverse of adding 12 is subtracting 12**

$2n = 6$

$\therefore \quad n = \frac{6}{2}$ **the inverse of multiplying by 2 is dividing by 2**

$\boldsymbol{n = 3}$

Verify the answer.

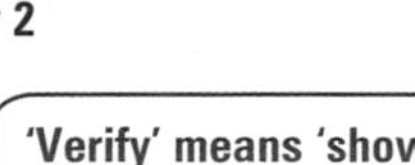

$2n + 12 = 2 \times \mathbf{3} + 12$ **substitute 3 for n**

$= 18$

The diagram can be filled in as shown.

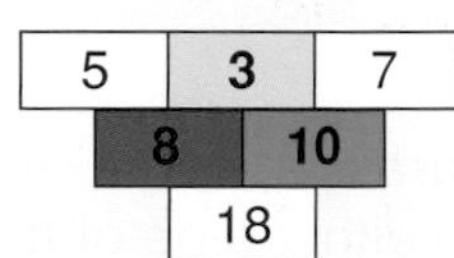

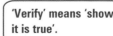

* **Exercise 13**

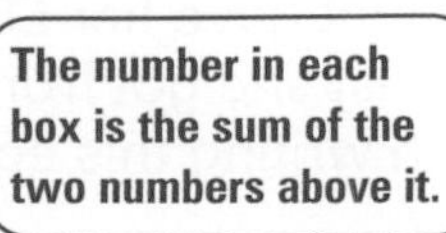

The number in each
box is the sum of the
two numbers above it.

1 Write and solve an equation to find the value of n.
Use this to find the missing numbers.
a and **b** have been started for you.

a

12	n	8
$12+n$	$8+n$	
32		

$$12 + n + 8 + n = 32$$

b

16	n	20
$16+n$	$n+20$	
60		

$$16 + n + n + 20 = 60$$

c

19	n	31
96		

d

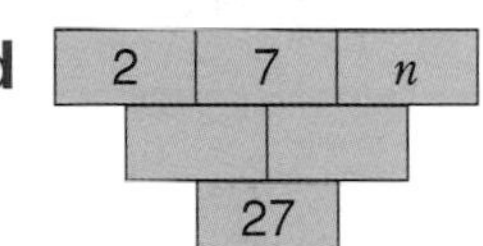

e

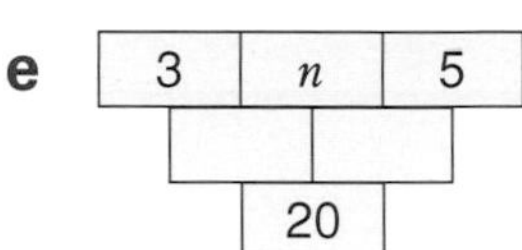

2 Write and solve an equation to find x.
a is started for you.

a

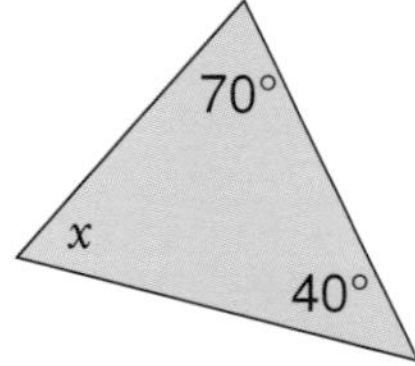

$$x + 70° + 40° = 180°$$
$$x + 110° = 180°$$

b

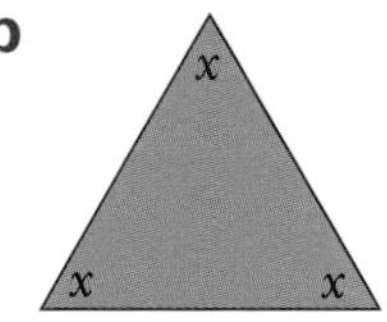

c

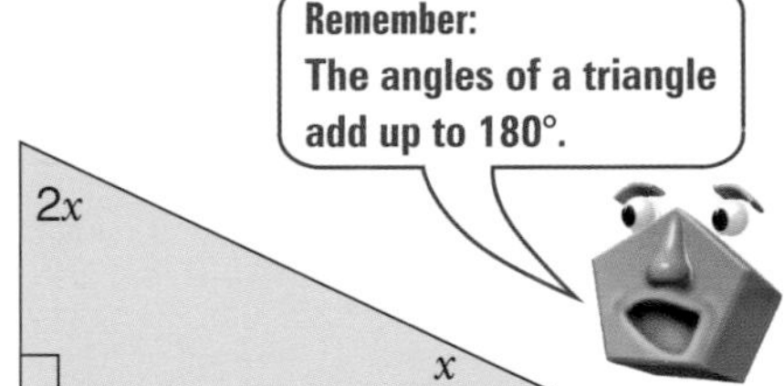

d

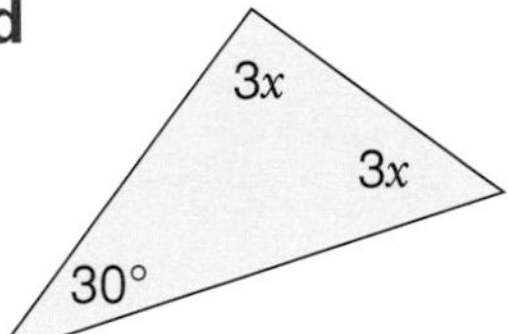

e

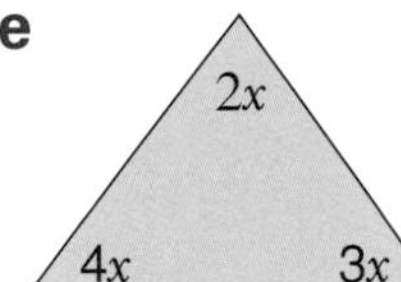

Investigation

Arithmagons

This is an arithmagon.
The number in each square is the sum of the numbers in the circles on either side of it.

What could the numbers A, B, C and D be?
Is there more than one answer? **Investigate**.

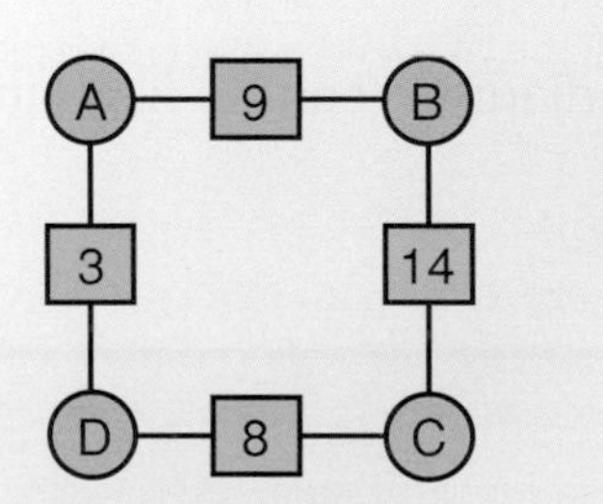

Summary of key points

$p-7$, $8n$, $7t+4$ are all **expressions**.

We write expressions as simply as possible.

Example Multiply a number by 2 then add 6 is written as $2n+6$.

Letters **follow the same rules as numbers**.

Examples $x+y=y+x$ $\quad pq=qp$ $\quad a(bc)=(ab)c$

$\mathbf{3}+\mathbf{4}=\mathbf{4}+\mathbf{3}$ $\quad \mathbf{8}\times\mathbf{9}=\mathbf{9}\times\mathbf{8}$ $\quad \mathbf{3}\times(\mathbf{4}\times\mathbf{5})=(\mathbf{3}\times\mathbf{4})\times\mathbf{5}$

We can **simplify** expressions by **collecting like terms**.

Examples $3n+6n=9n$

$8b-3b=5b$

$3x+8y+2x+y=3x+2x+8y+y$

$=5x+9y$

Write the like terms next to one another.

D

We can **simplify** expressions by **cancelling**.

Examples $\frac{8b}{2}=4b$ **divide numerator and denominator by 2**

$\frac{6a}{a}=6$ **divide numerator and denominator by *a***

E

To **write an expression without brackets** we use the rules of arithmetic.

Example $4(x+7)=\mathbf{4x}+\mathbf{28}$

	x	$+7$
4	**4x**	**+28**

We **evaluate an expression** by **substituting** values for the unknown.

Examples If $a=\mathbf{2}$, $b=\mathbf{3}$ and $c=\mathbf{5}$ then

$3a=3\times\mathbf{2}$
$=6$

$2c-b=2\times\mathbf{5}-\mathbf{3}$
$=10-3$
$=7$

A **formula** is a rule for working something out.

Examples $T=\frac{D}{S}$ is the formula for finding the time taken to travel a distance D at speed S.

If $D=20$ and $S=4$ then $T=\frac{20}{4}$
$=5$.

We can **write expressions and formulae** for practical situations.

$n + 4 = 12$ is an **equation**.
An equation always has an equals sign.
We can **solve equations** using inverse operations.

Example $2x - 4 = 8$ $x \rightarrow$ [multiply by 2] $\rightarrow$ [subtract 4] $\rightarrow 2x - 4$

$6 \leftarrow$ [divide by 2] $\overset{12}{\leftarrow}$ [add 4] $\leftarrow 8$

$\mathbf{x = 6}$

or $2x - 4 = 8$

$2x = 8 + 4$ **The inverse of adding 4 is subtracting 4.**

$= 12$

$x = 12 \div 2$ **The inverse of multiplying by 2 is dividing by 2.**

$\mathbf{x = 6}$

Test yourself

1 Write these without a multiplication sign. 
a $6 \times y$ **b** $c \times c$ **c** $4 \times (x + 3)$ **d** $(y - 4) \times 6$ **e** $p \times p$

2 Write an expression for these. A
Let the unknown number be n.
a subtract 4 from a number
b multiply a number by 7
c multiply a number by 2 then add 3
d add 3 to a number then multiply by 2
e multiply a number by itself

3 Simplify these. 
a $x + x + x$ **b** $5x + 4x$ **c** $9m - 3m$ **d** $10m + 3m + 2m$
e $5n + 3n - n$ **f** $10q - 3q - 2q$ **g** $3a + 5a + 4b + 5b$ **h** $5x + 2y + 3x + 2y$

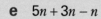

4 Simplify these expressions by cancelling. 
a $\frac{w}{w}$ **b** $\frac{20n}{5}$ **c** $\frac{28x}{7}$ **d** $\frac{30m}{m}$ **e** $\frac{15r}{r}$

5 Write these without brackets. 
a $5(x + 3)$ **b** $7(n + 4)$ **c** $8(a + 4)$ **d** $12(x + 2)$

6 Match each of these with an expression from the box. A B C D E

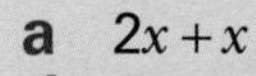
a $2x + x + 2x$ **b** $2x + 4 + x$ **c** $\frac{4x}{x}$
d $2(x + 2)$ **e** $x \times x$ **f** $\frac{16x}{4}$
g $(x + y) \times 3$ **h** $(x + y) + 2$

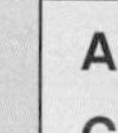

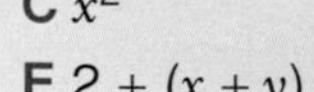
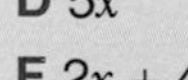

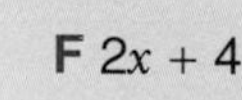
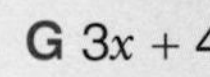

A $4x$	B $3(x + y)$
C x^2	D $5x$
E $2 + (x + y)$	F $2x + 4$
G $3x + 4$	H 4

7 If $x = 3$ and $y = 2$ find the value of these.

a $x + 7$ **b** $y - 1$ **c** $4x$ **d** $4 - y$ **e** xy
***f** $xy - 6$ ***g** $4(6 - y)$

8 $A = lw$ is a formula for finding the area of a rectangle.
Find A if $l = 6$ and $w = 3$.

9 $c = 80 + 50h$ is the formula for the cost to hire a wedding car.
c is the cost, in pounds, and h is the number of hours hired.
Find the cost to hire a car for

a 4 hours **b** 8 hours ***c** 5·5 hours.

10 Ben has p blue planes.

a Ben has twice as many red planes as blue planes.
How many red planes does he have?

b Ben has 4 more green planes than blue planes.
How many green planes does he have?

***c** How many planes does he have altogether?

11 Write a formula for these.

a the cost, c, of p packets of biscuits at £2 each $c =$ ____

b the total height, h, of a man of height m cm and his hat of height 12 cm
$h =$ ____

***c** the final length, l, of a 2 m piece of rope with r cm cut off $l =$ ____

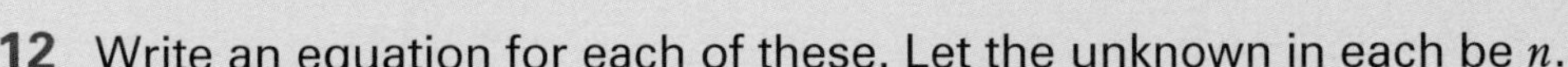

12 Write an equation for each of these. Let the unknown in each be n.

a I think of a number.
I subtract 5.
The answer is 7.

b I think of a number.
I multiply by 4.
The answer is 32.

c When the length of a fence, n metres, is divided by 6 the answer is 4 metres.

13 Solve these equations. Use inverse operations.

a $b + 6 = 15$ **b** $x + 7 = 20$ **c** $5x = 50$ **d** $\frac{y}{9} = 4$

14 Solve these equations. Use inverse operations.

a $2n + 4 = 12$ **b** $4y - 8 = 28$ **c** $8p + 12 = 52$

***15** Write and solve equations to find the answers to these.

a I think of a number.
When I multiply by 4 and add 9 the answer is 21.
What is the number?

b Find the value of x.

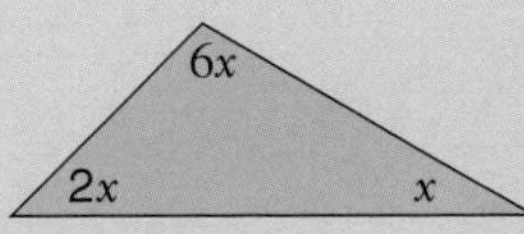

9 Sequences and Functions

You need to know

✓ sequences page 136
✓ functions page 136

Key vocabulary

continue, flow chart, function, function machine, input, inverse, mapping, *n*th term, number sequence, output, predict, rule, sequence, term

Reductions

To get a *reduced number* add the digits of a number together.

Examples

		reduced number
16	1 + 6 =	7
32	3 + 2 =	5

If you get a two-digit number when you add, then repeat until you get a single digit.

Examples

			reduced number
59	5 + 9 = 14	1 + 4 =	5
78	7 + 8 = 15	1 + 5 =	6

1 Try to find a pattern.

a

	reduced number
$8 \times 1 = 8$	8
$8 \times 2 = 16$	7
$8 \times 3 = 24$	6
$8 \times 4 = 32$	5
$8 \times 5 = 40$	4
⋮	⋮

b

	reduced number
2	2
$2 \times 2 = 4$	4
$2 \times 2 \times 2 = 8$	8
$2 \times 2 \times 2 \times 2 = 16$	7
$2 \times 2 \times 2 \times 2 \times 2 = 32$	5
⋮	⋮

2 Try some other tables or multiplications to see if the reduced numbers give a pattern.

Counting on or counting back

Remember

1, 3, 5, 7, 9, ... is a **sequence**.

1st term — 4th term — This means the squence carries on forever.

Each number is called a **term**.

Sally is stacking books.
Each book is 0·5 cm thick.
She wrote down the height of the pile after each book had been stacked.

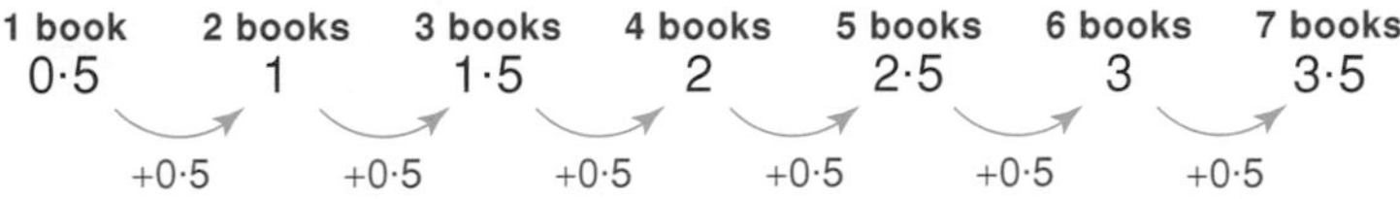

This sequence starts at 0·5.
It goes up in steps of 0·5.

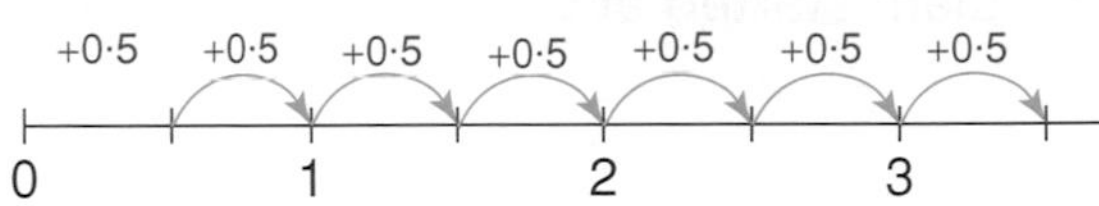

Worked Example
Write down the first six terms of this sequence.
Start at 19 and count back in steps of 3.
Describe the sequence in words.

Answer

The first six terms are **19, 16, 13, 10, 7, 4**.
We could describe the sequence like this:
It begins at 19 and goes down in steps of 3.
Each term is 1 more than a multiple of 3.

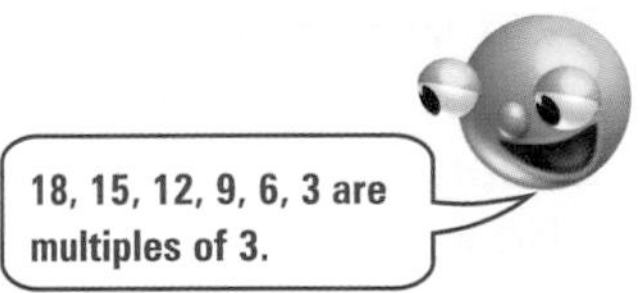

How else could you describe each term?

Exercise 1

1 Write down the first six terms of these sequences.
Use the number lines to help.

a Start at 5 and count on in steps of 3.
b Start at 73 and count back in steps of 4.
c Start at 5 and count on in steps of 0·5.
d Start at 2 and count back in steps of 0·2.
e Start at ⁻2 and count back in steps of 2.

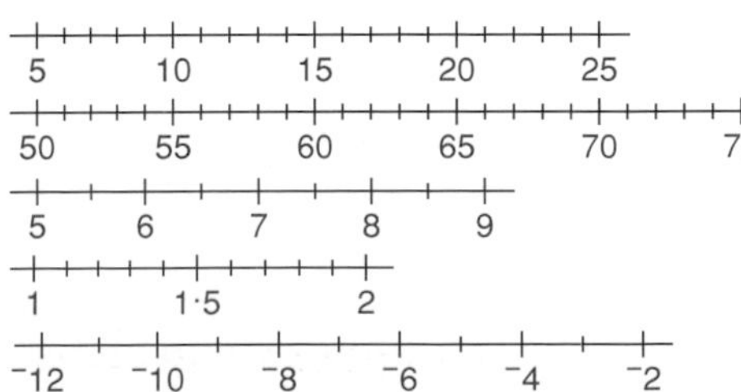

2 In which of the sequences you made in **question 1** are the terms getting bigger?

3 Write down the next 3 terms of these sequences.

a 7, 14, 21, 28, ... **b** 6, 11, 16, 21, 26, ... **c** 3, 7, 11, 15, 19, ...
d 50, 48, 46, 44, 42, ... **e** 1, 1·2, 1·4, 1·6, 1·8, ... **f** 78, 70, 62, 54, 46, ...

4 Look at **question 3**.
What goes in the gap?

a In part **a** the terms of the sequence are multiples of ___.
b In part **b** the terms are all ___ more than a multiple of ___.
c In part **c** the terms are all ___ less than a multiple of ___.

5 A bus leaves for the zoo every 10 minutes.
One leaves at 1:15 p.m.
Write down the times of the next five buses.

***6** Liam started at 0 and counted on in steps of 1, 2, 3, 4, ...

0 1 3 6 10 ...
+1 +2 +3 +4 ← **Each step is one more.**

What sequence would he get if he started at 2 and counted on in steps of 1, 2, 3, 4, ...?

* Practical

You will need a graphical calculator.

Susan used her graphical calculator to show 0·2, 0·6, 1, 1·4, 1·8, 2·2.
She keyed

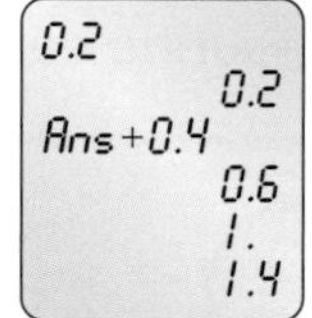

Susan then keyed

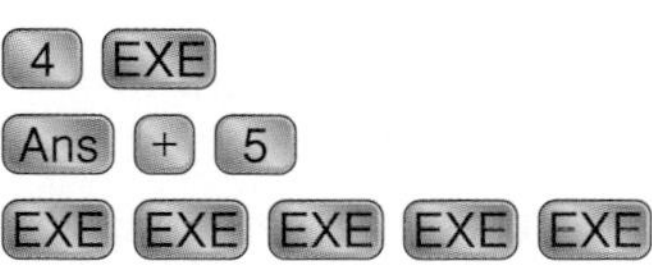

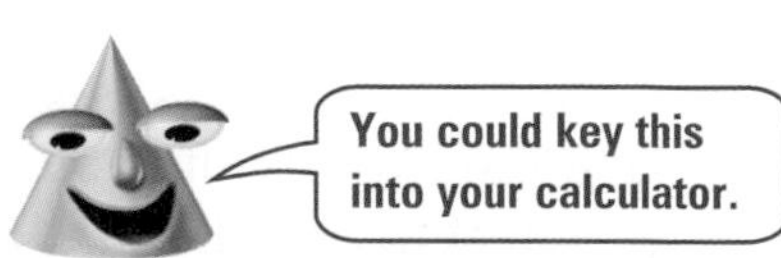

a Describe the sequence Susan will get on her screen.
b How many times would she have to press EXE after the 5 to get a number bigger than 50?
c Write down what you need to key to get a sequence which starts at 0·3 and goes up in steps of 0·3.

Writing sequences by multiplying and dividing

Maria swam one length today.
Each day she is going to swim twice as far as the day before.

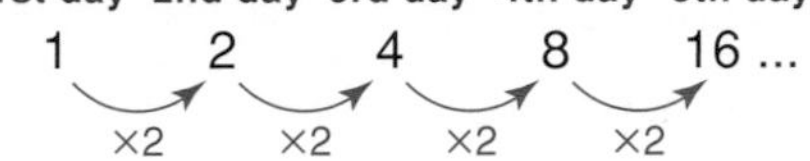

Example

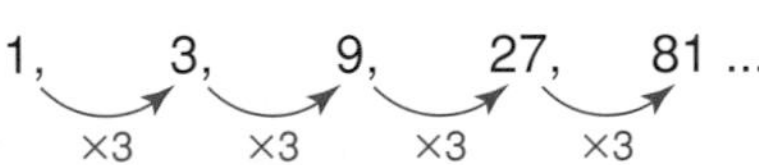

This sequence starts at 1. Each term is found by multiplying the previous term by 3.

Exercise 2

Only use a calculator if you need to.

1 Write down the missing terms.

a 2, 4, □, □, □, ... (×2 each time)

b 2, 6, □, □, □, ... (×3 each time)

c 5, □, □, □, □, ... (×10 each time)

d 1000, □, □, □, □, ... (÷10 each time)

e 80, □, □, □, □, ... (÷2 each time)

2 Write down the next term.

a 1, 2, 4, 8, ...
b 1, 3, 9, 27, ...
c 3, 6, 12, 24, ...
d 64, 32, 16, ...
e 100, 10, 1, ...

Discussion

- What do you think the answer to 33 333 × 11 will be?
  What do you think the answer to 33 333 333 × 11 will be? **Discuss.**
  Check using your calculator.

  3 × 11 = 33
  33 × 11 = 363
  333 × 11 = 3663
  3333 × 11 = 36 663

  How could you explain a 'rule' for finding the answers? **Discuss.**

Showing sequences with geometric patterns

Discussion

- These are the first three square numbers.

1 4 9

Draw the next two square numbers.
Can all the square numbers be shown using a diagram? **Discuss.**

- These are the first four triangular numbers.

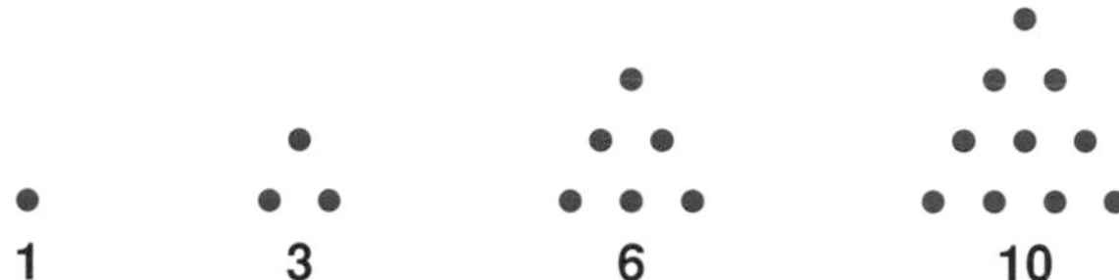

1 3 6 10

How else could the triangular numbers be drawn using dots?

Writing sequences from rules

Discussion

1, 2,

Matt spilt ink on his sequence.
What might the next few numbers have been. **Discuss.**

To write a sequence we need a **rule**.

Example **first term** 3, **rule** add 4
This rule gives the sequence
3, 7, 11, 15, 19, ...

Example **first term** 1, **rule** multiply by 2
This rule gives the sequence
1, 2, 4, 8, 16, ...

Exercise 3

Only use a calculator if you need to.

1 Write down the first five terms of these sequences.

- **a** **first term** 4, **rule** add 6
- **b** **first term** 4, **rule** multiply by 2
- **c** **first term** 80, **rule** subtract 5
- **d** **first term** 5000, **rule** divide by 5
- **e** **first term** 1, **rule** add 9
- **f** **first term** 20 000, **rule** divide by 2
- ***g** **first term** 2, **rule** multiply by 4
- ***h** **first term** 1000, **rule** subtract 25

2 We could describe the sequence with **first term** 4 and **rule** add 6 as 'the first term is 4 and each term is 6 more than the one before'.
Describe these in the same way.

- **a** **first term** 4, **rule** multiply by 2
- **b** **first term** 80, **rule** subtract 5
- **c** **first term** 5000 **rule** divide by 2
- **d** **first term** 64, **rule** add 6

3 Some of the terms of these sequences are smudged.
Find the missing terms.

- **a** 1600, ▢, ▢, ▢, 6·25 **rule** divide by 4
- **b** 1, ▢, 25, ▢, ▢ **rule** multiply by 5

4 Two sequences have been mixed up.
The rule for one is 'add 4'.
The rule for the other is 'subtract 3'.

7 15 11 15 21 9 3 12 19 18

What could the sequences have been?

5 Write down the first six terms of this sequence.

I am thinking of a sequence.
The 3rd term is 4.
The rule is 'multiply by 2'.

***6** Mr Jones asked his class to write a sequence with the rule 'add 4'.

Tom wrote 2, 6, 10, 14, ...
Bill wrote 15, 19, 23, 27, ...

- **a** Write down another possible sequence with the rule 'add 4'.
- **b** Is it possible to find a sequence with the rule 'add 4' for which
  - **i** all terms are multiples of 4
  - **ii** all terms are even numbers?

  If it is possible, give an example.

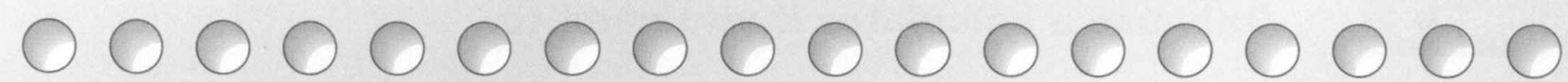

Investigation

Missing Terms

How many different ways can you fill in the missing terms? **Investigate**.

a ___, ___, ___, ___, 24

b 1, ___, ___, 10

We can show the sequence 2, 4, 6, 8, ... in a table.

Term number, n	1	2	3	4	5	...	n
Term	2	4	6	8	10	...	

We call the **term number**, n.

When n is **1**, this is the first term.
When n is **2**, this is the second term and so on.

We can write a rule for a sequence using n.

The rule for the nth term of the sequence in the table is $2 \times n$.

This tells us that each term is 2 times the term number.

The **20**th term would be $2 \times 20 = 40$.

Discussion

- For the sequence given in the screen above, what is the 50th term? **Discuss**. What about the 28th term?

- A rule for a sequence is given as

  'the rule for the nth term is $n + 3$'.

  What does 'n' stand for?
  How could you work out what the first five terms of this sequence are? **Discuss**.

  What if the rule for the nth term is $n - 1$?
  What about $3n$?

Worked Example
The rule for the nth term is $2n + 1$.
Write down the first 5 terms.

Answer
$2n + 1$ is $2 \times n + 1$

1st term ($n = \mathbf{1}$) $= 2 \times \mathbf{1} + 1$
$= 3$

2nd term ($n = \mathbf{2}$) $= 2 \times \mathbf{2} + 1$
$= 5$

3rd term ($n = \mathbf{3}$) $= 2 \times \mathbf{3} + 1$
$= 7$

4th term ($n = \mathbf{4}$) $= 2 \times \mathbf{4} + 1$
$= 9$

5th term ($n = \mathbf{5}$) $= 2 \times \mathbf{5} + 1$
$= 11$

Exercise 4

T

1 a The nth term of a sequence is $n + 1$.
Use a copy of this.
Fill it in.

1st term ($n = \mathbf{1}$) $= n + 1$
$= \mathbf{1} + 1$
$=$ ___

2nd term ($n = \mathbf{2}$) $= n + 1$
$=$ ___ $+ 1$
$=$ ___

20th term ($n = 20$) $= n + 1$
$=$ ___ $+ 1$
$=$ ___

b Find the first five terms of these sequences.

i $n + 3$ **ii** $n + 4$ **iii** $n - 1$ **iv** $2n$
v $2n + 2$ **vi** $3n$ ***vii** $20 - n$ ***viii** $3n - 4$

2 Look at the sequences you wrote in **question 1b**.
Describe each of the sequences in words.
The answer to **1bi** could be '**first term** 4, **rule** add 1'.

3

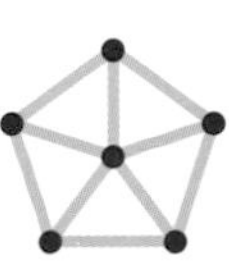

shape 1

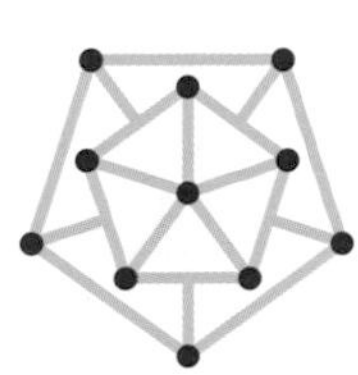

shape 2

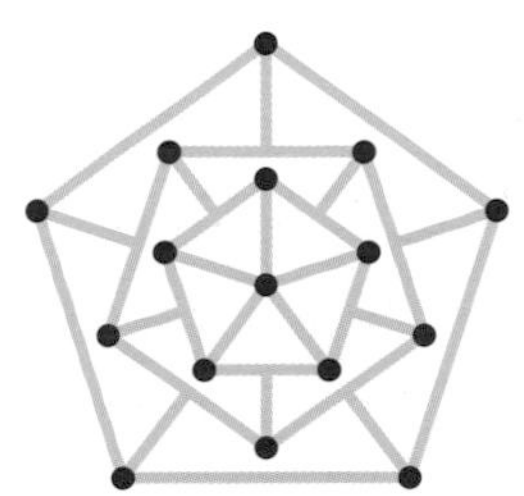

shape 3

The number of dots in the nth shape of this pattern is given by $5n + 1$.
Write down the number of dots in

a shape 5 **b** shape 10 **c** shape 20.

T

***4** Anna was told the nth term of a sequence was $n + 5$. She filled in this table for the sequence.

Term number	1 +5	2 +5	3 +5	4 +5	5 +5	6 +5	...	n
Term	6	7	8	9	10	11	...	$n+5$

Use a copy of these tables. Fill in the missing terms.

a

Term number	1	2	3	4	5	6	...	n
Term	0	1					...	$n-1$

b

Term number	1	2	3	4	5	6	...	n
Term	7	9					...	$2n+5$

T

* Practical

You will need a spreadsheet and a graphical calculator.

4, 8, 12, 16, 20, ...

The terms of this sequence are multiples of 4.
The rule for finding the next term is 'add 4'.
The nth term of the sequence is $4n$.

Using a spreadsheet we can find the first 20 terms of the sequence in two ways.

Using the rule for the next term

	A	B	C	D	E	
1	Term number	1	= B1+1	= C1+1	= D1+1	=
2	Term	4	= B2+4	= C2+4	= D2+4	=

Using the expression for the nth term

	A	B	C	D	E	
1	Term number	1	= B1+1	= C1+1	= D1+1	=
2	Term	= B1*4	= C1*4	= D1*4	= E1*4	= F

Use a spreadsheet to find the first 20 multiples of 5 in two different ways.

Use a spreadsheet to find the multiples of these numbers in two different ways.

7 11 15 24

Sequences in practical situations

Discussion

Raana made these photo frames with rods.

1 photo

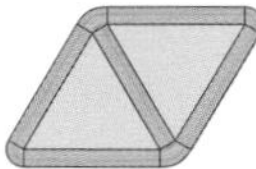
2 photos

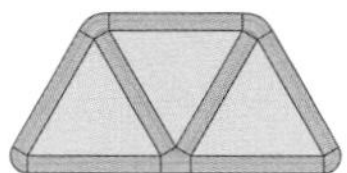
3 photos

Raana wanted to know how many rods he would need for 8 photos.

Each new photo frame has 2 more rods. But the first one has an extra 1 rod. So a frame for 8 photos will have 8×2+1 =
16 + 1
= 17 rods.

Is Raana right?

How could you work out the number of rods needed for
16 photos? 20 photos? n photos?
Discuss.

Worked Example

Pattern 1

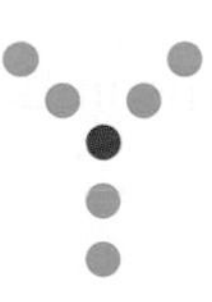
Pattern 2

Pattern 3

Jess made this pattern with buttons around the hem of her dress.

Pattern number	1	2	3	4	...
Number of buttons	4	7	10	?	...

a Draw shape 4.
How many buttons are in shape 4?
b Describe the pattern and how it continues.
c Explain how you can find the number of buttons in the nth shape.

Answer

a 

There are **13** buttons.

b **The first pattern has 4 buttons.**
3 more buttons are added each time the next pattern is made.

c The first pattern has 3 blue buttons, the second has 6 blue buttons, the third 9 blue buttons and so on.
The number of blue buttons is 3 times the pattern number.
Each pattern also has 1 purple button.
The number of buttons altogether in each pattern is 3 × pattern number + 1.

Exercise 5

T

1 Mr Hudson stacked boxes of films in different sizes in his shop.

Box 1

Box 2

Box 3

Box 4

a Use a copy of this table.
Fill it in.

Box number	1	2	3	4	5
Number of films	2	4	6		

b Describe the pattern for 'Number of films'.
How does it continue?

c Explain how you could find the number of films in Box n.

2 Maud's Magazines uses these for its logo.

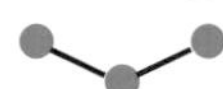

Shape 1

Shape 2

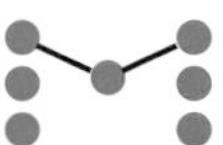

Shape 3

a Draw the 4th shape.

b Use a copy of this table.
Fill it in.

Shape number	1	2	3	4	5
Number of circles	3	5	7		

c Describe the pattern made by the number of circles.

d Explain how you would find the number of circles needed for the nth shape.

e How many circles will be used in the 10th shape?

3 Paul made these matchstick squares.

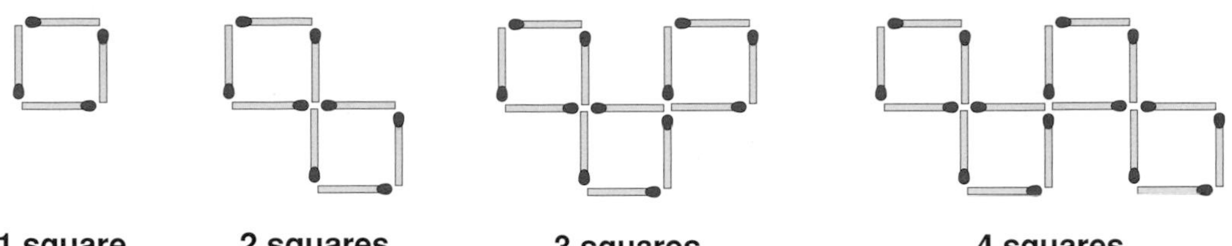

a Draw the shape with 5 squares

b What numbers go in the gaps in this table?

Number of squares	1	2	3	4	5
Number of matchsticks	4	8			

c How many matchsticks will be needed for 12 squares? Explain your answer.

d Will one of the shapes have 40 matchsticks?
Give a reason for your answer.

T **4**

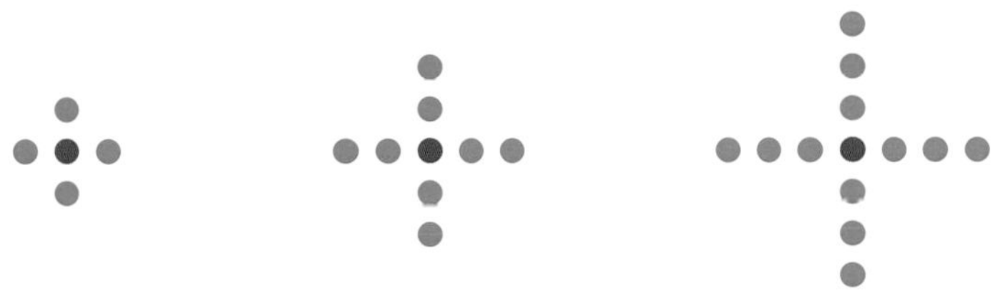

Pritesh drew these shapes on her bedroom wall.

a Draw shape 4.
Use a copy of this table.
Fill it in.

Shape number	1	2	3	4	5
Total number of circles	5	9			

b Describe the sequence made by the total number of circles.

*__c__ Explain how you could find the total number of circles needed for the nth shape by looking at the diagrams.

*__d__ How many circles are needed for shape 20?

T **5**

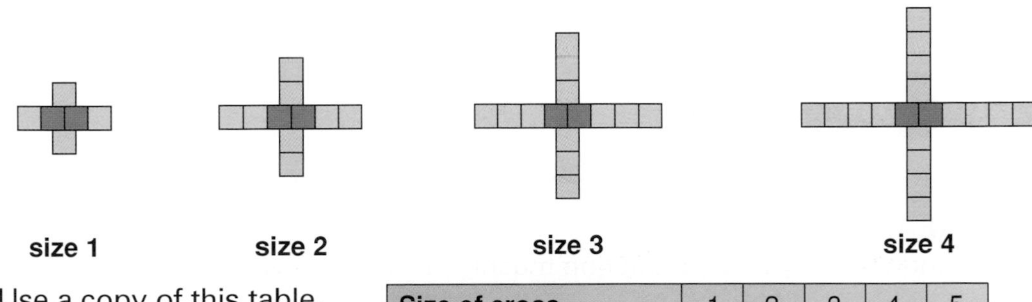

a Use a copy of this table.
Fill it in.

Size of cross	1	2	3	4	5
Number of squares	6	10			

b Describe the sequence made by the number of squares.

c Will one of the crosses have 40 squares?
Explain your answer.

d Explain how you could find the number of squares in cross size n by looking at the diagrams.

***6** Abigail made window hangers with coloured glass squares.

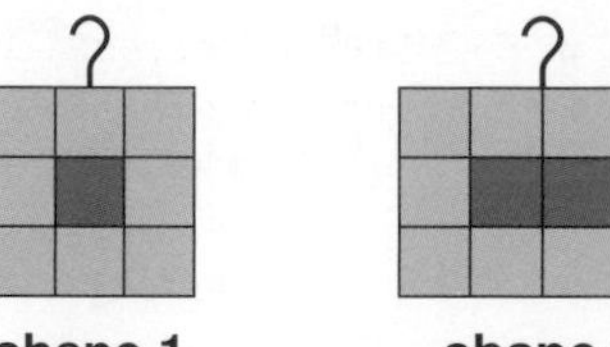
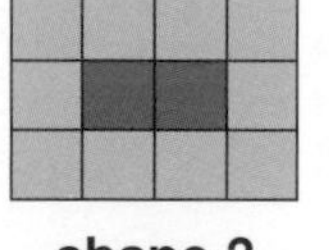
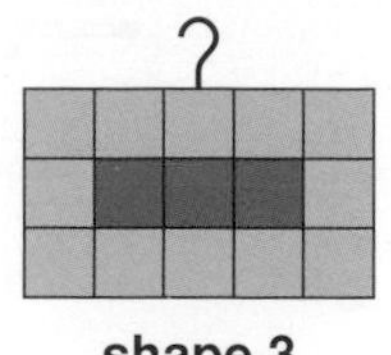
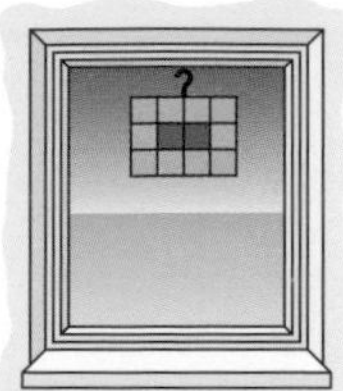

shape 1 shape 2 shape 3

a How many red and how many orange squares will there be in shape 8?
Explain how you worked this out.

b Will one of the shapes have 29 orange squares?
Give a reason for your answer.

Practical

You will need lego blocks as shown in the picture.

This table shows the number of ways of making blocks of length 1 to 5.

Total block length	**1**	**2**	**3**	**4**	**5**
Blocks needed	1	1+1 or 2	1+1+1 or 1+2 or 3	1+1+1+1 or 2+2 or 1+3 or 1+1+2	1+1+1+1+1 or 1+2+2 or 1+1+1+2 or 2+3 or 1+1+3
Number of ways	1	2	3	4	5

Predict the number of ways of making a block of length 6.
Check your prediction by making the blocks.

Functions

Remember

We can find the **output** of a function machine if we are given the **input**.

Example **input** **output**

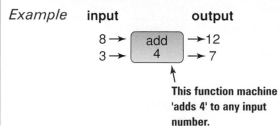

8 → [add 4] → 12
3 → [add 4] → 7

This function machine 'adds 4' to any input number.

Example **input** **output**

2 → [multiply by 3] → 6 → [subtract 4] → 2
3 → [multiply by 3] → 9 → [subtract 4] → 5

2 → **2 × 3** → **6** → **6 − 4** → 2
3 → **3 × 3** → **9** → **9 − 4** → 5

This function machine multiplies the input number by 3 then subtracts 4.

Exercise 6

1 Find the output for each of these.

a 8 → [subtract 6] → —

b 4 → [multiply by 4] → —

c 2 → [multiply by 2] → 4 → [add 1] → —

d 3 → [multiply by 3] → — → [subtract 4] → —

e 6 → [divide by 2] → — → [add 3] → —

f 10 → [subtract 5] → — → [multiply by 3] → —

2 Describe what each function machine in **question 1** does to the input.

Example **a** subtracts 6 from the input.

3 6 → [ ] → [ ] → output

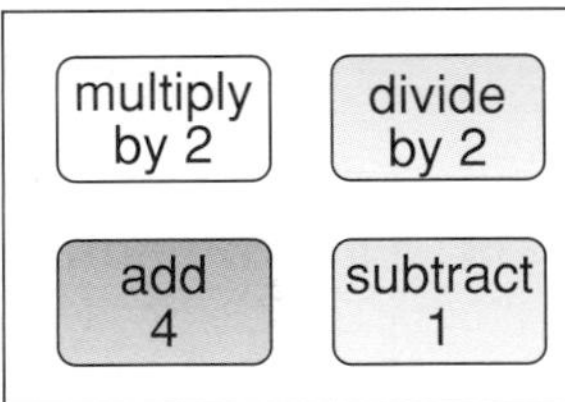

Choose operations from the box to put onto the machine.

a Which operations in which order give the biggest output?

b Which give the smallest output?

*__c__ Are the answers to **a** and **b** the same for any input?

Sometimes we show the inputs and outputs on a **table**.
We often call the input x and the output y.

Example x → [add 3] → [multiply by 2] → y

Input (x)	Output (y)
1	8
2	10
3	12
4	14
5	16

or

x	1	2	3	4	5	← **inputs**
y	8	10	12	14	16	← **outputs**

The outputs from the function machine form a sequence.

Sometimes the inputs and outputs are written like this.

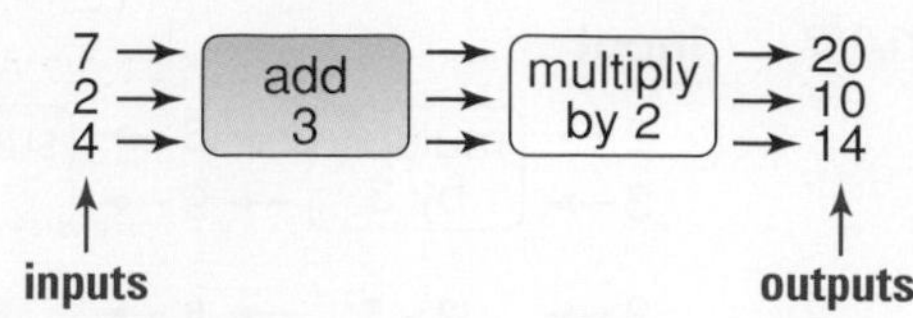

Exercise 7

T

1 Use a copy of this for each of these. Fill them in.

x	1	2	3	4	5	← inputs
y						← outputs

a x → multiply by 4 → y

b x → subtract 1 → y

c x → multiply by 3 → add 6 → y

d x → subtract 1 → multiply by 3 → y

2 Find the output for these.

a 3, 7, 8 → multiply by 2 → subtract 4 → __, __, __

b 18, 6, 24 → divide by 3 → add 1 → __, __, __

c 2, 1, 0 → add 4 → multiply by 2 → __, __, __

***d** 23, 49, 9·6 → subtract 3 → divide by 2 → __, __, __

3 Find the output for these.

a 8, 6, 3 → subtract 2 → multiply by 3 → __, __, __

b 10, 6, 2 → divide by 2 → add 4 → __, __, __

T

4 x → add 2 → multiply by 3 → y

a Use a copy of this table. Fill it in.

x	1	2	3	4	5
y					

Write in words what this function machine does.

b The order of operations is changed.

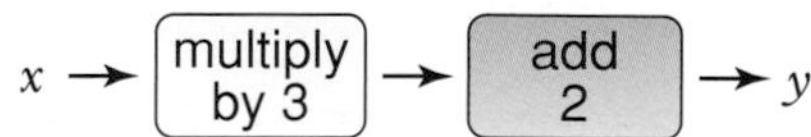

Use a copy of this table. Fill it in.

x	1	2	3	4	5
y					

Write in words what this function machine does.

c What happens when the order of the operations is changed?

We can show functions on a **mapping diagram**.

Example

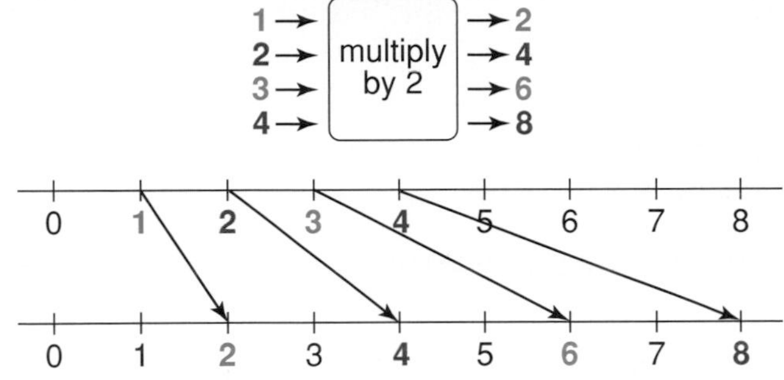

Exercise 8

T

1 Use a copy of these mapping diagrams.
Fill them in for the function machine and input given.
a is started for you.

a 0, 1, 2, 3, 4 → add 3 → y

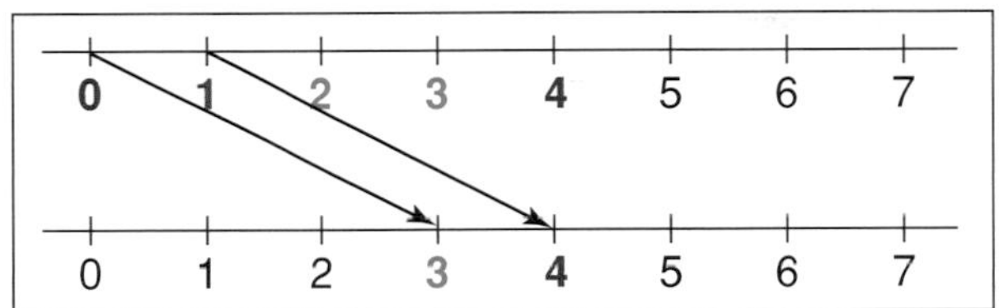

b 0, 1, 2, 3, 4 → subtract 2 → y

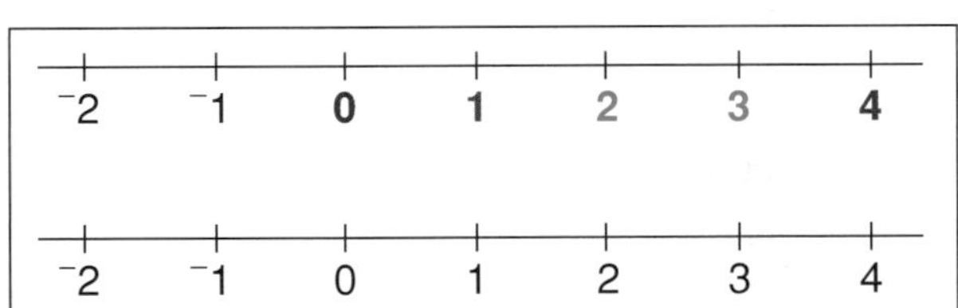

c 0, 2, 4, 6, 8 → divide by 2 → y

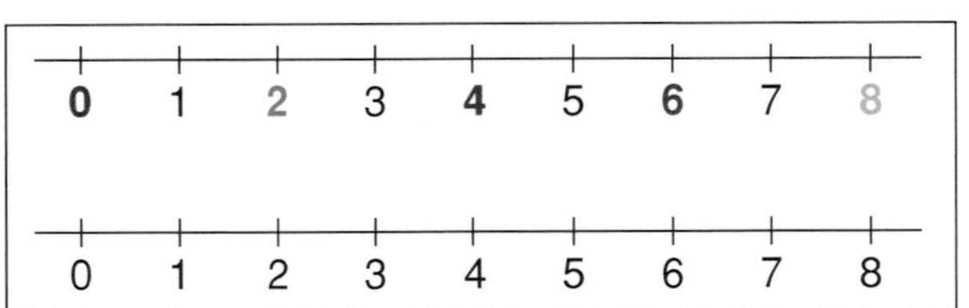

d 0, 1, 2, 3, 4 → multiply by 2 → add 1 → y

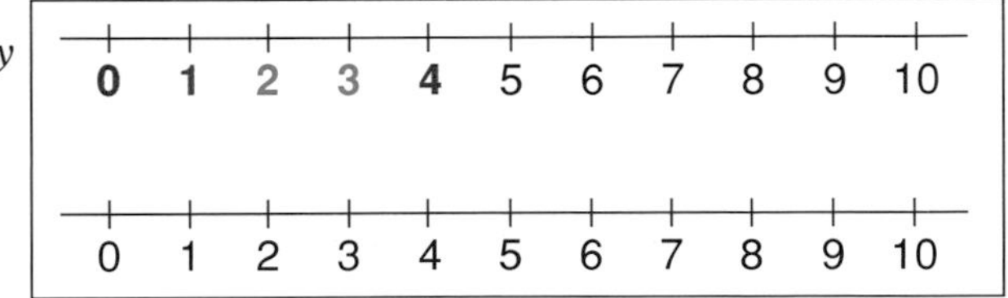

e 2, 3, 4, 5, 6 → subtract 2 → multiply by 3 → y

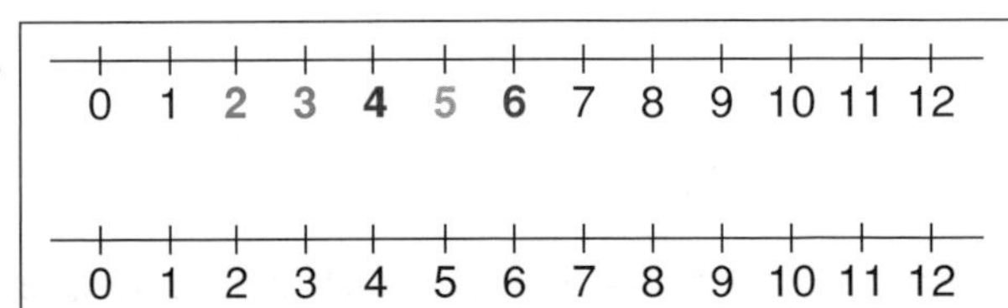

We can write a **rule for a function machine** using letters.

$x \rightarrow$ [multiply by 3] $\rightarrow$ [add 2] $\rightarrow y$

$x \quad \times 3 \quad +2 \quad = y$

We write the function as $x \times 3 + 2 = y$
or $y = 3x + 2$.

We sometimes write the rule using a mapping arrow. $x \longrightarrow 3x + 2$

Worked Example

Write the rule for this function machine as $x \longrightarrow$ ______

$x \rightarrow$ [divide by 2] $\rightarrow$ [add 4] $\rightarrow y$

Answer

x is divided by 2 and then 4 is added. $x \div 2 + 4$

$x \longrightarrow \frac{x}{2} + 4$

* Exercise 9

1 Write the rules for these function machines as $y =$ ___.

a $x \rightarrow$ [multiply by 2] $\rightarrow$ [add 4] $\rightarrow y$

$x \quad \times 2 \quad +4 \quad = y$

b $x \rightarrow$ [multiply by 8] $\rightarrow$ [subtract 7] $\rightarrow y$

$x \quad \times 8 \quad -7 \quad = y$

c $x \rightarrow$ [divide by 4] $\rightarrow$ [subtract 3] $\rightarrow y$

$x \quad \div 4 \quad -3 \quad = y$

***d** $x \rightarrow$ [add 3] $\rightarrow$ [multiply by 4] $\rightarrow y$

$x \quad +3 \quad \times 4 \quad = y$

2 Write the rules for these function machines as mappings. $x \longrightarrow$ ___.

a $x \rightarrow$ [multiply by 3] $\rightarrow$ [add 2] $\rightarrow y$

b $x \rightarrow$ [multiply by 5] $\rightarrow$ [subtract 2] $\rightarrow y$

c $x \rightarrow$ [divide by 3] $\rightarrow$ [add 2] $\rightarrow y$

***d** $x \rightarrow$ [add 2] $\rightarrow$ [multiply by 7] $\rightarrow y$

***3** $x \rightarrow$ [multiply by 4] $\rightarrow$ [multiply by 2] $\rightarrow y$

Mrs Patel asked her class to write the rule for this function machine as $x \longrightarrow$ ___.

Gemma wrote $x \longrightarrow x \times 4 \times 2$.
Anna wrote $x \longrightarrow x \times 8$.

Are both Gemma's and Anna's answers correct? Explain.

*4 Write the functions for these.
Simplify your answers as much as possible.

a x → multiply by 4 → multiply by 7 → y

b x → add 4 → add 6 → y

c x → add 9 → subtract 4 → y

d x → multiply by 8 → divide by 2 → y

Finding the function given the input and output

Discussion

- Pat drew this.

3 → ? → 15
5 → ? → 25
8 → ? → 40

What does the function machine do to each number? **Discuss**.

- Reece drew this.

4 → multiply by 2 → ? → 11
0 → multiply by 2 → ? → 3
7 → multiply by 2 → ? → 17

What is the missing operation? **Discuss**.

Exercise 10

1 Find the missing operations.

a 2 → ? → 6; 9 → ? → 27; 3 → ? → 9

b 9 → ? → 13; 1 → ? → 5; 15 → ? → 19

c 8 → ? → 2; 12 → ? → 6; 33 → ? → 27

d 24 → ? → 6; 16 → ? → 4; 100 → ? → 25

2 Find the missing operations.

a 3, 2, 1 → multiply by 2 → ? → 5, 3, 1

b 0, 1, 5 → multiply by 3 → ? → 1, 4, 16

c 4, 1, 6 → multiply by 3 → ? → 10, 1, 16

*d 1, 2, 3 → ? → ? → 3, 5, 7

Finding the input

Remember

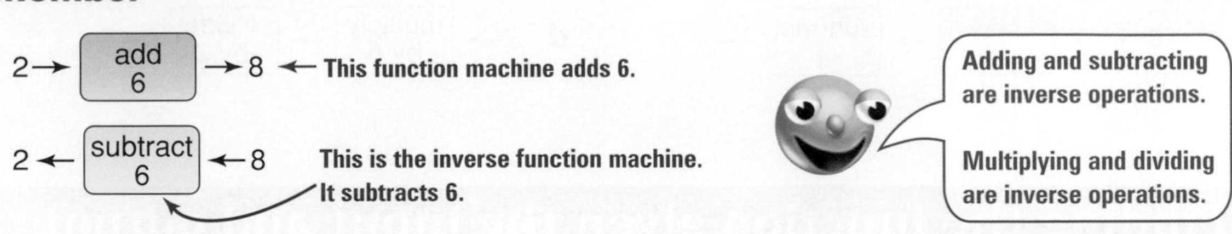

2 → add 6 → 8 ← This function machine adds 6.
2 ← subtract 6 ← 8
This is the inverse function machine.
It subtracts 6.
Adding and subtracting are inverse operations.
Multiplying and dividing are inverse operations.

We can use the **inverse function** machine to find the input.

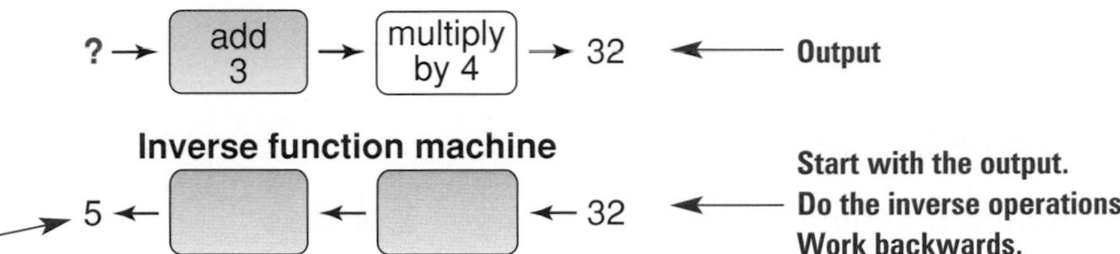

Exercise 11

T

1 Use a copy of these.
What numbers went into these function machines?
Use the inverse function machines to help you.

a
? → ? → ? → [multiply by 3] → 9, 15, 21

← ← ← [divide by 3] ← 9, 15, 21

b
? → ? → ? → [subtract 4] → 6, 12, 9

← ← ← [add 4] ← 6, 12, 9

c
? → ? → ? → [multiply by 2] → [add 1] → 11, 17, 41

← ← ← [divide by 2] ← [subtract 1] ← 11, 17, 41

d
? → ? → ? → [multiply by 3] → [subtract 1] → 11, 23, 29

← ← ← [ ] ← [add 1] ← 11, 23, 29

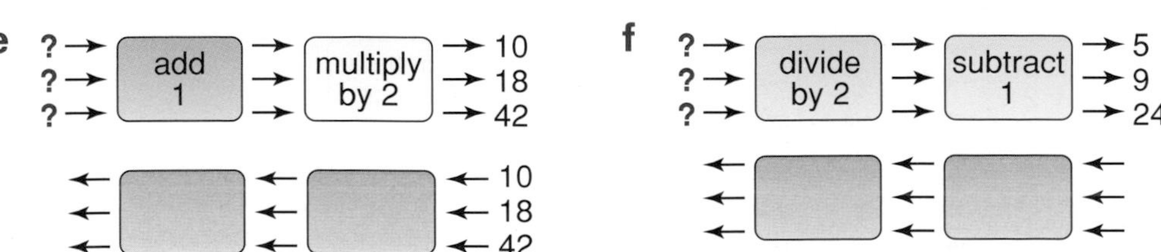

Summary of key points

We can **write a sequence** by **counting on** or **counting back**.

Examples Starting at 7 and counting on in steps of 4 we get

7, 11, 15, 19, 23, ...

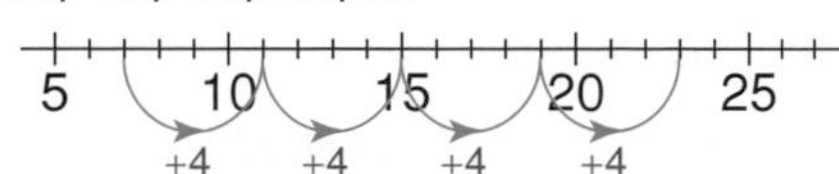

Starting at 2 and counting back in steps of 0·5 we get

2, 1·5, 1, 0·5, 0, ⁻0·5, ...

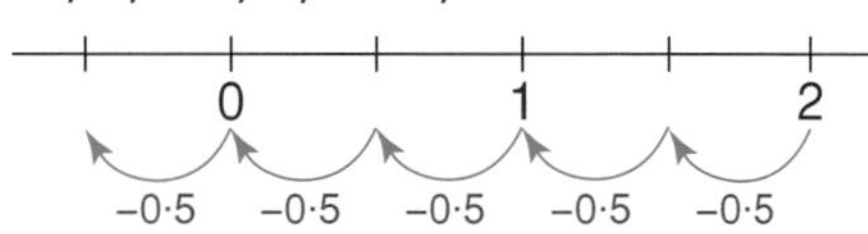

We can **write a sequence** by **multiplying** or **dividing**.

Example 1 4 16 64 256 ...

×4 ×4 ×4 ×4

We can **write a sequence** if we know the **first term** and the **rule for finding the next term**.

Example **first term** 6, **rule** subtract 2 gives 6, 4, 2, 0, ⁻2, ⁻4, ...

Each term is 2 more than the one before.

Sometimes the rule is given as a **rule for the nth term**.

Example The rule $2n + 1$ gives the sequence

3, 5, 7, 9, ...

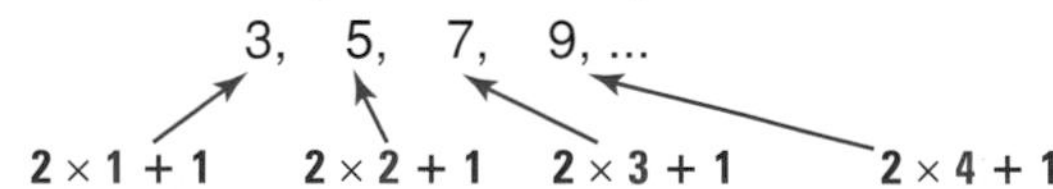

Sequences in practical situations

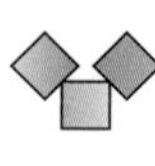

shape 1

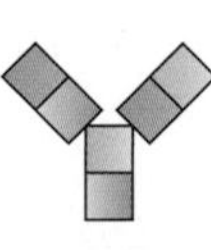

shape 2

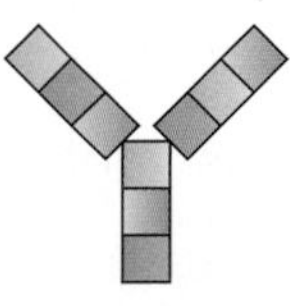

shape 3

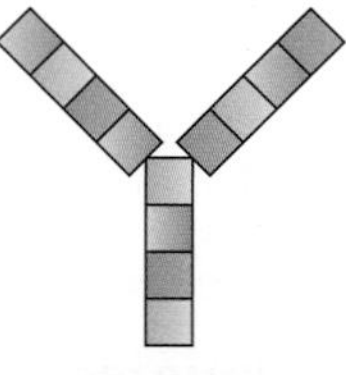

shape 4

Shape number	1	2	3	4
Number of squares	3	6	9	12

In the nth shape there are $3n$ squares.

There are **3** arms on each shape. The nth shape has **3** $\times n$ squares on the arms.

We can find the **output** of a function machine if we are given the **input**.

Example 3 → add 3 → 6
5 → add 3 → 8

This function machine 'adds 3' to any input number.

The inputs and outputs can be put in a **table**.

Example x → add 3 → multiply by 2 → y

x	1	2	3	4	5
y	8	10	12	14	16

We often call the input x and the output y.

A function can be shown on a **mapping diagram**.

Example
1 → add 3 → 4
2 → add 3 → 5
3 → add 3 → 6
4 → add 3 → 7

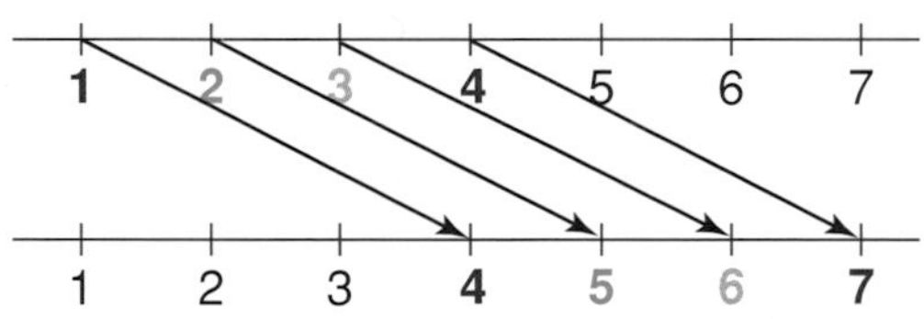

If we are given the input and output we can **find the function** for the machine.

Example 5 → ? → 15
10 → ? → 30
20 → ? → 60

$5 \times 3 = 15$
$10 \times 3 = 30$
$20 \times 3 = 60$

The rule for this machine is 'multiply by 3'.

We use **inverse operations** to **find the input** if we are given the output.

Example __ → multiply by 3 → subtract 4 → 20

We draw an inverse function machine.

8 ← divide by 3 ← 24 ← add 4 ← 20 ← Start with the output. Work backwards doing the inverse.

The input was 8.

Test yourself

1 Write down the first five terms of these sequences.

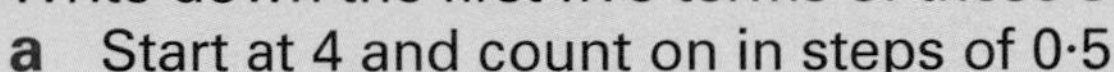

a Start at 4 and count on in steps of 0·5.

b Start at 1 and count back in steps of 3.

2 Write down the missing terms.

a

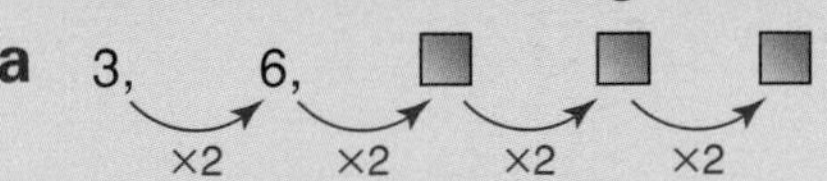

b

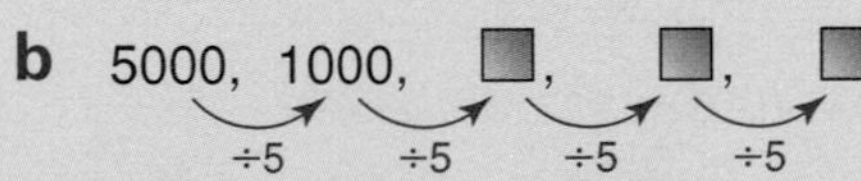

3 Match the descriptions with the sequences given in the box.

a The odd numbers from 9 to 21.

b The sequence begins at 9 and increases in steps of 3.

c Each term is a multiple of 4, plus 1.

d The sequence begins at 9 and decreases in steps of 2.

A 9, 12, 15, 18, ...	**B** 9, 13, 17, 21, ...
C 9, 7, 5, 3, ...	**D** 9, 11, 13, 15, ... 21

4 Write down the first four terms of these sequences.

a **first term** 1 **rule** add 5

b **first term** 1 **rule** multiply by 4

c **first term** 2000 **rule** divide by 2

5 Bob described the sequence he got in **question 4a** as 'The sequence begins at 1 and increases in steps of 5'. Describe the sequences you got in **4b** and **4c**.

6 Find the missing terms.

a 26, ⬭, ⬭, ⬭, 14 **rule** subtract 3

b 0·5, ⬭, ⬭, ⬭, ⬭ **rule** double

7 The nth term of a sequence is given. Find the first five terms.

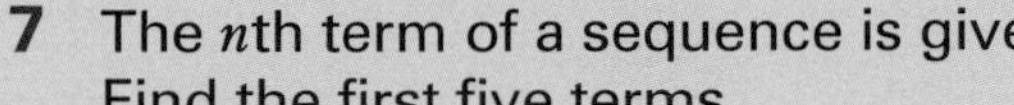

a $n + 5$ **b** $4n$ **c** $2n - 1$ **d** $5 - n$

8 Dylan made these dot diagrams. 

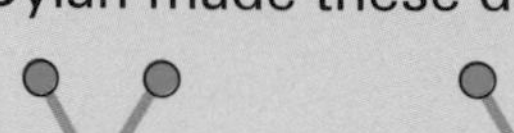

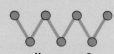

diagram 1 diagram 2 diagram 3

Diagram number	1	2	3	4	...
Number of dots	3	5	7	?	

a Draw diagram 4.
How many dots are in this shape?
b Describe the pattern and how it continues.
c Will one of Dylan's diagrams have 24 dots?
Give a reason for your answer.
d Explain how you can find the number of dots in the nth diagram.

9 Find the output for these. 

a 6 → subtract 4 → y

b 5 → multiply by 3 → y

c 4 → divide by 2 → add 5 → y

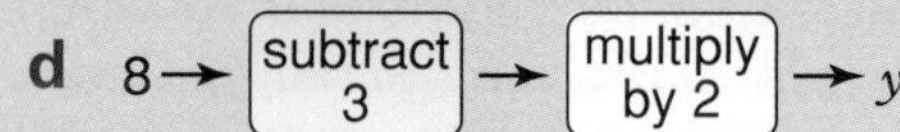

d 8 → subtract 3 → multiply by 2 → y

10 Find the output for these. 

a 12, 9, 27 → divide by 3 →

b 5, 8, 3 → multiply by 3 → add 4 →

T **11** Use a copy of this table.
Fill it in for the function machine.

x	1	2	3	4	5
y					

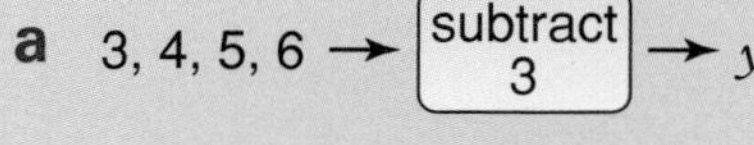

x → multiply by 2 → add 7 → y

T **12** Use a copy of these mapping diagrams.
Fill them in for these function machines.

a 3, 4, 5, 6 → subtract 3 → y

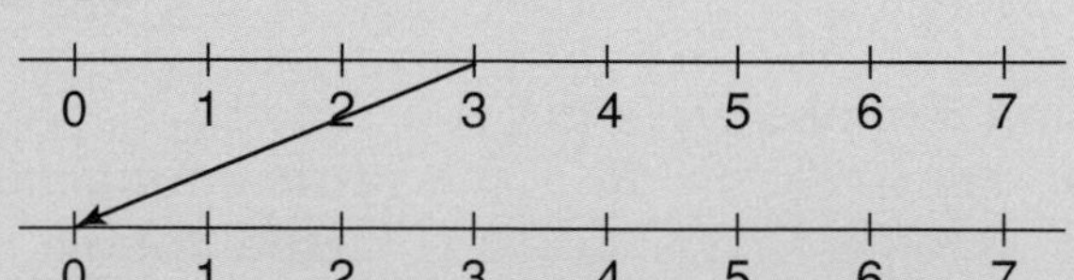

b 1, 2, 3, 4 → subtract 1 → multiply by 2 → y

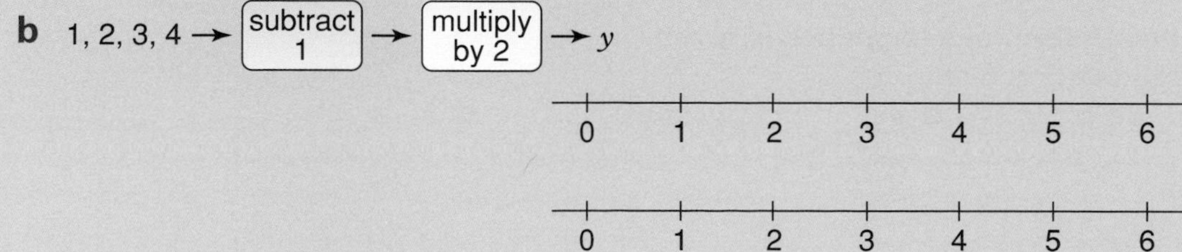

13 What is the missing operation? ◆ I

a 27 → [?] → 9
6 → [?] → 2
24 → [?] → 8

b 5 → [multiply by 3] → [?] → 17
1 → [multiply by 3] → [?] → 5
8 → [multiply by 3] → [?] → 26

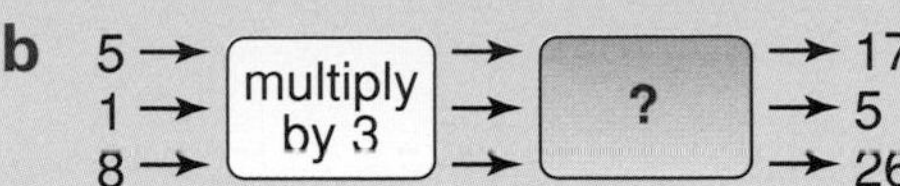

T **14** Use a copy of these. ◆ J
What numbers went into these function machines?
Use the inverse function machines to help you.

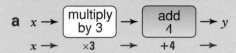

a ? → [multiply by 2] → 8
? → [multiply by 2] → 20
? → [multiply by 2] → 16

← [?] ← 8
← [?] ← 20
← [?] ←

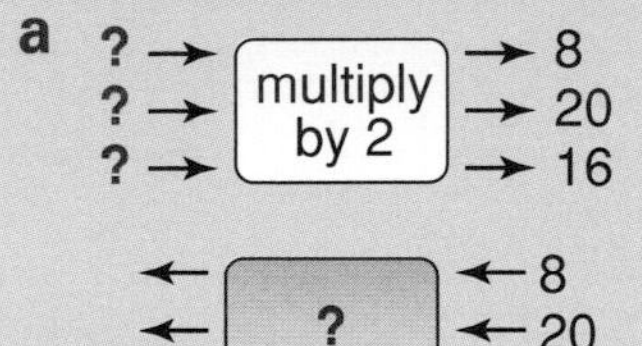

b ? → [multiply by 3] → [add 4] → 10
? → [multiply by 3] → [add 4] → 7
? → [multiply by 3] → [add 4] → 19

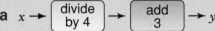

← [?] ← [?] ← 10
← [?] ← [?] ←
← [?] ← [?] ←

***15** Write the rules for these function machines in words. ◆ G
Then write the rule as $y =$ ___.

a x → [multiply by 3] → [add 4] → y
x → ×3 → +4 →

b x → [divide by 2] → [add 3] → y

***16** Write the rules for these function machines as a mapping, $x \rightarrow$ ___. ◆ G

a x → [divide by 4] → [add 3] → y

b x → [add 2] → [multiply by 5] → y

10 Graphs

You need to know

✓ coordinates page 136
✓ graphs page 137
✓ real-life graphs page 137

Key vocabulary

coordinate pair, equation (of a graph), horizontal axis, intersect, negative slope, origin, positive slope, slope, steepness, straight-line graph, vertical axis

It's a puzzle

You will need a piece of graph paper with 1 cm squares.

Draw a set of axes with both x- and y-values from $^-6$ to 6.

Mark these points: A(6, 6) B(6, $^-6$) C($^-6$, $^-6$) D($^-6$, 6) E($^-6$, 0) F(0, 6) G($^-3$, 3) H(3, 3) I($^-3$, $^-3$)

Join A to B, B to C, C to D, E to F, A to C, B to G, G to H, D to A, E to I.

Cut out the shapes you have drawn.

Make this picture using your shapes.

Graphing functions

Remember

(2, ⁻3) is a **coordinate pair**.

x-coordinate *y*-coordinate

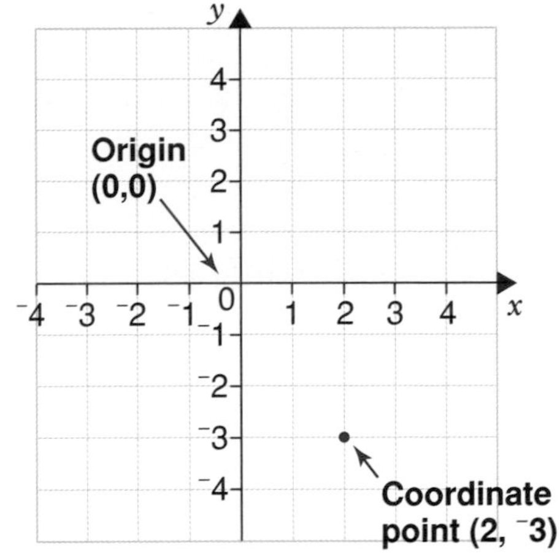

We can find coordinate pairs that all follow the same rule.

Example (1, 4) (2, 5) (3, 6)

+3 +3 +3

In each of these the *y*-coordinate is 3 more than the *x*-coordinate.
The rule is $y = x + \mathbf{3}$.

Sometimes we are given the rule.
Then we can find and plot **coordinate pairs**.

Example $y = x - 2$
We find some coordinate pairs that follow this rule.
We find the value of *y* for the *x*-values given.

Subtract 2 from *x*

x		*y*
0	0 − 2 →	⁻2
2	2 − 2 →	0
4	4 − 2 →	2

We can write this in a table

x-coordinates	0	2	4
y-coordinates	⁻2	0	2

or write them as coordinate pairs.
(0, ⁻2), (2, 0), (4, 2)

Exercise 1

T **1** The rule is $y = 3x$.
The y-coordinate is 3 times the x-coordinate.
Use a copy of this table.
Work out what y is for each x-value.

x-coordinate	1 ×3	3 ×3	4 ×3	7 ×3
y-coordinate	3			

T **2** Use a copy of this.
Fill in the coordinate pairs so they follow the rule.

a $y = x + 1$ (0, __), (1, __), (2, __), (3, __)
+1 +1 +1 +1

b $y = 2x$ (1, __), (2, __), (3, __), (4, __)
×2 ×2 ×2 ×2

c $y = x + 5$ (3, __), (2, __), (1, __), (0, __), ($^-$1, __),

***d** $y = 10 - x$ (0, __), (1, __), (2, __), (3, __), (4, __)

T **3** Use a copy of these tables.
Fill in the gaps.

a $y = x - 1$

x	$^-$1	0	1	2
y	$^-$2			

***b** $y = 5 - x$

x	3	4	5
y			

4 The coordinate pairs (3, 6), (4, 8) and (10, 20) all follow the rule $y = 2x$.
Does (8, 16) follow the same rule?
Explain your answer.

There is more than one answer.

***5** Which of these coordinate pairs follow the rule $y = x + 4$?

A (1, 5) **B** (10, 6) **C** (20, 24) **D** ($^-$4, 0) **E** ($^-$1, $^-$5) **F** ($\frac{1}{2}$, $4\frac{1}{2}$)

We can **draw a graph** if we are given the rule.

Example $y = x + 3$

1 We find the y-values by adding 3 to each x-value given.

x-coordinate	$^-$1 +3	0 +3	2 +3
y-coordinate	2	3	5
coordinates	($^-$1, 2)	(0, 3)	(2, 5)

2 We draw a straight line through the points ($^{-}1$, 2), (0, 3), (2, 5).

3 We label the line $\boldsymbol{y = x + 3}$.

4 All other points on the line will follow the same rule.

Example The point (1, 4) is on the line.

It follows the rule $y = x + 3$.

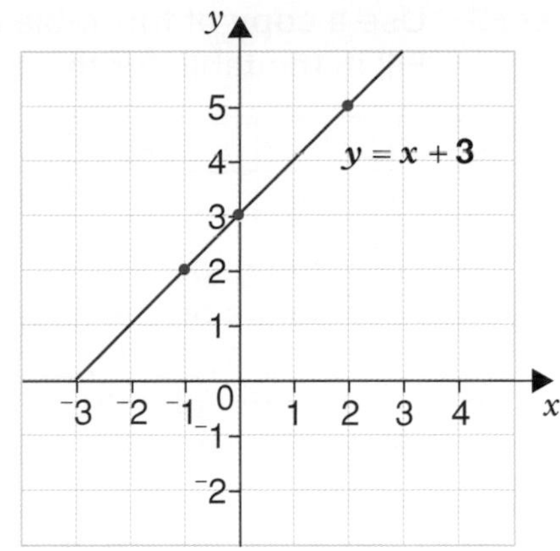

Exercise 2

T **1 a** Use a copy of this table and grid.
Fill in the table for this rule.
$y = x - 1$

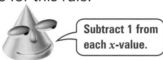

x-coordinate	1	2	3	4
y-coordinate	0			
coordinates	(1, 0)	(2,__)	(3,__)	(4,__)

Subtract 1 from each x-value.

b On the grid, plot the four points from the table.
Draw a line through them.
Label it $y = x - 1$.

Draw your line carefully.

c Does the point (5, 6) lie on this line?

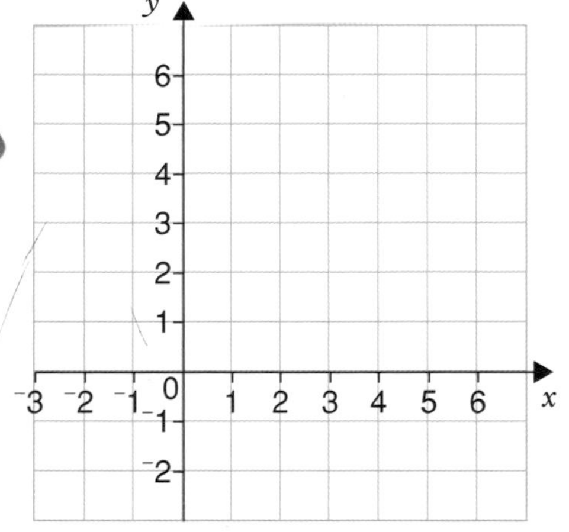

T **2 a** $y = x + 1$
Use a copy of this table and grid.
Fill in the table for the rule.

x	$^{-}3$	$^{-}1$	0	2
y	$^{-}2$			

b Fill in the gaps.
Four points on the line $y = x + 1$ are ($^{-}3$, $^{-}2$), ($^{-}1$, __), (0, __), (2, __).

c On the grid, plot these four points.
Draw a line through them.
Label it $y = x + 1$.

***d** Does the point ($^{-}2$, $^{-}1$) lie on this line?

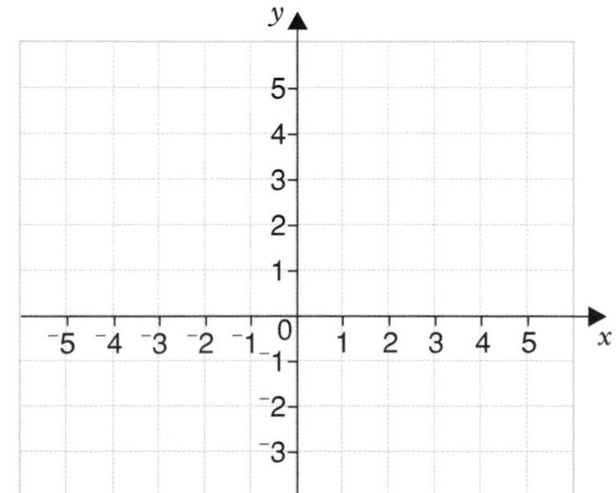

3 **a** $y = x + 4$.
Use a copy of this table and grid.
Fill in the table for the rule.

x	$^{-}5$ +4	$^{-}1$ +4	0 +4	1 +4
y	$^{-}1$			

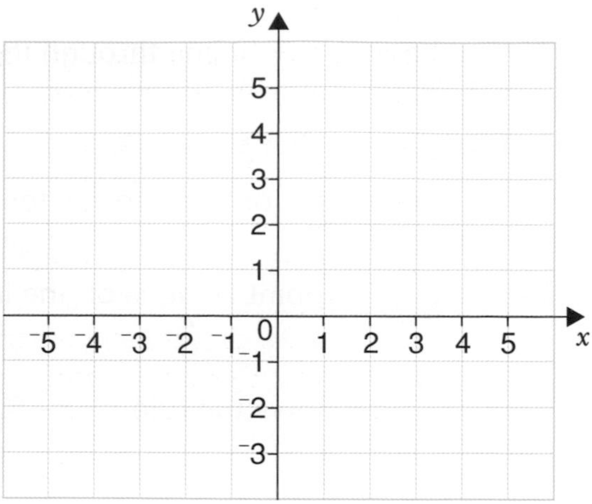

b Fill in the gaps.
Four points on the line $y = x + 4$ are
($^{-}5$, $^{-}1$), ($^{-}1$, __), (0, __) and (1, __).

c On the grid, plot these four points.
Draw a line through them.
Label it $y = x + 4$.

d Does the point ($^{-}4$, 0) lie on this line?

4 $x \rightarrow$ [×3] $\rightarrow y$

a Use a copy of this table for the given function machine.
Fill it in.

x	0	1	2	3	4
y	0				

There is more about function machines on page 178.

b Copy and finish the coordinate pairs from the table.

(0, __), (1, __), (2, __), (3, __), (4, __)

c On a grid, plot the five points.
Do the five points lie in a straight line?

T

***5** **a** $y = 5 - x$ Work out the y-values for the x-values, 0, 2 and 4.

$x = 0$
$y = 5 - 0$
$= \_\_$

$x = 2$
$y = 5 - 2$
$= \_\_$

$x = 4$
$y = \_\_ - 4$
$= \_\_$

b (0, __), (2, __), (4, __)

Copy these.
Fill them in using your answers to **a**.

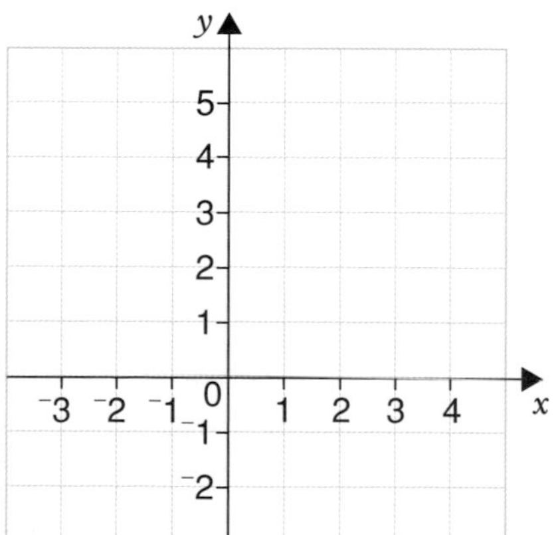

c Use a copy of the grid.
Plot the three points.
Draw the line $y = 5 - x$.
Label it.

d Which of these points lie on the line $y = 5 - x$?
(0, 5), (5, 1), (3, $^{-}2$)

e Will $y = 5 - x$ go through the point (6, $^{-}1$)?

T

*6 **a** $y = 2x + 1$
Use a copy of this table and grid.
Fill in the table for the rule.

x	$^-1$	0	1	2
y	$^-1$			

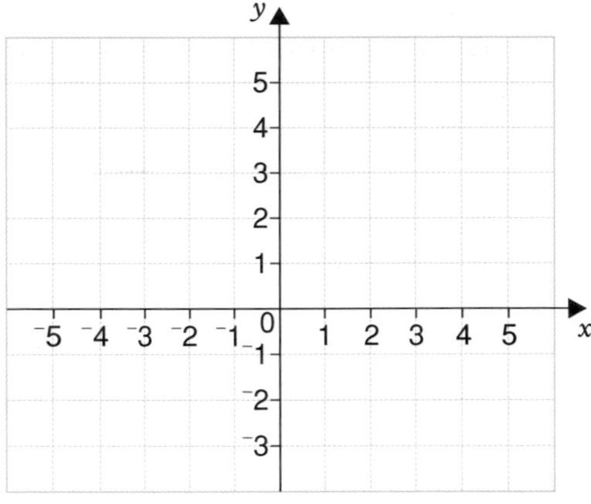

b Four points on the line $y = 2x + 1$ are ($^-1$, $^-1$), (0, __), (1, __) and (2, __).

c On the grid, plot these four points.
Draw a line through them.
Label it.

d Does the point (4, 7) lie on this line?

T

Investigation

Families of Graphs

You will need copies of the tables and some axes or a graphical calculator or a graph plotter.

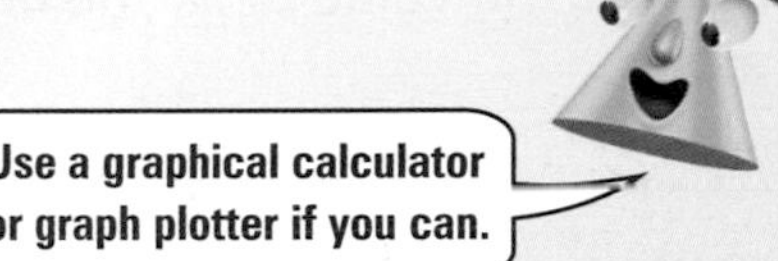

Use a graphical calculator
or graph plotter if you can.

1 a Use a copy of these tables and some axes with x-values from $^-5$ to 5 and y-values from $^-12$ to 12.

$y = x$

x	$^-4$	0	4
y	$^-4$		

$y = 2x$

x	$^-3$	0	3
y	$^-6$		

$y = 4x$

x	$^-2$	0	2
y	$^-8$		

On your axes draw and label the graphs of
$y = x$,
$y = 2x$ and
$y = 4x$.
What do you notice?
Which point do all the graphs have in common?

b Would $y = 3x$ have a steeper slope than $y = 5x$?

2 a Use a copy of these tables and some axes.

$y = x + 1$

x	$^-3$	0	3
y	$^-2$		

$y = x + 4$

x	$^-6$	0	3
y	$^-2$		

$y = x + 5$

x	$^-2$	0	2
y	3		

On your axes draw and label the graphs of
$y = x + 1$,
$y = x + 4$,
$y = x + 5$.
What do you notice about the slopes of these graphs?

b What do you notice about where each intersects the y-axis and the equation of its line?

c Where would $y = x + 3$ cross the y-axis?
What about $y = x + 7$?

'Intersects' means 'crosses'.

***3** Repeat questions **2a** and **2b** but replace the tables and equations with these.

$y = 8 - x$

x	0	2	5
y	8	6	

$y = 5 - x$

x	0	1	4
y	5		

$y = 4 - x$

x	0	1	3
y	4		

$y = mx$ is the equation of a **straight line** which goes **through the origin**.
m can have any value.

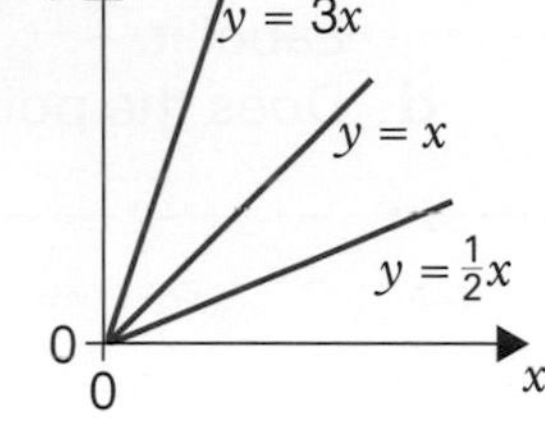

$y = 3x$ has a steeper slope than $y = x$.

$y = \frac{1}{2}x$ has a slope which is not as steep as $y = x$.

The bigger the value of m, the number multiplying x, the steeper the slope.

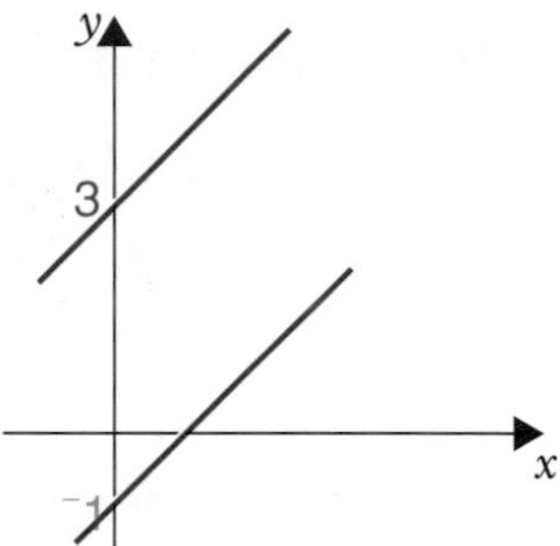

$y = x + \mathbf{3}$ crosses the y-axis at **3**.
$y = 2x - \mathbf{1}$ crosses the y-axis at **⁻1**.

These lines have a **positive** slope.

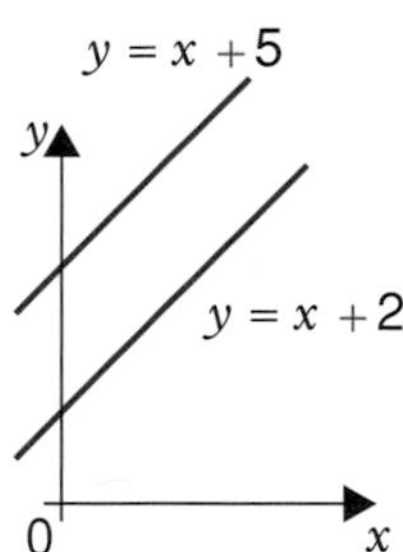

These lines have a **negative** slope.

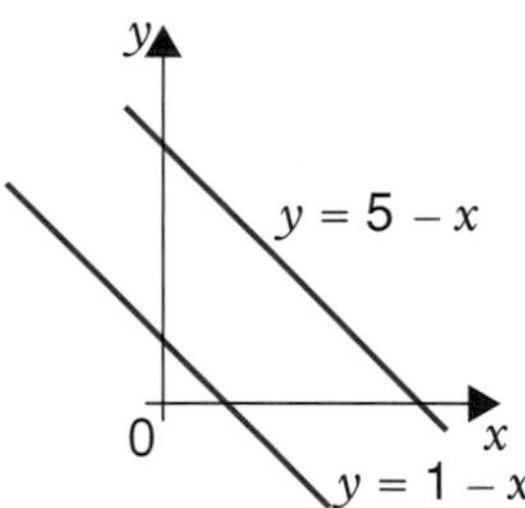

Exercise 3

1 Choose from the box.

$y = 2x$	$y = 3 - x$	$y = x - 3$	$y = \frac{1}{2}x$	$y = 3x$

Which graph will
a have the steepest slope
b have a negative slope
***c** cut the y-axis at (0, ⁻3)?

2 Will these have a positive or negative slope?
a $y=x+3$ **b** $y=2x$ **c** $y=x-4$ **d** $y=6-x$ **e** $y=8-x$

**3* Which of these graphs will cut the y-axis at $^{-}5$?
A $y={}^{-}5x$ **B** $y=5-x$ **C** $y=x-5$ **D** $y=x+5$

Lines parallel to the x- and y-axes

$y=a$ is a straight line **parallel to the x-axis.**
It cuts the y-axis at a.

$x=b$ is a straight line **parallel to the y-axis.**
It cuts the x-axis at b.

Examples

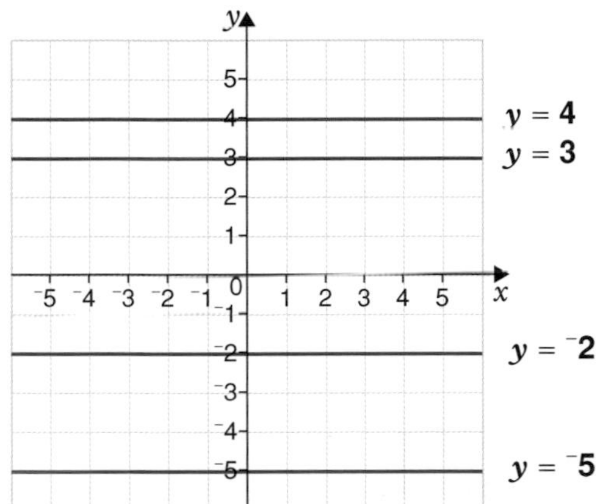

lines parallel to the x-axis

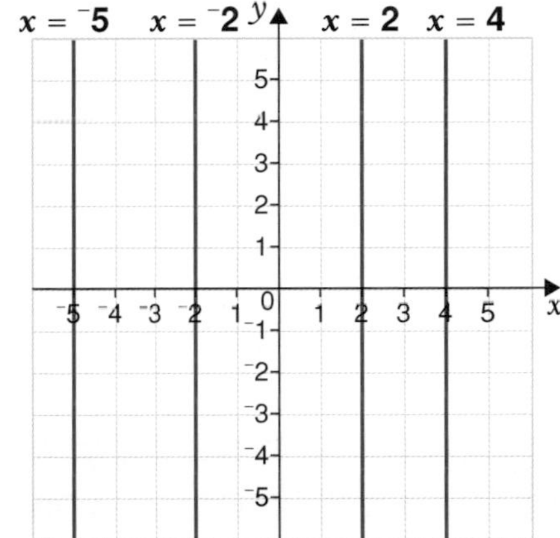

lines parallel to the y-axis

Exercise 4

1 Match these equations to the lines.
a $y={}^{-}1$
b $x=2$
c $x={}^{-}2$
d $x={}^{-}1$
e $y=2$
f $y={}^{-}2$

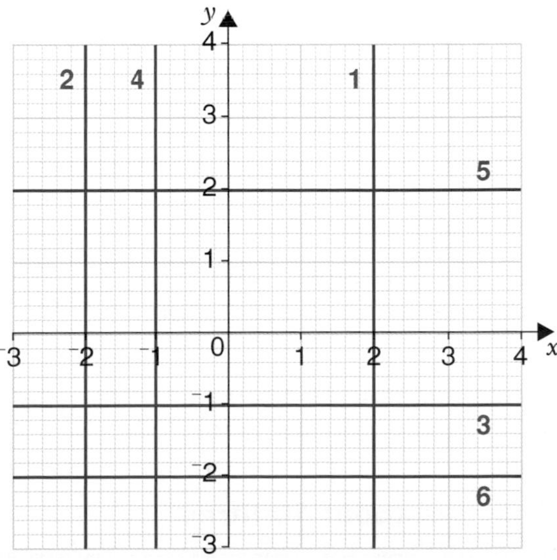

T

2 Use a copy of this grid
On your grid, draw and label these graphs.

a $x = 4$ **b** $y = {}^{-}2$ **c** $x = {}^{-}4$
d $y = 2$ ***e** $x = 1{\cdot}5$ ***f** $y = {}^{-}3{\cdot}5$

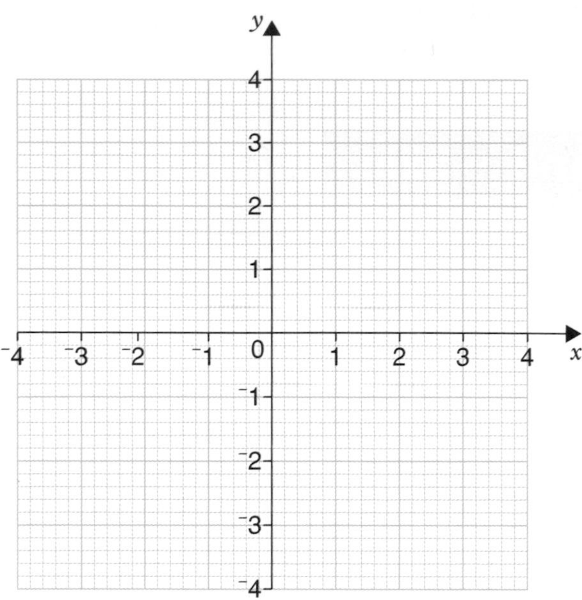

3 Write down the equation of a line which is
a parallel to the y-axis
b parallel to the x-axis.

Reading and plotting real-life graphs

Reading graphs

We can **estimate** values from a graph.

This graph can be used to change between pints and litres.

A large vase holds about 16 pints.
We can estimate how many litres this is using the graph.

Each small square on the horizontal axis represents four pints.

Each small square on the vertical axis represents four litres.

16 pints is **about 10 litres**.

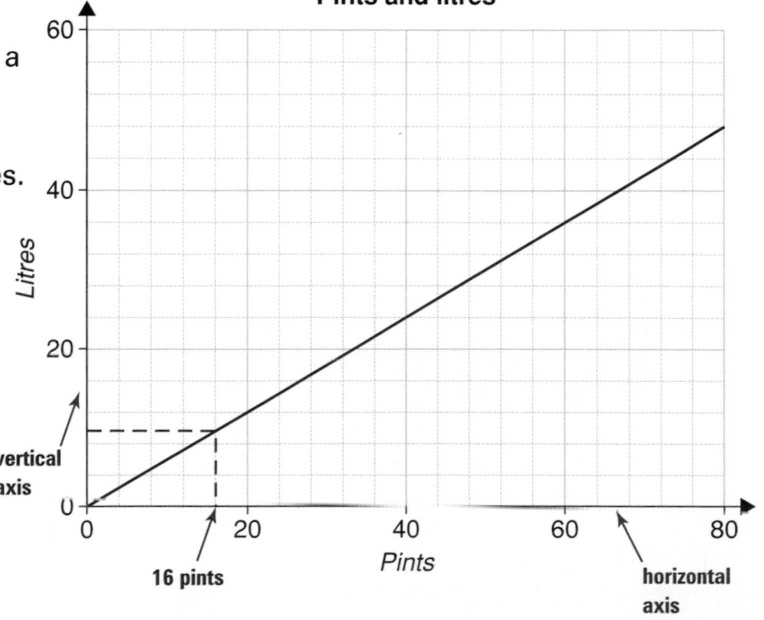

Exercise 5

1 **a** What does each small square on the kilograms axis represent?
b What does each small square on the pounds axis represent?
c Convert these to pounds.
i 30 kg **ii** 10 kg
d Convert these to kilograms.
i 60 lb **ii** 24 lb
e Anita weighed 28 kg.
How many pounds is this?
***f** Anita stands on the scales holding her cat.
The cat weighs 10 lb.
What do the scales read, in kg?

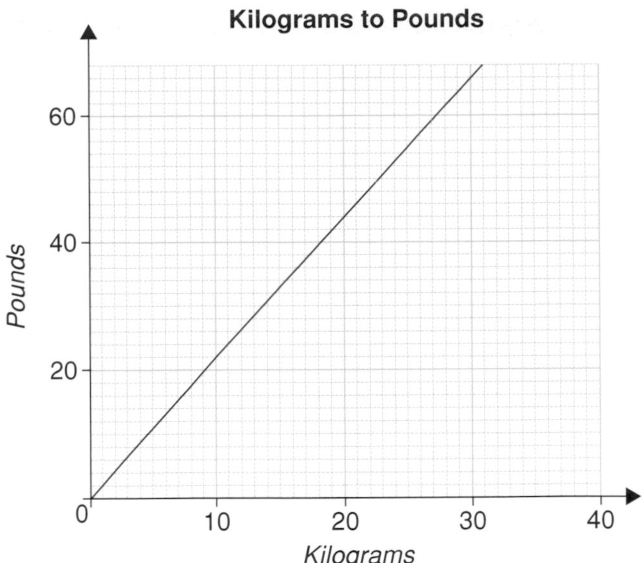

2

Energy Conversions

Kilojoules (kJ): 0, 50, 100, 150, 200, 250, 300, 350

Calories: 0, 10, 20, 30, 40, 50, 60, 70, 80

a How many calories does each small square on the Calories axis represent?
b How many kilojoules does each small square on the Kilojoules axis represent?
c Convert these to calories.
i 50 kJ **ii** 210 kJ
d Convert these to kilojoules.
i 60 calories **ii** 74 calories
e Allaf ate a pear (250 kJ).
How many calories were in this?
f Debbie ate a piece of cheese (50 calories).
How many kilojoules were in this altogether?
***g** Jake is on a special diet.
He must each 280 kJ for breakfast and 40 kJ for morning tea.
How many calories is this?
***h** A milkshake has 800 calories.
How many kilojoules is this?

3 This graph shows how much petrol two cars use.

- - - - - -	Tom's Car
————	Kim's Car

a Tom's car went 60 km. How many litres of petrol did it use?
b Kim's car went 100 km. How many litres of petrol did it use?
c Tom's car used 6 litres of petrol one day. How far did it go?
d How much more petrol does Tom's car use than Kim's car when each car travels 60 km?

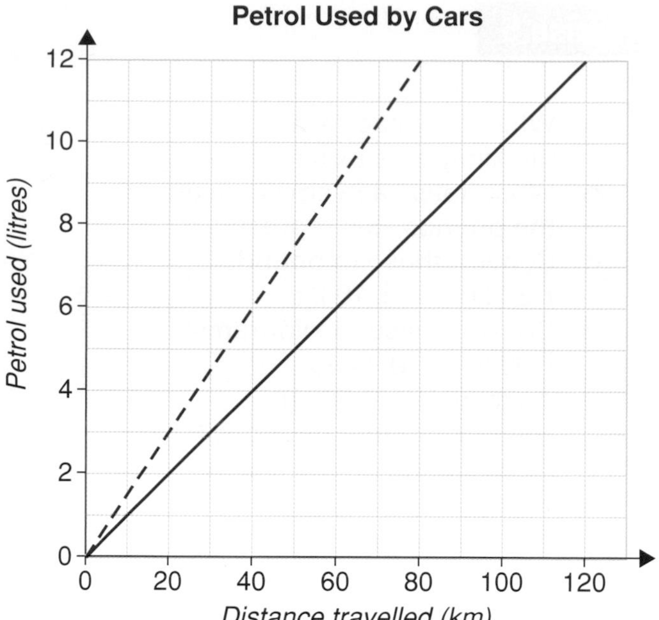

4 The graph gives the shortest distance that should be between cars at different speeds.
a Ed is driving in bad weather at 40 miles per hour. What is the shortest distance he should be from the car in front?
b Fay is driving in good weather at 55 miles per hour. What is the shortest distance she should be from the car in front?
***c** Mr Shaw is driving 70 metres behind another car. The weather is bad. What is the fastest he should be driving?

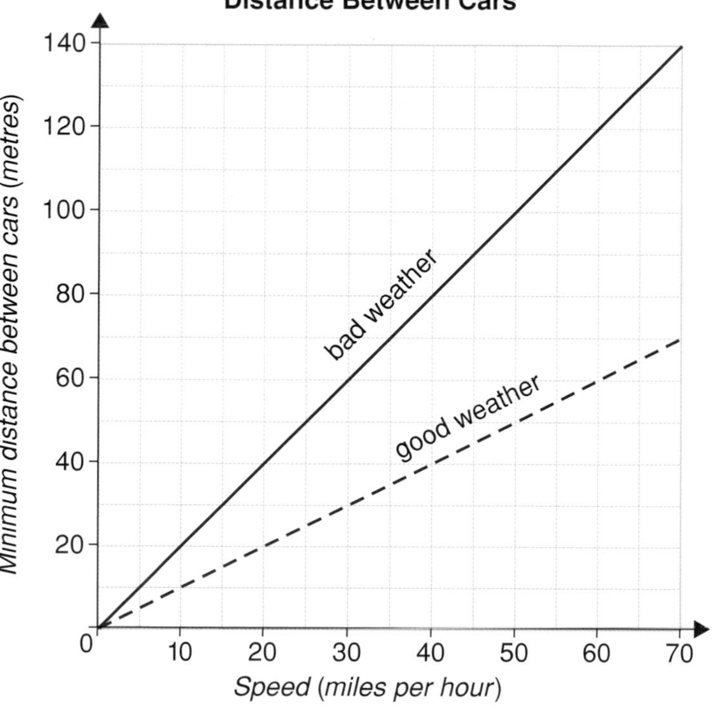

Plotting graphs

Example Marcel worked out how far a plane was from Hedgend after t minutes. He filled in this table.

Time in minutes	0	2	5
Distance in km	10	20	35

He drew this graph by plotting these points.

(0, 10) (2, 20) (5, 35)

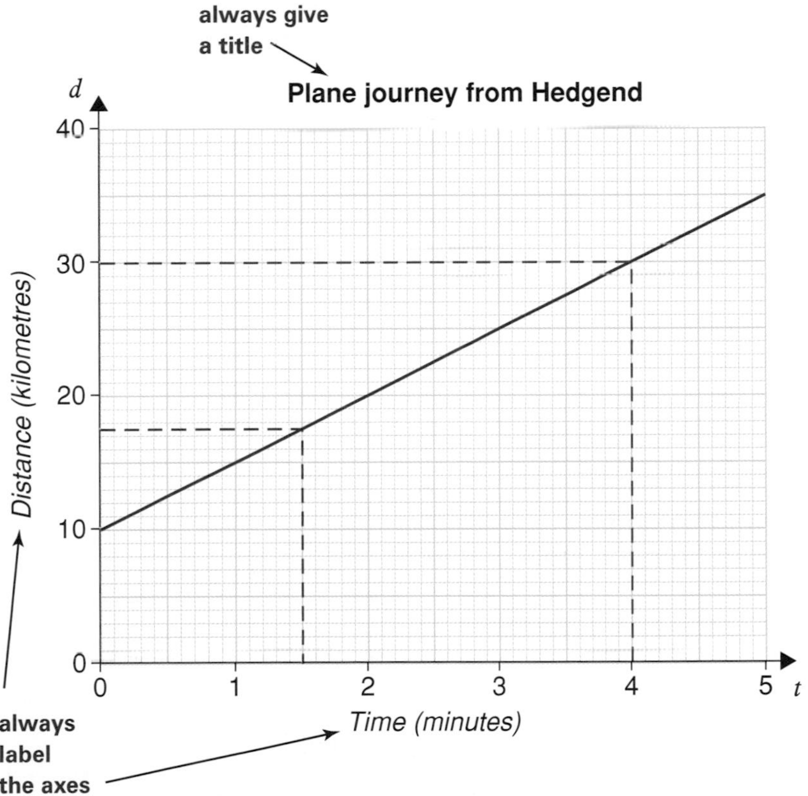

We can use the graph to estimate how far the plane is from Hedgend after 4 minutes. The pink dashed lines show that it was about **30 km**.

Katherine lives 17·5 km from Hedgend.

We can use the graph to estimate how long it takes until the plane is flying over her house.

The blue dashed lines show that it took about **1·5 minutes**.

Exercise 6

T

1 Ingrid travelled to Scotland in her car.
She used 5 ℓ of petrol for every 50 km she travelled.
She filled in this table.

ℓ	5	10	25
km	50	100	250

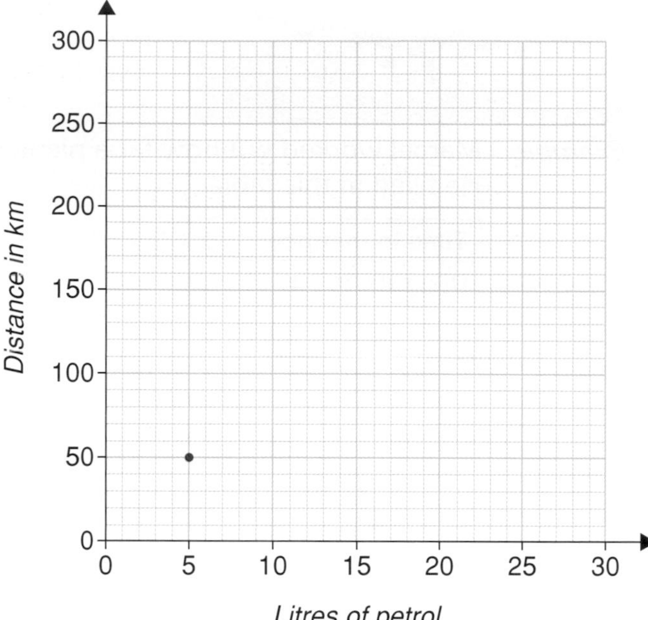

a Use a copy of this grid.
Plot the points from the table on it.
Draw a straight line through the points.
Finish labelling the graph.

b Ingrid drove 150 km to visit her aunt.
About how much petrol did Ingrid's car use?

c One week Ingrid's car used 28 ℓ of petrol.
About how far did it travel?

T

2 The cost to hire a computer is £100 + £20 × the number of weeks hired.

a Use a copy of this table.
Fill it in.

Weeks	2	6	10
Charge (£)	140		

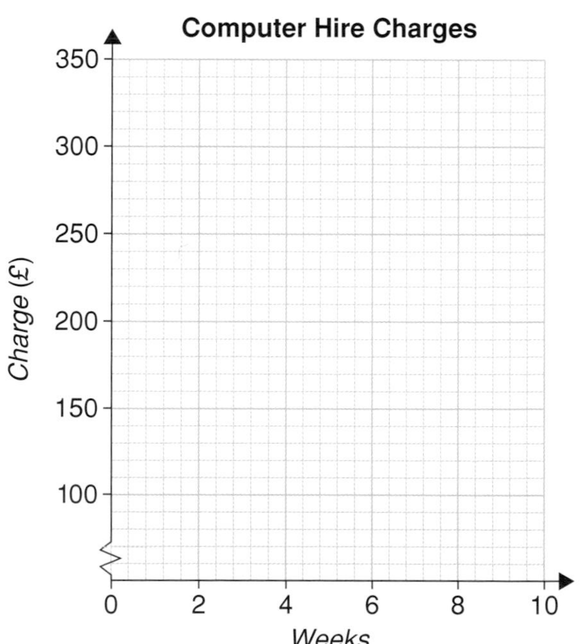

b Use a copy of this grid.
Plot the points from the table on the grid.
Draw a straight line through the points.

c Explain what the symbol ⌇ on the vertical axis means.

Show how to use your graph to answer these.

d How much does it cost to hire a computer for 9 weeks?

e Alison hired a computer and it cost her £240.
For how many weeks did she hire it?

T

3 Thomas wants to draw a graph to convert °C to °F.
He knows that 0 °C is 32 °F, 20 °C is 68 °F and 40 °C is 104 °F.

a Use a copy of this table.
Fill it in.

°C	0	20	40
°F	0		

b Use a copy of this grid.
Plot the points from the table on the grid.
Draw a straight line through the points.

*__c__ The temperature at sunset in Brighton was 11 °C.
What is this in °F?

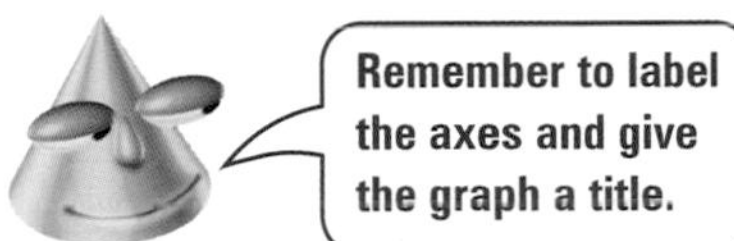

Remember to label the axes and give the graph a title.

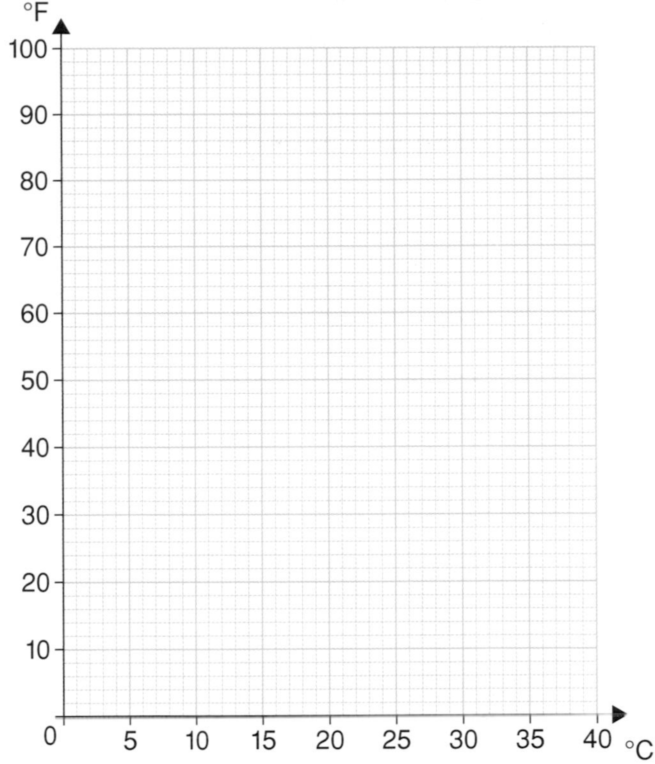

T

*__4__ A shop hires stereos.
The cost is £50 plus £5 for every hour.

a Use a copy of this table.
Fill it in.

Hours	0	4	8
Charge (£)	50		

b Use a copy of this grid.
Choose a scale for the vertical axis.
Plot the points from the table on the grid.
Draw a straight line through the points.
Label the vertical axis and give the graph a title.

c Raewyn hired a stereo for 9 hours.
Use your graph to find the cost of this.

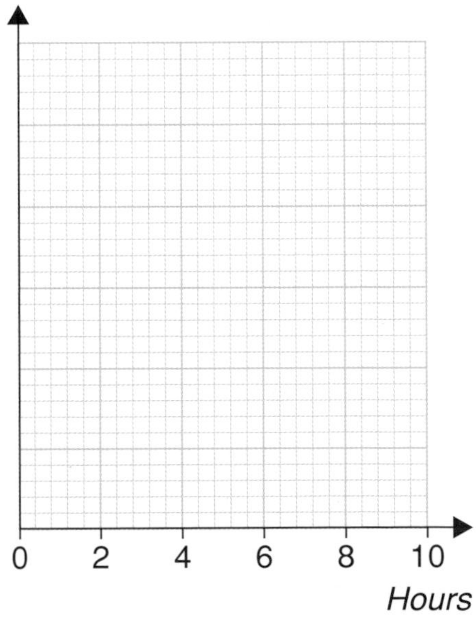

* Practical

You will need a spreadsheet.

Crocodile hunting in Australia
Rodeo riding in Canada
Cruising the Greek Islands
Skiing in Switzerland
Trekking in Nepal

Decide where you would like to go for a holiday abroad.
Find the exchange rate between British pounds (£) and the currency you would use on your holiday.
Use a spreadsheet to convert pounds to the currency of the country.

Example

	A	B	C	D
1	Pounds	£10	= B1+10	= C1+10
2	Australian Dollars	= B1*2.5	= C1*2.5	= D1*2.5

This spreadsheet changes £ to Australian dollars. The exchange rate is £1 = A$2.5.

Use the graph function of the spreadsheet to draw a graph to change pounds into the currency you chose.

Interpreting and sketching real-life graphs

Discussion

- 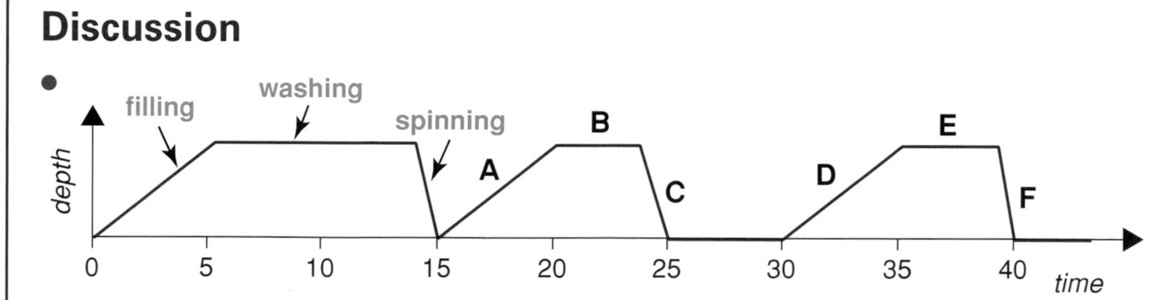

This graph shows the depth of water in a washing machine during one wash cycle.
Which of these matches A, B, C, D, E and F?

fill rinse spin drain

Exercise 7

1 Explain these graphs.
Use words like increases, decreases.

a

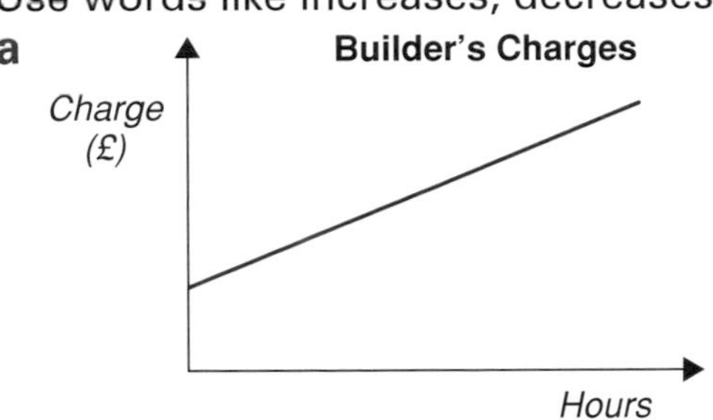

b

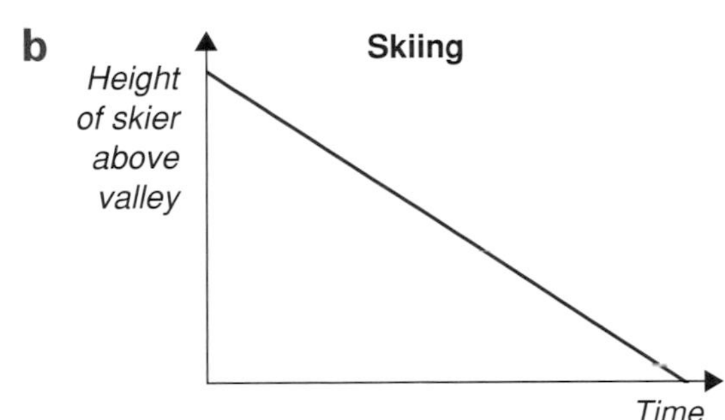

2 Which of these matches the graph shown?
- **A** A flashlight flashes once.
- **B** Cinema lights are dimmed slowly.
- **C** A car indicator flashes many times.
- **D** Car headlights flash three times.

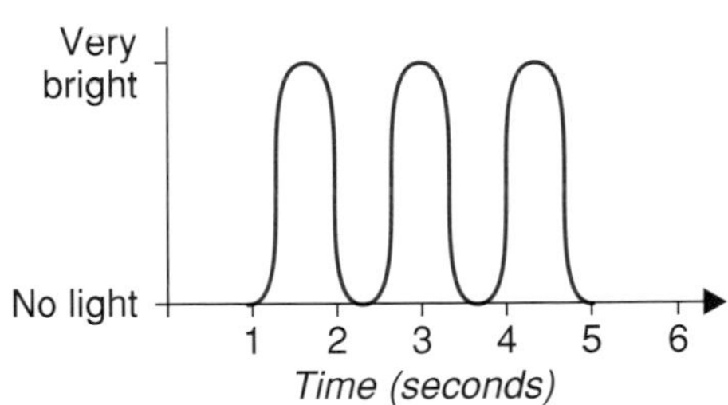

***3 a** Which of these best describes what this graph tells us?
- **A** The volume of air in the balloon increases then decreases then increases then decreases and so on.
- **B** The volume of air in the balloon increases as time goes by. The horizontal parts are when a breath is taken.
- **C** It takes less and less time to blow up a balloon.

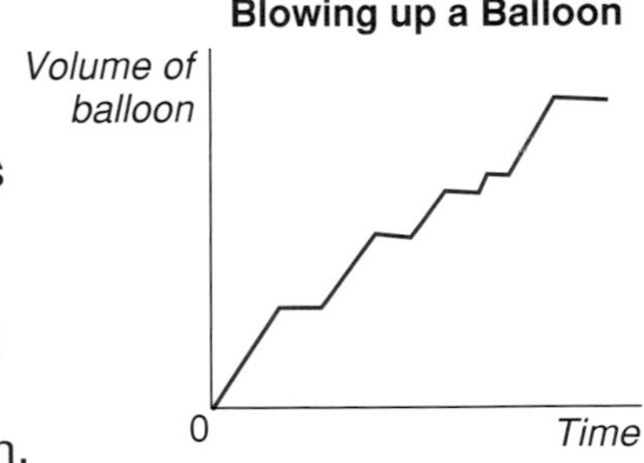

b Which of these best describes what this graph tells us?
- **A** The pulse rate is steady, then decreases then is steady.
- **B** The pulse rate increases, then stops, then decreases.
- **C** The pulse rate increases, then stays steady, then decreases with time.

c Which of these best describes what this graph tells us?

A The pasta is frozen so at first cools the water. Then, over time, it heats up. Eventually the temperature stays the same.

B The temperature starts off cold and over time increases.

C The temperature starts off hot, gets colder, then gets hotter and hotter.

Summary of key points

A To **graph a function**

find the y-value for the x-values given

plot the coordinate pairs

draw a straight line through the points.

Example $y = x - 1$

x	$0 \xrightarrow{^{-}1}$	$2 \xrightarrow{^{-}1}$	$4 \xrightarrow{^{-}1}$
y	$^{-}1$	1	3

The coordinate pairs $(0, {}^{-}1)$, $(2, 1)$ and $(4, 3)$ are shown plotted.

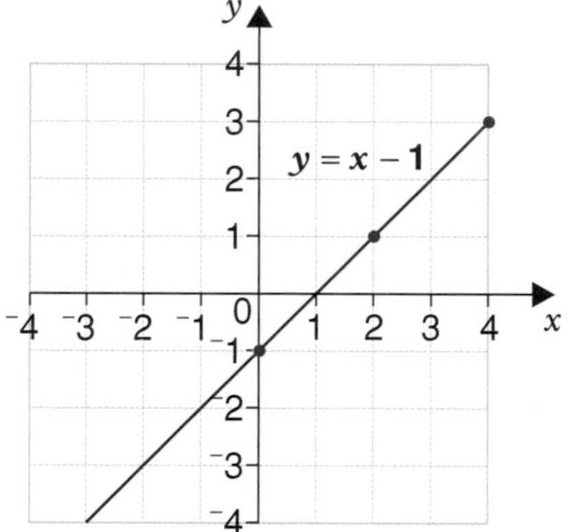

B $\boldsymbol{y = mx}$ is the equation of a straight line through the origin.

m can have any value.

The greater the value of m, the steeper the slope.

Example $y = 3x$ has a steeper slope than $y = x$.

$\boldsymbol{y = x + 2}$

This line has a **positive** slope.

$\boldsymbol{y = 4 - x}$

This line has a **negative** slope.

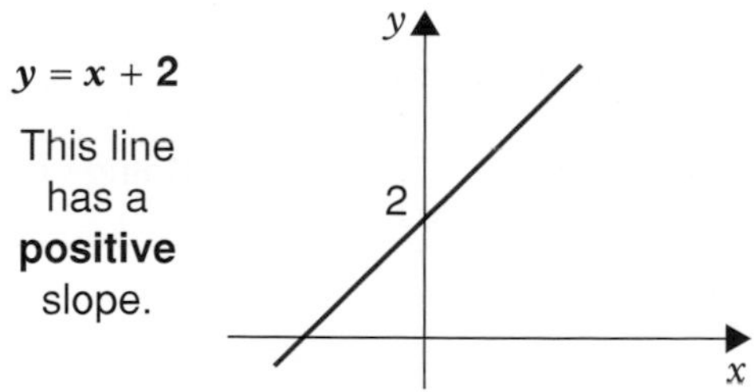

$y = x + \mathbf{2}$ crosses the y-axis at **2**.

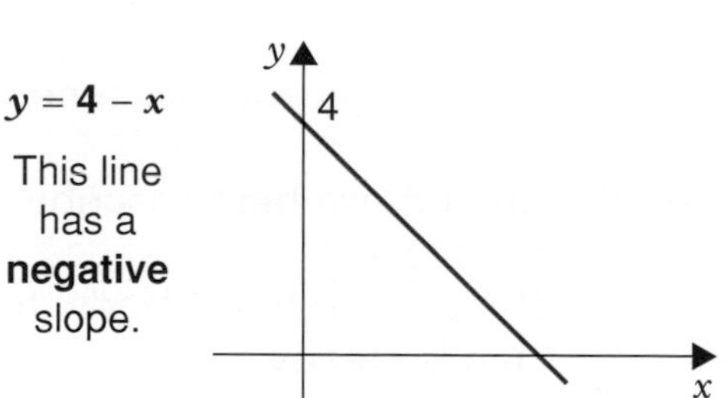

$y = \mathbf{4} - x$ crosses the y-axis at **4**.

Lines **parallel to the x-axis** all have equation $y = a$.
a is any number.
Examples $y = 7$ $y = {}^{-}1\frac{1}{2}$

Lines **parallel to the y-axis** all have equation $x = b$.
b is any number.
Examples $x = 4$ $x = {}^{-}3\frac{1}{2}$

We can **plot real-life graphs**.
Example

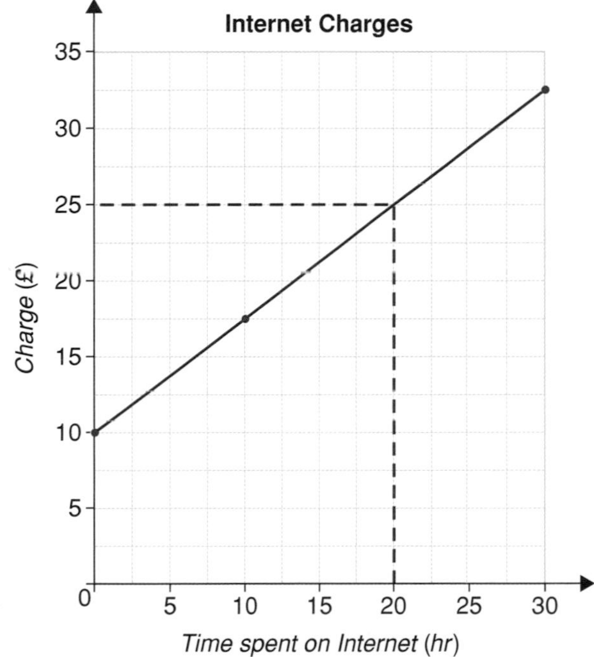

This graph shows monthly Internet charges.
The points (0, £10), (10, £17·50) and (30, £32·50) have been plotted and joined with a straight line.

We can **read graphs of real-life situations**.
We can estimate values from these graphs.
Example If I spend 20 hours on the Internet, the charge is about £25.

We can **interpret** straight-line graphs.

Test yourself

T **1** Use a copy of this. 
Fill in these coordinate pairs so they follow the rule.

(Each x-value has an arrow marked +2 to its y-gap in part **a**.)

a $y = x + 2$ (3, __), (2, __), (1, __), (0, __), ($^{-}1$, __)

b $y = 3x$ (0, __), (1, __), (2, __), (3, __)

***c** $y = 3 - x$ (0, __), (1, __), (2, __), (3, __)

 **2** Use a copy of these tables. A
Fill them in for the rules.

a $y = 4x$

x	1 ×4	3 ×4	5 ×4
y			

b $y = x - 4$

x	3	4	6
y			

c $y = 9 - x$

x	0	1	5
y			

T **3** Use a copy of this. A

a Fill in the table for $y = x - 1$.

x-coordinate	$^{-}2$ −1	0 −1	3 −1
y-coordinate			
coordinates			

b On the grid, plot these three points.
Draw and label the line $y = x - 1$.

c Does the point ($^{-}4$, $^{-}5$) lie on the line?

***d** Write down the coordinates of another point that lies on the line $y = x - 1$.

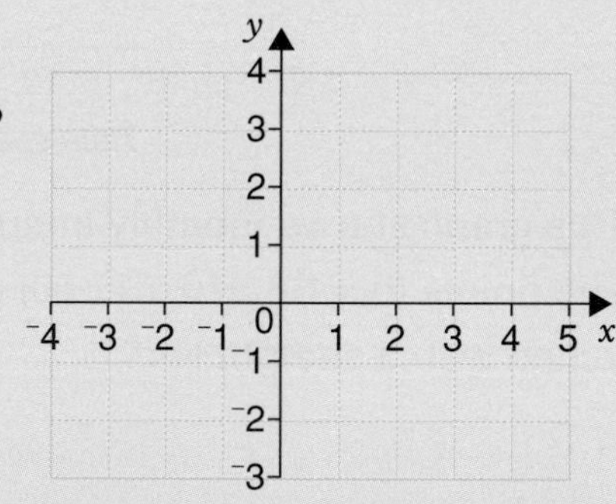

4 **a** $y =$ __x. What number could go in the gap to give the graph of a line which is steeper than $y = 2x$? 

b Which of these graphs has a positive gradient
$y = x + 3$ or $y = 5 - x$?

***c** Which of these graphs cuts the y-axis at $^{-}3$?
A $y = x + 3$ **B** $y = 3 - x$ **C** $y = x - 3$ **D** $y = 3x$

5 Which of these is the equation of a line parallel to the x-axis? 
a $y = 4$ **b** $x = {}^{-}4$ **c** $y = {}^{-}3$ **d** $y = x$

T

6 'Jones Electrical' charge a call out fee of £25 and then an hourly rate of £15. D

a Use a copy of this table.
Fill it in.

Hours	0	1	4
Charge (£)	25		

b Use a copy of this grid. Plot the points from the table on the grid.

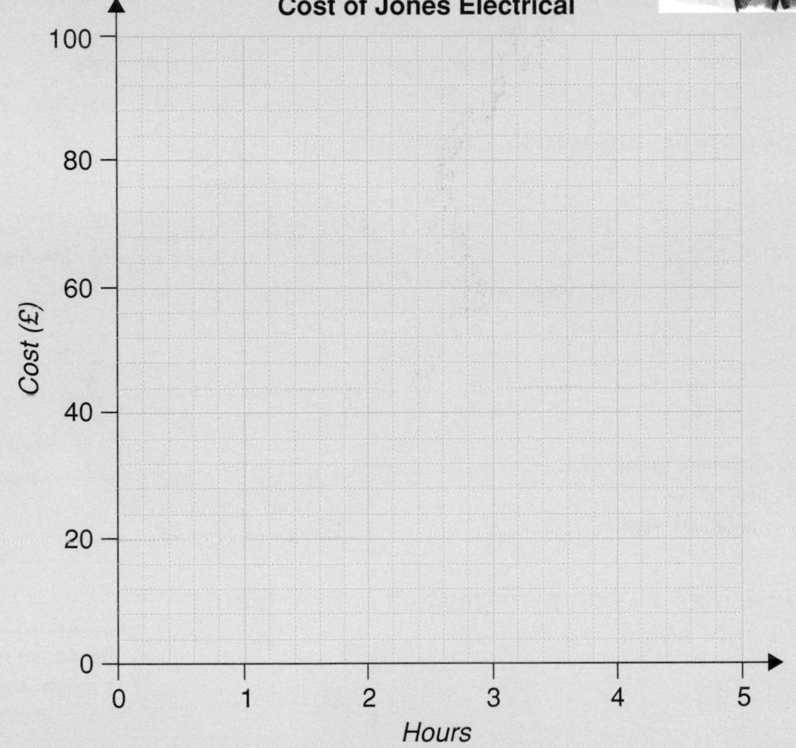

c Draw a straight line through the points.

d Use a graph to find the charge for 3 hours work.

e Mrs Cassidy was charged £55 for a job.
About how many hours did it take?

7 Which of these best describes what this graph tells us? E

A Tom starts by spending money straight away. Then he doesn't spend, then he spends, and so on.

B Over time, Sam has more and more money in his wallet.

C Sam started off not spending money. Then he spent some. Then he didn't for a while. Altogether he spent money three times.

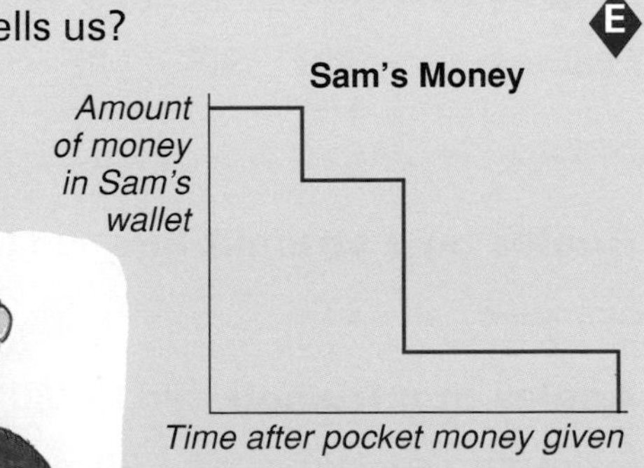

Shape, Space and Measures Support

Angles

We measure **angles** in degrees.

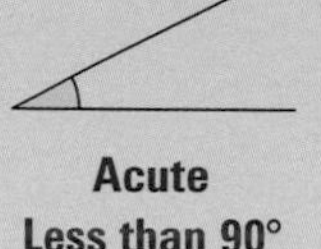

Acute
Less than 90°

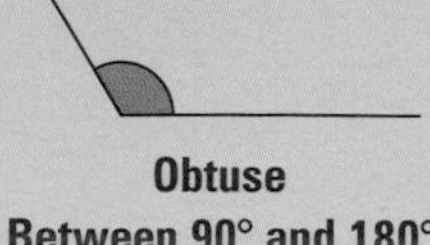

Obtuse
Between 90° and 180°

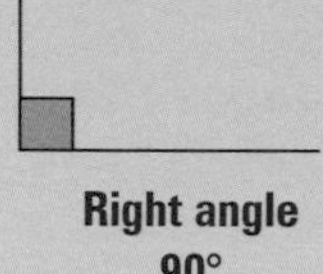

Right angle
90°

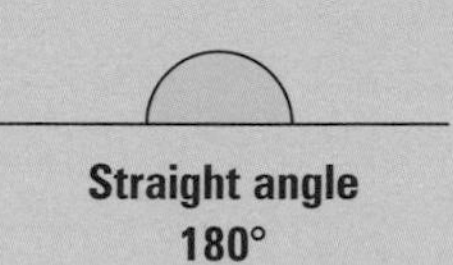

Straight angle
180°

We use a **protractor** or **angle measurer** to measure and draw angles.

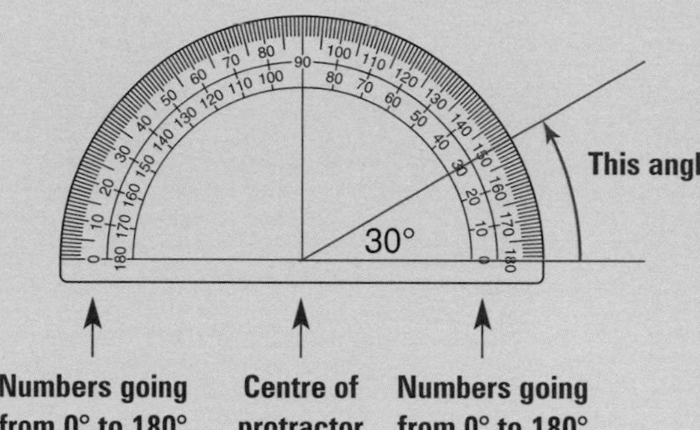

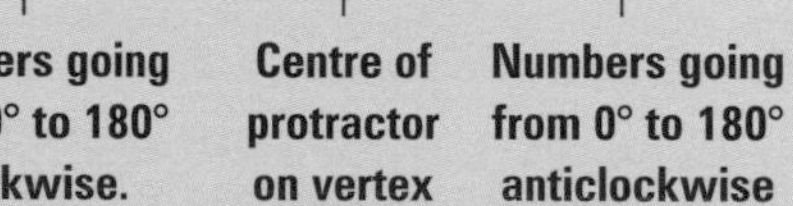

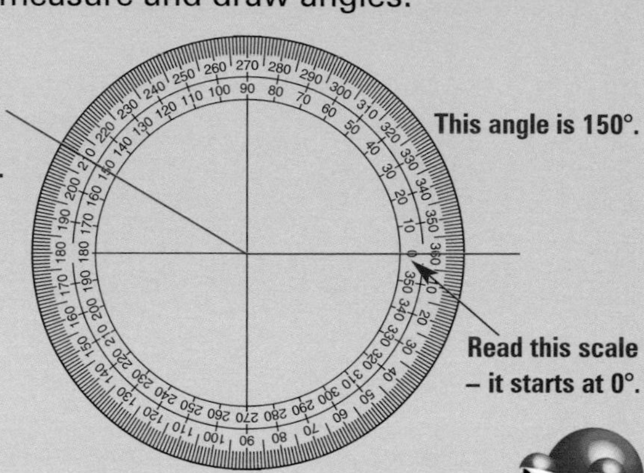

We can **estimate angle size** by comparing with a right angle.
Angle A is about $\frac{1}{3}$ of a right angle.
It is about 30°.

The corner of a page is a right angle.
A

Vertically opposite angles are equal.

Example $a = 100°$

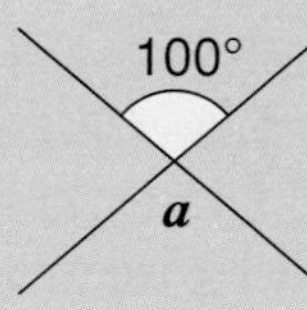

Angles at a point add up to 360°.

Example $a = 360° - 90° - 140°$
$= 130°$

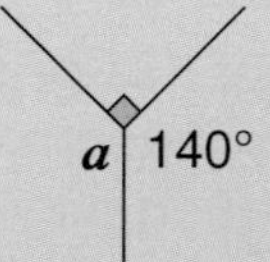

Angles on a straight line add to 180°.

Example $a = 30°$

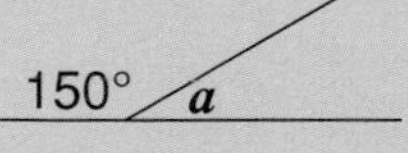

Angles in a triangle add to 180°.

Example $a = 180° - 90° - 30°$
$= 60°$

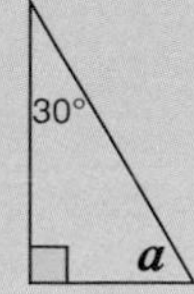

Practice Questions 5, 22, 27, 28

Lines

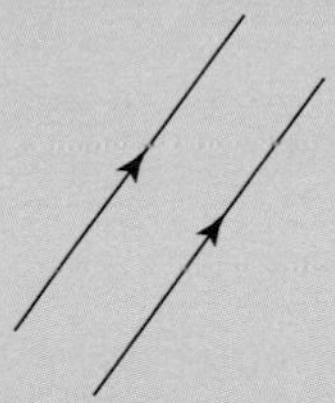

Parallel lines are always the same distance apart.

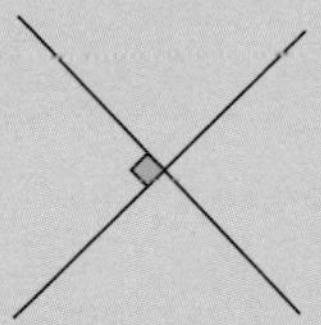

Perpendicular lines intersect (cross) at right angles.

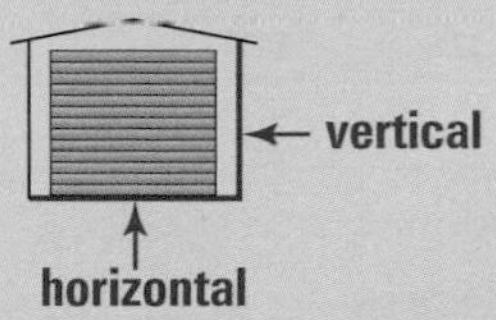

vertical

horizontal

We can **measure lines** using a ruler.
This line is 4·4 cm or 44 mm long.

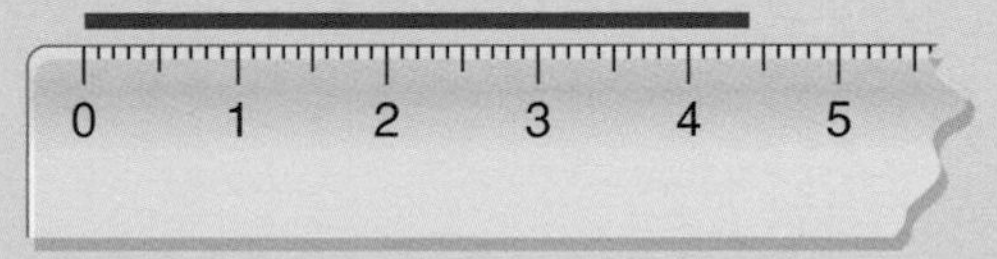

0 1 2 3 4 5

Practice Questions 2, 3

2-D shapes

Triangles

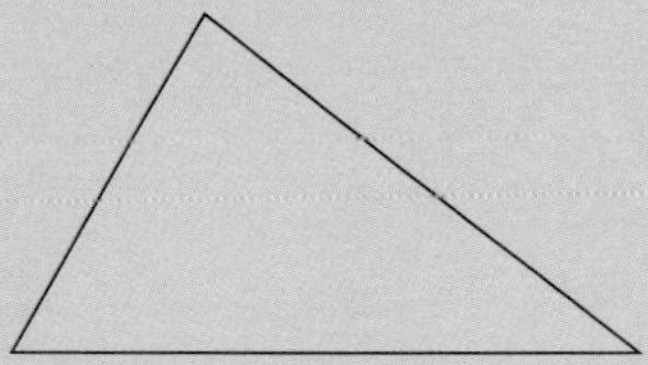

scalene
no equal sides
no equal angles

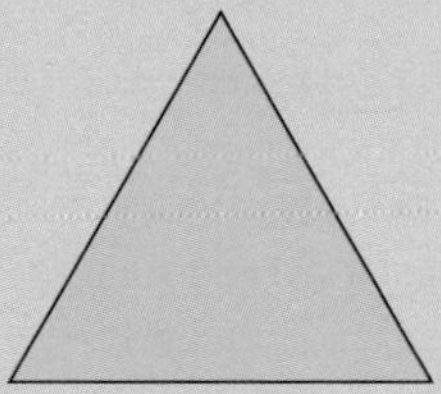

equilateral
3 equal sides
3 equal angles

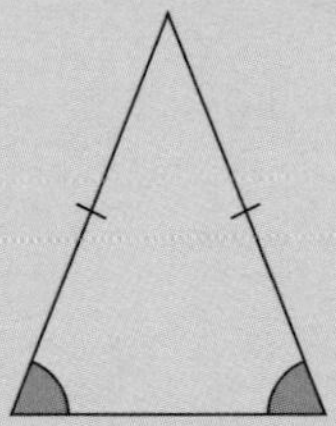

isosceles
2 equal sides
2 base angles equal

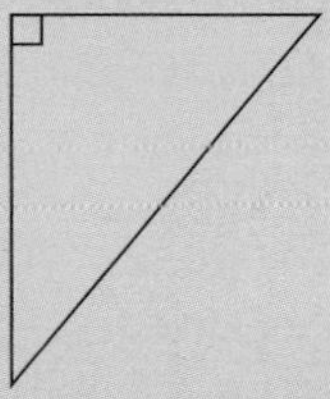

right angled

Quadrilaterals

A **quadrilateral** has four sides.

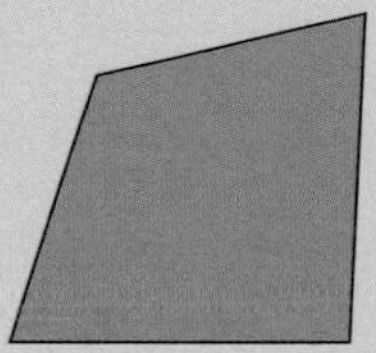

quadrilateral

These are some **special quadrilaterals**.

square
4 equal sides
4 right angles

rectangle 
2 pairs of opposite sides equal
4 right angles

parallelogram 
opposite sides equal and parallel

rhombus 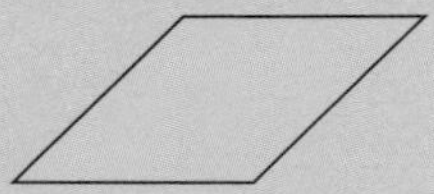
a parallelogram with 4 equal sides

trapezium 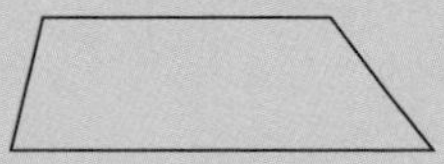
1 pair of opposite sides parallel

kite 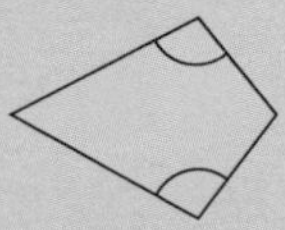
2 pairs of adjacent sides equal
1 pair of equal angles

Polygons

A 3-sided polygon is a **triangle**.
A 4-sided polygon is a **quadrilateral**.
A 5-sided polygon is a **pentagon**.
A 6-sided polygon is a **hexagon**.
A 7-sided polygon is a **heptagon**.
An 8-sided polygon is an **octagon**.

A **regular polygon** has equal sides and equal angles.

Practice Questions 1, 4, 8, 10, 45

3-D shapes

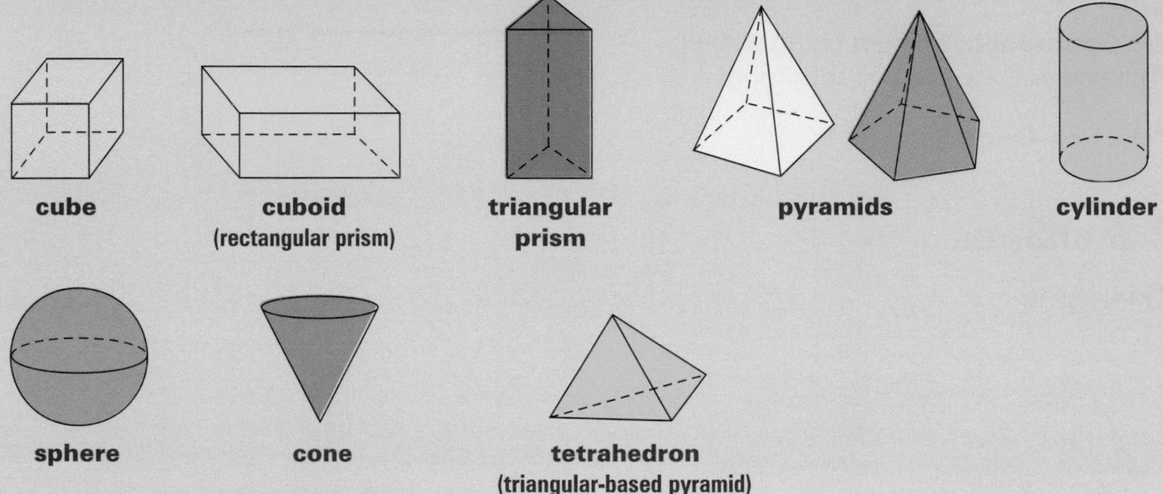

Faces, edges, vertices

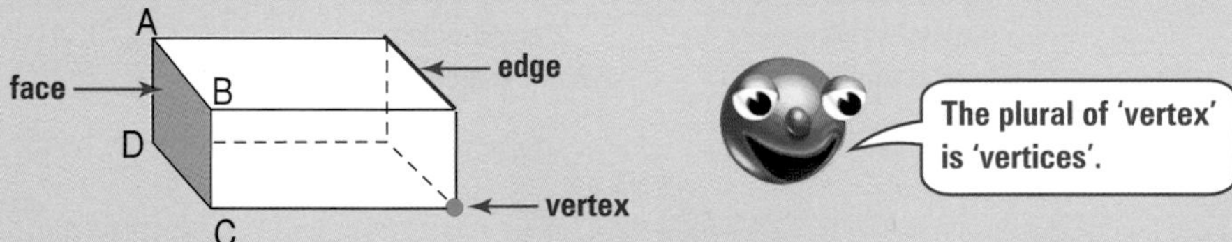

Practice Questions 9, 11

Nets

A **net** is a 2-D shape which folds to make a 3-D shape.
This net folds to make a cube.
The base is shown in yellow.

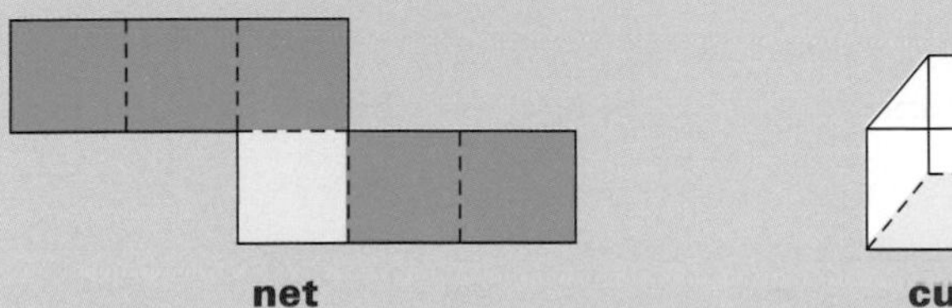

There are other nets which fold to make a cube.

Practice Questions 39, 43

Coordinates

The **coordinates** of P are (2, 4).

x-coordinate *y*-coordinate

We always write the x-coordinate first.
(x, y) is in alphabetical order.

Practice Question 14

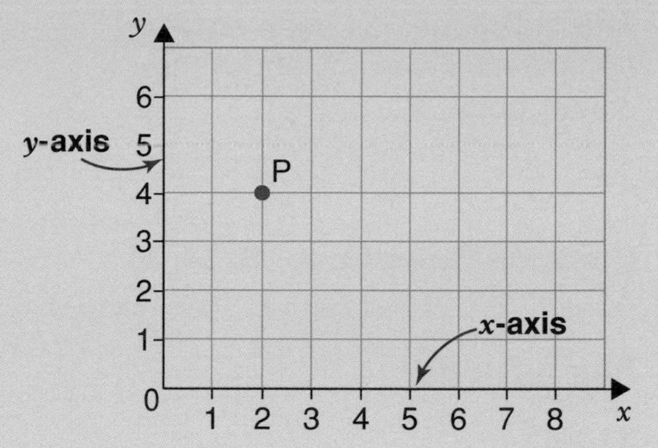

Symmetry

A shape has **reflection symmetry** if it can be folded so that one half fits exactly onto the other half.

Example Shape **A** is **symmetrical** about the dotted line.
The dotted line is called a line of symmetry.

Shape **B** is **not** symmetrical.

A

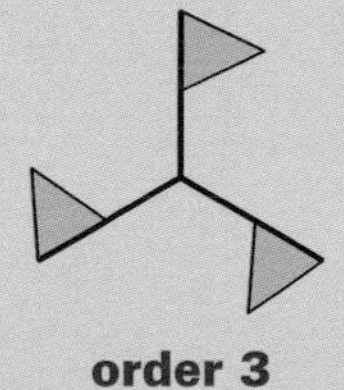

B

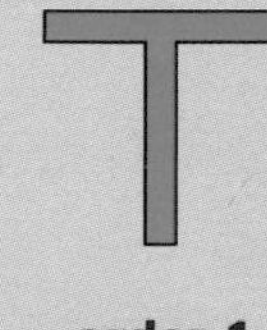

The **order of rotation symmetry** is the number of times a shape fits exactly onto itself during a complete turn.

A shape has rotation symmetry if it has order of symmetry greater than 1.

rotation symmetry **no rotation symmetry**

order 3 **order 1**

Practice Questions 7, 12, 20, 23, 25, 26

Transformations

The green shape has been **translated** 4 units to the left and 1 unit up to the red shape.

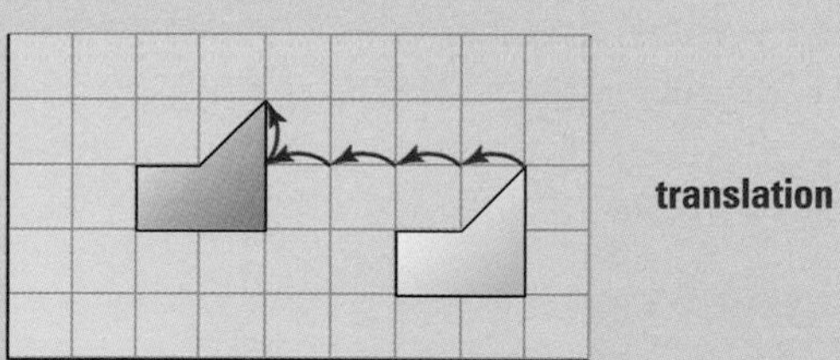

translation

The blue shape has been **reflected** in the mirror line, **m**, to get the pink shape.

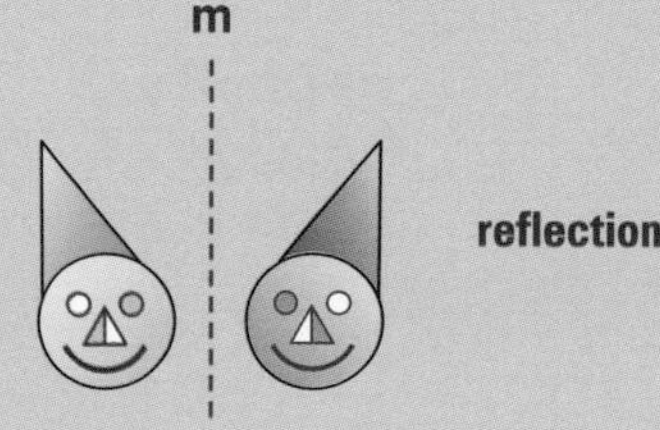

reflection

The red shape has been **rotated** 90° anticlockwise ↺ about the centre point, **X**.

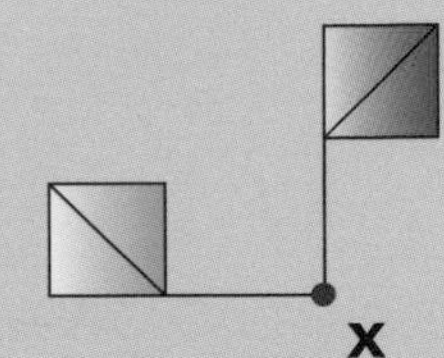

Practice Questions 18, 34, 36

Measures

Time

1 minute = 60 seconds
1 hour = 60 minutes
1 day = 24 hours

1 week = 7 days
1 year = 365 days
or 52 weeks
or 12 months
1 leap year = 366 days

1 decade = 10 years
1 century = 100 years
1 millennium = 1000 years

24-hour clocks number the hours from 0 to 23.

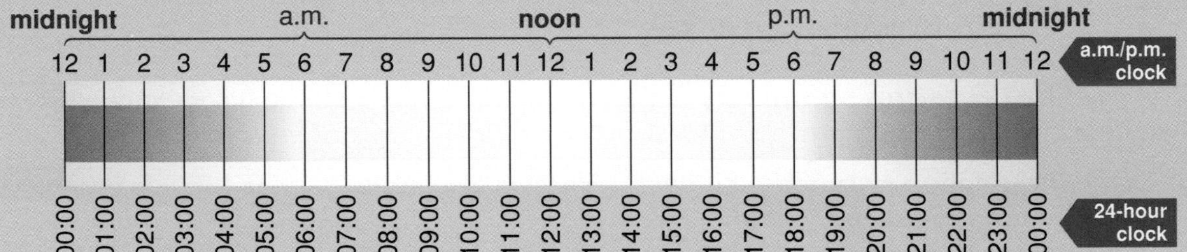

Metric measures

Length
1 kilometre (km) = 1000 metres
1 metre (m) = 1000 millimetres (mm)
1 metre (m) = 100 centimetres (cm)
1 centimetre (cm) = 10 millimetres (mm)

Capacity
1 litre (ℓ) = 1000 millilitres (mℓ)
1 centilitre (cℓ) = 10 millilitres (mℓ)
1 litre (ℓ) = 100 centilitres (cℓ)

Mass
1 kilogram (kg) = 1000 grams (g)

Examples 5 km = 5 × 1000 m
= 5000 m

300 cm = (300 ÷ 100) m
= 3 m

Imperial measures

These are rough metric and imperial equivalents.

length
8 km ≃ 5 miles

capacity
1 gallon ≃ 4·5 litres
1 pint is just over $\frac{1}{2}$ a litre.

mass
1 kg ≃ 2·2 pounds (lb)

Reading scales

To **read a scale** we must work out what each mark on the scale stands for.

Example On this scale, each mark stands for 10 mm.
The arrow is at about 35 mm.

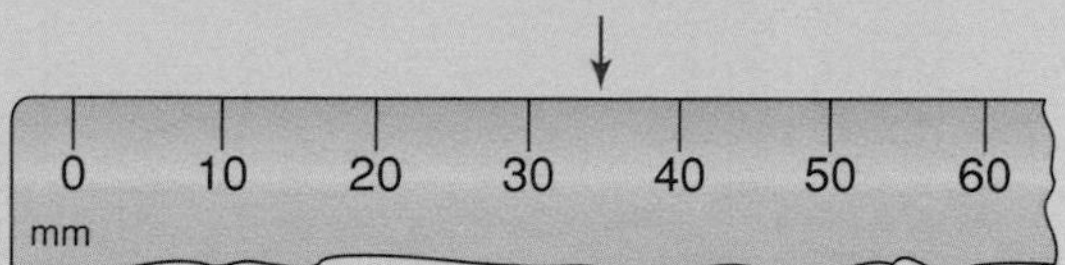

Practice Questions 6, 13, 15, 16, 17, 19, 21, 24, 30, 32, 33, 35, 41, 44

Perimeter and area

The distance round the outside of a shape is called the **perimeter**.
Perimeter is measured in mm, cm, m or km.

The amount of surface a shape covers is called the **area.**
Area is measured in square millimetres (mm^2), square centimetres (cm^2), square metres (m^2) or square kilometres (km^2).

The **area of a rectangle** is found by multiplying the length by the width.

length

width

Example Perimeter $= 2 \times 8 + 2 \times 4$
$= 16 + 8$
$= 24$ cm
Area $= 8 \times 4$
$= 32 \text{ cm}^2$

8 cm

4 cm

Practice Questions 29, 31, 37, 38, 40, 42

Practice Questions

1 Name these triangles as scalene, equilateral, isosceles or right-angled.

a 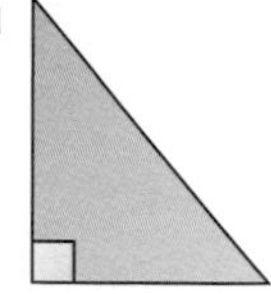

b 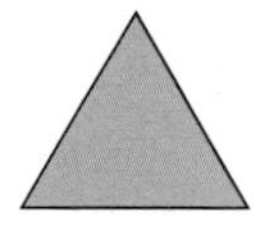

c 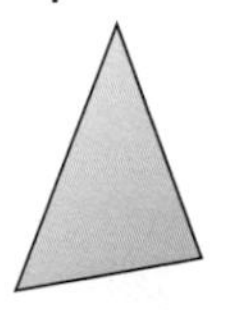

d 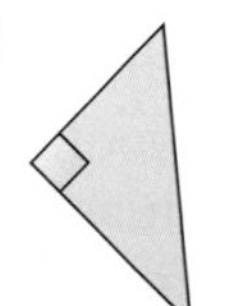

e 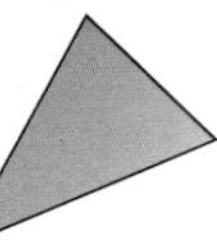

f 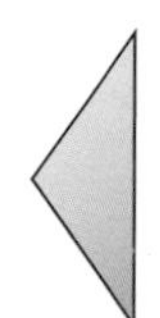

g 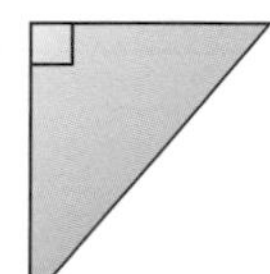

h 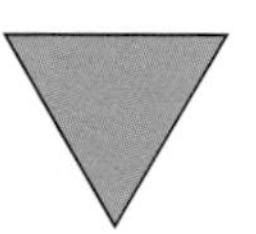

i 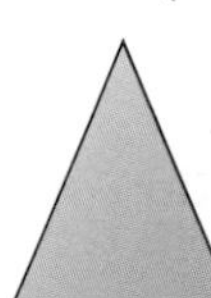

2

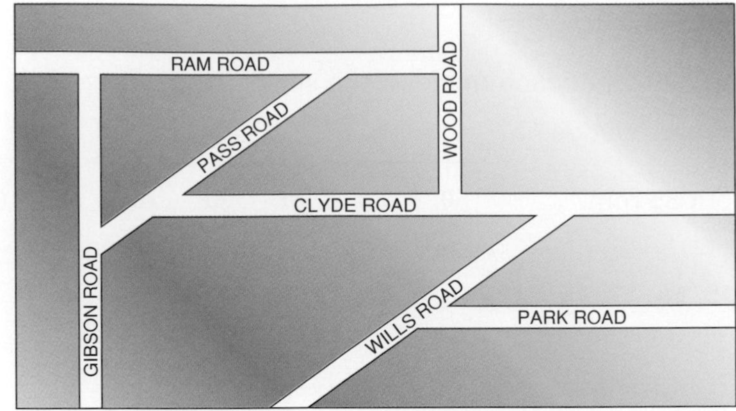

a Which road is parallel to Wood Road?

b Which road is perpendicular to Ram Road?
A Clyde Road **B** Pass Road **C** Gibson Road

c Is Pass Road parallel to Wills Road?

d Write down two other roads that are parallel.

3 Estimate the lengths of the sides of this quadrilateral to the nearest centimetre. Then measure them accurately.

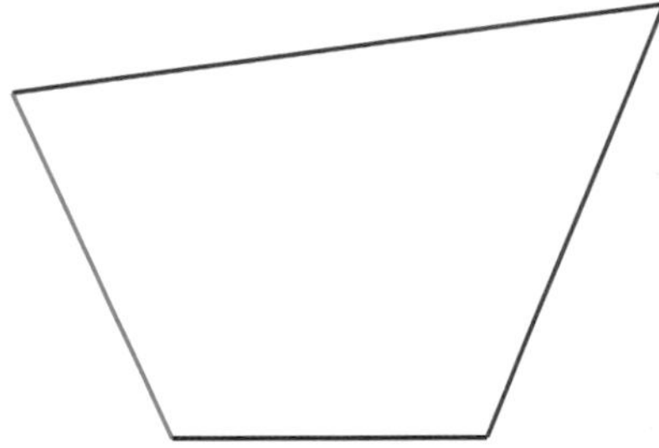

4 What shape am I?

a I have 4 equal sides.
I have 4 right angles.

b I have 3 sides.
2 of them are equal.

T **5** Use a copy of this.

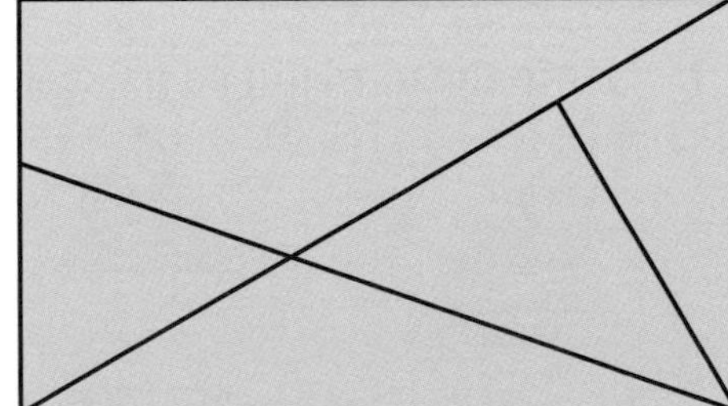

a Mark a right angle with a small square.

b Put a cross (x) in an acute angle.

c Put a dot (·) in an obtuse angle.

d How many triangles are there altogether?

6 **a** What unit would you use to measure these?

i the width of a book

ii the capacity of a small bowl

iii the mass of an egg

iv the length of a netball court

b What measuring instrument would you use to measure each of the above?

T

7 Use a copy of these.

a Draw all the lines of symmetry on each diagram.

i

ii

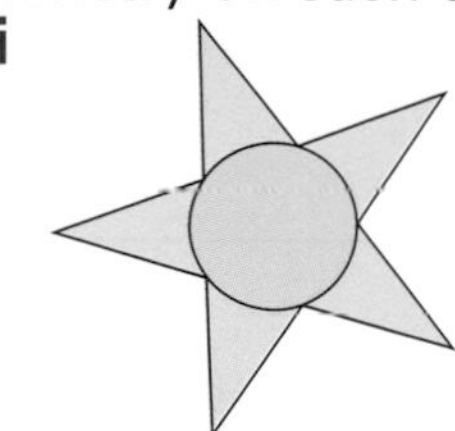

iii

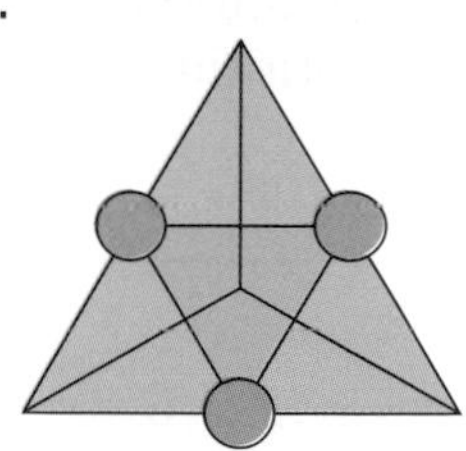

b What is the order of rotation symmetry of each shape?

8 Name these shapes.

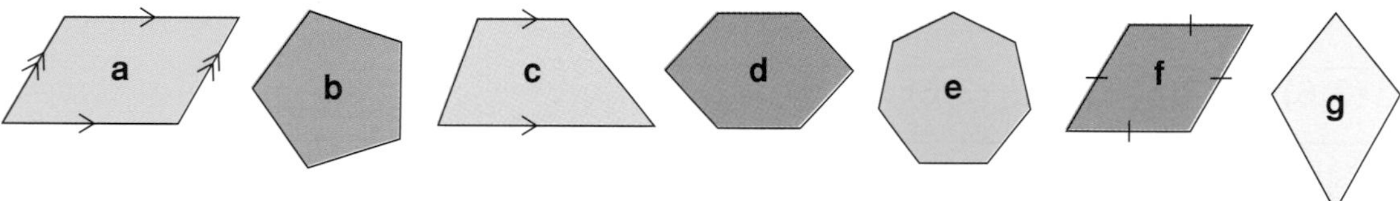

9 **a** How many edges does this shape have?

b How many vertices does this shape have?

c Three of the faces are rectangular.
How many other faces are there?
What shape are these?

d Name this shape.

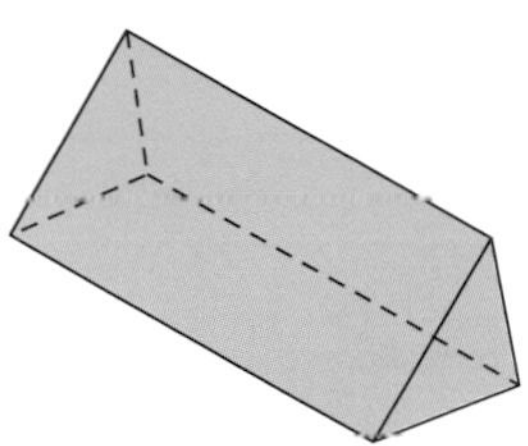

10 Which of these shapes are regular?

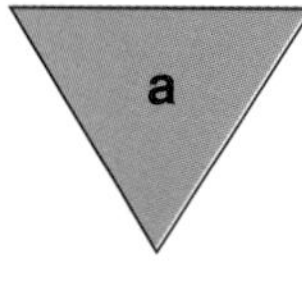

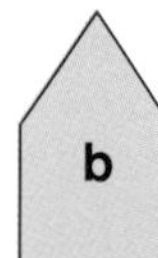

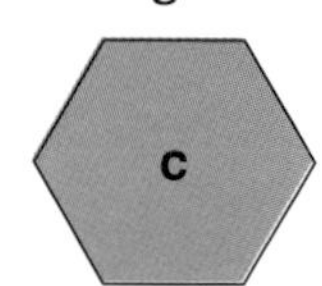

d

e

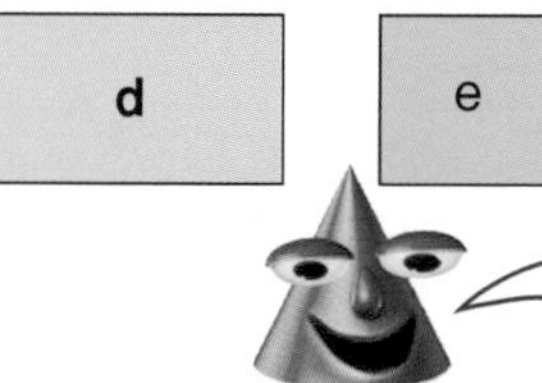

Remember: A regular shape has all sides and all angles equal.

11 Name these solids.

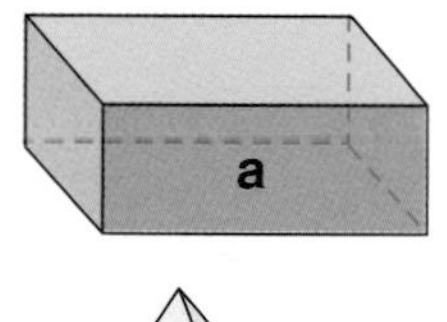

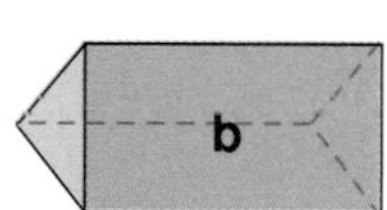

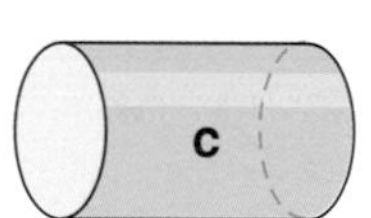

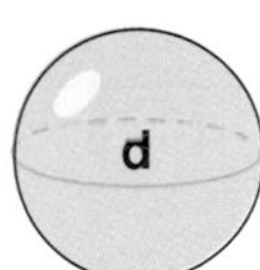

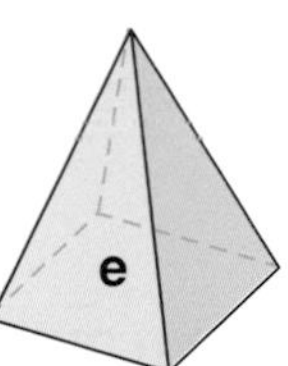

f

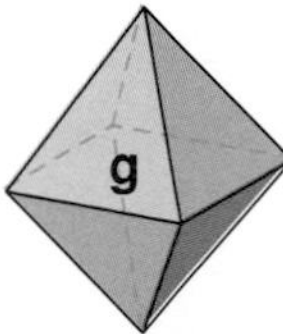

12 How many lines of symmetry do these shapes have?

a

b

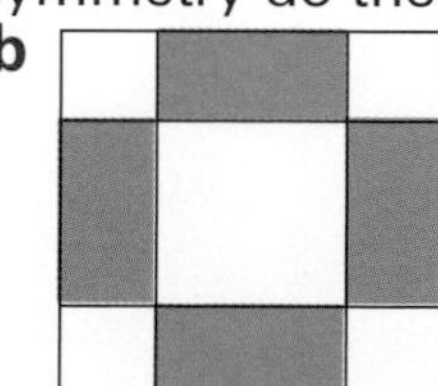

c

13 Ben missed the train by 12 minutes.
He got to the station at 2:23 p.m.
Write, in 24-hour time, the time the train left.

T **14** Use a copy of this.

T	___	___	___	___		___	___	___		___	___	___	___
(1, 7)	(5,0)	(2,3)	(6,8)	(2,3)		(8,4)	(6,8)	(2,3)		(4,4)	(2,0)	(6,8)	(2,3)

___	___	___	___	___	___	___	___		___	___
(3,2)	(5,0)	(0,5)	(3,2)	(6,5)	(2,3)	(5,6)	(8,6)		(2,0)	(5,6)

___	___	___	**T**	___		**T**	___	___	___
(2,3)	(8,4)	(6,8)	(1, 7)	(5,0)		(1, 7)	(5,0)	(8,4)	(5,6)

___	___	___	___	___	___
(3,6)	(2,3)	(2,0)	(3,6)	(6,3)	(2,3)

Fill in the words by finding the letter beside each coordinate.
T is filled in for you.

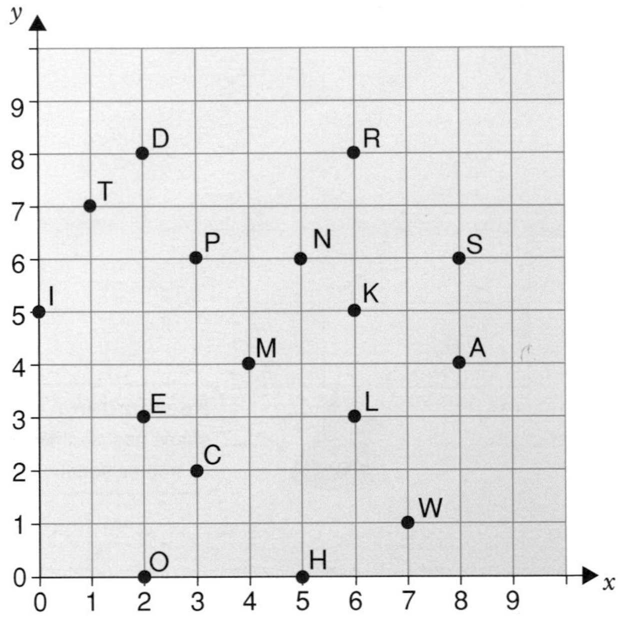

15 Robyn measured these in metric units.
What imperial unit could she have used instead?

a distance to the lake in kilometres
b mass of fruit in kilograms
c capacity of a bottle in litres

16 Last night the sun set at 19:30.
It rose this morning at 06:45.
How many hours of darkness were there?

17 What do each of these read?

a

b

c

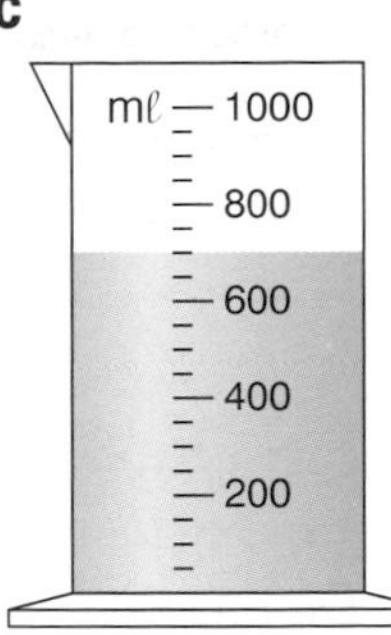

d

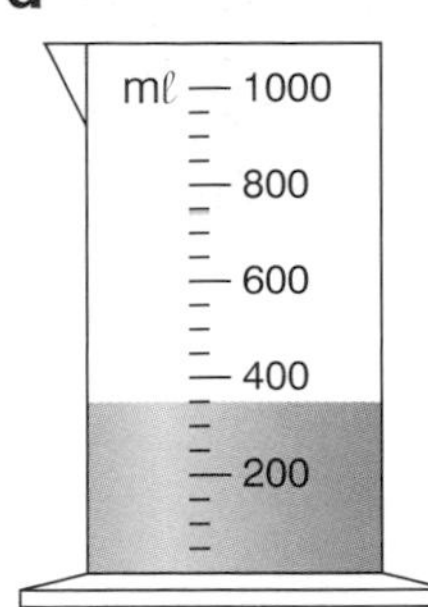

18 Describe how each of these shapes has been translated.

a

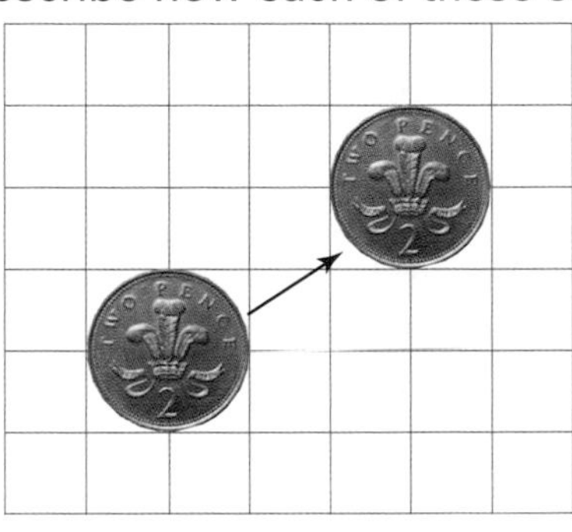

b

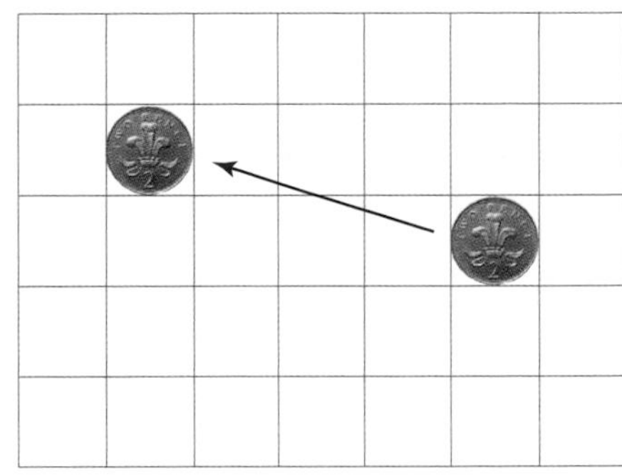

19 A medicine bottle holds 300 millilitres.
Robert is to have 15 millilitres twice a day.
How many days will the medicine last?

T **20** Use a copy of this.
Shade eight **more squares** so that both dotted lines are lines of symmetry.

a

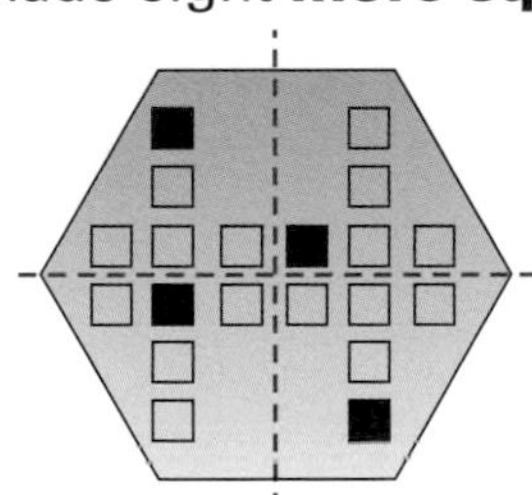

b

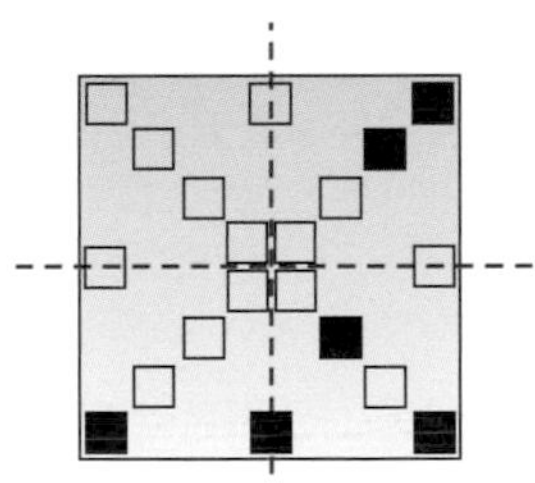

21 A sink holds 6 litres of water.
How many $\frac{1}{2}$ litre jugs full of water are needed to fill it?

22 Find the size of x in these.

a

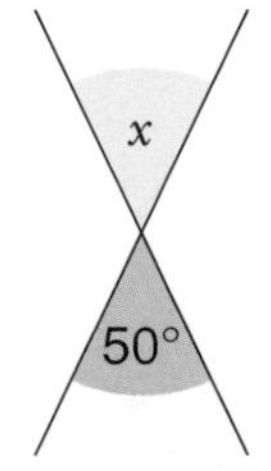

b

c

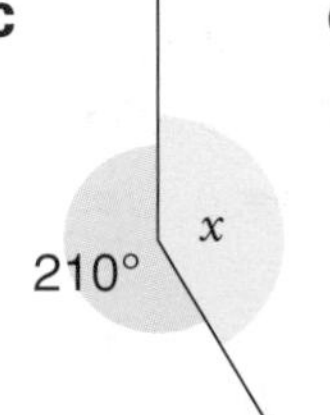

d

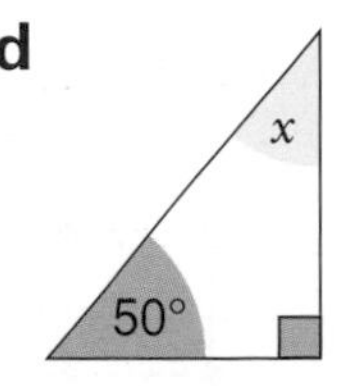

e

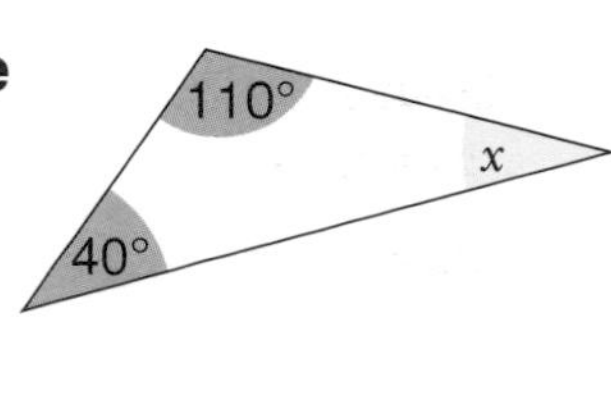

23 Which of the diagrams below shows this shape rotated through a

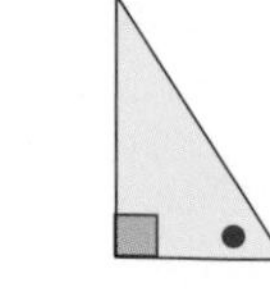

a half turn
b quarter turn
c full turn?

A  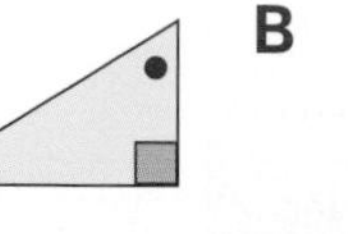 **B** **C** 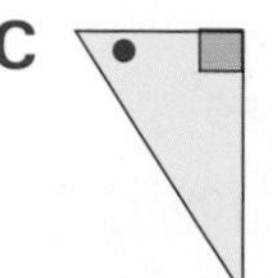 **D**

24 What goes in the gap?

a 7 cm = ___ mm	**b** 3 m = ___ mm	**c** 3 m = ___ cm
d 2 km = ___ m	**e** 6 cm = ___ mm	**f** 6 ℓ = 6000 ___
g 5 kg = 5000 ___	**h** 500 cm = ___ m	**i** 4000 g = ___ kg
j 3000 mℓ = ___ ℓ	**k** 7000 m = 7 ___	**l** 60 mm = 6 ___

25 Which of these shapes have rotation symmetry?

a  **b** 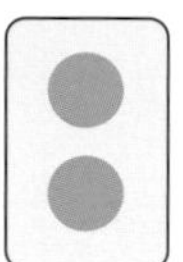 **c** 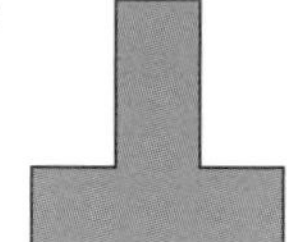 **d** 

26 Write down the order of symmetry of the shapes in question **25** which have rotation symmetry.

27 Estimate the size of each of these angles.
Use a protractor to check your estimate.

a 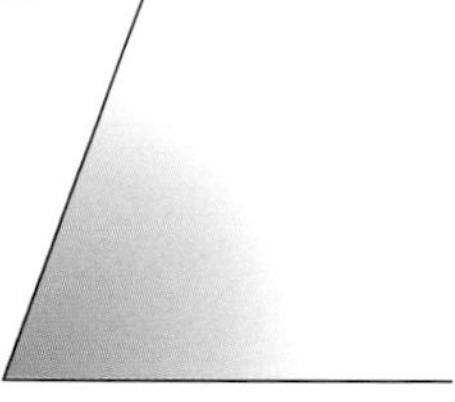 **b** 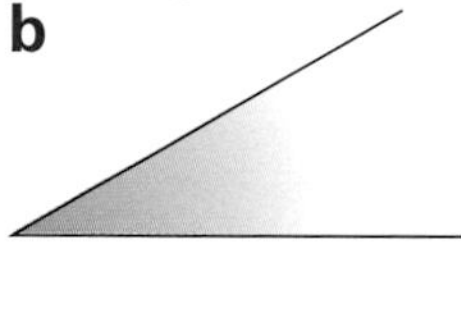 **c** 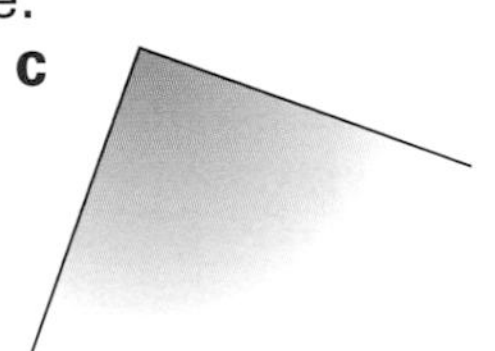 **d** 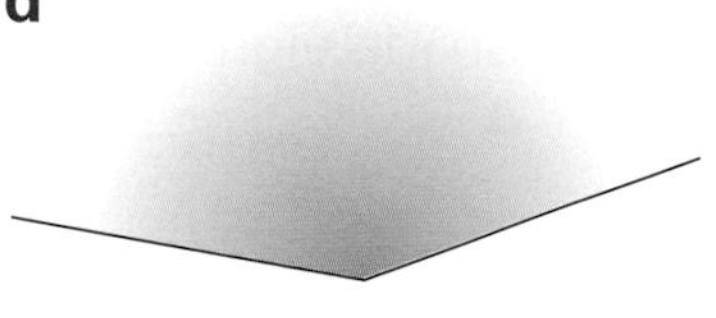

28 Name each of the angles in question **27**.
Choose from the box.

acute **obtuse** **right**

29 The distance between dots is 1 cm.
Without measuring, find the perimeters of the shapes.

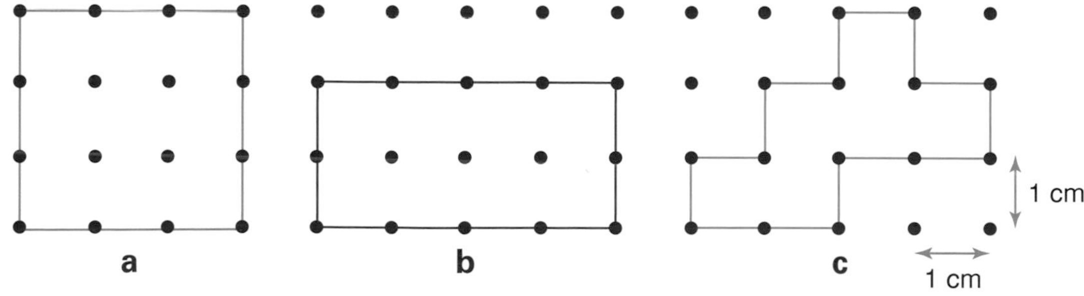

30 Which of these would you expect to be

a the amount of water needed to fill a kitchen sink?

A 50 ℓ **B** 0·5 ℓ **C** 15 ℓ **D** 1 ℓ

b the mass of a small dog?

A 10 kg **B** 1 kg **C** 100 kg **D** 100 g

c the length of a classroom?

A 70 cm **B** 70 m **C** 700 m **D** 7 m

31 Lucy used this pattern to make decorations. Count squares to estimate the area of each decoration.

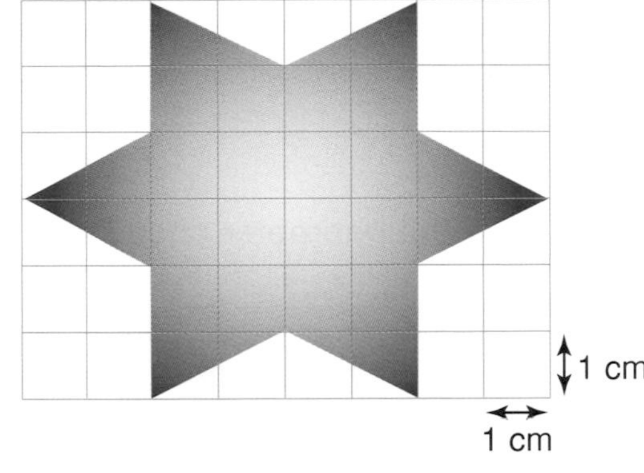

32 What reading is given by each of the pointers?

a

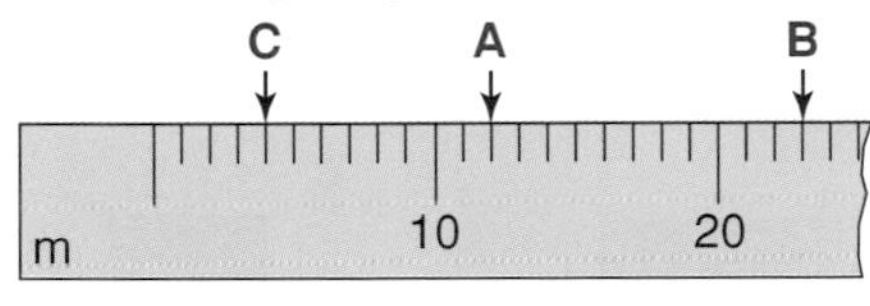

b

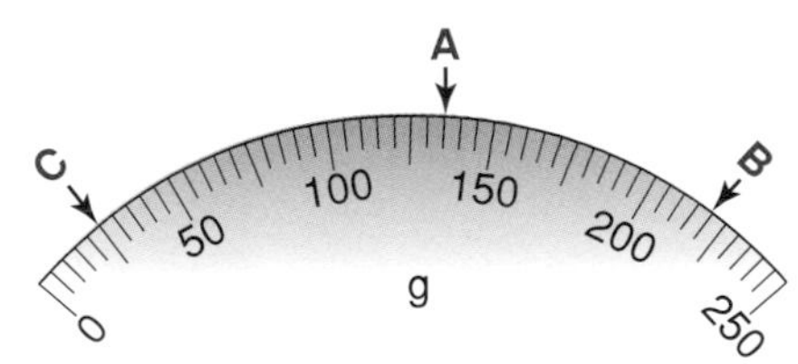

c

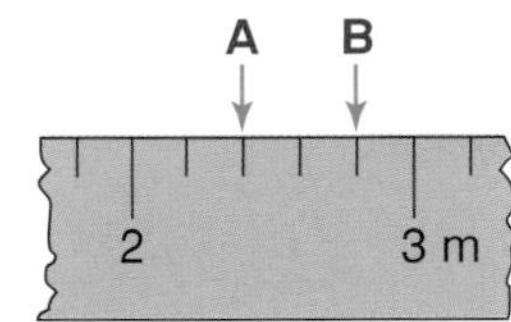

33 Tom took 3 hours 20 minutes and 15 minutes in a cycle race. How many minutes is this?

T **34** Use a copy of these. Draw the reflection in the mirror line, m.

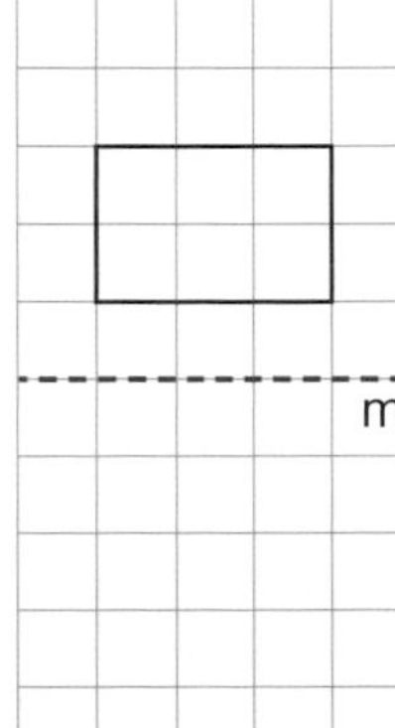

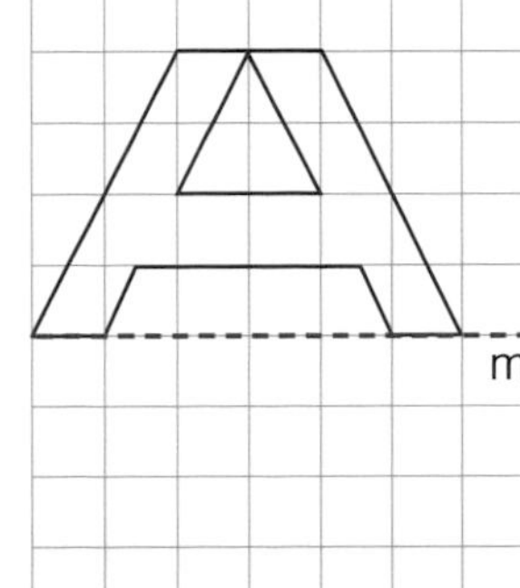

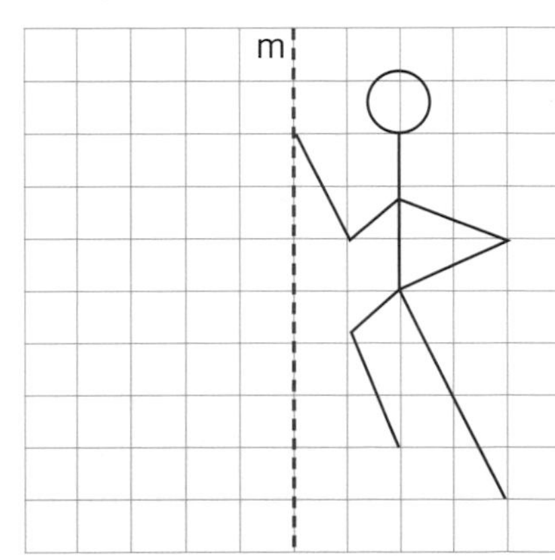

35 Ten apples weigh 2·5 kg.
How many grams is this?

36 Shape A has been translated to shape B.
Copy this sentence and fill in the gaps.
Shape A has been translated ___ units to the ___
and ___ units ___.

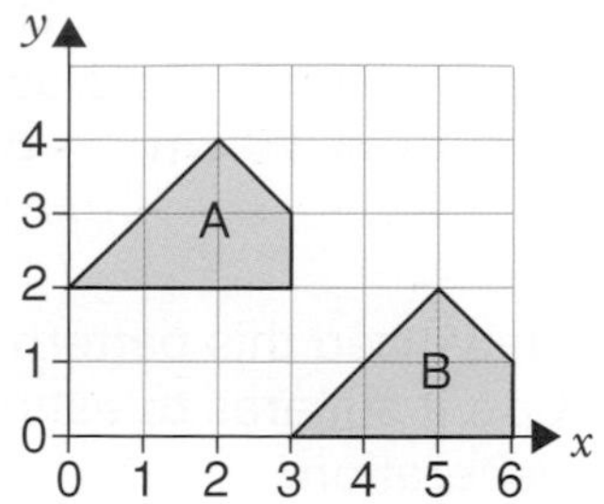

37 Find the perimeter of each of these.

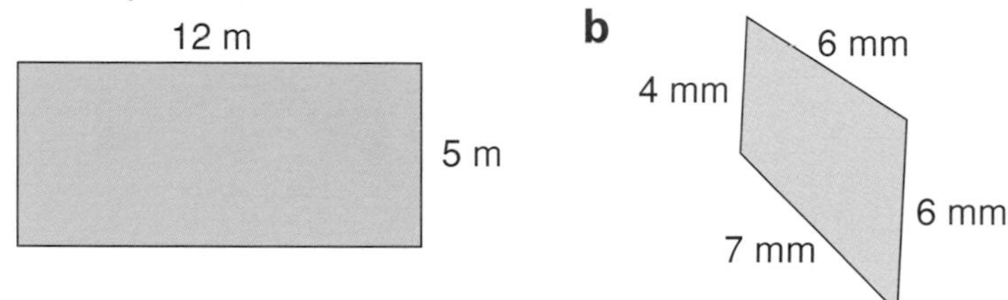

38 What is the area of each of these rectangles?

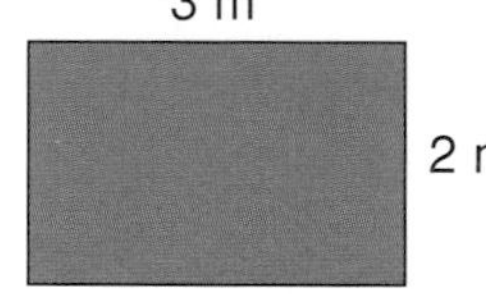

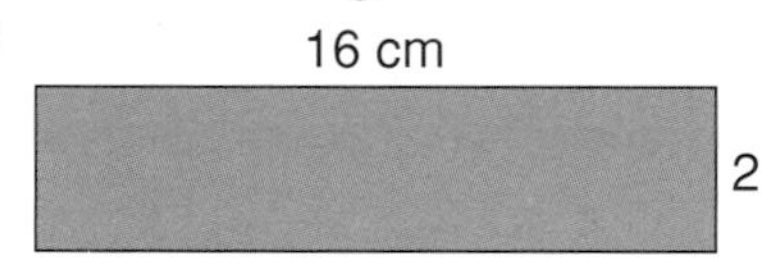

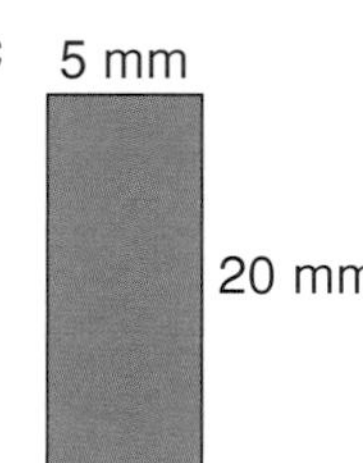

39 **a** Which of these nets will fold to make an open box?

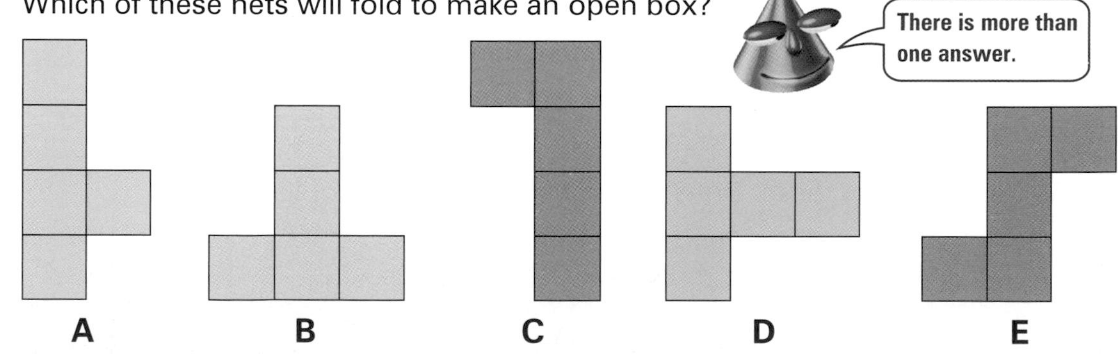

b Draw another two nets that fold to make an open box.

40 Choose a suitable unit to estimate the area of each of these.
Choose from the box.

a area of a classroom
b area of a book cover
c area of a calculator button
d area of a football field

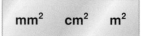

mm^2 cm^2 m^2

41 Mrs Samson bought 2 kg of sugar.
She used 400 g of sugar to make some fudge.
How many grams of sugar were left?

42 Nishi had 12 squares. She made three different rectangles with them.

a How many different rectangles could she make with 24 squares?

b How many squares does she need to make exactly five different rectangles?

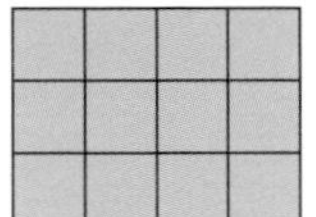
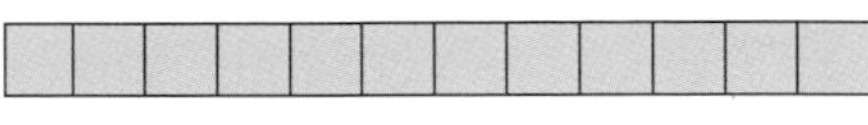

T

43 Use a copy of this.
Finish drawing the net for this cube.

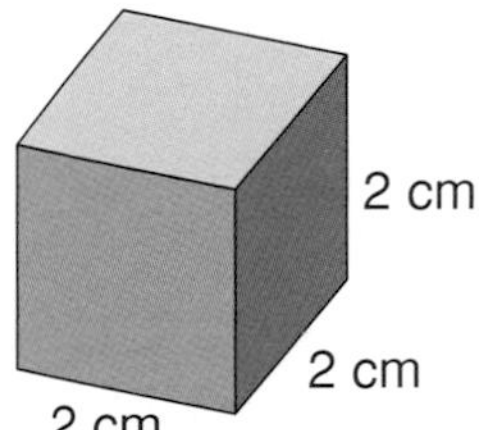

2 cm
2 cm

44 Jeff made 4 litres of punch for his birthday party.
How many 250 mℓ glasses could be filled?

45 Write true or false for each of these.

a A parallelogram has opposite sides equal and parallel.

b A kite has two pairs of opposite sides parallel.

c A trapezium has two pairs of parallel sides.

d An equilateral triangle has three equal sides and three equal angles.

e A rhombus has no equal angles.

f An arrowhead has two pairs of adjacent sides equal.

11 Lines and Angles

You need to know

✓ angles – measuring and drawing angles — page 210
- – vertically opposite angles
- – angles on a straight line
- – angles at a point
- – angles in a triangle

✓ lines — page 211

Key vocabulary

acute angle, adjacent, angle, angles at a point, angles on a straight line, base angles, degree(°), draw, isosceles triangle, line, line segment, measure, obtuse angle, parallel, perpendicular, protractor (angle measurer), reflex angle, right angle, ruler, set square, straight angle, vertex, vertically opposite angles

Picture perfect

1 This 'picture' has been drawn using a ruler and protractor.
It is made up of parallel and perpendicular lines.
Draw your own 'picture' using parallel and perpendicular lines.
Use a ruler and protractor.

Make your picture as interesting as possible.

2 Have a contest to see who can find a picture with the most parallel and perpendicular lines **or** the most acute, obtuse or reflex angles.

Naming lines and angles

This is a **line**.
It goes on forever in both directions.

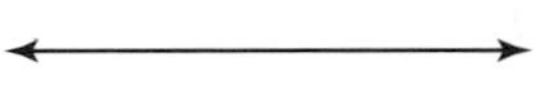

PQ is a **line segment**.
It has end points P and Q.

Discussion

A line has an infinite length.
Two straight lines are either parallel or they cross once.

Cameron **Holly**

Are Cameron and Holly right? **Discuss.**

Remember
When two line segments meet at a point, they make an angle.

We **name angles** in two ways.

1 Using the letter at the vertex.

Example This is ∠Q.

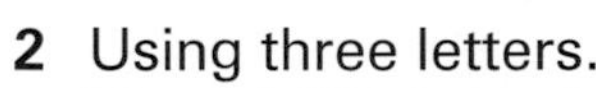

2 Using three letters.
The middle letter is at the vertex.

Example The shaded angle is ∠PQR or ∠RQP.

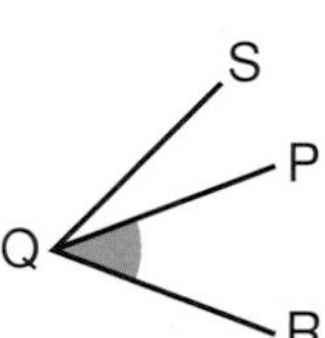

Discussion

- *An angle is the measure of turn from one arm to the other.*

What does this mean? Is it true? **Discuss.**

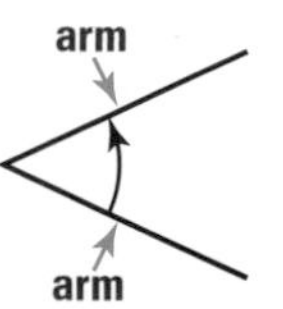

Exercise 1

1 Name the red line segment.

a

b

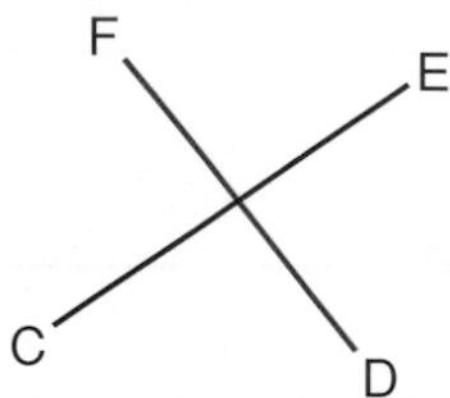

c

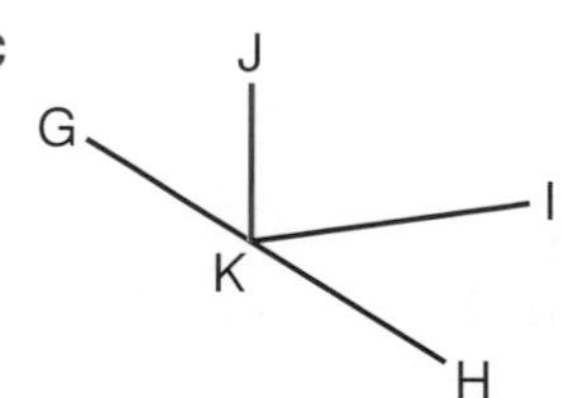

d

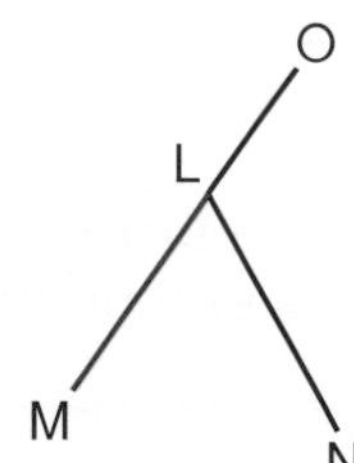

2 Use a single letter to name these angles.
The letters you write down make a word.
What is it?

a

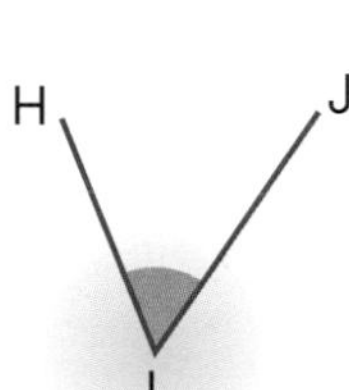

b

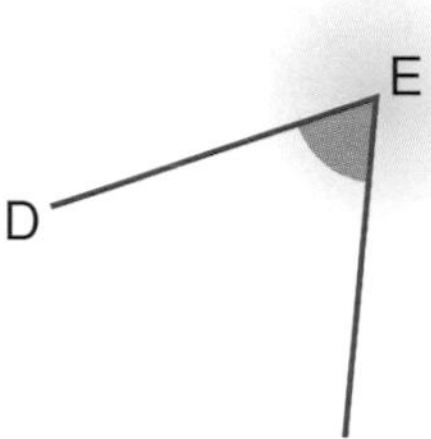

c

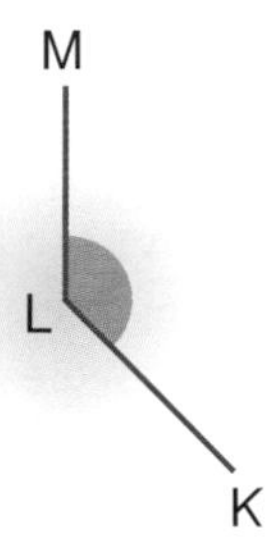

d

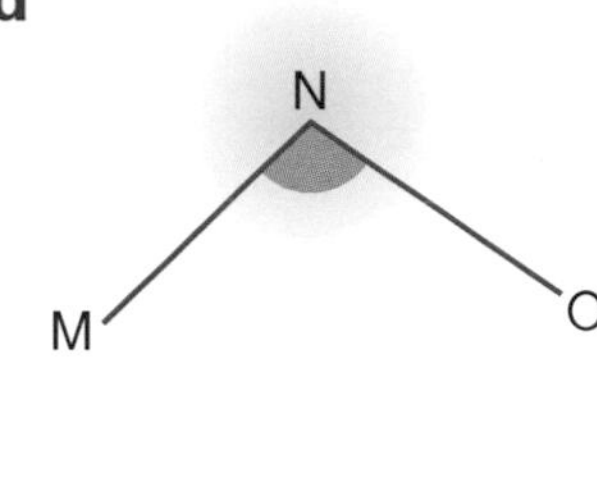

3 Josie named the shaded angle as ∠B.
Explain why this is not a good way to name it.
How should she name it?

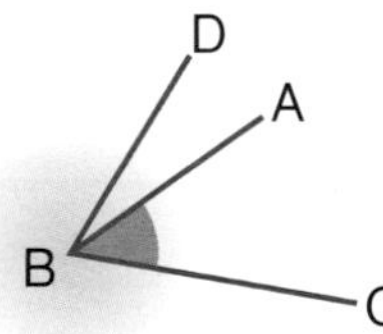

T

4 Use a copy of this.
Put the name of the angle in the box.
The first letter is there.
If you read down, what does the sentence say?

a 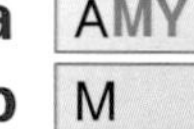

b M
c T
d F
e T

a

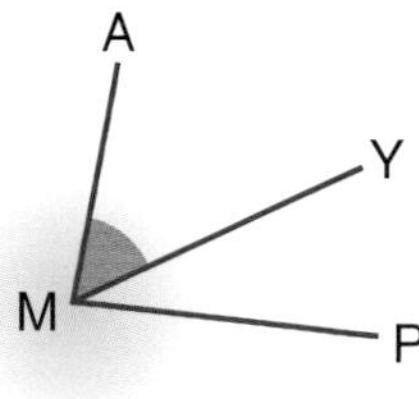

b

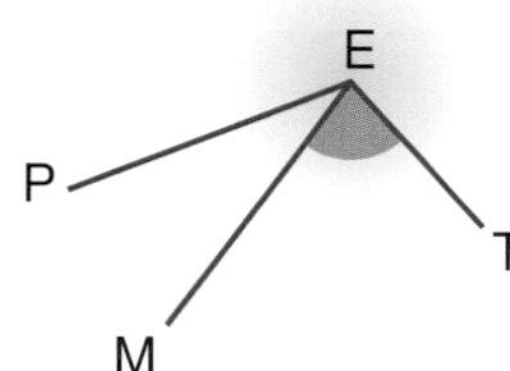

c

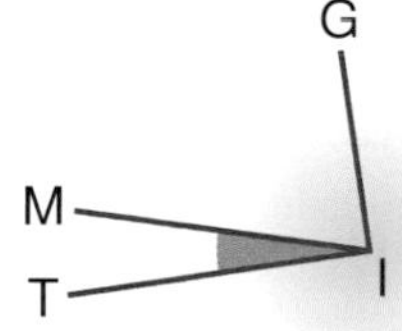

d

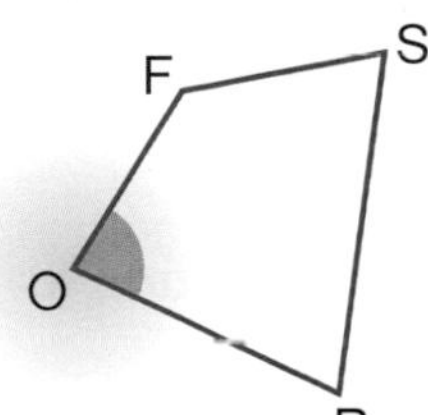

e

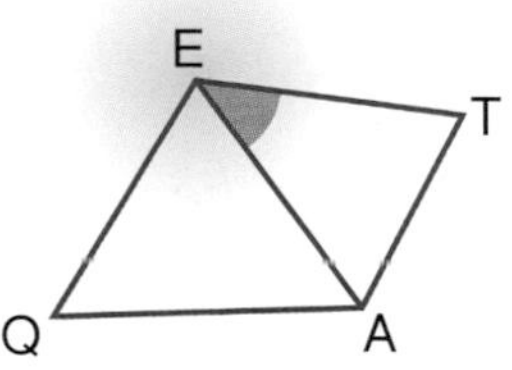

Special angles

Remember

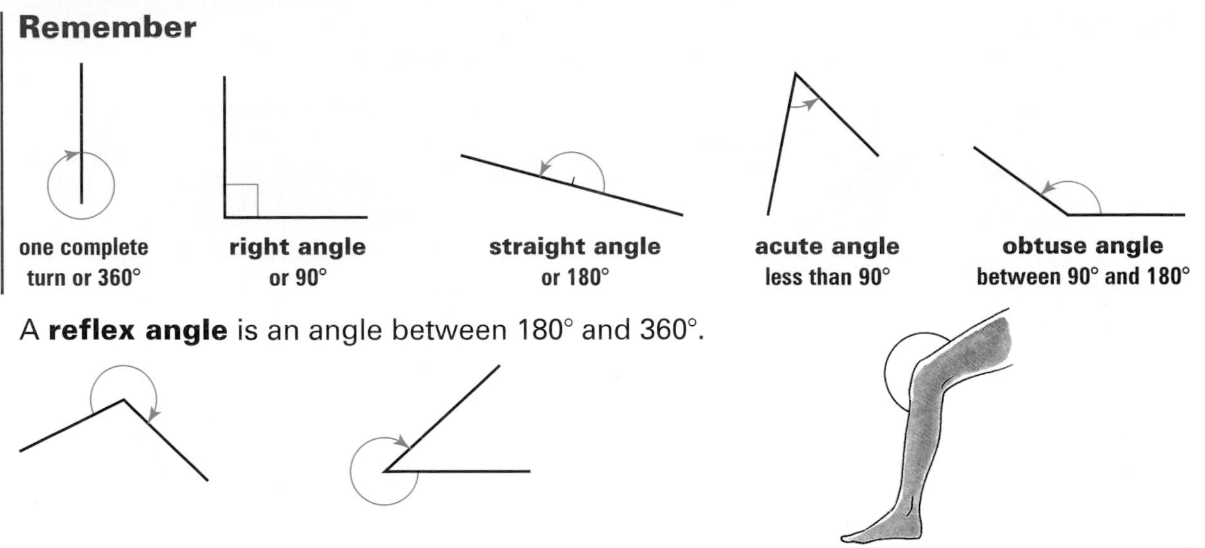

A **reflex angle** is an angle between 180° and 360°.

Exercise 2

1 Write down the colour of these angles in each diagram.
a obtuse **b** acute **c** right **d** reflex

diagram A

diagram B

2 Sketch a shape with
a 2 acute angles and 2 obtuse angles
b 1 reflex angle, 1 right angle, 2 acute angles and 1 obtuse angle.

***3** Is it possible to sketch a closed shape with 2 reflex angles in it?
If so, sketch one.

Measuring angles

Remember

To measure an angle to the nearest degree, use a **protractor**.

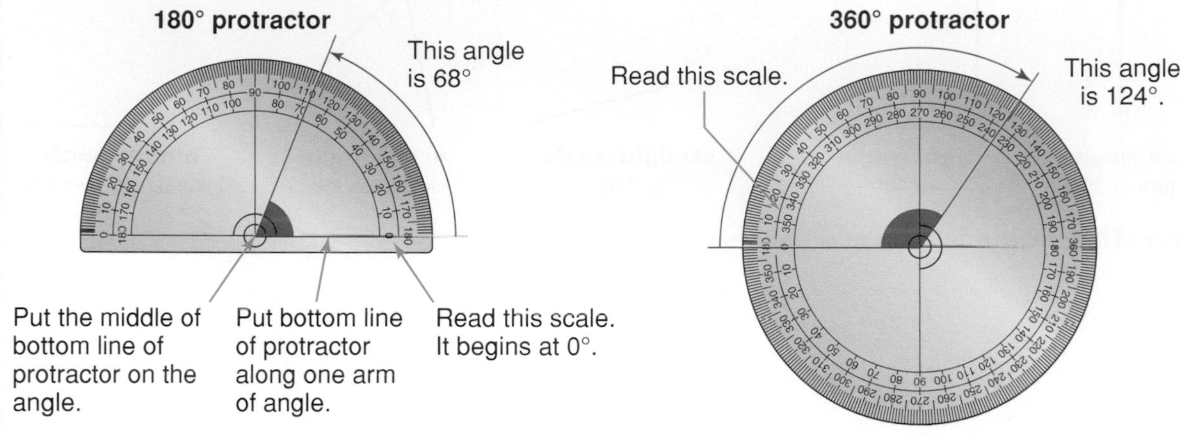
180° protractor
This angle is 68°
Put the middle of bottom line of protractor on the angle.
Put bottom line of protractor along one arm of angle.
Read this scale. It begins at 0°.
360° protractor
Read this scale.
This angle is 124°.

Measuring reflex angles

The easiest way to **measure a reflex angle** is with a 360° protractor (angle measurer).

This reflex angle is 316°.

To measure a reflex angle with a 180° protractor measure the acute or obtuse angle.
Subtract it from 360°.

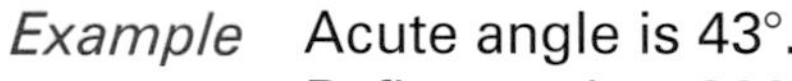

Example Acute angle is 43°.
Reflex angle = 360° − 43°
= 317°

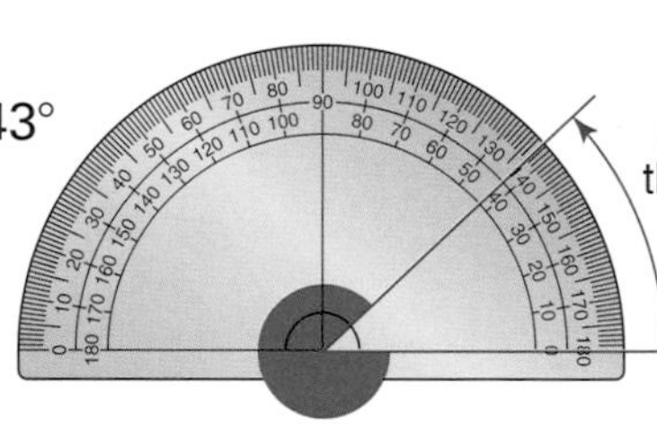

Measure this angle as 43°.

Before measuring, always **estimate** the size of the angle. Do this by comparing it with a right angle.

The corner of a sheet of paper is a right angle.

Example Estimate the size of the acute angle.
It is about 80°.
The reflex angle is about
360° − 80° = 280°.

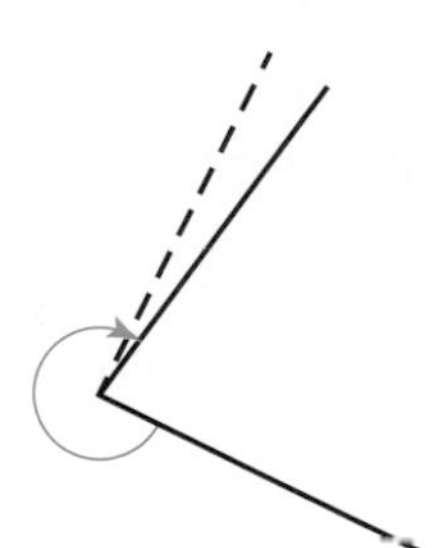

Exercise 3

T

1 Use a copy of this table.
Fill it in for these angles.

	Angle	Type	Estimate	Actual size
(a)	∠ABC	acute	40°	42°
(b)				
(c)				
(d)				
(e)				
(f)				
(g)				

a A C B

b D E F

c G H I

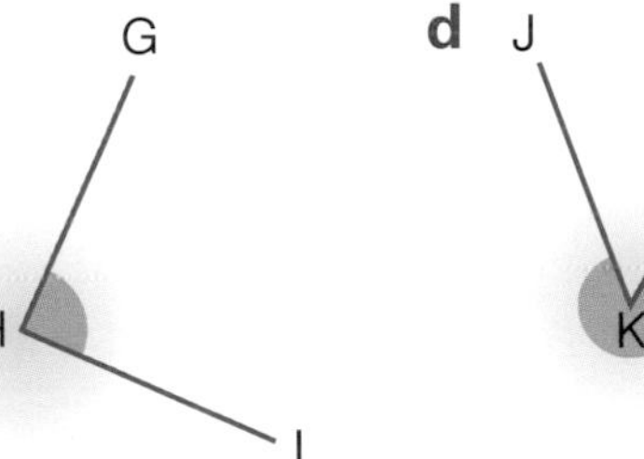

d J L K

e M N O

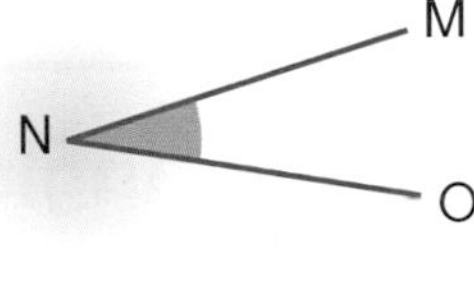

f P Q R

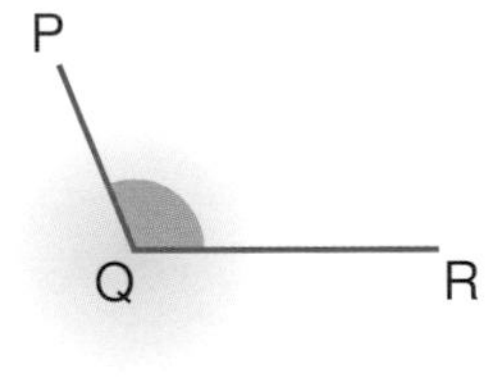

g T S U

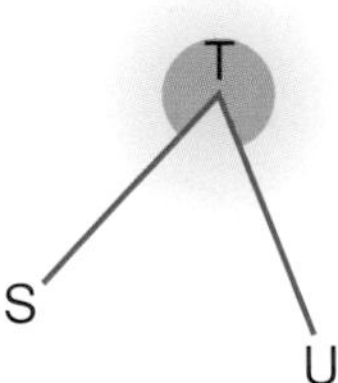

2 Estimate the size of each of the marked angles.
Check your estimate by using a protractor to measure them.

a

b

c

3 Measure the size of each of the marked angles.
As a check on the accuracy of your measurement, add all four angles together.
They should total 1080°.

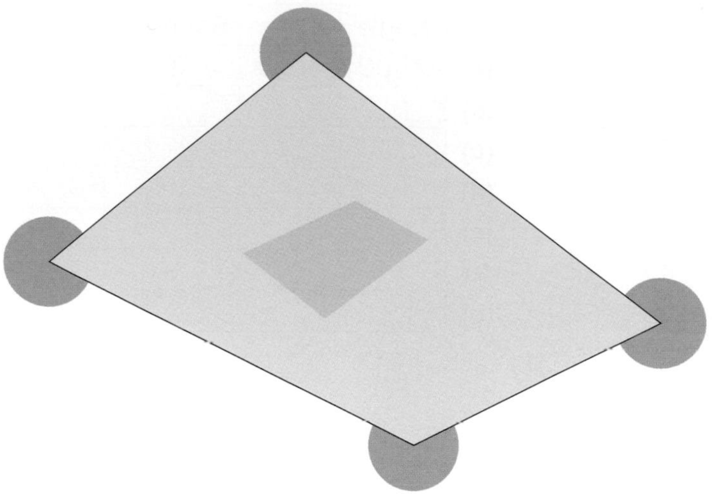

Drawing angles

Drawing a reflex angle

Using a 360° protractor

Example To draw 220°:

Step 1 Draw a straight line.

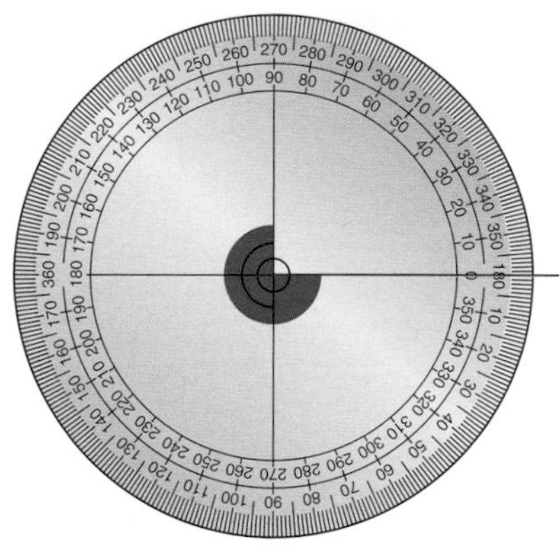

Step 2 Put the middle of the protractor on one end of the line. Put the bottom line of the protractor along the line.

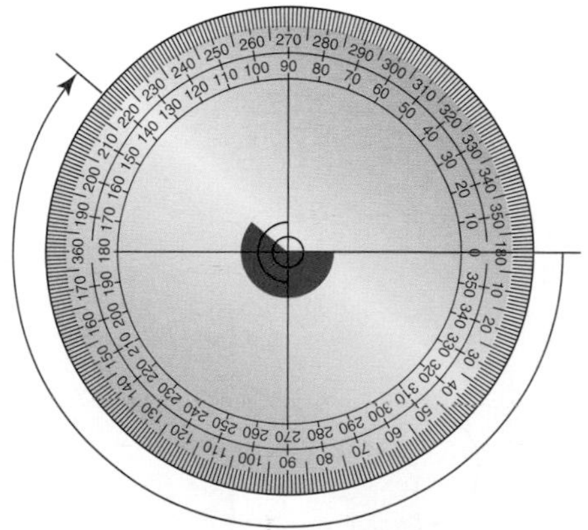

Step 3 Read the scale that begins at 0° on your line. Put a mark beside 220°.

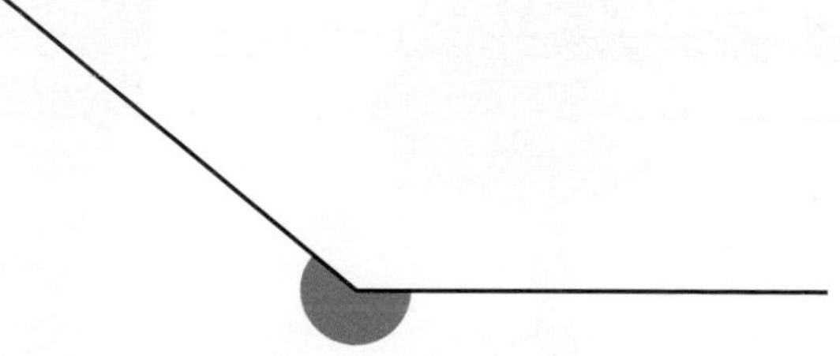

Step 4 Take the protractor away. Draw a line through the small mark you made.

Using a 180° protractor

Example To draw 220°:

Step 1 Subtract 220° from 360°. **360° − 220° = 140°**

Step 2 Draw the 140° angle.
The other angle in the diagram will be 220°.

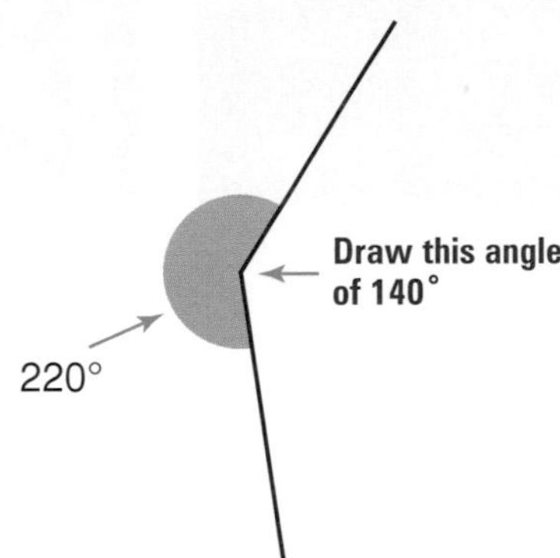
Draw this angle of 140°
220°

Guess my angle – a game for 2 players

You will need a protractor and a ruler.

Take turns to draw an angle.

Ask your partner to estimate the angle then measure it.

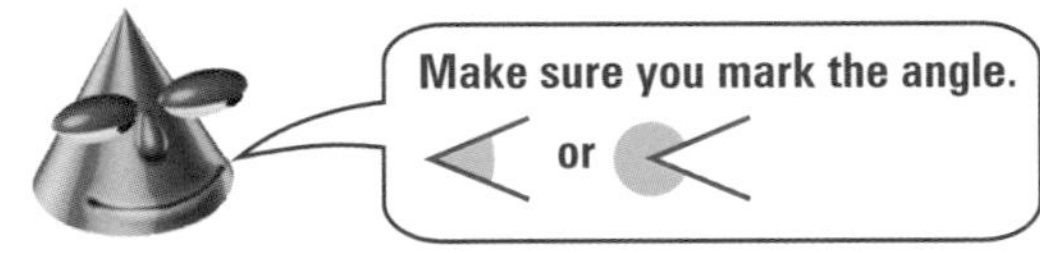
Make sure you mark the angle.
or

Give your partner 1 point if the estimate is within 10° of the measurement.

Give another point if the measurement is within 5° of the angle you drew.

Swap.

Have five turns each.

See who gets the most points.

Parallel and perpendicular lines

Remember
Parallel lines are always the same distance apart (equidistant).

Perpendicular lines intersect at right angles.

Practical

Point out the parallel lines in these pictures.
Point out the perpendicular lines.

Parallel lines never meet.
AB is parallel to CD.

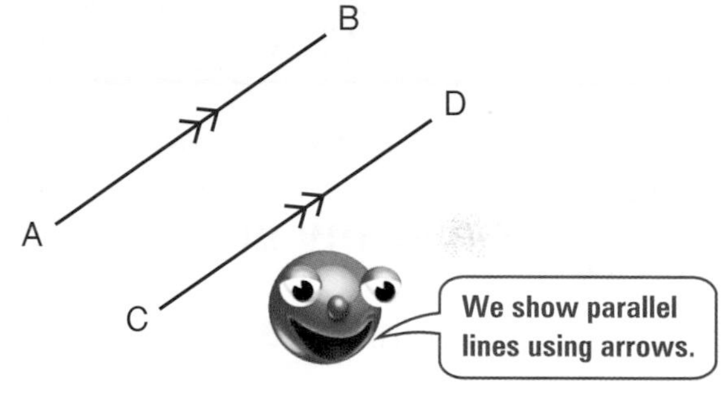

A
B
C
D
We show parallel lines using arrows.

Perpendicular lines cross at right angles.
XY is perpendicular to VW.

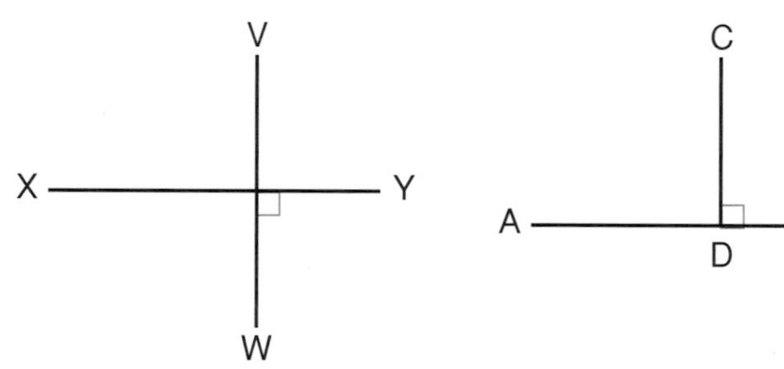

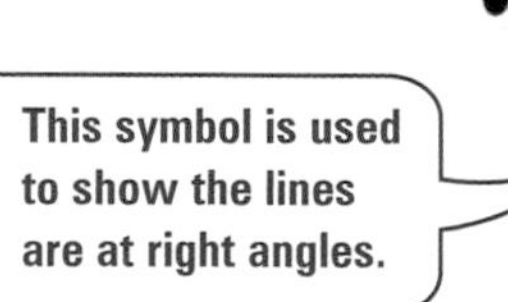

This symbol is used to show the lines are at right angles.

Exercise 4

T **1** Use a copy of these.
Mark the parallel lines with arrows.
Mark the perpendicular lines with ⊾.

a

rugby posts

b

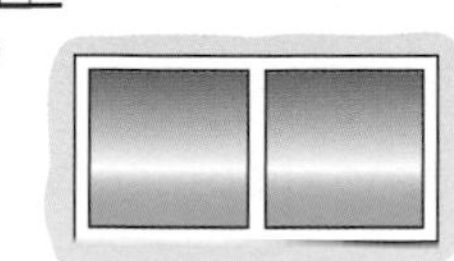

window

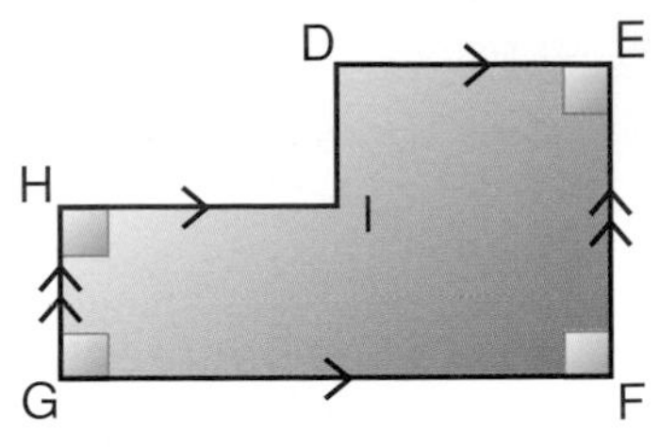

2 **a** Name the pairs of parallel lines.
b Name the pairs of perpendicular lines.

3  This is a drawing of a cuboid.

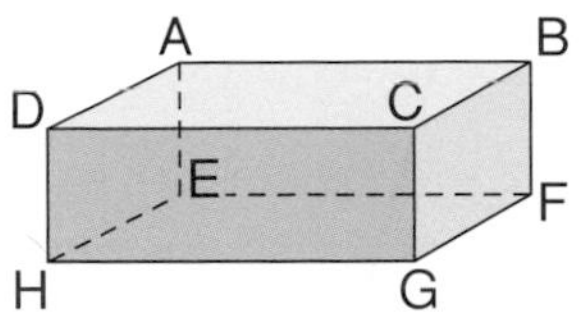

There is more about drawing 3-D shapes on page 255.

a Which edges are parallel to AB?
b Which edges are perpendicular to DH?

Practical

You will need paper and a stapler.

Make sure the edges don't move as you staple.

To make your own set square, follow these steps.

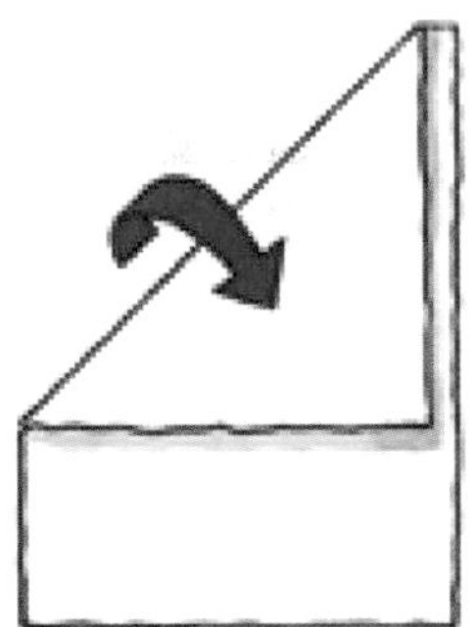

Fold one corner of the paper over to make a straight edge.

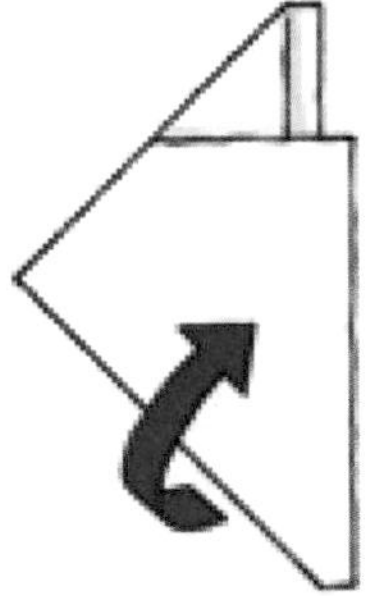

Fold the paper again so that half of the straight edge is *exactly* on top of the other half.

Staple the paper through all thicknesses.

Discussion

- How can you use your set square to find which of these lines are perpendicular? **Discuss.**

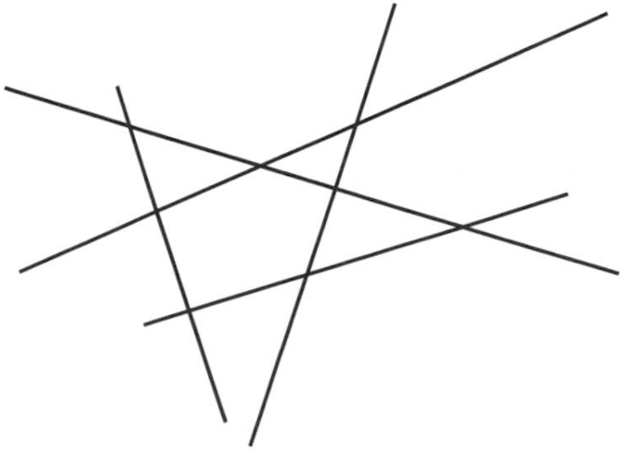

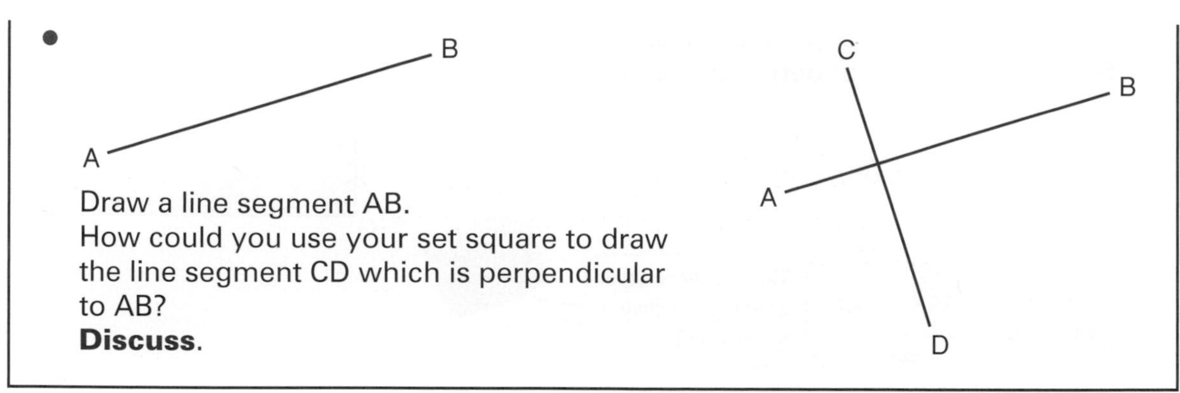

- Draw a line segment AB.
  How could you use your set square to draw the line segment CD which is perpendicular to AB?
  Discuss.

These diagrams show how to draw two parallel lines using a ruler and set square.

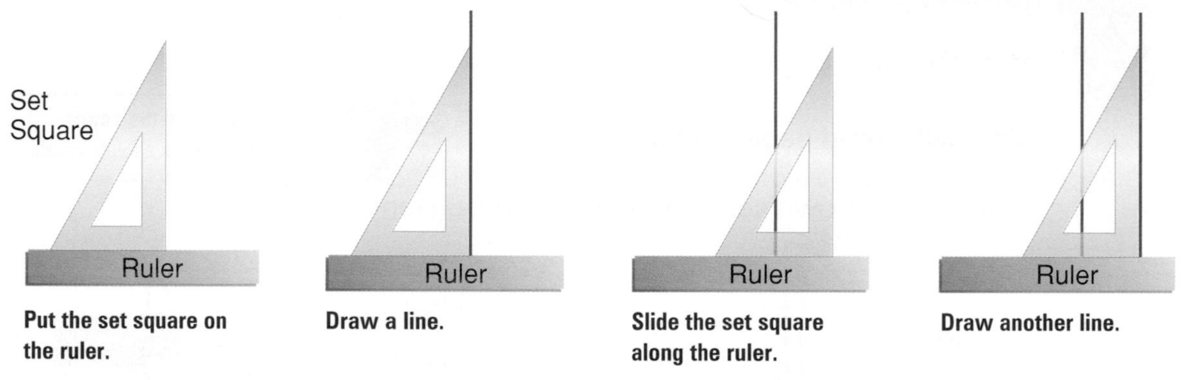

Put the set square on the ruler. **Draw a line.** **Slide the set square along the ruler.** **Draw another line.**

Discussion

The diagrams below show how to draw a line through a point C that is parallel to the line AB.

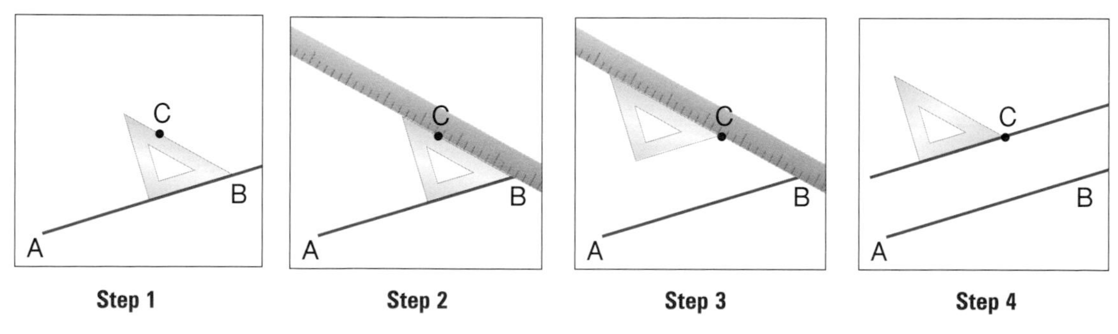

Step 1 **Step 2** **Step 3** **Step 4**

Discuss these steps.

Hint: in Step 3, the set square slides along the ruler.

Exercise 5

1 **a** Draw a line segment, AB.
b Mark a point, D, anywhere on the line segment.
c Use your set square to draw a line through D that is perpendicular to AB.

2 **a** Draw a line segment, CD.
b Mark a point, E, above the line.
c Use your set square to draw a line through E that is perpendicular to CD.

3 **a** Draw a line segment, PQ.

b Mark a point, R, below the line segment.

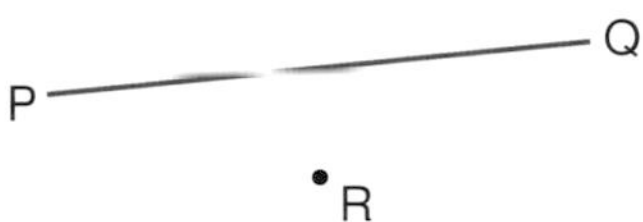

c Use your set square to draw a line through R that is perpendicular to PQ.

4 Draw a line segment GH.
Using your set square and ruler, draw a line that is parallel to GH.

5 **a** Draw a line segment PQ.
b Mark a point, S, above PQ.
c Use your set square and ruler to draw a line through S that is parallel to PQ.

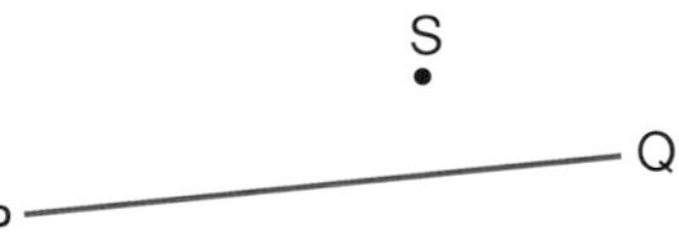

Practical

A new village is to be built.

Design a street plan for the village using parallel and perpendicular lines.

Give your village a name.

Calculating angles

T

Practical

You will need acetate sheets.

You could use a dynamic geometry package.

Draw a line segment AB. A———B

Draw another line segment CD on a separate sheet of acetate.

Lay it on top of the first piece so the lines cross.

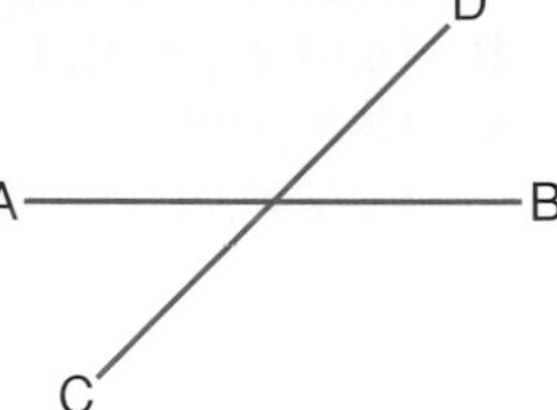

Move the line segment CD in a circle. Make sure that the lines still cross.

What can you find out about the size of the marked angles in each diagram below?

Which ones are equal?

Which ones add to 180°?

Which ones add to 360°?

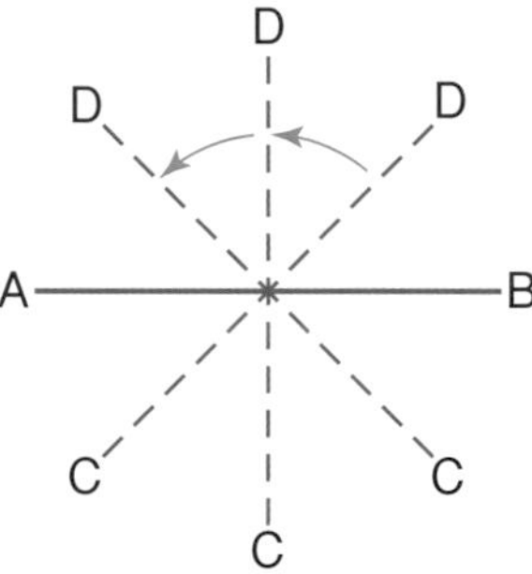

a

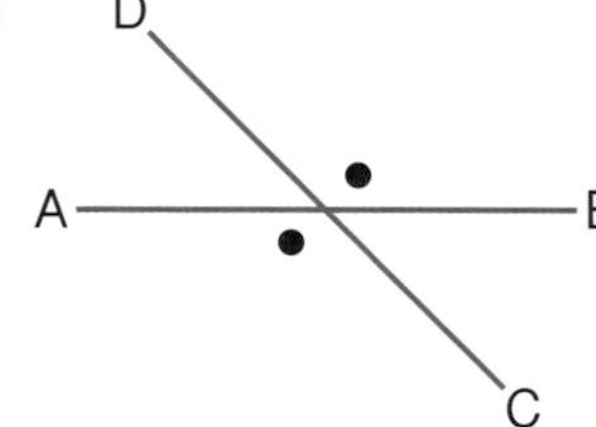

b

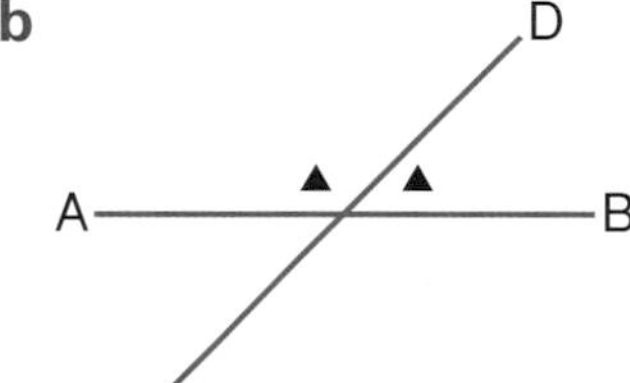

c

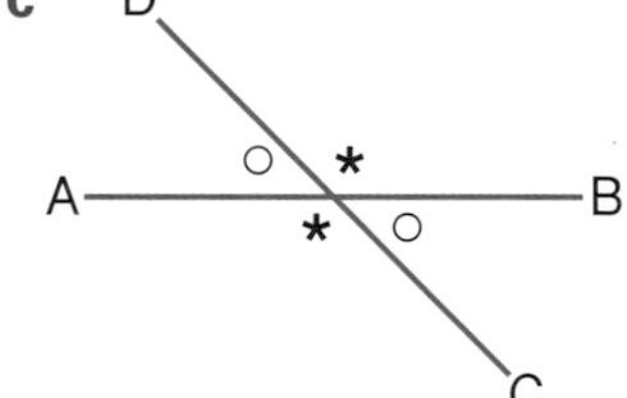

Remember

a and *b* are called **vertically opposite angles.**
They are opposite each other when two lines cross.
Vertically opposite angles are equal.

$a = b$
$c = d$

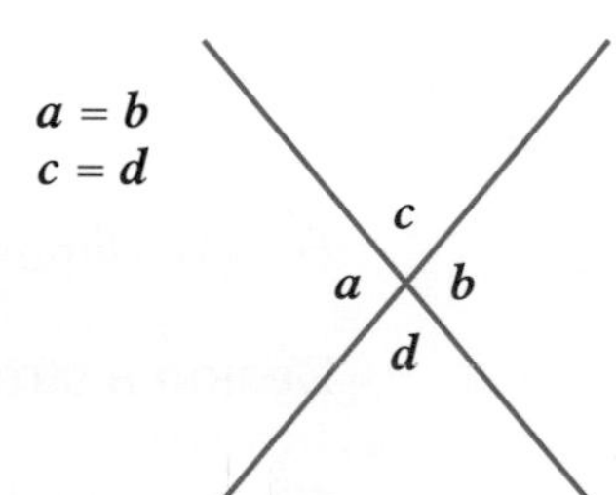

Examples

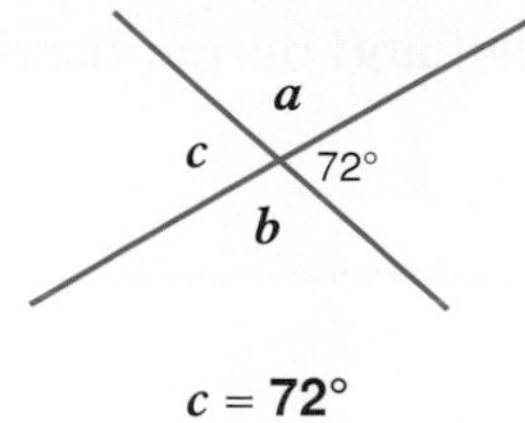

$c = $ **72°**

x 140°
a 40°

$a = $ **140°**
$x = $ **40°**

Remember

a, b, c and d are called **angles at a point**.
Together, a, b, c and d make a complete turn.
Angles at a point add to 360°.

$a + b + c + d =$ **360°**

Worked Example

Find the size of angle x.

a

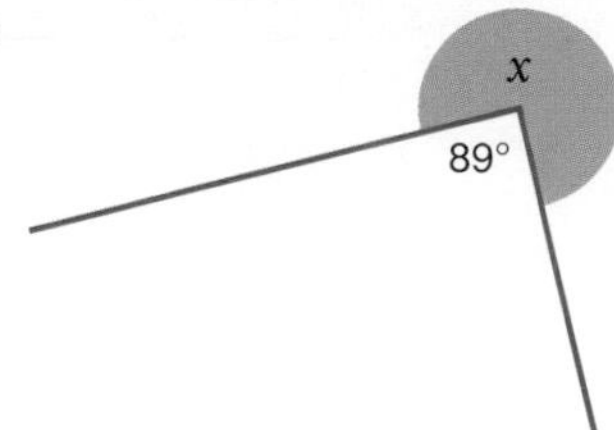

b

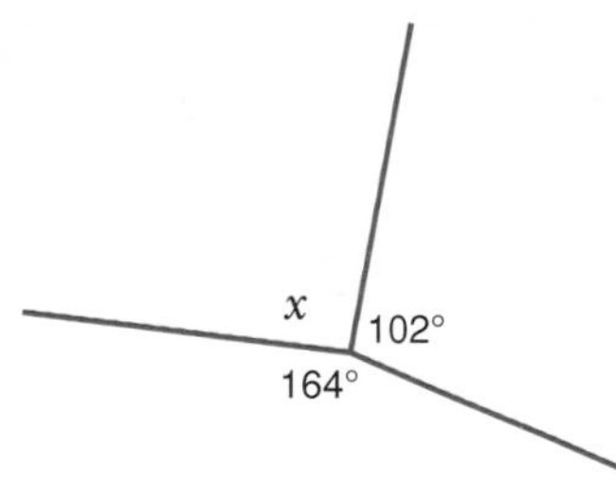

Answer

a $x = 360° - 89°$
$= \mathbf{271°}$

b $x = 360° - 102° - 164°$
$= \mathbf{94°}$

Exercise 6

1 Find the size of the angle marked with a letter.

a

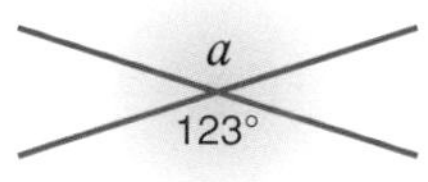

b

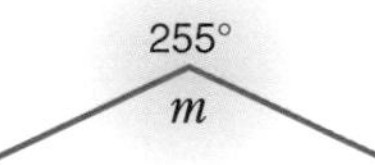

c

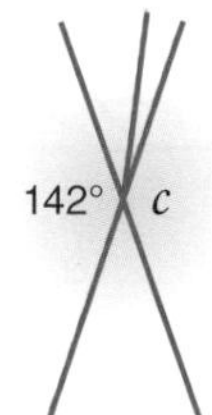

d

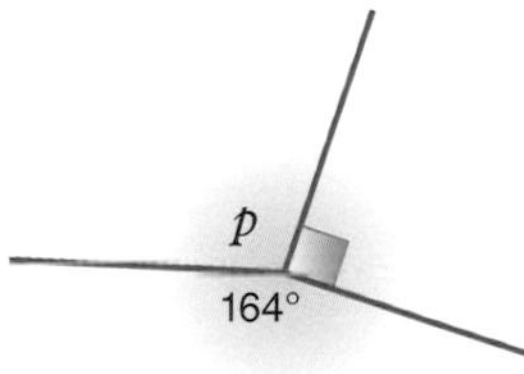

e

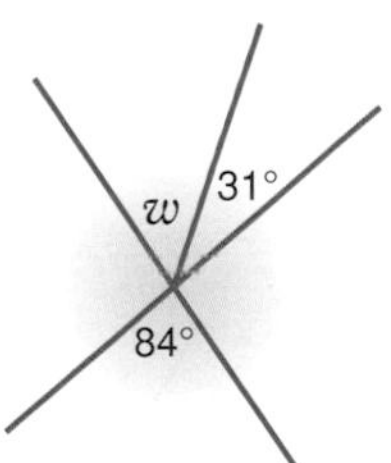

f

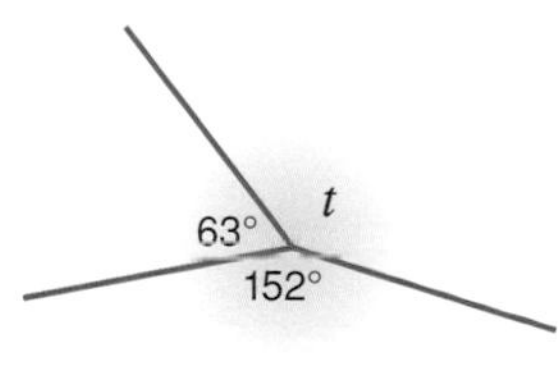

***g**

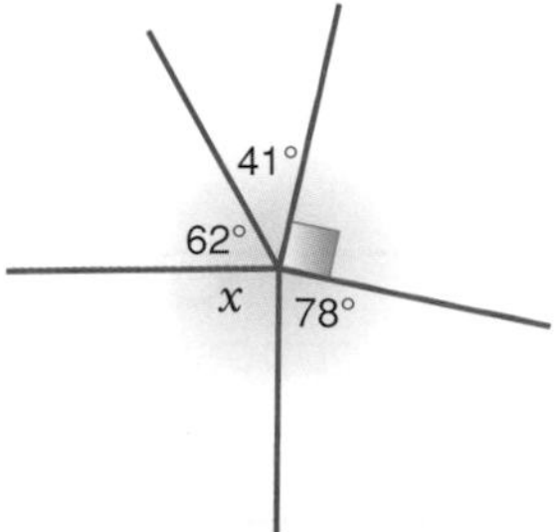

***h**

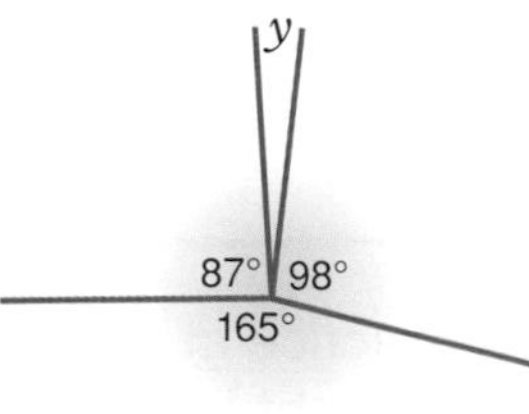

Remember
Angles on a straight line add to 180°

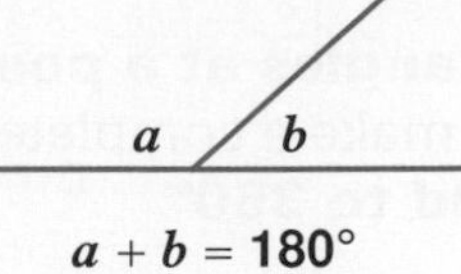

$a + b = 180°$

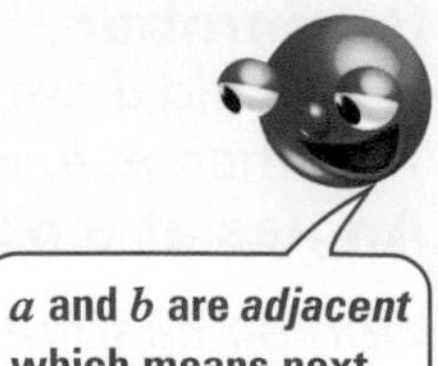

a and b are adjacent which means next to one another.

Worked Example
Find the size of angle a.

a

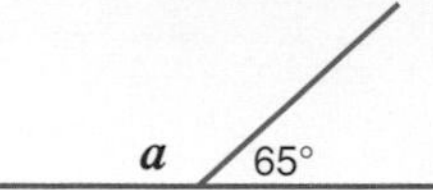

b

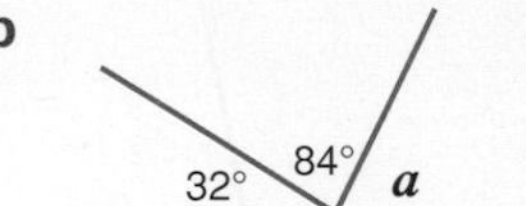

Answer

a $a = 180° - 65°$
$= \mathbf{115°}$

b $a = 180° - 84° - 32°$
$= \mathbf{64°}$

Exercise 7

1 Find the size of the unknown angle.

a

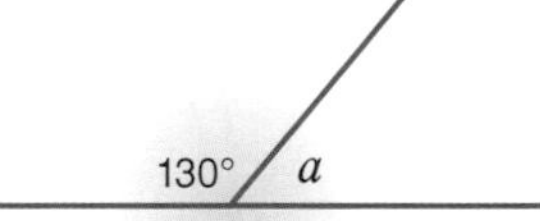

b

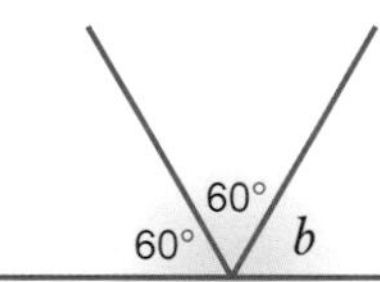

c

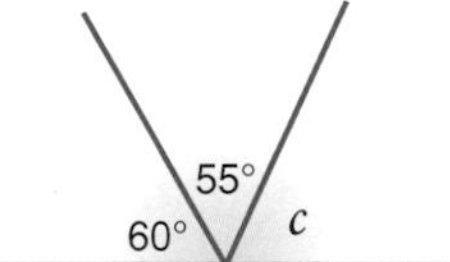

d

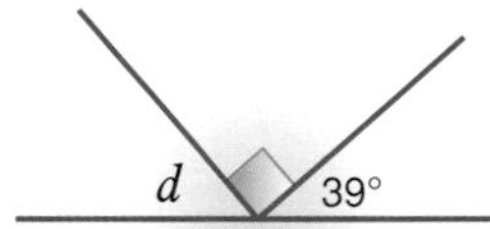

***e**

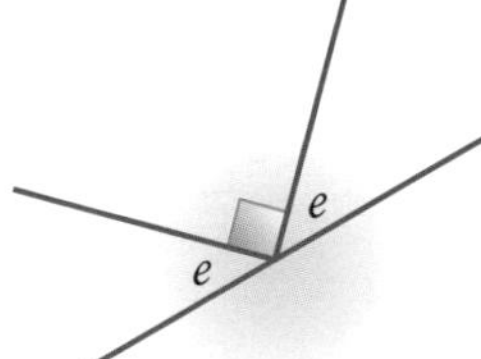

***f**

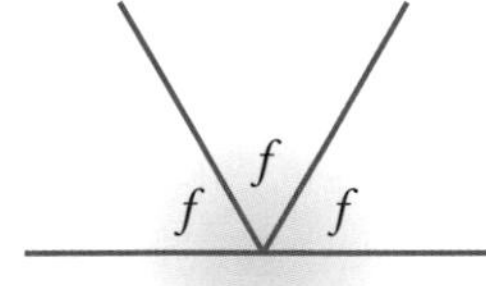

The following exercise gives you practice at calculating vertically opposite angles, angles at a point and angles on a straight line.

Exercise 8

T **1**

				H					
___	___	___	___	___	___	___	___		
110°	114°	118°	68°	140°	165°	47°	64°		

								H
___	___	___	___	___		___	___	___	___
64°	118°	61°	61°	68°		145°	165°	65°	140°

___	___	___		___	___	___		___	___	___	___
114°	47°	61°		61°	33°	61°		114°	68°	61°	47°

Use a copy of this box.
Calculate the shaded angles.
Put the letter that is beside each diagram above its answer.

H

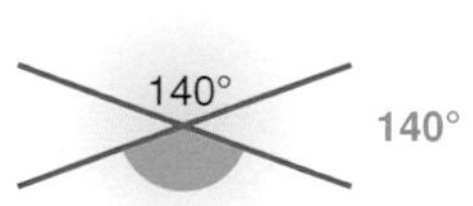

W

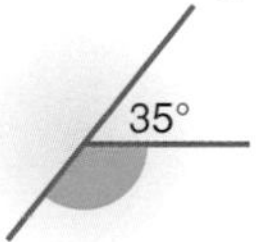

I

105°

T

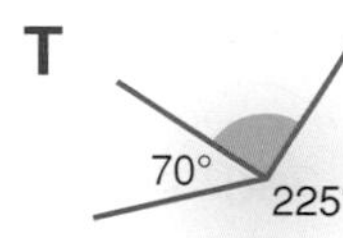

D

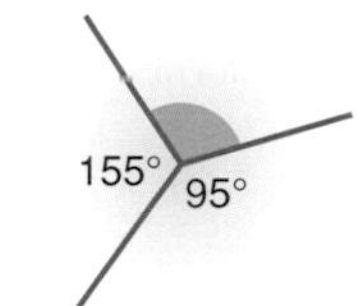

Y

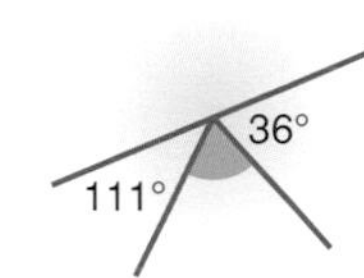

S

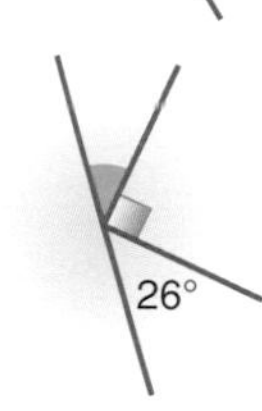

O

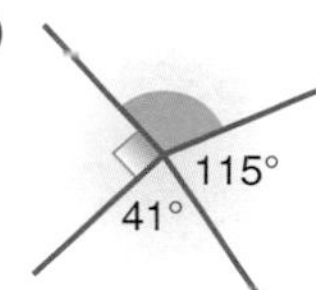

N

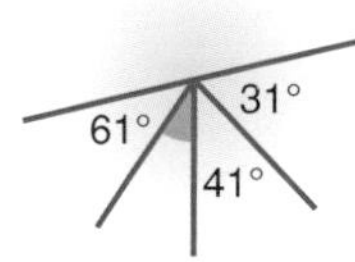

L

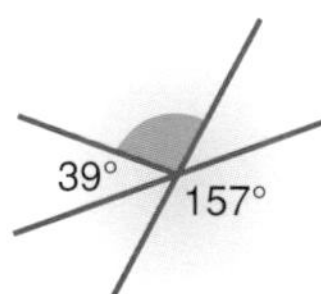

E

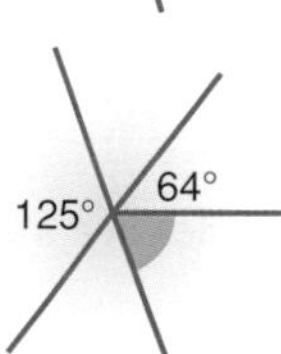

P

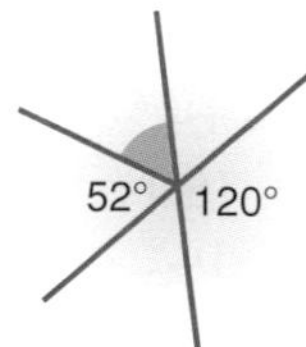

Angles in triangles

Remember
The three angles of a triangle add to 180°.

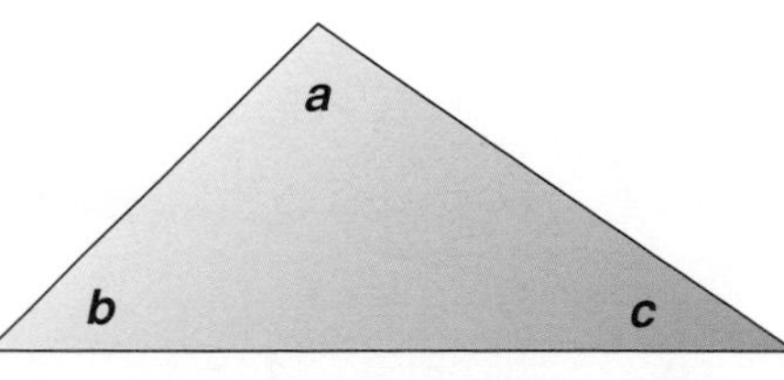

$a + b + c = 180°$

An **isosceles triangle** has two equal sides and two equal angles.

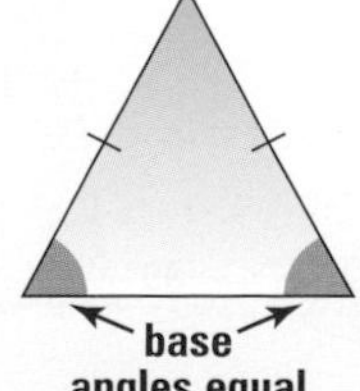

We mark equal sides with a dash.

Example

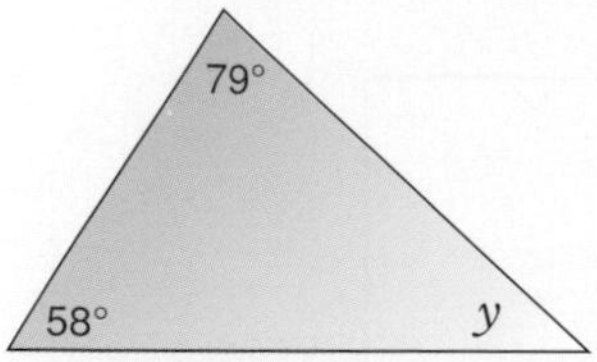
79°
58°
y

$y = 180° - 79° - 58°$ **angles in a triangle add to 180°**
$= \mathbf{43°}$

We always give a reason.

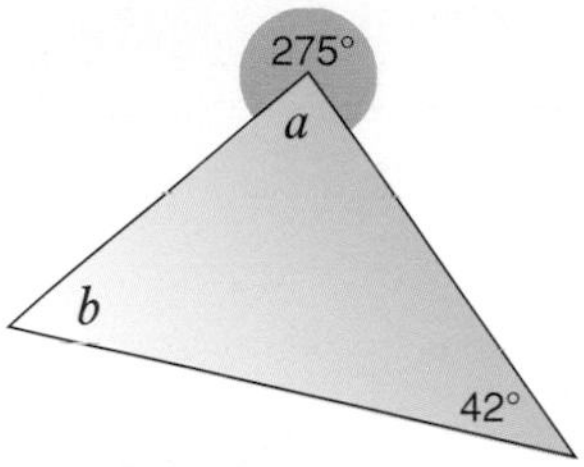
275°
a
b
42°

$a = 360° - 275°$ **angles at a point add to 360°**
$= \mathbf{85°}$

$b = 180° - 85° - 42°$ **angles in a triangle add to 180°**
$= \mathbf{53°}$

Worked Example
Find the size of n.

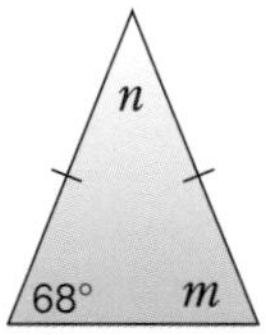
n
68°
m

Answer
m is one of the base angles of the isosceles triangle.
$m = 68°$
$n = 180° - 68° - 68°$ **angles in a triangle add to 180°**
$= \mathbf{44°}$

Exercise 9

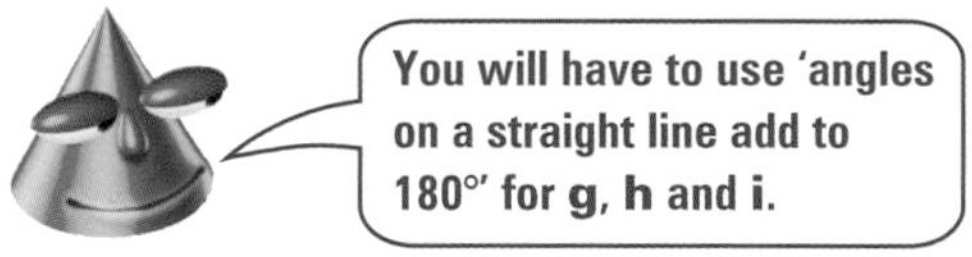
You will have to use 'angles on a straight line add to 180°' for g, h and i.

1 Find the size of x and y.

a
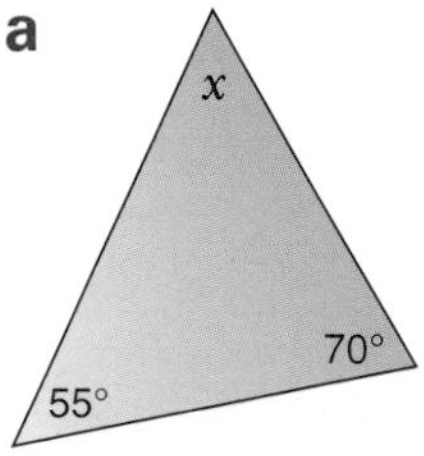
x
55°
70°

b
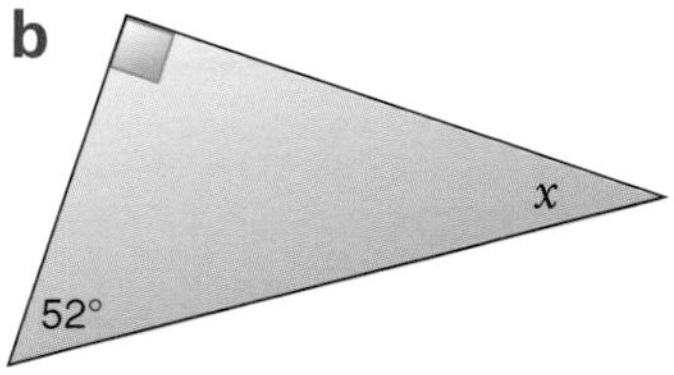
x
52°

c
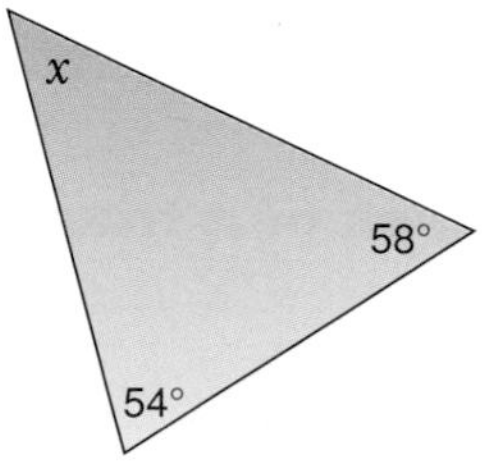
x
58°
54°

d
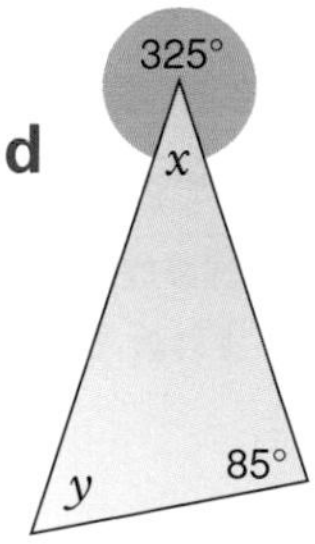
325°
x
y
85°

e
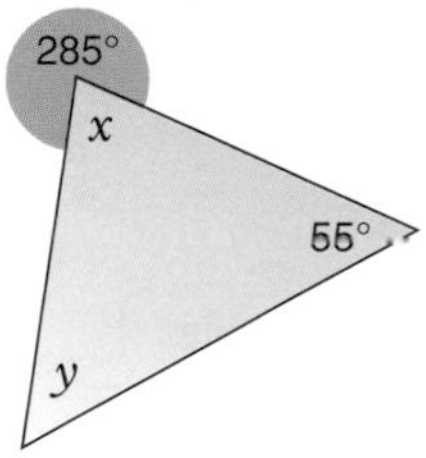
285°
x
55°
y

f
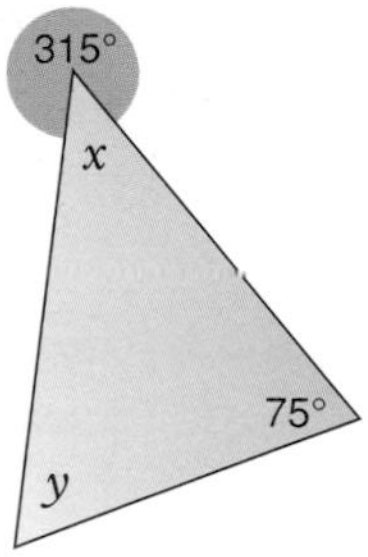
315°
x
75°
y

***g**
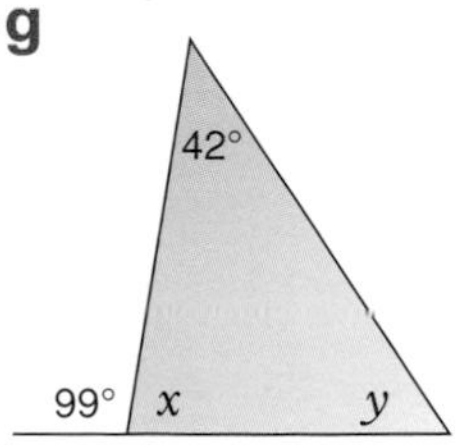
42°
99°
x
y

***h**
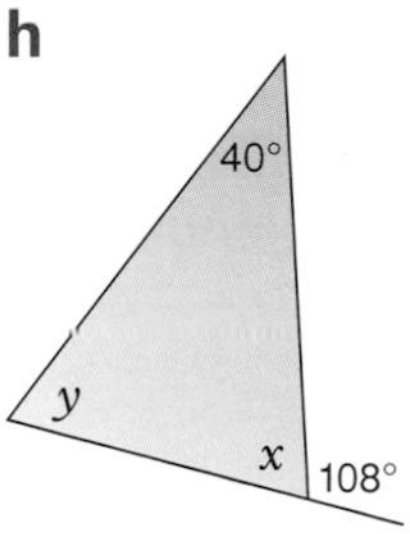
40°
y
x
108°

***i**
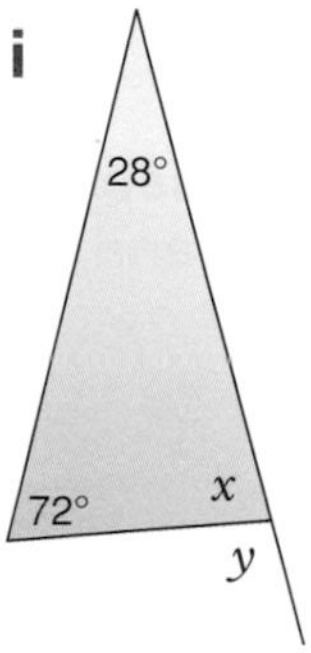
28°
72°
x
y

2 Find the size of a.

a

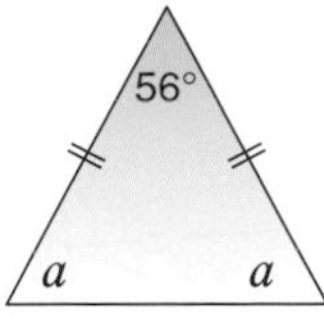

b

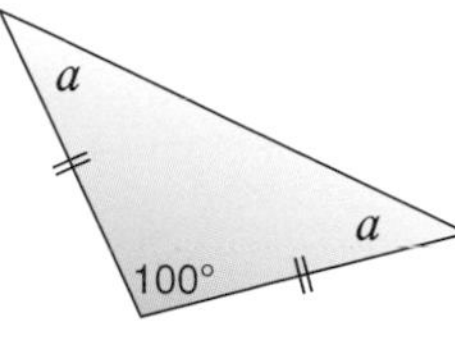

c

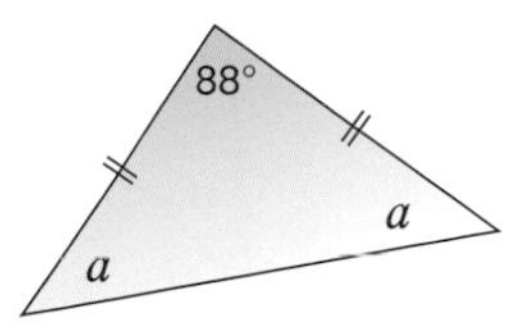

d

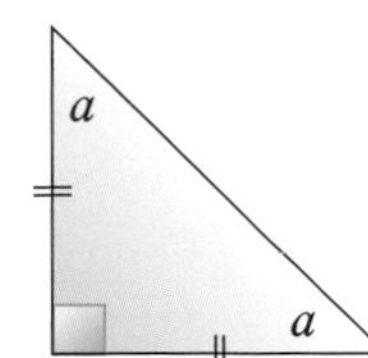

e

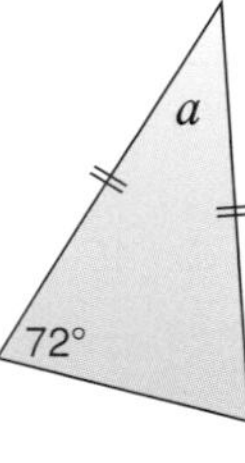

f

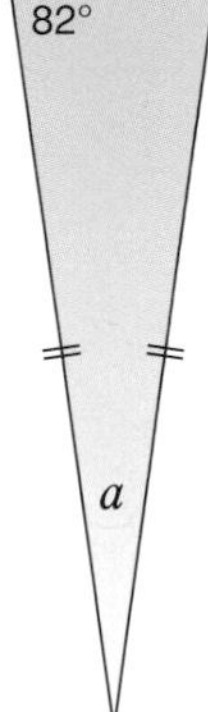

g

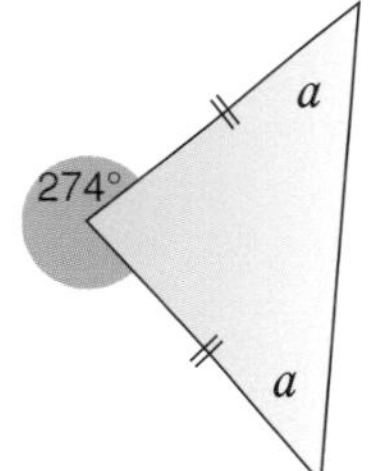

h

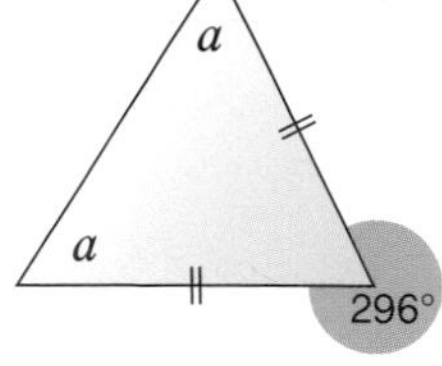

***3** Find the size of x, y and z.

a

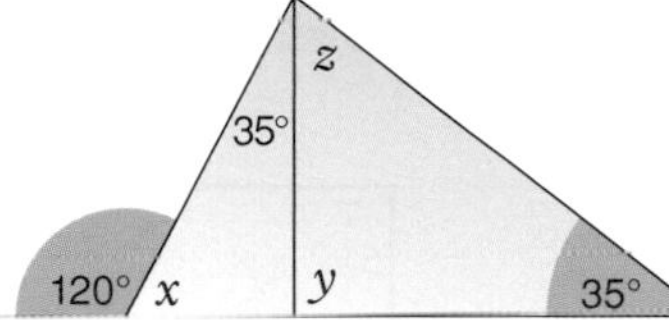

b

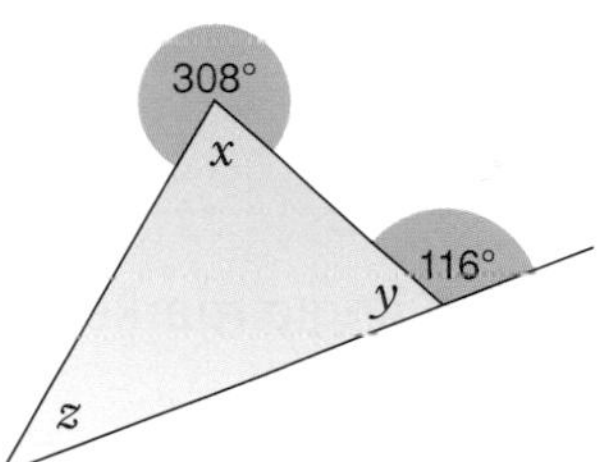

The next exercise gives you practice at calculating unknown angles.

Exercise 10

T

1 Use a copy of this.
Find the size of each unknown angle.
Use these to fill in the crossnumber.

Across	**Down**
1 c	**1** h
2 d	**3** e
5 g	**4** f
8 b	**6** a
9 i	**7** j

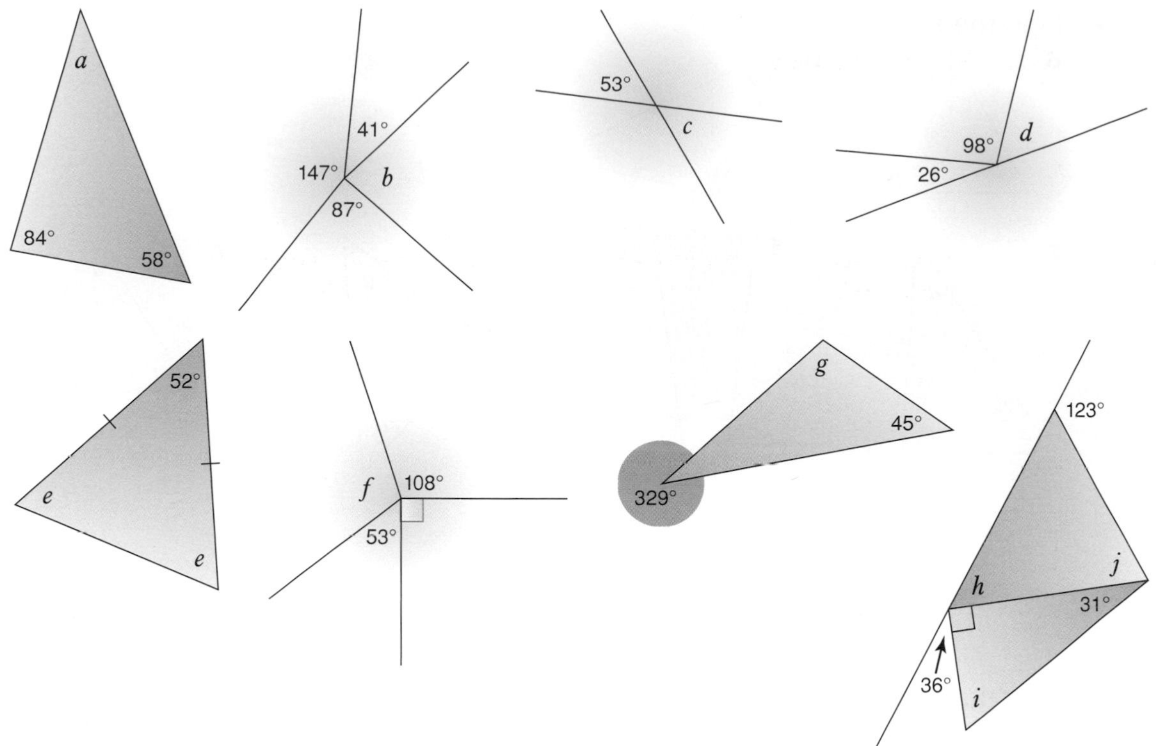

T

*2 Use a copy of this.
   a Find the size of each angle marked with a letter on the diagram.
   b If the size of the angle is less than 60°, shade the triangle with that angle.
   c What can you say about all the shaded triangles?

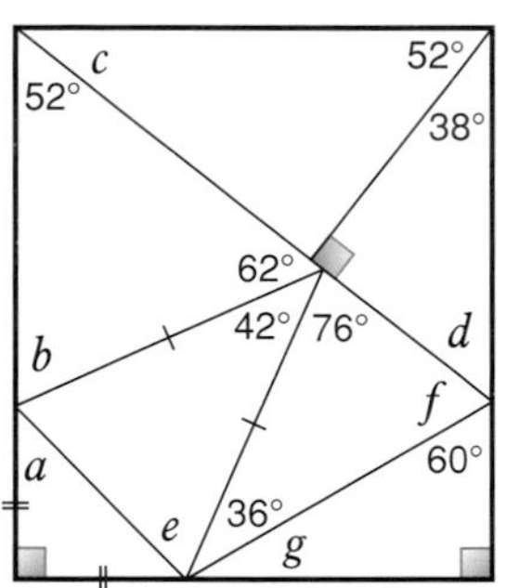

Summary of key points

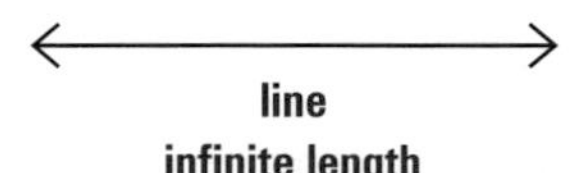

P **line segment** Q

We **name this angle**

1 using the letter at the vertex, ∠Q

or

2 using three letters.
The middle letter is at the vertex,
∠PQR or ∠RQP **or** $\hat{PQR}$ or $\hat{RQP}$

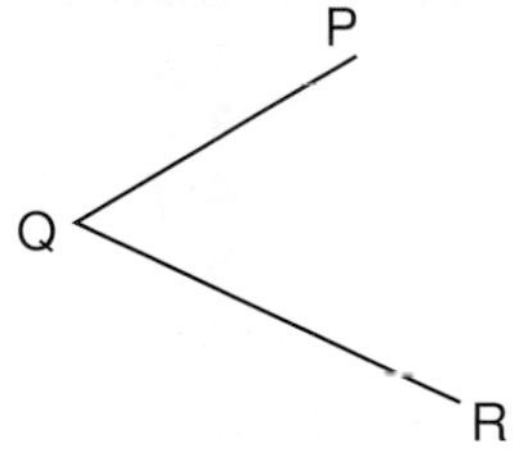

Special angles

one complete turn or 360°

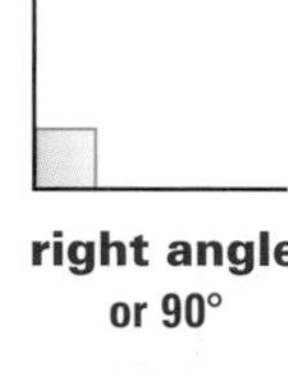

right angle or 90°

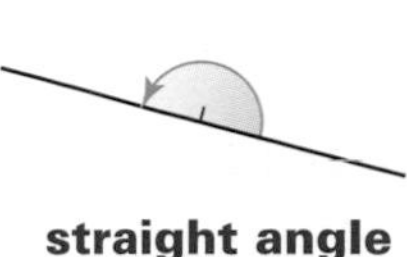

straight angle or 180°

acute angle less than 90°

obtuse angle between 90° and 180°

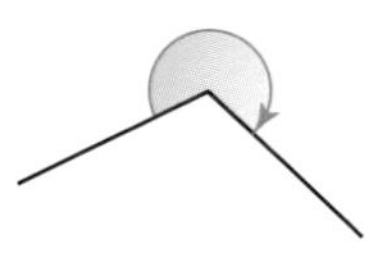

reflex angle between 180° and 360°

We **measure and draw angles** using a **protractor**.

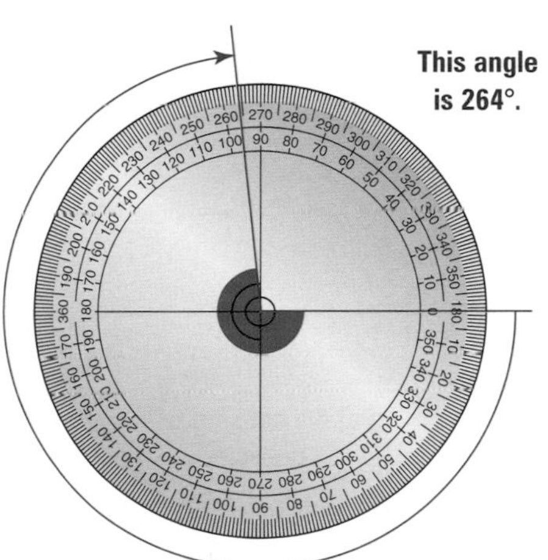

It is best to measure and draw reflex angles using a 360° protractor.

To measure a reflex angle with a 180° protractor

1 measure the acute or obtuse angle

2 subtract it from 360°.

Example Obtuse angle = 140°

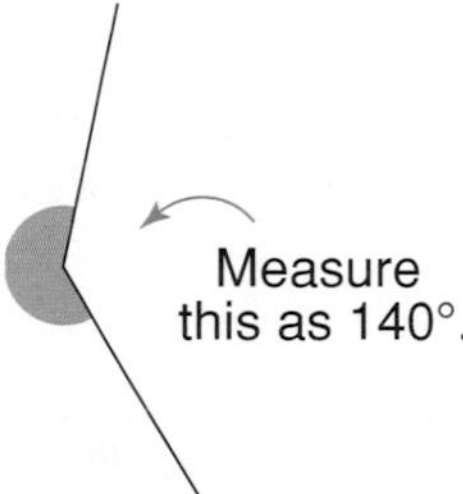

Reflex angle = 360° − 140°

= 220°

Always **estimate** the size of the angle first.

Do this by comparing the acute or obtuse angle to a right angle.

Parallel lines never meet.
We show parallel lines with arrows.
AB is parallel to CD.

Perpendicular lines cross at right angles.
MN is perpendicular to PQ.

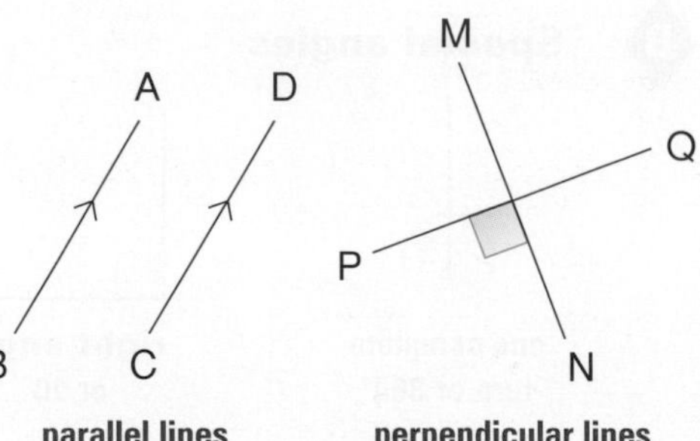

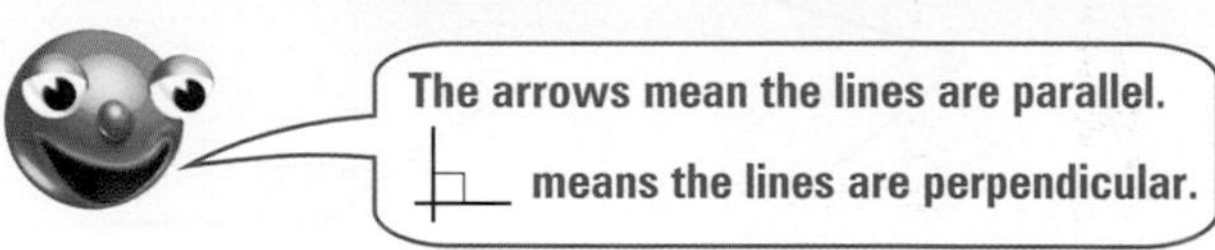

The arrows mean the lines are parallel.
means the lines are perpendicular.

Parallel and perpendicular lines can be drawn using a **ruler and set square**.

Example These diagrams show how to draw parallel lines.

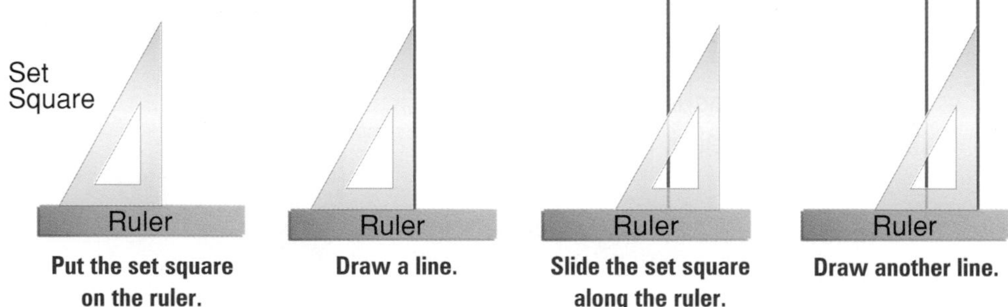

Put the set square on the ruler. **Draw a line.** **Slide the set square along the ruler.** **Draw another line.**

Calculating angles

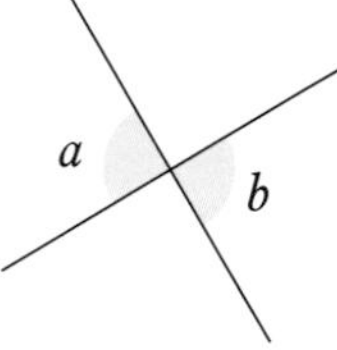

$a = b$
Vertically opposite angles are equal.

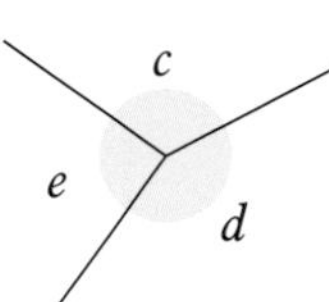

$c + d + e = \mathbf{360°}$
Angles at a point add to 360°.

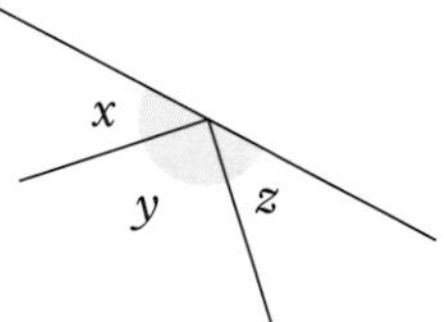

$x + y + z = \mathbf{180°}$
Angles on a straight line add to 180°.

The angles of a triangle add to 180°.

Example $m = 180° - 55° - 60°$
$= 65°$

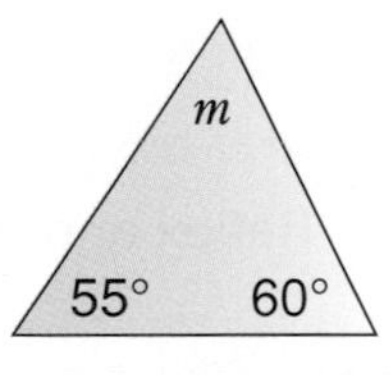

$m + 55° + 60° = 180°$

Test yourself

1 a Use a single letter to name these angles. 

i

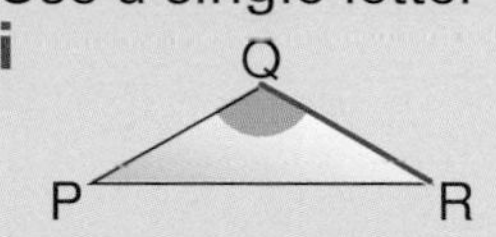

ii

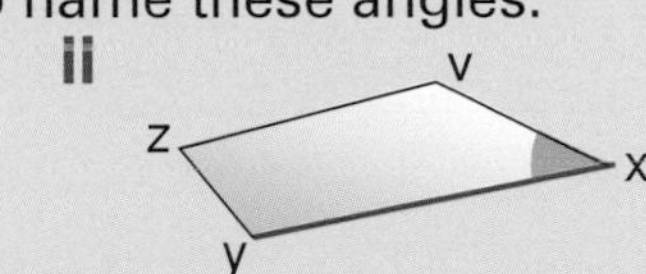

b Name the red line segments in the above diagrams.

c Name each marked angle as acute, obtuse or reflex.

2 Name the shaded angles. 

a

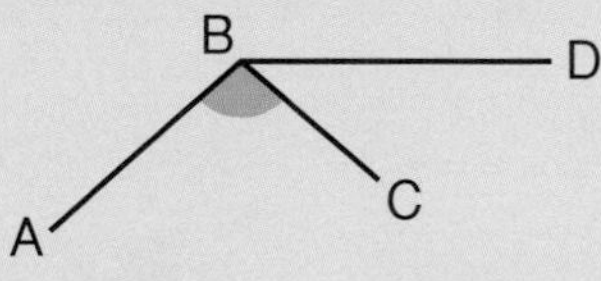

b

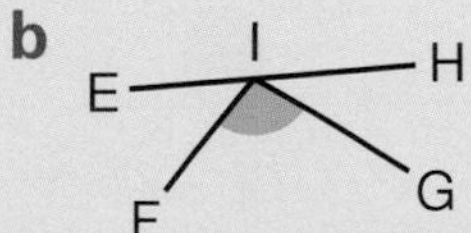

3 Sketch a shape which has 2 acute, 2 obtuse and 1 reflex angle. 

4 Jake started at the shop and walked to the pond to fish.
Measure the size of the red, green and blue reflex angles.

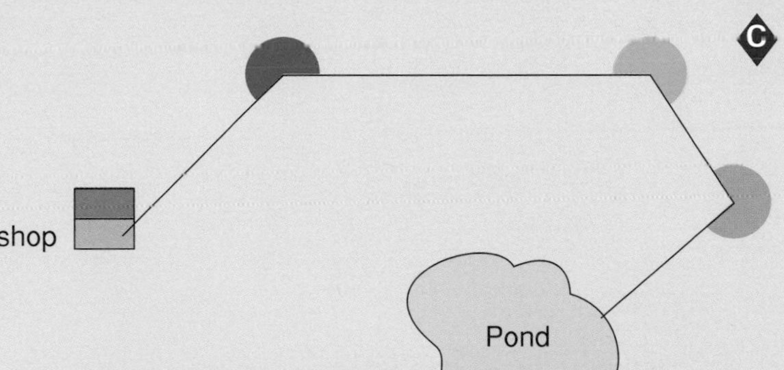

5 a Name the parallel lines in this shape. 

b Name the perpendicular lines.

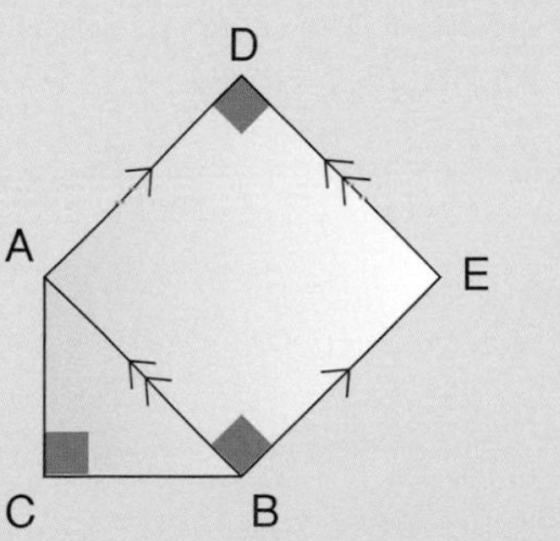

6 Use a copy of this diagram. 
Use your ruler and set square to draw

a a line through C that is perpendicular to AB

b a line through D that is parallel to AB.

What shape have you drawn?

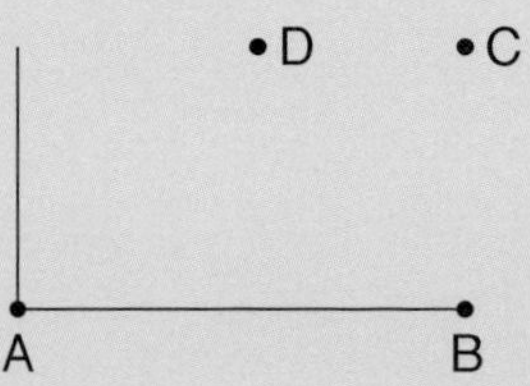

7 Find the size of x and y.

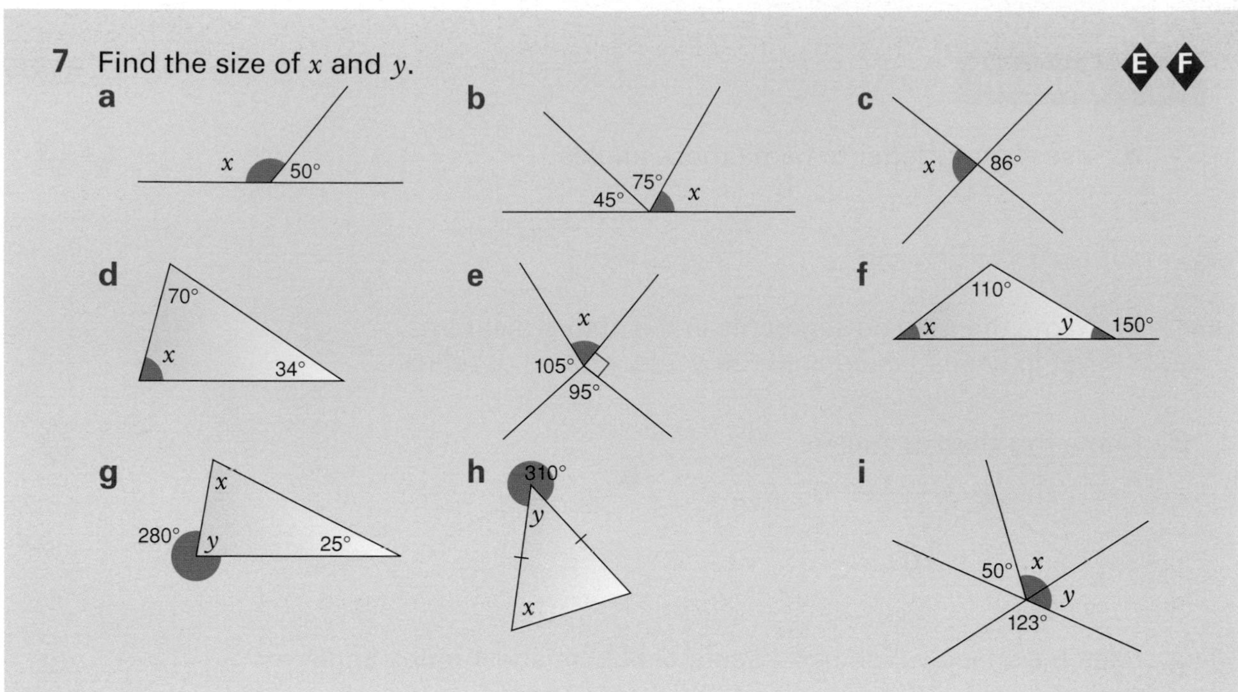

12 Shape and Construction

You need to know

Key vocabulary

adjacent, base (of solid), congruence, construct, diagonal, edge, face, isometric, mid-point, opposite, parallel, measure, net, tessellation

polygon: hexagon, pentagon, octagon

quadrilateral: arrowhead, delta, kite, parallelogram, rectangle, rhombus, square, trapezium

regular, shape, side

solid (3-D): cube, cuboid, pyramid, square-based pyramid, tetrahedron, three-dimensional (3-D)

symmetry: line of symmetry, order of rotation symmetry, reflection symmetry, rotation symmetry

triangle: equilateral, isosceles, right-angled, scalene

two-dimensional (2-D), vertex, vertices

T

Piecing it together

Ask your teacher for a set of tangram pieces or a large copy of this diagram.

Cut your diagram into 7 pieces.
Use all of your 7 tangram pieces to make these shapes.

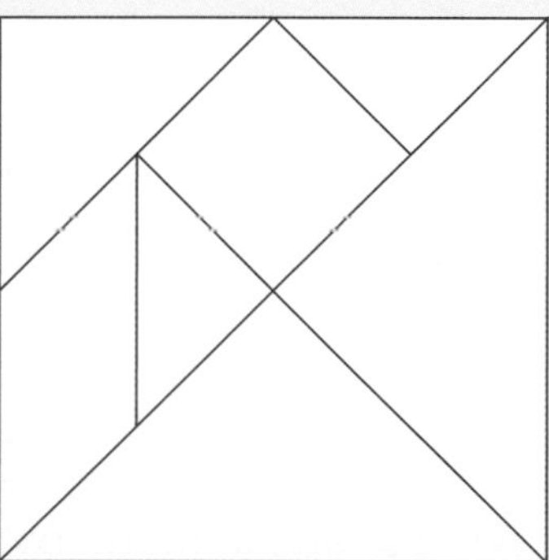

Visualising and sketching 2-D shapes

Practical

You will need a partner.
Describe a shape to your partner.
Can your partner name your shape?
Swap and get your partner to describe a shape to you.
What made it easy for you to name the shape?

Discussion

How might Max and Simone have got their shapes?

Any other shapes possible? **Discuss**.

Exercise 1

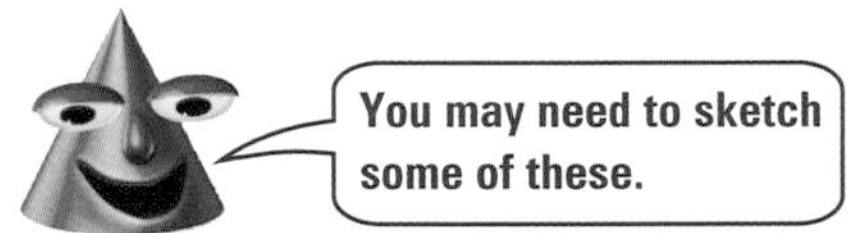

1 Imagine a square with both diagonals drawn on.
Remove one of the small triangles.
What shape is left?

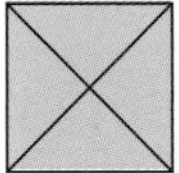

2 Imagine a regular hexagon.
Join the middle of one side to the middle of the next side.
Do this all the way round.
What shape is made by the new lines?

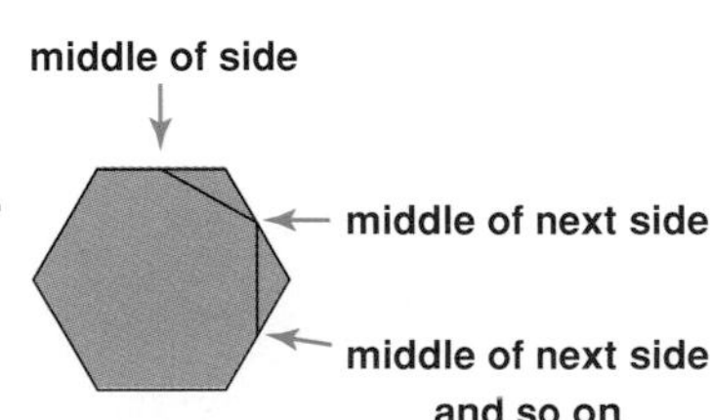

3 Imagine a rectangle with one corner cut off.
Describe the shape that you have left.

4 Imagine an equilateral triangle.
Fold it along one of its lines of symmetry.
What angles are in the folded shape? Explain your answer.

5 Imagine a square. Cut off all the corners.
What shape have you got left?
Is this the only possible shape?

6 Imagine a regular pentagon. Cut it into two pieces.
What shapes have you got?
Are these the only possible shapes?

Puzzle

1 Move two matchsticks to different places to make 5 equilateral triangles.

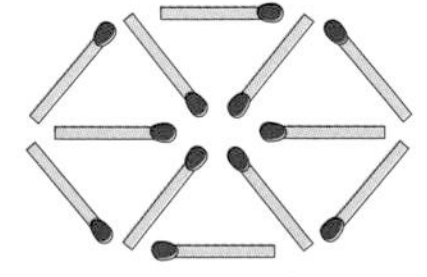

Remember:
An equilateral triangle has all sides equal.

2 Take away two matchsticks to leave 8 triangles.

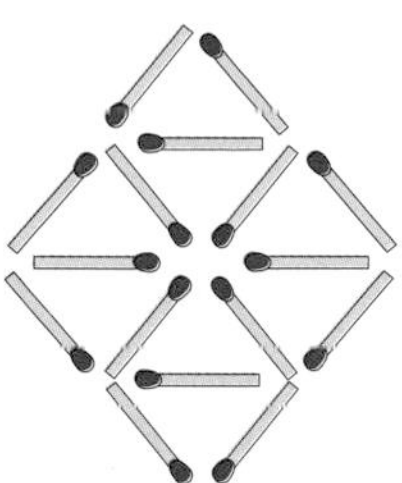

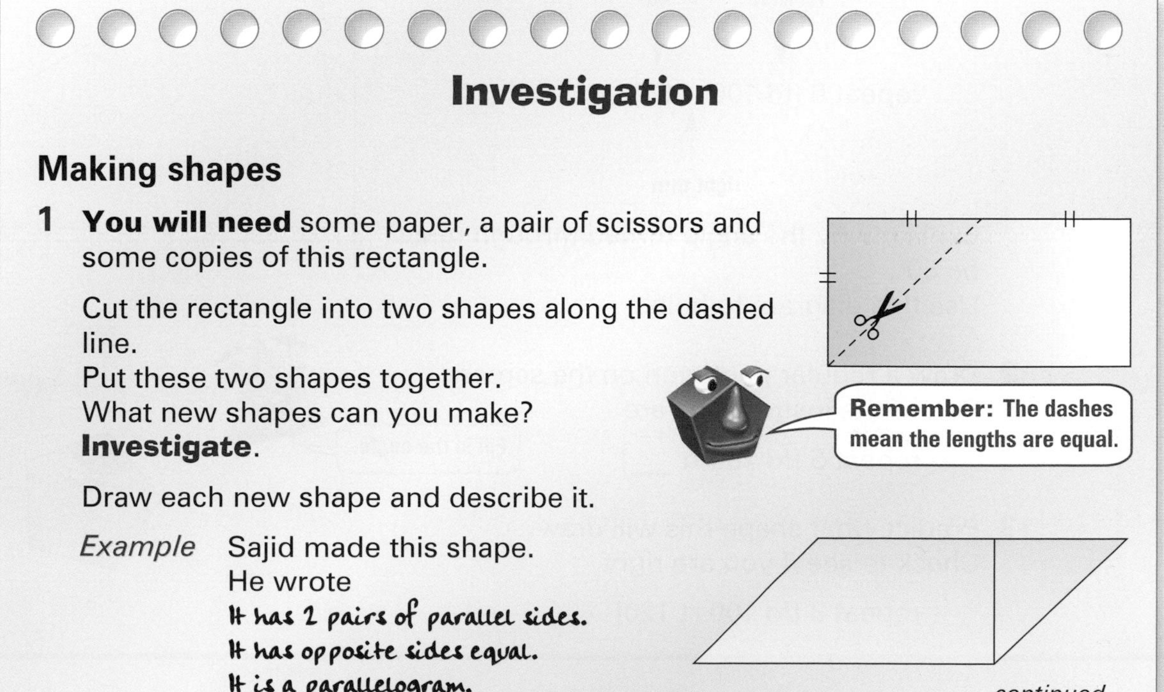

Investigation

Making shapes

1 **You will need** some paper, a pair of scissors and some copies of this rectangle.

Cut the rectangle into two shapes along the dashed line.
Put these two shapes together.
What new shapes can you make?
Investigate.

Remember: The dashes mean the lengths are equal.

Draw each new shape and describe it.

Example Sajid made this shape.
He wrote
It has 2 pairs of parallel sides.
It has opposite sides equal.
It is a parallelogram.

continued ...

*2 **You will need** two equal sized squares of acetate or tracing paper.

What shapes can you make by overlapping two squares? **Investigate**.

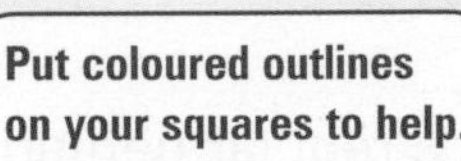

Put coloured outlines on your squares to help.

Example Rosemary made a quadrilateral and a pentagon.

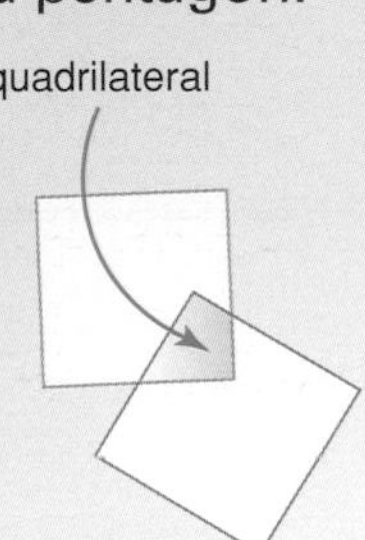

pentagon

*Which of these shapes cannot be made?
Explain why not.
rectangle, decagon, hexagon, kite, octagon, isosceles triangle, trapezium, rhombus

* Practical

You will need Logo.

1 This will draw a regular hexagon using Logo.

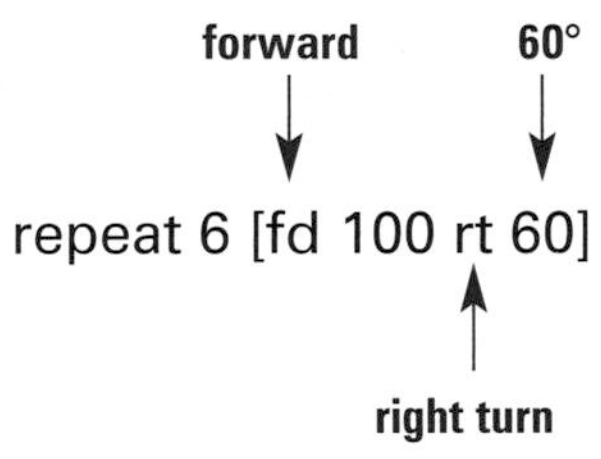

repeat 6 [fd 100 rt 60]
right turn

60°

120°

Explain why the angle turned through must be 60°.
Use this diagram to help.

2 Draw a regular pentagon on the screen.
Part of the instructions are

repeat 5 [fd 100 rt ___]

Fill in the angle.

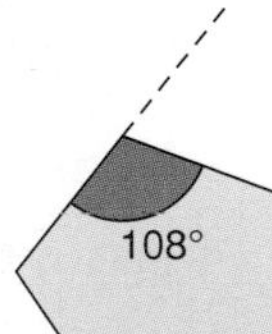

*3 Predict what shape this will draw.
Check to see if you are right.

repeat 3 [fd 100 rt 120]

Tessellations

Some shapes fit together with no gaps.
Sometimes we have to rotate or reflect the shape first.

Example This shape can be used to make a **tessellation**.

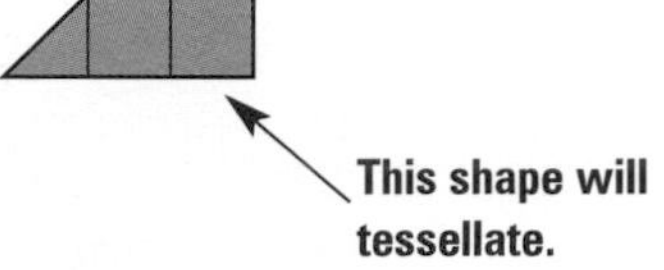
This shape will tessellate.

Exercise 2

T

1 Use a copy of this.
Garth started some tessellations.
Finish each for him.

a

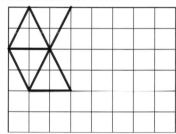

b

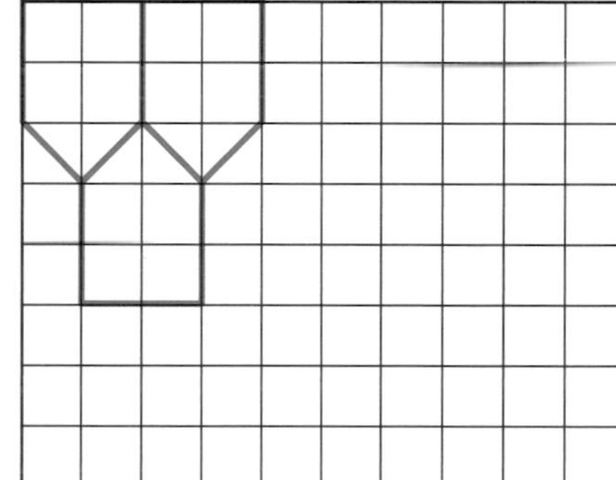

c

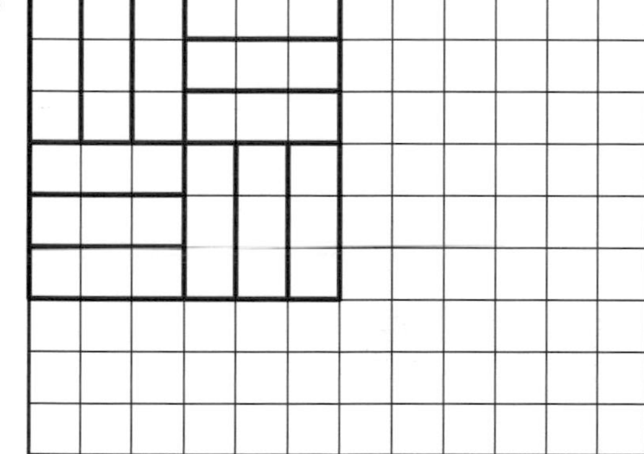

Congruence

Congruent shapes are exactly the same shape and size.
If two shapes are congruent, a tracing of one will fit exactly on top of the other.

Practical

You will need a copy of these shapes and some tracing paper.

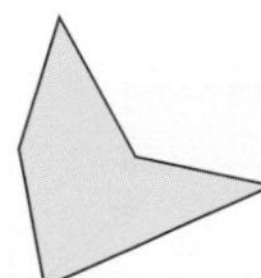 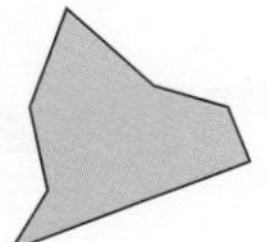 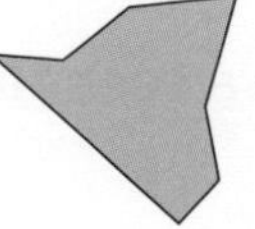 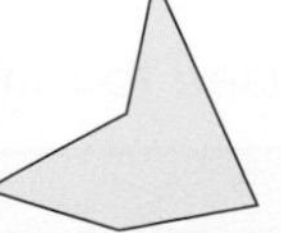  

Use tracing paper to find which of these shapes are congruent.

Exercise 3

1 Name all the shapes that are congruent to the red shape.

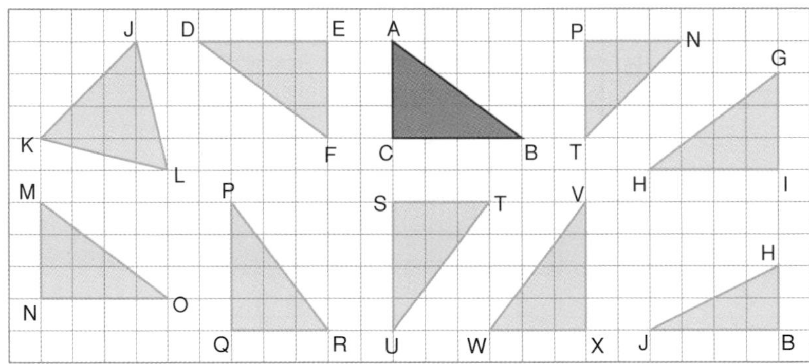

2 Name all the congruent shapes in this diagram.

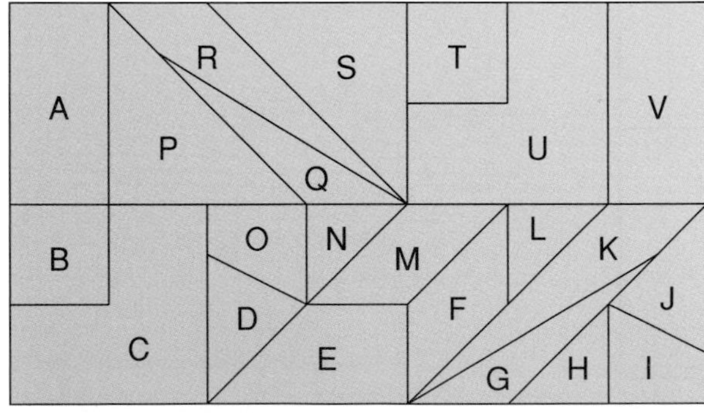

***3** Explain why these two shapes are not congruent.

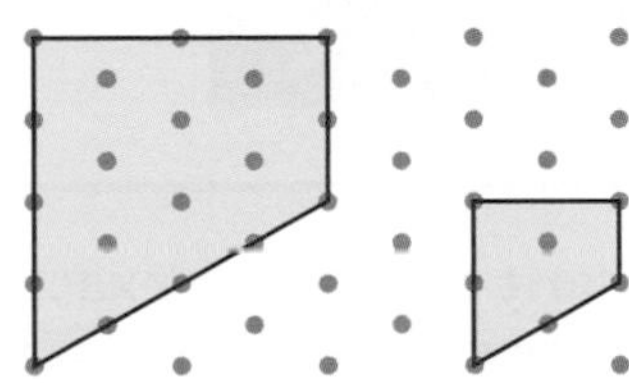

Constructing triangles

We can **construct triangles** using a **ruler** and **protractor**.

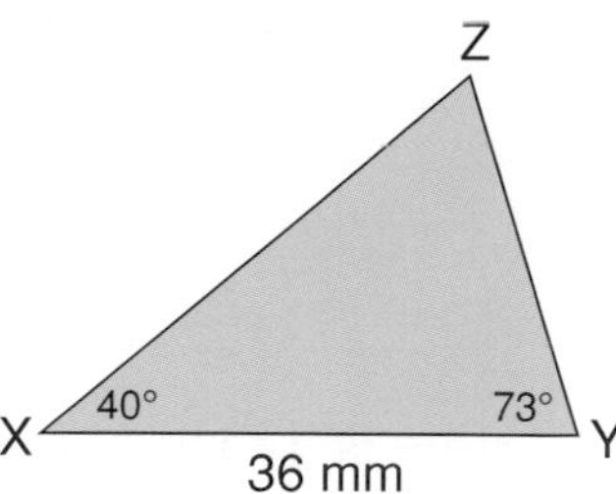

To construct this triangle follow the steps below.

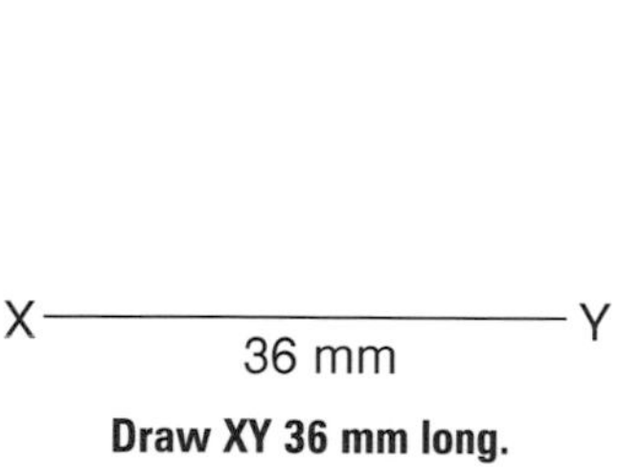

Draw XY 36 mm long.

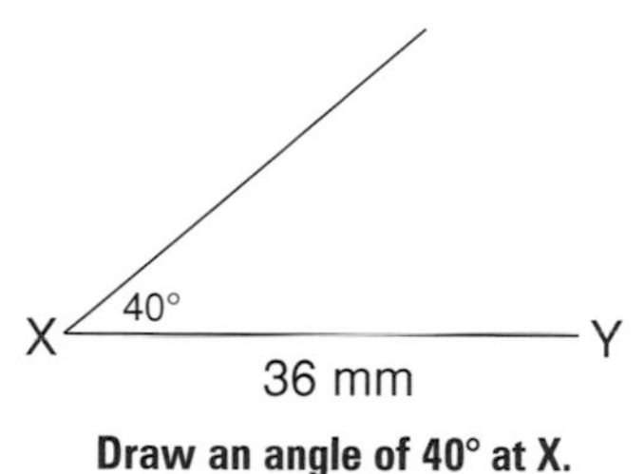

Draw an angle of 40° at X.
Use your protractor.

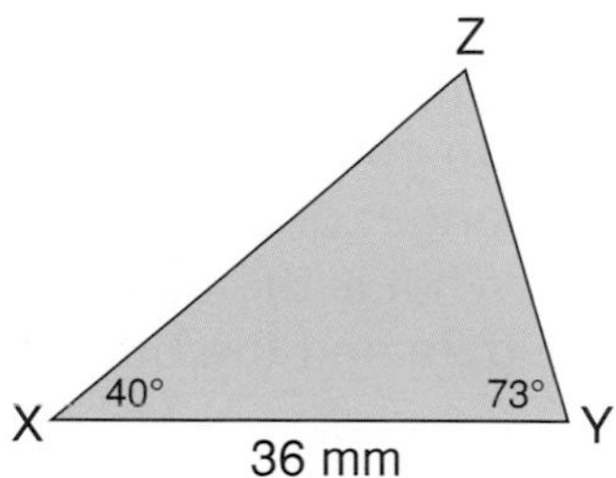

Draw an angle of 73° at Y.

Discussion

How could you construct triangle LMN?

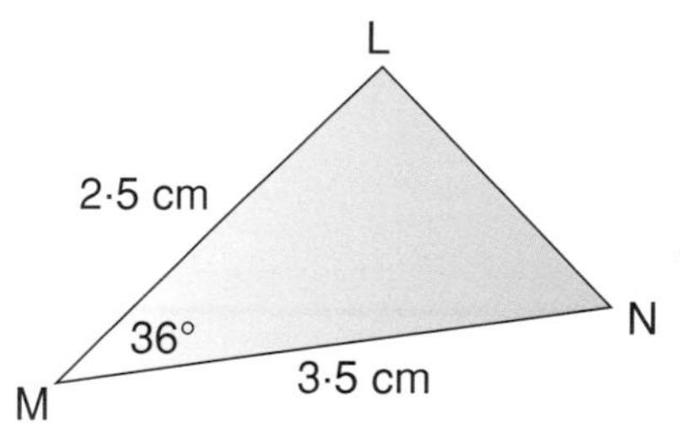

Exercise 4

1 Use your ruler and protractor to construct the sketched triangles.
On your triangle measure the size of angle B.

a

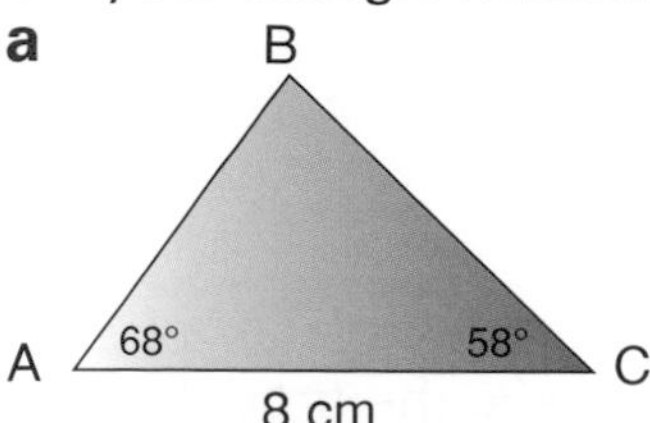

b

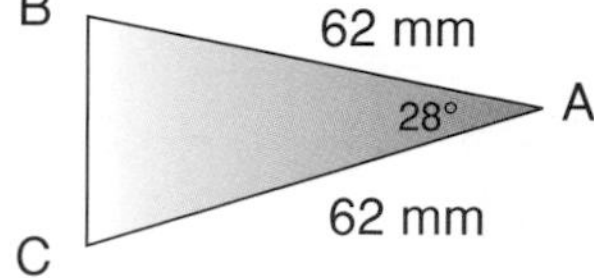

c

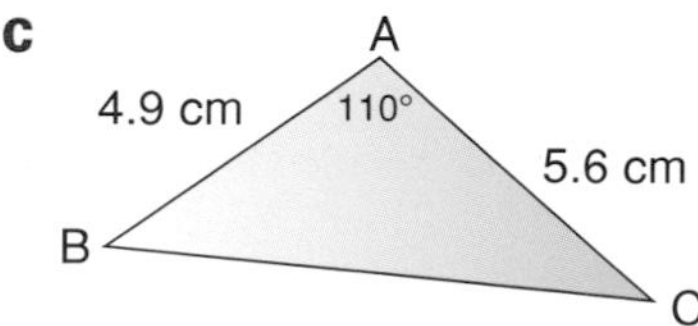

2 Construct triangle ABC.
Measure the size of the third angle in your triangle.
a CB = 74 mm, angle C = 60°, angle B = 50°
b AB = 68 mm, angle A = 72°, angle B = 39°

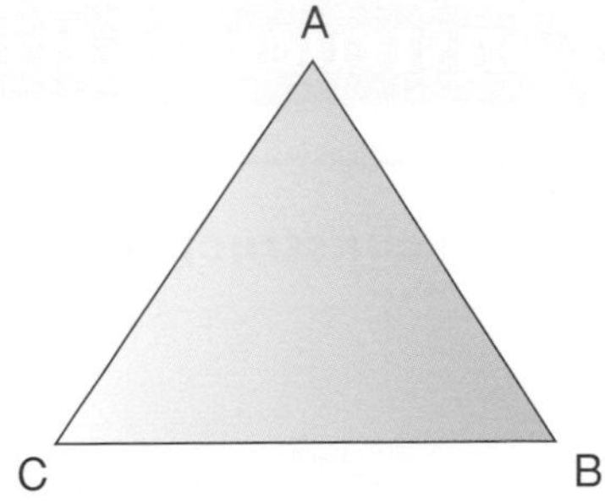

*__3__ Here is a plan of a pathway.
Construct the triangle.
Draw the 6 m line as 6 cm and the 8·7 m line as 8·7 cm.
On your triangle, measure the length of the third side.
What is the distance between the gate and the bus shelter?

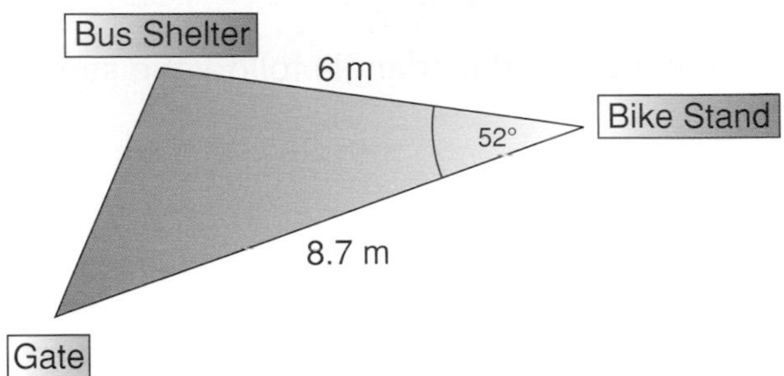

Describing and sketching 3-D shapes

Remember
3-D stands for **three-dimensional**
3-D shapes have length, width and height.

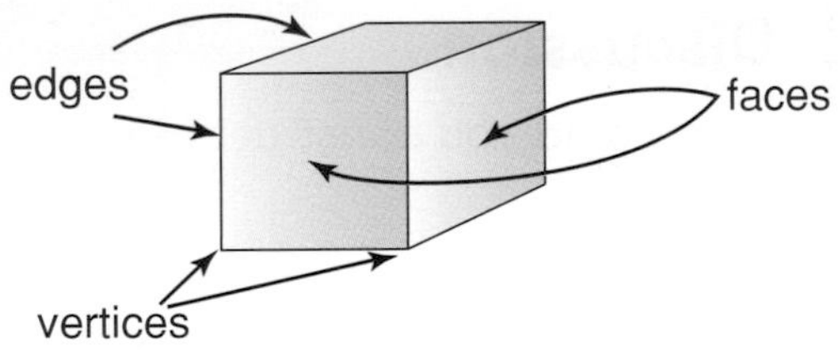

Practical

You will need some Multilink or centimetre cubes and a partner.

Sit back to back with your partner.
Without letting your partner see, make a model using 6 cubes at most.

Example Beth and Tony made these.

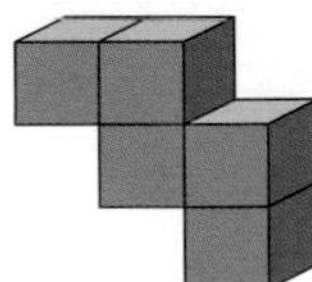

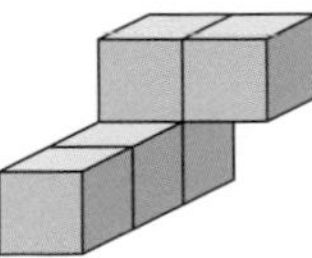

Take turns to tell your partner how to make the model.

Exercise 5

1 Imagine you have 2 identical cubes.
Put them together, matching face to face.

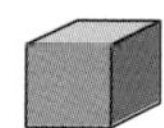
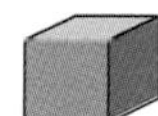

a Name the new solid.
b How many faces, edges and vertices does it have?

2 Imagine painting a dot on each face of 4 cubes.
a Imagine gluing the 4 cubes together in a row.
How many dots would be showing altogether?
b Imagine gluing the 4 cubes together in a shape like this.
How many dots would be showing altogether?

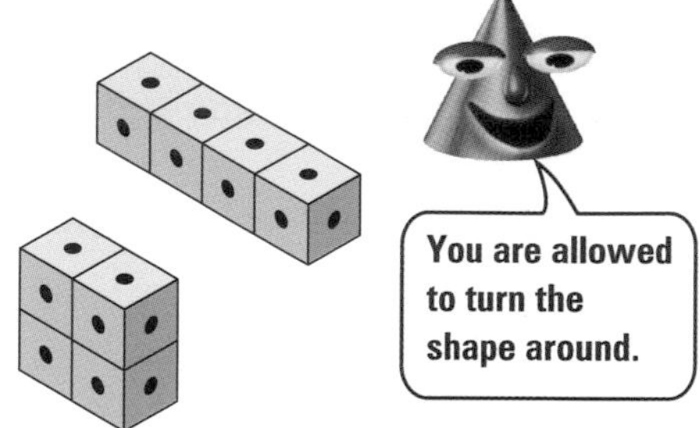

You are allowed to turn the shape around.

3 Imagine a pyramid with a square base.
Cut a slice off the top.
a Describe the new face created.
b How many faces, edges and vertices does the new solid have?

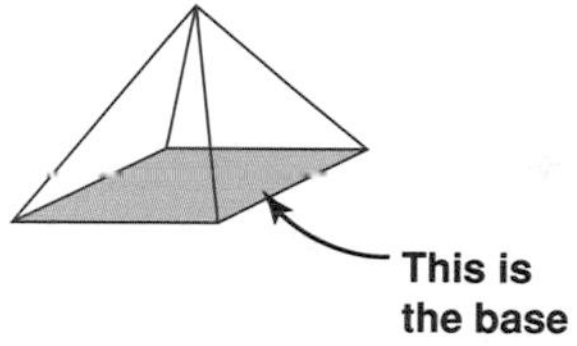

4 Imagine 2 square-based pyramids like the one in question **3**.
Put them together, matching the bases.
Describe the new solid.

***5** Imagine you are standing in front of a large square-based pyramid.
A genie gives you some magic and you shrink to the size of a mouse.
a If you walk around the pyramid, how many faces is it possible for you to see at one time?
b The genie now gives you wings to fly. You fly above the pyramid.
How many faces is it possible for you to see at one time?

Practical

You will need isometric paper and Multilink or centimetre cubes.

This shows you how to draw a cube on isometric paper.

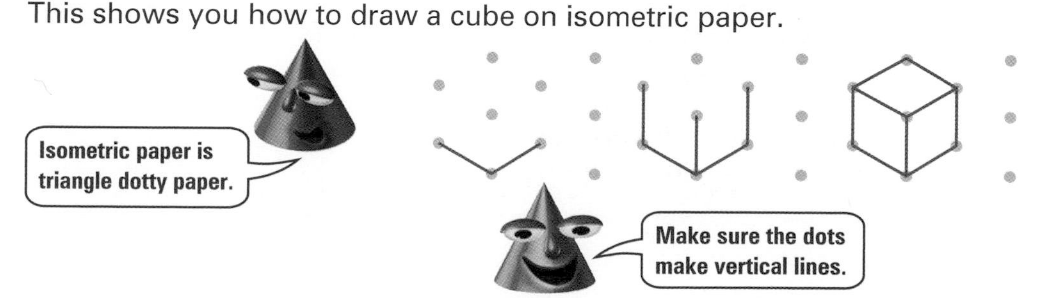

Isometric paper is triangle dotty paper.
Make sure the dots make vertical lines.

Simon wanted to know how many different ways 4 cubes could be put together.
He made this shape with 4 cubes.

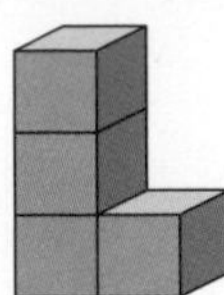

He drew it on triangle dotty paper (isometric paper).

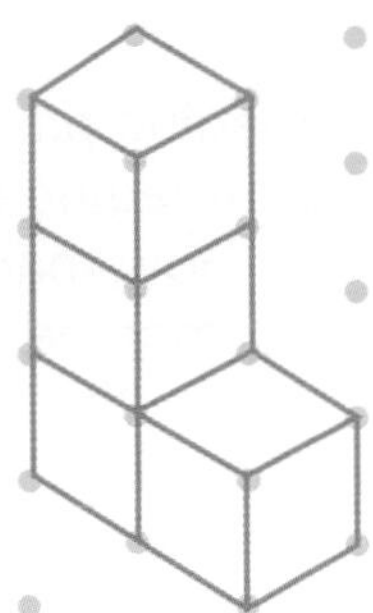

How many different shapes can you make with 4 cubes?

Draw your shapes on triangle dotty paper.

Note: This way is the same as the way above.

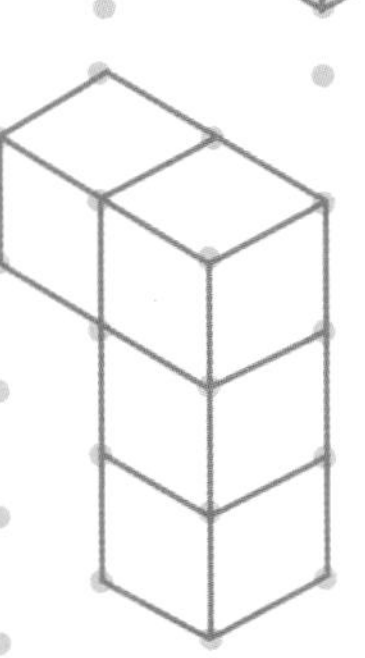

*How many different shapes can be made with 5 cubes?

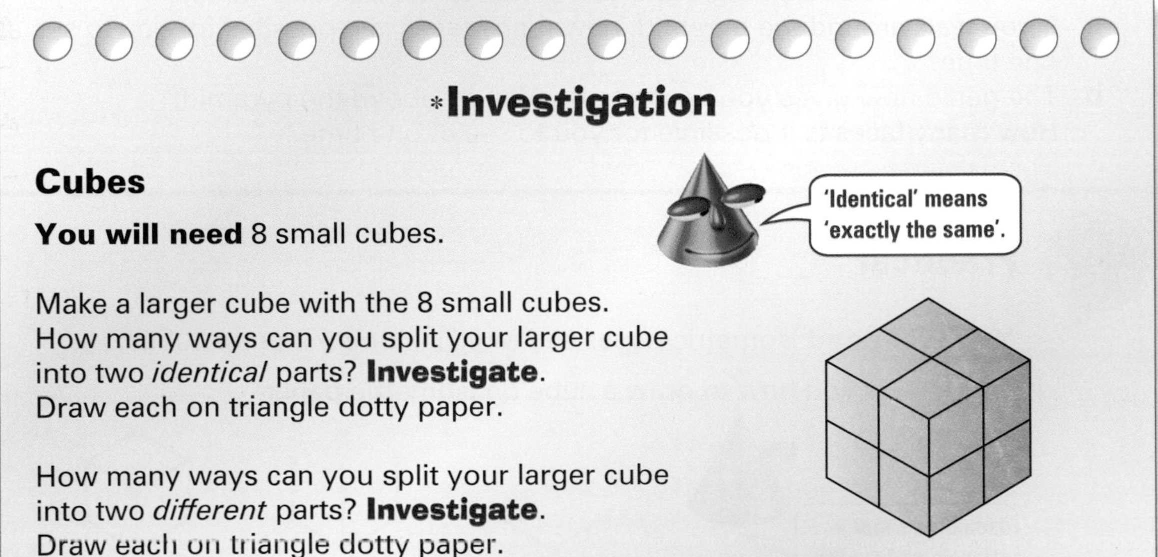

*Investigation

Cubes

You will need 8 small cubes.

'Identical' means
'exactly the same'.

Make a larger cube with the 8 small cubes.
How many ways can you split your larger cube into two *identical* parts? **Investigate**.
Draw each on triangle dotty paper.

How many ways can you split your larger cube into two *different* parts? **Investigate**.
Draw each on triangle dotty paper.

Nets

A 2-D shape that can be folded to make a 3-D shape is called a **net**.

Examples The net below folds to make the cuboid.

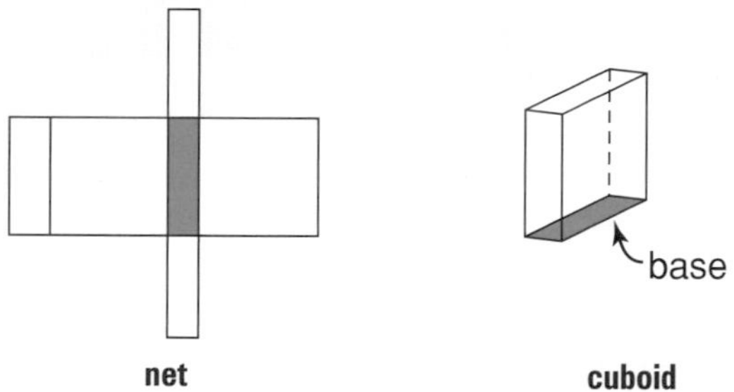

net **cuboid**

This net folds to make the tetrahedron.

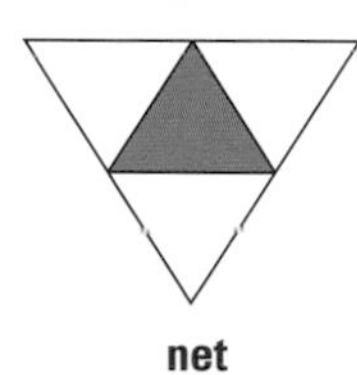

net

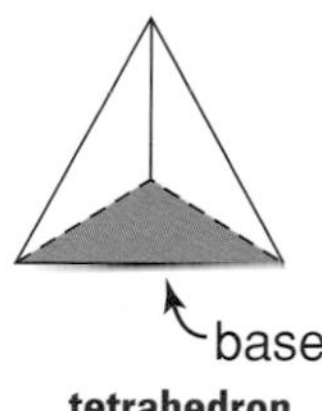

tetrahedron

Exercise 6

1 A

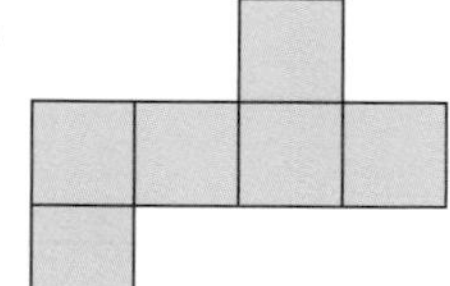

B

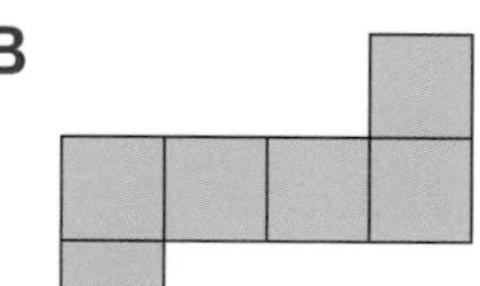

C

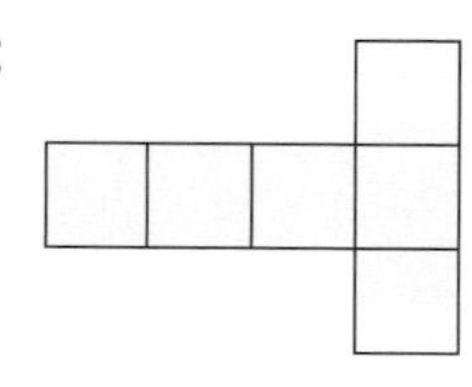

a Which of these nets will fold to make a cube?
b Draw another two nets that will fold to make a cube.

There are 11 different nets that fold to make a cube.

2 Which of the nets below will make this box?

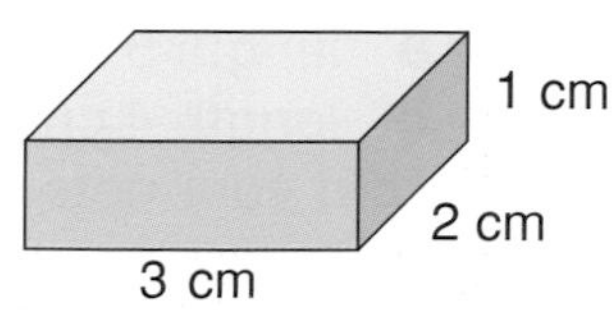

A

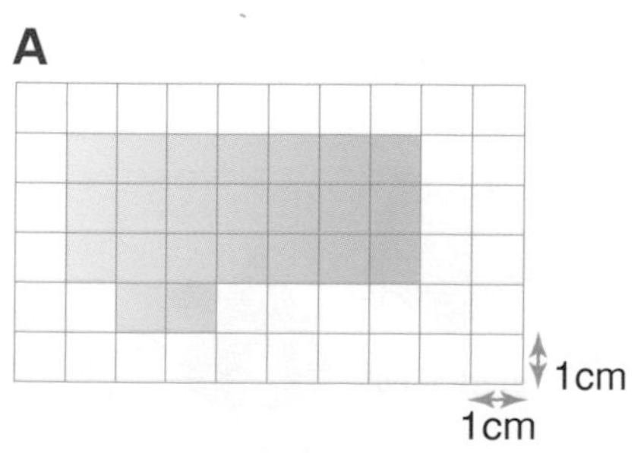

B

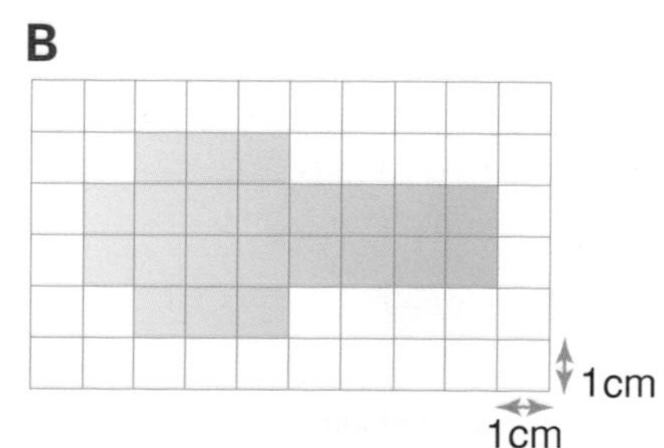

T

3 Imagine folding these nets.
Which ones will fold to make cuboids?

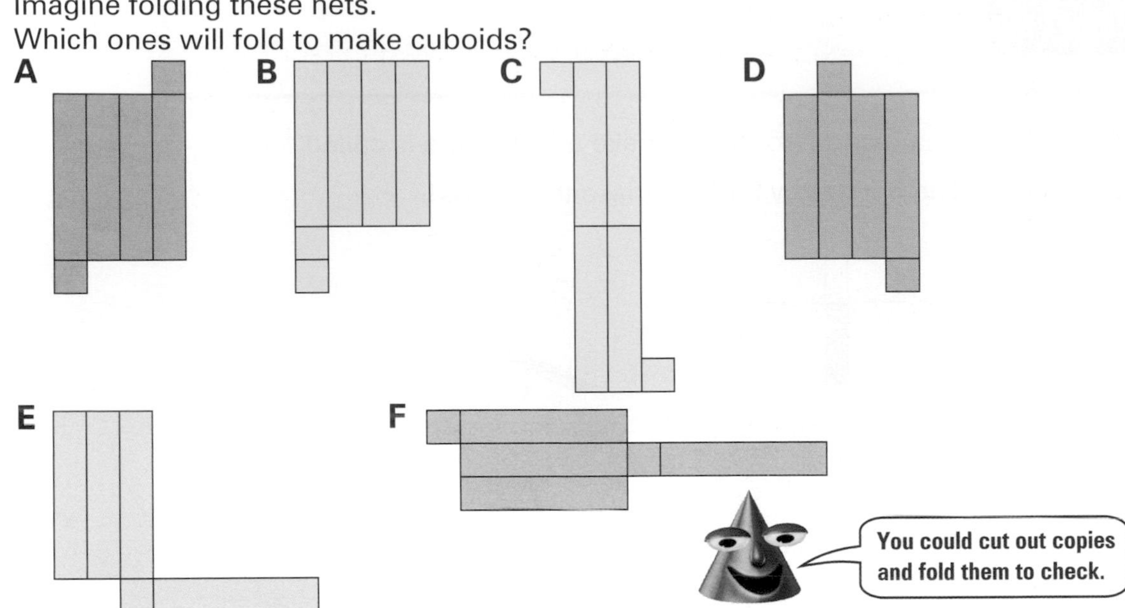

T

4 You will need squared paper, a ruler and a set square.

a Bobby wanted to make this box to display his medal.
He started the net below.
Use a copy of this.
Use your ruler and set square to finish it.
Put tabs on some of the edges.

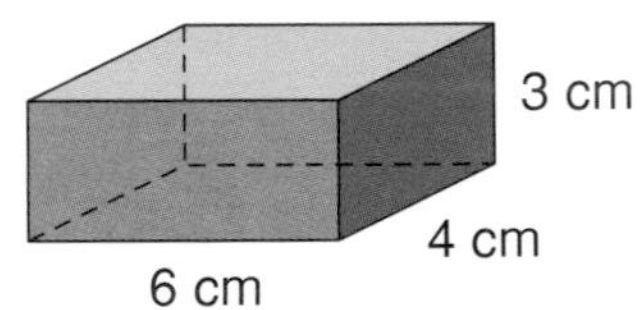

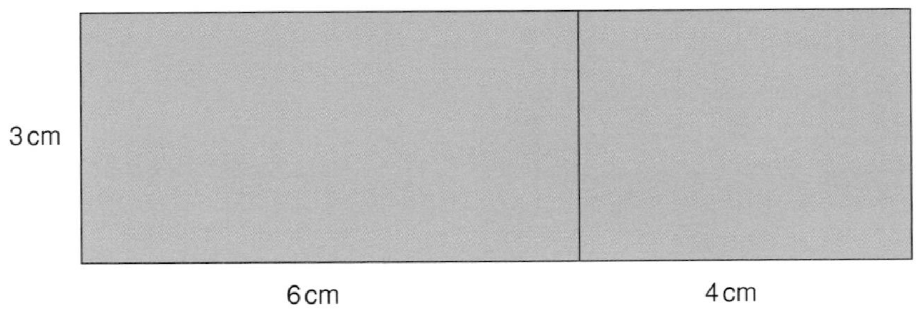

b Fold the net to make the box.

5 Use a ruler and set square to draw nets for these cuboids.

a length 5 cm, width 4 cm, height 2 cm

b length 4 cm, width 2 cm, height 3 cm

Fold your nets to make the cuboids.

6 Copy and finish sketching the nets for these shapes.

a

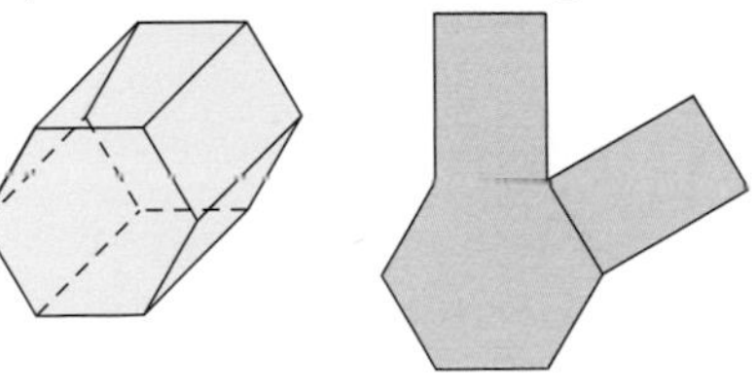

b

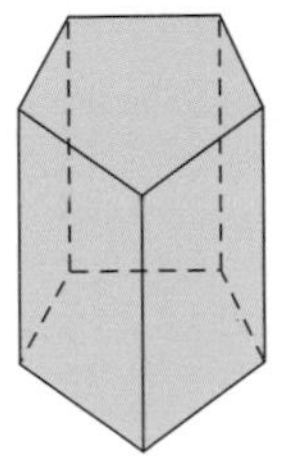

T

*7 Joanne started the net below for a tetrahedron.
Use two copies of this.
Use a ruler and protractor to finish the net in two different ways.

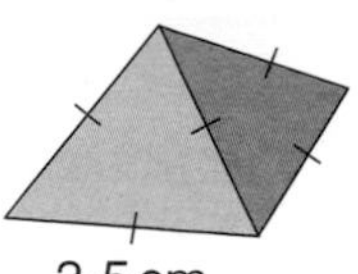

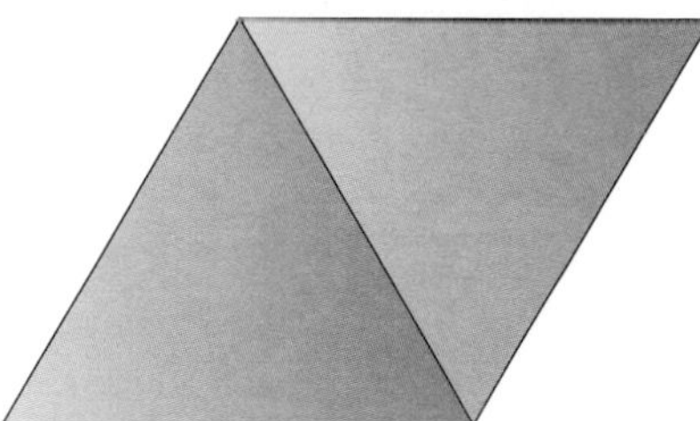

T

*8 Robyn made a pyramid-shaped box for an easter egg.
Part of her net is given below.
Use a copy of this.
Finish the diagram for the net accurately.

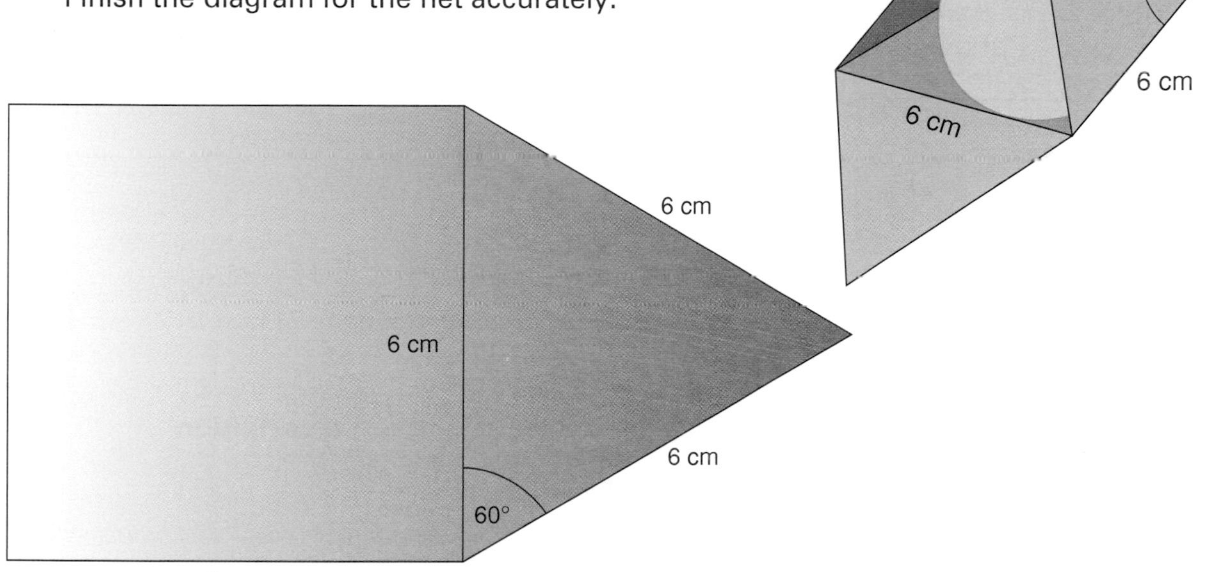

*9 David made some chocolates for his Aunt's birthday.
He designed a box with triangular ends.

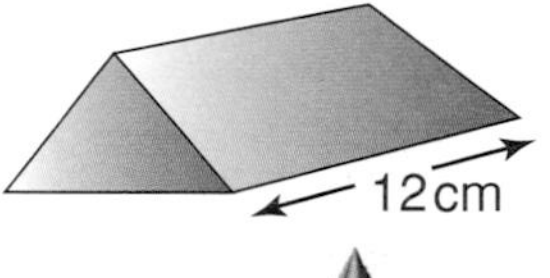

This shape is a *prism*.
It has two identical ends.

This sketch shows the triangular end.
Construct this triangle.
Using your triangle as part of the net for the box, finish the net.
Fold it to make the box.

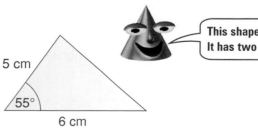

5 cm
55°
6 cm

Practical

You will need a ruler, set square, protractor and some sheets of paper.

The number of dots on opposite faces of a dice always add to 7.
This net can be used to make a dice.

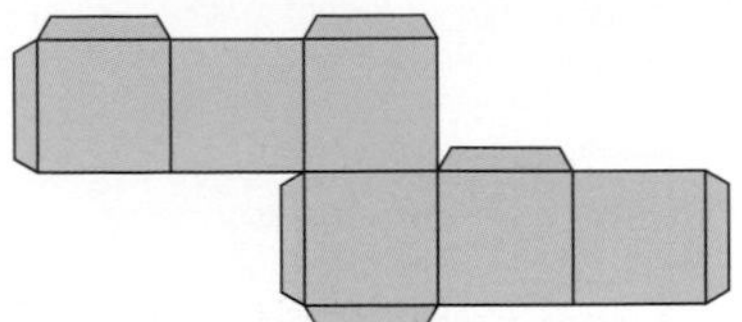

Use a larger copy of this net.
Draw the dots on the net, then make the dice.

Make other nets which fold to make a dice.
Put the dots on the faces before you fold your nets.

Summary of key points

We can **visualise and draw 2-D shapes**.
For the properties of some special 2-D shapes see page 211.

If shapes fit together leaving no gaps we can make a **tessellation**.

Example  will tessellate to give this.

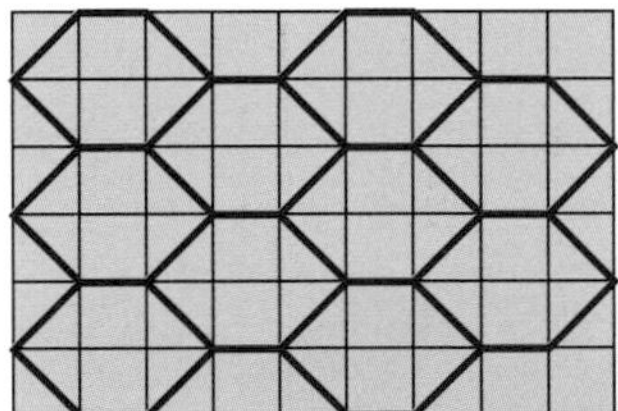

Congruent shapes are exactly the same shape and size.

Example A and B are congruent.

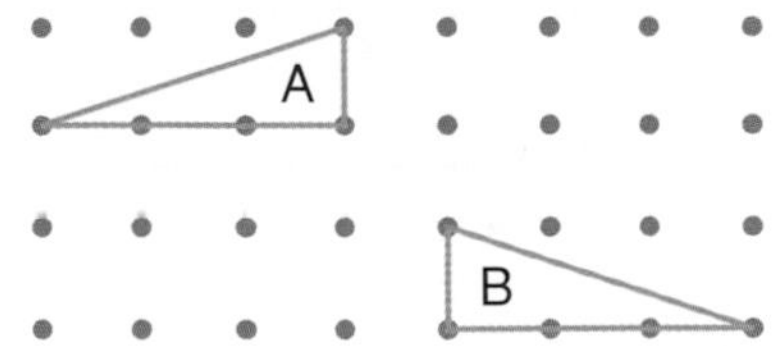

We can **construct triangles** using a ruler and protractor.

Example To construct this triangle
draw PR 2·6 cm long
draw an angle of 85° at R
draw an angle of 50° at P.

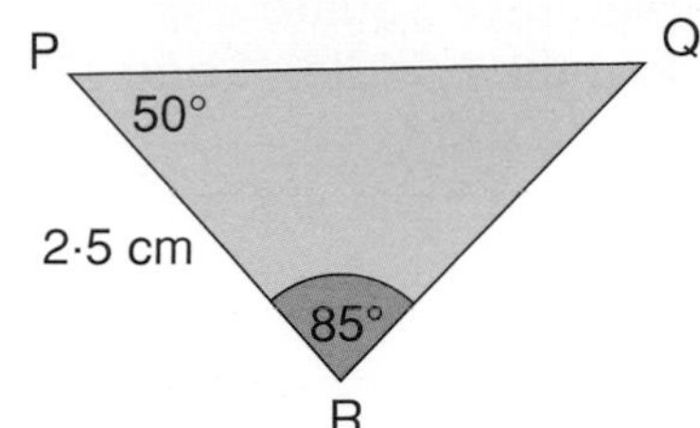

3-D shapes

'3-D' stands for 'three-dimensional'. 3-D shapes have length, width and height.

3-D shapes can be drawn on triangle dotty paper.

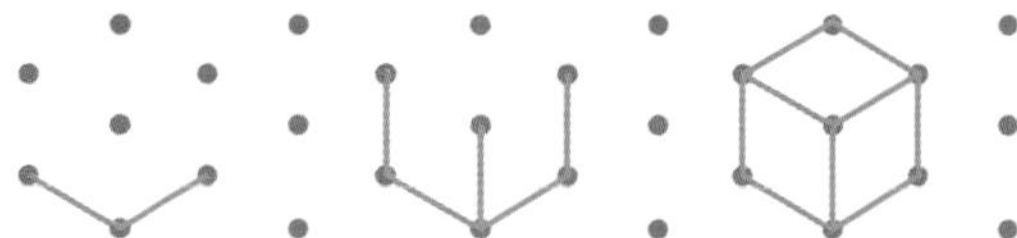

A 2-D shape that can be folded to make a 3-D shape is called a **net**.

Example The net below folds to make this cuboid.

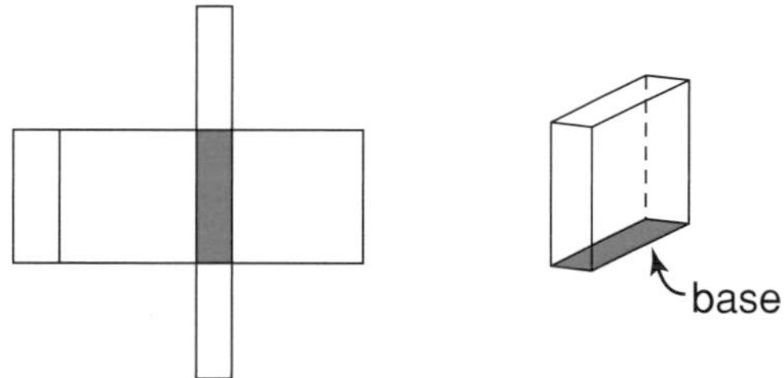

Test yourself

1 Use a copy of this.
Pru made a tessellation.
Finish it for her.

2 Which triangles are congruent to the red one?

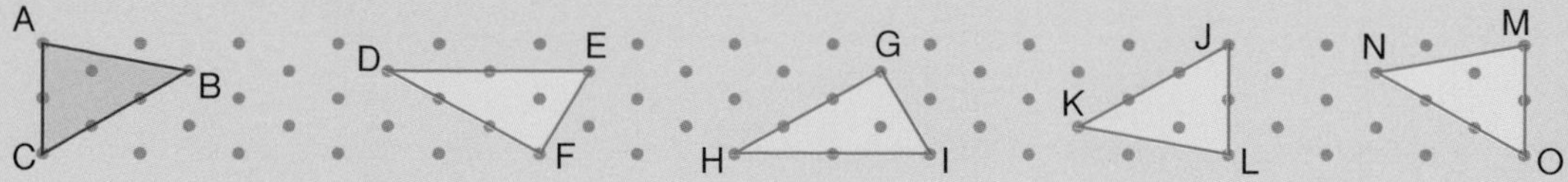

3 Imagine a square.
Join the middle of one side to the middle of the next side.
Do this all the way round.
What shape is made by the new lines?

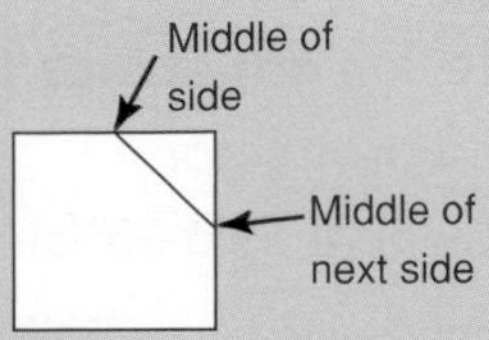

Middle of side

Middle of next side

A

4 Construct these triangles using a ruler and protractor.
Measure the size of angle B on your triangles.

a B, C, A; 38°, 62°, 8 cm

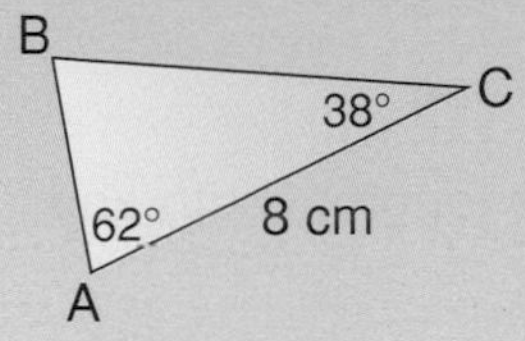

b B, A, C; 4·5 cm, 55°, 5 cm

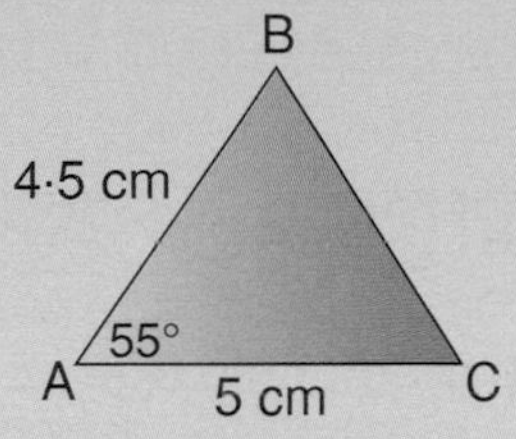

D

5 Imagine a cube. Cut off one corner as shown.

a Describe the new face created.

b How many faces, edges and vertices does the new solid have?

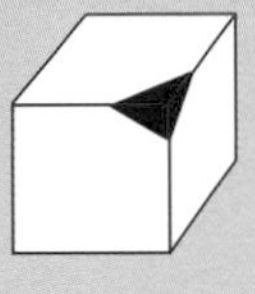

E

6 If you could fly over a triangular-based pyramid, how many faces would it be possible for you to see at one time?

E

T

7 Use a copy of these.
Use a ruler and set square to finish drawing the net for these.

a 3 cm, 4 cm, 6 cm

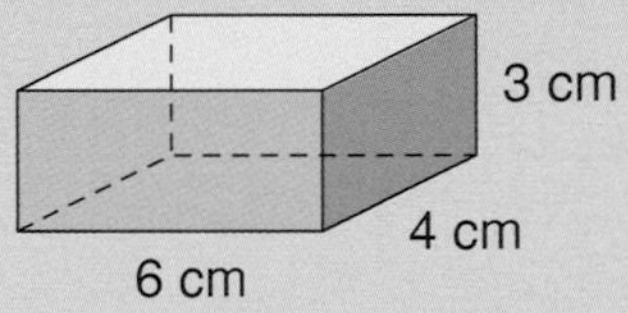

b 3·5 cm, 3·5 cm, 4 cm, 4 cm, 55°, 55°

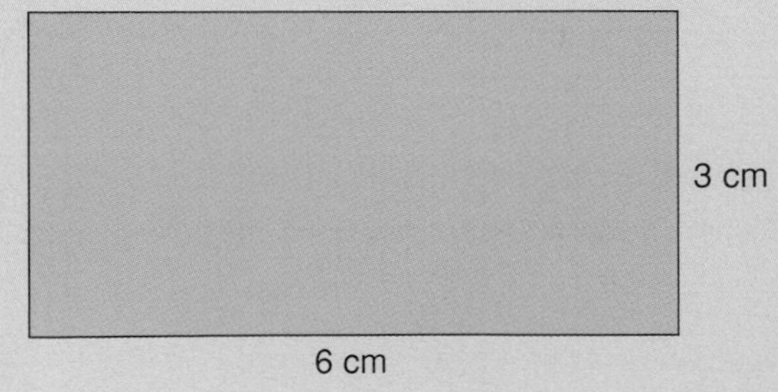

3 cm, 6 cm

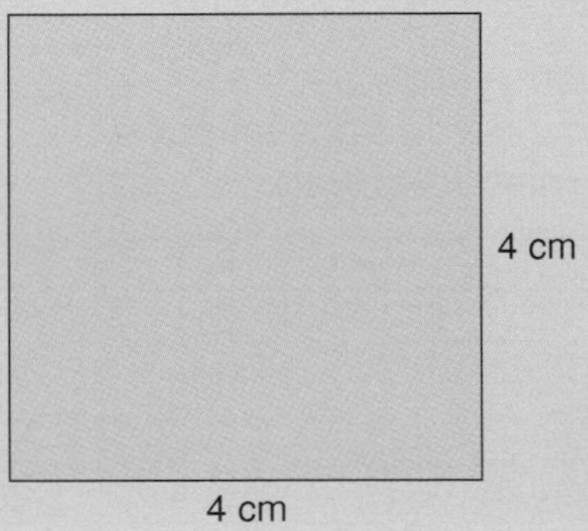

4 cm, 4 cm

F

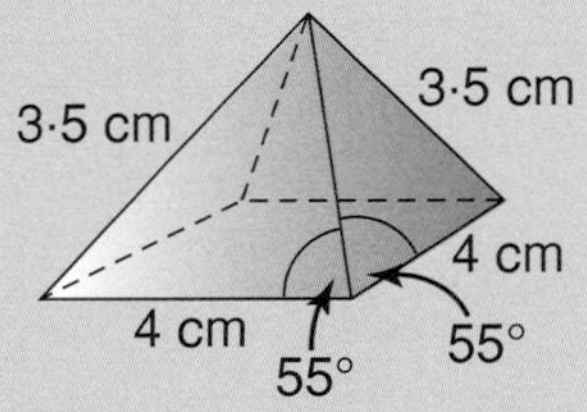

13 Coordinates and Transformations

You need to know

Key vocabulary

angle of rotation, centre of rotation, congruent, coordinates, grid, image, line of symmetry, line symmetry, mirror line, object, order of rotation symmetry, reflect, reflection, reflection symmetry, rotate, rotation, rotation symmetry, symmetrical, transformation, translate, translation, *x*-coordinate

Flag it up

- 

  These diagrams are made from two identical triangles.
  How else could you place these triangles?
  Which diagrams have line symmetry?

- 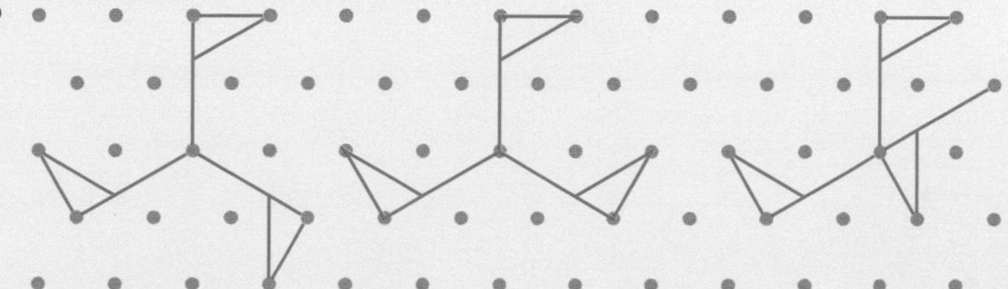

  These diagrams are made with three identical 'flags'.
  How else could these flags be placed?
  Which diagram has been made by rotating one of the flags?
  Do any of the diagrams have line symmetry?

- Make a pattern of your own with line symmetry.

Coordinates

Remember
The **coordinates** of A, B and C are:
A($^-4$, $^-3$), B($^-3$, 4), C(3, $^-2$).
We always write the x-coordinate first in the bracket.
We can remember this easily because x comes before y in the alphabet.

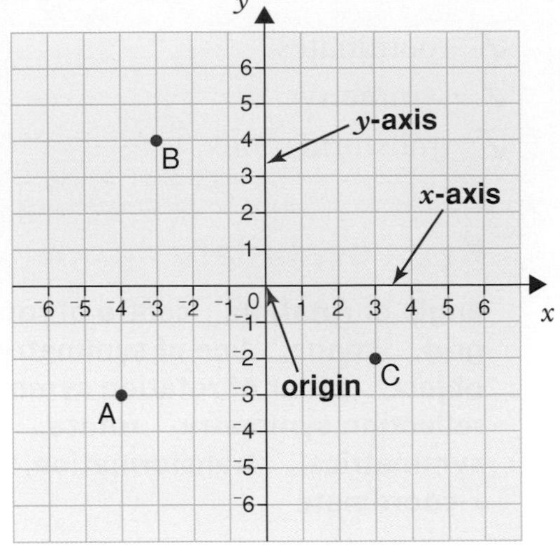

Worked Example
Plot these coordinates.
($^-2$, 2), (3, 2), ($^-1$, 4)

a Write down the coordinates of another point that will make a rectangle.
b Which of these points could you plot to make a parallelogram?
A (4, 5) **B** (4, 3) **C** (4, 4) **D** (5, 4)

Answer
a From the graph it can be seen that **(2, 0)** is a point which will make a rectangle.

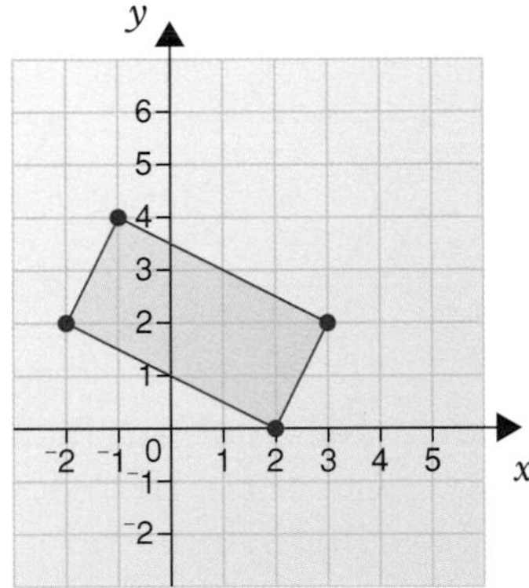

b C

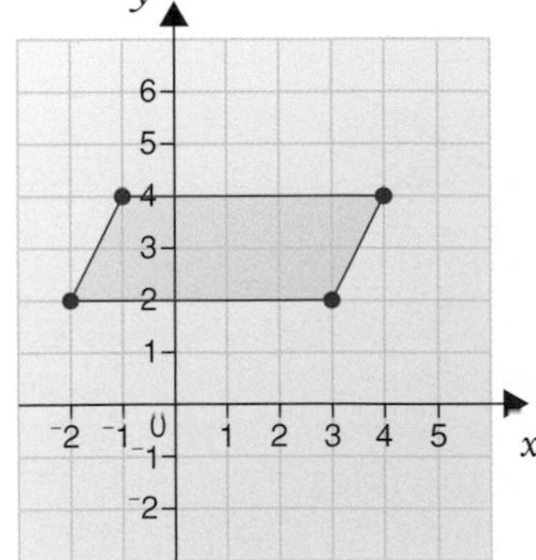

Exercise 1

T

1 Jake often visits the places shown on this graph.

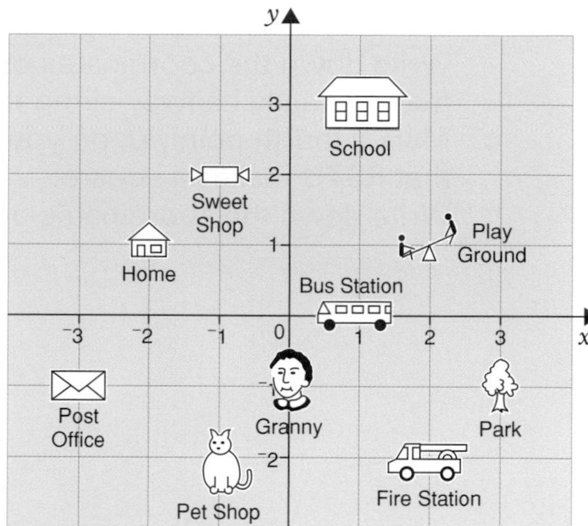

a Write down the coordinates of these.

school post office
bus station granny

b One morning Jake left home and walked to $(^-1, 2)$ then $(1, 0)$ then $(2, 1)$ then $(2, ^-2)$ then $(^-1, ^-2)$ and then $(0, ^-1)$ and then back home.
Write down all the places he visited in order.

c Use a copy of the graph.
Starting at home, join each point on Jake's walk with a straight line.

d The diagram for **c** should tell you which place Jake likes best.
Which place is this?

What does the arrow point to?

2 Write down the letters at each of these coordinates.
What does each sentence say?

$(3, 4)$ $(^-4, 4)$ $(2, 1)$
$(3, ^-3)$ $(^-4, ^-2)$ $(^-3, ^-4)$ $(^-2, 3)$
$(5, 2)$ $(^-4, 4)$ $(^-4, 1)$ $(^-2, 3)$
$(3, ^-5)$ $(^-2, 3)$ $(0, 0)$ $(0, 0)$

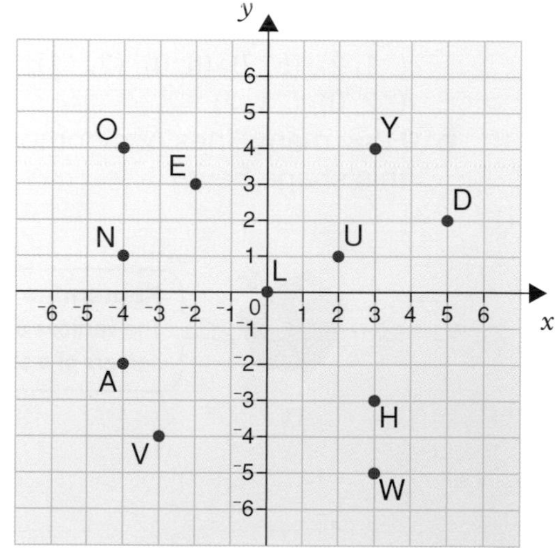

3 This shape was drawn by plotting and joining coordinates.
Copy and finish this list of the coordinates.

Head
$(^-4, ^-4)$, $(^-3, ^-1)$, $(^-4, 0)$, $(^-4, 3)$, ...

Ears
$(^-4, 0)$, $(^-4, ^-2)$, $(^-6, 0)$, $(^-6, 5)$, ...
and $(4, 0)$, $(4, ^-2)$, $(6, 0)$, $(6, 5)$, ...

Eyes
Put large dots at $(^-1{\cdot}5, 2.5)$ and ...

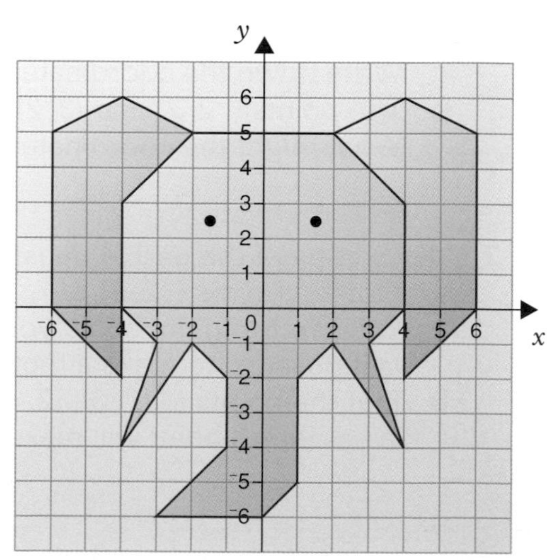

T **4** Use a copy of this grid.

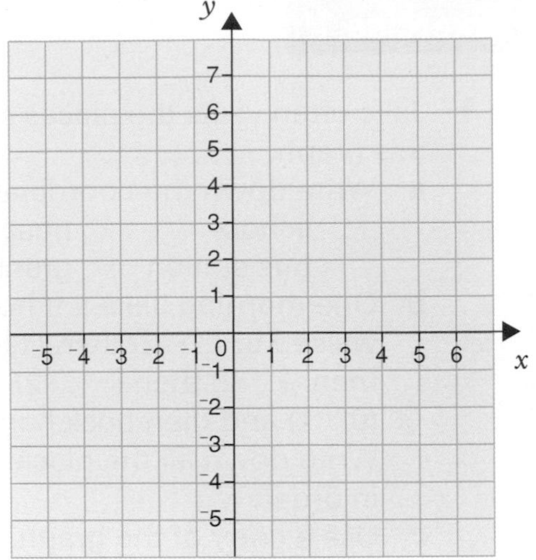

a On your grid plot these points.
R $(^{-}2, ^{-}1)$, S $(^{-}2, 5)$, T $(4, 5)$

b Join R and T with a straight line.
Write down the coordinates of the point that is exactly halfway along this line.

c Mark a fourth point, U, on your grid so that RSTU makes a square.
Write down the coordinates of U.

T **5** Use a copy of this grid.

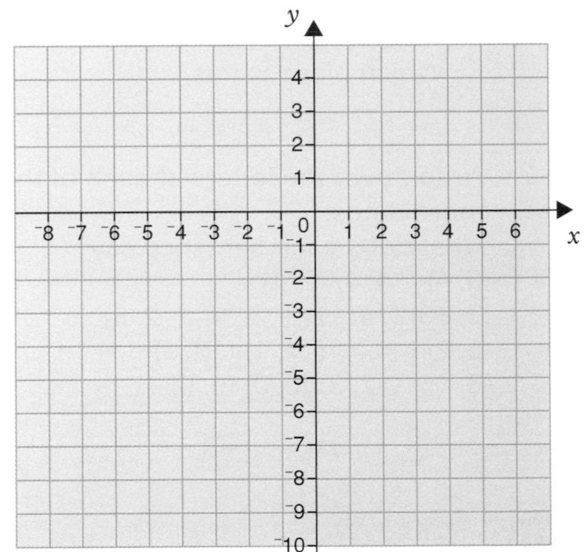

a These are the coordinates of the vertices of a shape.
Plot them on your grid.
Join them in this order.
$(^{-}1, 2)$, $(5, 2)$, $(6, 0)$, $(2, ^{-}1)$, $(^{-}2, 0)$, $(^{-}1, 2)$

b How many lines of symmetry does this shape have?

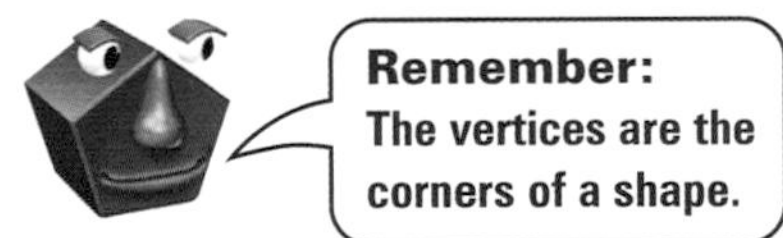

Remember:
The vertices are the corners of a shape.

T **6** Use a copy of the grid in question **5**.

a The points $(^{-}4, 0)$, $(1, 0)$, $(1, ^{-}3)$ are three of the vertices of a rectangle.
Write down the coordinates of the fourth vertex.

b The points $(^{-}2, 2)$ and $(3, 2)$ are two of the four vertices of a rectangle.
What might the coordinates of the other two points be?

T **7** Use a copy of the grid in question **5**.

a Plot the points $(^{-}2, 3)$, $(^{-}1, ^{-}2)$, $(^{-}6, ^{-}3)$.
What fourth point could you plot to make a square?
Is it possible to make a rectangle that is not a square?

***b** Plot the points $(^{-}4, ^{-}3)$, $(2, ^{-}1)$, $(^{-}2, 1)$.
What fourth point will make **i** a kite **ii** a parallelogram?

*8 a Which of the points could you join to make a
i square
ii parallelogram
iii trapezium?
b Which of the points shown could you join to make
i a right-angled triangle
ii an isosceles triangle without a right angle?

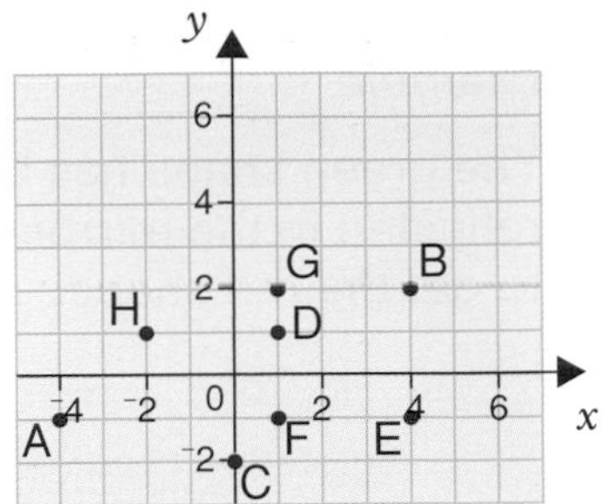

T

Puzzle

Use a copy of this grid.
Plot these points and join them in order.
(⁻7, 4), (⁻3, 6), (⁻1, 4),
(⁻1, 0) (⁻2, ⁻1), (7, ⁻1),
(2, ⁻4), (4, ⁻6), (⁻2, ⁻6),
(⁻5, ⁻4), (⁻5, 0), (⁻3, 2),
(⁻3, 4), (⁻7, 4)

Put a large dot at
(⁻3·5, 4·5).

What picture did you get?

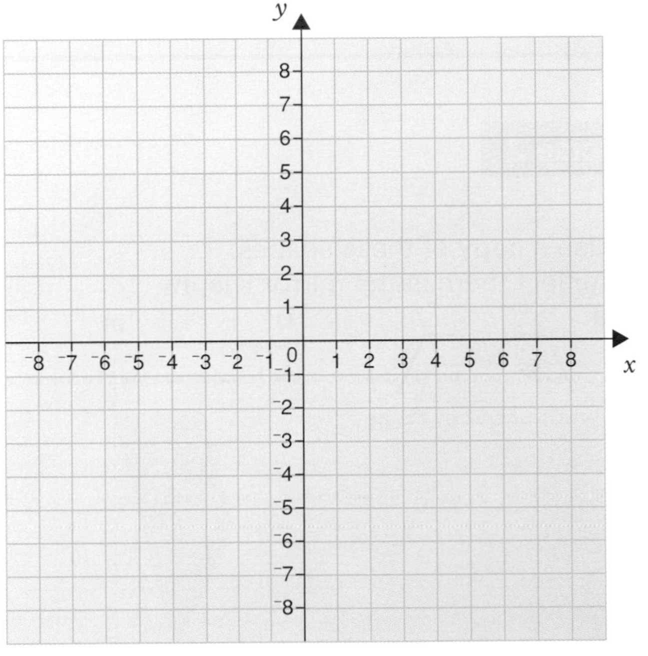

Reflection

We can use a mirror or tracing paper to help us draw the **reflection** of a shape in the mirror line.

Example

The orange shape has been reflected in the mirror line to get the blue shape.
The blue shape is called the **image**.

The image and the object are the same distance from the mirror line.

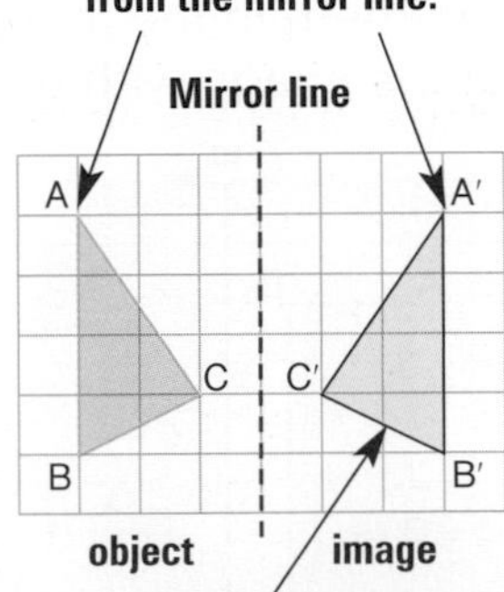

We label the image with dashed letters.

Example

The green shape has been reflected in the mirror line to get the red shape.

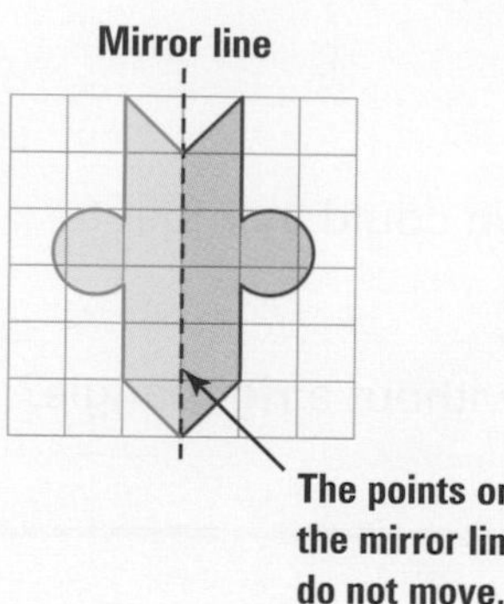

Exercise 2

T

1 Use a copy of these shapes.
Reflect them in the mirror line, **m**.

a

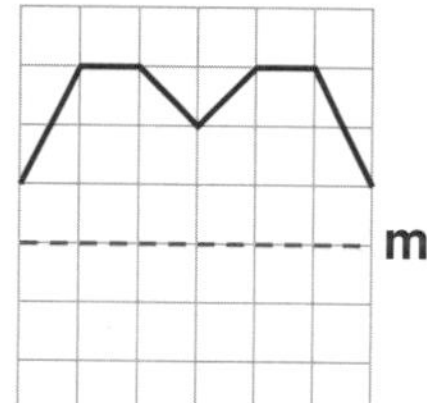

b

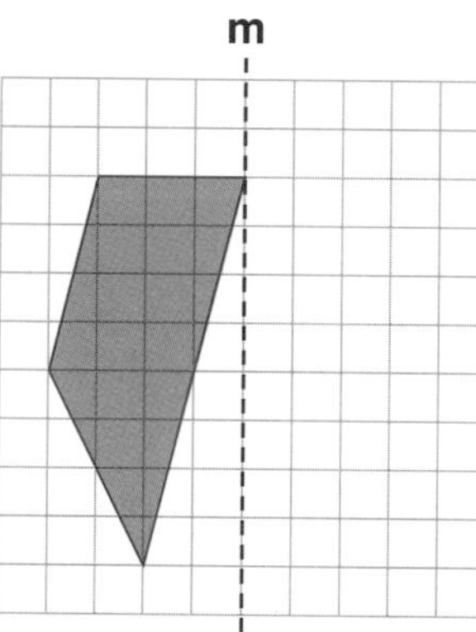

c

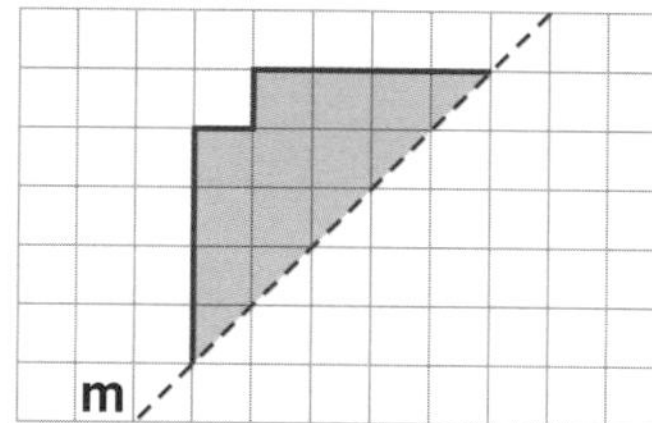

d

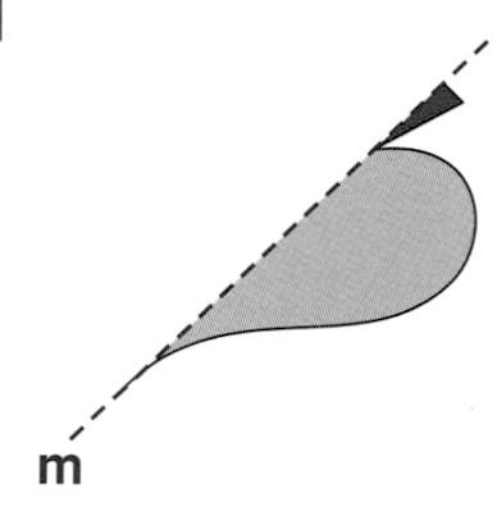

e

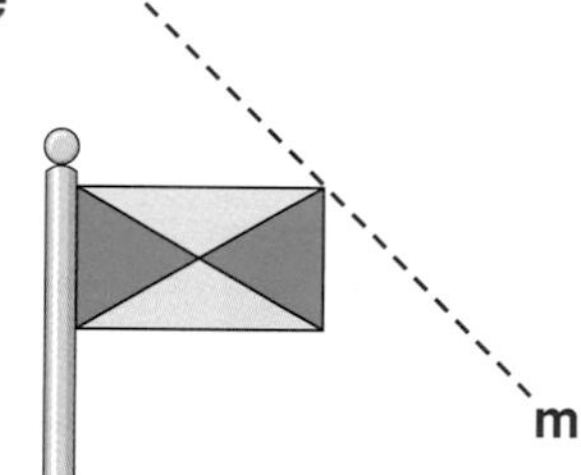

T

2 Use a copy of these.
Reflect them in the mirror line.
Label the image with dashed letters.

a

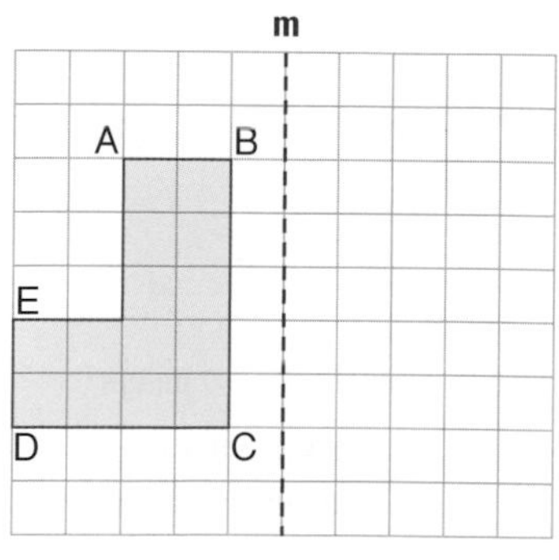

b

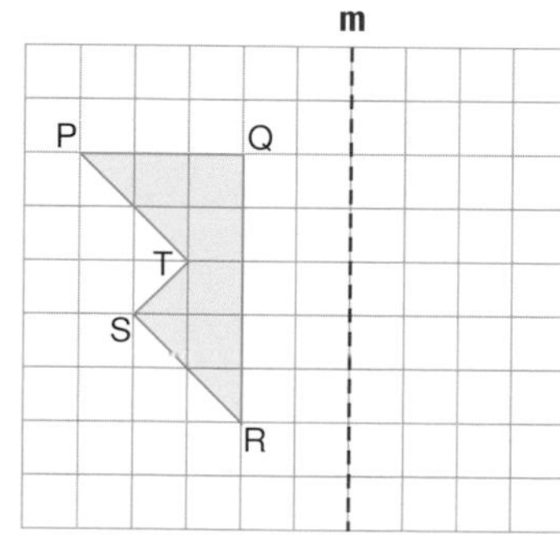

T

3 Use a copy of these.
Reflect the red shapes or lines in the x-axis to make a pattern.
Then reflect this new pattern in the y-axis.

a

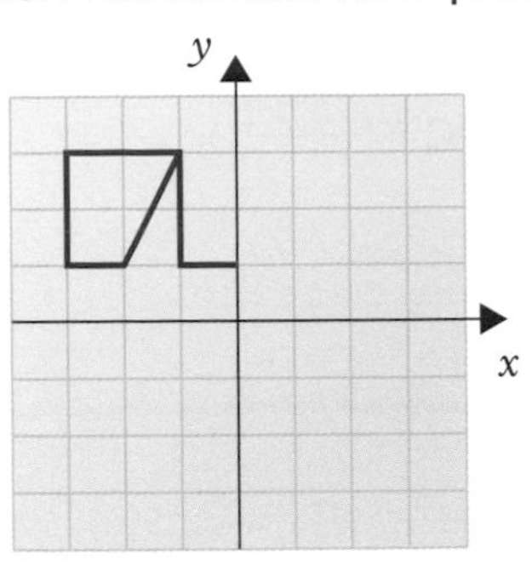

b

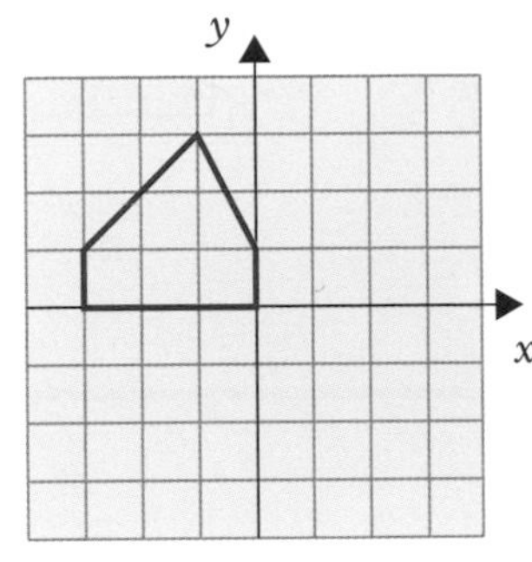

c

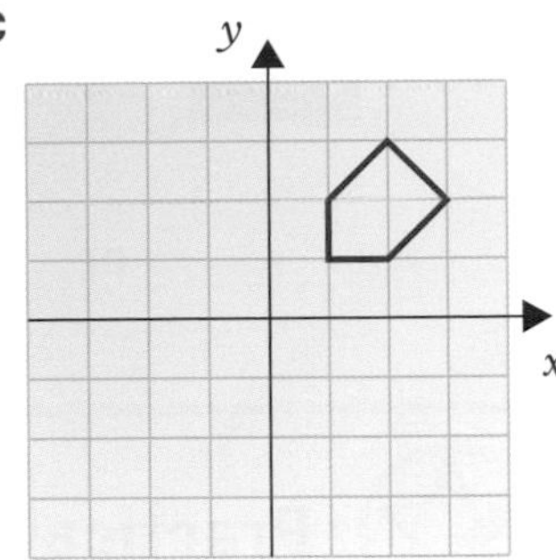

T

4 Use a copy of this.
Each diagram shows a shape and its image.
Draw the mirror line on each.

a

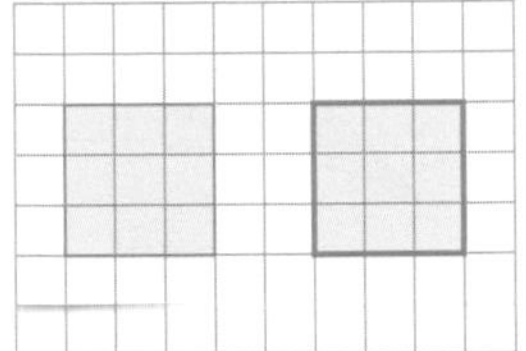

b

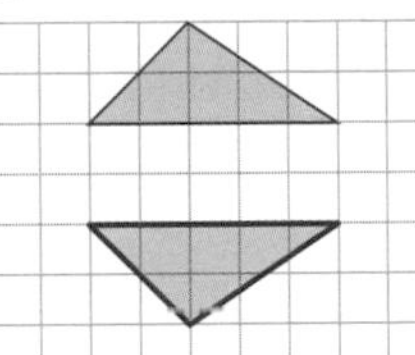

c

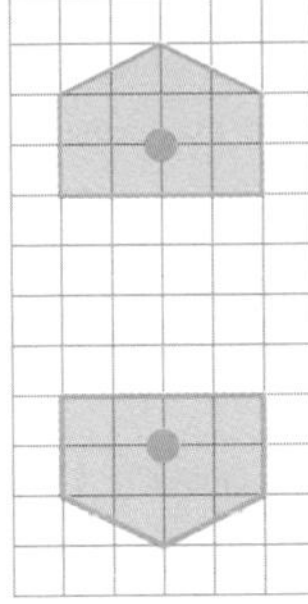

d

5 ABCD is reflected in the mirror line, **m**.

a Will the image also be a rectangle the same size?

b Which point will not move?

c B is $\frac{1}{2}$ cm from the mirror line.
How far will B′ be from the mirror line?

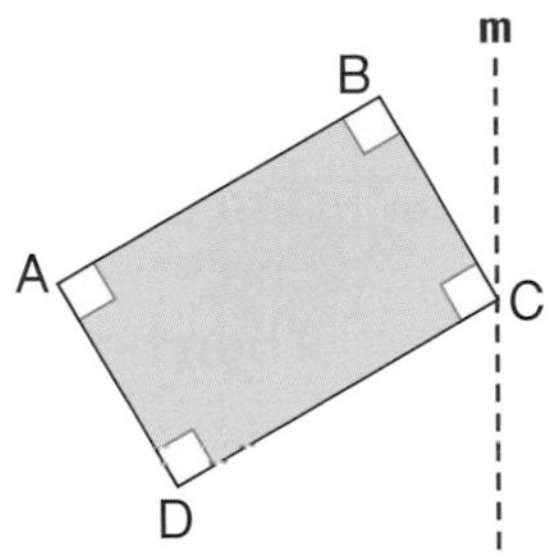

T

*__6__ Use a copy of this.
Reflect these words in the mirror line.

a

b

c

d

*7 Explain why A′B′C′D′ is not the reflection of ABCD in the mirror line **m**.

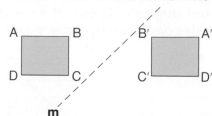

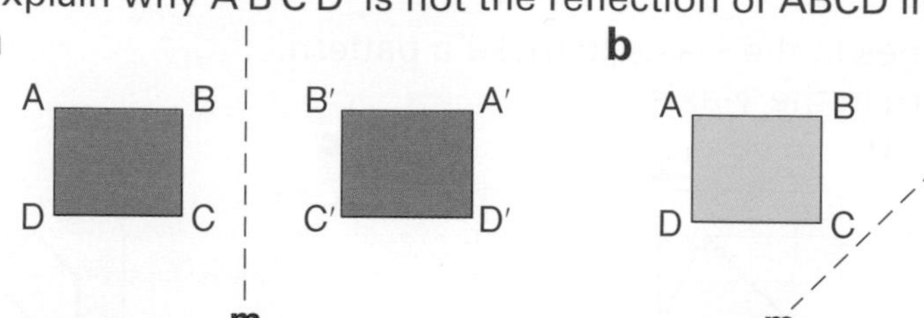

Practical

A You will need tracing paper.

This could be done using a dynamic geometry software package.

Draw a triangle.
Reflect it in one of its sides.
Name the shape that the image and object together make.

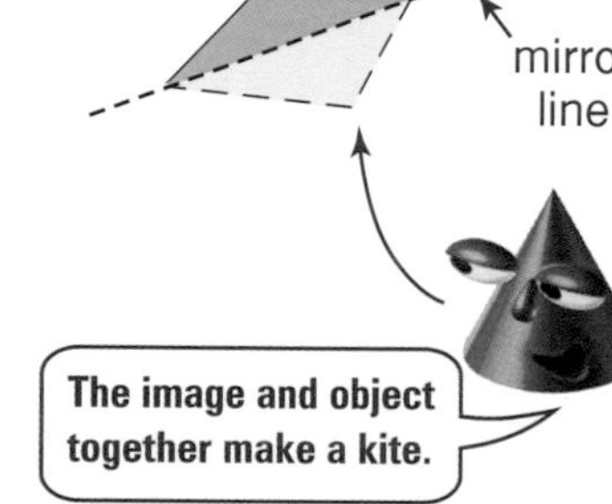

What if you reflect the triangle you drew in one of its other sides?

Try and make these shapes by reflecting a triangle in one of its sides. Which ones can you make?

rectangle	square	kite	parallelogram
arrowhead	rhombus	trapezium	

T **B You will need** a copy of the grid below.

Jon drew this pattern on one side of the line.
Then he reflected it.

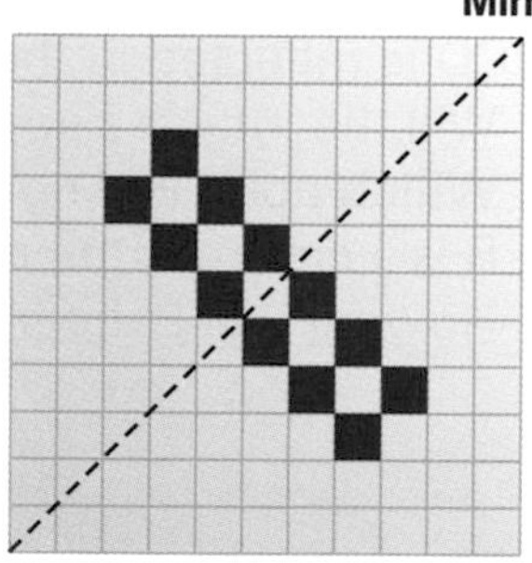

Draw a pattern on the grid by colouring squares on one side of the mirror line.
Reflect your pattern in the mirror line.

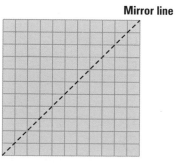

Mirror line

Rotation

Remember
A **rotation** is a movement around a centre point.

To rotate a shape you need to know the **centre of rotation** and the **angle of rotation**. The angle of rotation given is always in an **anticlockwise** direction.

Example Rotate ABCD 270° about (0, 0) means rotate ABCD anticlockwise 270°.

Example To rotate PQR a half turn (180°) about the origin, follow these steps.

1

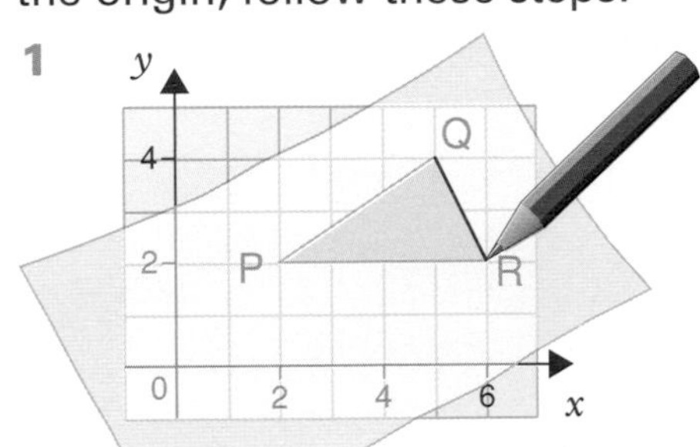

Trace the shape onto tracing paper.

2

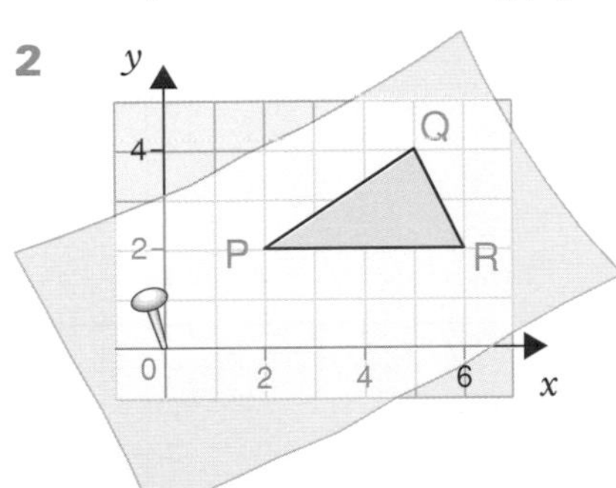

Put a pin or sharp pencil on the origin. Turn the tracing paper a half turn.

3

Press hard on the tracing paper to show where the image goes. Take away the tracing paper and draw the image.

Exercise 3

T **1** Use a copy of these.
Rotate each shape about X by the angle given below each grid.

a

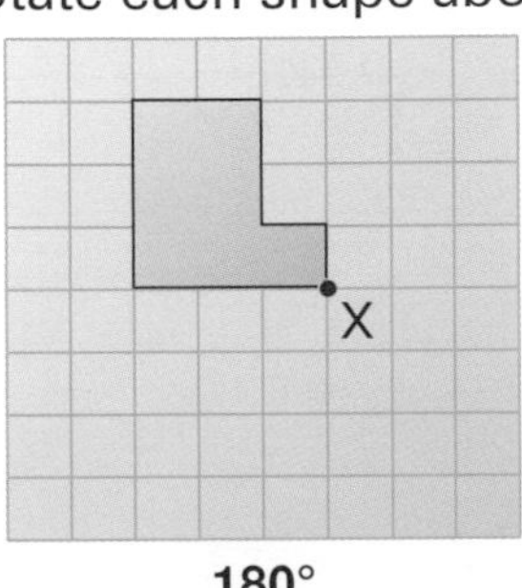

180°

b

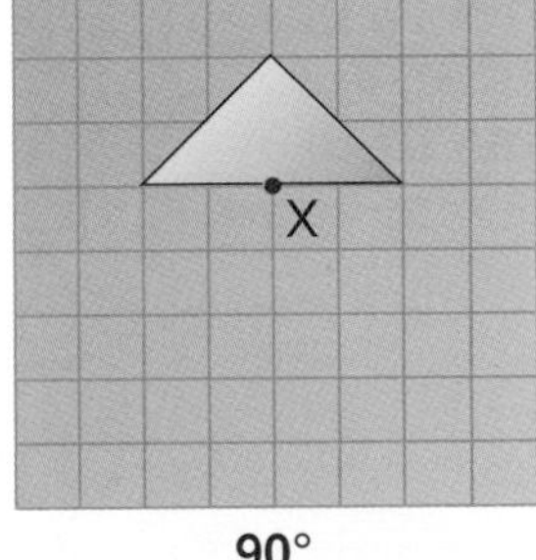

90°

c

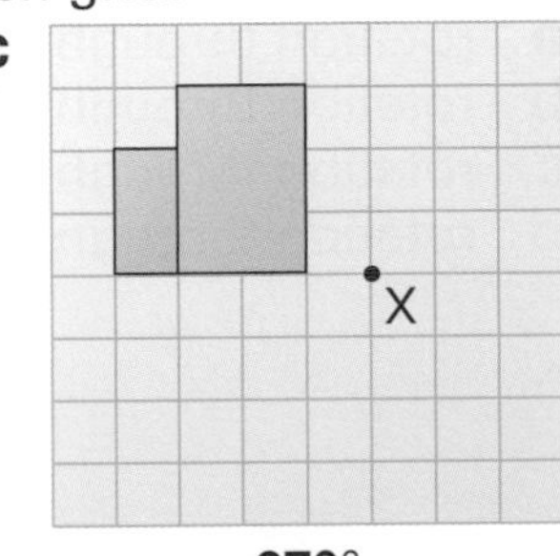

270°

T

2 Use a copy of these.
Rotate these shapes about (0, 0).
The angle of the rotation is given.

a

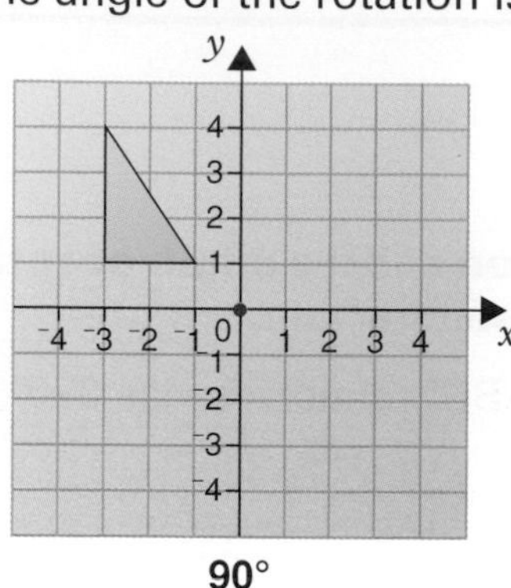

90°

b

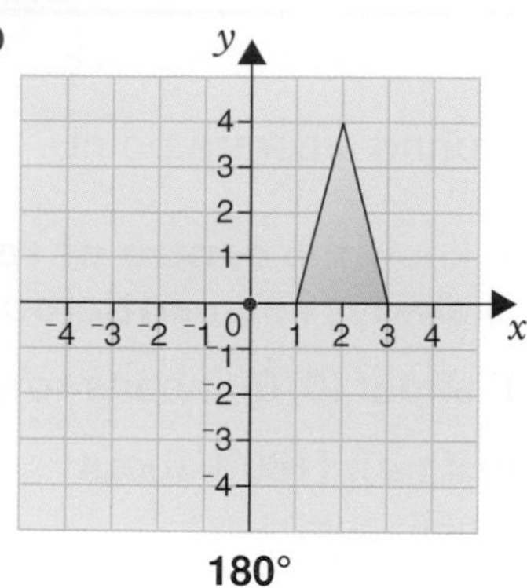

180°

c

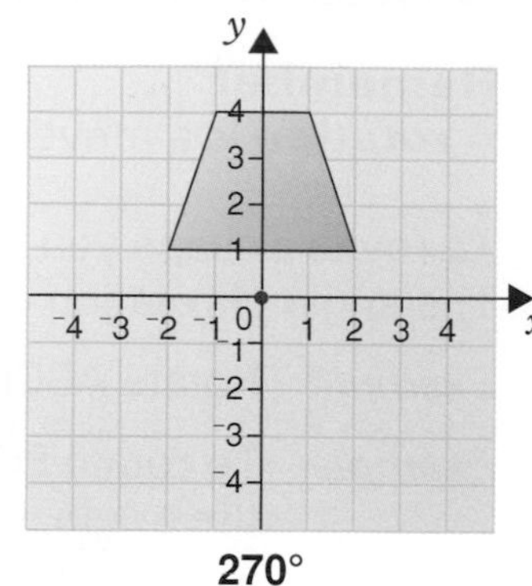

270°

T

3 Use another two copies of question **2a**.
Rotate the shape 90° about these points.
a $(^{-}1, 1)$ **b** $(^{-}2, 2)$

T

4 Use a copy of this grid.

a Plot these coordinate pairs on your grid.
(2, 1) (6, 1) (2, 3)
Join them to make a triangle.

b Rotate the triangle 90° about (0, 0).

c What are the new coordinates?

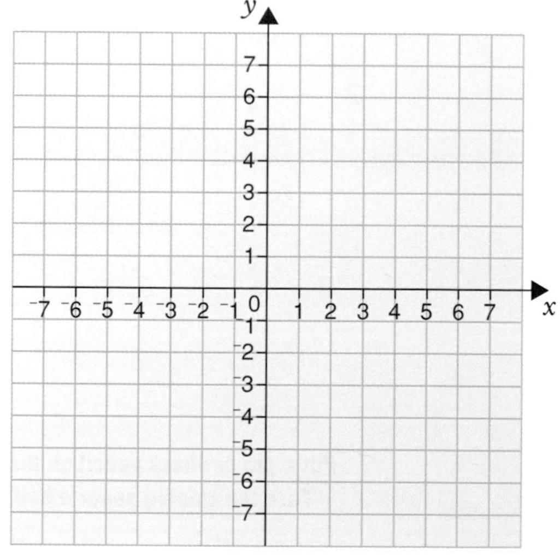

*__5__ A rotation through 90° about (0, 0) maps **A** onto **A**′.
Which of these rotations maps **A**′ onto **A**?
There are two correct answers.

a rotation through 180° about (0, 0)

b rotation through 90° about (0, 0)

c rotation through 270° about (0, 0)

d rotation through 90° clockwise about (0, 0)

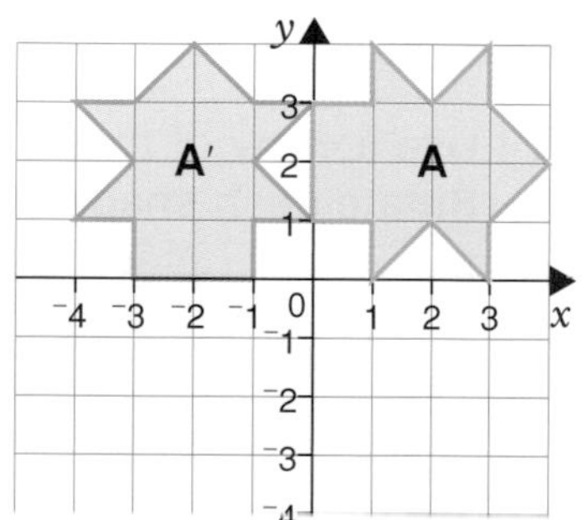

T

***6** Use a copy of this.
Rotate the shape 120° anticlockwise about the red dot.
Then rotate the image you get another 120° anticlockwise about the red dot.

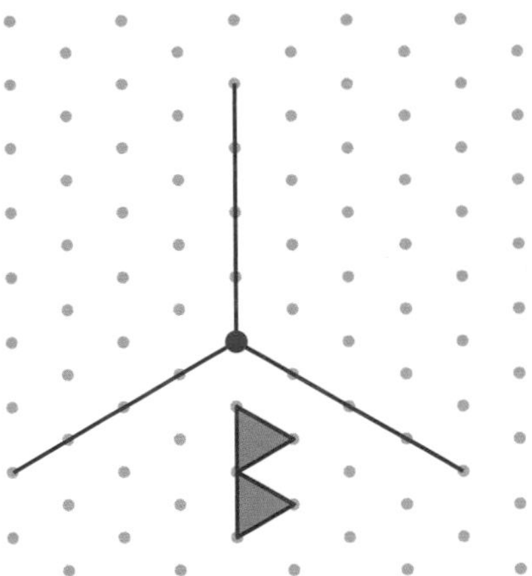

Translation

Remember
When we slide a shape without turning it we are **translating** it.

When a shape is translated, the image is **congruent** to the original shape.

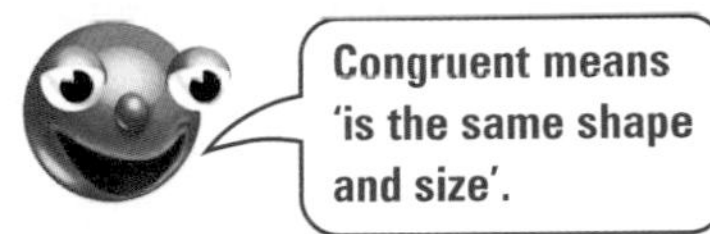
Congruent means 'is the same shape and size'.

Example The red shape has been translated 4 units to the left and 2 units down to give the blue shape.

To translate the blue shape back to the red shape we slide it in the opposite direction.
We translate it 4 units to the right and 2 units up.

This is called the inverse translation.

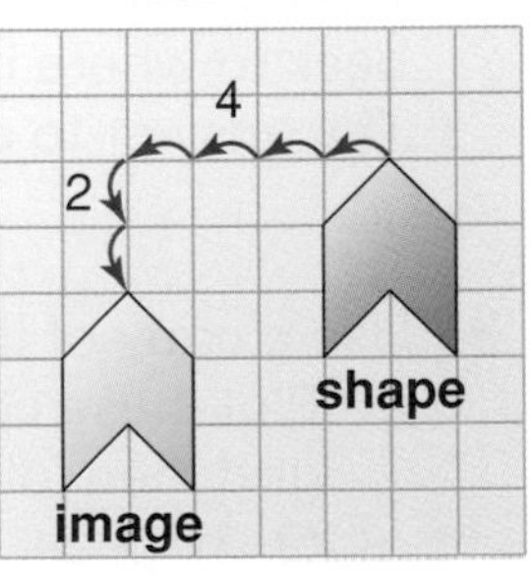
4
2
shape
image

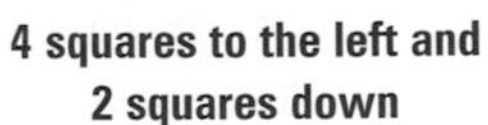
4 squares to the left and 2 squares down

Exercise 4

T

1 Use a copy of these.
Draw the image after these translations.

a
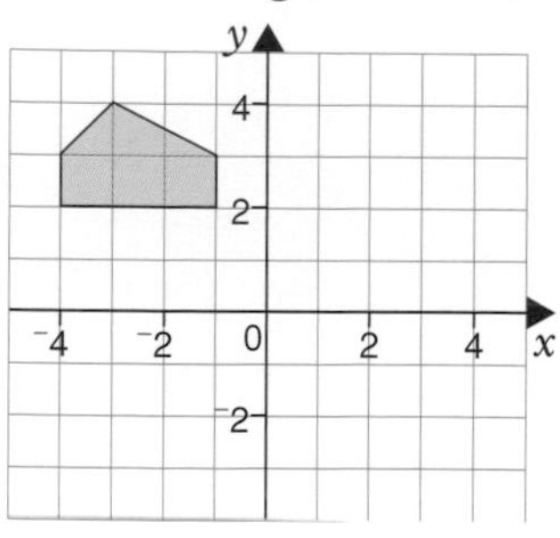
4 units down

b
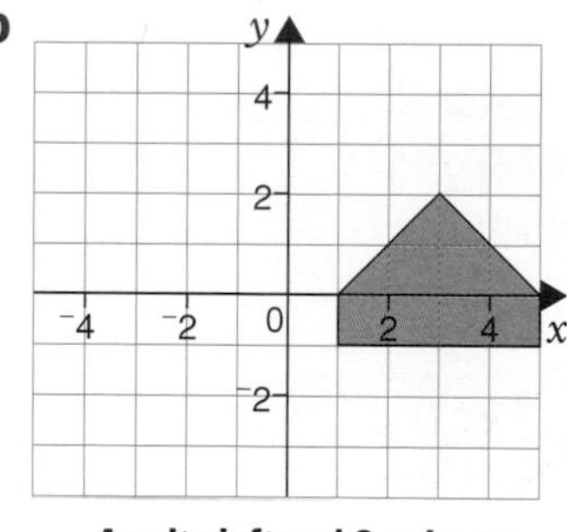
4 units left and 3 units up

c
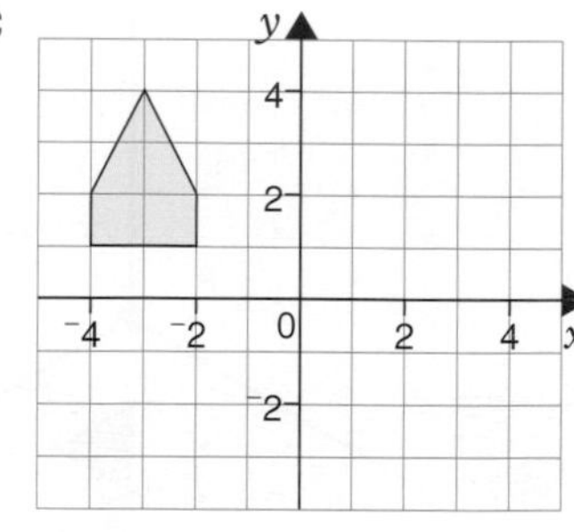
5 units right and 2 units down

d
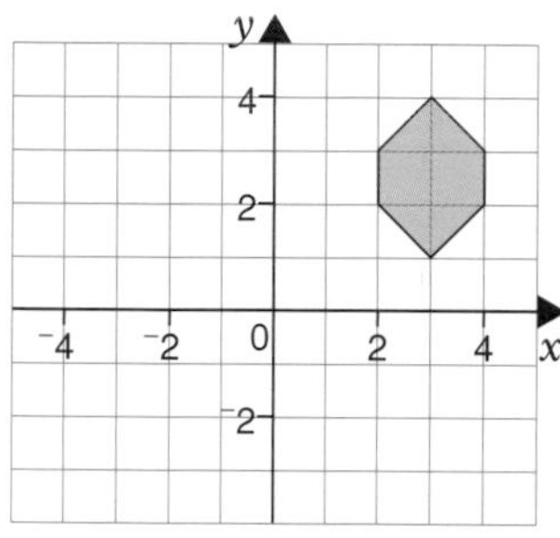
6 units left and 2 units down

e
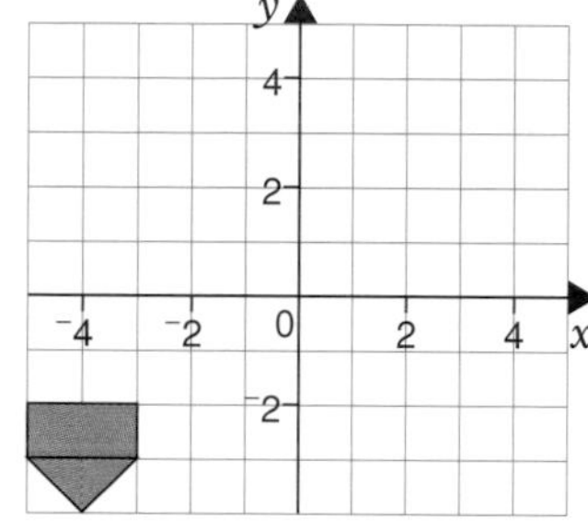
4 units right and 3 units up

2 What inverse translation is needed to translate each image you got in question **1** back to where it started?
The answer to **a** is 4 units up.

T

3 Use a copy of this.

a Plot these coordinate pairs on your grid then join them in order.
(3, 3), (3, 5), (5, 5), (5, 7), (7, 7), (7, 5), (5, 3), (3, 3)

b Translate your shape 4 squares to the left and 5 squares down.

c Write down the coordinates of the image.

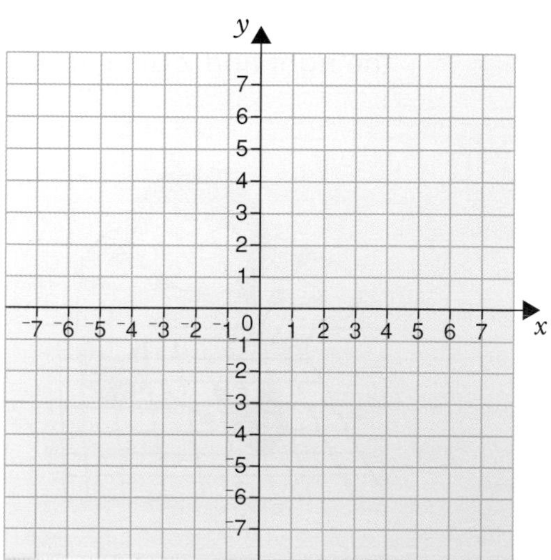

4 Which two of these give the same translation?
A 3 squares right, 4 squares down and 2 squares left
B 1 square right and 3 squares down
C 1 square right and 4 squares down

*__5__ Write down the inverse translation of
a 3 units right and 5 units down
b 7 units left and 2 units up.

* Combinations of transformations

Discussion

Sam reflected shape A in $\mathbf{m_1}$ to give shape B.
He then reflected shape B in $\mathbf{m_2}$ to give shape C.
He reflected shape C in $\mathbf{m_3}$ and so on.

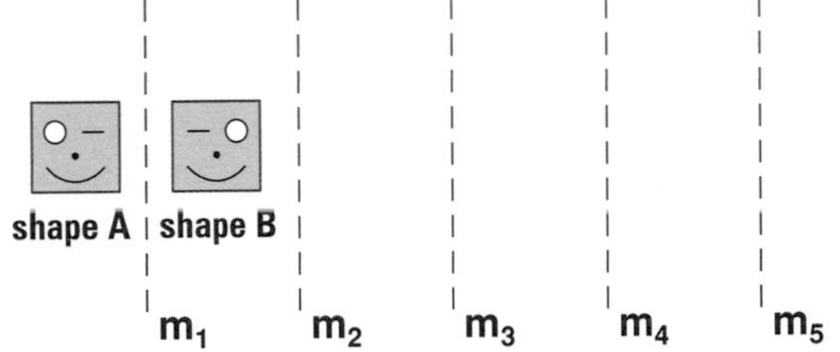

What happens when you keep reflecting a shape in parallel lines? **Discuss.**
You could try this again, starting with a different shape.

* Exercise 5

T **1** Use a copy of this.
a Reflect the purple shape in $\mathbf{m_1}$.
b Reflect the image you got in **a** in $\mathbf{m_2}$.

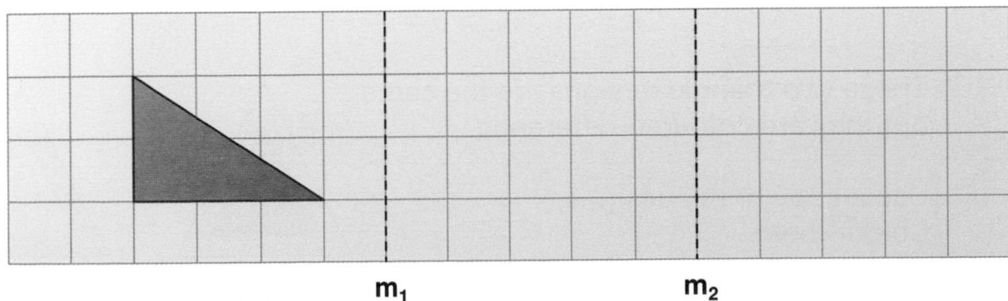

c What single transformation is the same as reflection in two parallel lines?
A translation **B** rotation **C** reflection

T

2 Rick reflects a shape in two perpendicular lines.
Use a copy of the diagram below.

a Reflect the shape in the x-axis.
b Reflect the shape you got in **a** in the y-axis.

What *single* transformation is the same as **a** and **b**?
A reflection **B** rotation of 180° **C** rotation of 90°

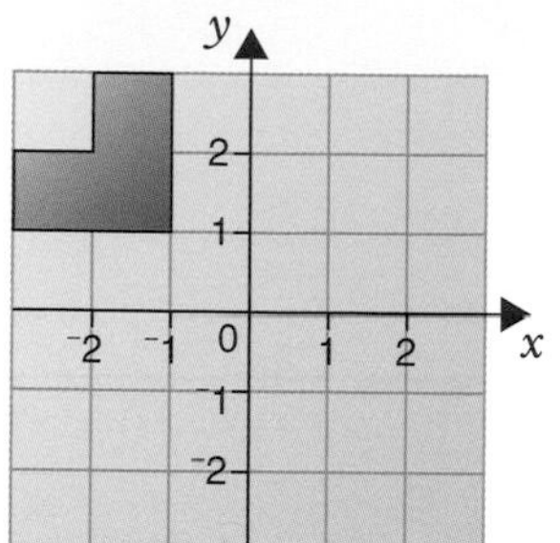

T

3 Use another copy of the diagram in question **2** for each part of this question.
Translate the shape 2 units right and 4 units up and **then** translate the image 1 unit left and 2 units down.
What single translation is the same as these two?

Symmetry

Practical

You will need

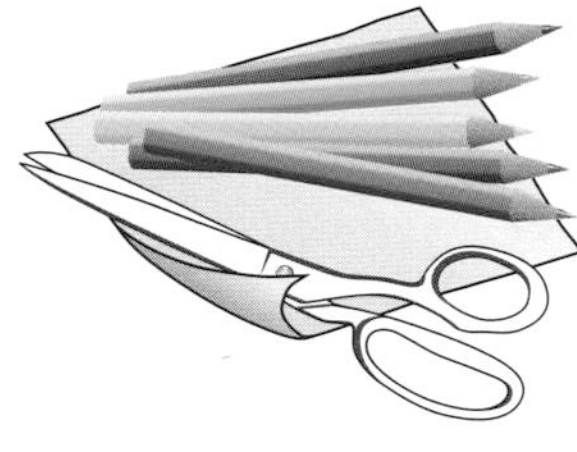

paper,
scissors and
colouring pens or pencils.

T

1 These two triangle designs are the same but they are coloured differently.

Use a copy of the designs.
Colour them.

Make a pattern by sliding or turning them or making symmetrical shapes with them.
You could cut each in half and make patterns with the halves.

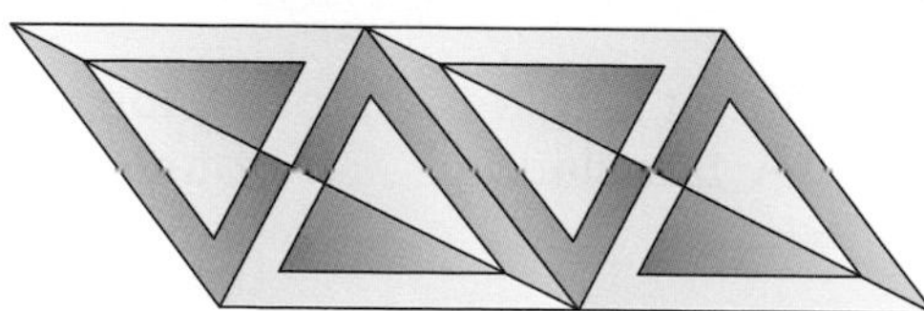

2 Do **1** again, starting with two other shapes that are coloured differently.
You could start with a hexagon,

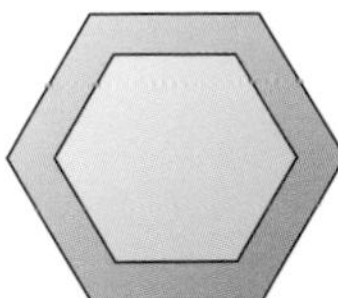
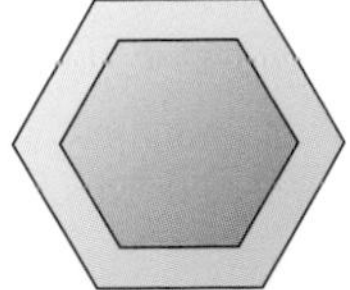

or you could start with a trapezium,

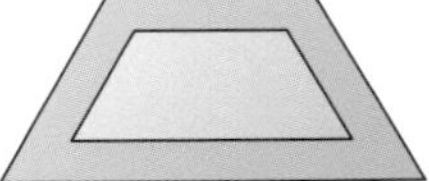
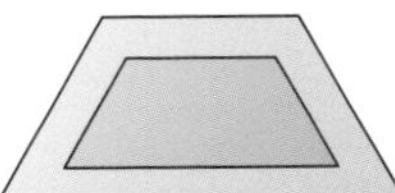

Reflection symmetry

A shape has **reflection symmetry** or **line symmetry** if a line can be found so that one half of the shape reflects onto the other half.
The line is a **line of symmetry**.

The line of symmetry is sometimes called the mirror line.

Examples Shapes A and C have reflection symmetry.

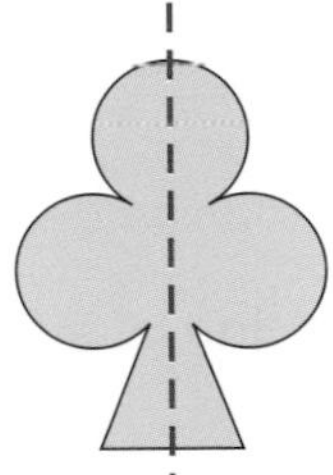

1 line of symmetry

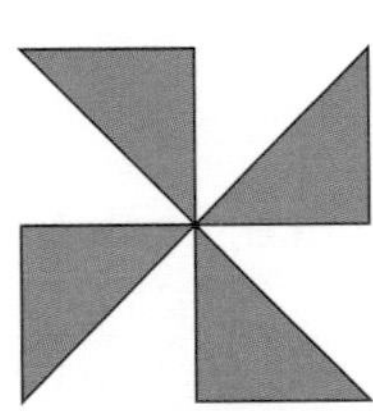

0 lines of symmetry

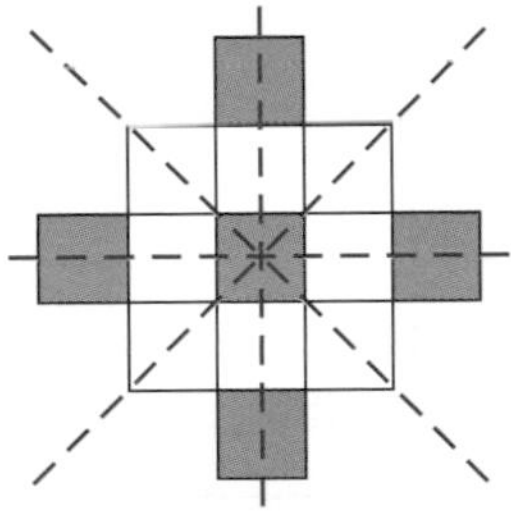

4 lines of symmetry

Which letters of your name have reflection symmetry?

Exercise 6

T

1 Use a copy of these.
Which of these patterns have reflection symmetry?
Draw the lines of symmetry on the ones that do.

a

b

c

T

2 Use a copy of these.
Shade **two more squares** to make the dashed line a line of symmetry.

a
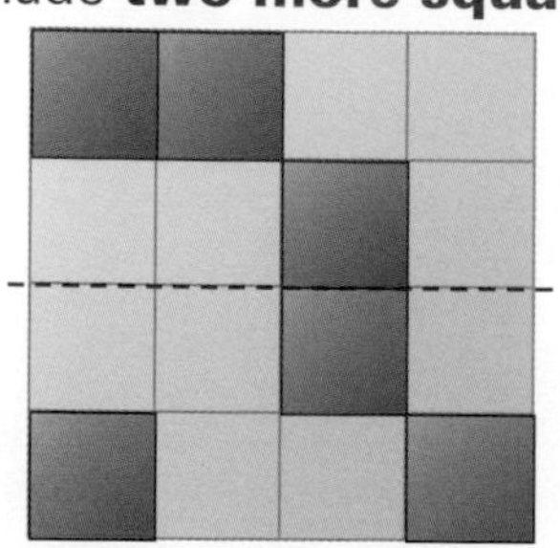
b
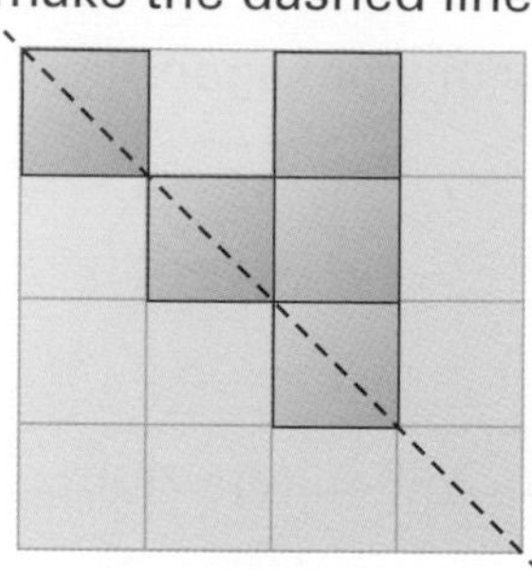
c
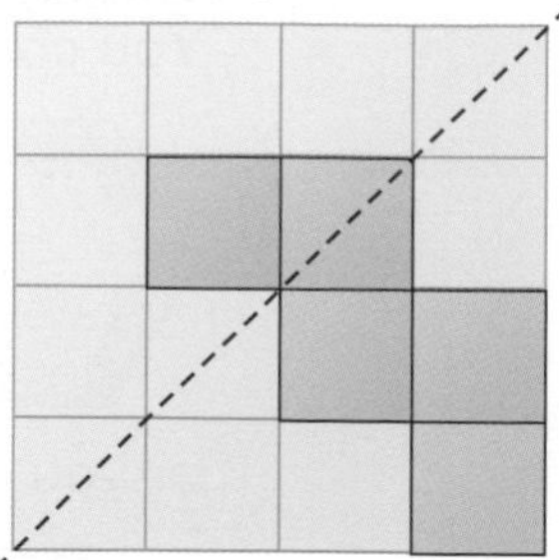

T

3 Use a copy of these.
Shade **more dots** so that the dashed lines are lines of symmetry.

a
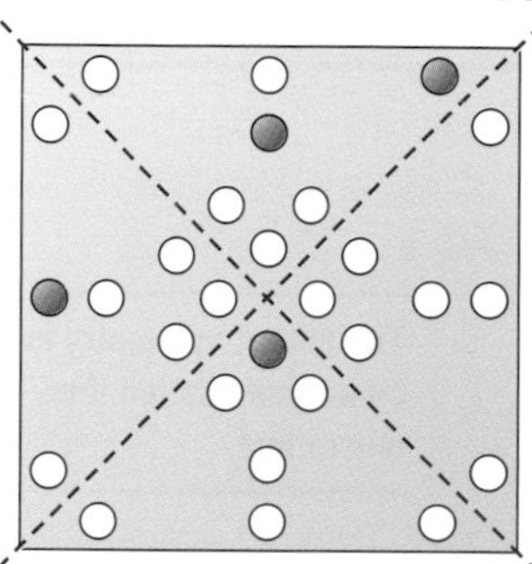
b
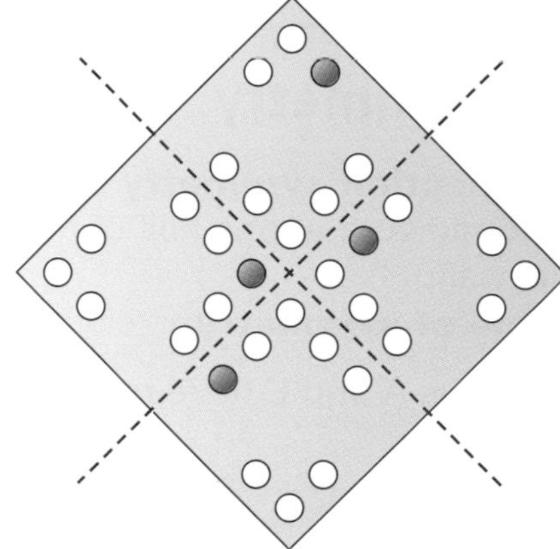

*4 A piece of paper has been folded twice, each time along a line of symmetry.
This is what it then looks like.

What shape might the piece of paper have been before being folded?
Is there more than one answer?

*5 Show how you can put these shapes together to make a single shape with reflection symmetry.
There is more than one way for each.
Find all the ways.

a
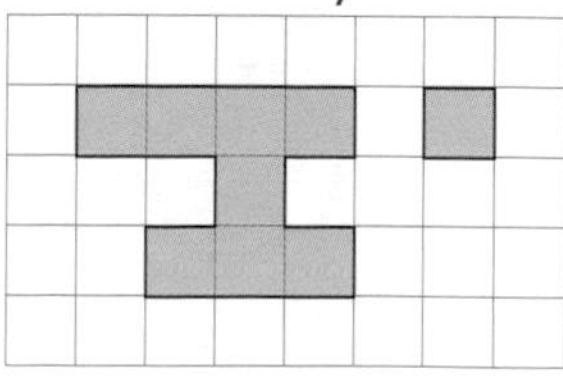
two ways

b
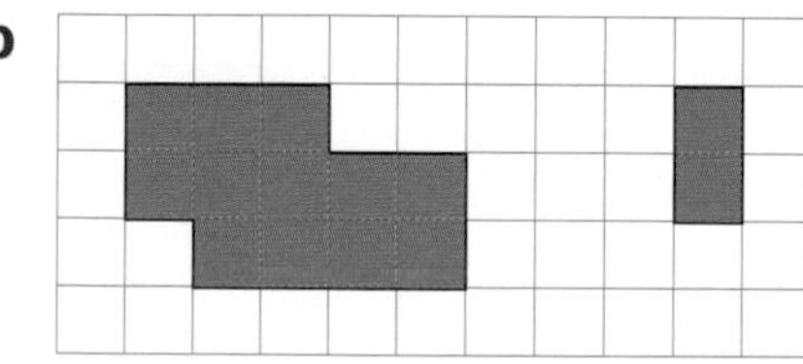
four ways

Practical

You will need squared paper.

Draw a pattern on squared paper that has

a 2 lines of symmetry
b 4 lines of symmetry
c 3 lines of symmetry.

Rotation symmetry

A shape has **rotation symmetry** if it looks the same in **more than one place** during a full turn.

The number of times it looks the same in a complete turn is called the **order of rotation symmetry**.

Examples

order 2

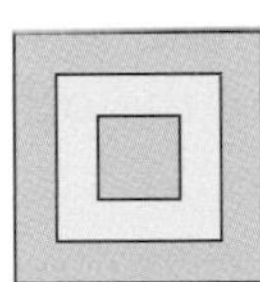

order 4

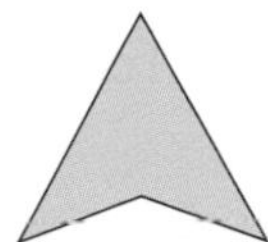

order 1
This shape has no rotation symmetry.

Exercise 7

1 Which of these shapes have rotation symmetry?

a 

b 

c 

d 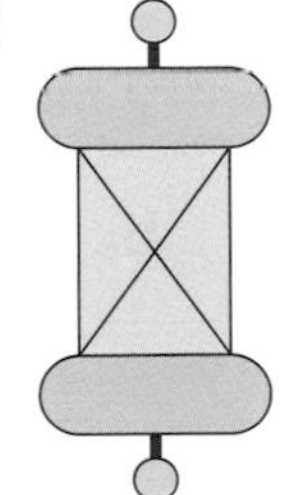

2 Write down the order of rotation symmetry of these shapes.

a 

b 

c 

d 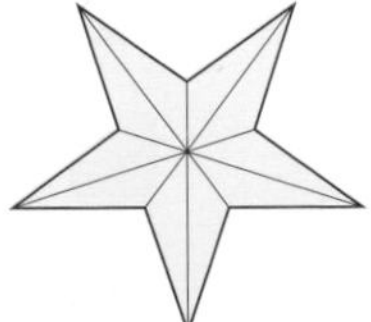

3

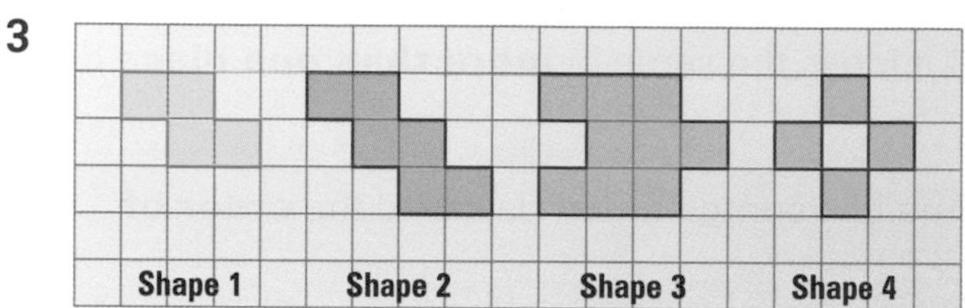

a Which of these shapes does *not* have rotation symmetry?
b What is the order of rotation symmetry of the other shapes?

4 Choose from the box.
Which special triangles and quadrilaterals have
a just 2 lines of symmetry
b 4 lines of symmetry
c no lines of symmetry
d no rotation symmetry
e rotation symmetry of order 2
f rotation symmetry of order 4?

> **square, rectangle, parallelogram, rhombus, trapezium, kite, arrowhead, scalene triangle, isosceles triangle, equilateral triangle, right-angled triangle**

***5 a** Rachel put these two shapes together, edge to edge. Her new shape had just 1 line of symmetry. Show two ways Rachel might have done this.

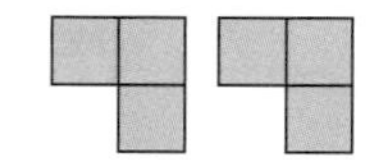

b Show a way of putting the two shapes together edge to edge to get a new shape with
i rotation symmetry of order 2 but no lines of symmetry (two ways)
ii 2 lines of symmetry *and* rotation symmetry of order 2.

***6** Show how you can put these shapes together to make a single shape with rotation symmetry of the order given.

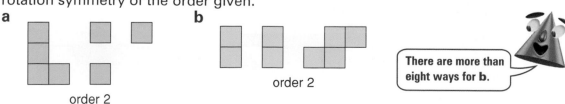

a

order 2

b

order 2

There are more than eight ways for **b**.

Investigation

Pentominoes

You will need some squared paper.

A pentomino is a shape made from 5 squares.
There are 12 pentominoes altogether.
Try to draw them all.

Which of the 12 pentominoes have line symmetry?
Draw the lines of symmetry on them.

Which of the 12 pentominoes have rotation symmetry?
Write down the order of rotation symmetry by each pentomino.

Practical

You will need coloured pencils or pens.

Use a copy of this.

Colour this shape so that it has rotation symmetry.

Use at least 2 colours.

*Practical

You will need Logo or a similar ICT package or a dynamic geometry package.

Make a shape on your screen with rotation symmetry of order
a 2 **b** 4 **c** 5 **d** 6 **e** 8 **f** 9.

Example Melanie made this shape by rotating a right-angled triangle through 45° angles. Her shape has rotation symmetry of order 8.

Enlargement

Discussion

- Jake had some photos enlarged.
  Think of some other everyday examples where the word 'enlarged' is used. **Discuss.**
- Binoculars are used to enlarge objects.
  Think of other things that can enlarge. **Discuss.**

The brown tree has been **enlarged** to the green tree.

Each length on the green tree is **2** times as long as it is on the brown tree.
The **scale factor** of the enlargement is **2**.

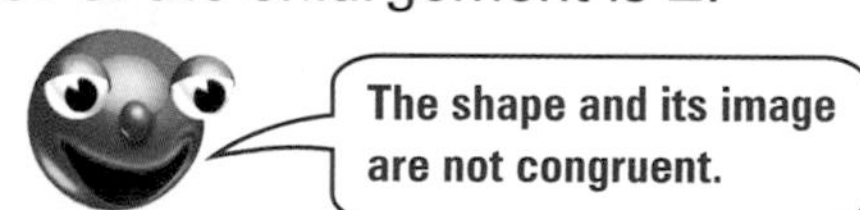

The shape and its image are not congruent.

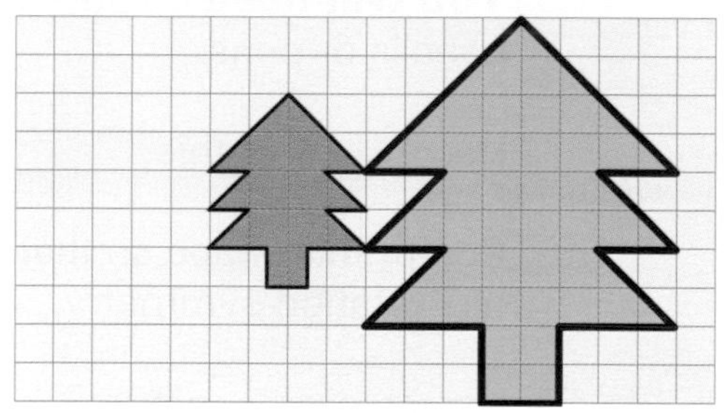

Exercise 8

1 Shape A has been enlarged to shape B.
What is the scale factor of the enlargement?

a

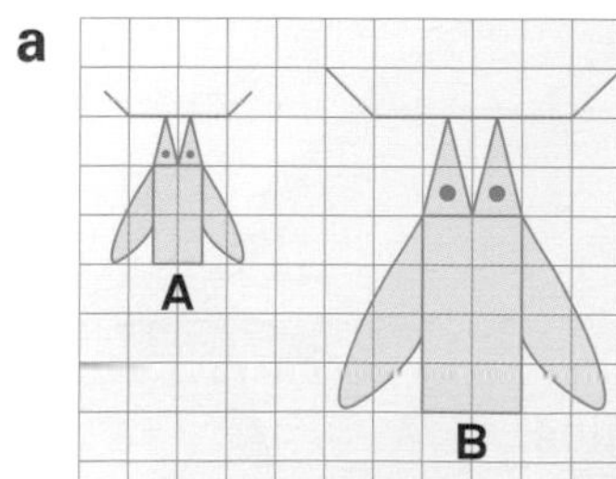

b

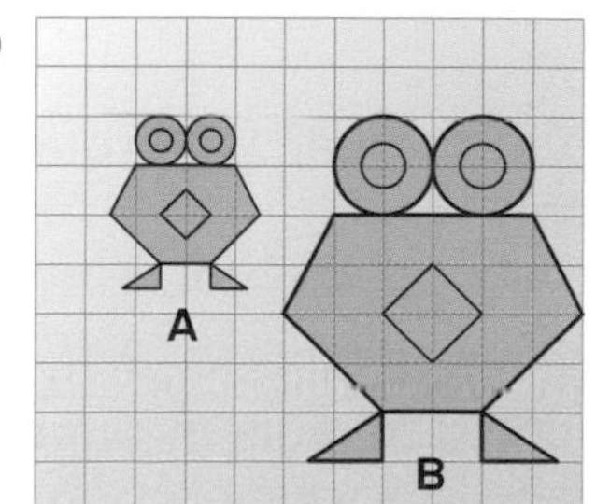

c

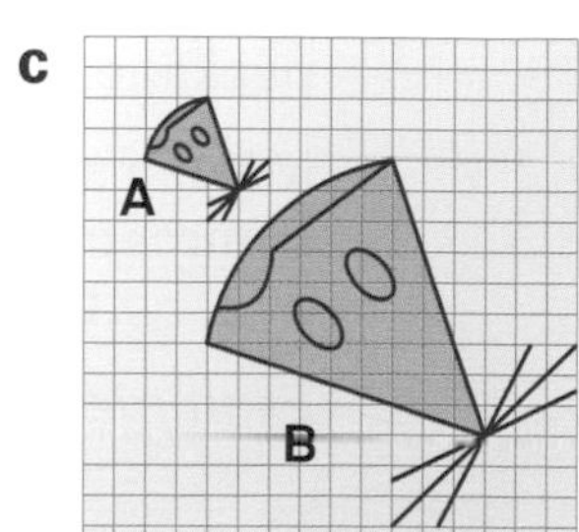

Summary of key points

We use **coordinates** to give the position of a point on a grid.
The coordinates of A are $(^{-}2, 1)$.
We always give the x-coordinate first.

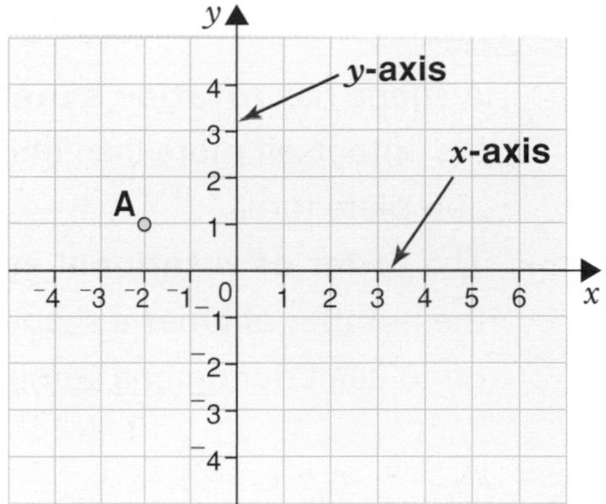

B **Reflection**

ABC has been reflected in the mirror line to get the **image** A′B′C′.

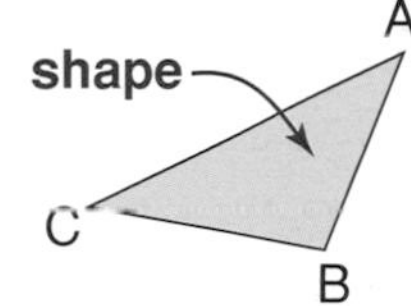

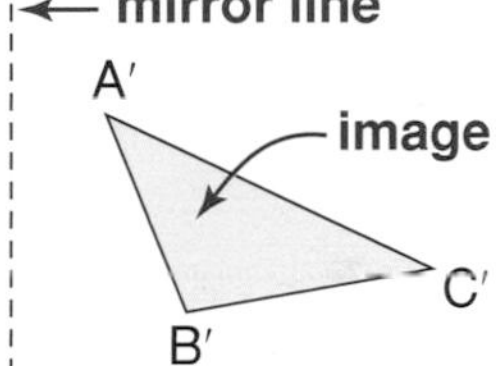

Points on the mirror line do not move under reflection.

To **rotate** a shape we need to know the **centre of rotation** and the **angle of rotation**.

Example ABC has been rotated 180° using (0, 0) as the centre of rotation.

The angle of rotation given is in an **anticlockwise** direction.
We can use tracing paper to do a rotation.

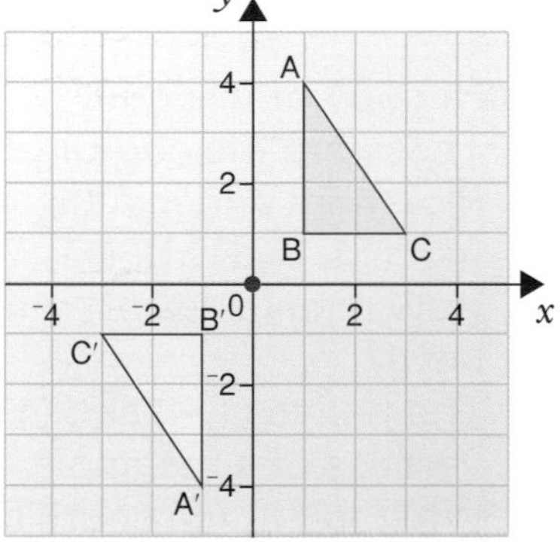

D To **translate** a shape we slide it.

Example This shape has been translated 4 units right and 3 units up.

The **inverse of a translation** is an equal move in the opposite direction.

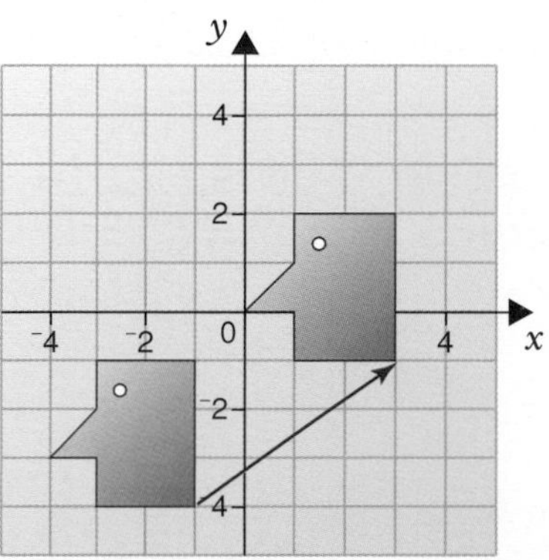

A shape has **reflection symmetry** if one half of the shape can be reflected in a line to the other half.
The line is a **line of symmetry**.

A shape has **rotation symmetry** if it fits onto itself more than once during a complete turn.
The **order of rotational symmetry** is the number of times a shape fits exactly on to itself during one complete turn.

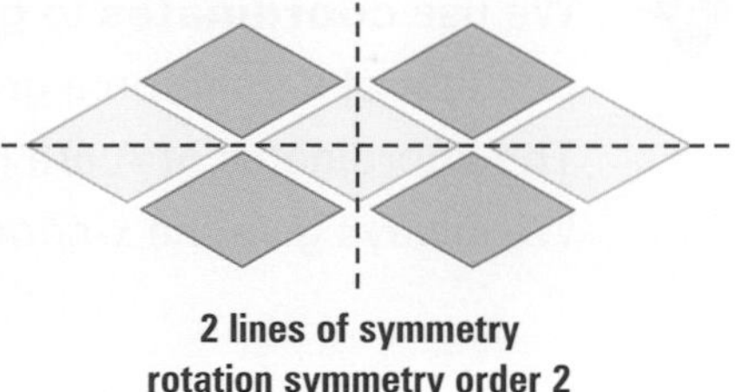

2 lines of symmetry
rotation symmetry order 2

The red F has been **enlarged** to give the blue F.
Each length on the blue F is **3** times as long as on the red F.
The **scale factor** of the enlargement is **3**.

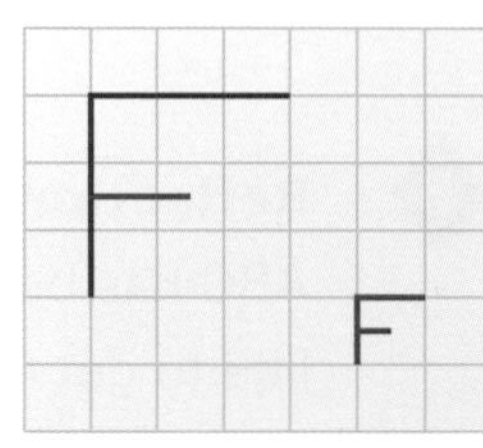

Test yourself

1 Use a copy of this grid.

a These are the coordinates of the vertices of a shape.
Plot them and join them in order.
$(^-1, 3), (1, 1), (^-1, ^-1), (^-3, 1), (^-1, 3)$

b How many lines of symmetry does the shape have?

c The points (1, 4) and (4, 2) are two of the four vertices of a rectangle.
What might the coordinates of the other two vertices be?
Is it possible to make a square?
Explain why or why not.

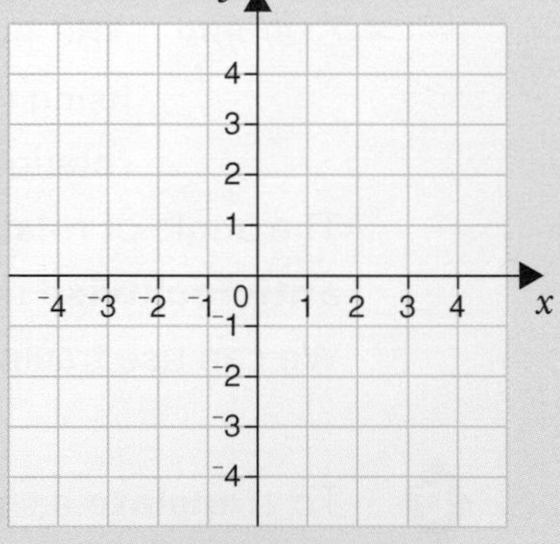

T **2** Use a copy of these.
Draw the reflection in the mirror line, **m**.

a

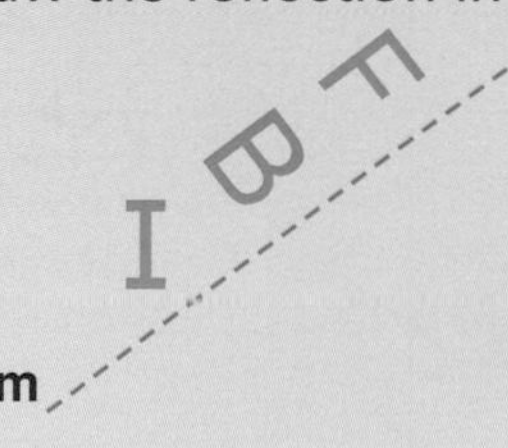

b

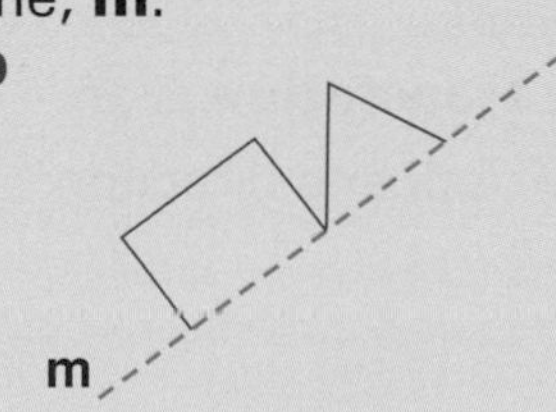

T

3 Use a copy of this. **B**
Reflect the shape in the x-axis to make a pattern.
Then reflect this new pattern in the y-axis.

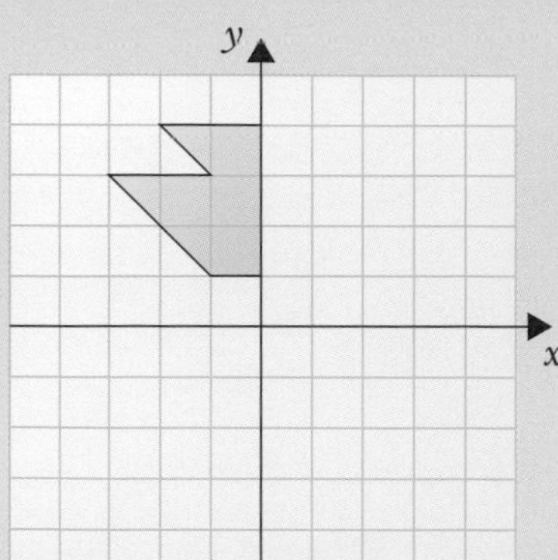

4 Explain why P′ is not the reflection of P in the line S. **B**

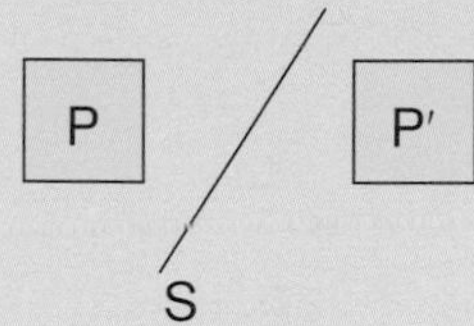

T

5 Use a copy of these. **C**
The centre of rotation and angle of rotation are given.
a Draw the image shapes.

i (0, 0) **90°**

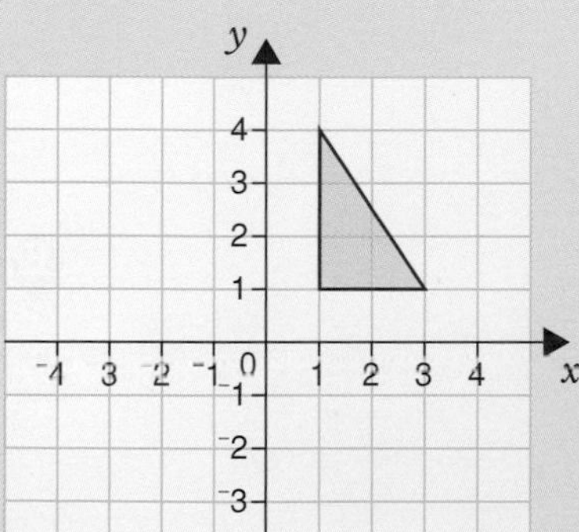

ii (0, 0) **180°**

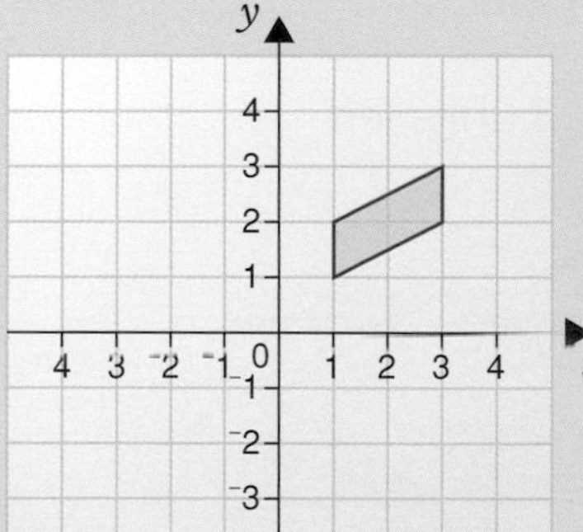

iii (2, 2) **270°**

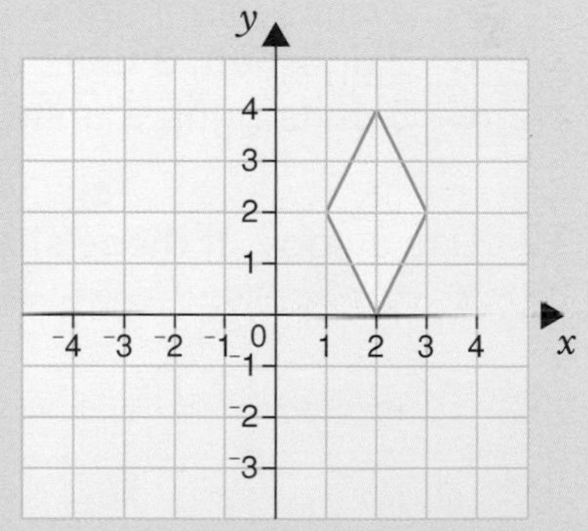

b Give the coordinates of the image shape in **i**.

6 I want to rotate the image I got in question **5i** back to where it started. **C**
What rotation do I need to do?

T

7 Use a copy of these.
Draw the image after these translations. 

a 3 units down

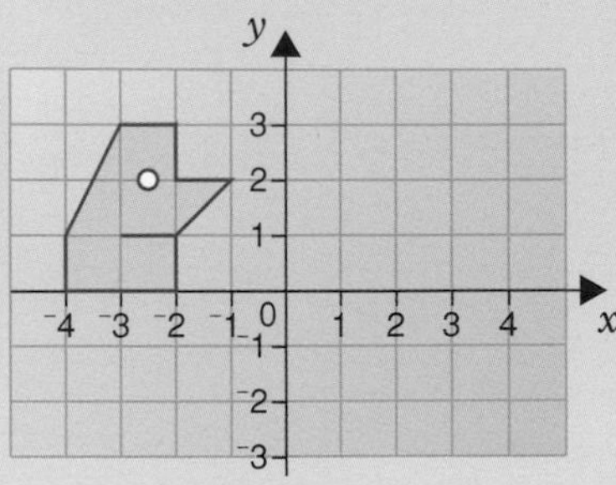

b 4 units right and 2 units down

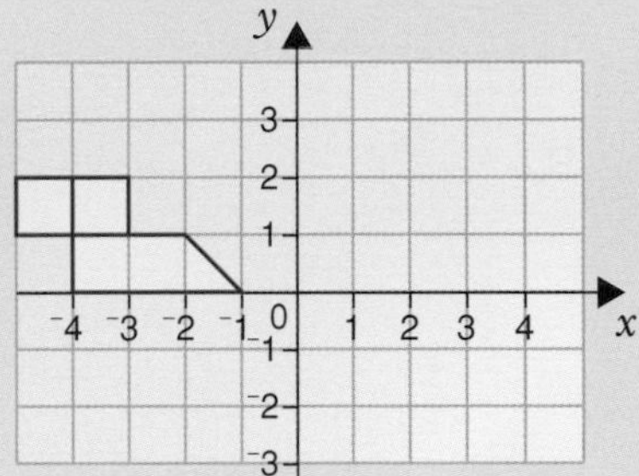

8 What translation is the inverse of these? 

a 3 units right and 1 unit up

b 5 units left and 3 units down

9 Which two of these give the same translation? 

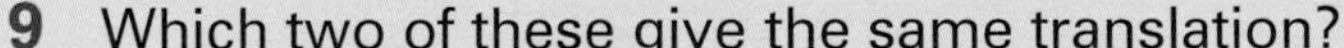

A 3 units left, 3 units up, 1 unit right

B 2 units left, 3 units up

C 5 units right, 3 units up, 3 units left

T

10 Use a copy of these shapes. 

a

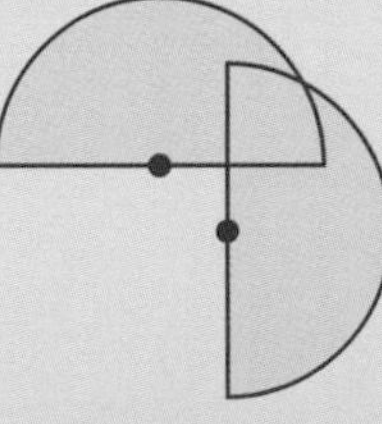

b

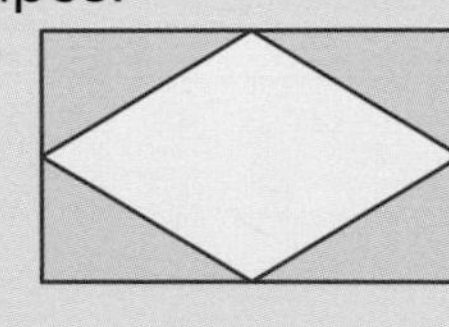

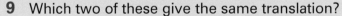

Draw on the lines of symmetry.

11 What is the order of rotation symmetry of these? 

a

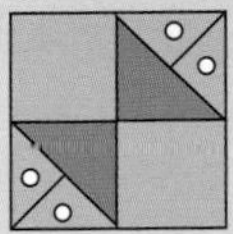

b

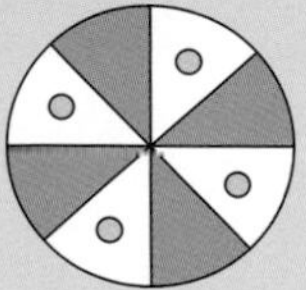

c

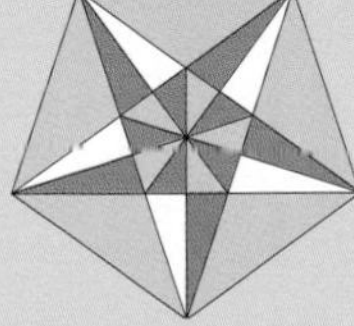

d

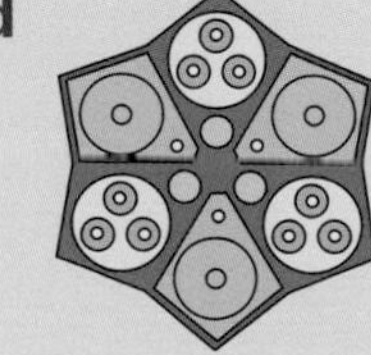

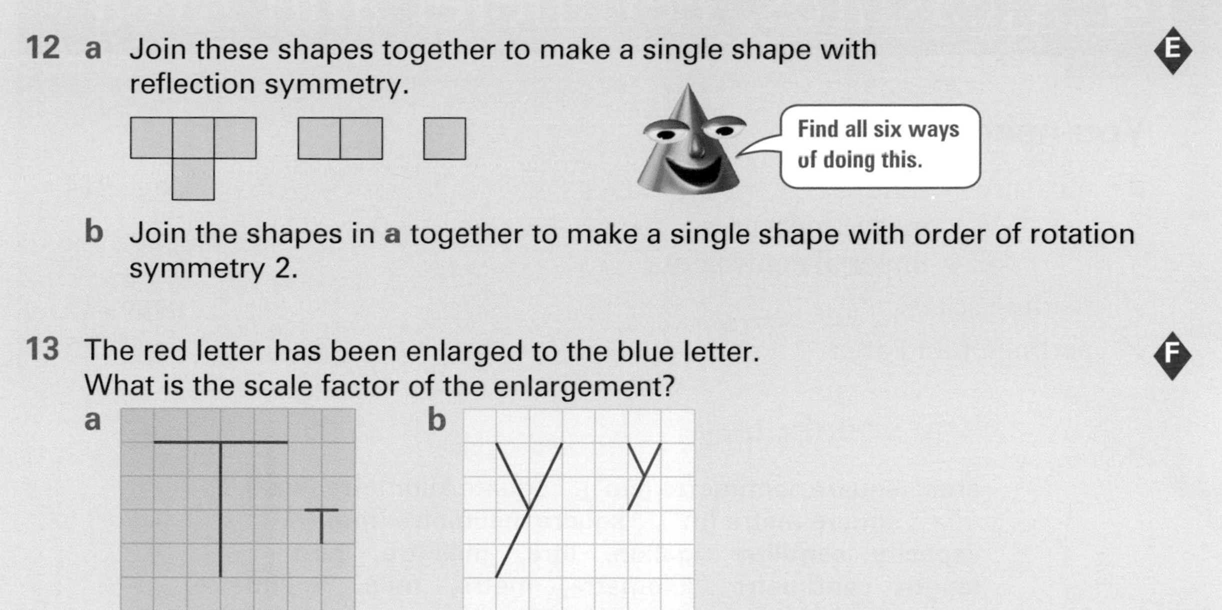
Find all six ways
of doing this.

12 a Join these shapes together to make a single shape with reflection symmetry. E

b Join the shapes in **a** together to make a single shape with order of rotation symmetry 2.

13 The red letter has been enlarged to the blue letter. F
What is the scale factor of the enlargement?

a

b

14 Measures. Perimeter and Area

You need to know

✓ measures – time — page 214
 – metric measures
 – imperial equivalents

✓ reading scales — page 215

✓ perimeter and area — page 215

Key vocabulary

area: square centimetre (cm^2), square kilometre (km^2), square metre (m^2), square millimetre (mm^2)
capacity: centilitre, gallon, litre, millilitre, pint
length: centimetre, kilometre, metre, mile, millimetre
mass: gram, kilogram, pound
temperature: degrees Celsius (°C), degrees Fahrenheit (°F)
time: century, day, decade, hour, millennium, minute, month, second, week, year
depth, distance, estimate, height, length, perimeter, range, surface area, width

Makeover

Paint Allow 1 litre of paint for every 8 m^2.

Curtain material Width needed: twice the width of the windows
Length needed: length of windows + 20 cm extra

Wallpaper

	WALLPAPER CHART														
height of room in metres	distance around the room in metres (m)														
	9	10	11	13	14	15	16	18	19	20	21	23	24	25	26
2·00 m – 2.30 m	4	5	5	6	6	7	7	8	8	9	9	10	10	11	12
2·31 m – 2.50 m	5	5	6	6	7	7	8	8	9	9	10	11	11	12	13
2·51 m – 2.70 m	5	6	6	8	8	8	9	10	11	11	12	13	13	13	14
2·71 m – 3.00 m	6	6	7	8	9	9	10	11	12	12	13	14	14	15	16
3·01 m – 3.20 m	6	7	8	8	10	10	10	12	12	13	13	14	15	16	16
	Number of rolls needed														

Use this information to do a project on decorating a room in your house or school.

As part of your project, take measurements, draw plans, work out how much paint, wallpaper, curtain material, etc. you will need.
Find the total cost.

Metric conversions

We often need to **change one metric unit into another.**

Remember

Length
1 kilometre (km) = 1000 metres (m)
1 metre (m) = 100 centimetres (cm)
1 metre (m) = 1000 millimetres (mm)
1 centimetre (cm) = 10 millimetres (mm)

Mass
1 kilogram (kg) = 1000 grams (g)

Capacity
1 litre (ℓ) = 1000 millilitres (mℓ)
1 centilitre (cℓ) = 10 millilitres (mℓ)
1 litre (ℓ) = 100 centilitres (cℓ)

kilo: means 1000 times
centi: means one hundredth
milli: means one thousandth.
These prefixes go in front of the base unit. The base unit for
length is metre
mass is gram
capacity is litre.

Discussion

- base unit ↓

Kilo			metre gram litre		centi	milli
1000	100	10	1	0·1	0·01	0·001

How could you use this chart to help you convert from one metric unit to another? **Discuss.**

Try using it to convert these.
5 kg to g   8 cm to mm   360 cm to m   840 mℓ to ℓ

- David worked out that he walked 2560 m to school each day.
He wanted to know how many kilometres this was.
Will the number of kilometres be more or less than the number of metres?

Changing larger to smaller units

Example

Jade put a 2·5 cm border around a poster.
She multiplied by 10 to change 2·5 cm to mm.

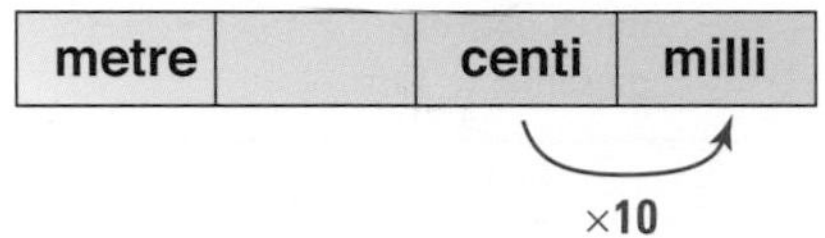

2·5 cm = 2·5 × 10 mm
= **25 mm**

Worked Example

Change **a** 0·42 kg to g **b** 14·2 ℓ to mℓ.

See page 21 for multiplying by 10, 100 and 1000.

Answer

a 0·42 kg = 0·42 × 1000 g
= **420 g**

b 14·2 ℓ = 14·2 × 1000 mℓ
= **14 200 mℓ**

Exercise 1

When changing larger units to smaller units, your answer will be a bigger number.

Kilo			metre gram litre		centi	milli

1 Change

a 7 cm to mm **b** 6·4 cm to mm **c** 3·5 km to m
d 2·6 m to mm **e** 0·8 cm to mm **f** 0·3 m to mm.

2 Change

a 3 kg to g **b** 5·7 kg to g **c** 8·7 kg to g
d 7·25 kg to g **e** 0·5 kg to g **f** 0·05 kg to g.

3 Change

a 4 ℓ to mℓ **b** 8·6 ℓ to mℓ **c** 6 ℓ to cℓ
d 1·4 ℓ to cℓ **e** 25 cℓ to mℓ **f** 4·6 cℓ to mℓ.

T

4

						G		
560	3·2	4·8	5200	52	6·4	5600	32	480

6·4	4·8	5200	4800	4800	32	320	15200	320	64	4·8

	G		
5200	5600	32	**30**

Use a copy of the box on the previous page.
What goes in the gap?
Write the letter beside each question above its answer.

G 5·6 ℓ = 5600 mℓ **O** 6·4 cm = __mm **R** 0·32 km = __m **T** 0·48 kg = __g
A 5·2 ℓ = __ mℓ **N** 0·52 ℓ = __ cℓ **F** 15·2 kg = __g **U** 0·32 cm = __mm
E 0·032 kg = __g **L** 4·8 kg = __g **H** 5·6 m = __cm **S** 0·64 cℓ = __mℓ
M 0·048 m = __cm

***5** What is the height of your classroom door in metres?
Change it to **a** cm **b** mm.

Changing smaller to larger units

Example Michael's bed is 190 cm long.
He divided by 10 then 10 again to change this to metres.

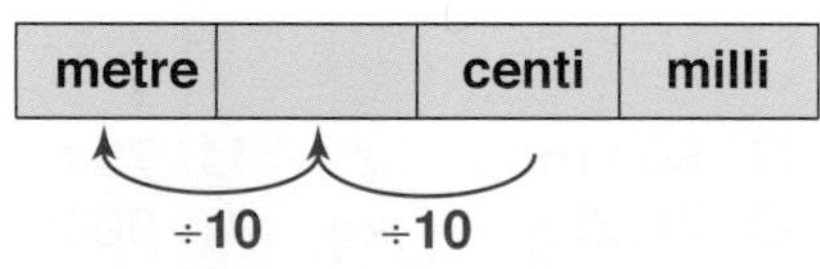

190 cm = 190 ÷ 10 ÷ 10 m
= 190 ÷ 100 m
= **1·9 m**

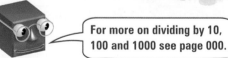

For more on dividing by 10, 100 and 1000 see page 000.

Worked Example
Change **a** 832 g to kg **b** 3 cℓ to ℓ.

Answer
a 832 g = 832 ÷ 1000 kg **move each digit 3 places to the right**
= **0·832 kg**
b 3 cℓ = 3 ÷ 100 ℓ **move each digit 2 places to the right**
= **0·03** ℓ

Exercise 2

1 Change

a 8000 cm to m **b** 400 cm to m **c** 160 cm to m **d** 185 cm to m
e 89 cm to m **f** 9 cm to m **g** 9200 mm to m **h** 180 mm to cm
i 720 mm to m **j** 4368 m to km **k** 864 m to km **l** 93 m to km.

2 Change

a 5000 mℓ to ℓ **b** 3400 mℓ to ℓ **c** 400 mℓ to ℓ **d** 2850 mℓ to ℓ
e 1396 mℓ to ℓ **f** 347 mℓ to ℓ **g** 54 mℓ to ℓ **h** 400 cℓ to ℓ
i 600 cℓ to ℓ **j** 750 cℓ to ℓ **k** 855 cℓ to ℓ.

3 Change

a 7000 g to kg **b** 4700 g to kg **c** 1860 g to kg **d** 75 g to kg

T **4**

3·25	7·5	4·65	3·25	5·2	7·5	75	5·2	0·05	9	0·36

0·9	75	4·65	0·75	T 5	**25 000**

T 5	0·05	0·465	7·5	0·075	0·9	0·5	0·9	3·6

Use a copy of the box.
What goes in the gaps?

T 5000 g = **5 kg** **N** 90 mm = __ cm **D** 500 mℓ = __ ℓ **U** 75 cm = __ m
S 75 mm = __ m **Y** 3600 m = __ km **O** 4650 g = __ kg **A** 90 cℓ = __ ℓ
L 520 cm = __ m **K** 360 g = __ kg **I** 50 m = __ km **E** 7500 mm = __ m
M 465 mℓ = __ ℓ **B** 750 mℓ = __ cℓ **P** 325 cℓ = __ ℓ

5 Chantelle's baby sister was very small.
She weighed just 855 g.
How many kg did this baby weigh?

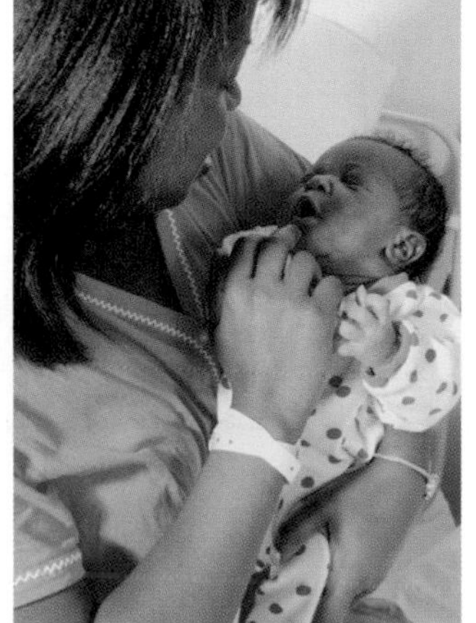

6 Find the missing numbers.

a __ m = 50 mm **b** 386 m = __ km
c 23 mm = __ cm **d** __ kg = 450 g
e 47 cm = __ m **f** __ ℓ = 385 mℓ
g __ ℓ = 420 cℓ

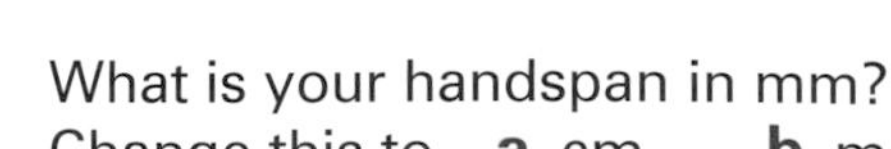

***7** What is your handspan in mm?
Change this to **a** cm **b** m.

Mixed conversions

Exercise 3

T

1 Use a copy of this crossnumber.
If decimal points are needed give them a full space.

Across
Write
1 1450 cm in m
4 37 mm in cm
6 2·8 cm in mm
7 0·048 ℓ in mℓ
10 0·707 kg in g
12 564 cm in m
14 7·35 m in cm
15 31·42 ℓ in cℓ
16 9090 g in kg
18 0·026 km in m
19 4100 mℓ in ℓ
20 3·4 cm in mm
22 0·523 kg in g
23 7070 mm in m.

Down
Write
1 0·12 ℓ in mℓ
2 0·048 m in mm
3 5·2 cm in mm
4 0·39 km in m
5 0·074 kg in g
8 8·05 kg in g
9 3460 m in km
10 7400 cℓ in ℓ
11 7·7 ℓ in mℓ
12 510 mm in cm
13 6·2 cm in mm
15 3·425 kg in g
16 9870 mℓ in ℓ
17 0·932 kg in g
21 4·3 m in cm
22 5·6 cm in mm.

1 1	2 4	•	3 5		4		5	
6							7	8
		9		10		11		
	12		13			14		
15								
				16			17	
18			19				20	21
						22		
	23							

2 Write

a 17·82 m in cm **b** 5·04 kg in g **c** 9461 mℓ in ℓ **d** 804 mm in cm
e 1842 cℓ in ℓ **f** 56 mℓ in ℓ **g** 542 m in km **h** 0·31 ℓ in cℓ.

Solving measures problems

Remember

1 minute = 60 seconds
1 hour = 60 minutes
1 day = 24 hours

1 week = 7 days
1 leap year = 366 days
1 year = 12 months or 52 weeks or 365 days

1 decade = 10 years
1 century = 100 years
1 millennium = 1000 years

Example Susie bought 500 g of nuts at £2·80 per kg.
She worked out how much they cost like this.

£2·80 = 280 p **She changed £ to p**
$\frac{1}{2}$ of 280p = 140 p **500 g is $\frac{1}{2}$ kg**
The nuts cost £**1·40.** **She changed p to £**

Exercise 4

Only use a calculator if you need to.

1 How many 5 mℓ spoons of medicine can be taken from a 0·2 ℓ bottle?

2 What is the total weight, in kg, of this fruit?

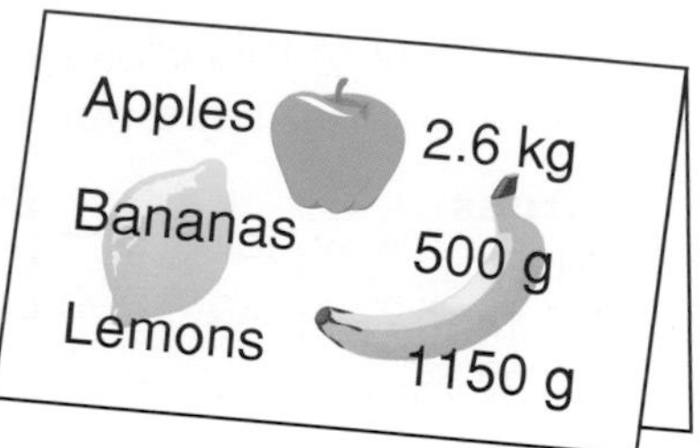

3 Hetty's baby sister is $4\frac{1}{2}$ hours old.
 a How many minutes is this?
 b How many seconds?

4 To keep in shape Charlotte swims 1 km twice a week.
If the pool is 40 m long, how many lengths does Charlotte swim each week?

5 Some books each weigh 760 g.
How many can be sent in this service lift?

6 Patty typed 10 pages in 1 hour 40 minutes.
How many minutes on average did it take to type each page?

7 Jamie made 2·2 ℓ of sauce.
He poured this into 4 jars of the same size.
How many mℓ of sauce was in each jar?

8 An art class made a poster using three sheets of paper with lengths 42 cm, 45 cm and 852 mm.
How long was the poster? (Answer in m.)

9 Tim is a tour guide for 'Lakes Tours'. Each tour takes 4 days.
Last year he guided 20 tours.
How many weeks and days did this take?

10 A skating track is 0·4 km long.
 a How many metres is this?
 b How many times does Joel need to skate round the track to travel 4 km?

11 Tanya went to the cinema at 4:30 p.m.
The film finished at 6:42 p.m.
 a Write the time the film started in 24-hour time.
 b How long was the film?

12 Tony walks 450 m to and from school each day.
How many kilometres is this each week?
(Tony goes to school 5 days a week.)

13 Ken bought 500 g of tomatoes at £1·89 per kilogram.
How much did the tomatoes cost to the nearest penny?

14 Kate's food in her hiking pack weighed 3·2 kg.
She ate a tin of soup which weighed 432 g.
How much did her food weigh, in kg, then?

15 A 1·2 kg box of cereal is enough for 25 servings.
How many grams is each of these servings?

16 Khalid made 450 cℓ of curry sauce.
How many 75 mℓ servings will he get from this?

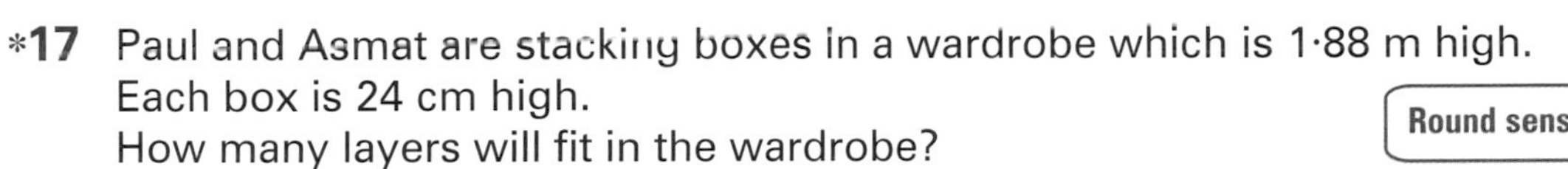

***17** Paul and Asmat are stacking boxes in a wardrobe which is 1·88 m high.
Each box is 24 cm high.
How many layers will fit in the wardrobe?

Round sensibly.

***18** A box weighs 800 g.
The box is filled with packets of crisps.
Each packet weighs 85 g.
The full box weighs a total of 4·88 kg.
How many packets of crisps are in the box?

***19** How many decades are there in a millennium?

* Puzzle

1 Each link of this chain is 24 mm from outside edge to outside edge.
Each link is made from brass 5 mm thick.
What is the length of the 6-link chain?

2 Rose needed to measure out exactly 2 ℓ of water.
She had two containers, one that held 8 ℓ and one that held 5 ℓ.
She began by filling the 5 ℓ container.
How did she continue?

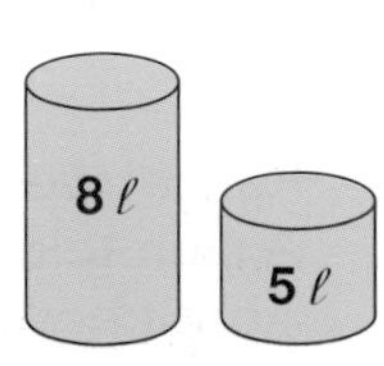

Metric and imperial measures

Remember

These are approximate **metric and imperial equivalents.**

1 gallon ≈ 4·5 litres 8 km ≈ 5 miles

1 pint is just over half a litre 1 kg ≈ 2·2 pound (lb)

≈ means "is approximately equal to."

Example A litre of orange drink costs 59p.
One gallon is about 4·5 litres.

4·5 litres would cost 4·5 × 59p = 265·5p
= £2·66 to the nearest penny.

One gallon would cost about **£2·66**.

Exercise 5

Only use a calculator if you need to.

1 About how many litres are these?
a 2 gallons **b** 4 pints **c** 8 pints **d** 3 gallons **e** 12 pints

2 About how many gallons are these?
a 9 litres **b** 18 litres

Try to use a mental method first.

3 About how many pounds are these?
a 3 kg **b** 12 kg **c** 4·5 kg

4 About how many kilograms are these?
a 2·2 lb **b** 6·6 lb **c** 11 lb **d** 22 lb

5 About how many kilometres are these?
a 10 miles **b** 25 miles

6 About how many miles are these?
a 16 km **b** 32 km **c** 64 km

7 Ruth weighs 50 kg.
About how many pounds does she weigh?

8 Rachel went to Germany.
A sign told her it was 56 km to Berlin.
About how many miles is this?

Berlin 56 km

9 Holly's sink holds about 18 ℓ.
About how many gallons is this?

10 2 litres of fruit juice cost £1·20.
About how much would 2 pints cost?

11 Tricia's aunt lives 30 miles south of Manchester.
About how many kilometres from Manchester does she live?

12 A tank holds 40 gallons of water.
About how many litres is this?

∗**13** A litre of petrol costs 93·6p.
About how much would a gallon cost?

Reading scales

There are ten spaces between 1 and 2.
Each space on this scale is
$1 \text{ m} \div 10 = \frac{1}{10} \text{ m} = 0{\cdot}1 \text{ m}$.

The pointer is at **1·4** m.

There are five spaces between 8 and 9.
Each space is
$1 \text{ cm} \div 5 = \frac{1}{5} \text{ cm} = 0{\cdot}2 \text{ cm}$.

The pointer is at **8·6** cm.

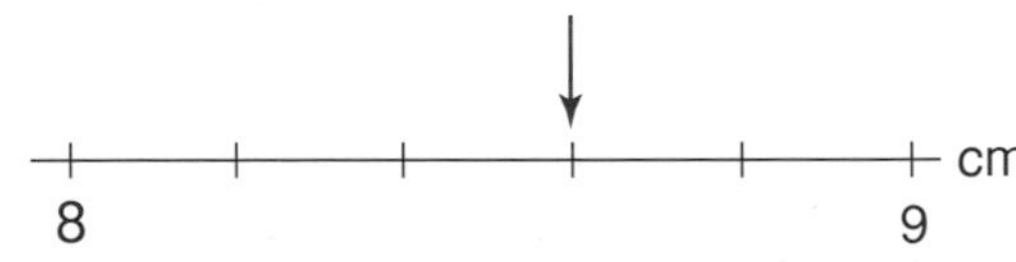

There are ten spaces between 0·1 and 0·2.
Each space on this scale is
$0{\cdot}1 \text{ kg} \div 10 = 0{\cdot}01$ or $\frac{1}{100}$ kg.

The pointer is at **0·14** kg.

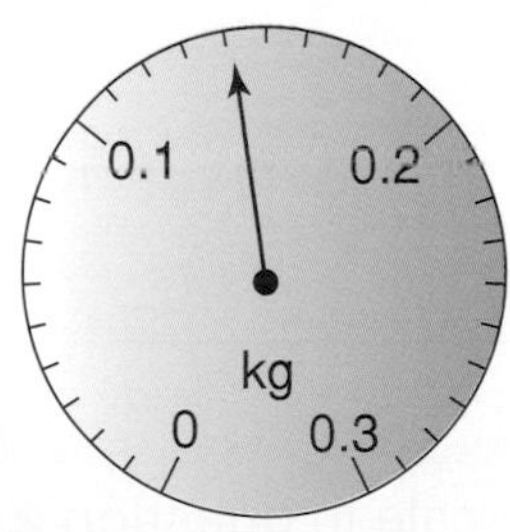

Sometimes we have to **estimate** the reading on a scale.
The pointer is about halfway between 5 ℓ and 6 ℓ or at about $5\frac{1}{2}$ ℓ.

Exercise 6

1 What measurement is given?

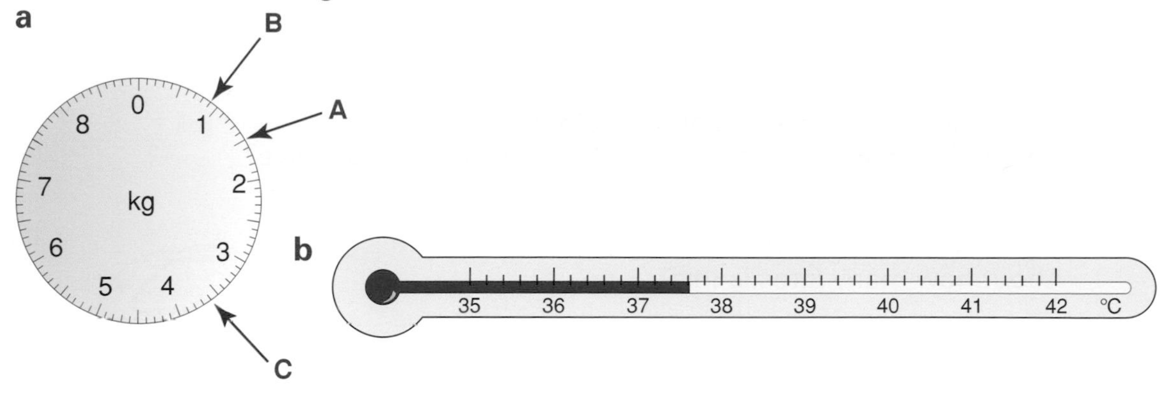

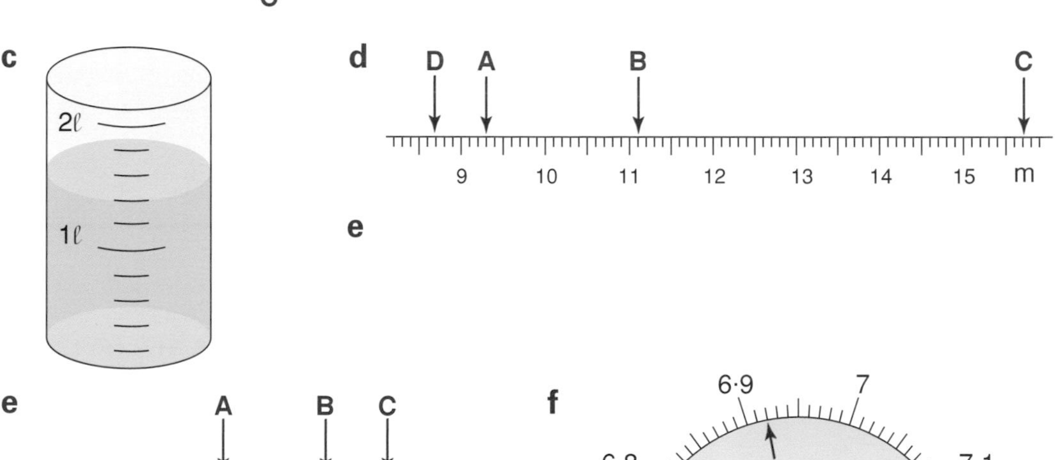

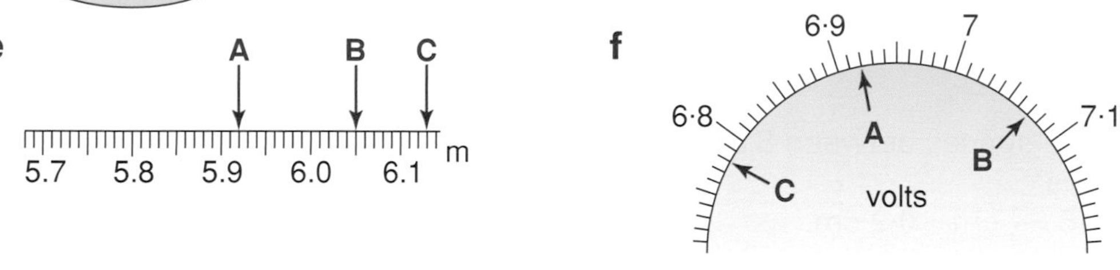

2 What reading, in mm, is given by the pointer?

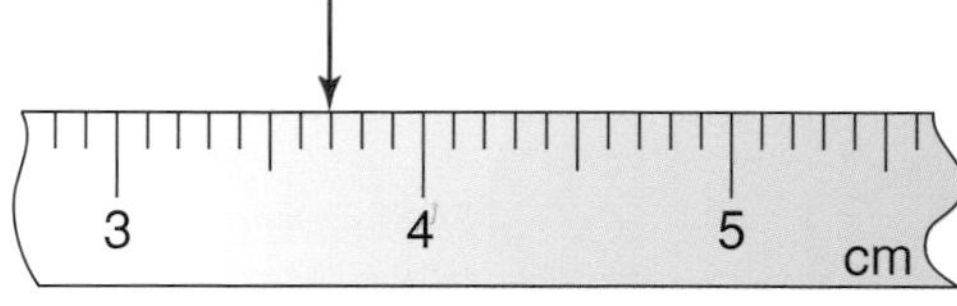

T

3 Use a copy of the scale in question **2**.
Use an arrow to show 4·6 cm.

4 Maria only had broken rulers.
Find the length of this.

5 Estimate the readings for A, B and C.

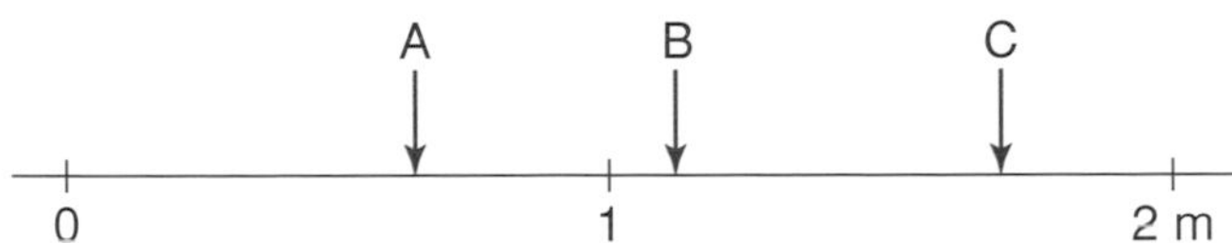

T

6 Use a copy of the scale in question **5**.
Use an arrow to show 1·6 m.

7 What is the volume, to the nearest 10 mℓ?

a **b** **c**

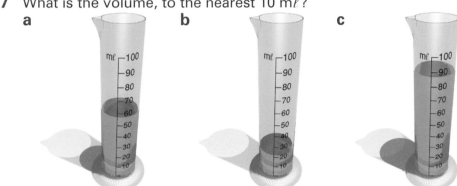

8 **a** What is the mass to the nearest 100 g?
b Estimate the mass to the nearest 10 g.

i **ii** **iii**

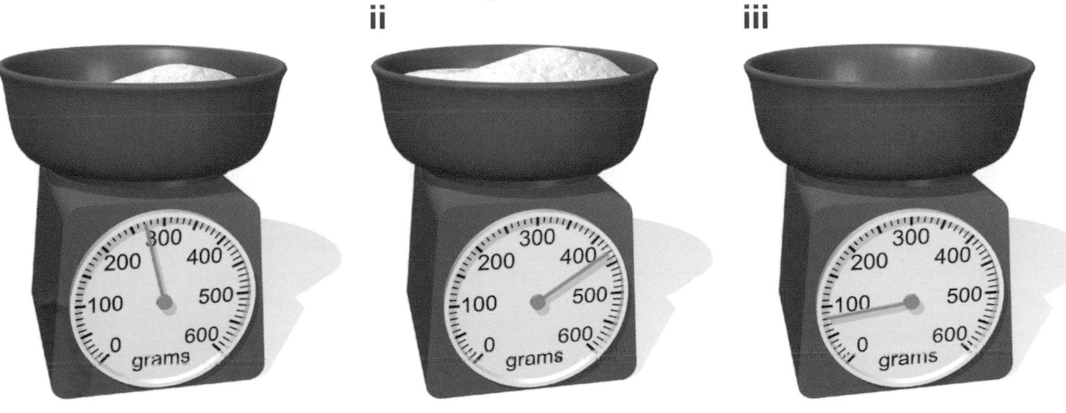

***9** Use this scale to convert these to °F.
a 40 °C **b** 100 °C **c** 0 °C

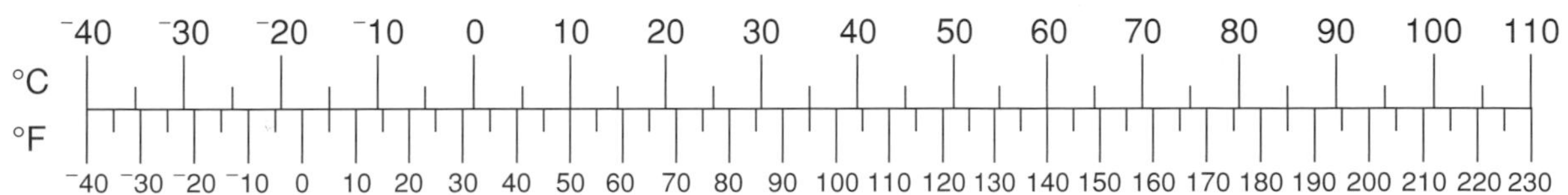

***10** Use the scale in question **9** to convert these to °C.
a 50 °F **b** 200 °F **c** 140 °F

Units and measuring instruments

Discussion

- What imperial or metric unit could you use to measure these? **Discuss.**

  mass of a nail
  width of a pencil
  distance from Mars to Jupiter
  mass of a car
  amount of petrol in a petrol tanker
  time to travel to the moon
  time to grow a water cress plant
  thickness of a hair
  diameter of a 20p coin

*Suggest a measuring instrument and a way to measure each. **Discuss.**

Exercise 7

1

kg	g	mg	km	m	cm	mm	ℓ	mℓ	min	sec

Which of the units in the box would you use to measure each of the following?

a length of a building
b time to eat dinner
c mass of a school bag
d amount of tea in a tea bag
e thickness of a ruler
f diameter of an aspirin tablet
g length of a Boeing 747
h time to run the length of a cricket pitch
i mass of a calculator
j distance around the Equator
k mass of a full suitcase
l amount of milk added to a cup of coffee
m time for eight heartbeats
n amount of water used in a shower

Estimating

When we **estimate a measurement** it is a good idea to give a **range** for it.

Jordan was asked to estimate the width of the teacher's desk.

He wrote this as $0{\cdot}8 \text{ m} < \text{width of desk} < 1 \text{ m}$.

Remember: < means 'is less than.'

Discussion

Kay wanted to paint one wall of her bedroom.
She estimated the length of the wall.
Then she could work out how much paint she needed.

Think of other times you might need to estimate a length, mass or capacity.
Discuss.
What unit would you use for each?

Practical

You will need a tape measure and chalk.

Estimate the length of some things such as the
length of a netball court,
width of a window,
length of a gymnasium,
length of a paper clip,
width of a book, ...

You could estimate by pacing.

Give a range for your estimate.

Measure the actual lengths.
You could draw a table like this one.

Estimate	Range	Actual
	_<_<_	

Exercise 8

1 Estimate the length of each coloured line.
Measure each line to the nearest 0·1 cm (nearest mm).

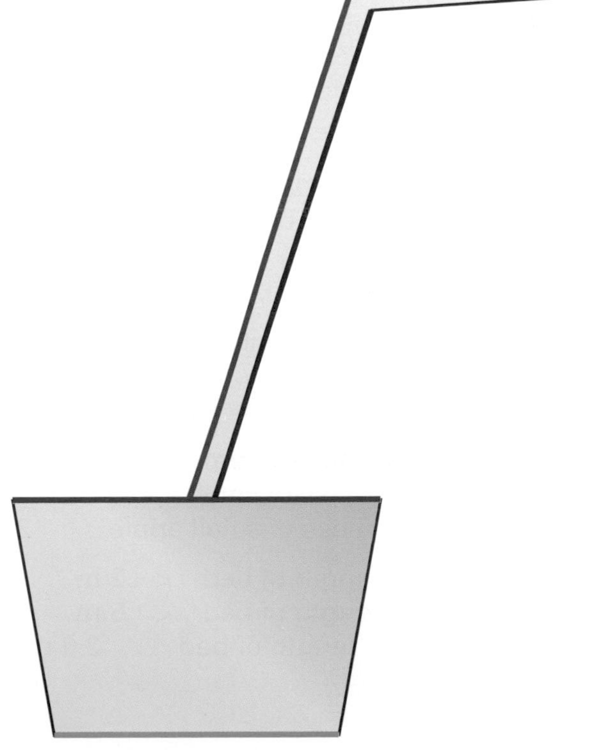

2 What should go in the gaps?
Choose from the numbers in the box below.
Use each number just once.

100	3500	250
2000	1·5	900
28		10
	60	100

a	temperature on a hot day	___ °C
b	capacity of a cup	___ mℓ
c	time to eat an apple	___ sec
d	length of a car	___ mm
e	amount of water in a bucket	___ ℓ
f	mass of a bag of onions	___ g
g	height of a boy	___ m
h	width of a door	___ mm
i	mass of an egg	___ g

3 **a** The length of an eyelash could be
A 3 mm **B** 20 mm **C** 30 mm **D** 10 cm.

b An apple has a mass of about
A 1 g **B** 10 g **C** 150 g.

c A man could have a mass of about
A 80 kg **B** 8 kg **C** 800 kg.

d A bottle of suntan cream could hold
A 10 mℓ **B** 200 mℓ **C** 1 ℓ.

e A pot full of soup could hold
A 100 mℓ **B** 3 ℓ **C** 100 ℓ.

4 Which of km, m, cm, mm is missing?

a A house is about 8___ high.
b John's thumb is about 50___ long.
c Brian can run about 250___ in 1 minute.
d London is about 350___ from Liverpool.
e Laura is 150___ tall.
f Louise walks 200___ to school.
g On her holiday abroad Rasha flew 920___ .

***5** Choose the best estimate.

a **A** 1 m < width of classroom door < 2 m
B 0·5 m < width of classroom door < 1 m
C 1·0 m < width of classroom door < 1·1 m

b **A** 100 mℓ < capacity of a cup < 300 mℓ
B 0 mℓ < capacity of a cup < 500 mℓ
C 500 mℓ < capacity of a cup < 1 litre

c **A** 500 g < mass of small apple < 1 kg
B 50 g < mass of small apple < 100 g
C 1 kg < mass of small apple < 2 kg

d **A** 1 m < length of bed < 2 m
B 1 m < length of bed < 5 m
C 1·5 m < length of bed < 2·6 m

*6 Write A, B or C for each item.

	Item	Mass between		
		A 10 g and 500 g	**B** 0·5 kg and 1·5 kg	**C** 1·5 kg and 5 kg
a	pen			
b	cup			
c	large cat			
d	ruler			
e	litre of milk			
f	pumpkin			

*7

	Item	Capacity between		
		A 0 mℓ and 100 mℓ	**B** 100 mℓ and 1 ℓ	**C** 1 ℓ and 10 ℓ
a	basin			
b	bucket			
c	shampoo bottle			
d	can of cola			
e	teaspoon			
f	perfume bottle			

Area of a triangle

Discussion

James made a triangular flag.
To do this he cut a rectangle in half.

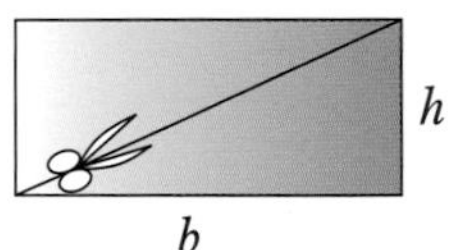

James said that the area of his flag was one half of the area of the rectangle.
Is he correct? **Discuss**.

Check by cutting rectangles yourself.

Do you always get a right-angled triangle when a rectangle is cut in half like this?

Can all right-angled triangles be made by cutting a rectangle in half? **Discuss**.

Remember

Area is the amount of space covered by a shape.

Area is measured in square kilometres (km^2), square metres (m^2), square centimetres (cm^2) or square millimetres (mm^2).

Area of a rectangle $= b \times h$

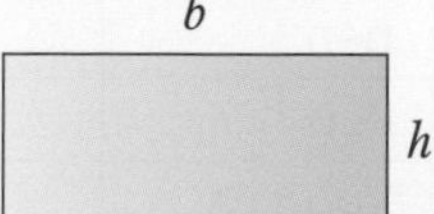

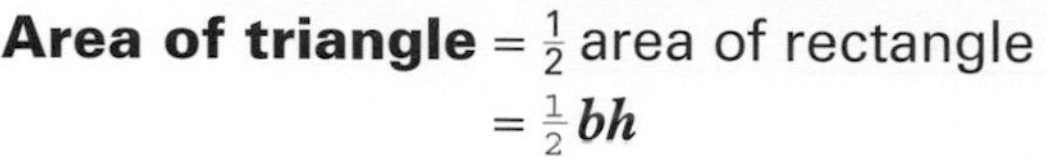

Area of triangle $= \frac{1}{2}$ area of rectangle

$= \frac{1}{2}bh$

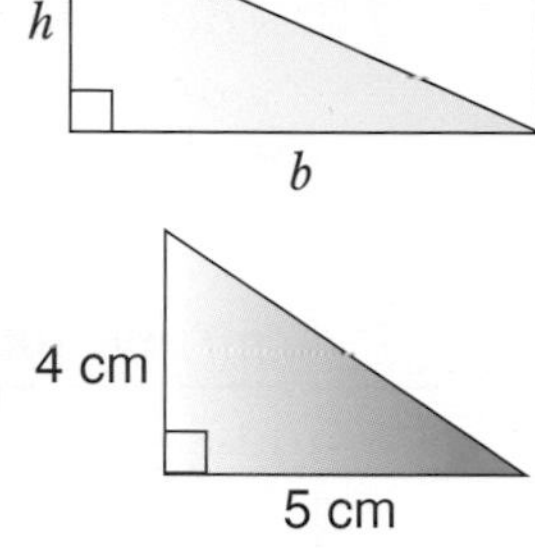

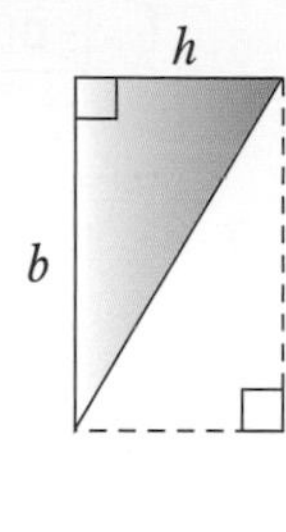

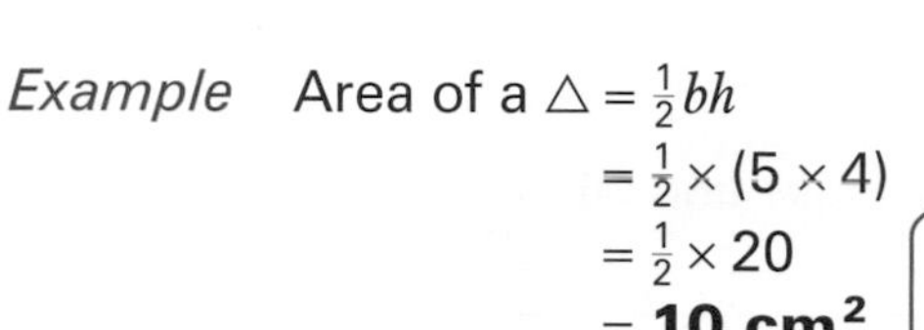

Example Area of a $\triangle = \frac{1}{2}bh$

$= \frac{1}{2} \times (5 \times 4)$

$= \frac{1}{2} \times 20$

$= \mathbf{10\ cm^2}$

Remember to put the units in your answer.

Exercise 9

Except questions 3 and 4.

1 Calculate the area of these triangles.

a

4 cm, 6 cm

b

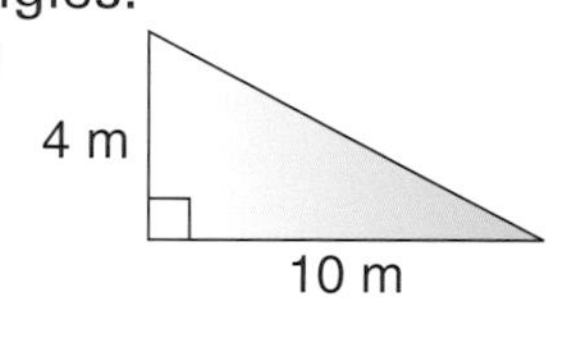

c

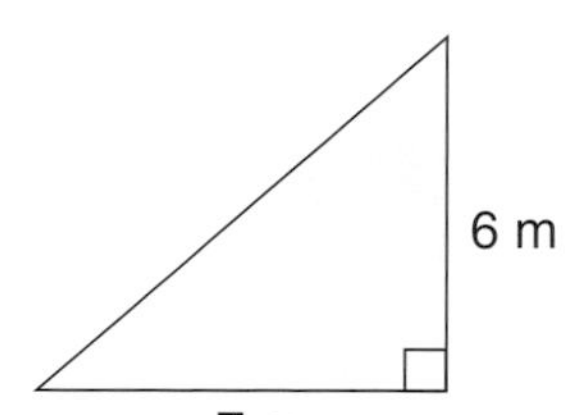

d

3 cm, 5 cm

e

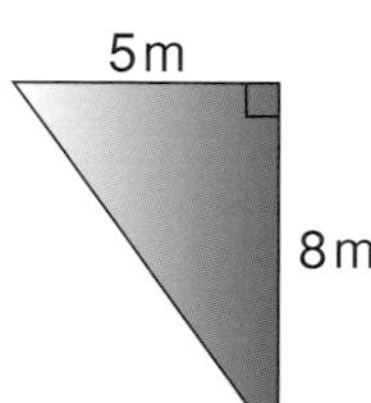

f

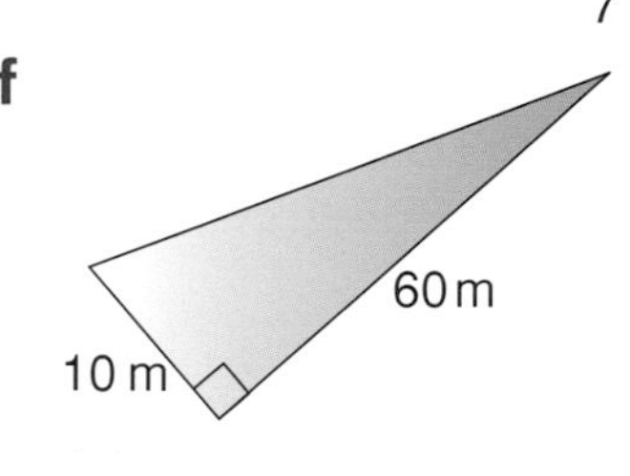

2 What is the area of this sail?

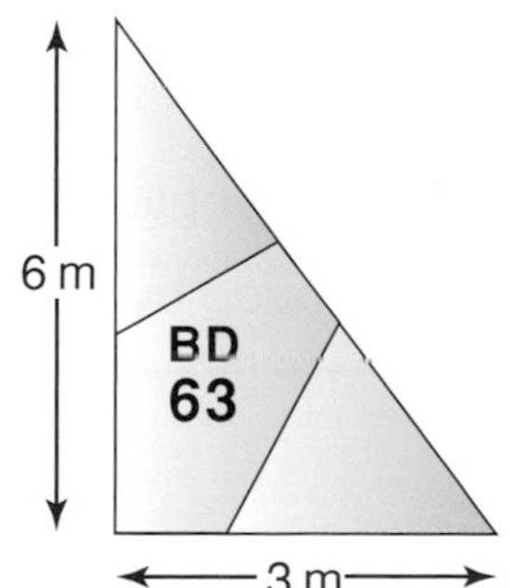

3 What are the areas of the tops of these spa pools?

a

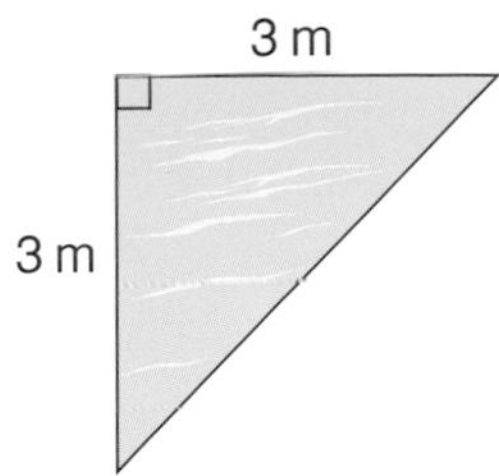

b

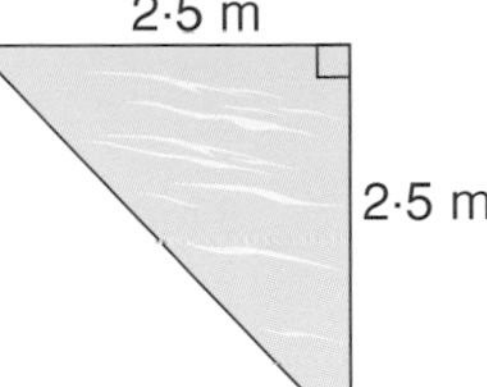

c

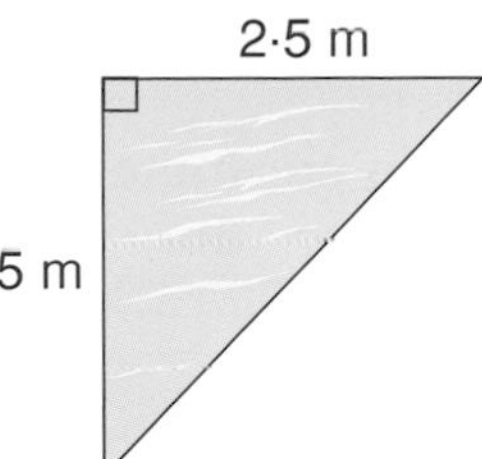

***4** **a** What is the area of this flower bed?
b Mary wants to fertilise the flower bed.
One box of fertiliser is needed for each 10 m^2.
How many boxes does she need?
c What fraction of a box will she have left?

***5** The area of this window hanging is 24 cm^2.
What might the lengths of **a** and **b** be?

Perimeter and area of shapes made from rectangles

Remember
Perimeter is the distance around the outside of a shape.
Perimeter is measured in km, m, cm, mm.

Put a dot to show where you start when finding perimeter.

Example To find the **perimeter** of this shape we need to find the missing lengths.

blue side = 14 − 8 = 6 cm
red side = 12 − 5 = 7 cm

Perimeter = 14 + 5 + 8 + 7 + 6 + 12
= **52 cm**

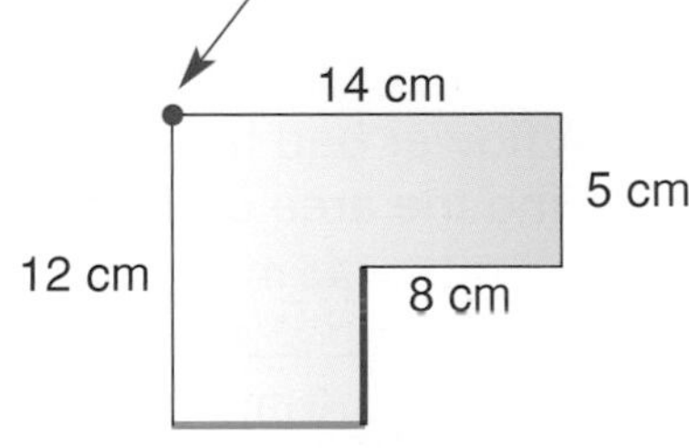

Example To find the **area** of this shape divide it into rectangles.
One way is shown.

Area of **A** = 12 × 6
= 72 cm^2
Area of **B** = 8 × 5
= 40 cm^2
Total area = **112 cm^2**

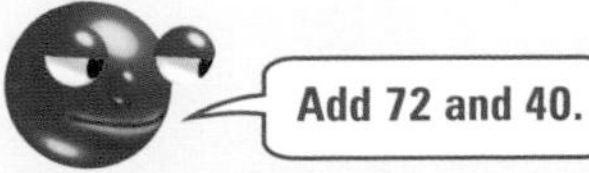

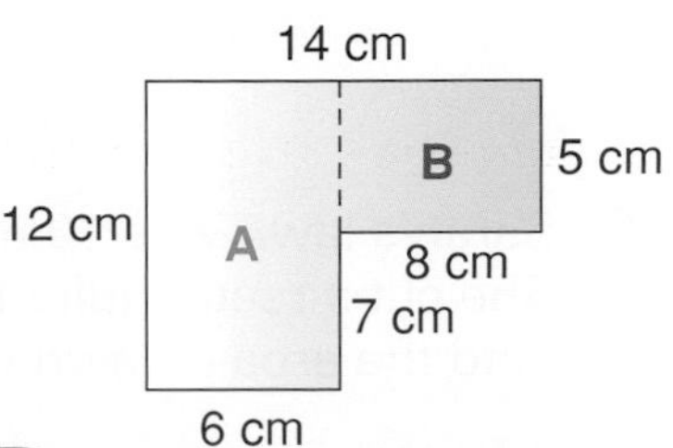

Exercise 10

Only use a calculator if you need to.

1 Find the perimeter of these shapes.

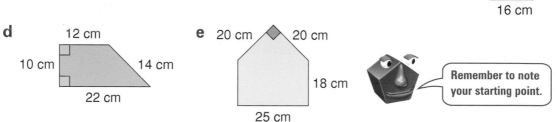

a 5m, 2m, 5m, 3m, 3m, 2m

b 8 mm, 4 mm, 2 mm, 9mm, 5 mm, 6 mm

c 28 cm, 10 cm, 12 cm, 30 cm, 16 cm

d 12 cm, 10 cm, 14 cm, 22 cm

e 20 cm, 20 cm, 18 cm, 25 cm

2 Find the area of each shape in question **1**.
a and **b** are started for you.

a

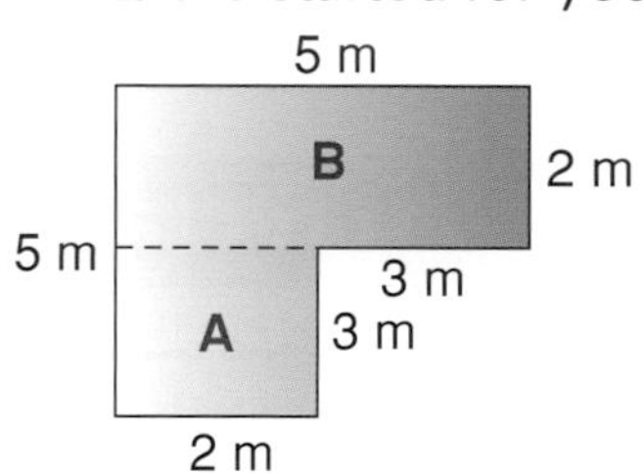

Area = area A + area B
$= 3 \times 2 + 5 \times 2$

b

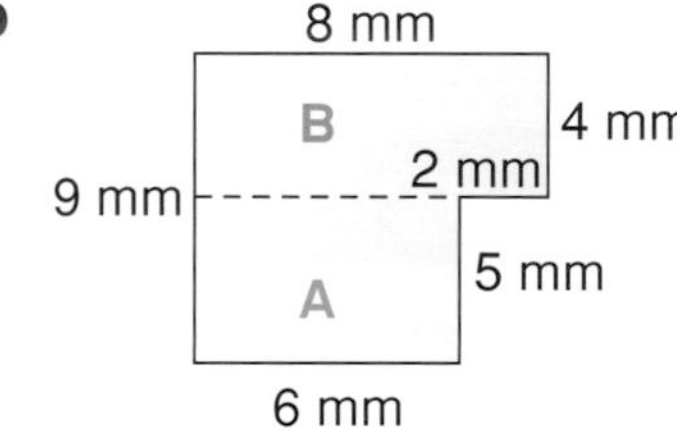

Area = area A + area B
$= 6 \times 5 + \ldots$

3 A flower bed has been cut out of each of these lawns.
Find the area of the remaining lawn.

a

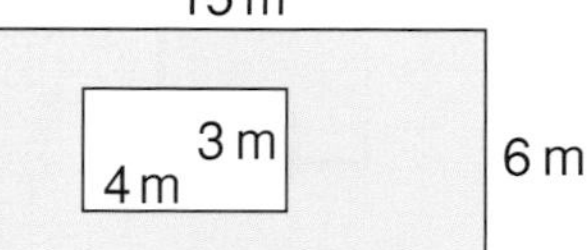

b

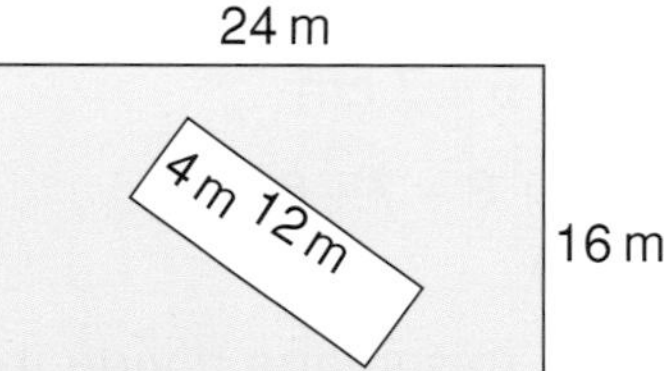

4 Sarah's lawn was 10 m by 12 m.
She cut a rectangular flower bed 2 m by 5 m, into the lawn.
Find the area of lawn left.

*5 This diagram shows a path through a courtyard.
Find the area of the path (shaded grey).

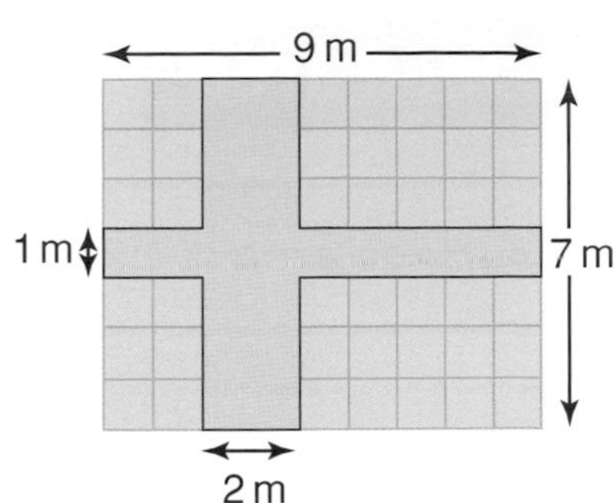

*6 A rectangular garden is 4 m by 6 m.
It is planted with flowers.
They cost £5·85 per square metre to plant.
How much does it cost to plant the garden?

Discussion

Pierre drew this red quadrilateral on square dotty paper.
The dots are 1 cm apart.
He found the area of the quadrilateral like this.

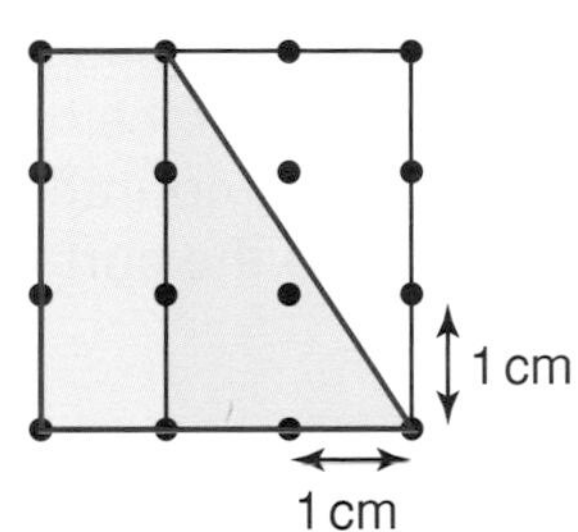

Area of blue rectangle = 3 cm^2
Area of green triangle = 3 cm^2

Discuss Pierre's method.
How else could Pierre have found the area of the quadrilateral?

How could you find the area of this pink quadrilateral? **Discuss**.

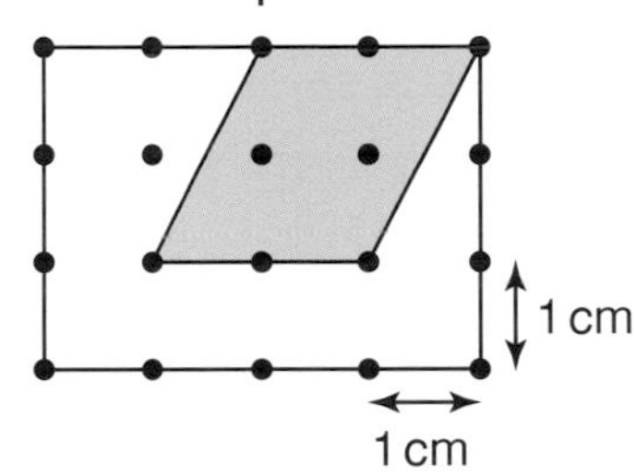

Investigation

Area and Perimeter

1 Five square paving slabs can be placed like this.
One plant can be planted along the edge of each slab.
How else could the slabs be placed?
A side of each slab must match at least one side of another slab.
How many plants could be planted? **Investigate**.
What if 4 square slabs were used?

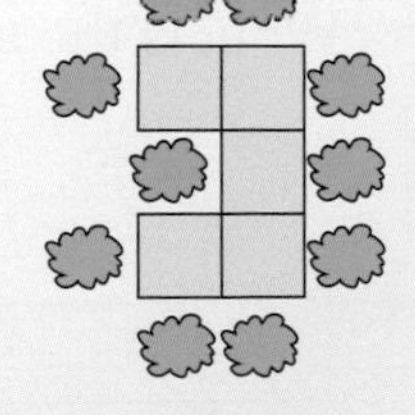

10 plants

2 **You will need** 1 cm squared paper.
Hayley drew this shape.
It has a perimeter of 16 cm.
Draw as many shapes as you can with a perimeter of 16 cm.
Which one has the greatest area?

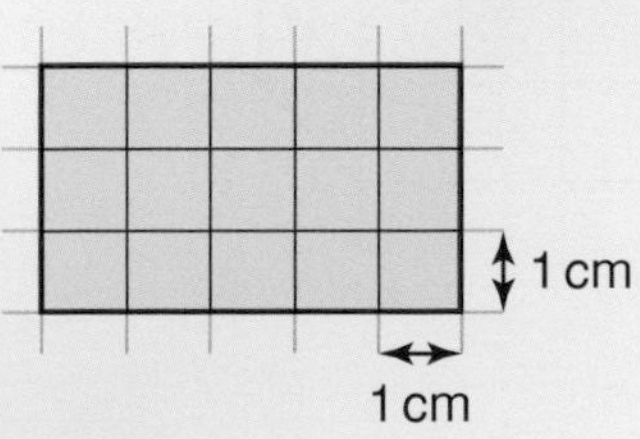

Surface area

The **surface area** of a 3-D shape is the total area of all the faces.

Practical

You will need some unit cubes or centimetre cubes.

Janet made this shape from centicubes.
Each face has an area of 1 cm^2.
She counted 18 faces.
So the surface area of her shape is 18 cm^2

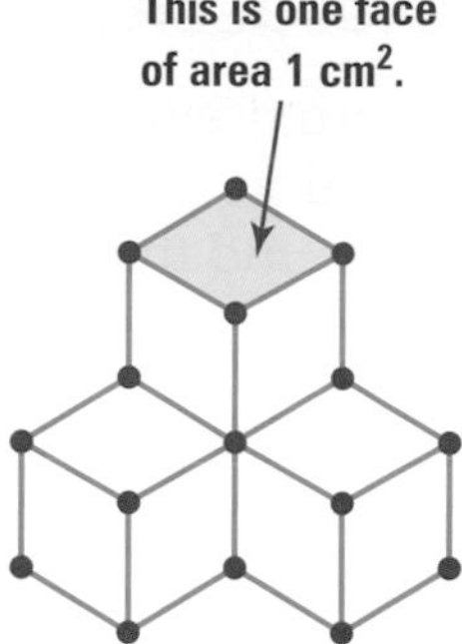

Make some other shapes using cubes.
Find the surface area of each.

Discussion

- The area of each square is 1 cm^2.
  The area of each face is 4 cm^2.

  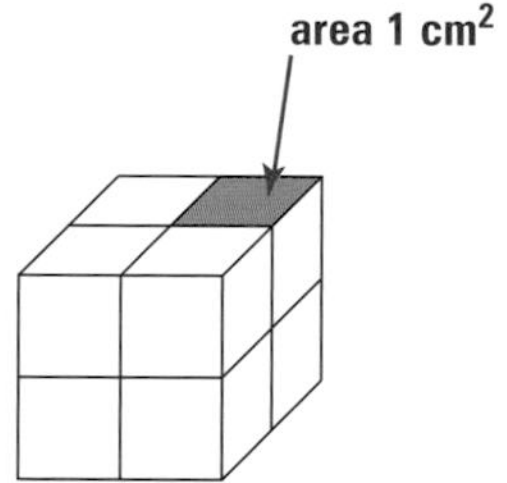

  Abbie said that for this cube

  Surface area $= 6 \times$ area of one face
  $= 6 \times 4$ cm^2

  What is the surface area of this cube? **Discuss**.

  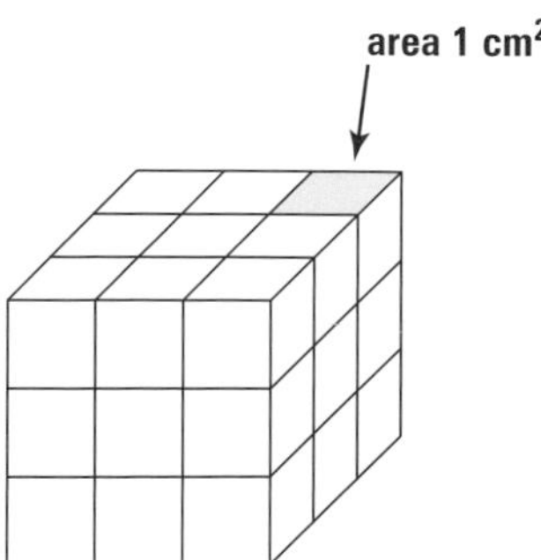

* ● This is a net for the cuboid shown.

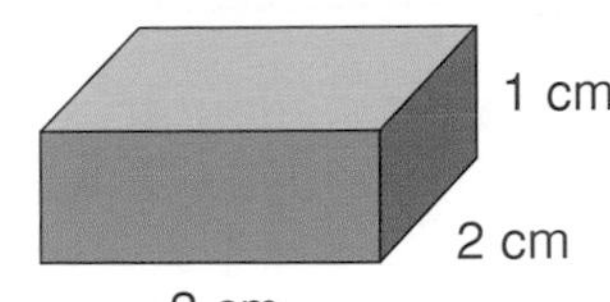

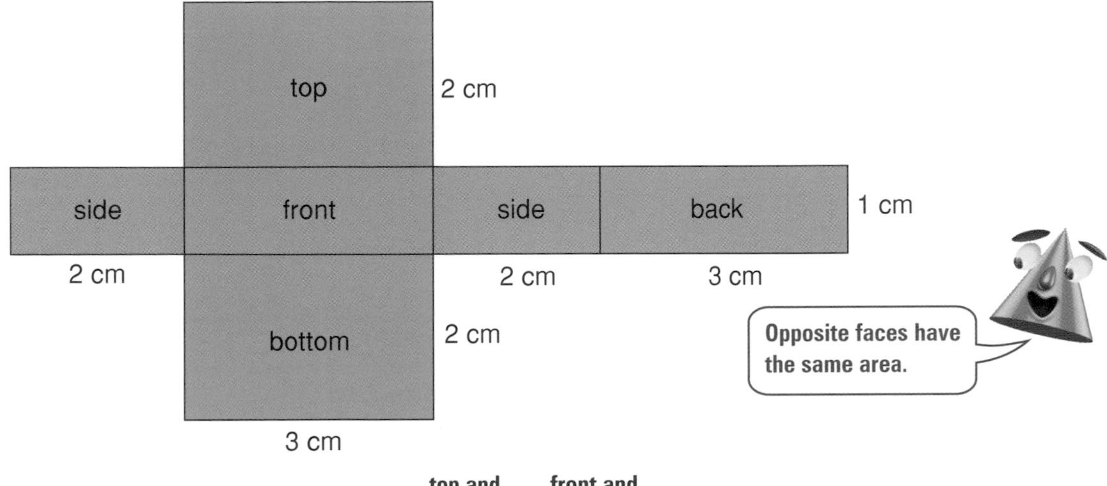

Brendon wrote

top and bottom ↓ front and back ↓ sides ↓

Surface area of cuboid = $2(3 \times 2) + 2(3 \times 1) + 2(2 \times 1)$

Will this give the right answer for the surface area? **Discuss**.

*How could you use this to write a formula for the surface area of a cuboid? **Discuss**.

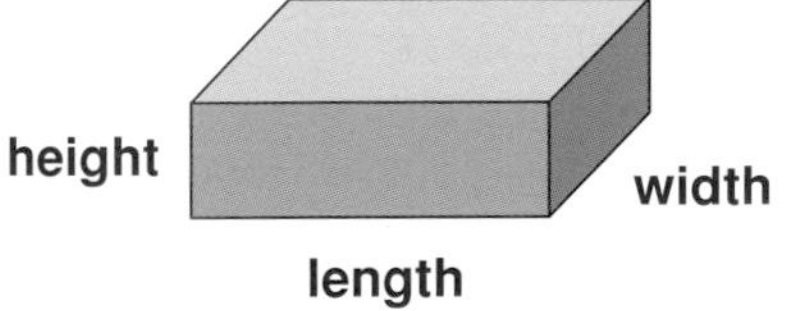

Practical

1 **You will need** some empty cuboid-shaped packets.

Unfold each packet until you have a net.
How could you use the net to find the surface area of the packet?

*2 **You will need** some cuboids such as a cereal packet, matchbox, tile, box, book.

Estimate the surface area of each cuboid.
Check by measuring the sides of each face and then calculating the surface area.

Surface area of a cuboid = 2(length × width) + 2(length × height) + 2(height × width)
$= \mathbf{2}\boldsymbol{lw} = \mathbf{2}\boldsymbol{lh} + \mathbf{2}\boldsymbol{hw}$

Worked Example
Brad wanted to glue green cardboard onto the surface of this wooden cuboid.
What area of cardboard will he need?

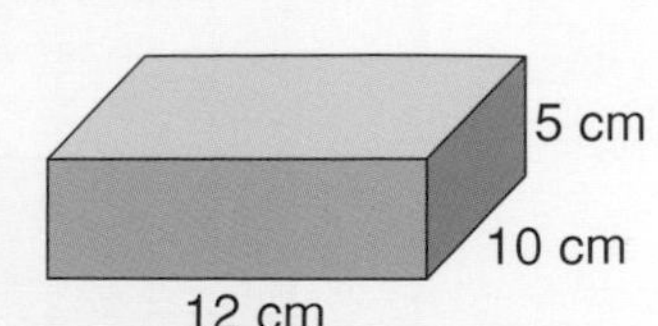

Answer
Total surface area $= 2lw + 2lh + 2hw$
$= 2(12 \times 10) + 2(12 \times 5) + 2(5 \times 10)$
$= 2 \times 120 + 2 \times 60 + 2 \times 50$
$= 240 + 120 + 100$
$= \mathbf{460\ cm^2}$

Exercise 11

Only use a calculator if you need to.

1 These shapes are made from unit cubes.
Find the surface area of each shape.

a
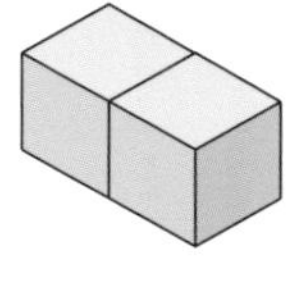

b
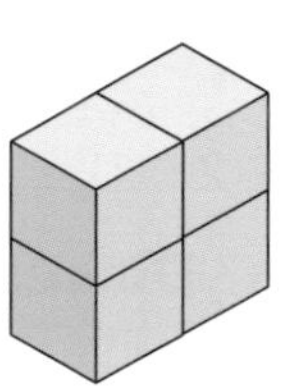

c

d
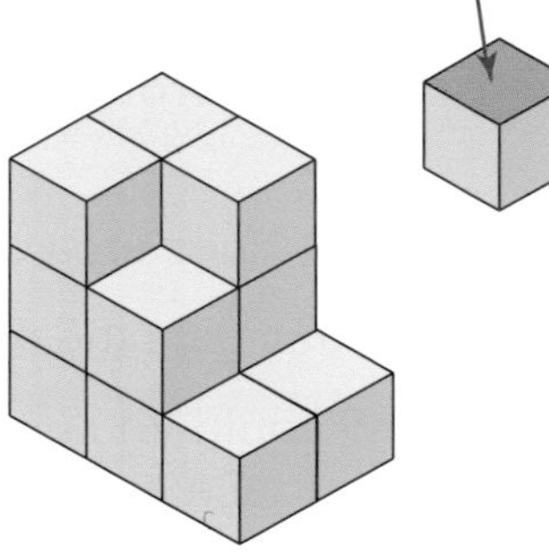

2 Copy and fill in the missing numbers in this for each cube.
surface area = 6 × area of 1 face
$= 6 \times \_\_\_ \text{ cm}^2$
$= \_\_\_$

a
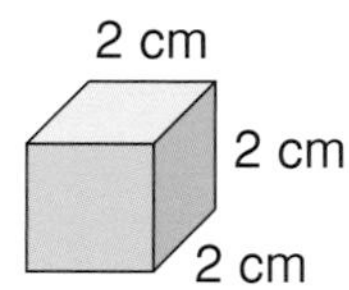

b
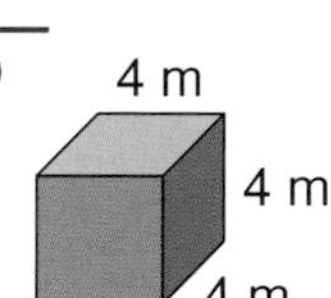

c
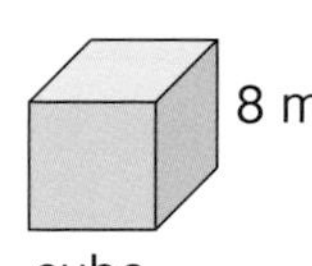

d
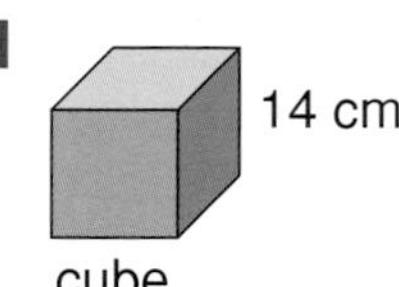

3 Calculate the surface area of each of these cuboids.
The first one is started.

a
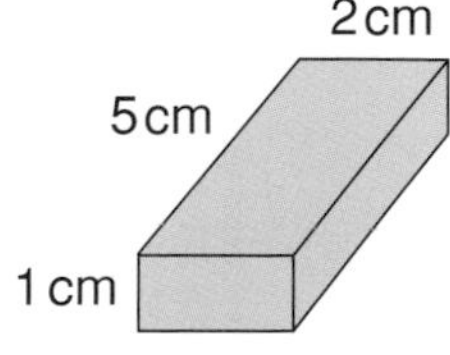

surface area $= 2lw + 2lh + 2hw$
$= 2 \times \_\_\_ \times \_\_\_ + 2 \times \_\_\_ \times \_\_\_ + 2 \times \_\_\_ \times \_\_\_$
$= \_\_\_ + \_\_\_ + \_\_\_$
$= \_\_\_$

b
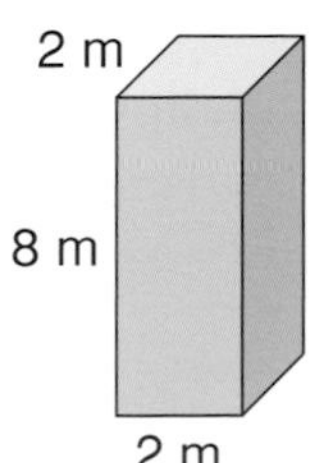

c
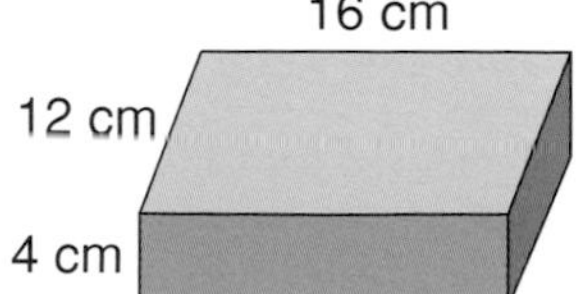

d
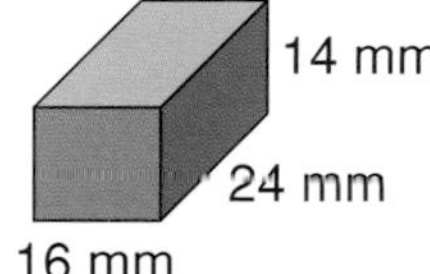

4 This small box is made from cardboard.

a If the box has a lid, how much cardboard is needed?

b How much cardboard is needed if the box has no lid?

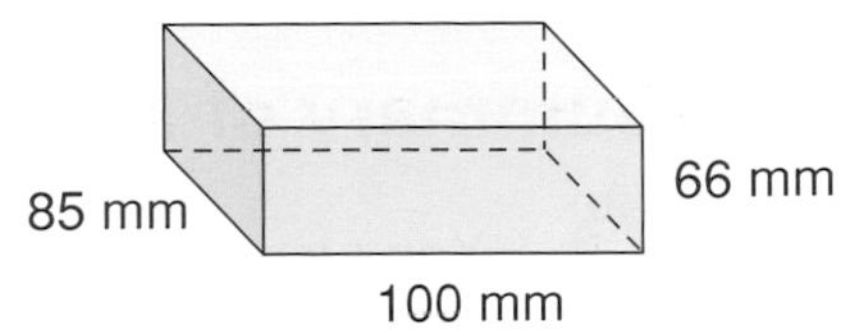

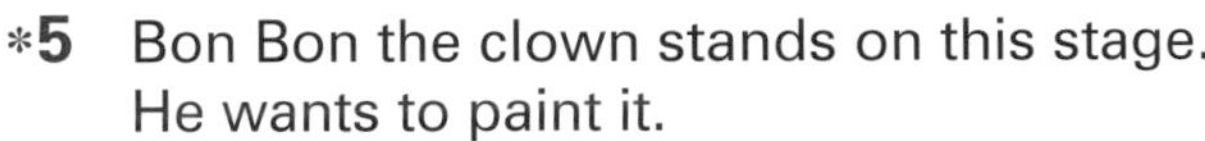

*__5__ Bon Bon the clown stands on this stage.
He wants to paint it.
He wants to paint all its surfaces.

a What is the surface area of the stage?

b Bon Bon buys 1 ℓ of red paint.
It will cover 24 000 cm^2.
Will he have enough paint?

*__6__ Sally places three cubes as shown to make a stand.
The top cube is in the middle of the other two.
She covers the stand with sticky paper.
Sketch the shapes of the sticky paper she could use and say how many of each are needed.

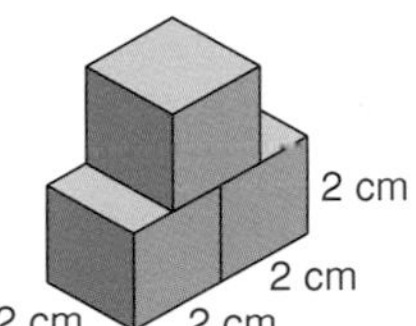

Investigation

* Surface area

You will need some unit cubes or centimetre cubes.

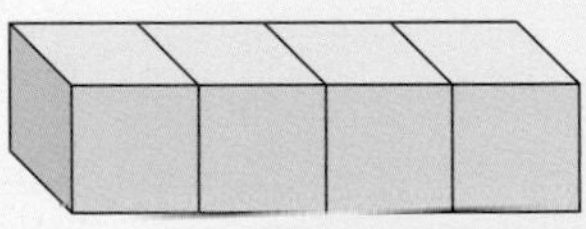

This shape is made with four centicubes.
The area of all of the surfaces (top, bottom, front, back and both sides) is 18 cm^2.

What is the surface area of these?
Can four centicubes be arranged in other ways?

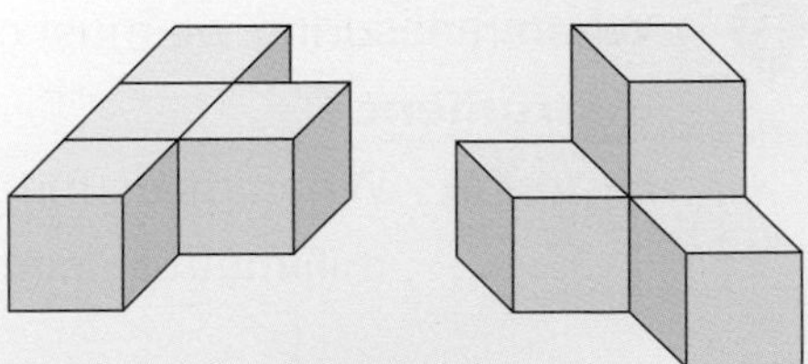

Investigate to find which way has the smallest surface area.

Investigate to find which way has the greatest surface area.

What if we began with three cubes?

Summary of key points

You need to know these **metric conversions**.

length	**mass**	**capacity (volume)**
1 km = 1000 m	1 kg = 1000 g	1 ℓ = 1000 mℓ
1 m = 100 cm		100 cℓ = 1 ℓ
1 m = 1000 mm		1 cℓ = 10 mℓ
1 cm = 10 mm		

Examples 0·62 kg = 0·62 × 1000 g
= 620 g

520 mℓ = 520 ÷ 1000 ℓ
= 0·52 ℓ

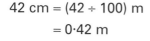

42 cm = (42 ÷ 100) m
= 0·42 m

You need to know these **metric and imperial equivalents.**

length	**mass**	**capacity**
8 km ≈ 5 miles	1 kg ≈ 2·2 lb	1 gallon ≈ 4·5 ℓ
		1 pint is just over $\frac{1}{2}$ ℓ

Example

×4 8 km ≈ 5 miles ×4
32 km ≈ 20 miles

When **reading scales** you need to work out the value of each small space.

Example There are five small spaces between 0 and 1.
Each small space is 1 ÷ 5 = $\frac{1}{5}$ or 0·2 kg.
The pointer is at 1·6 kg.

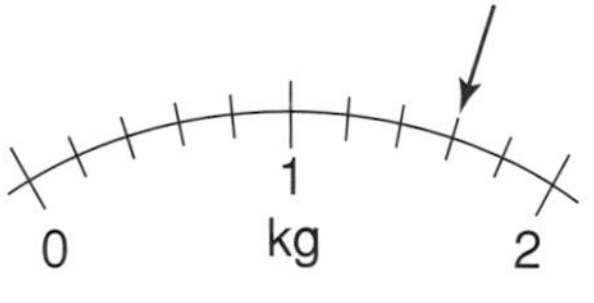

When measuring we must choose a **unit** to use and a **measuring instrument**.

Example When measuring the length of a pin we could measure in millimetres using a ruler.

We we **estimate** we often give a **range** for the estimate.

Example 200 g < mass of calculator < 500 g.

Area is the amount of space covered by a shape.
Area is measured in km^2, m^2, cm^2, mm^2.

Area of a rectangle = length × width
$= \boldsymbol{lw}$

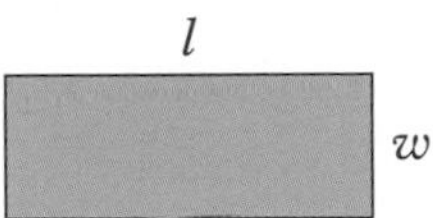

Area of a triangle = $\frac{1}{2}$ area of rectangle
$= \frac{1}{2} \times$ base length × height
$= \frac{1}{2}\boldsymbol{bh}$

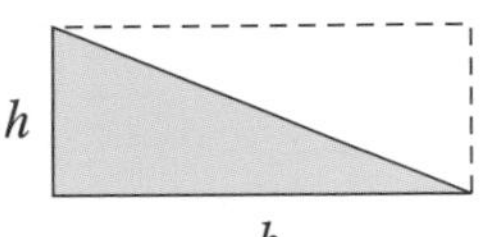

We can find the **perimeter** and **area** of a **shape made from rectangles**.

Examples To find the perimeter, we find the missing lengths.

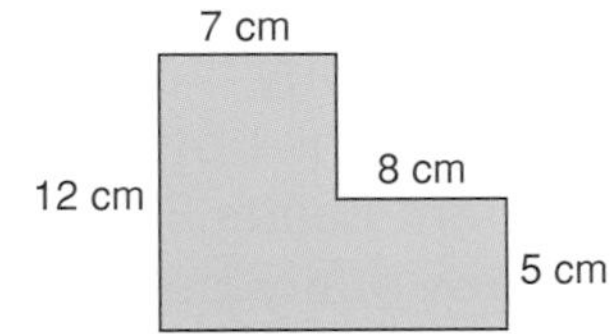

Perimeter = 7 + 7 + 8 + 5 + 15 + 12
= 54 cm

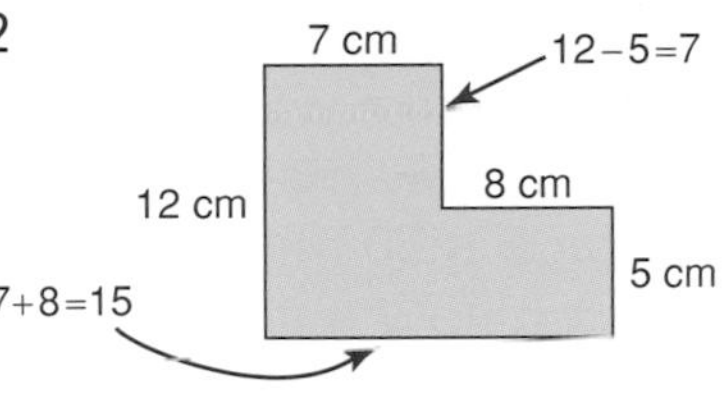

To find the **area** we divide the shape into two rectangles.
Total area = area of A + area of B

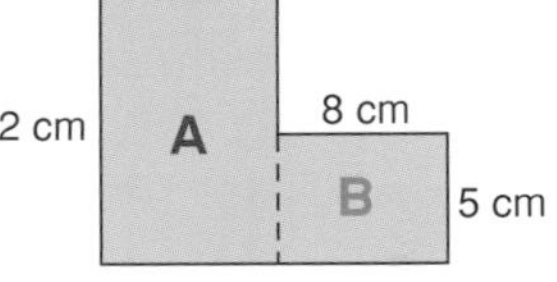

Area of **A** = 12 × 7
$= 84\ cm^2$

Area of **B** = 8 × 5
$= 40\ cm^2$

Total area $= 84\ cm^2 + 40\ cm^2$
$= 124\ cm^2$

The **surface area of a cube**
= 6 × area of one face
$= 6 \times 4\ cm^2$
$= 24\ cm^2$

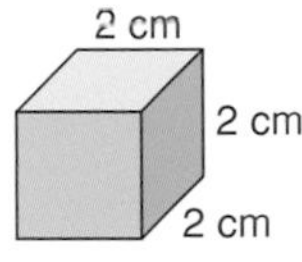

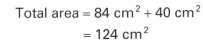

The **surface area of a cuboid**

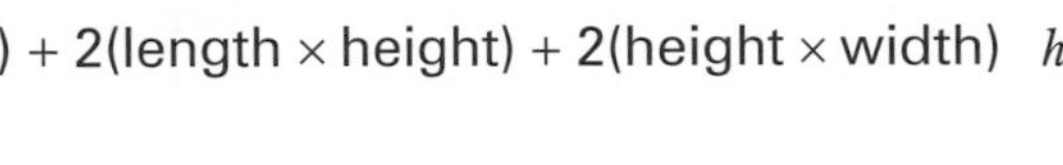

= 2(length × width) + 2(length × height) + 2(height × width)
$= 2lw + 2lh + 2hw$

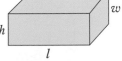

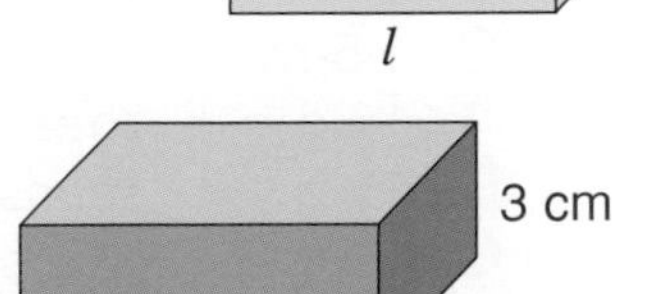

Example Surface Area $= 2lw + 2lh + 2hw$
$= 2(6 \times 5) + 2(6 \times 3) + 2(3 \times 5)$
$= 60 + 36 + 30$
$= 126\ cm^2$

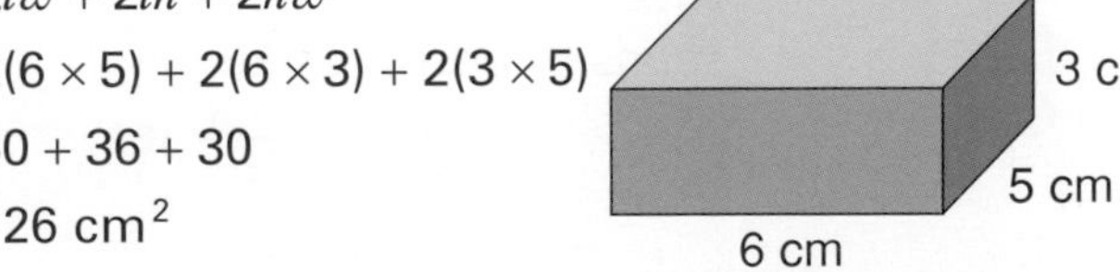

Test yourself  **Except for questions 7, 8 and 9.**

1 Find the missing numbers. **A**

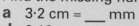

a	3·2 cm = ___ mm	**b**	4·7 km = ___ m	**c**	3·6 km = ___ cm
d	0·18 m = ___ mm	**e**	0·6 ℓ = ___ mℓ	**f**	476 g = ___ kg
g	86 m = ___ km	**h**	285 mℓ = ___ ℓ	**i**	75 cm = ___ m
j	5·2 mm = ___ cm	**k**	864 mm = ___ m	**l**	0·06 kg = ___ g
m	5·85 cℓ = ___ ℓ	**n**	386 cℓ = ___ mℓ	**o**	6·2 ℓ = ___ cℓ

2 Grant is training for cycling. **A B**

a He trains on a 2500 m track.
Yesterday he travelled 40 km on the track.
How many laps did he do?

b One drink bottle holds 750 mℓ.
Grant needs 300 cℓ.
How many bottles will he need?

c A road race is 56 km.
About how many miles is this?

d Grant's bike weighs 10 kg.
About how many lb is this?

e A race is 50 miles long.
About how many kilometres is this?

3 Find the measurements given by pointers A, B and C. **C**
In **c** you will need to estimate.

a

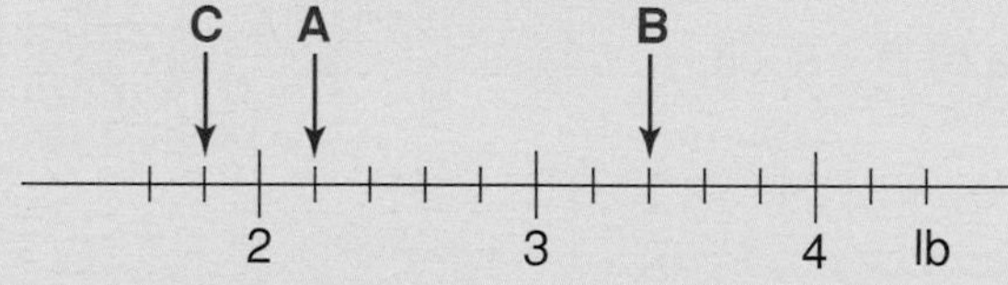

b

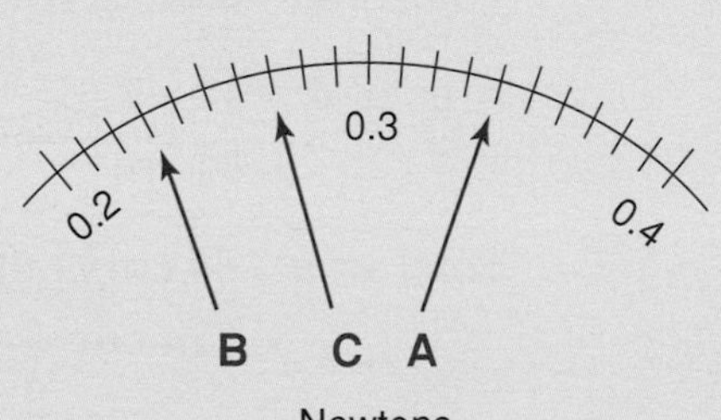

c

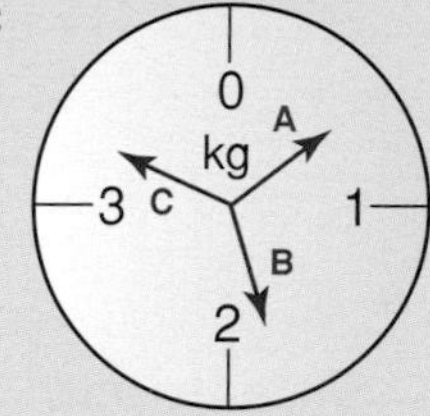

4 Choose the best range. 

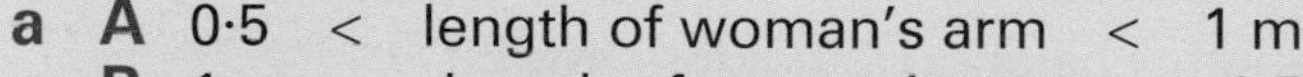

a **A** 0·5 < length of woman's arm < 1 m
B 1 m < length of woman's arm < 1·5 m
C 1·5 m < length of woman's arm < 2 m

b **A** 10 g < mass of pen < 1 kg
B 10 g < mass of pen < 20 g
C 10 g < mass of pen < 200 g

5 Find the area of these flags.

a

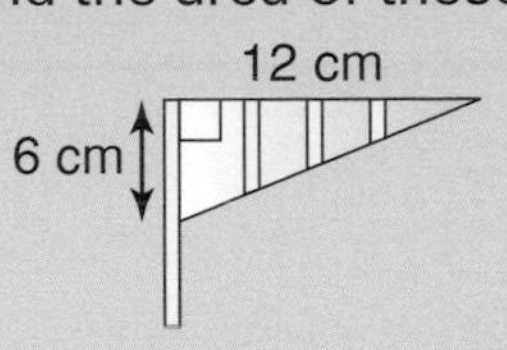

b

2 m

2 m

c

6 Find the perimeter of these shapes.

a

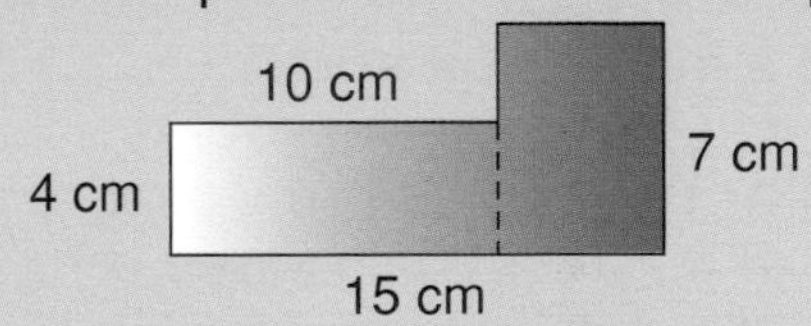

***b**

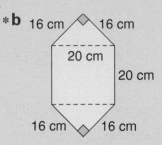

16 cm 16 cm

20 cm

20 cm

16 cm 16 cm

7 Find the area of the shapes in question **8**.

8 What is the total surface area of these boxes? **a** has been started.

a

3 m

3 m 3 m

side end

b

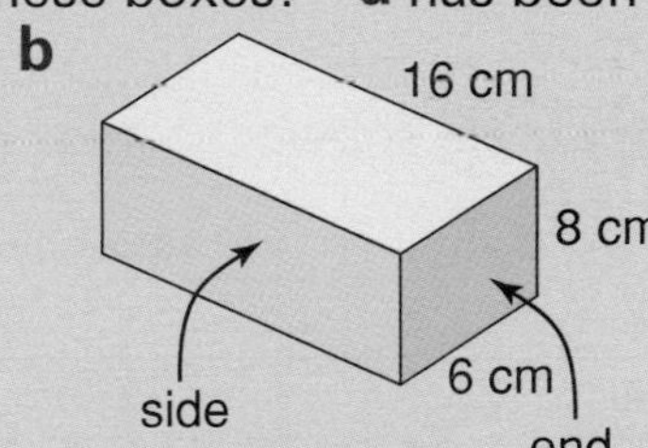

surface area = 6 × area of 1 face

= 6 × ___ cm^2

= ___ cm^2

***9** Patrick built a courtyard with a garden in the middle.

a What is the area of the courtyard?

b Patrick wants to put a wooden border along the outside of the courtyard.
How many pieces of wood, 125 cm long, will he need?

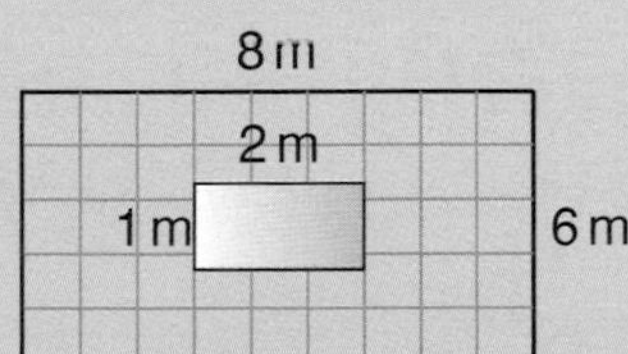

Handling Data Support

Planning and collecting data

We use these steps to **plan a survey**.

Step 1 **Decide what you want to find out.**
Step 2 **Decide what data you need to collect.**
Step 3 **Decide how to collect the data.**

Once a survey has been planned you need to make a **collection sheet**.

Example Julia wrote down the colour of her friends' bedrooms.

Colour	Tally	Frequency
White	~~IIII~~	5
Cream	~~IIII~~ II	7
Blue	IIII	4
Yellow	III	3
Green	II	2

Frequency table

Some data is best **grouped**.

Example This frequency table shows the ages of singers in a show.

Age	Tally	Frequency
1–5	I	1
6–10	III	3
11–15	~~IIII~~ III	8
16–20	~~IIII~~ ~~IIII~~ ~~IIII~~ II	17
21–25	~~IIII~~ ~~IIII~~ ~~IIII~~ ~~IIII~~ IIII	24

Practice Questions 1, 6, 18

Displaying and interpreting data

These show some ways of **displaying data**.

Pictogram

Ways of getting to school

cycle	
walk	
train	
car	
bus	
= 10 people	

35 come by train

Bar chart

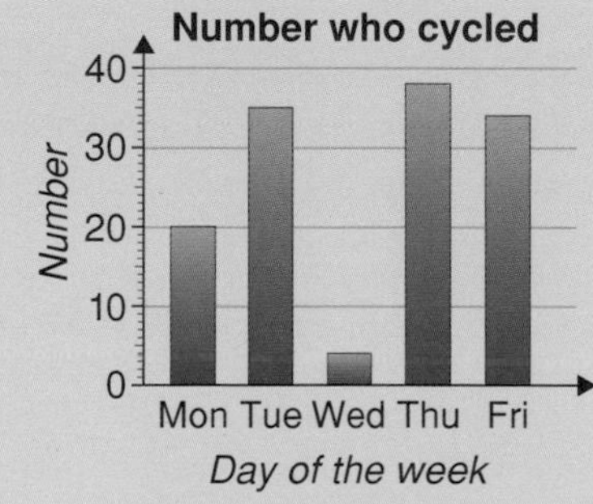

38 cycled on Thursday

Always give your graph a title and label the axes.

Line graph

Jane's Temperature

Temperature (°C): 35, 36, 37, 38

Time: 8 a.m., noon, 4 p.m., 8 p.m.

At 8 a.m. it was 37 °C, at noon it was 38 °C, at 4 p.m. it was 37·5 °C and at 8 p.m. it was 37·8 °C.

Pie chart

Colour of balloons

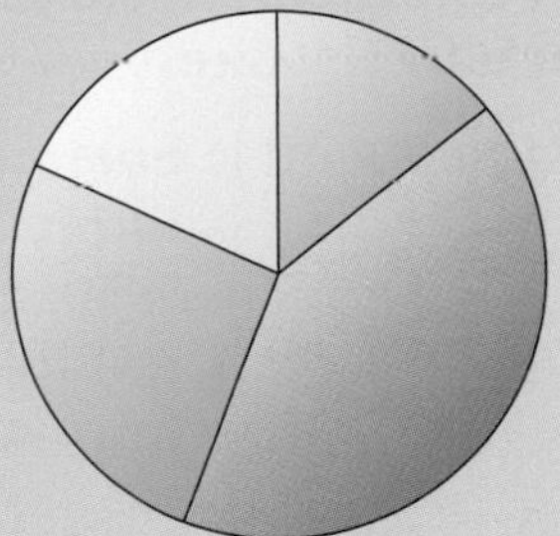

There are more red balloons than any other colour.

Practice Questions 3, 4, 9, 10, 13, 15, 17

Range, mode, mean and median

The **range** is one way of measuring the spread of data.

Range = highest value − lowest value

Example Eric wrote down the weights of some parcels he was posting for Christmas.

500 g 750 g 860 g 940 g 625 g 910 g

The range is 940 − 500 = 440 g.

(940: highest value; 500: lowest value)

The range is 440 g.

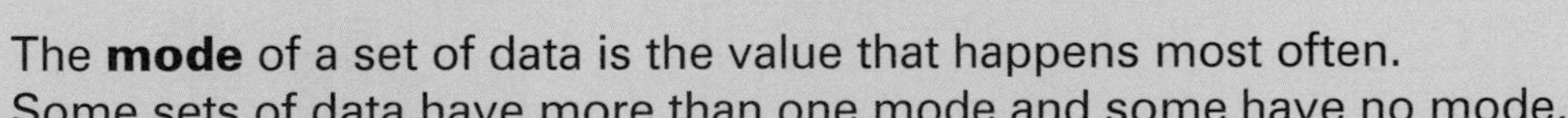

The **mode** of a set of data is the value that happens most often.
Some sets of data have more than one mode and some have no mode.

Example Julie wrote down the sizes of tins of cat food bought.

450 g	750 g	250 g	450 g	450 g	750 g
250 g	750 g	450 g	750 g	450 g	750 g

This data has two modes, 450 g and 750 g.

$$\textbf{Mean} = \frac{\textbf{sum of data values}}{\textbf{number of data values}}$$

Example 4, 8, 6, 2, 3, 9, 3, 5

$$\text{Mean} = \frac{4+8+6+2+3+9+3+5}{8} = \frac{40}{8} = 5$$

The **median** is the middle value when a set of data is arranged in order of size.

Example 1, 3, (8), 11, 13 These are already in order.
8 is the median.

Practice Questions 7, 8, 12

Probability

We can describe the **probability** of an event happening using one of these words.
certain **likely** **even chance** **unlikely** **impossible**

Examples It is **certain** that June follows May.
It is **likely** that you will eat breakfast tomorrow.
There is an **even chance** of getting a head when you toss a coin.
It is **unlikely** that you will see the Queen in person tomorrow.
It is **impossible** to draw a triangle with 4 sides.

We sometimes use a **probability scale** to show probability.

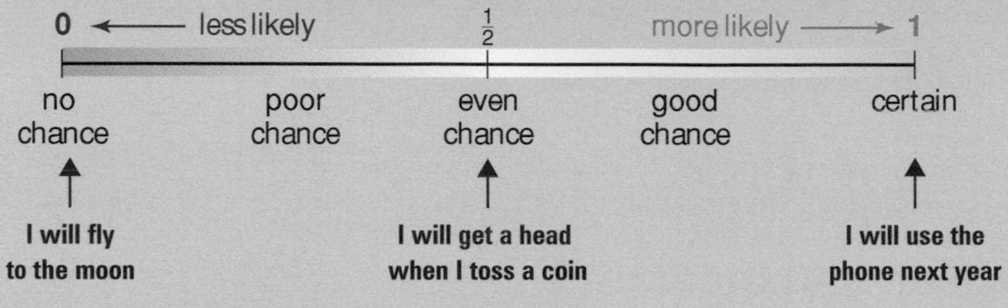

Practice Questions 2, 5, 11, 14, 16

Practice Questions

T **1** Sunhats come in sizes 1 to 6.
Bryn wrote down what size sunhat he sold to each customer.

	Size of sunhat sold										
Monday	1	1	2	2	3	1	1	4			
Tuesday	1	1	3	3	6	5					
Wednesday	6	4	3	5	3	2	4	1			
Thursday	1	4	6	3	2	2	2	1	4	1	1

a Use a copy of this frequency table.
Fill it in for the data above.

Size of sunhat	Tally	Frequency
1		
2		
3		
4		
5		
6		

b Which size sunhat did Bryn sell most of?

2 Put these events in order of likelihood.
Put the most likely first.

A A lion will eat you tomorrow.
B The sun will rise tomorrow.
C The Prime Minister will visit you this year.
D You will fly to Hollywood some day.
E Someone in your class will be sick tomorrow.
F You will eat breakfast tomorrow.

3 This bar chart shows the number of times Mia went for a run.

a How many times did Mia run in week 1?
b In which week did she run the most times?
c She was sick one week. Which week do you think this was?

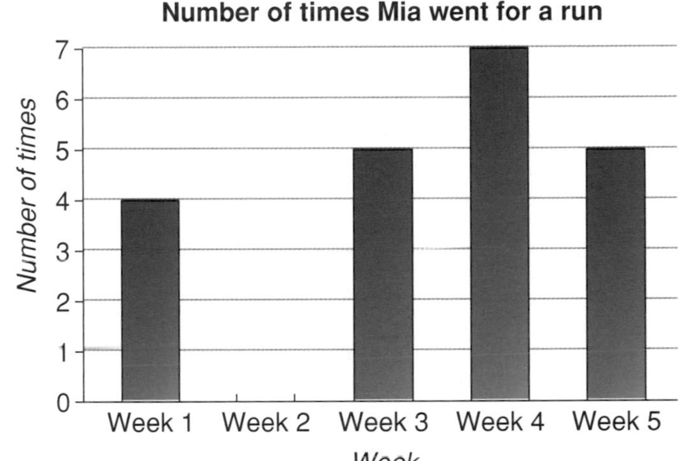

4 This pictogram shows the number of goals scored by some players in a hockey team.

a How many goals were scored by
i Hayley
ii Anna?
b Who scored the most goals?

Player	Goals
Meg	
Hayley	
Anna	
Emma	
Shenaz	
Key: represents 2 goals	

5 Write **impossible**, **unlikely**, **likely** or **certain** for each of these.

a A lorry will turn into a car.
b Tomorrow someone in your class will speak.
c You will sleep sometime in the next month.
d Someone in your class will eat a takeaway next week.
e Everyone in your class will eat a takeaway tomorrow.

T

6 Mick wrote down how many CDs each of his friends had.

4	8	5	7	16	3	11	15	20
14	17	12	13	14	16	7	9	12

Use a copy of this frequency table.
Fill it in.

Number of CDs	Tally	Frequency
1–5		
6–10		
11–15		
16–20		

7 5, 5, 7, 8, 16, 24, 47

Find the

a mode **b** range **c** mean **d** median.

8 These are the masses of 5 mice.

85 g 96 g 110 g 98 g 101 g

a What is the range of the masses?
b What is the mean mass?
c What is the median mass?

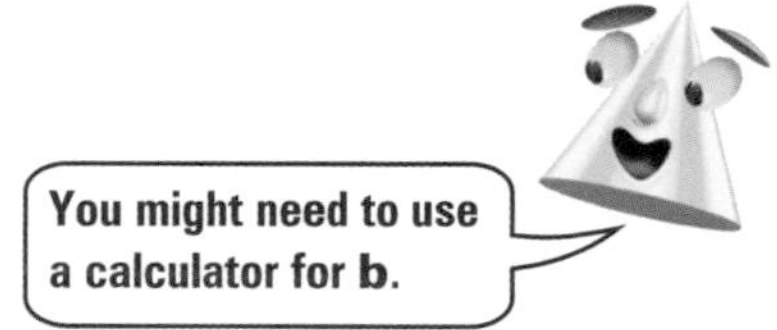

You might need to use a calculator for **b**.

9 The pictogram shows the number of animals in a game park.

a How many elephants are in the park?
b How many lions are in the park?
c Lyn looked at the pictogram.
She thought there were 45 monkeys in the park.
Explain why Lyn was wrong.
d 22 snakes are brought into the park.
Show what you would draw on the pictogram to show this.

Animals in a game park	
Lions	🦁 🦁 (part)
Monkeys	🐒 🐒 🐒 🐒 (part)
Elephants	🐘 🐘 🐘
Snakes	
Each picture = 10 animals	

10 For one week Sam plotted the midday temperatures.
He drew this graph.

a What was the midday temperature on Saturday?
b On which day was the midday temperature 8 °C?
c Which was the coldest day?

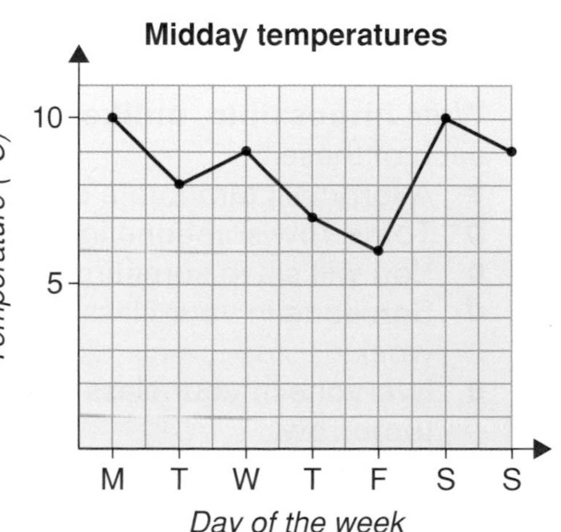

11 Which of these have an even chance of happening?

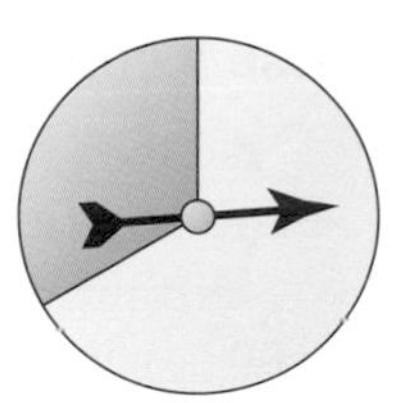

a The next baby born will be a girl.
b The next time you go to the beach you will swim.
c The next time you roll a dice you will get an odd number.
d When this spinner is spun it will stop on yellow.

12

Temperatures in °C							
	Mon	Tue	Wed	Thu	Fri	Sat	Sun
Manchester	15	15	12	13	13	15	8
Bath	18	20	16	13	15	17	14
Brighton	24	20	19	15	22	22	20

a Calculate the range of temperatures for each city.
b Which city had the greatest range?
c What is the mode of all the temperatures?
d Calculate the mean temperature for Manchester.
e What was the median temperature for Bath?

13 This pie chart shows the ages of people at a concert.

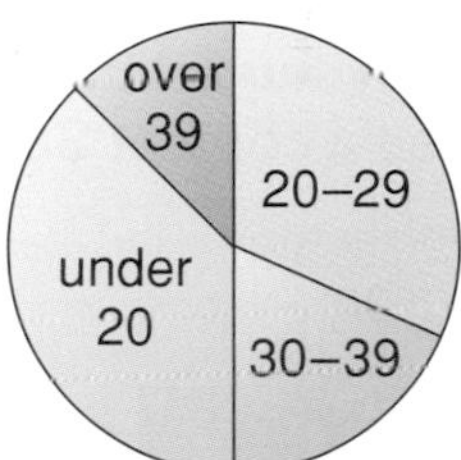

a About what fraction were aged from 20–39?
b Do you think the concert was more likely to be
A a pop band **B** a 70s music concert?
Explain why you think this.

14 Sue spins this spinner.
Write **impossible**, **poor chance**, **even chance**, **good chance**, **certain**, for each of these.

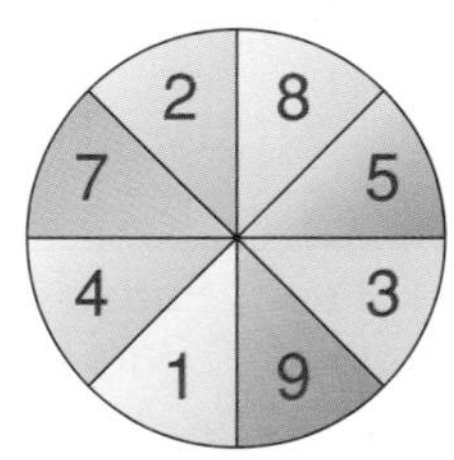

a Sue will spin a number less than 10.
b Sue will spin an even number.
c Sue will spin the number 12.
d Sue will spin a number less than 8.

T

15 Reece measured the height of a plant each week.
These are his results.

Week	1	2	3	4	5	6
Height (mm)	10	26	34	40	42	46

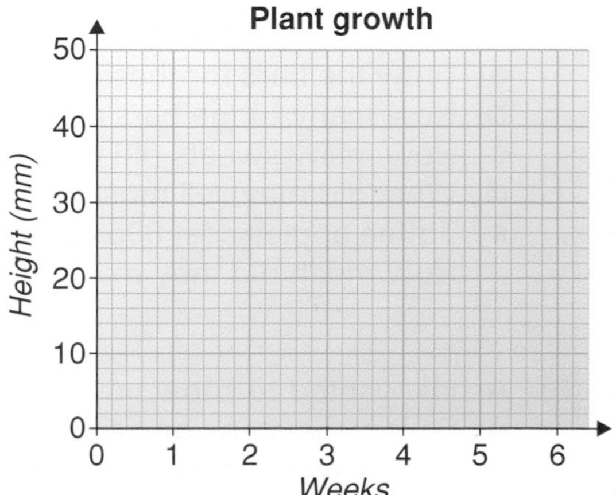

a Use a copy of the grid.
Draw a line graph.
b How tall was the plant after 1 week?
c How tall was the plant after 6 weeks?
d How long did it take the plant to grow to 40 mm?

T

16 Use a copy of this scale.

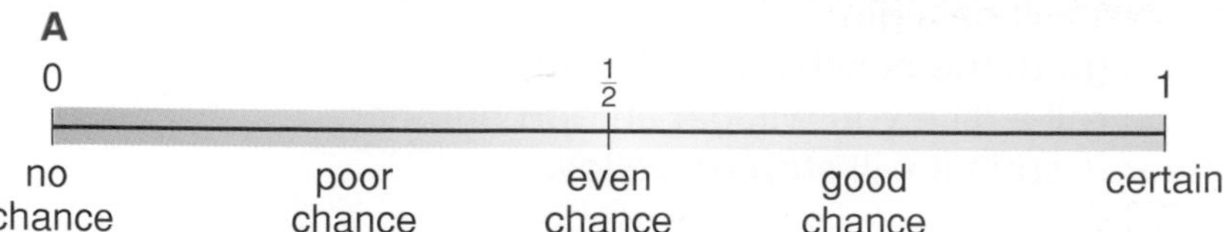

Write the letter which is beside each of these on the line to show how likely it is to happen.
A is done for you.

A A seal will drive a car down your street.
B You will watch TV tonight.
C It will snow next Christmas.
D You will grow taller.
E There will be no clouds in the sky tomorrow morning.
F You will visit a relative this weekend.
G You will see the city or town where you were born this year.

T

17 Sam's class made food to sell at sports day.
Sam started this bar chart of what they sold.
Use a copy of Sam's bar chart.

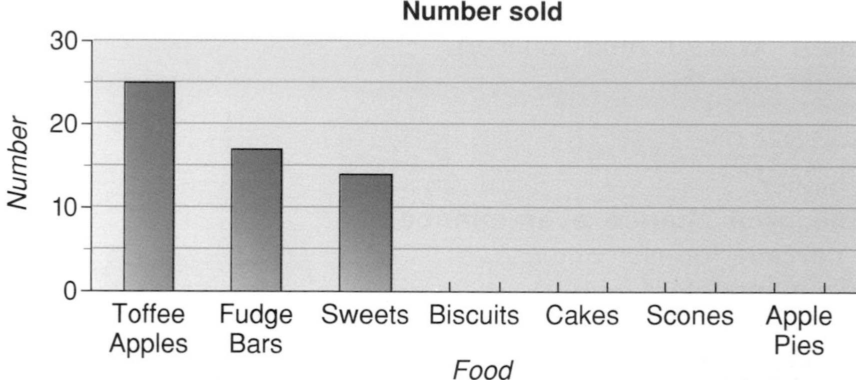

They sold 29 biscuits
19 cakes
23 scones
17 apple pies.

a Draw the bars for these on your bar chart.
b How many fudge bars did they sell?
c How many sweets did they sell?
d What did they sell most of?
e Toffee apples cost 80p each.
How much did they make on these altogether?

18 Ashok wanted to know how the pupils in his class liked to travel to school.
a Follow the steps on page 316 to plan a survey for Ashok.
b Design a collection sheet to collect the data.

15 Data Collection

You need to know

✓ planning and collecting data page 316

Key vocabulary

class interval, collection sheet, data, experiment, frequency, frequency chart, grouped data, interval, primary source, questionnaire, secondary source, survey, table, tally

At the Polls

Step 1 At election time, surveys are often used to sway voters.
Think of some other examples where the results of surveys are used to change people's ideas.

Step 2 The 'Deseat Party' rang twelve people and asked if they were going to vote for them.
Nine said they would.
In their advertisement in the paper the next day the headline said:

75% of people say they will vote for Deseat. Join the majority!

Is this a reasonable thing to say? Explain.

Grouping data

Ben was doing a survey on how much people spent at the canteen.
He wrote down the amounts spent one lunchtime.

£4·95	£2·50	£3·90	£1·30	£10	£3·50
£3	£5	£8·50	£2	30p	£6·99
£9	£4·60	£5	£1·50	£9	£5·20

It is best if this data is grouped.
The groups must be of **equal width**.

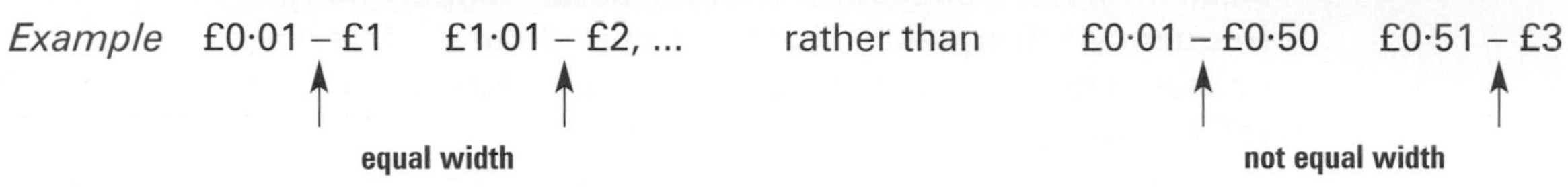
Example £0·01 – £1 £1·01 – £2, ... rather than £0·01 – £0·50 £0·51 – £3
equal width
not equal width

The groups are called **class intervals**.
We can group the data in a **frequency table**.

Example

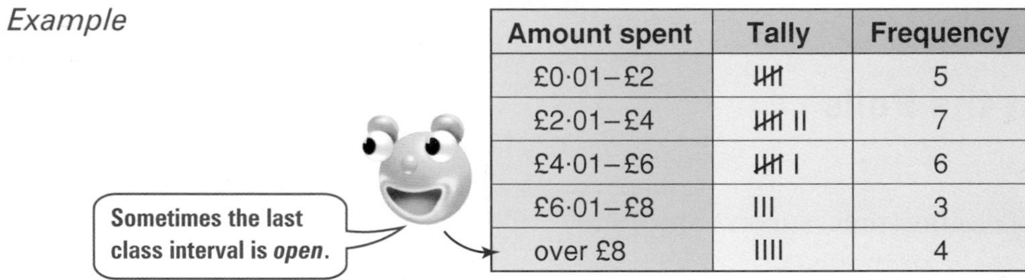
Sometimes the last class interval is *open*.

Amount spent	Tally	Frequency
£0·01–£2	卌	5
£2·01–£4	卌 II	7
£4·01–£6	卌 I	6
£6·01–£8	III	3
over £8	IIII	4

Discussion

In the above example, would it have been more useful if Ben had grouped the data like this? **Discuss.**

£0·01–£1 £1·01–£2 £2·01–£3, ...

What about like this? **Discuss.**

£0·01–£5 £5·01–£10 £10·01–£15, ...

What about like this? **Discuss.**

£0·01–£0·50 £0·51–£1 £1·01–£1·50, ...

Which class intervals are the most useful and why? **Discuss.**

Exercise 1

T

1 Charles wrote down the ages of the people who came to the class play.

28 62 34 29 32 47 68 17 37 48
37 70 49 43 32 82 61 29 38 64

Use a copy of this frequency table.
Fill it in.

Age	10–19	20–29	30–39	40–49	50–59	60–69	70 or over
Tally							
Frequency							

T

2 This data gives the points scored in a radio competition.

2·9 1·9 2·5 2·8 2·6 2·1 3·7 2·5
2·4 2·9 4·2 2·7 2·8 3·2 3·5 4·1
1·8 2·0 2·7 4·8 2·2 1·7 2·8 2·9

"How long can you not say 'Yes' for?"
Radio FM 3

a Use a copy of this frequency table.
Fill it in for the data.

Points scored	1·5–1·9	2·0–2·4	2·5–2·9	3·0–3·4	3·5–3·9	4·0–4·4	4·5–4·9
Tally							
Frequency							

b Use a copy of this frequency table.
Fill it in for the data.

Points scored	1·5–2·4	2·5–3·4	3·5–4·4	4·5–5·4
Tally				
Frequency				

c Which table shows the data better? Explain.

***3** Nick wrote down how much money he banked each week for 30 weeks.

£27 £30·50 £16 £23·15 £22·70 £19 £20·20
£16·50 £43 £8 £20·50 £14 £11·25 £24·50
£24 £15·50 £30 £16·80 £9·40 £21·20 £21
£32·80 £12 £17·75 £20 £15 £19·30 £24·20
£17·80 £21

a Draw a frequency table.
Use these class intervals.

£5·01–£10, £10·01– ··· £20·01–£25 over £25

b What other class intervals could you use?

Surveys – the problem or question

Remember
Before you begin a survey you need to **plan it** using these steps.

Step 1 **What do you want to find out?**

Example What music do 12-year-olds like?

Step 2 **Decide what data you need to collect.**

Example The number of 12-year-olds who like different sorts of music.

It is helpful to think of some possible answers you might get.

Step 3 **Decide where to collect the data from.**
Decide how much data to collect.

You could collect data from

a a **survey** (primary source)
Sometimes it isn't possible to ask every person.
We ask a **sample** of people.

You have to decide how many people to ask.

Example If we want to know what music 12-year-olds like we can't ask every 12-year-old.

b an **experiment** where you count or measure something (primary source)

Example If we want to know if boys or girls have longer arms, we have to measure.

c **other sources** such as reference books, newspapers, Internet websites, historical records, databases, CD-ROMs, ... (secondary source)

Discussion

Look at the questions below.

Use **steps 1**, **2** and **3** in the screen above to plan a survey for each. **Discuss**.

- Which is your better catching hand?
- Does your school need more sports gear? If so what?
- How much pocket money do pupils in your class get?
- What sort of films do your classmates like going to?

Collecting the data

You will need to design a **collection sheet** or a **questionnaire**.

Example **Collection sheet**

Time taken to get to school

Time (min)	Tally	Frequency
0–9	𝍸 𝍸 III	13
10–19	𝍸 IIII	9
20–29	𝍸 II	7
30–39	IIII	4
40+	II	2

Example **Frequency chart**
Survey on ways of travelling to school

You need to decide what units to use for any measurements.

Name	Year	Form of travel	Distance (m)	Time taken (minutes)

Example

Questionnaire

How do you travel to school? Tick one box.

Walk ☐ Bus ☐ Car ☐ Train ☐ Bicycle ☐ Other ☐

How long does it take you (in minutes)?

1–10 ☐ 11–20 ☐ 21–30 ☐ 31–40 ☐ > 40 ☐

Discussion

Discuss how to design a collection sheet for each of these.

- Which is your better catching hand?
- Does your school need more sports gear? If so what?
- How much pocket money do pupils in your class get?
- What sort of films do your classmates like going to see?

Exercise 2

1 

Ryan wanted to know how many of each flavour milkshake a shop sold.
These were the flavours sold.

chocolate strawberry caramel orange vanilla

a Write down some possible results Ryan might get.
b Design a collection sheet Ryan could use.

2 Choose *one* of the questions below.
Design a collection sheet or questionnaire to collect the data.
a How often do people go to the cinema?
b Which items does the canteen run out of most often?
c What sport do people in your class watch most often?
d Is the height of most people about the same as three times the distance round their head?
*__e__ Do most people in your class have a reaction time of less than $\frac{1}{2}$ second?

*3 Suki wanted to know what people in her school buy at the canteen.
a Write down some possible results Suki could get from this survey.
b What data does she need to collect?
c Design a collection sheet to collect this data.
d About how many people do you think she should ask? Explain your answer.
e How could she collect the data?

Planning a survey

Remember
Before you carry out a **survey** you must

1 decide what you want to find out
2 decide what data you must collect
3 decide how you will collect the data and how much data to collect.

Practical

Choose one of the questions below.
You could use one of your own.
Check with your teacher.
Follow the steps on the previous page and plan a survey.
Design a collection sheet or questionnaire.

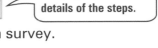

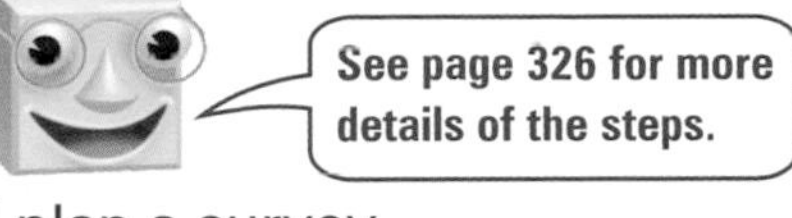

See page 326 for more details of the steps.

Questions
What after school activities do the pupils in your class do?
Where do pupils in your class go for their holidays?
What do pupils in your class buy as presents for friends/parents?
In which month does it rain most?

You could use the Internet.

Summary of key points

Some data is best if it is **grouped**.
The groups are called **class intervals**.
They must be of equal width.

A tally chart or frequency table can be used to collect grouped data.

Example This frequency table shows amounts of money pupils spent last weekend.

Money spent	£0·01–£1	£1·01–£2	£2·01–£3	£3·01–£4	over £4
Tally	III	𝍸 III	𝍸 𝍸 I	𝍸	III
Frequency	3	8	11	5	3

Use these steps to **plan a survey**.

Step 1 **Decide what you want to find out**.

Step 2 **Decide what data needs to be collected**.
Think of possible results you might get from your survey.

Step 3 **Decide where to collect the data from, and how much to collect**.
You could collect data by

a doing a **survey** using a questionnaire or collection sheet **(primary source)**

b doing an **experiment** where you count or measure something **(primary source)**

c gathering data from other sources such as books, newspapers, the Internet, historical records or a database. **(secondary source)**

Once a survey has been planned a **collection sheet** or **questionnaire** has to be designed.

Test yourself

T

1 Angus wrote down how many minutes his phone calls lasted. 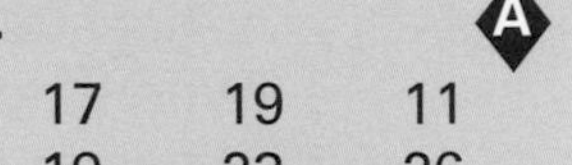

8 10 16 3 1 24 25 30 36 17 19 11
16 18 4 3 7 2 1 4 17 19 23 26

Use a copy of this frequency table.
Fill it in.

Number of minutes	Tally	Frequency
1–10		
11–20		
21–30		
>30		

open class interval (arrow pointing to >30)

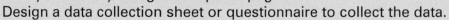

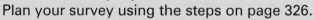

2 For *one* of the questions below, design a collection sheet or questionnaire to collect the data. 

a Which fast food is the most popular?
b How far can classmates jump, to the nearest centimetre, from a standing start.
c Do boys or girls have longer big toes?

3 Choose a survey topic. 
Plan your survey using the steps on page 326.
Design a data collection sheet or questionnaire to collect the data.

16 Analysing Data, Drawing and Interpreting Graphs

You need to know

Key vocabulary

average, bar chart, bar-line graph, frequency, interpret, mean, median, modal class/group, mode, pie chart, range, represent, statistic, survey, title

Watch it!

Television viewing: by gender and age
United Kingdom
Hours per person per week

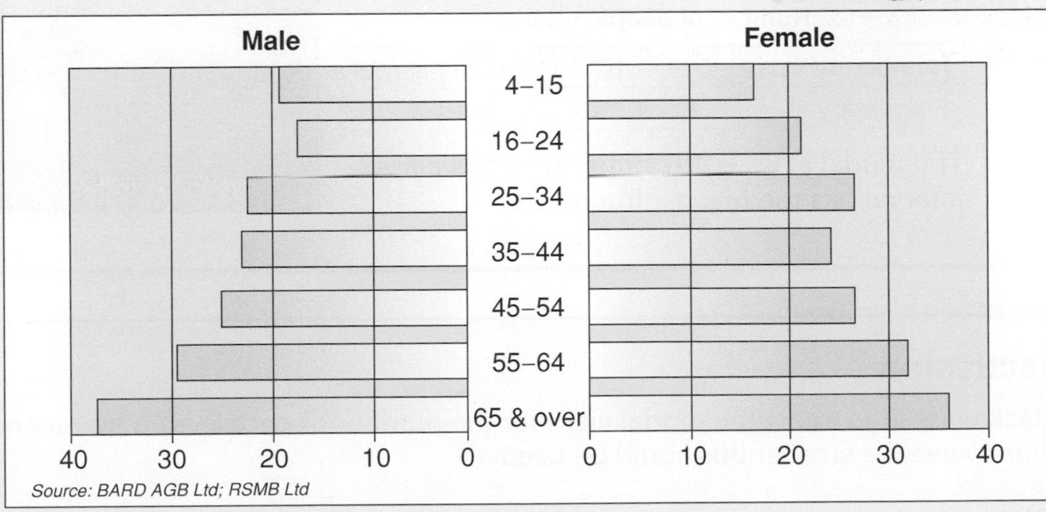

What does this graph tell you about

– the differences between male and female TV viewing
– the differences in TV viewing between age groups?

Mode and range

Sometimes there is more than one mode

Remember

The **mode** is the most commonly occurring data value.

Example For 8, 10, 12, 12, 12, 14, 15 the mode is 12.
For 3, 6, 4, 7, 6, 8, 2, 3, 6, 3 the modes are 3 and 6.

Example

Shoe size	Tally	Frequency
5	𝍸 III	8
6	𝍸 I	6
7	𝍸	5
8	III	3

The **modal** shoe size is 5 because this has the highest frequency.

The **range** is the difference between the highest and lowest values.

Example 8, 16, 4, 25, 17, 23, 36

36 − 4 = 32

The range of this data is 32

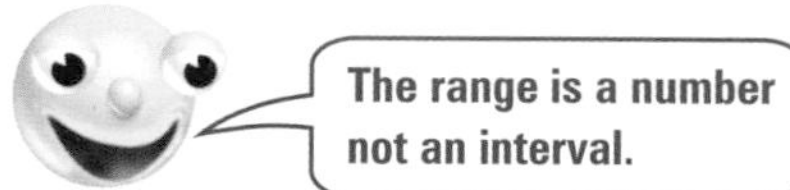

If a frequency table has grouped data we find the **modal class** or **modal group**.

Example This frequency table shows the number of people on a bus each morning.

Number of people on bus

Number on bus	0–9	10–19	20–29	30–39
Frequency	8	16	5	2

The modal class is 10–19 because this class interval has the highest frequency.

Discussion

- Jack wanted to know the modal class for the number of people who travel on a bus to see if a smaller bus could be used.

  Think of another example when it would be useful to know the modal class. **Discuss.**
- What does the range tell us about data? **Discuss.**

Exercise 1

1 Olivia wrote down the number of books she got from the library on her last eight visits.

4 3 6 2 7 3 3 3

a What is the modal number of books she borrowed?
b What is the range of the number of books she borrowed?

2 This table gives the time spent on homework by six girls on two nights.
a What is the modal time spent on homework over both nights?
b What is the modal time spent on Wednesday?
c What is the modal time spent on Thursday?
d What is the range of the times spent on Wednesday?

Time spent on homework

Wednesday	Thursday
50 min	20 min
45 min	15 min
50 min	10 min
50 min	15 min
30 min	30 min
45 min	25 min

3 This table gives the results Sally's class got in maths.
Write down the modal class.

Maths

Score	Tally	Frequency
1–10	III	3
11–20	~~IIII~~ I	6
21–30	~~IIII~~ II	7
31–40	~~IIII~~ ~~IIII~~ II	12
41–50	III	3

4 This table gives the percentages Sam's class got in a fitness test.
Write down the modal class.

Percentage	Tally	Frequency
41–50	~~IIII~~ I	6
51–60	~~IIII~~ ~~IIII~~	10
61–70	I	1
71–80	~~IIII~~ ~~IIII~~	10
> 80	III	3

5 50 students each tossed a dice 100 times.
This table shows the number of sixes tossed.
What is the modal class?

Number of sixes	0–4	5–9	10–14	15–19	20–24	25–29
Frequency	3	8	12	18	7	2

Mean

Remember

mean = $\frac{\text{sum of data values}}{\text{number of values}}$

Example The mean of 15, 7, 28, 19, 23 and 16 is

$$\frac{15 + 7 + 28 + 19 + 23 + 16}{6} = \frac{108}{6}$$
$$= \mathbf{18}$$

See page 317 for more about the mean.

Exercise 2

Only use a calculator if you need to.

1 Find the mean for each of these.
a 0, 2, 2, 3, 4, 4, 6
b 12, 15, 19, 26, 28
c 24, 12, 16, 28, 32, 46, 52, 30

2 Matthew weighed himself five times.
These are the five readings.
61·3 kg, 61·2 kg, 60·9 kg, 61·0 kg, 61·1 kg
Find the mean of the five readings.

3 **Maths test marks**

Callum	68	73	55	74	65
Dylan	93	39	65	73	70

a Who has the highest mean mark? By how much?
***b** After the next test Callum's mean was 67.
What did he score in this test?

***4** Asad got these marks in four mental tests.
8 7 9 8
The mean is 8.
After his fifth test, the mean of his marks was still 8.
What mark did he get in his fifth test?

***5** Jack has four number cards.
Their mean is 5.
Jack picks another card.
The mean of his five cards is 6.
What number is on the new card?

Data is sometimes given in a **frequency table**.
We can find the mean from the table.

Example This frequency table shows how many sick days Pamela's friends had last term.

Number of sick days	Frequency	Total number of sick days
1	4	**1 × 4 = 4**
2	4	**2 × 4 = 8**
3	2	**3 × 2 = 6**
4	1	**4 × 1 = 4**

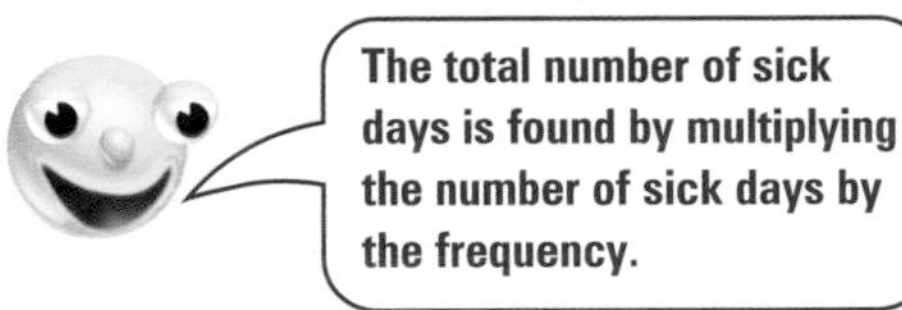

The total number of sick days is found by multiplying the number of sick days by the frequency.

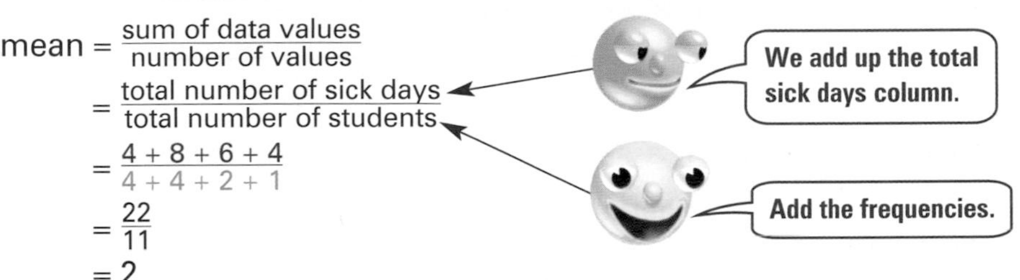

We add up the total sick days column.
Add the frequencies.

$$\text{mean} = \frac{\text{sum of data values}}{\text{number of values}}$$
$$= \frac{\text{total number of sick days}}{\text{total number of students}}$$
$$= \frac{4+8+6+4}{4+4+2+1}$$
$$= \frac{22}{11}$$
$$= 2$$

The mean number of sick days is **2**.

Exercise 3

1 The number of goals scored by a hockey team are given in this table.
Find the mean.

Number of goals	0	1	2	3
Frequency	1	3	3	5
Total goals	0 × 1 = 0	1 × 3 = 3	2 × 3 = 6	3 × 5 = 15

Copy this and fill in the gaps.

$$\text{mean} = \frac{\text{sum of total goals}}{\text{sum of frequency}}$$
$$= \frac{0+3+\_\_\_+\_\_\_}{1+3+\_\_\_+\_\_\_}$$
$$= \_\_\_$$
$$= \_\_\_$$

Remember: To find the sum, we add.

2 This frequency table gives the class sizes at Amy's school.
Find the mean class size.

Class size	28	29	30	31	32
Number of classes	1	0	2	5	2
Total number of pupils	28 × 1 = 28	29 × 0 = 0	30 × 2 = 60	_____	_____

3 This table shows the marks scored in a 'parents quick quiz' at a school quiz evening.
  a What was the range of marks?
  b What was the modal mark?
  c What was the mean mark?

Number of marks	Number of parents	Total marks
0	2	
1	7	
2	5	
3	2	
4	3	
5	1	

Median

Remember
The median is the middle value when a set of data is put in order of size.

Example This list gives the number of squares of pizza eaten by 9 friends.

2, 5, 6, 6, (7), 10, 11, 12, 15

The values are already in order of size.
The middle value is 7. The median is **7**.

When there is an even number of values, the median is the mean of the two middle values.

Worked Example
Find the median of these values.

21, 10, 72, 15, 43, 20, 56, 83

Answer
Put the values in order.

10, 15, 20, (21), (43), 56, 72, 83

There are two middle values, 21 and 43.
The median is the mean of these two values.

mean of two values $= \frac{21 + 43}{2}$
$= \frac{64}{2}$
$= 32$

The median is **32**.

Exercise 4

1 Find the median for each of these.
  a 1, 5, 8, 12, 16, 24, 29
  b 3, 9, 5, 12, 16, 12, 7
  c 13, 24, 16, 33, 17, 31, 28
  d 80, 20, 30, 50, 40, 30
  e 4, 9, 5, 9, 7, 12
  f 42, 38, 16, 57, 32, 41, 28, 52

2 In a mental test, a group of students got these marks:

17 16 11 16 18 12 16

What was the median mark?

3 This shows Vic's basketball team.
What is the median height?

4 Jon collected this data from his friends.

	Jon	Rajiv	Tim	Caleb	Tom	Isabel
Number of sisters	0	1	3	1	2	2
Science mark	82	64	85	72	76	71

a What is the median number of sisters?

***b** Jon thinks he has the median science mark. Is he correct?

***c** What is the median science mark?

***5** This bar chart shows the number of pupils who were late to school each day one week.
What is the median number of pupils late per day?

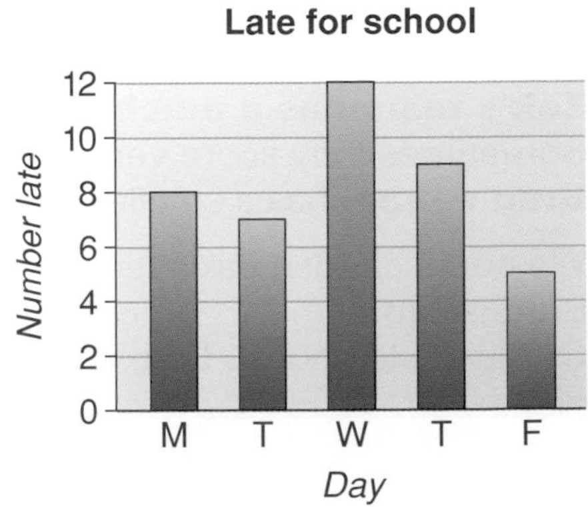

Mean, median, mode, range

The next exercise gives you practice at finding the **mean, median, mode and range**.

Exercise 5

1

Team	Scores							
Green Valley	35	17	33	35	36	16	27	41
Red Ferns	16	24	22	31	29	15	31	32
St Peters	18	21	31	22	12	39	20	19
Albion	14	16	18	31	31	32	30	22

This table gives the scores for the last eight games of four basketball teams.

a Find the modal score, range, mean and median for each team.
b Put the teams in order using their mean scores.
c Put the teams in order using their median scores.
d Which team has the greatest range?

Comparing data

To **compare data** we use the **range** and either the **mean**, the **median** or the **mode**.

Worked Example
The mean and range of two rugby teams is given.

	Mean	Range
Brad's team	24	13
Zak's team	24	60

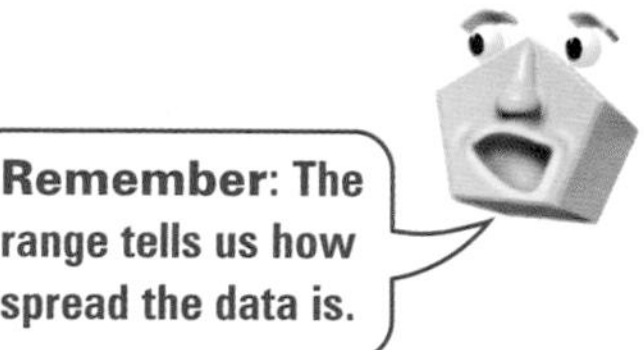

Remember: The range tells us how spread the data is.

Which team would you choose to play a visiting team?
Explain your answer.

Answer
Both teams have the same mean.

Zak's team has a much greater range.
Sometimes they score very high points and sometimes very low points.
Brad's team has a smaller range.

We could choose Zak's team because there is more chance of a high score than with Brad's team.
Or we could choose Brad's team beause it has more consistent scores.

Exercise 6

1 This table gives the mean and range of the scores of two girls in a gymnastics competition.

	Mean	Range
Jackie	7·9	0·8
Elaine	8·1	4·3

Only one girl can be chosen to go to a national competition.
Use the mean and range to decide which girl you would choose.
It doesn't matter who you choose but you must explain why you have chosen her.

2 Ross could catch either the 83 or the 64 bus home.
He caught the 83 one week and the 64 the next.
This table shows the time for the journeys.

	M	T	W	T	F
83 Bus (time in min)	25	28	26	25	26
64 Bus (time in min)	20	34	19	40	17

a Find the median of the 83 bus times.
b Find the median of the 64 bus times.
c Find the range of each set of data.
d Decide which bus it would be more sensible to catch. Explain why.

3 This table gives the mean and range for the rainfall each month at two different places in the world.

	Mean	Range
Rainfall at A (mm)	340	650
Rainfall at B (mm)	348	16

Use the mean and range to choose in which place you would rather live.
It doesn't matter which place you choose but you must use the mean and range to explain why you would rather live there.

***4** A 100-word sample was taken from two newspapers.
The number of letters in each word was counted.
This table gives the mean and range of the number of letters per word.

Newspaper type	Mean	Range
Tabloid	4·2	8
Sunday	4·0	15

Write two sentences comparing the results.

***5** Ryan did an experiment to see which was his better catching hand.
He threw five cubes in the air 100 times.
He wrote down how many of these he caught each time.

	Mode	Range
Left hand	3	3
Right hand	2	5

Which do you think is Ryan's better catching hand?
Give a reason.

* 

Practical

Collect two sets of data you can compare.
Find the mean, median or mode of the data and the range.
Use these to compare the data.

Suggested data

- midday temperatures at two different places each day for a week
- tries scored, in matches last season, by two rugby teams

- prices of cars for sale at two different car dealers
- numbers of goals scored by first and second division teams throughout the season
- hours of TV watched by two different classes or by two different year groups or by two different ages each day for a month
- numbers of fast-food meals eaten each week by two different age groups

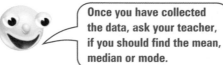

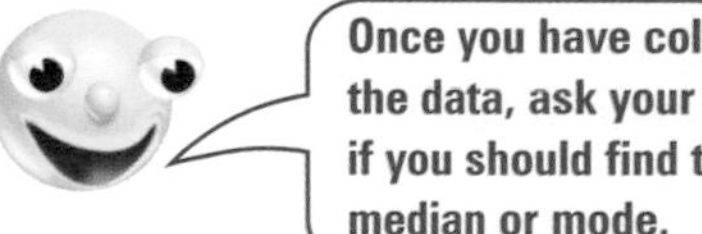

Once you have collected the data, ask your teacher, if you should find the mean, median or mode.

Bar charts and bar-line graphs

Bar-line graphs

Remember
A **bar-line graph** is like a bar chart but it has lines instead of bars.

Example

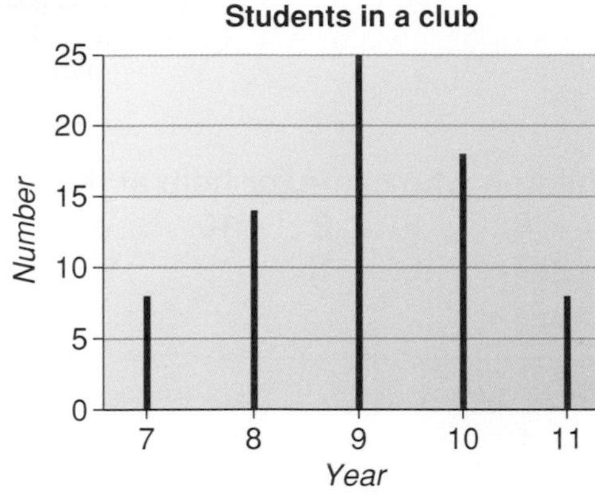

Exercise 7

T

1 Use a copy of this.
Kim wrote down how much he spent each day on holiday.

£4 £3 £5 £4 £8 £7 £3 £4 £8 £4 £4
£4 £8 £4 £8 £5 £7 £3 £1 £8 £2 £1

a Fill in the frequency chart.

Amount spent (£)	1	2	3	4	5	6	7	8
Tally								
Frequency								

b Draw the bar-line graph.

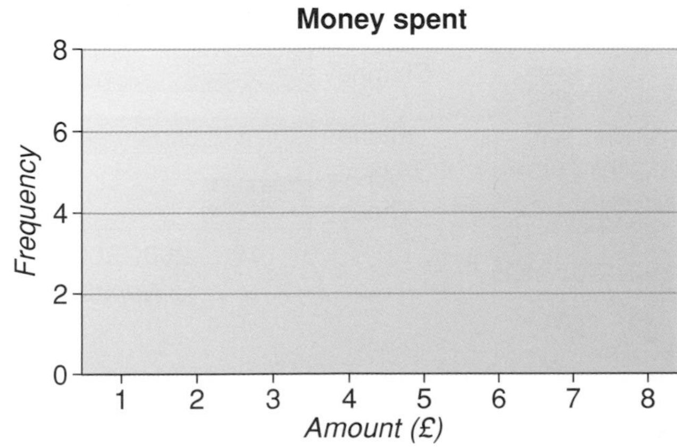

T

2 This table gives the number of people in the families of pupils at Bill's school.

Number in family	3	4	5	6	7
Frequency	19	28	27	18	12

Use a copy of the grid.
Draw a bar-line graph of the data.

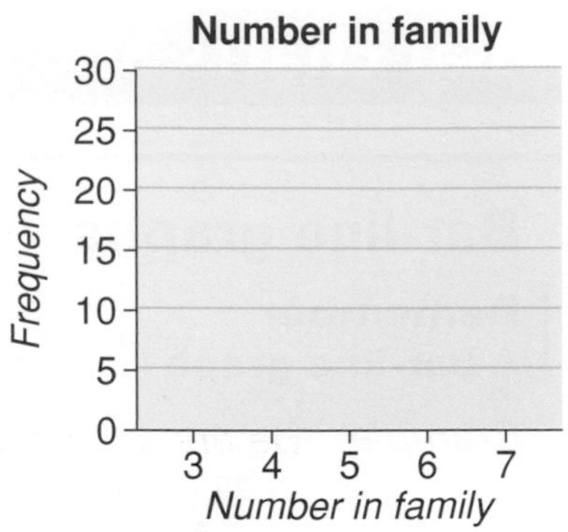

T

3 Use a copy of this.
Tandy wrote down the ages of the children who came for help at the library.

8 7 9 10 7 7 8 8 8 10 9 7
10 6 9 7 8 8 7 10 8 9 10 8

a Fill in the frequency table.

Age	6	7	8	9	10
Tally					
Frequency					

b Finish the bar-line graph.

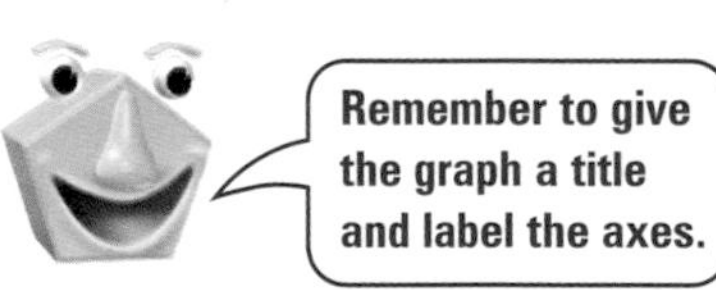

Remember to give the graph a title and label the axes.

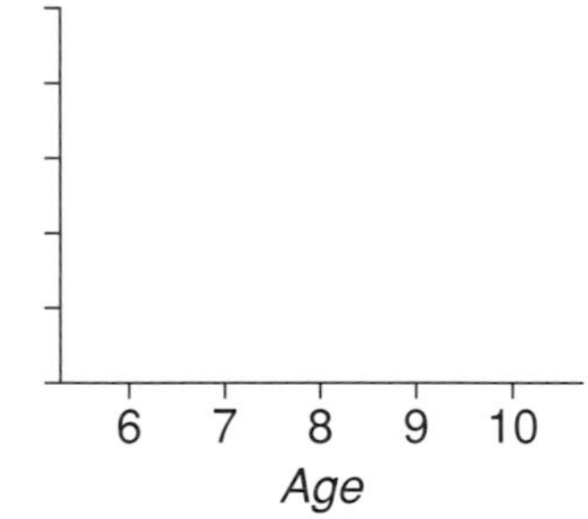

Bar charts

Bar charts can have vertical or horizontal bars.

Examples

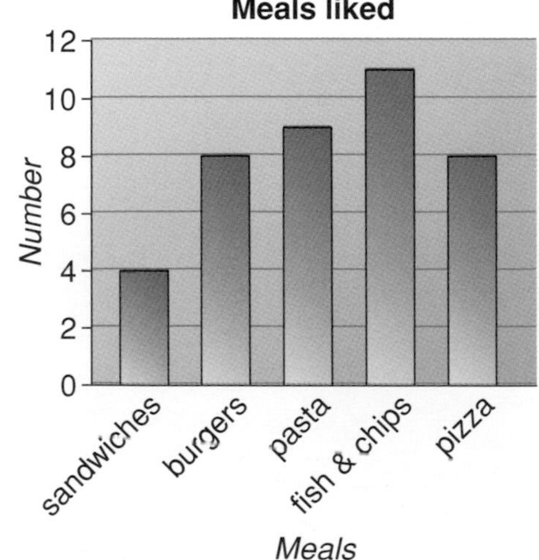

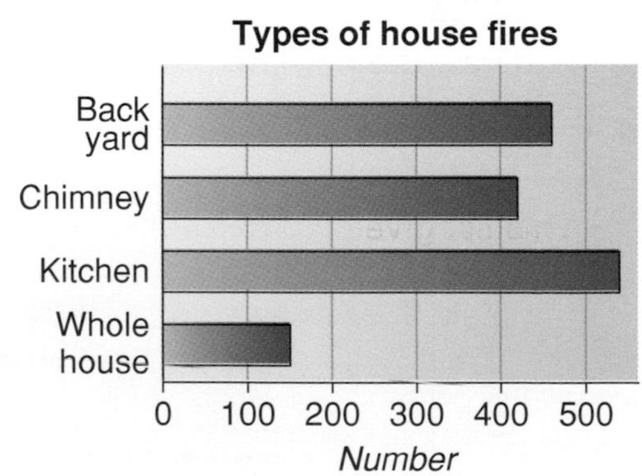

We can use a **bar chart** to show some sorts of **grouped data**.

Example The owner of a supermarket wrote down how many items each customer bought.
This frequency table shows his results.
He drew this bar chart

Number of items	Tally	Frequency
1–5	𝍸 IIII	9
6–10	𝍸 III	8
11–15	𝍸 II	7
16–20	𝍸 III	8
21–25	𝍸 I	6
26–30	IIII	4

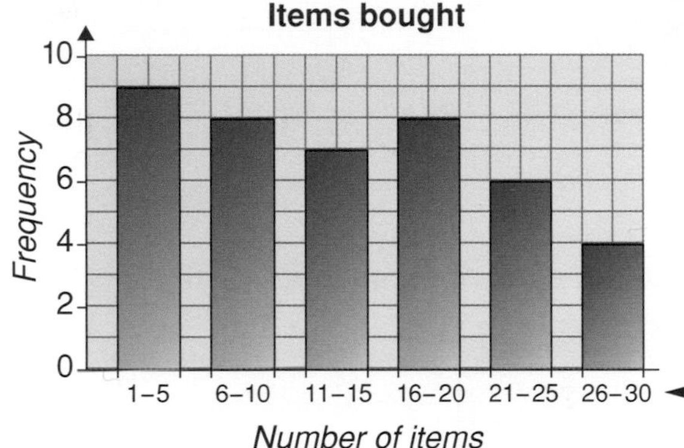

The class interval is written under each bar.

Sometimes we show two sets of data on a bar chart.

Example

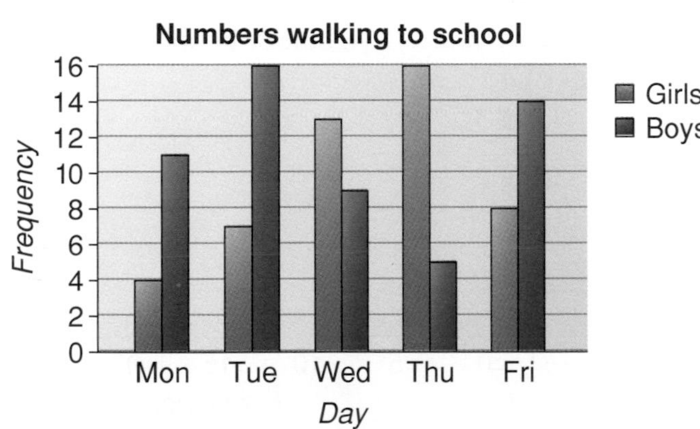

Exercise 8

T

1 This list gives the number of votes five pupils got for class captain.

Zak 3 Katie 11 Jody 6
Ross 5 Avid 7

Use a copy of this bar chart.
Finish it.

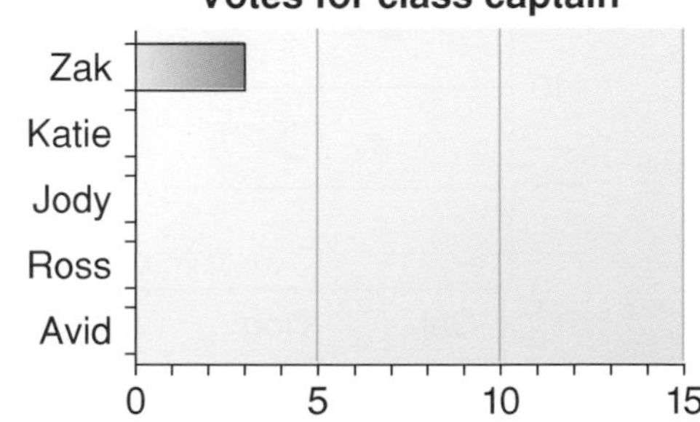

T

2 Some of Tammy's class entered a contest. This table shows the marks.
Use a copy of this bar chart.
Finish it.

Marks	Tally	Frequency
1–3	IIII	4
4–6	~~IIII~~ II	7
7–9	III	3

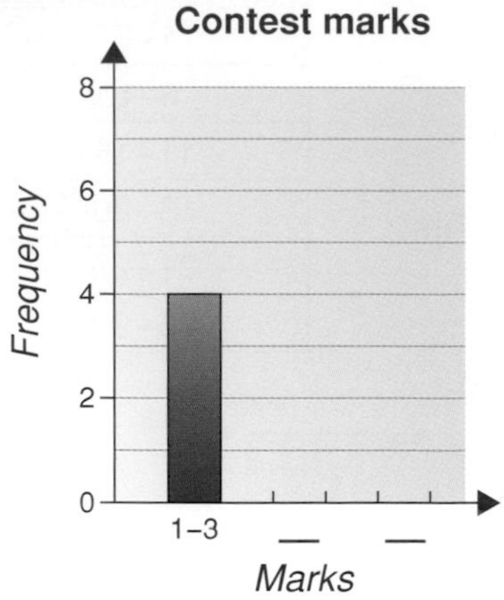

T

3 Penny wrote down the colour of the eyes of the players in all the sports teams.

Colour	Tally	Frequency
Blue	~~IIII~~ ~~IIII~~ ~~IIII~~ ~~IIII~~ ~~IIII~~	25
Brown	~~IIII~~ ~~IIII~~ ~~IIII~~ ~~IIII~~ ~~IIII~~ ~~IIII~~ I	31
Grey	~~IIII~~ ~~IIII~~	10
Hazel	~~IIII~~ ~~IIII~~ ~~IIII~~ II	17

Use a copy of this grid.
Draw a bar chart.

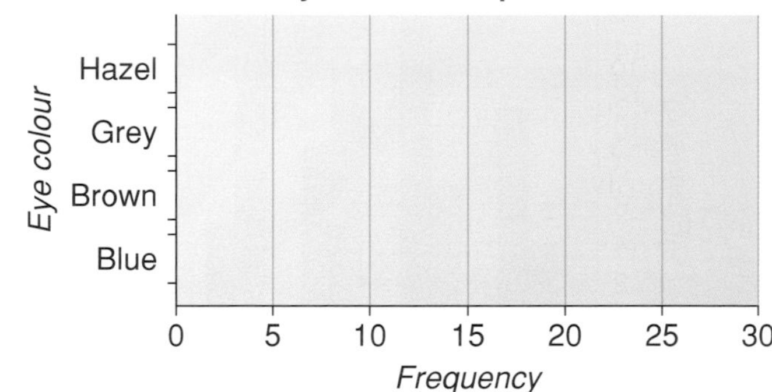

T

4 The frequency chart shows what animals were at the vets one weekend.
Use a copy of the bar chart below.
Finish it.

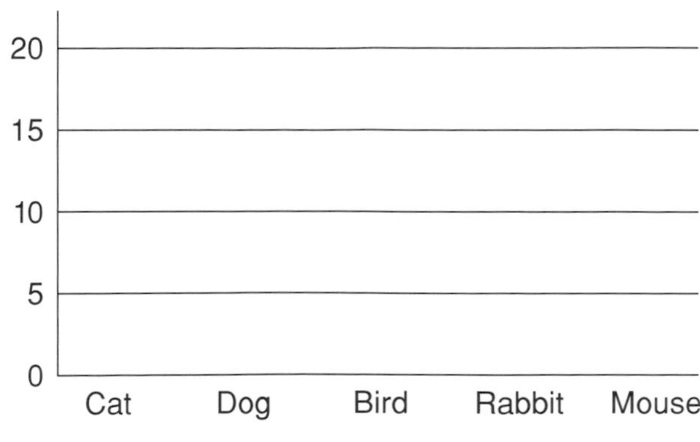

☐ Saturday
☐ Sunday

	Frequency	
Animal	Saturday	Sunday
Cat	13	19
Dog	16	17
Bird	1	3
Rabbit	0	2
Mouse	4	1

T

5 A nurse asked 23 people how much fruit they ate in one month.
These are his results.

5	26	7	31	37	25
6	10	8	24	36	33
39	18	29	16	12	39
38	40	24	1	15	

a Use a copy of this table. Fill it in.
b Draw a bar chart for the data.

Number of pieces	Tally	Frequency
1–10		
11–20		
21–30		
31–40		

T

6 Matt asked what the birth month of boys and girls in his class were.
This frequency chart shows his results.

Month	Jan	Feb	Mar	Apr	May	Jun	Jul	Aug	Sept	Oct	Nov	Dec
Boys	1	1	0	0	1	2	0	3	0	5	1	2
Girls	2	1	0	1	0	4	0	0	2	2	3	0

Draw a bar graph.
Put boys and girls on the same grid.

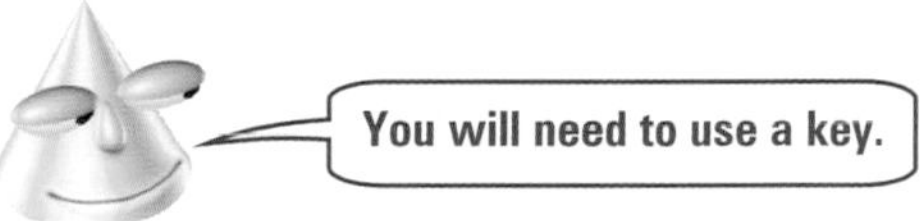

Practical

Choose one of the ideas below.
Collect some data about it.
Make up a collection sheet to use.
Graph your data on a bar chart.

Ideas: favourite colour of your classmates
sports that girls and boys watch on TV
how girls and boys travel to school
favourite singer of boys and girls
highest temperature each day one month

Drawing pie charts on the computer

A **pie chart** is a circle graph.
It shows how something is shared or divided.
The bigger the section, the bigger the proportion it shows.

Example This pie chart shows the proportion of kilojoules in a Big Mac Combo.

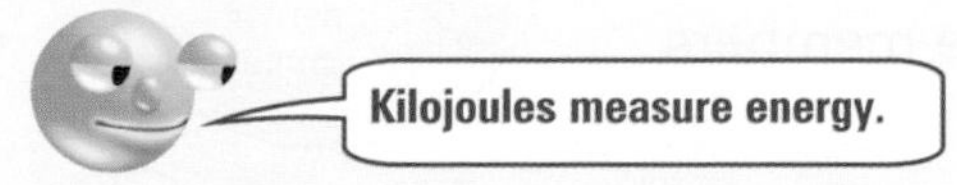

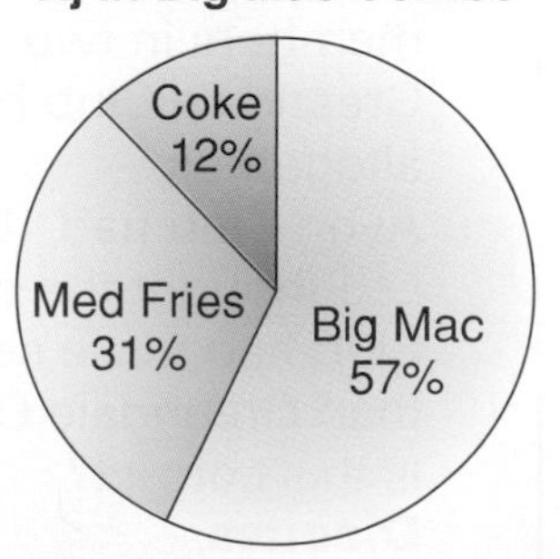

* Practical

You will need a spreadsheet program.

1 This frequency table shows the percentage of pupils who have 0, 1, 2, 3 and 4 brothers.

Number of brothers	0	1	2	3	4
Percentage	20	40	27	10	3

Put this data into a spreadsheet.

	A	B	C	D	E	F
1	Number of brothers	0	1	2	3	4
2	Percentage	20	40	27	10	3

Use the graph function of your spreadsheet to draw a pie chart.

2 Choose some other data that could be displayed on a pie chart.
Put the data into a spreadsheet.
Use the graph function to draw a pie chart.

Interpreting graphs and tables

Discussion

- A school has five year-groups.
  Sixty pupils raised money for a new computer.
  Look at the graph.
  Does Year 7 have fewer pupils than year 9?
  Discuss.

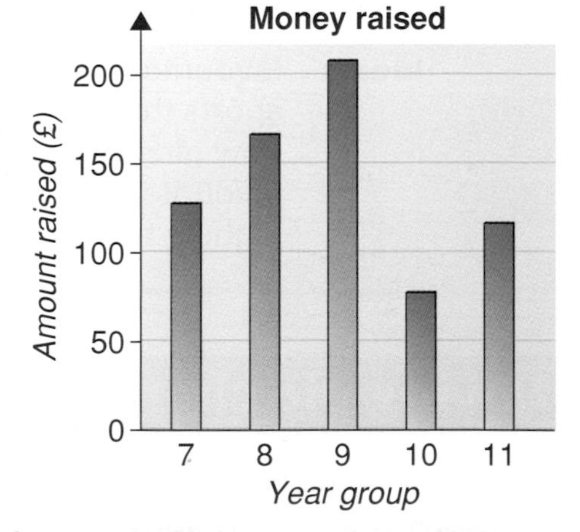

- These pie charts show the number of members in two tennis clubs.
  Greendale Club had 250 members altogether.
  Avon Club had 100 members altogether.
  Lee thought the charts showed that Avon Club had more senior female members than Greendale Club.
  Is this correct?
  Discuss.

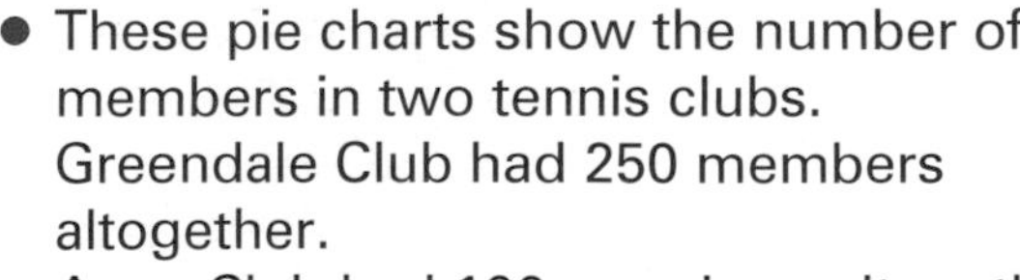

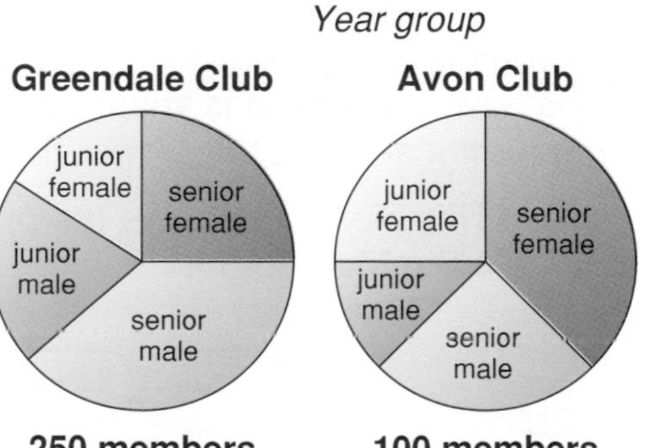

Exercise 9

Only use a calculator if you need to.

1 These graphs show the temperatures for three weeks of the year.
Match these sentences to the bar charts.

a It was very warm at first, then suddenly it got much colder.
b Every day was colder than the day before.
c Each day was hotter than the day before.

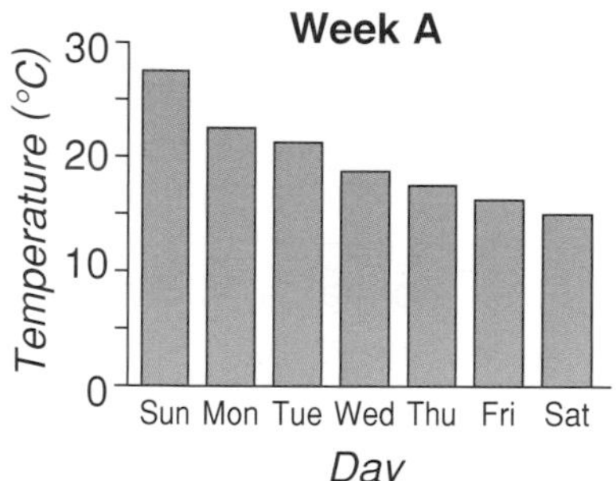

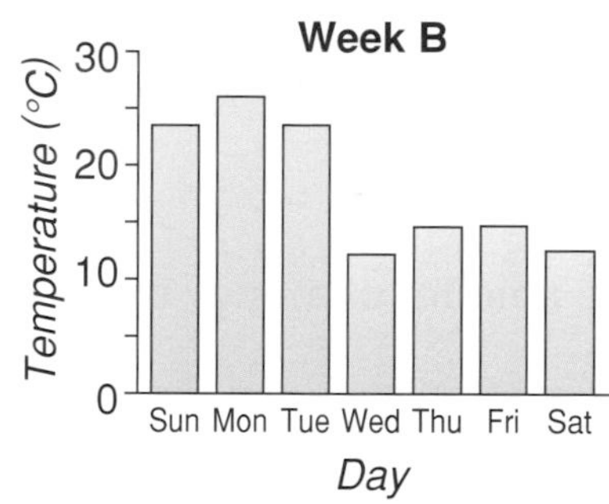

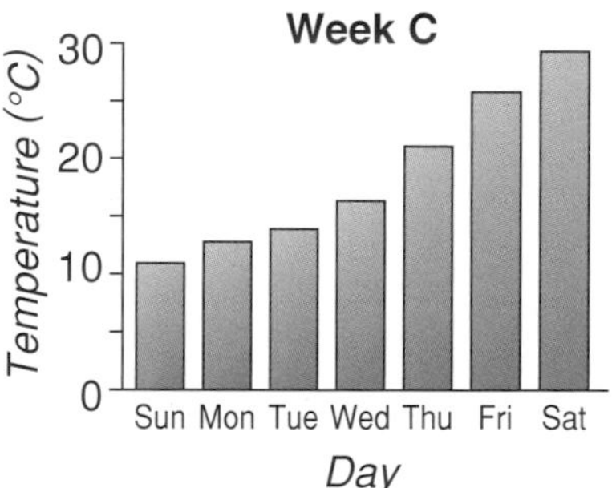

2

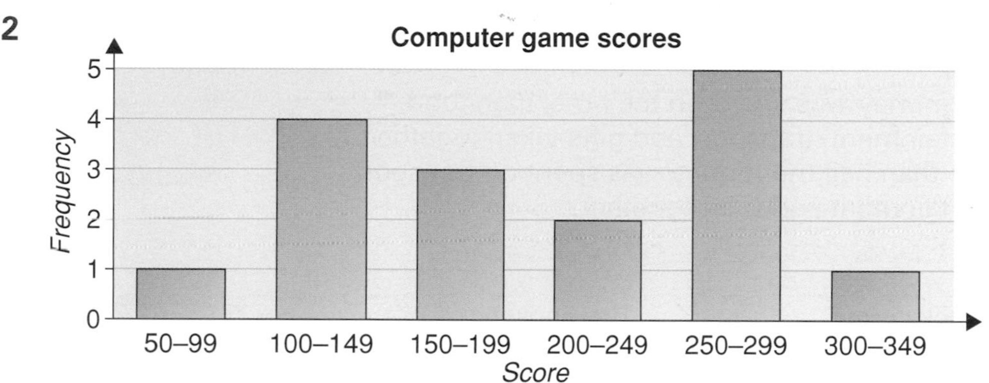

This graph shows scores in a computer game.

a Scores of 250 or more won a prize.
How many people won a prize?
b How many people played altogether?
c A paper said that
'Five people scored between 270 and 300 points.'
Is this correct?
Choose one of these answers.
A Yes **B** No **C** Can't tell

3 A red and a blue dice were each tossed 100 times.
This bar chart shows the results.
One of the dice is fair and the other unfair.
Which do you think is the fair dice?
Why?

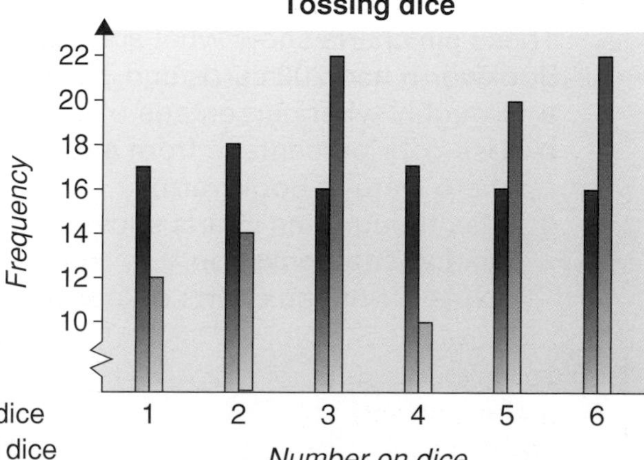

4 This graph shows the amount of pocket money Julia's friends get.
Julia gets £1·50 pocket money.
She asked her mother to increase it to £3.
She told her mother that most of her friends got between £2 and £4.
Is Julia's request reasonable?
Give a reason.

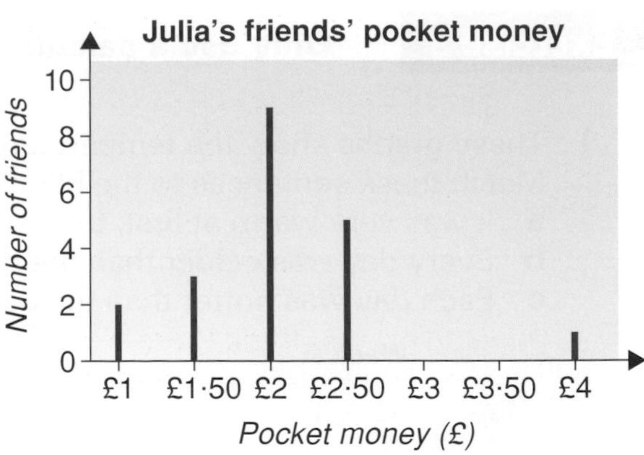

5 This pie chart shows the amount of money spent on a holiday.

a On which item was the most money spent?

b What two items had over half of the money spent on them?

c Which of these sentences are true?

1 More money was spent on the hotel than on air travel.

2 Less money was spent on the hotel than food, entertainment, transport and gifts taken together.

3 More than half the money was spent on transport, entertainment and food together.

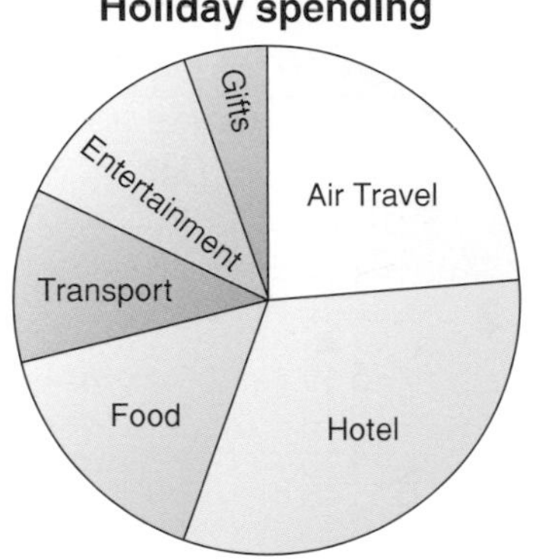

***6**

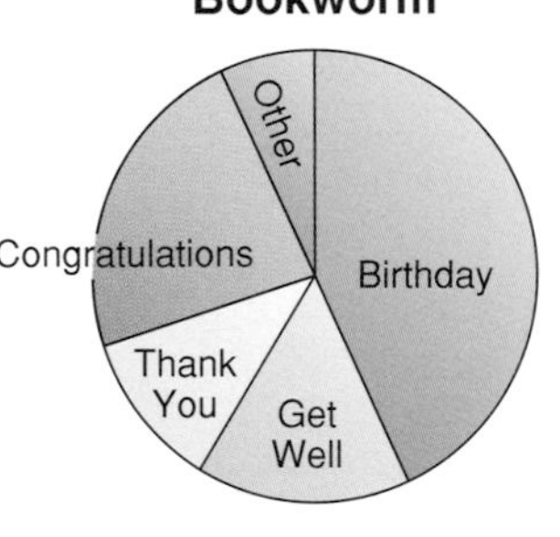

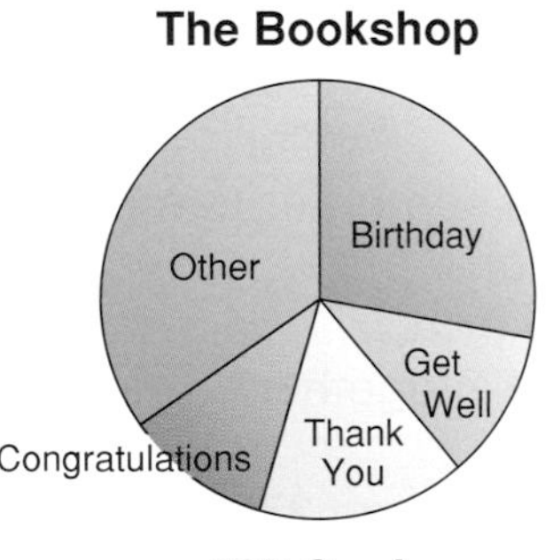

These pie charts show what sorts of cards were in two bookshops.
Bookworm had 200 cards and The Bookshop had 600.

a Roughly what percentage of cards at Bookworm were birthday cards?

b Use your percentage from **a** to work out roughly how many birthday cards there were at Bookworm.

c Max thought the charts showed there were more birthday cards at Bookworm than at The Bookshop.
Explain why the charts do not show this.

*7 **a** There were 1200 people at a concert. Jill worked out the number of 12–15 year olds like this.

$$14\% \text{ of } 1200 = \frac{14}{100} \times 1200$$
$$= 0{\cdot}14 \times 1200$$
$$= 168$$

How many are in each of the other age groups?

b Why do you think there were fewer 30+ people at the concert than other age groups?

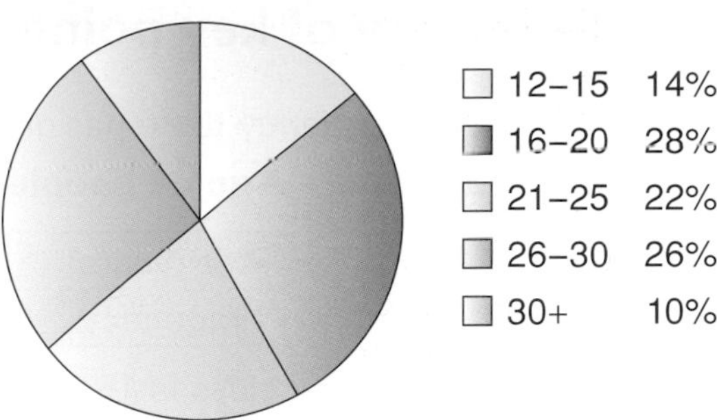

*8 This bar-line graph shows the average monthly temperature at 12 p.m. Christine draws a dotted line on the chart. She says 'the dotted line shows the mean for the four months'. Use the chart to explain why Christine cannot be correct.

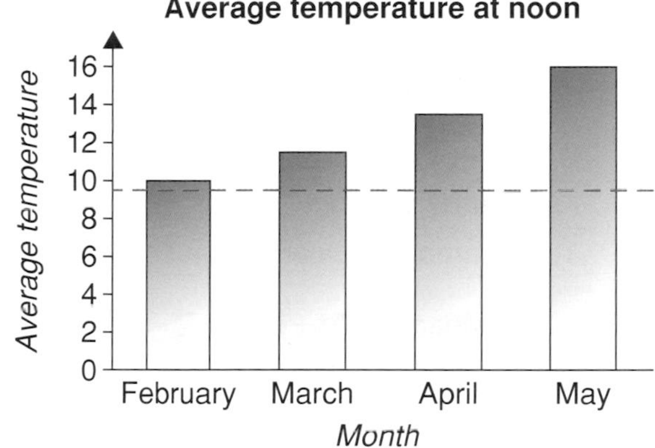

Practical

Find some published graphs.
Good places to look are newspapers, books or the Internet.
Choose a graph to interpret.
Write some sentences about what the graph tells you.

Example

This graph tells us the time that burglaries happened. We can see that a burglary is more likely to be carried out during the evening or night than during the day. What else can we tell?

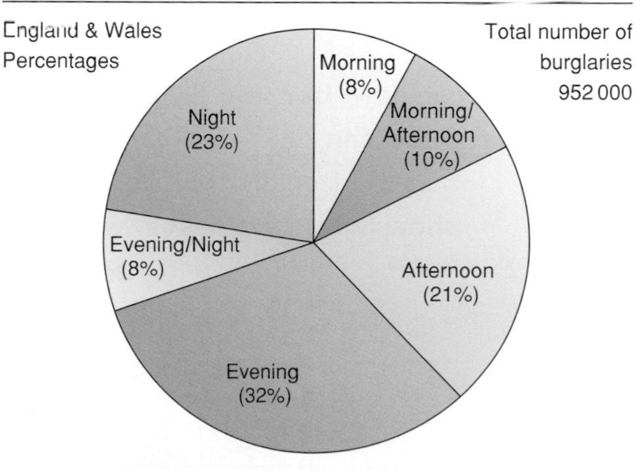

Source: British Crime Survey, Home Office

Summary of key points

If a frequency table has grouped data we find the **modal class**.

Example **Age of people at Internet café**

Age (years)	0–4	5–9	10–14	15–19	20–24
Frequency	2	3	19	26	21

The modal class is 15–19 because this class interval has the highest frequency.

Mean = $\frac{\textbf{sum of data values}}{\textbf{number of data values}}$

Sometimes the data is given in a **frequency table**.

Example **Number of scars on Tom's friends**

Number of scars	0	1	2	3	4
Frequency	14	8	4	2	2
Total number of scars	$0 \times 14 = 0$	$1 \times 8 = 8$	$2 \times 4 = 8$	$3 \times 2 = 6$	$4 \times 2 = 8$

Multiply the number of scars by the frequency to get the totals.

Mean $= \frac{0+8+8+6+8}{14+8+4+2+2}$ ← **sum of total number of scars** / **sum of frequencies**

$= \frac{30}{30}$

$= \mathbf{1}$

The **median** is the middle value when a set of data is arranged in order of size.

When there is an even number of values, the median is the mean of the two middle values.

Example 5, 8, 3, 7, 9, 2, 1, 10

In order of size these are 1, 2, 3, **5, 7,** 8, 9, 10

There are two middle data values.

median $= \frac{5+7}{2}$

$= 6$

We can draw **bar-line graphs** and **bar charts**.

Bar charts can

have horizontal or vertical bars

show two sets of data.

Example

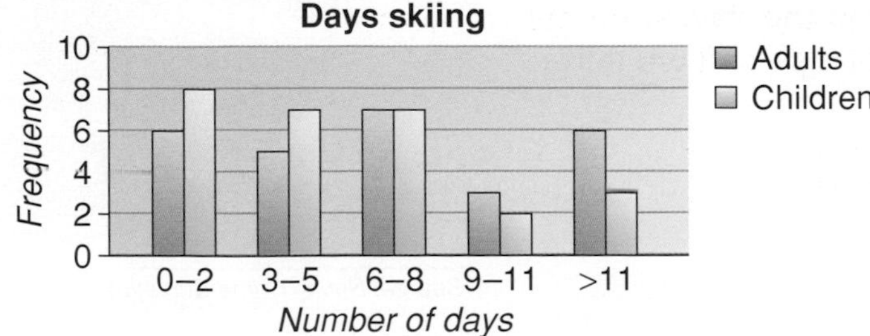

A **pie chart** is a circle graph.
It tells us proportions.

Example This pie chart tells us the country of birth of Year 7 students at a school.

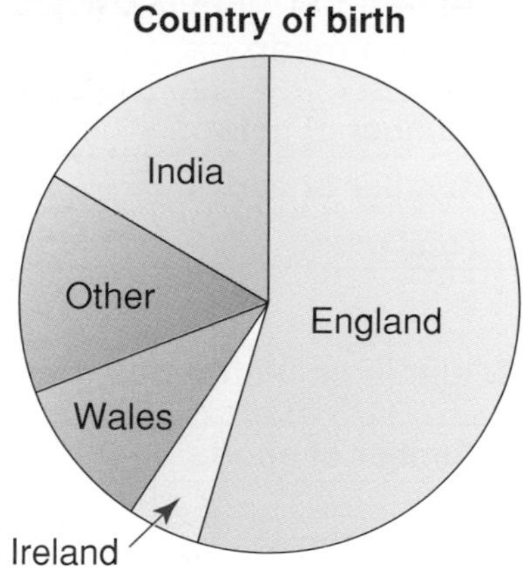

We often use a graph to help us **interpret data**.

Example This bar chart tells us that Year 10 students watch more television than Year 7 students.

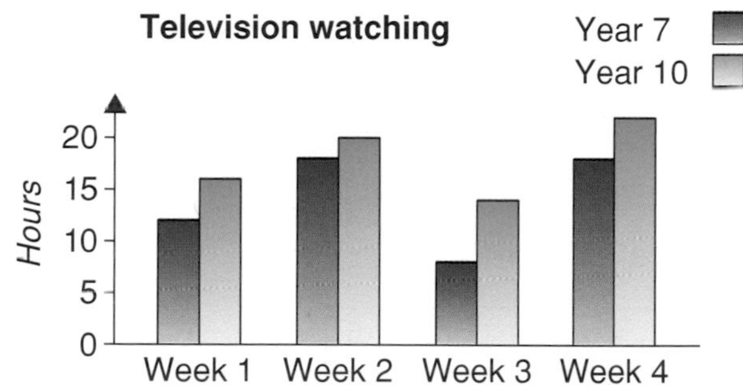

Test yourself

Only use a calculator if you need to.

1 This table shows the marks that class 9L got in a test.
What is the modal group?

Mark	Tally	Frequency
31–40	II	2
41–50	IIII	4
51–60	~~IIII~~ II	7
61–70	~~IIII~~ ~~IIII~~ III	13

2 The heights of some students are given.

158 cm 172 cm 159 cm 164 cm 167 cm

a What is the mean height of these students?
b What is the range of the heights?
c What is the median height?

3 The number of pets owned by pupils is given in this table. 
Find the mean.

Number of pets	1	2	3	4	5
Number of pupils	5	4	5	3	1
Total pets	$1 \times 5 = 5$	$2 \times 4 = 8$	______	______	______

T **4** Melanie collected data on the number of sports played by some pupils.

Number of sports	0	1	2	3	4	5	6
Tally	||||	𝍸 ||	𝍸 𝍸 ||||	𝍸 𝍸	𝍸 |	|	|
Frequency	4	7	14	10	6	1	1

Use a copy of the grid.
Draw a bar-line graph for the data.

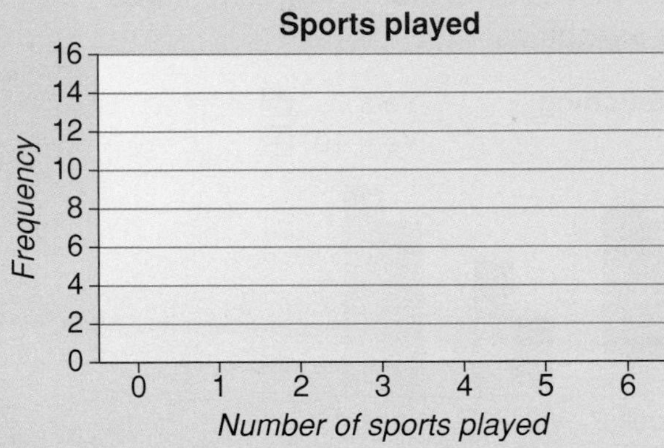

T **5** Omar's class got these marks for a project.

19 16 45 43 40 39 36 30 28 42 35 40
32 38 41 48 27 18 29 38 42 26 41 35

a Use a copy of this table. Fill it in.

Mark	11–20	21–30	31–40	41–50
Tally				
Frequency				

b Draw a bar chart for this data.

6 This frequency chart shows the number of boys and girls away from school one week. 

Day	Monday	Tuesday	Wednesday	Thursday	Friday
Boys	6	10	3	9	8
Girls	4	5	6	7	12

Draw a bar chart for this data.
Have separate bars for boys and girls. Use a key.

F

7 This bar chart shows what people at a sports centre did on Saturday and Sunday.

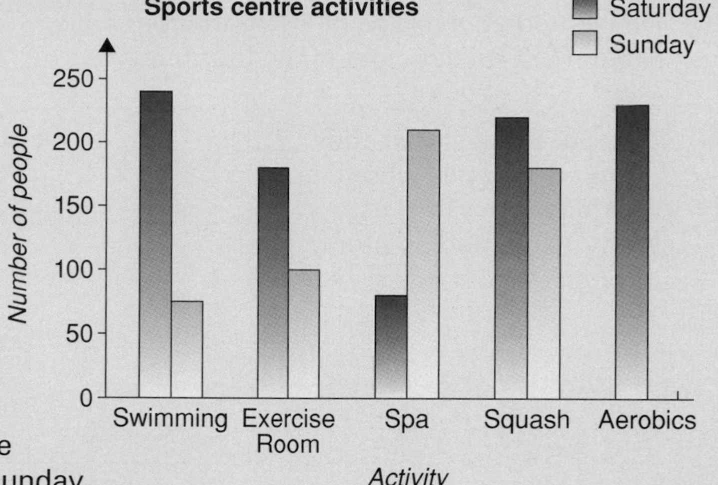

a One day the weather was warm and on the other day it was cool. Which day do you think was warm? Explain.

b Which of these is the most likely reason nobody did aerobics on Sunday?

A Everyone slept in.
B The centre didn't have aerobics classes on Sunday.
C An earthquake destroyed the aerobics room.

E

8

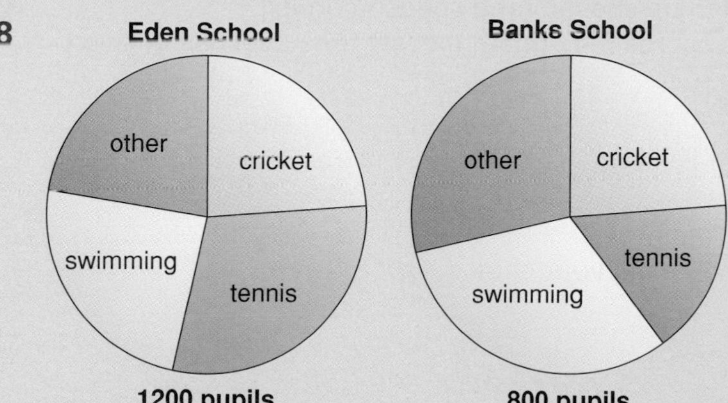

Erin was trying to organise a summer sports contest between Eden School and Banks School.
She said 'Cricket will be easy to organise because both schools have the same number of cricketers.'
Explain why Erin is wrong.

E

9 Kirsty's drama school is putting on a play for families.
This pie chart shows the ages of the children coming.

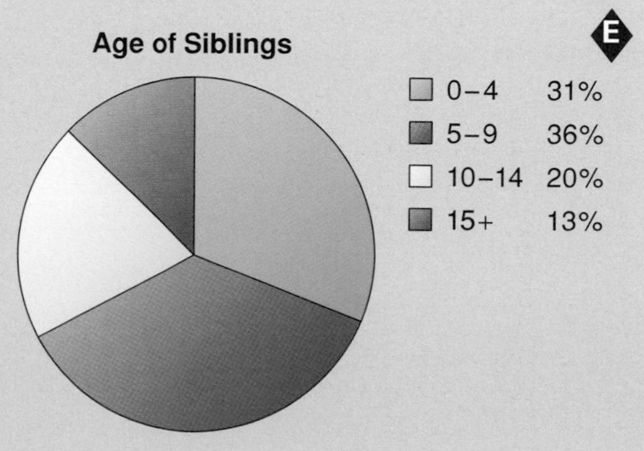

a Do you think it would be better to start the play at 6 p.m. or 8 p.m.? Explain your answer.

***b** There are 200 children coming altogether.
How many of each age group are there?

***10** Paul got these marks in three tests: 72, 80 and 82. **B**
He had one more test to sit.
He wanted an average of 80 for the four tests.
What mark must he get in the fourth test?

***11** This bar chart shows the number of pupils who missed their exams. **C**
What is the median number of pupils who missed exams?

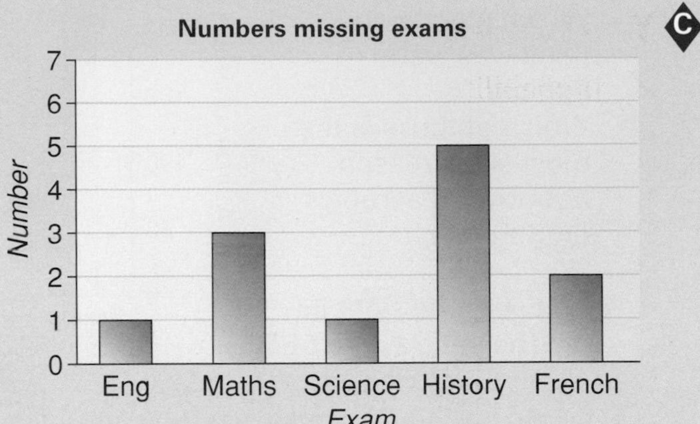

***12** Pete and Kishan both want to be chosen for a speech contest. **B**
The mean and range of the scores they got in the last ten speeches is given.

	Mean	Range
Pete	73	15
Kishan	73	35

Who would you choose?
Use the mean and range to explain your choice.

17 Probability

You need to know

✓ probability page 318

Key vocabulary

certain, chance, dice, equally likely, even chance, event, fair, impossible, likely, outcome, possible, probability, probability scale, random, spin, spinner, unfair

In a spin

You will need thin card and 2 paper fasteners (split pins).

Step 1 Design a spinner that has these probabilities.

stopping on green $\frac{1}{4}$
stopping on red $\frac{1}{2}$
stopping on blue $\frac{1}{8}$
stopping on yellow $\frac{1}{8}$

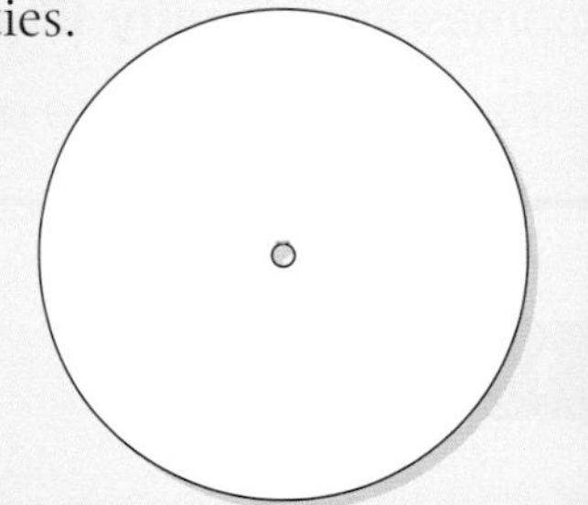

Step 2 Design another spinner that has these probabilities.

stopping on red $\frac{1}{5}$
stopping on blue $\frac{1}{10}$
stopping on green $\frac{3}{10}$
stopping on yellow $\frac{2}{5}$

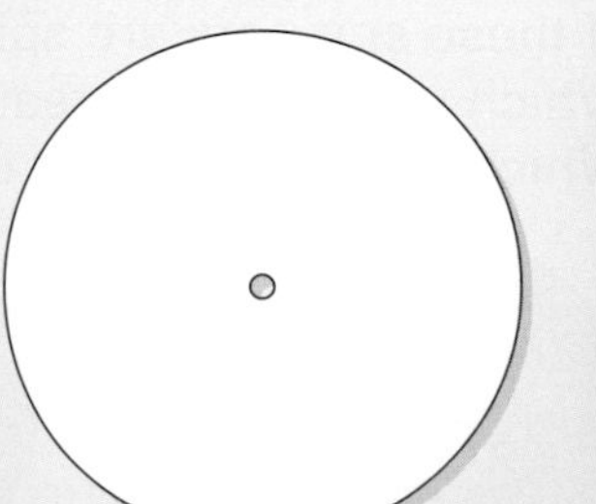

Language of probability

Discussion

- Is there more chance of having a road accident at certain times of the day? **Discuss**.
  What about at certain times of the year?

You could find out if this is true using the library, Internet, CD-ROM, ...

- In some countries there is a higher chance of dying before you are 70 than in other countries.
  Is this true? **Discuss**.
- What is the chance of these happening in England? **Discuss**.
  an earthquake   a cyclone
  a meteorite crashing
  Which do you think is most likely to happen? **Discuss**.
- Think of an **event** where the outcome
  a is certain   **b** is impossible
  c has an even chance of happening.
  Discuss.

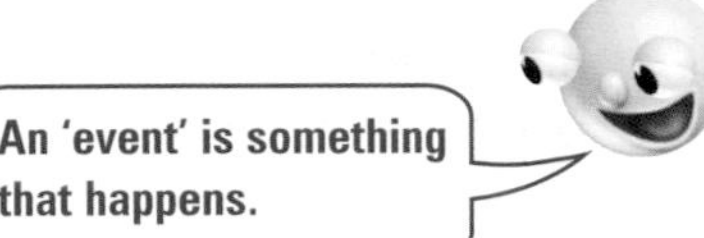
An 'event' is something that happens.

Some events are **more likely** to happen than others.

Example When this spinner is spun it is more likely to stop on yellow than on red.

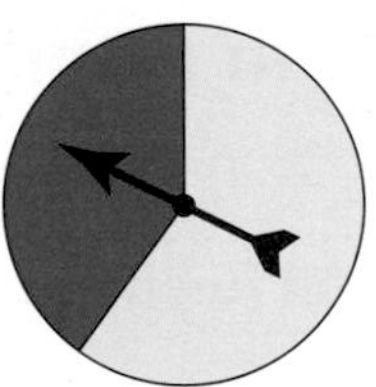

Some outcomes are **equally likely** to happen.

Example If a dice is rolled, the outcomes 1, 2, 3, 4, 5 and 6 are all **equally likely**.

Exercise 1

1 All of these spinners are spun at the same time.
  a Which one has the greatest chance of stopping on red?
  b Which has the greatest chance of stopping on green?

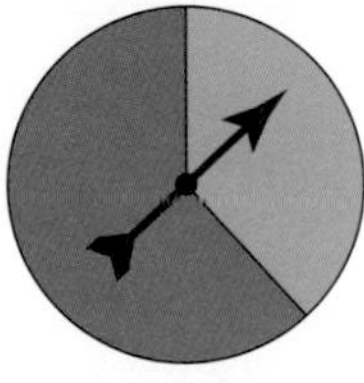
Spinner A

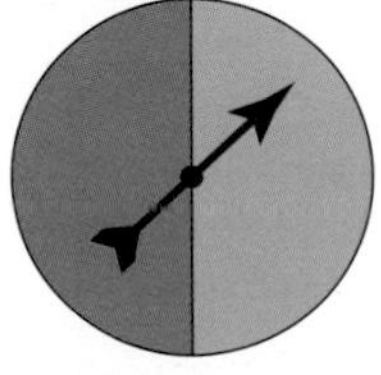
Spinner B

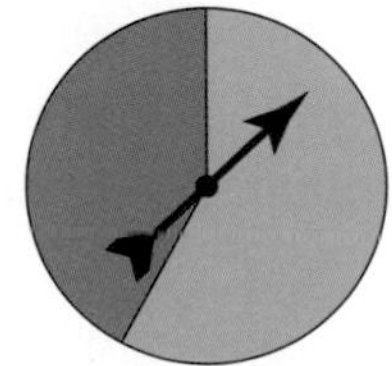
Spinner C

2 A class is divided into two groups, yellow and blue.
This spinner is spun.

If it stops on yellow, the yellow group gets a point.
If it stops on blue, the blue group gets a point.

Which group is more likely to win?
Why?

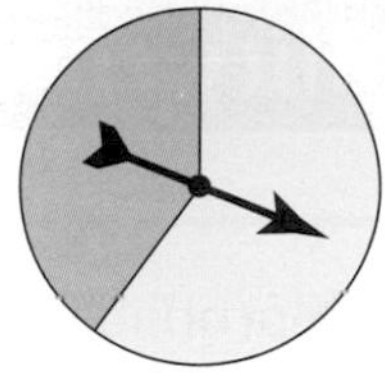

3 Anton, Fiona and Kirsty play a game of **TOSS 6**.

The first to toss 10 sixes wins.

Anton's cube has	5, 6, 6, 3, 4, 2	on it.
Fiona's cube has	4, 4, 4, 6, 6, 6	on it.
Kirsty's cube has	6, 3, 4, 1, 1, 2	on it.

Is this a fair game?
How could you make this game fair?

4 ③ △7 ④ △9 ⑤ ① △11 ⑧

a Nina takes a card without looking.
Is she more likely to get a triangle or a circle?

b Is Nina's card more likely to have an odd or an even number on it?

* **c** Sam mixes the cards up and turns them face down.

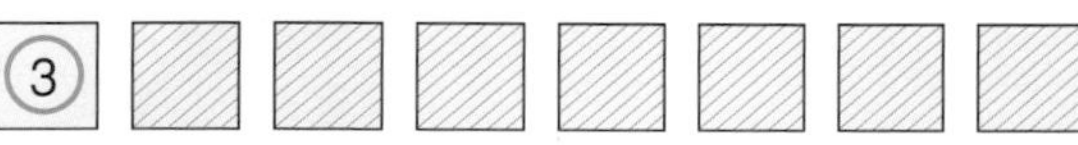

He turns one over.
It has a ③ on it.
He turns another card over.
Is it more likely he will get a number smaller than 3 or a number bigger than 3?
Explain.

5 Which of these events will have equally likely outcomes?

a tossing a coin

b taking one of these cards without looking 1 2 3 4

c spinning this spinner

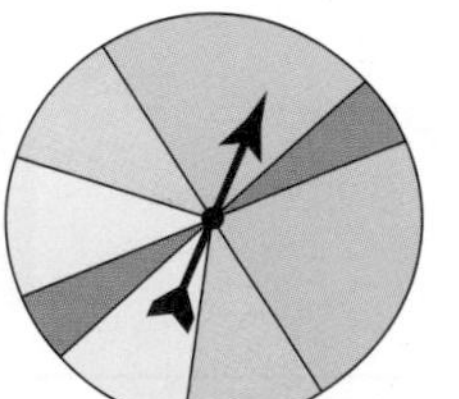

Probability scale

We can show probabilities on a **probability scale**.

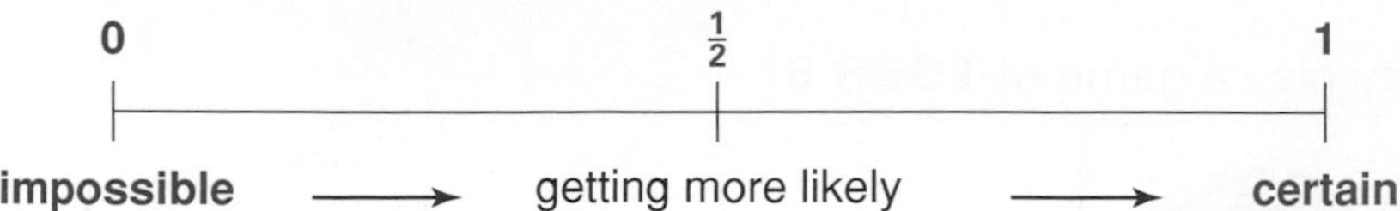

All events have a probability somewhere from 0 to 1.

Example This probability scale shows the probability of some events.

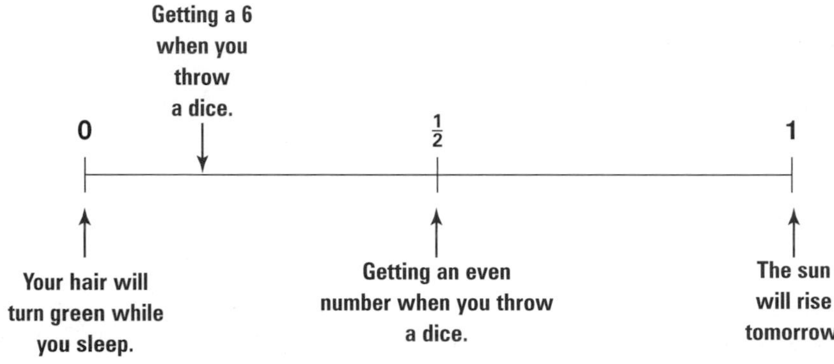

Discussion

- Jane thinks there is a 50% chance that this spinner will stop on an even number.
  Is she right? **Discuss**.

  Where would she put an arrow to show the probability on this scale?

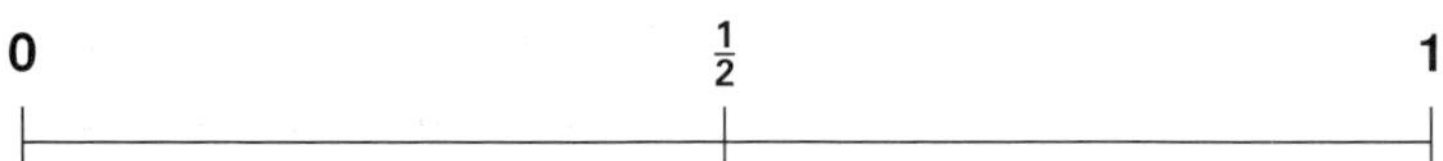

- **Discuss** where to put the probability of these events on the scale.
  - sliding on ice next time you are in a car
  - breaking your arm next week
  - seeing some blue sky tomorrow
  - the first person you see tomorrow being female

Exercise 2

T **1** Use a copy of this probability scale.

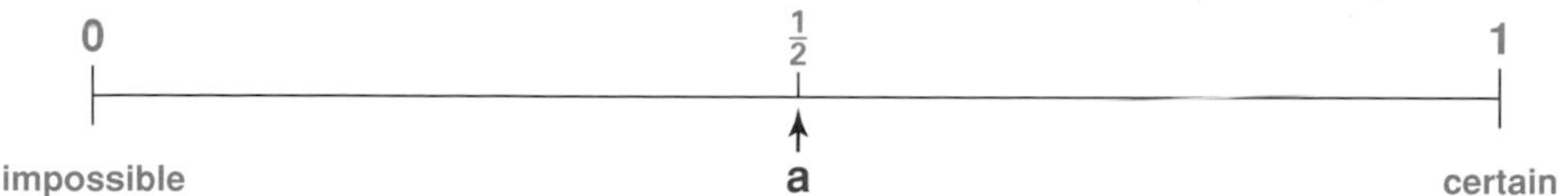

Show where each of these might be on the scale.
The first one is done.

a You will get a tail when you toss a coin.
b Someone in the world will tell a joke tomorrow.
c You will find a £100 note on Saturday.
d You will get out of bed tomorrow.

T **2** Use a copy of this probability scale.

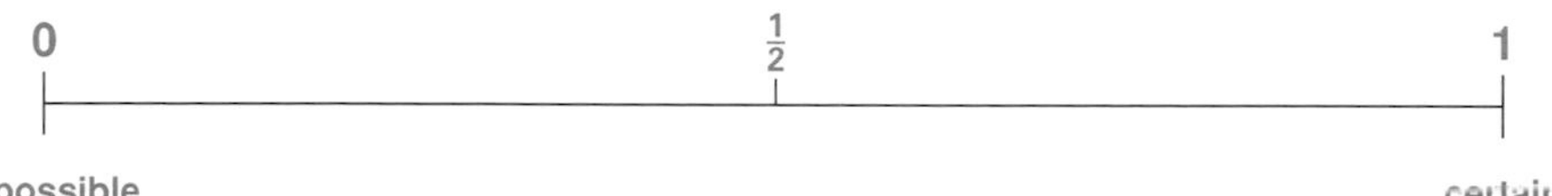

Put an arrow on the scale to show the probability of these.

a the spinner shown stopping on red
b the spinner shown stopping on green
c the next baby born being a boy
***d** a black bead being taken, without looking, from the bag

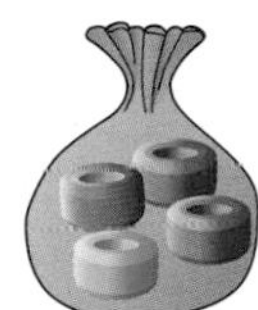

T **3** The arrow on the probability scale shows the chance of spinner A stopping on purple.

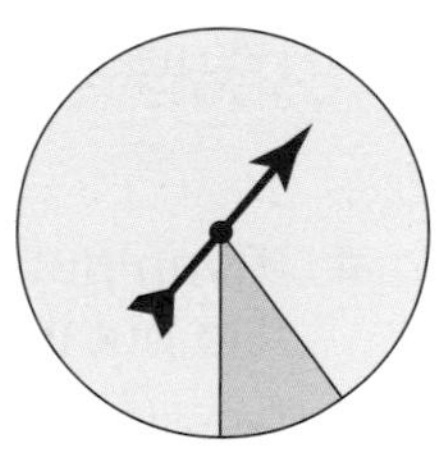

Use a copy of this.
Put an arrow on the scale to show the chance of spinner B stopping on purple.
Explain why you put your arrow here.

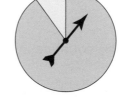

***4** These discs were put in a bag.
Kim took one without looking.

This probability scale shows the probability of her getting each colour.

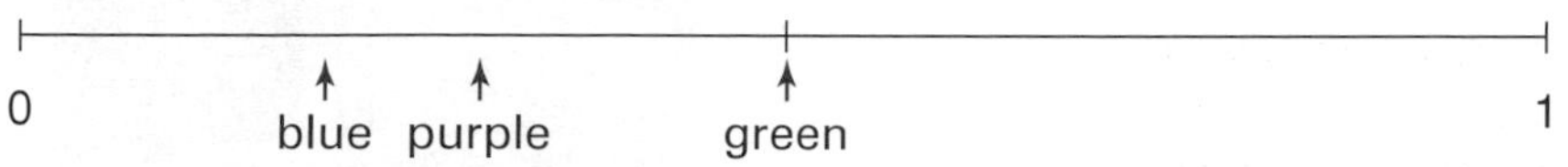

Draw a probability scale to show the probability of taking each colour if these discs were put in a bag.

Outcomes

A bead is taken from this bag without looking.
It could be red or green or blue or yellow or purple.

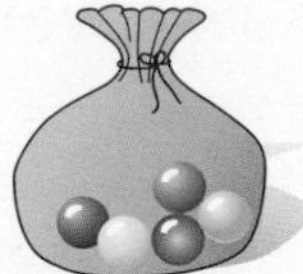

These colours are called the **possible outcomes**.

Exercise 3

1 Mel spins this spinner.
Write down the possible outcomes.

2 Alex put these letters in a bag.

A L E X

She pulled one out without looking.

a Copy and finish this list of possible outcomes.

A, ___, ___, ___

b Do each of the letters have the same chance of being chosen?

3 The letters of the word WINNER are put in a box.
One is chosen without looking.
Write down the list of possible outcomes.

4 Ryan put some counters in a bag.
He put in

7 green   8 red   1 yellow   2 blue   1 black counter.

He took one without looking.
Copy and finish this list of possible outcomes for the colour.

green, ...

5 A pack of crisps has 4 salt and vinegar, 3 ready salted, 2 barbecue and 3 sour cream and chives.
Kanta takes one without looking.
Write down the list of possible outcomes.

Calculating probability

Some outcomes are **equally likely**.

Example Harry spins this spinner.
He is equally likely to get each colour.
There is the same amount of each colour.

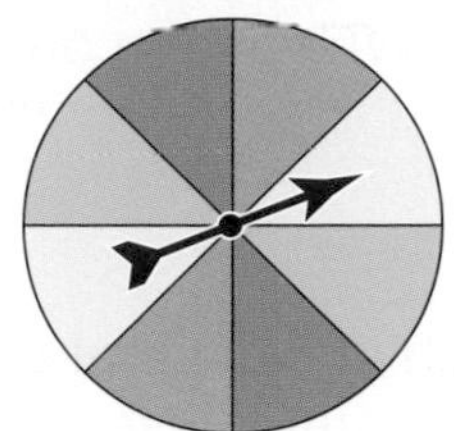

We can **calculate the probability** of getting each colour.
For **equally likely outcomes**,

$$\textbf{probability of an event} = \frac{\textbf{number of ways event can happen}}{\textbf{number of possible outcomes}}$$

For the example above

probability of Harry getting red = $\frac{2}{8}$ ← **number of ways it could stop on red** / ← **total number of sections it could stop on**

= $\frac{1}{4}$ or 25% or 0·25

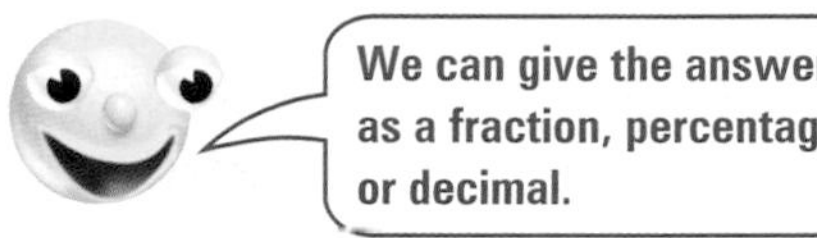

We can give the answer as a fraction, percentage or decimal.

Worked Example
The letters of the word CHANCE are put in a bag.
Hein took one without looking.
What is the probability it is the letter **a** E **b** C?

Answer

a There is one way the letter E can be chosen.
The total number of possible outcomes is 6.
So the probability is $\frac{1}{6}$.

b There are two ways the letter C can be chosen.
The total number of possible outcomes is 6.
So the probability is $\frac{2}{6}$ or $\frac{1}{3}$.

Hein didn't look when she chose a letter.
We could have said 'Hein chose a letter at random'.

Choosing **at random** means every item has the same chance of being chosen.

Exercise 4

Only use a calculator if you need to.

1 What is the probability of getting a tail when a fair coin is tossed?

A fair coin is equally likely to land on heads as on tails.

2 The arrow is spun.

a The probability it will stop on red = $\frac{}{}$ ← number of red parts / ← total number of parts

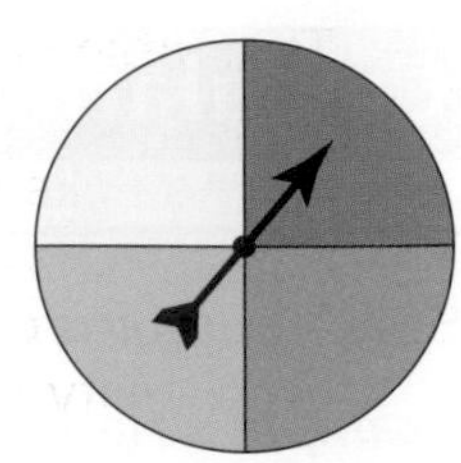

b What is the probability it will stop on grey?

3 Robyn can't make up her mind what to do one Saturday.
She puts these four pieces of paper in a box.
She takes one without looking.

a Write down all the possible outcomes.

b What is the probability Robyn's piece of paper will have 'bike ride' on it?

4 A letter of the word IMAGINATION is picked at random.
What is the probability of getting these?
The first one is started.

a M

Probability (M) = $\frac{}{}$ ← number of Ms / ← total number of letters

= ____

b N **c** A **d** I

5 Colin spins this spinner.
Use the formula below to find the probability it will stop on

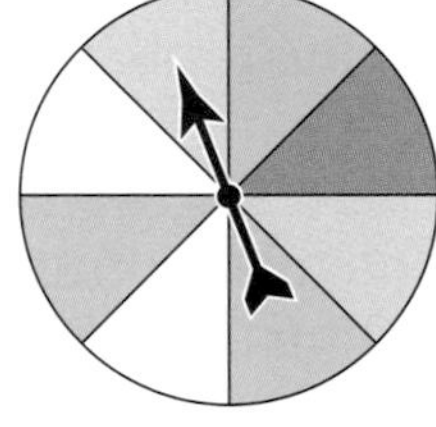

a purple **b** white **c** blue **d** red.

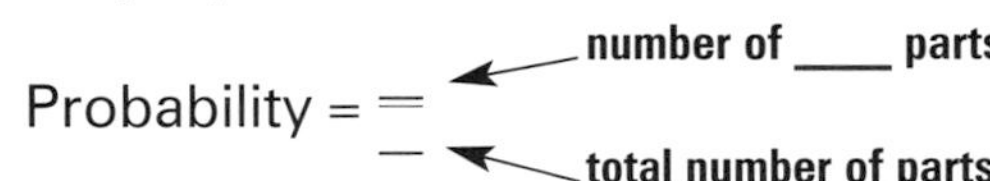

6 There are 50 pieces of chalk in a box.
All of them are white.
Mrs Patel chooses one piece at random.
What is the probability that this piece of chalk is

a white **b** yellow?

***7** The letters of the alphabet are put in a bag.
One letter is chosen at random.
What is the probability it is

a the letter T

b a vowel

c a consonant?

T

∗8 This table shows the colours of 100 tickets sold in a raffle.
All the tickets were put in a hat.
One ticket was pulled out without looking.
The arrow on this probability scale shows the probability that the ticket pulled out was pink.

green	20
pink	60
blue	5
yellow	15
Total	100

0 impossible ↑ pink 1 certain

Use a copy of this line.

a Put an arrow on the line to show the probability that the ticket pulled out was green.
Explain why you put the arrow here.

b Put an arrow on the line to show the probability that the ticket pulled out was blue.

c Put an arrow on the line to show the probability that the ticket pulled out was yellow.

∗9 A fair dice is rolled.
What is the probability of rolling

a a 6
b an odd number
c a number greater than 4
d a factor of 8
e a prime number
f zero
g 7
h a number between 0 and 7?

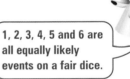

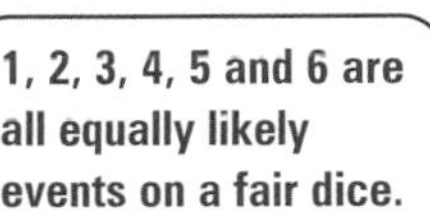

1, 2, 3, 4, 5 and 6 are all equally likely events on a fair dice.

∗10 Ben and Sarah are playing a word game.
Letters are chosen at random from a bag.
There are 4 letters left in the bag.

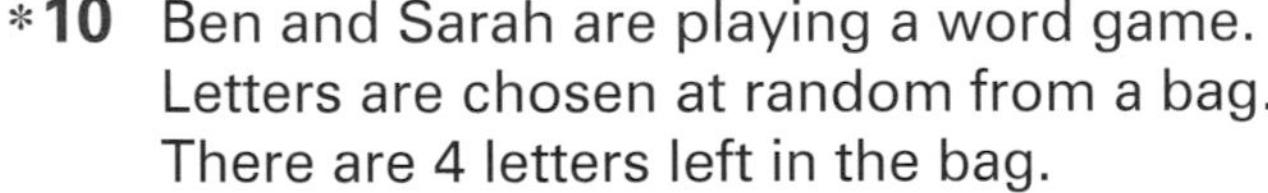

Ben needs the T to make a word.
Sarah needs the A or the E.
What is the probability that the next letter chosen will be

a the letter Ben needs
b one of the letters Sarah needs?

One letter is chosen at random.
It is **not** T.
What is the probability that the letter chosen is

c the one Ben needs
d one of the letters Sarah needs?

Estimating probability from experiments

Discussion

Rose made a biased dice.

She wanted to know the probability of throwing a 6 with her dice.

Can she use this formula to find the probability of throwing a 6?

$$\text{probability} = \frac{\text{number of ways event can happen}}{\text{number of possible outcomes}}$$

Discuss.

A biased dice is not fair.
Each number does not
have an equal chance of
being thrown.

Often we cannot calculate the probability of an event happening.
Instead, we **estimate the probability** by doing an **experiment**.

Example If we want to know the probability of someone catching a ball we need to do an experiment to find out an estimate.

Example Owen tossed a ball 100 times.
He caught it 47 times.
He estimated the probability of catching the ball.

$$\text{probability of catching ball} = \frac{\text{number of times ball was caught}}{\text{total number of throws}}$$

$$= \frac{47}{100}$$

He said 'The probability of my catching the ball is just under $\frac{1}{2}$.'

If Owen wanted a more accurate estimate he would need to toss the ball more times.

Practical

T **A** **You will need** a bag and some red and green counters.

1 Ask someone to put 10 of the counters in the bag.
2 Without looking, take a counter out of the bag.
3 Use a copy of the tally chart.
Record its colour.
Put the counter back.
4 Repeat **2** and **3** fifty times.

Colour	Tally	Frequency
red		
green		

5 Use this formula to estimate the probability of getting a red counter.

$$\text{probability} = \frac{\text{number of times red taken from bag}}{50}$$

6 Estimate the probability of getting a green counter.

B **You will need** some thin card and some Blu-Tack.

T

Make a biased dice like this.

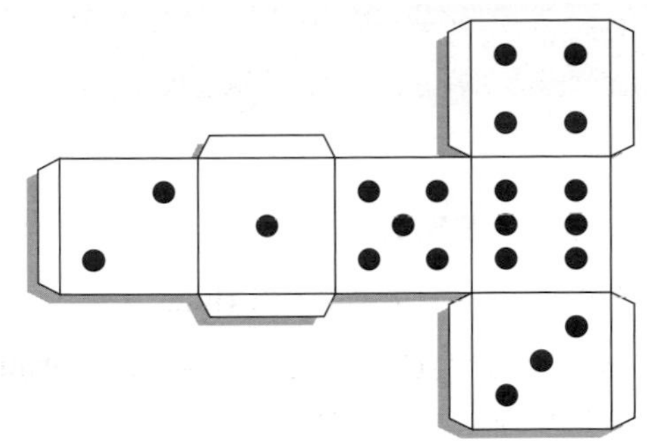

1 Use a larger copy of this net and cut it out.
2 Tape a small piece of Blu-Tack to the inside of one face.
3 Tape your dice together.
Roll your dice 100 times.
Record the results in a tally chart.
Use your results to estimate the probability of getting each number on your dice.

Number	Tally	Frequency
1		
2		
3		
4		
5		
6		

Investigation

Coin flips

Someone once told me that if a coin was placed tails up on the thumb nail, then flicked into the air, it was likely to land tails up!
Investigate.

Comparing calculated probability with experimental probability

Discussion

There is a 50% chance of getting a head when a coin is tossed.

Does this mean you would get exactly five heads if you tossed a coin 10 times?

Would you get exactly 50 heads if you tossed it 100 times?

What about 1000 times? **Discuss**.

Practical

A **You will need** a coin.

The calculated probability of getting a head is $\frac{1}{2}$.

1 Toss a coin 10 times.
How many heads did you get?

2 Toss a coin 100 times.
Record your results in a tally chart.
How many heads did you get?
Is the probability of getting a head closer to $\frac{1}{2}$ in **1** or **2**?

T *B **You will need** a computer software package that simulates tossing a coin or a dice.

'Simulates' means 'mimics'.

Simulate tossing a coin 50 times.
How many heads do you get?
How many heads would you expect to get using calculated probability?

Repeat the simulation.
Did you get the same result?

You could use the random (RND) function on a spreadsheet.

Simulate tossing a coin 1000 times, then 2000 times, then 3000 ...
What do you notice?

Exercise 5

1 Brian spins a fair coin four times.
He gets a head three times.
Brian says that if he spins it another four times, he'll get three heads again.
Explain why Brian is wrong.

2 Olivia, Ben and Joshua each rolled a different dice 360 times.
Only one of the dice was fair.
Whose was it?
Explain your answer.

Number	Olivia	Ben	Joshua
1	27	58	141
2	69	62	52
3	78	63	56
4	43	57	53
5	76	56	53
6	67	64	5

*3 There are 100 sweets in a box.
Eric takes a sweet without looking.
He writes down what sort it is and then **puts it back**.
He does this 100 times.
This chart shows Eric's results.

toffee	20
mint	38
jelly	14
choco	25
caramel	3

a Eric thought there must be exactly 20 toffees in the box.
Explain why he is wrong.
b What is the smallest number of caramels that could be in the box?
c Is it possible there is any other sort of sweet in the box?
Explain.
d Eric starts again and does the same thing another 100 times.
Will his chart have exactly the same numbers on it?
e Eric's friend takes a sweet. What sort is he most likely to get?

Boxes – a game for a group

You will need a 'box' like this.

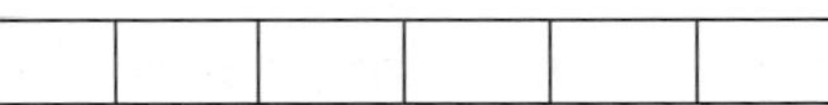

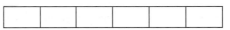

To play
- Choose a leader.
- The leader calls out six digits from 0 to 9, each one different.
- As each digit is called, write it in one section of your 'box'.
- The winner is the person who has made the largest possible number.
- The winner is the leader for the next round.

Remember place value on page 17.

Summary of key points

Some events are **more likely** to happen than others.

Example Ben took one of these cards without looking.
He is more likely to get a blue card than a red card.

We can show probabilities on a **probability scale**.

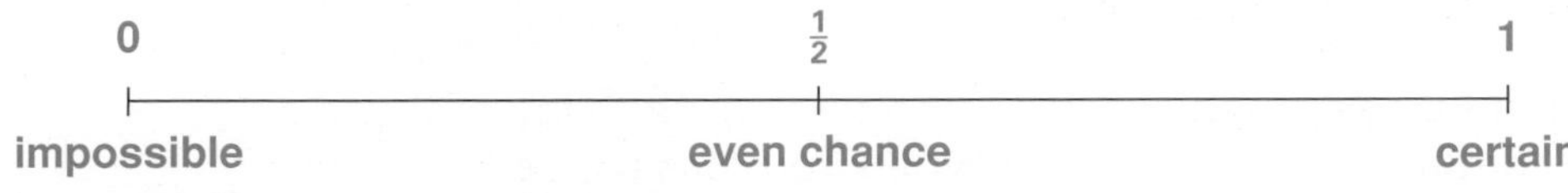

All probabilities lie from 0 to 1.

This spinner is spun.
It could stop on **A, B, C** or **D**.
These are called the possible **outcomes**.

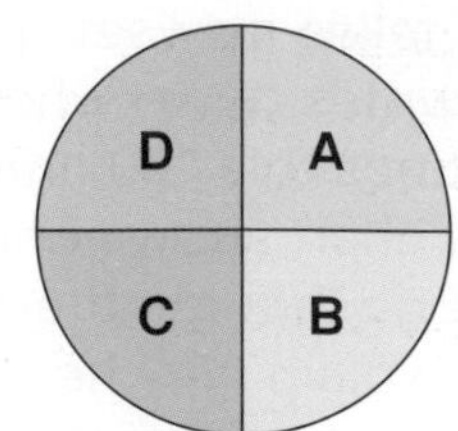

They are **equally likely** because they have an equal chance of happening.

For equally likely outcomes

$$\textbf{probability of an event} = \frac{\textbf{number of ways event can happen}}{\textbf{number of possible outcomes}}$$

Example The names of 5 boys and 3 girls were put in a box.
Tim took one at random.
Probability (girl) = $\frac{3}{5}$ ← **3 ways of getting a girl** / ← **total number of possible outcomes**

Sometimes we cannot calculate the probability, but we can **estimate** it by **doing an experiment**.

Example If we wanted to know the probability that a car at a corner will turn right we would need to do an experiment.
We could find out how many out of 1000 cars turned right at the corner.
From this we could estimate the probability using this formula.

$$\text{probability} = \frac{\text{number of cars that turned right}}{1000}$$

If we want a **more accurate estimate we should survey more cars**.

Test yourself

1 Jake puts these shapes in a bag.
He takes one without looking.
Which shape is he more likely to get?
Explain why. A

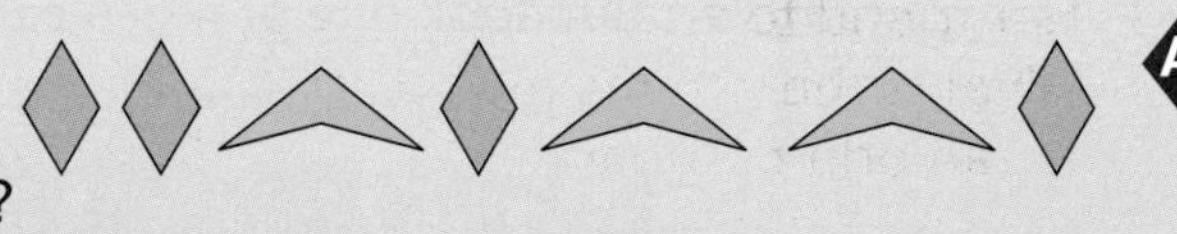

T **2** Use a copy of this probability scale. B

0 ——— $\frac{1}{2}$ ——— 1

Put an arrow on the scale to show the probability of these.

a getting an even number when you toss a dice
b getting a 2 when the spinner is spun
c getting a number more than 4 when the spinner is spun
d Friday coming straight after Thursday

3 Peter put the letters of his name in a bag. **C**
He takes one out without looking.
Write a list of the letters it might have been.

4 What is the probability the letter Peter takes in question **3** is **D**
a P **b** E?

Probability (P) = — ← number of Ps
— ← total number of letters
= —

5 There are 16 counters in a bag. **D**
Five of them are black.
Miranda chooses a counter from the bag at random.
What is the probability that Miranda chooses a black counter?

Probability (black) = — ← total number of black
— ← total number of counters
= —

6 Bill put eight purple counters and eight black counters in a bag. **E**

He took a counter without looking and then **put it back**.
He did this 16 times.
Bill took out purple counters 10 times and black counters 6 times.
Bill said 'I must have made a mistake and put 10 purple and 6 black counters in the bag.'
Explain why Bill is wrong.

***7** Ellie had these ten number cards. **D**

1 2 4 6 7 8 9 11 13 15

Her friend took one card without looking.
What is the probability the card will have

a an odd number
b an even number
c a number less than 10
d the number 3
e a number less than 16
f a number greater than 6?

D

***8** Raffle tickets are numbered 1 to 300.
Lena buys five tickets and gets the numbers 8, 9, 10, 11 and 12.
Freddie buys five tickets and gets the numbers 18, 29, 182, 207, 234.
One ticket is chosen at random.
Is Lena or Freddie more likely to have the winning number?
Explain your answer.

Test Yourself Answers

Chapter 1 page 31

1 **a** 7 hundreds or 700 **b** 7 units or 7 **c** 7 tenths or 0·7 **d** 7 hundredths or 0·07
e 7 thousandths or 0·007
2 650·4
3 **a** Twenty-five point zero eight **b** Seventy-two point zero one eight
c Six and three hundredths **d** Four and two hundred and seventy-three thousandths
4 **a** 49·06 **b** 3002·35 **c** 610·025 **5** **a** 8·8 **b** 13·96 **c** 3·99 **d** 4·99
6 **a** 28·252 kg **b** 8·657 km **c** 17·972 ℓ
7 SHARKS ARE THE ONLY FISH THAT CAN BLINK
8 **a** 0·13 minutes **b** £4·50 **9** **a** 8·6 **b** 7·527 **c** 4·231 **d** 8·36
10 **a** 3·99, 4·1, 4·12, 4·214
b 0·684, 0·846, 0·86, 0·864, 0·87
11 **a** Tim **b** £2.05, £1.50, £1.25, £1.10
12 **a** 600 **b** 800 **c** 100 **d** 1200 **e** 3200 **13** **a** £15 400 **b** £15 000
c Yes, if the figure is rounded to the nearest ten thousand.
It would have been more reasonable to say that just over £15 000 was raised.
d largest amount is £15 499 and smallest amount is £14 500
14 **a** B. Smith 17, R. Johns 20, M. Carter 17, S. Patel 20, M. Read 18
b B. Smith 17·2, R. Johns 20·5, M. Carter 16·6, S. Patel 20·0, M. Read 18·0
15 **a** 6 **b** 8 **c** 13 **16** **a** 2 **b** 5 **c** 12

Chapter 2 page 53

1 $^-6$, $^-4$, $^-1$, 0, 1, 3 **2** **a** $^-8$ °C **b** 6 °C
3 **a** 5 **b** $^-2$ **c** 3 **d** $^-1$ **e** $^-6$ **f** $^-6$ **4** $^-8$, $^-2$, $^-1$, $^-5$, 4, 5, 6, 2, 1
5 **a** 75, 150, 220, 235, 240 **b** 75, 150, 240, 336, 522
c 188, 220, 240, 336 **d** 150, 220, 240
e 150, 188, 220, 240, 336, 522 **f** 150, 240, 336, 522
g 240, 336 **h** 522
6 **a** 18 **b** 28 **c** 15 **d** 20 **7** 11, 13, 17, 19, 23
8 **a** No **b** Yes **c** No **d** Yes **9** 5 and 19 or 7 and 17 or 11 and 13
10 A rectangle **11** **a** 8 **b** 5 **12** 21
13 **a** 8 **b** 5 **c** 9 **d** 16 **e** 3 **f** 36 **14** **a** 16 **b** 10 **c** 49 **d** 7
15 **a** 46·24 **b** 841 **c** 2·9 **d** 6·3 **16** **a** 4·6 **b** 5·7 **c** 10·4

Chapter 3 page 73

1 **a** 21 **b** 70 **2** **a** 40 **b** 50 **c** 24 **d** 100 **e** 117 **f** 225 **g** 429 **h** 32 **i** 4816
3 **a** 1·7 **b** 1·9 **c** 9·8 **d** 1·7 **e** 13·6 **f** 11·6 **g** 5·1 **h** 13·2
4 **a**

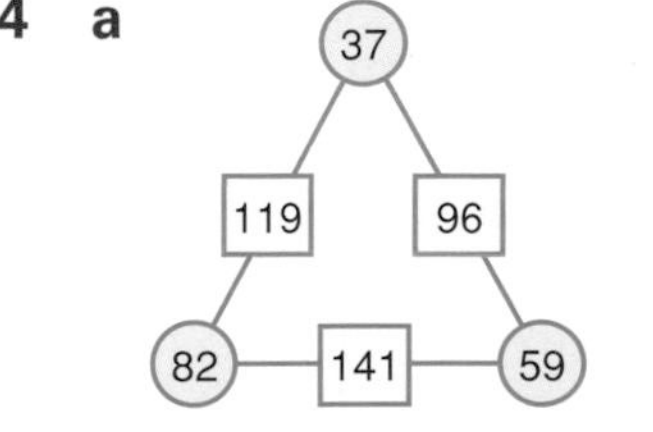

b

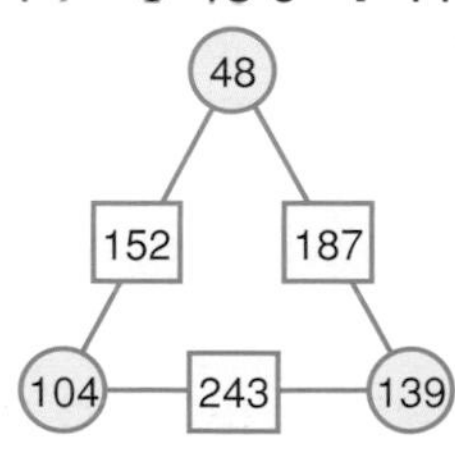

5 **a** $8 \times 90 = 720$ **b** $56 \div 8 = 7$
$8 \times 900 = 7200$ $560 \div 8 = 70$
$8 \times 9000 = 72\,000$ $5600 \div 8 = 700$
$56\,000 \div 8 = 7000$

6 **a** 60 **b** 410 **c** 450 **d** 39 **e** 32 **f** 800 **g** 3600 **h** 902 **i** 130 **j** 1800
7 **a** 2·6 **b** 21·5 **c** 2·4 **d** 0·7 **e** 2·4 **f** 5·4 **g** 0·6 **h** 129 **i** 265 **j** 61·1
8 **a** 12·4 **b** 382 **c** 595 **9** 6·2 kg
10 **a** 52 m **b** 130 m **c** 208 m **d** 1560 m **11** 24
12 **a** 8 **b** 26 **c** 14 **d** 60 **e** 3 **f** 4 **g** 50 **h** 24 **i** 4 **j** 6 **k** 18 **l** 24
13 Exact **14** **a** C **b** B
15 Possible answers are:
a $500 + 200 = 700$ or $450 + 200 = 650$
b $3 \times 5 = 15$ or $3{\cdot}5 \times 5 = 17{\cdot}5$
c $1000 - 400 = 600$ or $950 - 350 = 600$

Chapter 4 page 93

1 **a** 7288 **b** 16·26 **c** 25·72 **d** 42·59 **e** 9412 **f** 1·36 **g** 295.06 **h** 796·81
2 **a** 65·49 **b** 20·8 **3** £84·32 **4** **a** 1530 **b** 4984 **c** 15 568 **d** 16 910
5 £9·45 **6** **a** 421·6 **b** 13·89 **c** 22·96 **d** 182·4 **7** 2310
8 **a** 6·2 **b** 15·3 **c** 32·4 **9** 12·3 g **10** **a** 15 **b** 14 **c** 37 **d** 15 **11** No
12 **a** The answer is wrong. The answer should be bigger than 5·2 because we have multiplied by a number bigger than 1.
b The answer is wrong. The answer should be bigger than 8·3 because we have divided by a number smaller than 1.
c The answer is wrong. The answer should be smaller than 89 because we have divided by a number bigger than 1.
13 **a** $35\,112 \div 42 = 836$ or $35\,112 \div 836 = 42$ **b** $192 \times 1{\cdot}9 = 364{\cdot}8$
c $28{\cdot}08 - 19{\cdot}72 = 8{\cdot}36$ or $28{\cdot}08 - 8{\cdot}36 = 19{\cdot}72$
14 **a** 5550 **b** 10·13 **c** 1·5 **d** 2·2
15 **a** 7 days 18 hours **b** 6 minutes 13 seconds

Chapter 5 page 112

1 $\frac{7}{10}$ **2** **a** About $\frac{1}{4}$ **b** About $\frac{1}{3}$ **3** **a** $\frac{51}{100}$ **b** $\frac{49}{1000}$ **c** $\frac{43}{60}$
4 **a** $\frac{3}{5} = \frac{6}{10} = \frac{9}{15} = \frac{12}{20}$ **b** $\frac{5}{8} = \frac{10}{16} = \frac{15}{24} = \frac{20}{32} = \frac{25}{40}$ **c** $\frac{2}{7} = \frac{4}{14} = \frac{6}{21} = \frac{8}{28} = \frac{10}{35}$
5 There are many possible answers. Some possible answers are:
a $\frac{4}{6}, \frac{6}{9}, \frac{8}{12}, \frac{10}{15}$ **b** $\frac{6}{8}, \frac{9}{12}, \frac{12}{16}, \frac{15}{20}$ **c** $\frac{2}{16}, \frac{3}{24}, \frac{4}{32}, \frac{5}{40}$
6 **a** $\frac{1}{3}$ **b** $\frac{3}{4}$ **c** $\frac{4}{5}$ **d** $\frac{2}{3}$ **e** $\frac{3}{4}$ **f** $\frac{3}{8}$ **7** **a** $\frac{1}{3}$ **b** $\frac{3}{4}$
8 **a** $\frac{1}{2}$ **b** $\frac{3}{10}$ **c** $\frac{3}{5}$ **d** $\frac{43}{100}$ **e** $\frac{9}{20}$ **f** $\frac{7}{25}$
9 **a** 0·2 **b** 0·75 **c** 0·79 **d** 0·04 **e** 0·24 **f** 1·5
10 **a** 0·5 **b** 0·6 **c** 0·7 **11** **a** $\frac{3}{4}, \frac{2}{5}, \frac{3}{8}, \frac{1}{4}, \frac{1}{6}$ **b** $1\frac{7}{8}, 1\frac{4}{5}, 1\frac{3}{4}, 1\frac{5}{8}$
12 **a** $\frac{4}{5}$ **b** $\frac{5}{8}$ **c** $\frac{1}{4}$ **d** $\frac{1}{2}$ **e** 1 **13** **a** $\frac{3}{10}$ **b** $\frac{3}{8}$ **c** $1\frac{1}{2}$ **d** $\frac{1}{8}$
14 **a** £24 **b** 35 cm **c** 9 m **d** 150 g **15** 6
16 **a** 8 **b** 4 **c** 12 **d** $\frac{2}{5}$

Chapter 6 page 122

1 **a** $\frac{3}{10}$ **b** $\frac{27}{100}$ **c** $\frac{3}{4}$ **d** $\frac{7}{20}$ **2** **a** 0·3 **b** 0·27 **c** 0·75 **d** 0·35
3 $\frac{12}{25}$ **4** 0·85
5 **a** 40% **b** 71% **c** 16% **d** 90% **e** 29% **f** 55% **g** 90% **h** 4% **i** 100%

6 **a** $\frac{3}{10}$ **b** 30% **c** 70% **7** 45%
8 **a** 40% **b** 30% **c** 45%
9 **a** 8 **b** 10 **c** 4 **d** 9 **e** 40 **f** 9 **g** 63 **h** 264
10 12 **11** £48
12 **a** 1008 kg **b** 2771 m **c** 1347·2 mm **d** £2574·80 **13** **a** 136 cm **b** 169·2 cm

Chapter 7 page 134

1 **a** £12 **b** £18 **c** £30 **d** £48 **2** 375 g
3 **a** 1 : 3 **b** 1 : 6 **c** 2 : 5 **d** 3 : 5 **4** 2 : 3
5 **a** 3 : 2 **b** 60% **c** 0·4 **6** 15 litres
7 8 **8** **a** $\frac{3}{4}$ **b** 60 **9** 21 cm

Chapter 8 page 164

1 **a** $6y$ **b** c^2 **c** $4(x+3)$ **d** $6(y-4)$ **e** p^2
2 **a** $n-4$ **b** $7n$ **c** $2n+3$ **d** $2(n+3)$ **e** n^2
3 **a** $3x$ **b** $9x$ **c** $6m$ **d** $15m$ **e** $7n$ **f** $5q$ **g** $8a+9b$ **h** $8x+4y$
4 **a** 1 **b** $4n$ **c** $4x$ **d** 30 **e** 15
5 **a** $5x+15$ **b** $7n+28$ **c** $8a+32$ **d** $12x+24$
6 **a** D **b** G **c** H **d** F **e** C **f** A **g** B **h** E
7 **a** 10 **b** 1 **c** 12 **d** 2 **e** 6 **f** 0 **g** 16 **8** 18
9 **a** £280 **b** £480 **c** £355 **10** **a** $2p$ **b** $p+4$ **c** $4p+4$
11 **a** $c=2p$ **b** $h=m+12$ **c** $l=200-r$
12 **a** $n-5=7$ **b** $4n=32$ **c** $\frac{n}{6}=4$
13 **a** 9 **b** 13 **c** 10 **d** 36 **14** **a** 4 **b** 9 **c** 5
15 **a** $4n+9=21$; $n=3$ **b** $9x=180°$; $x=20°$

Chapter 9 page 187

1 **a** 4, 4·5, 5, 5·5, 6, 6·5 **b** 1, ⁻2, ⁻5, ⁻8, ⁻11, ⁻14
2 **a** 12, 24, 48 **b** 200, 40, 8
3 **a** D **b** A **c** B **d** C
4 **a** 1, 6, 11, 16 **b** 1, 4, 16, 64 **c** 2000, 1000, 500, 250
5 **a** The sequence begins at 1. Each term is 4 times bigger than the one before.
b The sequence begins at 2000. Each term is half the term before.
6 **a** 23, 20, 17 **b** 1, 2, 4, 8
7 **a** 6, 7, 8, 9, 10 **b** 4, 8, 12, 16, 20 **c** 1, 3, 5, 7, 9 **d** 4, 3, 2, 1, 0
8 **a** 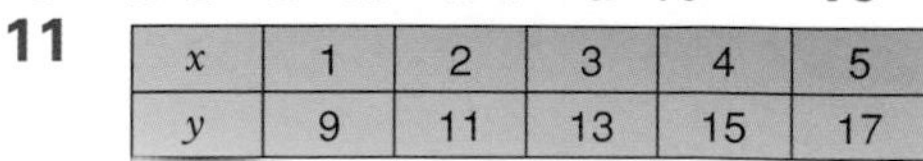 There are 9 dots in this diagram.
b The first diagram has 3 dots and 2 dots are added for each additional diagram.
c No because 24 is an even number and all of the diagrams have an odd number of dots.
d One possible answer is: Shape n has n dots along the bottom and $n+1$ dots along the top. The nth shape will have $n+n+1=2n+1$ dots.
9 **a** 2 **b** 15 **c** 7 **d** 10 **10** **a** 4, 3, 9 **b** 19, 28, 13
11

x	1	2	3	4	5
y	9	11	13	15	17

12 **a** **b**

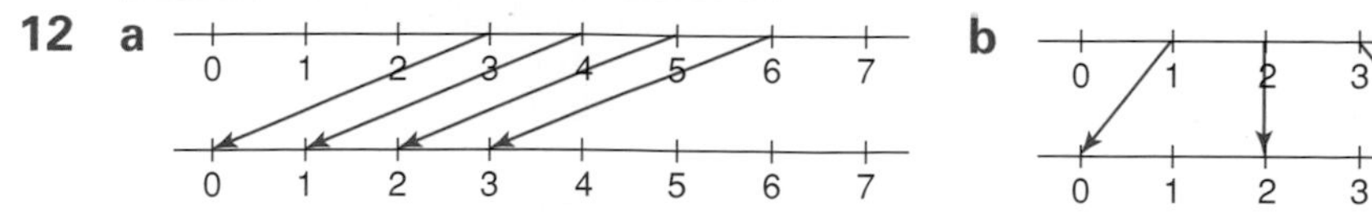

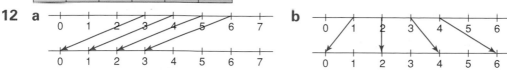

13 **a** Divide by 3 **b** Add 2 **14** **a** 4, 10, 8 **b** 2, 1, 5

15 **a** x is multiplied by 3 then 4 is added; $y = 3x + 4$
b x is divided by 2 then 3 is added; $y = \frac{x}{2} + 3$

16 **a** $x \longrightarrow \frac{x}{4} + 3$ **b** $x \longrightarrow (x + 2) \times 5$ or $x \longrightarrow 5(x + 2)$

Chapter 10 page 208

1 **a** (3, 5), (2, 4), (1, 3), (0, 2), (⁻1, 1) **b** (0, 0), (1, 3), (2, 6), (3, 9) **c** (0, 3), (1, 2), (2, 1), (3, 0)

2 **a**

x	1	3	5
y	4	12	20

b

x	3	4	6
y	−1	0	2

c

x	0	1	5
y	9	8	4

3 **a**

x-coordinate	⁻2	0	3
y-coordinate	⁻3	⁻1	2
coordinates	(⁻2, ⁻3)	(0, ⁻1)	(3, 2)

b

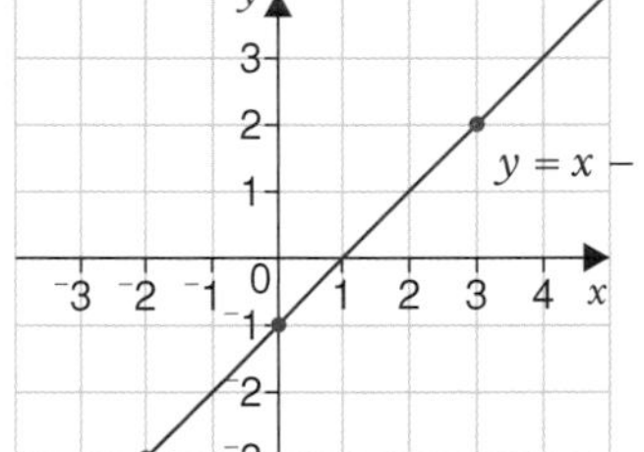

c Yes

d There are many possible answers. Two are (5, 4) and (⁻10, ⁻11).

4 **a** Any number greater than 2 is correct. **b** $y = x + 3$ **c** C

5 **a** and **c**

6 **a**

Hours	0	1	4
Charge (£)	25	40	85

b and **c**

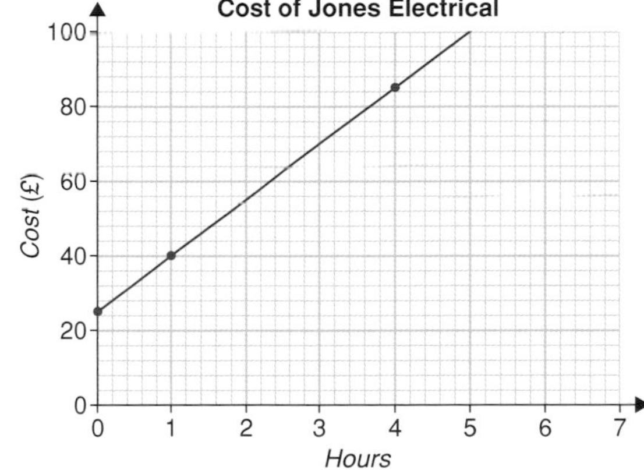

d £70

e 2 hours

7 C

Chapter 11 page 245

1 **a** **i** ∠Q **ii** ∠X **b** **i** QR **ii** XY **c** **i** Obtuse **ii** Acute **2** **a** ∠ABC **b** ∠FIG

3 A possible answer is:

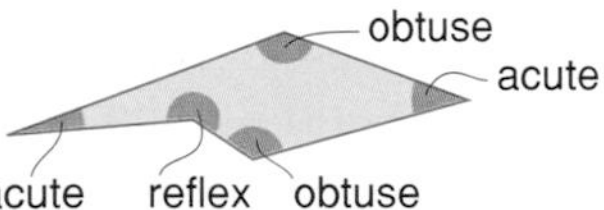

4 red 225°, green 237°, blue 262°

5 **a** AD and BE, AB and DE **b** AC and CB, AB and BE, AD and DE, BE and ED, AB and AD

6 A rectangle

7 **a** 130° **b** 60° **c** 86° **d** 76° **e** 70° **f** $y = 30°$, $x = 40°$ **g** $x = 75°$, $y = 80°$
h $x = 65°$, $y = 50°$ **i** $x = 73°$, $y = 57°$

Chapter 12 page 261

1 A possible answer is: 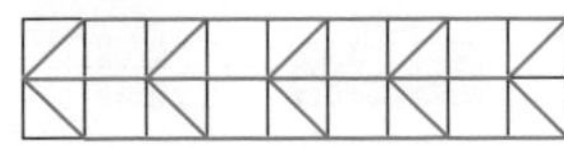

2 JKL and MNO **3** A square **4 a** 80° **b** 68°
5 a It is a triangle. **b** 7 faces, 15 edges, 10 vertices **6** 3
7 Possible answers are given
The nets are not full size.
a

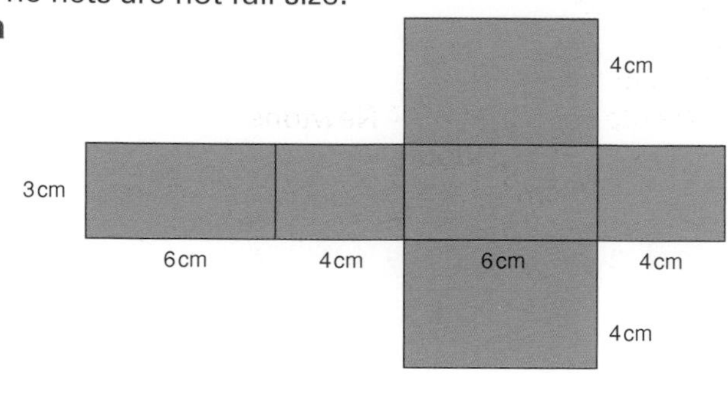

b

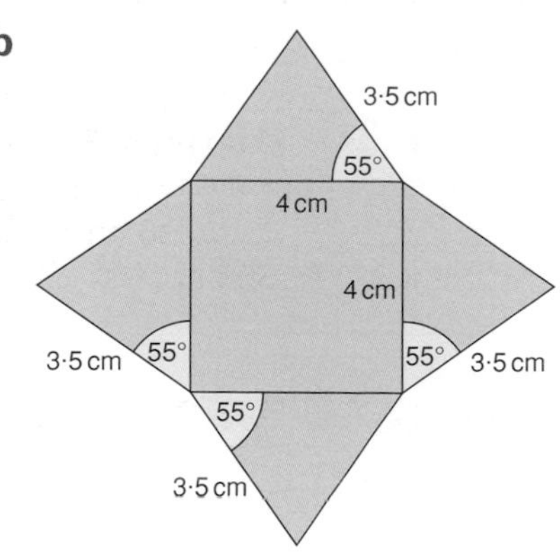

Chapter 13 page 284

1b 2 **c** There are many answers. Two are (0, 3) and (3, 1) or ($^-$2, 0) and (1, $^-$2). Yes it is possible to make a square because only two points are given. We can plot two more points at ($^-$1, 1) and (2, $^-$1) to make a square.
2 Use a mirror to check your answers. **3** Use a mirror to check your answers.
4 P and P′ are not the same distance from the mirror line S.
5 a i

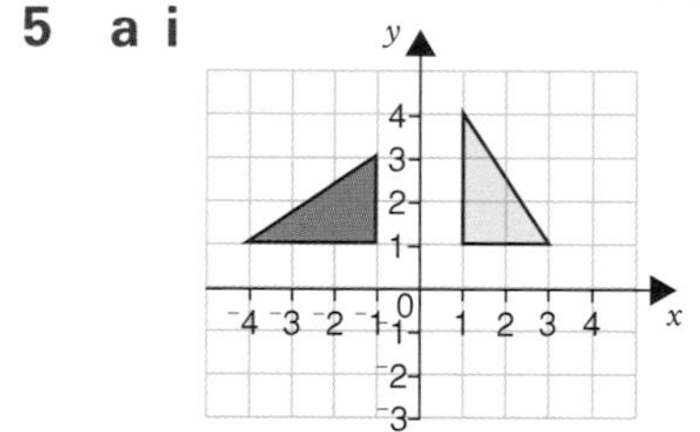

ii

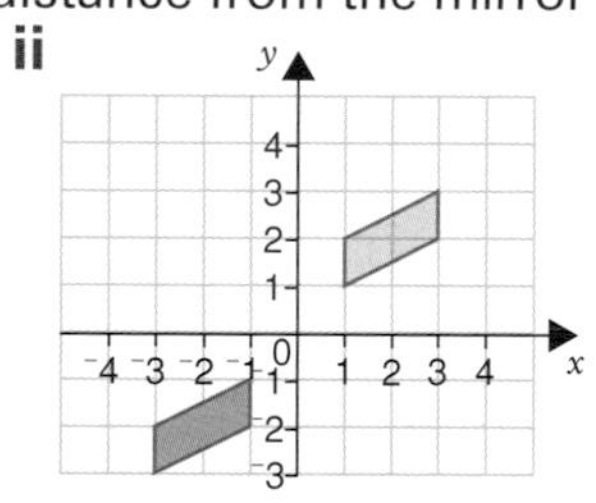

iii

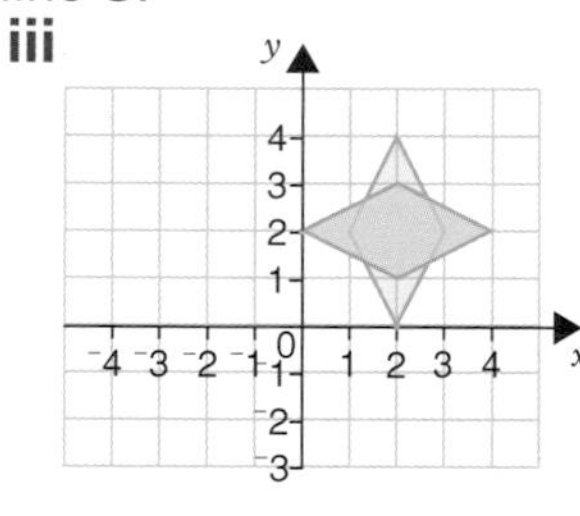

b ($^-$1, 1), ($^-$1, 3), ($^-$4, 1)
6 Rotation 90° clockwise about (0, 0) or 270° about (0, 0)
7 a

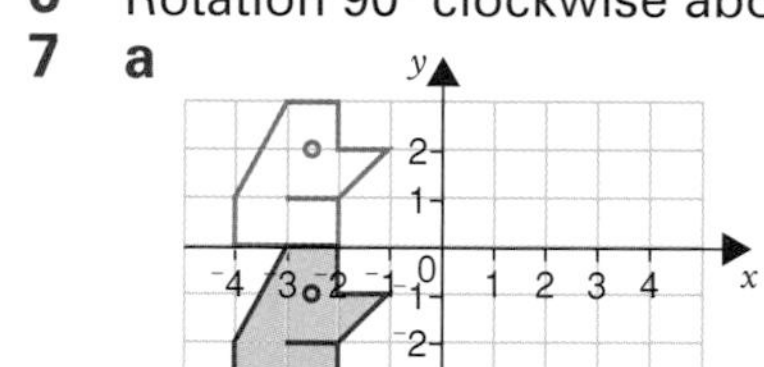

b

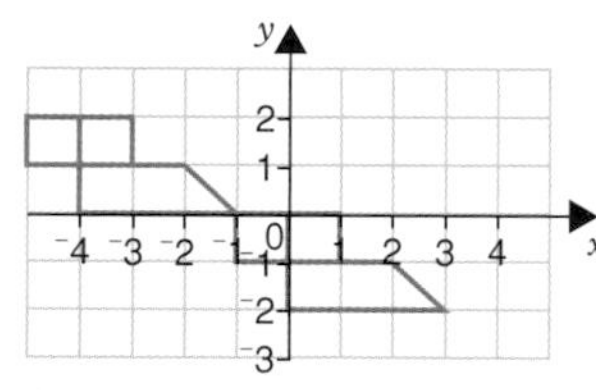

8 a 3 units left and 1 unit down **b** 5 units right and 3 units up **9** A and B
10 a

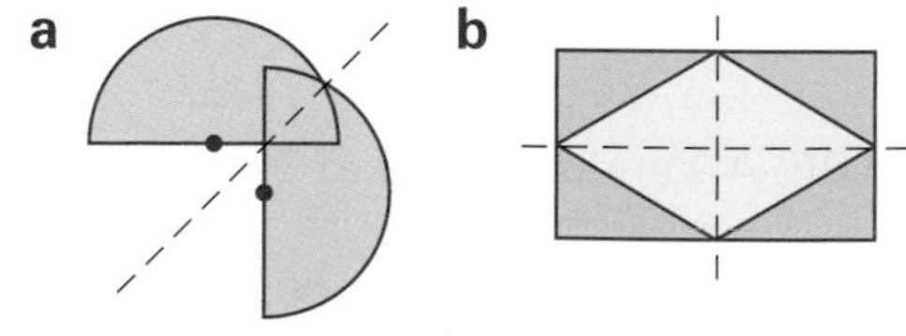

b

11 a 2 **b** 4 **c** 5 **d** 3
12 a

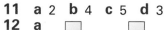

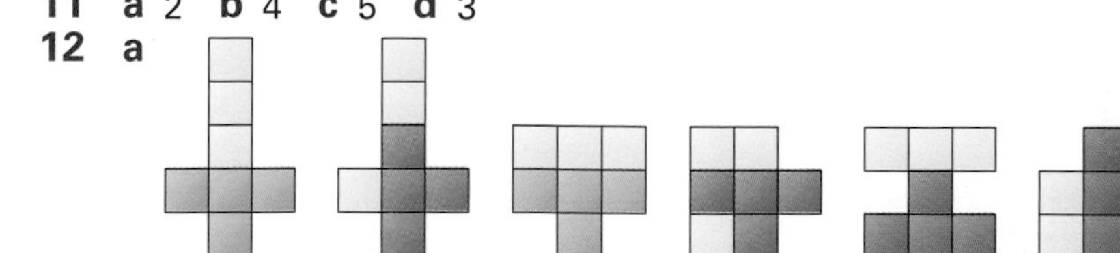

b

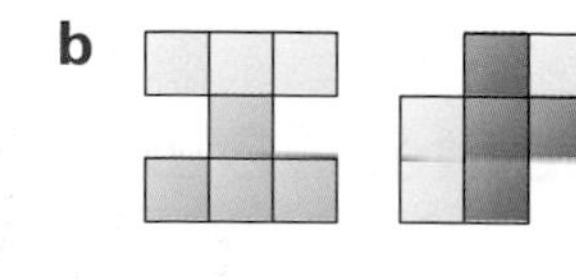

13 a 4 **b** 2

Chapter 14 page 314

1 **a** 32 **b** 4700 **c** 360 **d** 180 **e** 600 **f** 0·476 **g** 0·086 **h** 0·285 **i** 0·75 **j** 0·52 **k** 0·864 **l** 60 **m** 0·0585 **n** 3860 **o** 620
2 **a** 16 **b** 4 **c** 35 **d** 22 **e** 80 km
3 **a** A is at 2·2 lb, B is at 3·4 lb, C is at 1·8 lb
b A is at 0·34 Newtons, B is at 0·23 Newtons, C is at 0·27 Newtons
c A is at about 0·5 kg, B is at about 1·8 kg, C is at about 3·2 kg
4 **a** A **b** B **5** **a** 36 cm^2 **b** 2 m^2 **c** 160 cm^2 **6** **a** 44 cm **b** 104 cm
7 **a** 75 cm^2 **b** 656 cm^2 **8** **a** 54 m^2 **b** 544 cm^2 **9** **a** 46 m^2 **b** 23

Chapter 15 page 330

1

Number of minutes	Tally	Frequency
1–10	ЖЖ ЖЖ	10
11–20	ЖЖ III	8
21–30	ЖЖ	5
>30	I	1

2 Possible answers are:

a

Fast food liked best	Tally	Frequency
McDonalds		
KFC		
Pizza		
Fish and chips		
Other		

b

Distance jumped (cm)	Tally	Frequency
1–25		
26–50		
51–75		
76–100		
101–125		
126–150		
151–200		
More than 200		

c Are you male ☐ female ☐ ?
Length of big toe (in mm) ____

Chapter 16 page 351

1 61–70 **2** **a** 164 cm **b** 14 cm **c** 164 cm **3** 2·5
4

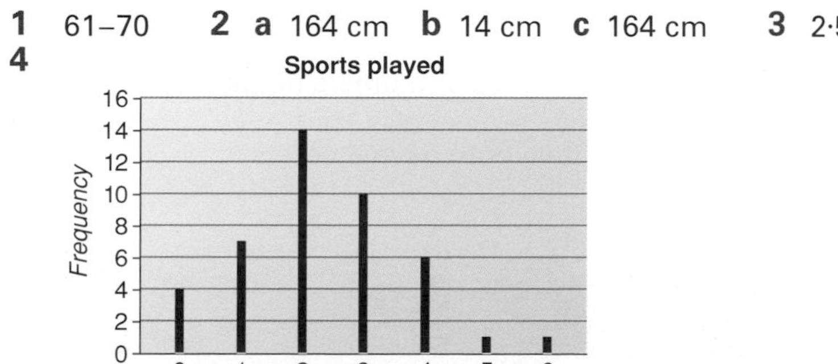

5 a

Mark	11–20	21–30	31–40	41–50
Tally	III	卌	卌 IIII	卌 II
Frequency	3	5	9	7

b

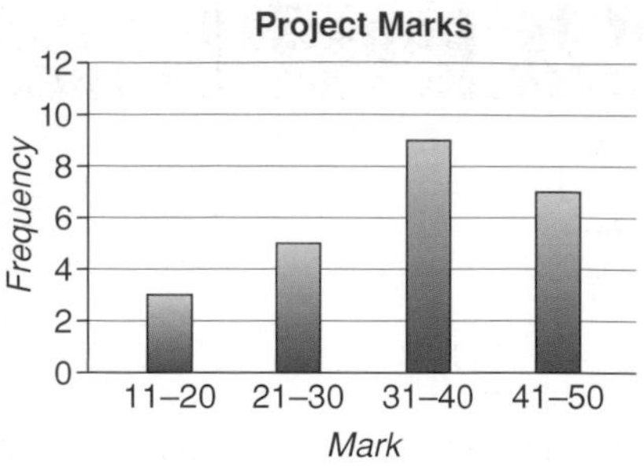

6

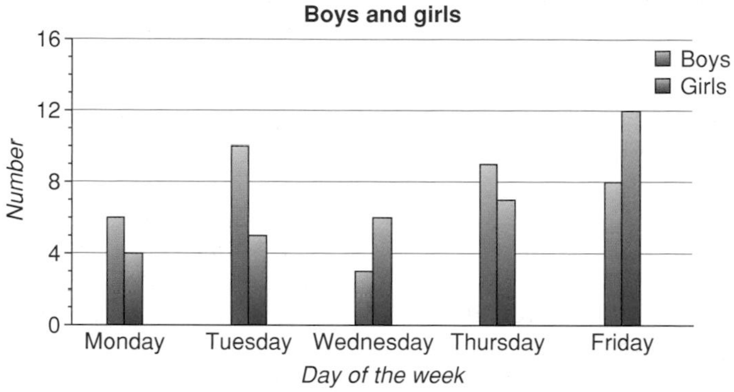

7 **a** Saturday because more people went swimming and fewer had a spa. This is what you would expect on a warm day.
b B.

8 The charts show the proportion who play each summer sport and not the actual numbers. There are 1200 pupils at Eden School and only 800 at Banks School. Eden School will have more cricketers.

9 **a** 6 p.m. because most of the children coming are under 10 and 8 p.m. would be too late for young children. **b** 0–4, 62; 5–9, 72; 10–14, 40; 15+, 26

10 86 **11** 2

12 One possible answer is: I would choose Pete because he has the same mean as Kishan but his range is much smaller which means he is more likely to get a mark fairly close to 73. Kishan has a larger range so he might get a mark much higher than 73 but he also might get a mark much lower than 73.

Chapter 17 page 368

1 A rhombus (diamond) because there are more of them.

2

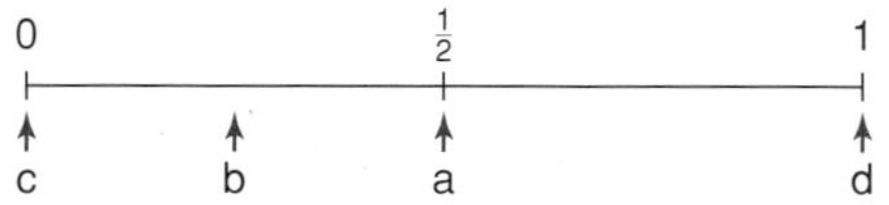

3 P, E, T, R **4** **a** $\frac{1}{5}$ **b** $\frac{2}{5}$ **5** $\frac{5}{16}$

6 Although each colour has an equal chance of being selected it does not mean they will be selected equally.
Bill might have taken out some counters more than once and others not at all.

7 **a** $\frac{6}{10}$ or $\frac{3}{5}$ **b** $\frac{4}{10}$ or $\frac{2}{5}$ **c** $\frac{7}{10}$ **d** 0 **e** 1 **f** $\frac{6}{10}$ or $\frac{3}{5}$

8 They have the same chance of winning because they both have 5 tickets.

Index